33
20
13
25

AGING | Tenth Edition

Editor

Harold Cox
Indiana State University

Harold Cox, professor of sociology at Indiana State University, has published several articles in the field of gerontology. He is the author of *Later Life: The Realities of Aging* (Prentice Hall, 1993). He is a member of the Gerontological Society of America and the American Sociological Association's Occupation and Professions Section and Youth and Aging Section.

Annual Editions
A Library of Information from the Public Press

Cover illustration by Mike Eagle

The Dushkin Publishing Group, Inc.
Sluice Dock, Guilford, Connecticut 06437

The Annual Editions Series

Annual Editions is a series of over 65 volumes designed to provide the reader with convenient, low-cost access to a wide range of current, carefully selected articles from some of the most important magazines, newspapers, and journals published today. Annual Editions are updated on an annual basis through a continuous monitoring of over 300 periodical sources. All Annual Editions have a number of features designed to make them particularly useful, including topic guides, annotated tables of contents, unit overviews, and indexes. For the teacher using Annual Editions in the classroom, an Instructor's Resource Guide with test questions is available for each volume.

VOLUMES AVAILABLE

Africa
Aging
American Foreign Policy
American Government
American History, Pre-Civil War
American History, Post-Civil War
Anthropology
Archaeology
Biology
Biopsychology
Business Ethics
Canadian Politics
Child Growth and Development
China
Comparative Politics
Computers in Education
Computers in Business
Computers in Society
Criminal Justice
Developing World
Drugs, Society, and Behavior
Dying, Death, and Bereavement
Early Childhood Education
Economics
Educating Exceptional Children
Education
Educational Psychology
Environment
Geography
Global Issues
Health
Human Development
Human Resources
Human Sexuality
India and South Asia

International Business
Japan and the Pacific Rim
Latin America
Life Management
Macroeconomics
Management
Marketing
Marriage and Family
Mass Media
Microeconomics
Middle East and the Islamic World
Money and Banking
Multicultural Education
Nutrition
Personal Growth and Behavior
Physical Anthropology
Psychology
Public Administration
Race and Ethnic Relations
Russia, the Eurasian Republics, and
   Central/Eastern Europe
Social Problems
Sociology
State and Local Government
Urban Society
Violence and Terrorism
Western Civilization,
   Pre-Reformation
Western Civilization,
   Post-Reformation
Western Europe
World History, Pre-Modern
World History, Modern
World Politics

Cataloging in Publication Data
Main entry under title: Annual editions: Aging. 10/E.
    1. Gerontology—Periodicals. 2. Gerontology—United States—Periodicals. 3. Aged—United States—Periodicals. 4. Aging—Periodicals. I. Cox, Harold, *comp.* II. Title: Aging.
ISBN 1–56134–342–0   301.43 5′0973   78–645208

Tenth Edition

Printed in the United States of America

To the Reader

In publishing ANNUAL EDITIONS we recognize the enormous role played by the magazines, newspapers, and journals of the *public press* in providing current, first-rate educational information in a broad spectrum of interest areas. Within the articles, the best scientists, practitioners, researchers, and commentators draw issues into new perspective as accepted theories and viewpoints are called into account by new events, recent discoveries change old facts, and fresh debate breaks out over important controversies.

Many of the articles resulting from this enormous editorial effort are appropriate for students, researchers, and professionals seeking accurate, current material to help bridge the gap between principles and theories and the real world. These articles, however, become more useful for study when those of lasting value are carefully *collected, organized, indexed,* and *reproduced* in a *low-cost format*, which provides easy and permanent access when the material is needed. That is the role played by *Annual Editions.* Under the direction of each volume's *Editor,* who is an expert in the subject area, and with the guidance of an *Advisory Board,* we seek each year to provide in each *ANNUAL EDITION* a current, well-balanced, carefully selected collection of the best of the public press for your study and enjoyment. We think you'll find this volume useful, and we hope you'll take a moment to let us know what you think.

The decline of the crude birth rate in the United States and other industrialized nations combined with ever-improving food supplies, sanitation, and medical technology have resulted in keeping most people alive and healthy well into their retirement years. The result is a shifting age composition of the populations in these nations who now find their population comprised of fewer people under age 20 and more people 65 years old and older.

In 1900 approximately 3 million Americans were 65 years old and older, and they comprised 4 percent of the population. Currently, there are 31 million persons 65 years old and older, and they represent 12.5 percent of the total population. The most rapid increase in older persons is expected between 2010 and 2030 when the "baby boom" generation reaches 65. Demographers predict that by 2030 there will be 66 million older persons representing approximately 22 percent of the total population. The growing number of older persons in the population has made many of the problems of aging immediately visible. These problems have become widespread topics of concern for political leaders, government planners, and the average citizen.

Moreover, the aging of the population has not only become a phenomenon of the United States and the industrialized countries of Western Europe, but it is also occurring in the underdeveloped countries of the world as well. An increasing number and percentage of the world's population are now defined as aged.

Today almost all middle-aged people expect to live to retirement age and beyond. Both the middle-aged and the elderly have pushed for solutions to the problems confronting older Americans. Everyone seems to agree that granting the elderly a secure and comfortable status is desirable. Voluntary associations, communities, and state and federal governments have committed themselves to improving the lives of older persons.

The change in the age composition of the population has not gone unnoticed by the media or the academic community. The number of articles appearing in the popular press and professional journals concerning the problems and opportunities confronting older persons has increased dramatically over the last several years. While scientists have been concerned with the aging process for some time, in the last two decades there has been an expanding volume of research and writing on this subject. This growing interest has resulted in the tenth edition of *Annual Editions: Aging.*

This volume is representative of the field of gerontology in that it is interdisciplinary in its approach, including articles from the biological sciences, medicine, nursing, psychology, sociology, and social work. The articles are taken from the popular press, government publications, and scientific journals. They represent a wide cross section of authors, perspectives, and issues related to the aging process. They were chosen because they address the most relevant and current problems in the field of aging and present a variety of divergent views on the appropriate solutions to these problems. The topics covered include demographic trends, the aging process, longevity, social attitudes toward old age, problems and potentials of aging, retirement, death, living environments in later life, and social policies, programs, and services for older Americans. The articles are organized into an anthology useful for both the student and the teacher.

The goal of this edition was to choose articles that are pertinent, well written, and helpful to those concerned with the field of gerontology. Comments, suggestions, or constructive criticism are welcomed to help improve future editions of this book. Please fill out the article rating form on the last page of this volume. Any anthology can be improved. This one will continue to be—annually.

Harold Cox

Harold Cox
Editor

Contents

Unit 1

The Phenomenon of Aging

Six selections examine the impact of aging on the individual, the family, and society

The concepts in bold italics are developed in the article. For further expansion please refer to the Topic Guide and the Index.

Unit 2

The Quality of Later Life

Eight selections consider the implications of living longer, as well as the physiological and psychological effects of aging.

The concepts in bold italics are developed in the article. For further expansion please refer to the Topic Guide and the Index.

Unit 3

Societal Attitudes toward Old Age

Five selections discuss societal attitudes of discrimination toward the elderly, sexuality in the later years, and institutionalization.

Unit 4

Problems and Potentials of Aging

Five selections examine some of the inherent medical and social problems encountered by the aged, including the dynamics of poverty and elder abuse.

The concepts in bold italics are developed in the article. For further expansion please refer to the Topic Guide and the Index.

Unit 5

Retirement: American Dream or Dilemma?

Three selections look at the broad social implications of the continuing trend toward early retirement and examine the necessity of reassessing and reshaping policies to keep valuable elderly employees in the workforce.

The concepts in bold italics are developed in the article. For further expansion please refer to the Topic Guide and the Index.

Unit 6

The Experience of Dying

Five selections discuss how increased longevity will affect support programs and the family and consider the effects of death and terminal illness of the family.

Unit 7

Living Environments in Later Life

Five selections examine the problems of maintaining a positive living environment for the increasing number of elderly people.

The concepts in bold italics are developed in the article. For further expansion please refer to the Topic Guide and the Index.

Unit 8

Social Policies, Programs, and Services for Older Americans

Four selections consider the necessity of developing effective and positive support programs, policies, and services for older citizens.

The concepts in bold italics are developed in the article. For further expansion please refer to the Topic Guide and the Index.

The concepts in bold italics are developed in the article. For further expansion please refer to the Topic Guide and the Index.

Topic Guide

This topic guide suggests how the selections in this book relate to topics of traditional concern to students and professionals involved with gerontology. It is useful for locating articles that relate to each other for reading and research. The guide is arranged alphabetically according to topic. Articles may, of course, treat topics that do not appear in the topic guide. In turn, entries in the topic guide do not necessarily constitute a comprehensive listing of all the contents of each selection.

TOPIC AREA	TREATED IN:	TOPIC AREA	TREATED IN:
Abuse	20. How to Take Care of Aging Parents	**Employment**	7. New Life for the Old
Alcoholism	21. Older Problem Drinkers 23. Older Persons and the Abuse and Misuse of Alcohol and Drugs	**Environmental Stress**	35. From 'Our Town' to 'Ghost Town'?
Alzheimer's Disease	38. Canada's Health Insurance & Ours	**Euthanasia**	29. Right Way to Die 31. Physician-assisted Dying
Attitudes Toward Aging	4. Why We Will Live Longer 15. Saved by the Hand That Is Not Stretched Out 16. Search of a Discourse on Aging 17. Getting Older Is Getting Better 26. School Days for Seniors 30. Is Dying Young Worse Than Dying Old?	**Exercise**	2. Exercise Isn't Just for Fun
		Family Relations	11. Remarriage among the Elderly
		Gender Gap	14. Men and Women Aging Differently
		Gentrification	36. Room of One's Own
Autonomy	34. Board and Care Versus Assisted Living 39. Can We Afford Old Age? 40. Heading for Hardship	**Health Care/ Health Problems**	2. Exercise Isn't Just for Fun 4. Why We Will Live Longer 10. Roles for Aged Individuals in Post-Industrial Societies 12. Women in Our Aging Society 29. Right Way to Die 30. Is Dying Young Worse Than Dying Old? 38. Canada's Health Insurance & Ours
Baby Boomers	4. Why We Will Live Longer 27. Rethinking Retirement		
Biology of Aging	3. Why We Get Old 8. Sexuality and Aging	**Life Expectancy/ Longevity**	1. Can You Live Longer? 4. Why We Will Live Longer 14. Men and Women Aging Differently
Death and Dying	28. Coping with Dying 29. Right Way to Die 32. Family Bereavement Groups	**Living Will**	31. Physician-assisted Dying
Dementia	37. Group Homes for People with Dementia	**Migration Patterns**	22. American Maturity
Demography	22. American Maturity	**Mortality Rate**	12. Women in Our Aging Society 18. What Doctors and Others Need to Know
Economic Status	7. New Life for the Old 25. Retirement Prospects of the Baby Boom Generation 39. Can We Afford Old Age? 40. Heading for Hardship	**Nutrition**	1. Can You Live Longer?
		Physiology of Aging	8. Sexuality and Aging 12. Women in Our Aging Society 13. Live and Learn 19. Amazing Greys
Education	13. Live and Learn 26. School Days for Seniors		

The Phenomenon of Aging

The process of aging is complex and includes biological, psychological, sociological, and behavioral changes. Biologically, the body gradually loses the ability to renew itself. Various body functions begin to slow down, and the vital senses become less acute. Psychologically, aging persons experience changing sensory processes; perception, motor skills, problem-solving ability, and drives and emotions are frequently altered. Sociologically, they must cope with the changing roles and definitions of self that are imposed by society. For instance, the role expectations and the status of grandparents are different from those of parents, and the roles of the retired are quite different from those of the employed. Being defined as "old" may be desirable or undesirable, depending on the particular culture and its values. Behaviorally, aging individuals may move slower and with less dexterity. Because aging individuals are assuming new roles and are viewed differently by others, their attitudes about themselves, their emotions, and, ultimately, their behavior can be expected to change.

Those studying the process of aging often use developmental theories of the life cycle—a sequence of predictable phases, which begins with birth and ends with death—to explain behavior at various stages of a person's life. A person's age, therefore, is important only because it provides clues about his or her behavior at a particular phase of the life cycle, be it childhood, adolescence, adulthood, middle age, or old age. There is, however, the greatest variety of health and human development among older persons than among any other age group. While every three-year-old child can be predicted to experience certain developmental tasks, there is a wide variation in the behavior of 65-year-old persons. Some are in good health, employed, and performing important work tasks. Others are retired and in good health. Still others are retired and in poor health, while others have died before reaching the age of 65.

The articles in this unit are written from a biological, psychological, and sociological perspective. These disciplines attempt to explain the effects of aging, the resulting choices in lifestyle, and the wider cultural implications of an older population.

In the article "Can You Live Longer? What Works and What Doesn't," *Consumer Reports* examines what are and what are not reasonable ways to boost the odds of a longer life. This is followed by "Exercise Isn't Just for Fun," which advises that adjusting one's lifestyle through diet, exercise, and personal habits can affect not only longevity but the quality of life. The essay "Why We Get Old" explains the aging process and how it affects each of the basic biological functions.

In "Why We Live Longer . . . and What It Will Mean," Richard Kirkland explains why he believes the baby boom generation will be the longest living generation in U.S. history. In the next essay, "Over *What* Hill?" the lives of well-known public figures over age 65 who have chosen to remain as active in their later years as they were throughout their adult lives are examined. The final article, "Undercover among the Elderly," reveals a number of negative treatments and insults older people receive from others merely because they are old. The author presents the experiences of Patricia Moore, a young woman who had disguised herself as an older person and traveled throughout the country. Moore describes how differently others reacted to her as an older woman.

Looking Ahead: Challenge Questions

What accounts for most behavior changes during the aging process: biological, psychological, or sociological factors?

Biological, psychological, sociological, and behavioral researchers usually work independently to explain the aging process. Do you think it would be possible to combine these disparate perspectives into one single theory of aging? Explain your answer.

Will it ever be possible to slow down the aging process? Would this be desirable? Why, or why not?

What is meant by the concept of "successful aging"?

CAN YOU LIVE LONGER?
What works and what doesn't

May your hands always be busy
May your feet always be swift
May you have a strong foundation
When the winds of changes shift
May your heart always be joyful
May your song always be sung
May you stay forever young.
"Forever Young," by Bob Dylan

Two decades after writing those lyrics, Bob Dylan is 50 and the generation he sang to has begun the inexorable march into middle age. Even advertising executives, long obsessed with youth, are shifting focus from yuppies to "grumpies"—Grown-Up Mature Professionals.

Among the markets caught up in the accelerating generational flow is the market for products and services that promise to keep us forever young. In 1990, for example, Americans spent an estimated $3- to $4-billion on cosmetic surgery and another billion dollars on moisturizers. Beyond those superficial attempts to *look* young, more and more people are turning to medications, vitamins, and programs that they hope will actually slow the aging process itself.

The scientific basis for some of those treatments is provocative but limited—often only suggestive studies in animals or cell culture. Other treatments have no real basis at all. And some nostrums are illegal, hazardous, or both.

Sales and science

Ironically, sales of useless anti-aging treatments have blossomed just as scientific researchers have come closer to developing effective ones. Hormone cocktails to maintain bone and muscle, and nerve-growth factors to ward off Alzheimer's disease, are among the new treatments poised for serious testing. Last June, a three-year study by the National Academy of Sciences' Institute of Medicine concluded that such prospects are promising enough to boost Federal funding of aging research to nearly $1-billion annually. Even such once-scorned regimens as vitamin supplements and extremely low-calorie diets are drawing new attention from legitimate researchers.

But while serious scientists pursue research in aging, the entrepreneurs have jumped far ahead of the evidence. Even preliminary studies have quickly been exploited by what's loosely termed the life-extension movement, an assortment of supplement packagers, mail-order houses, and anti-aging doctors. As monkey-gland injections give way to plausible (if not yet proven) nutrients and drugs, the line between science and hokum is blurring.

Take the case of deprenyl, used to treat Parkinson's disease. Deprenyl drew attention early in 1989 when Canadian researchers announced they had used it to extend the lifespan of rats. Supporters soon proposed that the drug might do the same for people.

Jozseph Knoll, the 66-year-old Hungarian pharmacologist who developed the drug—and who says he takes low doses regularly himself—has reported that the drug not only lengthens the lives of rats, but boosts their libido. At a medical symposium in mid-1990, according to Medical World News, Knoll

Longevity merchants are turning a germ of provocative research into costly, irrational treatments. But there are some reasonable ways to boost your odds of a longer life.

claimed that deprenyl "can shift the lifespan of the human from 115 years to 145." Several physicians in attendance said that they or their colleagues were taking the drug as a preventive. Longevity, a magazine on anti-aging strategies with a circulation of about 300,000, ran a substantial interview with Knoll headlined "An Anti-Aging Aphrodisiac." The Wall Street Journal gave deprenyl front-page coverage.

Today, there is still no direct evidence that deprenyl can slow the aging process in human beings. Nevertheless, physicians can legally prescribe it—as some are doing—to anyone who wants to try it in an attempt to prolong youth. The theory that it can "is worth further

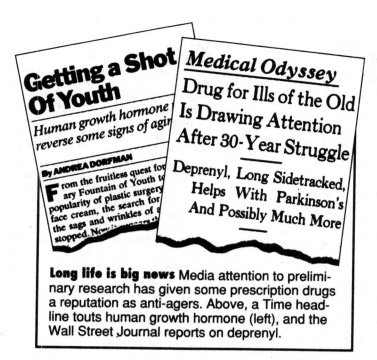

Long life is big news Media attention to preliminary research has given some prescription drugs a reputation as anti-agers. Above, a Time headline touts human growth hormone (left), and the Wall Street Journal reports on deprenyl.

investigation," says Dr. William Langston, the president and research director of the California Parkinson's Foundation in San Jose. "But whether the theory will turn out to be true is a whole other question."

A second touted aging retardant, human growth hormone, is much more restricted in its use than deprenyl; it's available only through 500 approved medical specialists. But it could become another big youth drug. When a report on the hormone was published late in 1990 in the New England Journal of Medicine, it touched a national nerve. Twelve elderly men injected with the hormone for six months shed an average of 14 percent of their body fat. Their muscle mass bulked up by almost 9 percent, and their skin regained a youthful firmness—a transformation, as the researchers wrote, "equivalent in magnitude to the changes incurred during 10 to 20 years of aging."

Although aging experts called the findings very preliminary, the public simply called. Spurred by exuberant headlines, hundreds of people besieged the study investigators and their own physicians with requests for the miracle drug. Overlooked were the caveats beyond the bold type: The effects of long-term growth-hormone replenishment are unknown; an excess of the hormone can cause arthritis, diabetes, high blood pressure, and heart failure; and a year's treatment runs $14,000. (Despite all that, the hormone has

already found a black market among athletes and body-builders, who are now using it as an undetectable alternative to steroids.)

Banking on pills

The current surge of interest in thwarting the clock dates back to the 1982 publication of the book "Life Extension—A Practical Scientific Approach," by Durk Pearson and Sandy Shaw. They confidently proclaimed the aging process can be slowed and even partially reversed with an array of vitamins, minerals, amino acids, food additives, and prescription drugs. The regimen seemed almost irresistibly easy. If you took the right dietary supplements, Pearson and Shaw said, you could stay young, stay slim without dieting, and build strapping muscles with 30 seconds of exercise a day.

"Life Extension" and its two sequels sold 1.7 million copies. Pearson and Shaw became media stars, making frequent television appearances to promote their ideas and posing for photographers in scanty bathing suits to show off their youthful physiques (both are nearing 50).

Although the book included all the appropriate cautions about self-experimentation, the American public signed on as guinea pigs. Sales of multinutrient, megadose supplements shot up. Among the beneficiaries were Pearson and Shaw, who designed and licensed several supplement formulas.

Pearson's and Shaw's ideas are based on the free-radical hypothesis

of aging, which does have a respectable scientific pedigree. It holds that the body's cells age under ongoing attack from free radicals, highly reactive compounds formed when the body converts food into energy. Each free radical has an unpaired electron that desires a mate. The free radical will steal an electron from another compound, rendering that compound unstable and setting up a chain reaction that damages vital cell structures. By one estimate, each cell sustains more than 10,000 of these hits a day, and not all the damage is repaired. According to the free-radical theory, cumulative cell damage produces the hallmarks of senescence, such as wrinkled skin and decline in kidney function.

Support for that theory, proposed in 1956 by University of Nebraska chemist Denham Harman, is now trickling in. But it's not yet clear whether aging can be forestalled, as Pearson and Shaw believe, by taking "antioxidants"—substances that can prevent some of the damage caused by free radicals. (Vitamins C and E and beta-carotene are familiar antioxidants.) Harman himself, who stands staunchly by his theory, stops short of recommending a specific regimen to hold the aging process at bay. "A lot of people," he says, "may be making promises they can't substantiate."

Pearson and Shaw, however, are less reserved; by their own account,

A drug with longevity Over the past two decades the U.S. Food and Drug Administration has taken several actions against companies marketing Gerovital, but the drug always resurfaces. Despite lavish health claims, its main ingredient has been shown only to have mild antidepressant effects. In some brands tested by the FDA, even that ingredient was missing.

STRETCHING THE LIFESPAN

LESS FOOD, MORE YEARS?

All over America, rodents are dieting for science. As a reward, they're living healthier and longer—up to 50 percent longer than the eldest members of their species on typical laboratory diets. Caloric restriction is the only strategy shown to extend maximum lifespan, and some scientists believe it can work for you. The idea is to slash calories while maintaining healthful levels of vitamins and other nutrients.

Usually, restricted animals are served about 40 percent fewer calories than a control group. With age, the big eaters follow a typical path of illness and infirmity, but the dieters are remarkably spared. Heart disease, cataracts, and kidney failure occur less frequently. Cancers develop later, if at all. And, while fully fed mice survive to 38 months at most, the dieters live up to 55 months.

It's the same story with fish, flies, water fleas, and protozoa. Now the Federal Government is supporting a key experiment to see whether caloric restriction can work in primates. In a facility in Poolesville, Md., 30 squirrel monkeys and 120 rhesus monkeys are being tracked for age-related behavioral, physiologic, and biochemical changes, an alternative to waiting out their 20- and 40-year lifespans. Half the animals get generous helpings of monkey chow; the others, on a restricted diet, get 30 percent fewer calories.

The study is in its fourth year, too soon to show differences in aging between the groups, say National Institute on Aging researchers. But the restricted monkeys are already showing maturational delays—in the onset of puberty, for instance—similar to those seen in restricted mice. And the leaner monkeys appear to be in good health, a prerequisite for testing the technique in people.

If the primate studies pan out, "you'd have to be a real stubborn purist to doubt that caloric restriction can work in humans," says Dr. Roy L. Walford, a professor of pathology at the University of California at Los Angeles and a pioneer in caloric-restriction studies. Dr. Walford,

who is now 67 years old, says he has followed a restricted diet himself for the past five years. He has also written three books counseling others how to do the same. Extrapolating from animal data, he believes we can increase the human lifespan to about 140 years or so if serious calorie-cutting starts by early adulthood. Although the benefits seem to increase with the number of calories banished (up to a point), even moderate restriction gains extra years, he says.

Instead of counting calories, Dr. Walford focuses on weight loss, which is safest when it takes place gradually over four to six years. He advises a target weight that's 10 to 25 percent below your "setpoint," the amount you weigh when you neither undereat nor overindulge. He also recommends a nutrient-packed diet reinforced with supplementary vitamins and minerals, most at officially recommended levels.

Although Walford has done well-respected immunological research, he's a scientific maverick. In addition to his life-extension theories, he's just begun a two-year stint as the medical officer for Biosphere 2—the controversial self-enclosed ecosystem in the Arizona desert that's been criticized as having more showmanship than science.

When asked for human data, Walford—who has shed 12 percent of his body weight so far—cites the Okinawan population. Okinawans eat 30 percent fewer calories than the average Japanese, and boast 5 to 40 times as many centenarians as other parts of Japan. But despite that and other anecdotal human evidence, most scientists are waiting for the primate research to show results before they make up their minds. Dr. Richard Cutler, co-director of the primate study at the National Institute on Aging, is the first to say it may not work. It's possible, he says, that evolution has already lengthened the human lifespan "to the hilt," leaving us less room for improvement than other species.

That's speculation, but so is every other

discussion of how caloric restriction works. More than half a century after the life-extending effect of caloric restriction was discovered, scientists have few clues about what makes it so. Attempts to juggle the composition of the diet—changing the balance of fats and protein, for instance—point to calorie-cutting and nothing else as the basis for success. But no one knows why it should work. The only hint comes from the finding that caloric restriction increases the activity of certain protective genes, some of which regulate enzymes that inactivate destructive free radicals.

In addition to being mysterious, the low-calorie life-extension findings seem to contradict other recent research in nutrition and health. Dr. Reubin Andres, clinical director of the National Institute on Aging, believes we should add a few pounds as we age. By reanalyzing reams of data from the Metropolitan Life Insurance Company—which has periodically devised the "desirable" weight tables—and from other sources, he has determined that in middle age and beyond, people with higher weights have a survival advantage. By Dr. Andres's calculations, it's desirable to gain about a pound a year after age 30, as most people do naturally.

Critics say that's contrary to what we know about the health effects of overweight, which has been linked to heart disease, diabetes, and high blood pressure. They also charge that the thinner people in his studies, who had higher death rates, may have been cigarette smokers (who are typically thinner) or people who were already ill and losing weight. Dr. Andres replies that even when those groups are excluded, the weight advantage persists. After a decade of controversy, Government health authorities have agreed and incorporated his suggestions into the "Dietary Guidelines for Americans," a handbook of nutrition and health.

It's hard to compare the issues of weight gain and caloric intake. But in any case, the evidence on caloric restriction is too preliminary and the regimen too rigorous to warrant a lifetime of serious calorie-cutting. The theory's greatest contribution may be to trigger more research on how the aging process works, and on ways to develop more palatable approaches.

---

they each take dozens of pills a day. While the pair have based their program on an exhaustive review of anti-aging research, their interpretation of that research, says one gerontologist, is "grotesquely optimistic." Other researchers have charged Pearson and Shaw with carelessly

applying results of animal tests to humans, ignoring negative data, and endorsing an uncharted and potentially harmful course of pill-popping.

Pearson says that he and Shaw believe "we have probably increased our life expectancy by at least one year for every year we've been at

this." At that rate, of course, they and presumably anyone else who follows their example will live forever—or, as Pearson says, "until you get croaked by an accident."

Warnings for self-starters

Taking a cue from the success of

Read all about it Prominently displayed in health-food stores and other vitamin outlets, booklets like these spread the gospel about a wide array of anti-aging supplements. This allows marketers to avoid health claims on supplement labels, which in legal terms would make them unapproved new drugs.

Buying time? As early as 1984, Congress estimated sales of questionable "youth cures" at $2-billion a year, calling it the fastest growing and most profitable segment of the medical quackery market.

Pearson and Shaw, enterprising doctors, health-food stores, and mail drops listed in the back pages of magazines such as *Longevity* and *American Health* now cater to those modern-day Ponce de Leons in search of the fountain of youth.

From the magazine ads it would seem that all roads lead to long life. A hair-analysis lab offers a nutritional profile "for life extension." Details of a free-radical scavenger "50 times more powerful than Vitamin E" can be had for five dollars, applied to your first order. (It proves to be pine-bark extract, unheard of by researchers on aging.) An offer for "youthful ideas" from the Fountain of Youth International turns out to be just that: inspirational prose to help you think young. And a vaguely worded anti-aging ad leads to an Iowa doctor practicing homeopathy, the unproven use of extremely diluted herbs and other substances to stimulate the body's defenses.

Catalog-shopping is another way to buy (most major credit cards accepted). From *Super Selenium Complex* to *Spots Begone* age-spot cream, catalogs brim with the promise of youth and good health.

In most cases, the products deliver far less than the catalogs promise. We asked two nutrition scientists to comment on *Life Extension Mix*, a popular brew of vitamins, minerals, amino acids, and other nutrients.

Both faulted the supplements on many counts; one, Dr. Jeffrey Blumberg of Tufts University, called it "a not fully rational product."

The doses of some nutrients are ridiculously high, Dr. Blumberg notes, and in some cases may cause adverse effects. For example, a day's dosage of the mix contains 200 milligrams of vitamin B6—100 times the U.S. Recommended Dietary Allowance, and twice the level shown to cause neurologic symptoms, lethargy, and headache in sensitive people. Other nutrients in the formula, such as calcium and Vitamin D, don't meet minimum recommended levels. Health benefits claimed in promotional material correspond only weakly to scientific fact. Finally, taking the recommended nine tablets daily requires self-discipline and about $600 a year, compared with $42 for a run-of-the-mill multivitamin-and-mineral supplement that meets the U.S. RDAs.

Few of these objections ruffle those in the life-extension fold. "People are willing to make themselves guinea pigs," observes William Falloon, vice president of the Life Extension Foundation in Hollywood, Fla., a group that promotes anti-aging products and research. "We don't want to grow old waiting for studies to be done."

Even without further studies, however, there's reason to think many popular life-extension pills are useless, dangerous, or both. Consider four current best-sellers:

Coenzyme Q10 (CoQ10). An enzyme produced in the body, CoQ10 is riding the free-radical wave. Preliminary studies suggest it acts as an antioxidant in blood lipid particles, which carry cholesterol in the bloodstream, and may help keep atherosclerotic plaque from forming. But its anti-aging activity remains speculative, and there's not even good evidence that oral CoQ10 supplements will increase enzyme levels in the body's tissues.

Superoxide dismutase (SOD). This is another natural enzyme with strong antioxidant activity. As a supplement, however, it's worthless: Like other proteins, SOD is broken down in the digestive tract. The "protective" coating on some products only means it's disassembled farther down the line.

Ribonucleic acid (RNA). Present in all body cells, RNA plays a critical role in communicating the genetic code. Supplements of RNA are claimed to rejuvenate old cells,

improve memory, prevent wrinkling. But long before reaching the cells, the supplement is broken down by digestion, like the RNA in chicken and beef.

Dehydroepiandrosterone (DHEA). This adrenal hormone declines dramatically after young adulthood, leading scientists to speculate that declining levels play a role in aging. Experimentally, it has blocked tumors in certain strains of mice and helped others avoid weight gain. Studies in humans show that naturally high DHEA levels may be associated with a lower risk of heart disease. However, adverse effects of experimental use of DHEA have included unwanted hair—it's an androgen steroid—and an enlarged liver, reasons that no responsible voices are recommending its use.

High-priced longevity

The mail-order ads make it easy to spend your money on risky and unproven treatments without ever leaving your home. But if you venture to explore any of the life-extension clinics now springing up, the costs and risks are even higher.

At the deluxe end of the longevity mart is the Lee-Benner Institute of Aging Control & Nutritional Medicine in Newport Beach, Calif. The Institute's program—which costs $3500 for as little as one or two days of consultation and testing—is being marketed as state-of-the-art medicine. It includes a battery of tests to determine "biological age" (which most scientists believe is still unmeasurable), advice on diet and exercise, and nutritional supplements. (See next page.)

For about $2600, you can spend a week at L'Aqualigne in St. Maarten, where the price tag includes a body peel, acupuncture, whole-body massage, and vitamin therapy. The resort's revitalization program features injections of *Gerovital H3*, a famous Romanian therapy. (John F. Kennedy, Marlene Dietrich, and other celebrities were reputed to have used it.) The drug's active agent is procaine hydrochloride, better known as *Novocain*, a local anesthetic. In the body, procaine breaks down into a substance that can quench free radicals. But claims of anti-aging effects—relief from arthritis, heart disease, and baldness, to name a few—have never been substantiated. In the U.S., despite the lack of FDA approval, *Gerovital* tablets can be obtained by mail—minus the revitalizing benefits of

HIGH-PRICED PROMISES

TWO DAYS WITH A LONGEVITY DOCTOR

For $3500 you might expect some pampering, perhaps a massage. But the Lee-Benner Institute of Aging Control & Nutritional Medicine is all business, beginning with the $5 charge for a slim information packet. The cost of the program must be paid in advance by cashier's check. Health insurance may cover some of the fee, advises a cover letter; otherwise, you should "look at it as an investment in your future."

The payoff, according to a promotional brochure, is escape from the "health problems and diseases that can wrinkle, disfigure, impair, restrict and depress you." Practically all aging symptoms can be "erased, delayed or reversed," it assures, leaving "a youthful you." A CU reporter decided to sign on.

The Institute occupies a small suite of offices in a medical plaza in affluent Newport Beach, California. A waiting-room display case sports an autographed photo of well-muscled Joe Antouri, Mr. USA 1990 and a Lee-Benner client. On the mint-green walls hangs a flattering profile of the center, published in Longevity magazine. The video shown to first-time patients, set against John Lennon's "Imagine," extols the "proven effects" of the Lee-Benner method and closes with customers' testimonials.

The program's best advertisement may be Dr. Lord Lee-Benner himself, the medical director. Trim and well-toned, he looks remarkably youthful for age 57. (Biologically he's in his "early thirties," he says, and getting younger.) A neurologist and psychiatrist by training, Dr. Lee-Benner is in fact the only physician at the "Institute," notwithstanding the brochure description of a staff of "nationally recognized neurologists, cardiologists, physiologists, nutritionists" and other medical professionals. (Other physicians in the office suite actually handle workers' compensation cases under Dr. Lee-Benner's direction, according to his receptionist.)

The first morning our reporter (whose affiliation with CONSUMER REPORTS was not revealed) took a battery of tests that would be used to calculate her biological age: tests of exercise endurance, muscle strength, near vision, body composition, and the ability to absorb and exhale oxygen. Next came an extensive "rate of aging" questionnaire, on topics ranging from how much refined flour she ate to how much aerosol spray she used.

The next morning, Dr. Lee-Benner gently broke the news: Despite general good health and normal lab values, the 38-year-old reporter was told, she inhabits a body that's 42.6 years old and is aging eight years for every five. "You got here in the nick of time," Lee-Benner said.

For the next two hours the doctor detailed the hows and whys of his method, which he says he fashioned from the work of some 4000 investigators. At its heart is the free-radical theory of aging, which holds that highly volatile molecules formed during metabolism damage cells and thus age the body. Lee-Benner recommends a sustained reduced-calorie diet to slow the formation of free radicals, and supplements to head off their damaging blows.

Theory aside, there's no proof these strategies work. Although Lee-Benner says he "keeps up" with patients through follow-up visits (at $1500 for further tests and $500 an hour for consultation), he has never published data for scrutiny by his peers.

We asked researchers studying nutrition and aging to evaluate the Lee-Benner program. It earned high marks for increasing patient awareness of good health habits and for emphasizing exercise.

The diet, however, received mixed reviews. "It has some very reasonable elements and authentic advice mixed in with some marginal science and outlandish claims," says Dr. Jeffrey Blumberg, associate director and senior scientist at the USDA Human Nutrition Research Center on Aging at Tufts University. It's extremely restrictive, limiting total fat to 10 percent of calories—a very difficult target, especially for nonvegetarians. Some of the advice is questionable: Adding the preservative BHT to cooking oils to prevent rancidity borders on the "paranoid," according to Dr. Blumberg. And other information—such as the claim that fruit juices contain no vitamins—is just wrong.

The experts in aging we consulted dismissed the use of various tests to determine a patient's "biological age" as so much hocus-pocus. Although many aspects of physiologic function change with age—lung capacity declines, for instance—none has been shown to be a valid measure of how the whole person is aging. Furthermore, "different organ systems within the individual age at different rates, and the important thing is how each one ages over time," explains Dr. David Harrison, a biologist at The Jackson Laboratory at Bar Harbor, Maine. "Throwing functional measures into a formula to get a single biological age is worthless." Nor can a questionnaire determine a person's rate of aging. "That makes assumptions about what causes aging, and we just don't know."

Hardest to swallow were the three formulas of nutritional supplements designed by Dr. Lee-Benner and sold by a company called Responsible Health Inc. *Perfect Balance*, a mix of antioxidants and other vitamins and minerals, proved to be unbalanced—too low in certain elements, such as folic acid, and too high in others. *Perfect Mind* purports to ward off mental decline with precursors to an important nerve-cell messenger, though supporting evidence is slim. And *Perfect Body* is built on the premise—also shaky—that certain amino acids stimulate the release of growth hormone.

The three supplements, which together cost $50 a month, may benefit Dr. Lee-Benner far more than they benefit his patients. Although he seems to have taken pains to hide his connection to Responsible Health Inc. (the company's address is a post-office box), the company's phone rings in his office. Public documents show Responsible Health's chief executive officer, chief financial officer, and apparent owner is Blake Wagner, Lee-Benner's wife. According to the California Medical Association, that arrangement may run afoul of its ethical guidelines on several counts, including a physician's obligation to inform patients of any finanical interest in a therapy.

Some people might benefit from the diet and exercise components of the Lee-Benner method, if they are overweight and sedentary, have unhealthy diets, or suffer from high blood cholesterol. But any primary-care physician with an interest in nutrition could provide the same testing, evaluation, and guidance for about $600. It's called preventive medicine.

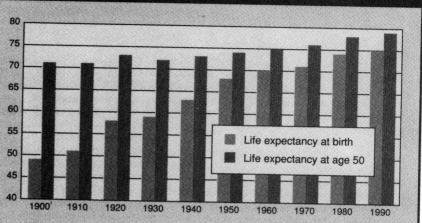

LIFE EXPECTANCY- WHAT'S THE LIMIT?

Most of the dramatic rise in life expectancy since 1900 reflects major reductions in infant and maternal mortality and the conquest of many deadly childhood diseases. A baby born today, on average, will live to age 75—half again as long as a newborn in 1900. But advances against midlife killers have been more modest. Today's 50-year-old can expect to live to age 79, only eight years longer than his or her turn-of-the-century counterpart. Few will reach the theoretical maximum lifespan for humans, estimated at 110 to 120. In fact, even with major inroads against heart disease and cancer, some experts expect life expectancy to top out at age 85—unless the fundamental rate of aging can be slowed.

- Life expectancy at birth
- Life expectancy at age 50

Drugs by mail Foreign mail-order firms sell potent and potentially harmful prescription drugs, as well as some drugs unapproved by the FDA. Agents favored by life-extension enthusiasts include drugs used to treat epilepsy and Parkinson's disease.

Strengthening the FDA A bill to enhance the FDA's enforcement authority now stands before a House of Representatives committee. The bill would enable the FDA to recall or embargo supplements that make false health claims before going through the courts. Its sponsors dismiss opponents' claims that the legislation will turn vitamins into prescription drugs.

basking in the warm Caribbean sun.

A remarkably enduring renewal technique is live-cell therapy, which for a half century has drawn the rich and famous to tony clinics in Switzerland and other parts of Europe. These days, Americans can go to Tijuana for the same dubious treatment at half the price (but still nearly $4000 for a week's stay). The goal is to "regenerate the tired, exhausted glands and tissues that accelerate the aging process," explains biochemist Jacob Swilling, who directs the post-clinic support program at Tijuana's Institute GenesisWest-Provida. Fetal sheep cells—flash-frozen, flown in from Munich, and thawed to bring them back to life—are supposed to revive "depleted resources that keep the body from responding to stress," Swilling says.

The guiding principle of fetal-cell therapy is that "like heals like." Swilling claims that injected sheep thyroid cells, for instance, travel to the human thyroid to conduct repair and rejuvenation, a phenomenon as yet undocumented. Sheep-cell advocates contend that injected fetal cells escape immune-system reaction. American scientists are uniformly skeptical. "Even when we go to great lengths to match human tissues for transplantation, many get rejected," says Dr. William Adler, chief of the immunology program at the National Institute on Aging. "Imagine the reaction from a different species."

Most troubling is the potential for serious harm. Animal cells can spread viral disease and set off severe, even fatal allergic reactions.

Literature from the Institute GenesisWest-Provida assures potential clients that all safety precautions are taken. But that claim, like the Institute's vague claims of rejuvenation, must be taken on faith.

The youth doctors

Some of the more extreme anti-aging treatments thrive outside the reach of American law. But it's now fairly easy to find a doctor in the U.S. who claims to be an expert in life extension—even though it's an ill-defined "specialty" unrecognized by any certifying board.

The Life Extension Foundation publishes a list of physicians who specialize in anti-aging treatments. According to Foundation vice-president William Falloon, they are "knowledgeable about preventive medicine and open to innovative therapies." Among them are doctors who offer hair analysis and chelation therapy—techniques that have become hallmarks of fringe medical practitioners—as well as those using blatantly fraudulent treatments like coffee enemas. Also on the list is one physician who limits himself to selling nutritional supplements, having lost his medical license. (Falloon and Life Extension Foundation president Saul Kent are now under Federal indictment in Florida, charged with importing and selling unapproved new drugs and mis-branded prescription drugs.)

Others on the list, like a New York City doctor consulted by a 38-year-old CU reporter, maintain conventional practices but oblige patients eager to experiment with "anti-aging" drugs. At our reporter's request, the

doctor explained the alleged benefits of a half-dozen such drugs. He then took a brief medical history (a blood test was "recommended but not required"), pulled out his prescription pad, and wrote prescriptions for two drugs currently popular in life-extension circles. One was deprenyl, the anti-Parkinsonism drug. The other was the generic equivalent of *Hydergine*, an agent once widely used to improve memory and mental clarity in patients with Alzheimer's disease and milder brain disorders.

Many clinicians have abandoned *Hydergine* after disappointing results, including a study last year showing that the drug is ineffective against Alzheimer's and may even worsen some symptoms of the disease. Longevity-seekers still believe the drug's antioxidant properties can hold back mental decline. Even so, one anti-aging doctor conceded that "its clinical effects are subtle. You have to take this one on faith."

Other prescription drugs held in esteem by life-extensionists include L-dopa, another anti-Parkinsonism agent; lypressin (*Diapid*), a nasal spray used to treat diabetes insipidus, a disease characterized by excessive urination; and *Dilantin*, an anti-seizure drug. All have no benefits in healthy people and potentially serious side effects, and most clinicians say it's premature for healthy people to take them in the hope of slowing the aging process.

Another stop on the road to long life brought our reporter to medicine's outer fringe. The purpose of her visit was to consult with Dr. Vladimir Dilman, a Soviet gerontologist with a provocative theory of

THE SUPPLEMENT STORY
CAN VITAMINS HELP?

For a long time, the only voices endorsing nutritional supplements belonged to the people who sold them. In the opposite camp stood the guardians of the nation's well-being, including the Surgeon General, the National Research Council, and the U.S. Department of Health and Human Services (HHS). Their position remains that a balanced diet provides all the nutrients needed for good health.

In recent years, however, some scientists have jumped ship. They point to mounting evidence that certain vitamins and other nutrients may offer protection against cancer, cataracts, Parkinson's disease, and other disorders. They speculate that extra doses of those nutrients may slow the aging process. And, while few go so far as to make public recommendations, they freely admit that popping pills has become part of their own daily routine.

The pills they take are antioxidants—for the most part, vitamin C, vitamin E, and beta-carotene, a substance partially converted to vitamin A in the body. (Vitamin A itself does not have antioxidant activity.) Antioxidants are thought to be protective largely because they can inactivate free radicals, destructive molecules that can damage cells.

Those who take antioxidants to slow the aging process admit they're on somewhat shaky ground. "It's banking on an aging mechanism that hasn't been proven," says biologist David Harrison of The

Jackson Laboratory in Bar Harbor, Maine. Nonetheless, like several scientists we contacted, he takes a supplement regimen that includes vitamins C and E, beta-carotene, and a multiple-vitamin tablet. "I'm not sure it does any good, but I'm certainly not sure that it doesn't."

The case for antioxidants as an anti-aging remedy is still speculative. Attempts to use them to extend lifespan in animals have been largely unsuccessful. But several converging lines of evidence suggest antioxidants may help stave off diseases of aging.

Free-radical damage has been implicated by some studies in diseases such as cancer, rheumatoid arthritis, cataracts, and cardiovascular disease. High levels of antioxidants—measured both in the diet and in the blood—have been associated with lower rates of these illnesses. "Whether we look at animal or cell culture studies, at population comparisons or intervention trials, we see the same relationship between antioxidants and protection from disease," says Dr. Jeffrey Blumberg, associate director of the U.S. Department of Agriculture Human Nutrition Research Center on Aging at Tufts University.

Moreover, he notes, it appears that the higher the antioxidant level, the lower the risk of disease, and vice-versa. In some studies of diet and cancer, for instance, people with the lowest intake of beta-carotene had up to seven times the

lung-cancer risk of those with the highest intake. In other reports, people with the diets richest in vitamin C were at the lowest risk for cancer of the stomach, oral cavity, and esophagus. And in a large study of 16 European populations, there was a strong correlation between high blood levels of vitamin E and a lower risk of death from coronary disease.

The next step is to give volunteers antioxidants in experimental programs and see whether their rates of disease are lower than average. Many such trials, including a dozen sponsored by the National Cancer Institute, are now attempting to provide that link.

The Physicians Health Study, a major ongoing project administered by Harvard Medical School, recently turned up an unexpected, hopeful finding about beta-carotene and heart disease—a finding the researchers stumbled on while testing beta-carotene as a cancer preventive. The investigators gave beta-carotene to half of the 22,000 physicians in the study. After six years, the researchers found that in a subgroup of 333 men who had signs of coronary disease before entering the study, those receiving beta-carotene experienced half as many cardiovascular "events" such as heart attack and stroke. It's premature to conclude that beta-carotene protects the heart, but the study offers a tantalizing lead for further testing.

aging. But first she was seen by Dr. Pavel Yutsis, a Brooklyn, N.Y., physician with whom Dr. Dilman is currently affiliated. Dr. Yutsis's specialty is clinical ecology, the study of disease due to "chemical hypersensitivity"—a field based on principles the American Medical Association and the American College of Physicians consider unproven.

The reporter (whose affiliation with CONSUMER REPORTS was not disclosed) asked only about anti-aging treatment and offered no complaints. By the end of the first session, however, she had a tentative diagnosis of candida (yeast) infection and was warned about the mercury from her dental fillings. (For more on dental amalgams, see CONSUMER REPORTS,

May 1991.) She was also sold $125 worth of anti-aging nutritional supplements, conveniently stocked by Dr. Yutsis. And she was scheduled for a six-hour oral glucose-tolerance test for "metabolic dysfunction."

The test—involving hourly blood samples after ingestion of a bottle of glucose syrup—revealed a "problem": The patient's insulin level dur-

In another promising intervention study, at Tufts University, healthy elderly individuals given vitamin E supplements showed significant improvements in immune function, which typically declines with age.

How much is enough?

Even at this early stage, the evidence raises important questions about how much of those nutrients we need and the best way to get them. Traditionally, vitamins have been recommended in amounts sufficient to prevent deficiency diseases such as scurvy and rickets. Those levels, determined by a National Academy of Sciences committee, are the Recommended Dietary Allowances (RDAs).

While the RDAs vary by age and sex, the U.S. RDA—the number used on most food and supplement labels—gives the level that should be enough to prevent deficiency in most healthy people. The U.S. RDA for vitamin C is 60 milligrams; for vitamin E, 30 I.U. (international units). While there is no U.S. RDA for beta-carotene, the U.S. RDA for vitamin A is 5000 I.U.—which can also be provided by about six milligrams of beta-carotene.

Current work on antioxidants suggests to some researchers that doses higher than the RDAs may be best for disease prevention. Most clinicians advise that we get those extra nutrients from our diets, because most studies have examined antioxidants in foods rather than supplements. "We know that vegetables high in beta-carotene are protective, but we don't know if the benefit is from the beta-carotene or some other component," explains Dr. Judith Hallfrish, research leader of the carbohydrate nutrition lab at the U.S. Department of Agriculture.

Loading up on fruits and vegetables is certainly good advice. Yellow and green leafy vegetables, such as carrots, sweet potatoes, squash, cantaloupe, spinach, and broccoli, are rich in beta-carotene; green leafy ones are also high in vitamin E. Good sources of vitamin C include citrus fruits and juices, strawberries, broccoli, brussels sprouts, and sweet red peppers.

The Dietary Guidelines for Americans, a joint effort of the Department of Agriculture and Health and Human Services, recommends at least three daily servings of vegetables and two of fruit. By one estimate, those intakes can provide as much as two to four times the U.S. RDAs for vitamins E and C, plus five or six milligrams of beta-carotene. However, some researchers believe even those levels are too low to afford optimal protection from disease.

Moreover, for most Americans, obtaining those nutrients from food alone would entail a profound dietary change. In one large national food-consumption survey, only 9 percent of participants met the fruit and vegetable guidelines cited above. Other surveys indicate a substantial gap between the typical daily intake of antioxidants and the levels Dr. Blumberg estimates may be optimal for disease prevention, based on the scientific literature. The average intake of beta-carotene is approximately two milligrams, well below the 25-mg level that he believes may be protective and that other researchers are using in clinical trials. The average intake of vitamin C, about 100 mg, is also well below the 500 mg Blumberg says may be optimal.

It's virtually impossible to get what appears to be an optimal dose of vitamin E—between 100 I.U. and 400 I.U. daily—by diet alone. In some population studies, notes Dr. Blumberg, individuals with the lowest risk of disease had blood levels of vitamin E high enough to suggest they were taking supplements.

"It may be true you can get the RDAs if you improve your diet," says Dr. William Pryor, a biochemist at Louisiana State University, Baton Rouge, and a prominent free-radical researcher. "But if you believe pharmacologic levels of vitamins can protect against disease, you're talking about supplements."

What to do?

A growing number of researchers now believe that, in addition to loading your diet with fruits and vegetables, taking antioxidant pills may be a reasonable move. Even the relatively high doses used by these scientists appear to be safe; the levels of vitamin C, vitamin E, and beta-carotene they consider optimal have not been associated with adverse effects. (In contrast, higher doses of vitamin C—more than 1000 milligrams a day—may cause diarrhea and other problems. And high doses of some other vitamins, notably vitamin A and vitamin D, have been shown to cause harm.)

As for price, an RDA-level multivitamin and mineral supplement, plus additional doses of vitamins E and C and beta-carotene, totals about a quarter a day.

Nevertheless, CU's medical consultants are not yet ready to recommend supplements for the general population. No one has yet proven the theory that antioxidants slow aging and fight disease by protecting the body from free radicals, although evidence is accumulating. Very few studies so far have examined the effects of supplement intake directly, and prospective clinical trials are still essential.

In addition, there's the nagging fact that the vitamin industry remains completely unregulated: No Government safeguard guarantees that the doses in pills match what's promised on the label. Researchers have found many vitamin supplements contain lower doses than the label claims.

---

ing the test, while well within the normal range, was high by the two doctors' standards. So was her blood-sugar level. According to Dr. Dilman's theory of aging, increases in insulin and glucose account in part for the decline in immune function that occurs with advancing years. Moreover, immune-system decline influences overall aging and the incidence of age-related disease.

"Your health is great," said Dr. Dilman, "but your insulin level shows you have started to age." Ordinarily, he said, he treats immune-system aging with phenformin, a glucose-lowering drug not available in the U.S. (It was taken off the market in 1977 after it was found to produce dangerous levels of lactic acid in diabetics; Dilman claims he no longer gives it to people at risk.) This time, instead, the doctors prescribed a form of the B-vitamin niacin.

CU's medical consultants find little basis for such anti-aging testing and treatment, which cost our reporter $650. The six-hour glucose tolerance test has been all but abandoned by physicians as an artificial stress that sheds little light on how glucose is naturally metabolized. Moreover, the test was improperly administered and used capillary blood (obtained by finger-stick), which gives a less accurate reading than blood from a vein. In a subsequent three-hour glucose-tolerance test administered by our senior medical consultant, the staffer showed no indication of troubled glucose metabolism. A good thing, too: Niacin has no known glucose-lowering effect.

Most doctors in this country who are familiar with Dr. Dilman's theory consider it intriguing, but no more. It is virtually untested in healthy people and, in our opinion, is not ready for prime-time patient care.

Who's minding the store?

The popularity of life-extension potions—whether obtained through the mail, in a health-food store, or through a doctor's prescription— sends a collective shudder through scientists doing research on aging. "Peculiar things happen when you dump chemicals in your body," warns Caleb Finch, professor in the neurobiology of aging at the University of Southern California. "Each has its own effect, and there's no way to predict the interactions or the long-term consequences."

Despite the potential for harm, the U.S. Food and Drug Administration has paid scant attention to life-extension products because, under existing law, few of them are legally "drugs." A substance becomes a drug, as defined by law, when its marketer claims a therapeutic effect for it. That's why most products available in health-food stores are labeled only as a "dietary supplement." Smart marketers have learned to place their health claims elsewhere, in pamphlets stacked nearby or in books placed conveniently for browsing.

The exuberant prose of some life-extension catalogs may seem like a clear case of health peddling. But the FDA must prove in court that the distributor of the product actually made a specific claim, sometimes a difficult task. And even in the clearest cases, the agency has held back.

"Anti-aging claims are frankly not a very high priority in our health-fraud arena," acknowledges Daniel L. Michels, director of the office of compliance at the FDA's Center for Drug Evaluation and Research. Products making false claims for cancer, heart disease, or AIDS are more likely to face regulatory action, because of the risk that patients will use them in place of proven therapies.

Coenzyme Q10 and ginseng, both popular with longevity buffs, have faced FDA sanctions because they were sold with specific health claims beyond the anti-aging promise. But the agency can target only one offending distributor at a time. Both compounds are still available, marketed by companies other than those originally targeted by the FDA.

Strict adherence to FDA regulations would place many more products at risk. Any nutritional claim— even instructions to "use as a nutritional supplement"—can be deemed "false and misleading" if the substance isn't recognized as having nutritional value. Coenzyme Q10, bee pollen, and superoxide dismutase fall into that category. Other substances—notably, some amino acids touted as growth-hormone releasers—have been approved as food additives but not as freestanding products. Observes an FDA spokesman: "It's safe to say that many items on health food store shelves aren't authorized to be on the market. But neither have they been challenged."

Adding life to years

Beyond drugs, supplements, treatments, and the marketing hype, a major scientific question remains unanswered: Can *any* intervention slow the body's basic aging process?

The free-radical theory, like some others, holds that aging is the result of random damage caused by the environment, lifestyle factors, and our own internal workings—a process of cellular wear and tear that, presumably, could someday be slowed down. But there are also signs that the aging process is influenced by a genetic program that may be difficult to change.

Researchers who favor the genetic view are trying to understand just how the body might be programmed to age. Some are looking for answers in the immune system, whose function declines with age. In another approach, Dr. Richard Cutler, a research chemist at the National Institute on Aging, has postulated "longevity determinant genes" that control production of free-radical-quenching enzymes—a marriage of the wear-and-tear and genetic theories of aging.

Ultimately, the various theories may be integrated into a comprehensive understanding of how aging occurs. But even if that happens, few researchers expect in the near future to be able to increase the maximum human lifespan—the theoretical limit for the species, the greatest age that a person living under ideal conditions would be able to reach. (For human beings, maximum lifespan is estimated at 110 to 120 years.)

While we may be unable to extend lifespan, we can improve life *expectancy*—the average age that a person in a given time and place, like late-20th-century America, can expect to reach. One approach is to develop better ways to prevent and treat the diseases that come with aging. Preventing age-related diseases—including chronic, disabling conditions such as arthritis—would also extend what gerontologists call the "healthspan," the years of vim and vigor. Ultimately, a better basic understanding of how the body ages should help extend both life expectancy and healthspan.

Gerontologists predict that the next decade or two will bring advances that allow us to better weather the vagaries of age. Many post-menopausal women already use estrogen replacement to prevent debilitating bone loss and reduce the risk of heart disease. (See CONSUMER REPORTS, September 1991.) The restitution of other dwindling hormones and enzymes could improve the health of minds, muscles, and joints, preventing many disabling conditions and enhancing the quality of our later years.

Meanwhile, you can maximize your shot at longevity by following familiar risk-reduction strategies: Eat a well-balanced, low-fat, high-carbohydrate diet, exercise regularly, refrain from smoking and alcohol abuse, and avoid obesity.

Some of those tactics produce the same effects claimed for life-extension products. Aerobic exercise, for instance, has been shown to build muscle effectively even in elderly people, without the potential side effects of human growth hormone. A diet high in fruits and vegetables will give you plenty of antioxidants.

Research into the aging process may one day find a true way to turn back the hands of time. Meanwhile, a prudent diet and exercise program now might just keep you around long enough to benefit.

Successful aging Volunteers in a National Institute on Aging study show milder age-related changes than expected. Researchers think this may be because they are unusually health-and-fitness conscious. Men in this study also live eight years longer on average than a comparable group of white American males.

Exercise Isn't Just For Fun

Study after study showing benefits even for the very old

Only one older person out of four exercises regularly or maintains anything like the level of physical activity recommended by specialists on aging. Yet study after study shows the positive health effects of regular physical activity—even for the very old.

Exercising for a half hour twice a week significantly increased the health and mobility of men and women with serious chronic ailments in a program and study conducted by University of Michigan public health specialists. All participants were deemed at high risk for placement in nursing homes.

Most of the 75 men and women in the study were overweight and had never exercised regularly. All but a few were over 75 years of age.

Arthritis, hypertension, heart disease and diabetes were among the health problems—all of them worsened by inactivity—that the men and women in the study suffered from. Many reported at least three chronic health problems, the University of Michigan School of Public Health researchers said.

Easy to Master

The exercises employed were gentle and easy to master. They included neck and shoulder rolls, spinal twists and side stretches, arm and leg flexes and extensions, and pelvis rocks. While seated on chairs, participants leaned backward and forward to flex abdominal muscles. Slow deep-breathing exercises were also part of the routine.

Even minor physical improvement often made major differences in the participants' functioning, the researchers said.

Participants said they could "get around and move faster" or "felt less stiff in the joints" or "had more energy and were able to walk longer distances." One woman said she could hold her cards better. Another said, "It has helped lift my spirits."

Reduces Heart Risks

Another study suggests that moderate exercise may be important in preventing and delaying the onset of heart diseases in older persons.

Heart disease occurred later and less frequently in the group of older persons who exercised than in the non-exercising control group in a 2-year study conducted by the Medical College of Pennsylvania. A total of 184 persons were included in the trial, all of them healthy non-exercisers previously.

About 800,000 Americans over age 65 die annually from major cardio-vascular diseases, the nation's leading cause of death.

The medical college estimates that about 27 percent of older Americans exercise regularly. A 1990 goal of 50 percent has been set by the U.S. Public Health Service (PHS) for all ages of the population.

At Duke University Medical Center, supervised exercise programs play a key role in intercepting the downward health spiral of persons suffering from chronic lung disease such as emphysema, bronchitis and asthma.

"Many people with chronic lung disease descend to their level of breathlessness," said Neil MacIntyre, M.D., director of Duke's Comprehensive

From *Aging*, No. 362, 1991, pp. 37-40. © 1991 by the Administration on Aging, Washington, DC. Reprinted by permission.

RESOURCES FOR Shaping Up

TV Helps

Over the past few years, exercise programs for older persons have been getting increasing amounts of broadcast time.

Billie Kirpich's series of half-hour programs was one of the groundbreakers in this field. Called **Exercise with Billie**, the 12-part series was developed by the Dade County Area Agency on Aging and distributed to 185 educational television stations nationwide in 1987. The programs start with exercises that home-bound elderly persons can do while seated, gradually working up to others that can be done standing.

Kirpich is a professional dancer in the senior citizen age bracket who says, "People were designed to move and keep active." She sees exercise as a gateway to other activities—"discussing, socializing, writing, getting involved in literature and history, where older people are finding they can do more than anyone imagined."

Last summer, her new 12-part *Exercise with Billie* series began to be aired by a still larger number of educational and public broadcasting stations. And a 1-hour video cassette of five progressive sessions is now available from Exercise with Billie, 20 Island Ave., Suite 1418, Miami Beach, FL, 33139 at $29.95 plus $2.50 shipping.

Other exercise programs for senior citizens have begun to show up in some video stores, to fill the demand of seniors who have become aware of the benefits of exercise. Two popular ones are:

Angela Lansbury's Positive Moves, 50 mins., which presents warm-ups and exercises that beginners will find easy to follow, and, *Richard Simmons and the Silver Foxes*, 60 mins., a classic beginner's aerobic workout involving celebrity parents Jackie Stallone, Sal Pacino, Harry Hoffman and Pauline Fawcett.

Chair Exercises

Other videos for more specialized use include the following:

Armchair Fitness, has three 20-minute stretching and strengthening low-impact aerobic workouts of increasing difficulty, set to music, all together on one cassette. They can be performed sitting erect in a chair. Leader's and user's guide included, for $39.95 plus $2.50 shipping from CC-M Productions, P.O. Box 15707, Chevy Chase, MD 20825-1707.

Senior Shape-Up is a 50-minute program designed to improve flexibility, coordination and cardiovascular endurance, choreographed to old favorites and show tunes. It includes both chair and standing exercises. Video VHS and audio cassette versions are available for $22.95 which includes shipping, from Yablon, Inc., P.O. Box 7475, Steelton, PA 17113.

ACE-Aerobic Chair Exercises is designed for frail persons or those using wheelchairs and persons with arthritis or cardiovascular conditions. It is $22.95 shipping included from Yablon, Inc., address given above.

Three exercise videos for seniors from Terra Nova Films are **Arthritis Exercise, Senior Shape Up,** and **Tai Chi**. The arthritis tape, developed with guidance from the Arthritis Foundation, helps take each joint through a full range of motion. Movements are designed for all arthritis sufferers, from those with infrequent pain and stiffness to the chronically disabled. The price of the 35-minute cassette is $79.95, rental $55. The shape-up tape is a combination workout consisting of 20 minutes sitting and 20 minutes standing exercises for flexibility, strength-building, endurance, coordination and balance. The Tai Chi cassette presents some basic movements of the art of exercise, meditation and defense through the experience of seniors, in a 45-minute tape produced by White Crane Senior Center. The Tai Chi and shape-up tapes are $89.95 each, $55 for rental from Terra Nova at 9848 S. Winchester Ave., Chicago, IL 60643, phone 312-881-8491.

Manuals for Leaders

Elder Fit is a 66-page guide to comprehensive exercise and fitness programs for older adults. It includes instructions for eight sessions of chair exercises, standing exercises and dance activities, as well as notes on precautions to be taken, evaluation procedures and equipment resources. Edited by Diane Penner, it is published by the American Alliance for Health, Physical Education, Recreation and Dance (AAHPERD). Eighty senior centers run by the New York City Office for the Aging have implemented the *Elder Fit* program as part of their Project Stay Well. The book can be ordered at $13.95 by calling 800-321-0789. Other books from the Alliance include **Mature Stuff: Physical Activity for the Older Adult**, a 245-page update of health and exercise related knowledge for older adults, with new ideas for fitness program leaders and participants. It is $30 plus shipping from the 800 number above.

Reach For It is an expanded second edition of a handbook of health, exercise and dance for older adults by University of Nebraska aging specialists David E. Corbin, Ph.D., and Josie Metal-Corbin, M.Ed. Its 324 pages contain new chapters on nutrition, sexuality, drugs, the aging body and water exercises, and include sample medical forms and fitness assessments as well as updated information on audio-visual programs and publications. The price is $29.95, shipping included, from Eddie Bowers Publishing Co., 2600 Jackson St., Dubuque, IA 52001.

Pulmonary Rehabilitation Program. "When they feel breathless, they reduce their activity even more, which in turn lowers their level of breathlessness. It's a vicious downhill cycle. But if you can intercept the downward spiral and increase the level of activity, their breathlessness becomes less noticeable and easier to cope with," he said. At the conclusion of the hospital-based program, each patient gets an individual exercise "prescription" to follow at home, building on the progress achieved in the program.

About two-thirds of the patients in the Duke program maintained or increased their functional abilities, and their scores of psychological tests stayed the same or increased, MacIntyre said. The report covered about 400 patients.

Dramatic differences in death rates have been found between physically fit women with blood pressure below 120 **and women in the lowest physical fit**ness level with diastolic resting blood pressure above 140, in research reported by the Journal of the American Medical Association.

The relative death risk of women in the group with the highest blood pressure and lowest fitness is rated 43.4 times greater—4,338 percent higher—than for the high-fitness, low blood pressure group. The study was based on data from more than 13,000 women, and it was published in the November 3, 1989 issue of the Journal.

Fewer Hip Fractures

Older people who engage in active exercise one or more hours a day have about half the risk of hip fracture as older people who exercise less than a half hour daily or not at all. This was among the findings of a University of Southern California study begun in 1981, of the life-style practices of 13,649 men and women living in Leisure World, a retirement community in Lagura Hills, Calif.

The findings on hip fractures, which were 40% less likely in women who did active exercise daily, were reported in the January, 1991 issue of *Epidemiology*. Identified as active exercise were such activities as swimming, bik-

ing, tennis, jogging, vigorous walking, dancing and indoor exercise programs. Less vigorous activities such as golfing, gardening and household chores don't substantially reduce the risk of hip fractures, the findings suggest.

Evaluation of other risk factors showed that cigarette smokers had a significantly increased risk of hip fracture (which disappeared in ex-smokers) and that women who were taking estrogen had a lowered risk of fracture.

Promotes Mental Health

The Public Health Service recommends regular physical exercise not only as heart disease and cancer prevention but also in delaying the onset or preventing hypertension, obesity, osteoporosis, diabetes and some mental health problems. It may also reduce the incidence of stroke and help to maintain the mobility and independence of older people, the PHS's Office of Disease Prevention and Health Promotion states.

Aerobic exercise improved cardiorespiratory fitness, lowered cholesterol and increased bone mineral content in older men and women studied in 1989

by Duke University Medical Center and North Carolina Spine Center.

Participants did aerobics for 60 minutes three times a week over a 4-month period. At the end of the study the participants reported that they had more energy and endurance and were sleeping better. They also reported better family relations, better sex life, less loneliness, improved mood and greater self-confidence.

Physical Exam

Although most older people are able to participate, to some extent, in a structured, progressive exercise program, they should have a physical examination before beginning, advises Richard Lampman, director of the University of Michigan Medical Center's Cardiac Fitness and Exercise Research program. The examination should include a stress test or exercise tolerance test, to gauge current level of fitness, and an evaluation of medication being used, to determine whether they should be altered to allow for increased activity levels. Blood testing for glucose and cholesterol levels should also be part of the comprehensive examination.

Why We Get Old

In the grand scheme of things, we humans are a lot like the Energizer bunny. As the only species whose life span is known to extend decades past the reproductive years, we keep going and going as other creatures fall by the wayside, succumbing to predators or disease while still in their prime. Yet such longevity is a mixed blessing. By outliving our biological utility, we are subject to aging, a process that experts grimly define as "the autonomous deterioration that adults undergo with increasing chronological age."

Our inexorable decline is compounded by the anguish of recognition. Although the old gray mare ain't what she used to be, she isn't aware of it. Humans alone are thought to be cognizant of aging and its physical effects.

Until the late nineteenth century, even that awareness didn't seem to bother us much. Scientists gave little thought to the aging process because they were more concerned with getting people to — rather than beyond — middle age. It was not until the early 1900s, when antibiotics and maternity care pushed the average life span into the sixth decade, that gerontology emerged as a new scientific discipline.

Gerontology was dedicated to exploring all aspects of the aging process and was expected to help physicians distinguish normal aging from the effects of illness. It has only recently begun to do so. Although gerontologists are still debating the biological underpinnings of growing older, they agree that the major organ systems change in certain ways as a natural consequence of age. Researchers attribute many of these alterations to the effects of cell death.

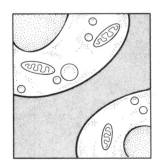

The cell
Before 1960 most scientists thought that the body itself imposed a death sentence on the cell — and that, once freed from its corporeal confines, the cell could live and divide indefinitely.

In the 1960s biologist Leonard Hayflick pulled the rug out from under this theory by showing that normal cells growing under stringent laboratory conditions divide a finite number of times and then die off. He also found that fibroblasts (connective-tissue cells) extracted from fetal tissue divided twice as many times as those from adults' organs, an observation that other investigators later verified.

Scientists generally accept the notion that the life span of a cell, like most bodily functions, is genetically programmed and environmentally influenced. However, they are still looking for the genes and the environmental agents responsible.

Among the prime suspects are reactive oxygen species, including oxygen free radicals (OFRs). The products of a variety of chemical reactions, OFRs are oxygen molecules or compounds in an incomplete state. Because electrons are missing from their outer shell, they operate with the zeal of a roué in a singles bar, eagerly seeking to pair with the first available molecule from any part of the cell. This attachment is often destructive to the radical's chosen mate, which is kept from performing its designated function in the cell.

Fortunately, the cell has its own network of molecular bouncers called antioxidants, substances entrusted with the task of apprehending OFRs and inactivating them. Some scientists believe that this network becomes less effective as the cell ages, allowing more OFRs to disrupt cellular processes. Others think that the network may simply become overworked, causing a cumulative energy drain on the cell.

In addition to the disorderly conduct of OFRs, the normally peaceful glucose molecules also start to act up in aging cells. They mimic OFRs' style, but with a strong preference for proteins. Once formed, a glucose-protein union is almost impossible to tear asunder. The bulky complex lolls about, obstructing cellular business and successfully resisting the enzymes dispatched to break it up.

These obstreperous molecules aren't the only players in the drama of cellular decline. As the cell ages, its housekeeping goes to pot. Stores of sugars, fats, proteins, and RNA (the molecule entrusted with translating the genetic message into proteins) increase, while the amount of DNA (which programs cellular activity) shrinks. The mitochondria (the cells' powerplants) become misshapen, and the number of ribosomes, which are instrumental in protein manufacture, decreases.

As form declines, so does function. Mitochondrial slowdowns produce cellular brownout, and molecular debris accumulates. Some scientists now suspect that in a cleanup frenzy, lysosomes (which break down waste products) digest proteins faster than the cells can make them.

The death toll mounts as a result of these intracellular goings-on. On average, by age 75 the number of cells in the human body has declined by as much as 30% — and has thus exacted a toll on every major system.

The skin

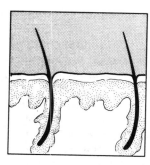

The creases and lesions that the cosmetics commercials dub "age lines" and "age spots" are actually caused by ultraviolet radiation rather than the passing years. In studying buttock skin that has not been exposed to the sun, dermatologists have concluded that "photoaging" and normal aging are two different processes, and that the latter is the kinder and gentler of the two.

That's not to say that protected skin gets off scot-free. Aging takes a toll on the dermis (the second layer of skin) as the number of fibroblasts, its principal constituent cell, declines. Molecules of collagen, the connective protein that forms the dermis's supportive matrix, link together in rigid rods. And the fine skeins of elastic fibers that criss-cross the dermis are replaced by thicker tubules. As a result, the skin loses the resilience of youth, eventually taking on the appearance of tissue paper that has been crumpled and ironed flat.

The nervous system

By age 30, the brain begins to lose thousands of neurons a day. When these cells die, they are not replaced. Thus, by the time we reach 80, our brains will weigh about 7% less than they did in our prime. Some areas of the brain shrink more than others, with the cerebral cortex (the gray matter that handles higher mental skills, behavior, and perception) losing as much as 45% of its cells.

The production of neurotransmitters (chemical messengers that carry impulses to and from cells in the brain) also slows down. With fewer agents available to carry information, translating the brain's message into action takes longer. That's why we may find that we don't volley a tennis ball — or a witty rejoinder — as readily as we once did.

A loss of peripheral nerves blunts our sense of touch and our perceptions of heat and cold and decreases our sensitivity to pain. And we may become dizzy or find it hard to keep our balance, perhaps because of changes in the inner ear.

The cardiovascular system

The heart is the only organ that grows bigger with age. But bigger is not better in this case: enlargement occurs because as the cells of the myocardium (cardiac muscle) die, they are replaced by fat and connective tissue. The myocardium loses some of its contractile might and some of its ability to relax. During exercise, contractions become less frequent as well as less forceful. The heart loses about 1% of its reserve pumping capacity each year after age 30, reducing the amount of oxygen delivered to the tissues by red blood cells.

Red cells and other blood components are deployed less efficiently because the vessel walls, thickened with rigid collagen deposits, lose their ability to dilate and contract in response to the heart's pumping action.

The respiratory system

As the lungs age, they become less elastic and are no longer able to inflate or deflate completely. They can't take in as much oxygen, so there's less available for passing red cells to snatch up and carry through the circulatory system to needy tissues.

The linking of collagen molecules (similar to what is happening in the aging skin) and the loss of muscle fibers render the chest wall and the diaphragm weaker and more rigid, making it harder to cough deeply enough clear mucus from the lungs.

The musculo-skeletal system

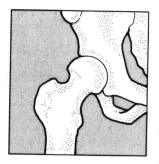

While other systems are tooling down, vigorous remodeling continues in the skeleton. Bone consists mainly of a collagen matrix inlaid with crystals of calcium and phosphorus. It is continually maintained by two teams of cells: osteoclasts cart off old bone, and osteoblasts replace it with new.

The volume of new bone formed depends on the body's demands for skeletal support. When weight-bearing requirements decrease because someone is confined to bed, dispatched by NASA into space, or inactive, the unneeded skeletal calcium is excreted in urine. Calcium may also be stolen from bone by other tissues that need it for normal cell maintenance.

Both men and women tend to lose bone mass as they age. The process usually begins earlier and proceeds more rapidly in women due to a reduction in estrogen levels as menopause nears. Although no one knows exactly how estrogen acts on bone maintenance, it is thought to play a role in calcium metabolism.

Muscle mass and strength also decline, due to a loss of muscle fibers and the nerves that stimulate them. There is some evidence that, at least in men, a natural decline in human growth hormone levels may accelerate muscle attrition (see *Harvard Health Letter,* June 1992).

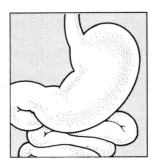

The digestive system

The digestive system holds up better than most body systems. Like all muscular structures, though, the alimentary organs (esophagus, stomach, small intestine, and colon) lose tone with age. So the regular contractions that propel food through them become less frequent. The esophagus channels food into the stomach less speedily, and some research indicates that the stomach takes longer to process it.

Although the production of several digestive enzymes begins to decline in middle age, the loss is usually not great enough to have a noticeable effect. Some nutrients — such as calcium, vitamin B-12, and zinc — are not fully absorbed.

The other digestive organs also begin to slow down. The gallbladder becomes sluggish in releasing bile into the small intestine, increasing the likelihood of gallstones. The liver shrinks with age and receives a smaller blood supply than in earlier times. Although it still performs most of its vital functions, such as producing blood-clotting factors, as well as ever, it needs more time to metabolize drugs and alcohol.

The immune system

Immune function is hampered by the gradual degeneration of the thymus, a small gland in the neck once responsible for educating T-lymphocytes to coordinate the body's defense system. The thymus reaches its maximum size early in childhood, begins to shrink shortly after puberty, and virtually disappears by old age. As the gland fades away,

T-cells decline in number; the remaining ones don't function as well as their predecessors did.

B-lymphocytes, the other major immune players, also lose their edge. Each B-cell is trained to apprehend a particular molecular invader by means of a pincerlike molecule (an antibody) on its surface. Every time that adversary appears, the preprogrammed cell produces hundreds of identical copies bearing antibodies set to attack the invader. Both the capacity to form clones and the ability to release antibodies are diminished in the B-cells of an elderly immune system. Moreover, an increasing percentage of the antibodies that are produced are directed at the body's own tissues, raising the risk for autoimmune diseases such as arthritis.

The reproductive system

By middle age, a woman's reproductive clock is winding down. Her ovaries, which at birth contained about two million eggs, have resorbed or shed all but the last few. For reasons not fully understood, there is a growing risk that these eggs will contain the genetic defects responsible for Down's syndrome and other hereditary disorders.

Sex-hormone levels decline with age for both men and women. During menopause a woman's ovaries stop producing estrogen and progesterone. In men testosterone output diminishes steadily after age 65 or 70.

Changes in hormone balance are thought to be responsible for the enlargement of the prostate gland, which contributes most of the fluid in semen. As the prostate expands, it may press upon the urethra (the tube that carries urine from the bladder out through the penis), making urination more difficult.

Sperm production declines in tandem with testosterone levels, yet men may remain fertile well into old age. The semen of elders may not be the prized commodity it once was, however: recent research suggests that as men age, their sperm are more likely to carry certain genetic defects.

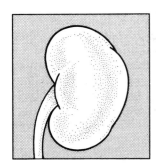

The excretory system

The gradual reduction of blood flow to the kidneys, coupled with a reduction in nephrons (filtering units), impairs the organs' ability to extract wastes from the blood and concentrate them into urine. Just when the kidneys require more water to excrete the same amount of waste, bladder capacity also declines.

Thus, the older we get, the more we appreciate having a bathroom right down the hall.

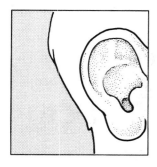

The sensory organs

As anyone beyond a certain age knows all too well, our five senses dim with the passing decades. In the eye, the lens is not as elastic and is thus less able to change focus as we redirect our gaze from distant to near objects. This condition, called presbyopia (from the Greek words for "elder" and "eye"), is what brings most of us to the ophthalmologist for reading glasses in middle age.

As it loses elasticity, the lens also becomes thicker, which decreases the efficiency of light transmission. The pupil, whose size is controlled by a doughnut-shaped sphincter muscle, expands less readily when ambient light dims. The amount of light reaching the retina is reduced as the diameter of the pupil narrows and the opacity of the lens increases. When the deep purple falls, older people may find it more frustrating than romantic.

Presbycusis (age-related hearing decline) is caused principally by the attrition of nerve cells that conduct sound signals to the brain. This first produces a gradual decline in the ability to hear high-pitched sounds and eventually makes lower frequencies harder to detect as well.

The sense of taste is also diminished by age. As the number of taste buds declines, our gustatory range narrows and we may no longer appreciate subtle flavors as keenly as we once did. Although no definitive studies have been conducted on the sense of smell in aging humans, biologists suspect that we may become similarly oblivious to delicate fragrances.

The endocrine system

And now the good news. Although hormone-secreting glands shrink as we grow older, their performance doesn't seem to be affected. Age alone does not perceptibly change our output of thyroid hormone, which regulates metabolism; adrenaline, which orchestrates the body's response to stress; or pituitary hormones, which stimulate the thyroid, adrenal glands, and ovaries. And the aging pancreas, which secretes insulin to regulate glucose metabolism, can respond to sudden increases in blood sugar as readily as a younger organ, even though a higher glucose level is required to jolt it into action.

Staving off senescence

The picture would be pretty bleak if all of our systems declined at the same rate. We'd find ourselves slouching into our sunset years, our wrinkled, fatty flesh hanging from our atrophied frames. Short of breath and faint of heart, we'd probably be too pooped to pursue any sensual pleasures we could still appreciate.

Fortunately, each system ages according to its own timetable, and these schedules vary dramatically from person to person. Nowhere is this variety more evident than at a 30-year high-school reunion, where the recipient of the "bald guy" trophy recounts his tennis triumphs to a bushy-haired classmate who has just received a new cardiac pacemaker.

While a full head of hair isn't an adequate trade-off for coronary disease, systems that age slowly can often compensate for those declining at a faster clip. For example, a durable digestive system may process calcium efficiently enough to ward off bone loss, and a good set of lungs can cover for a declining circulatory system.

Although we can't reverse the effects of age, we can avoid accelerating the process by taking the "wellness" mantra to heart. Avoid sun and cigarettes, limit alcohol and fat consumption, eat lots of vegetables, and embrace exercise.

The logic is simple. The sun's ultraviolet radiation exacerbates skin aging. Smoking speeds bone and lung deterioration. Excessive alcohol consumption disturbs metabolism. And fat promotes weight gain. On the other hand, vegetables are good sources of the antioxidant vitamins C and E and beta carotene. Aerobic exercise increases lung capacity, and weight-bearing activities enhance bone and muscle mass.

For the present, these commonsense guidelines for healthy aging seem to be the only points of medical accord. While much has been made of the fact that "undernourished" laboratory rats have extended life spans, there have been no studies to demonstrate whether the same is true for humans. Although research indicates that postmenopausal estrogen replacement averts osteoporosis, the benefits of that treatment may not outweigh its risks for every woman. And investigators have just begun to explore the effects of growth-hormone and antioxidant supplementation.

These days, there's a disingenuous ring to the familiar lament, "If I had only known I was going to live so long, I'd have taken better care of myself." Now that we know that we're likely to keep going and going — presumably well into our eighth decade — we can't plead ignorance any longer.

— *BEVERLY MERZ*

WHY WE WILL LIVE LONGER... AND WHAT IT WILL MEAN

The one-two punch of healthier habits and biomedical breakthroughs could push life expectancy past 90. Get ready for a brave new world.

Richard I. Kirkland Jr.

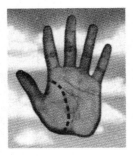

Hope I die before I get old.
PETE TOWNSHEND
1966

The generation that once rocked to that mocking line from the Who is within bifocal range of 50. And guess what? Baby-boomers have to find a new tune. The 76 million Americans born between 1946 and 1964 not only are the largest generation, but are set to become the longest-lived in U.S. history as well. No other change due in the 21st century will so profoundly alter the way we live.

This upheaval-in-the-making didn't begin with the boomers, of course. The two age cohorts just ahead of them will push the old limits too. In 1900, average life expectancy from birth in the U.S. was a mere 47 years. By 1970 it had climbed to around 71. Since then, while most of us were looking elsewhere, it has gone up again, to 76. To be precise, that's 72.7 years for American men and 79.6 for women.

Even if this remarkable upward trajectory ended tomorrow, more than half of you reading these words could still expect to live past 81. That's because the longer you live, the better your odds. But it's not going to flatten out. Among experts on aging, even the most conservative agree we should be able to add three or four years to life expectancy over the next five decades. Others think we can do far better than that. Says Dr. Edward Schneider, 53, who heads the Andrus Gerontology Center at the University of Southern California: "If we do things right over the next few decades, at least half the baby-boomers might expect to live into their late 80s and 90s."

A few wild-eyed optimists even contend that by cracking the secrets of our genetic code we can live much, much longer. For all you restless baby-busters and aspiring fortysomethings with one eye on the corner office, here's a terrifying illustration of the sort of paradigm-shattering change they have in mind. Four words: *100-year-old CEOs!*

How many oldsters? Social Security projections are the most conservative. Epidemiologist Jack Guralnik at the National Institute on Aging assumes recent big gains in life expectancy will continue. Kenneth Manton, a demographer at Duke University, thinks they may well accelerate.

REPORTER ASSOCIATE *Rosalind Klein Berlin*

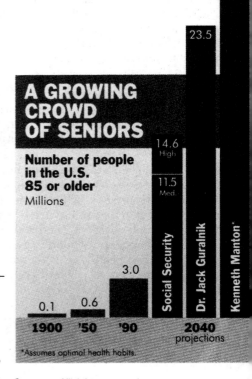

A GROWING CROWD OF SENIORS

Number of people in the U.S. 85 or older
Millions

1900	0.1
'50	0.6
'90	3.0
2040 (Social Security)	11.5 Med.
2040 (Dr. Jack Guralnik)	14.6 High / 23.5
2040 (Kenneth Manton*)	43.0

2040 projections

*Assumes optimal health habits.

Who's right? In FORTUNE's view, the way to bet is on lives that will increasingly stretch out toward 90 and beyond in the years ahead—with considerable potential on the upside. A host of consequences adhere to that extraordinary prospect. Many are already beginning to be felt, though the biggest shocks are a few decades away.

Among them: Inheritances will get smaller, as long-lived elders consume capital that once flowed to the next generation. (Priced a nursing home for your folks lately? One upscale nursing home in Westchester County, New York, prefers to see that Mom or Dad has $500,000 in liquid assets before it considers taking one of them in.) Extended and multiple careers will become the norm, and the prevailing retirement age (now around 60) will creep back toward 70 as a growing number of older workers choose—some from necessity, some for fulfillment—to remain in the labor force. When Social Security was enacted in 1935 and the retirement age was set at 65, average life expectancy was around 61. The system won't stay afloat unless it is rebuilt into a means-tested welfare program for only the poorest of the elderly.

Are we ready for this? Are you kidding? According to recent polls, most Americans do not expect to live into their 80s. So far, the age at which most of us retire continues to go down, not up. Most taxpayers are acutely aware that America's aging will impose a huge burden on Social Security—after all, isn't that one of the main reasons payroll taxes have been rising steadily since the late 1970s? What they don't realize—as the chart reveals—is that if life expectancy reaches 80 in the next few decades and keeps on climbing, Social Security's bean counters will have woefully underestimated the future size of America's older population. Richard Suzman, the respected chief of demography at the National Institute of Aging (NIA), believes that by 2040 the number of Americans over 85 could top 30 million, up from 3.3 million today.

For an upbeat glimpse of what could be in store, consider the long and still unfolding career of John Marks Templeton, 81: author (eight books), father (five children), grandfather (16 grandkids, so far), great-grandfather (two), and world-beating stock-picker. Sixteen months ago, after 53 years in the investment business, he finally retired, selling his wildly successful Templeton fund group and its $21 billion in assets under management to Franklin Resources of San Mateo, California, for $913 million. His share: $400 million.

Now the Tennessee-born Templeton,

who became a British citizen in 1963 after he moved permanently to Lyford Cay, Nassau, and collected a knighthood for his philanthropic work, jets around the globe supervising more than 30 charitable projects backed by the four foundations he has established. "I'm working as hard as I ever did," he reports, with no plans to slow down. Last year Templeton edited and contributed to a collection of essays, by various experts, called *Looking Forward: The Next Forty Years*. "It's such a joy to learn about the new things going on in the world," he says. "This is the most exciting era in history. I wake up every morning fairly sizzling with enthusiasm."

MOST OF US will enter our 80s with considerably less capital than Sir John—and simmering, not sizzling. But since most of us *will* enter them, we'd better start thinking hard about how we aim to spend that extra time. Because the whole world is rapidly aging, this adjustment will ultimately pose a global challenge. When it comes to average life expectancy, the U.S. is outpaced by more than 15 countries, led by Japan, where at birth it's now 79 years. Still, two things put America in the vanguard of the longevity revolution:

the unrivaled vigor and duration of its postwar birth explosion, which guarantees it an unrivaled cohort of octogenarians, nonagenarians, and centenarians four decades from now; and its role as planetary hotbed for the biomedical and genetic research that's likely to produce major breakthroughs in our ability to add years to life and—most important—quality to those extra years.

What are the advances that will make us live longer and healthier? They range from the marvelous to the mundane.

■ More targeted medical weaponry.
"Many who used to get sent to heart transplant centers can now be put on medical management and handled outside a hospital without surgery," says Kenneth Manton, director of Duke University's Center for Demographic Studies. "That's the difference biomedical research is delivering and will continue to deliver." No group will benefit from this difference more than older persons, since 80% of fatal heart attacks occur among those over 64 and 80% of cancers appear after age 50.

Take hypertension. The diuretics of the 1950s lowered blood pressure and deaths from cardiovascular disease by draining the body of salt. This often had nasty side ef-

Proof that pumping iron fights frailty: Mauro Rio, 94, works out daily in his South Boston apartment.

"If curing heart disease and cancer means we get to die of Alzheimer's, we'll look back on them as our friends."

fects, such as raising the risk of diabetes. Each subsequent advance in treatment—beta-blockers in the 1960s, calcium channel blockers in the 1970s, and so-called ACE inhibitors in the 1980s, which work by blocking the kidney's production of the hormone that causes blood vessels to constrict—has improved the treatment of hypertension with fewer side effects.

Like those first diuretics, most cancer treatments are still the medical equivalent of using carpet bombing rather than smart bombs. But over the next two decades, rather than blast patients with massive overdoses of radiation or chemotherapy—killing healthy cells as well as malignant ones—doctors will learn how to fire computer-designed compounds directly into affected organs. That should translate into lower doses and longer, higher-quality life.

■ Better brains through chemistry.

For most people, the greatest terror old age holds is the fear of losing one's mind. It's most cheering then to hear this prediction from Zaven Khachaturian, who directs the lion's share of the $200-million-a-year research program on Alzheimer's disease at the NIA: "Within six years we should come up with treatments that will slow the brain's deterioration enough to enable Alzheimer's victims to function for another decade. In ten to 15 years, we might even be able to prevent this disease."

According to the NIA, some four million Americans today are afflicted with Alzheimer's, a virulent form of dementia that riddles the brain with clumps of protein plaques and tangles and brings on a relentless slide into mental oblivion. This epidemic could explode as America ages. According to recent estimates, 6% of people ages 65 to 74 have the disorder, and nearly half of those over 85 show signs of it. More than 100,000 Americans die of Alzheimer's each year, putting it right up there with the nation's major killers: heart disease (800,000 annual deaths), cancer (200,000), and strokes (150,000). Lucky sufferers expire within five years; the unfortunate stay alive up to two decades. "If curing heart disease and cancer

means we get to stick around and die of Alzheimer's," says medical researcher Roderick Bronson of Tufts University, "we'll look back on them as our friends."

The war against Alzheimer's is progressing on two fronts. Warner-Lambert has just begun marketing Cognex, a limited treatment that works in a handful of cases and then succeeds only in allowing the patient to function for an extra six to nine months. But several major drugmakers, notably Bayer, are testing in animals a more effective second-generation treatment that works by blocking the accumulation in neurons of toxic levels of calcium—one of the ways those tangles are formed. Researchers in Sweden are even testing on humans what may become the third-generation treatment, compounds that stimulate nerve-cell growth.

Geneticists in the mid-1980s pinpointed the location of the genes connected to an inherited form of Alzheimer's, which tends to strike much earlier, in the 40s and 50s.

And last fall a team led by Dr. Allen Roses of Duke University Medical Center announced it had identified a gene—called ApoE 4 and ensconced on human chromosome 19—that is strongly linked with the onset of late-stage Alzheimer's. Doctors will use such genetic markers to identify people most at risk and start them on preventive treatments as these become available. Eventually, healthy nerve cells may be injected directly into the brain, where they will grow, make the right connections, and replace dead neurons. "That's pretty futuristic stuff," says Khachaturian. "But it's definitely coming down the pike, perhaps in 20 years."

Such treatments, along with new memory-enhancing drugs, would also benefit stroke victims and those suffering from spinal injuries or Parkinson's disease and other neurologic disorders. In the not-too-distant future, people may chew pills to fend off dementia the way middle-aged men now munch baby aspirin to prevent heart attacks.

■ Beefed-up bug fighters.

Body parts don't age at the same rate. But one universal characteristic of getting older—and the reason we become increasingly vulnerable to everything from cold viruses to cancer—is a steady falloff, starting around age 30, in the effectiveness of our immune systems. Part of the problem seems to reside in a class of lymphocytes, known as T-cells, that

Volunteerism's funny face: Jean Harper, 71 (middle), teaches juggling in New York City.

attack infected cells directly and also serve as messengers to mobilize the rest of the immune system. As we age, the number of T-cells produced by the thymus gland declines, while the percentage of them already in the bloodstream but no longer functioning rises. Getting rid of these so-called effete T-cells, one theory holds, should encourage the thymus to get cracking and put the immune system back in fighting trim.

Gerontologist Edward Schneider believes a drug to do that will be developed in five years—and he's hoping to get there first. Schneider and some colleagues launched a biotech startup, Rejuvon, last year and are currently chasing venture capital.

■ **Hormone cocktails.** Remember hormones? These are the body's chemical messengers that turn genes on or off and regulate how tissues and organs grow and repair themselves. They're also what, in our early teens, made our shoe sizes surge from eight to 11, our pores gush oil, and even not-so-close encounters with the opposite sex a dizzying experience.

As the years accumulate, many of us stop pumping out enough of this bodacious stuff. Levels of human growth hormone, which helps keep us lean as well as make us taller, decline with age in about half of all adults. Researchers have also learned that, just as women during menopause experience a sharp drop in production of the female sex hormone estrogen, most men aged 60 and older manufacture markedly lower amounts of the male sex hormone testosterone.

The linkage between hormone levels and health, though still poorly understood, is formidable. Estrogen replacement therapy dramatically slows the bone thinning that develops into osteoporosis and cripples millions of older women. It also significantly reduces in most females the risk of heart attack and stroke. In men, testosterone injections can strengthen muscles and counter anemia, while a related hormone, known as DHEA, has been shown in animal tests to revive aging immune systems and even deter cancer.

In the most dramatic display yet of hormonal firepower, Daniel Rudman of the Medical College of Wisconsin in 1990 injected human growth hormone into elderly men whose levels of it were unusually low. Within months their fat shrank by 14%, their lean body mass expanded by 9%, and their skin increased in thickness by 7%. The overall effect on physique, he reported, was equal to shedding ten to 20 years. These remark-

able results have since been confirmed by other researchers. They have also spawned a cottage industry of Mexican longevity clinics that supply American and European clients with doses of the high-priced drug, which costs $13,000 for a year's supply.

The real problem with hormone treatments, however, isn't their expense; it's their potentially devastating side effects. Use of growth hormone over long periods—and to be effective it must be taken continually, or else the magical results vanish in a Dorian Gray–style reversal—often results in carpal tunnel syndrome, other kinds of joint inflammation, and diabetes-like symptoms. Estrogen and testosterone may increase the risk of cancer in some recipients.

Still, as more research leads to a better understanding of what dosages are proper—and how best to deliver them—such therapies could become more widespread. Within five years Rudman believes that physicians may be allowed to use growth hormone for short-term therapies—to accelerate healing of wounds, say, or to enhance the ability of some underweight elderly to absorb nutrients. Further down the road, he says, older patients in 20 years may well visit doctors to have their hormone levels checked and get prescriptions for "custom-tailored cocktails" that will help them stay fit.

■ **New, improved, fat- and smoke-free lifestyles.** "No drug in current or prospective use holds as much promise for sustained health as a lifetime program of physical exercise," says Dr. Walter Bortz of Stanford University Medical School, a 20-miles-a-week jogger at age 63. That view, backed by a growing body of evidence, can no longer be dismissed as the raving of fanatics on perpetual endorphin overdoses. "Exercise is one of the real breakthrough areas in the research," agrees Dr. John Rowe, 49, president of Manhattan's Mount Sinai Medical School and Hospital, who was a 1988 recipient of a MacArthur Foundation grant to develop ways to encourage successful aging.

Studies have shown, for example, that in addition to its familiar cardiovascular benefits, working out stimulates the body's production of growth hormone and improves the functioning of the immune system, especially among older people. Says Bortz: "Exercise for young people is an option, but for older people it is an imperative."

In addition to lacing on those jogging shoes, don't neglect to eat your spinach—and your carrots, kale, broccoli, oranges, and bananas as well, all of which are high

in vitamins E and C, as well as beta-carotene. Why? It has long been known that as the human body merrily goes about its basic business of converting glucose and oxygen to energy, it spews out a torrent of so-called free-radical molecules. These cause damage to proteins, membranes, and ultimately the DNA in cell mitochondria—the place where the energy we run on is generated. Free radicals have been implicated in many of the changes that accompany aging and appear to play a role in cancer, arteriosclerosis, cataracts, and nerve damage. To defend against such wanton self-destruction, however, the body also produces antioxidants that react with and disarm free radicals. Some are enzymes. The other natural antioxidants are, yes, good old vitamins C and E, and beta-carotene. (For more on what *you* can do to live long and well, see box on next page.)

A final arresting fact for anyone still skeptical about the efficacy of this get-a-lifestyle mumbo jumbo: Since the mid-1960s, the death rate from heart disease in the U.S. has plummeted by 50%. And do we owe this boon to the huge increase over that time in the balloon angioplasties and triple bypasses performed by gifted, dedicated, and highly compensated surgeons? No. Instead, almost every medical and epidemiological expert credits three sweeping changes. First and most important is the sharp decline in smoking—the single most effective, legal way to shorten your life, and now practiced by only 25% of the adult population, vs. 40% in 1965. Second is the rise in exercise, especially among men. Third are dietary changes that have lowered the typical American's cholesterol count.

■ **Putting on new pairs of genes.** "I'm not interested in adding three or four years to life expectancy," says evolutionary biologist Michael Rose, 38, a professor at the University of California's Irvine campus. "I'm interested in 200-year-old humans."

Say what? Since our ancestors got up off their four feet a couple of million years ago, the longest any human has ever lived, depending on which old coot or cootess you believe, is between 115 and 120 years. That barrier is our species' maximum life span. Breaking it, as Rose contemplates, will require more than simply fighting the manifold disorders of aging one disease at a time, as we now do. It will take nothing less than what gerontologists call "a magic bullet," a fundamental assault at the molecular level on the upward sweep of mortality itself.

If such a bullet is ever made, genetic engineering will supply the ordnance. Consid-

HOW YOU CAN LIVE WELL AND LONG

First, a brief disclaimer from one of the country's top experts on aging. "Life's a crapshoot," says the NIA's Dick Sprott. "There aren't any guarantees."

The odds get better, though, the longer you stick around. Based on current mortality rates, if you're 40 and male, you're already a good bet to make it to 75, three years beyond an-American's average life expectancy at birth. A man who's 65—an age more than 70% of the population now reaches—can expect to live until 80. Women can expect to make 85.

The real way to beat the house is by extending your health span, not just your life span. Personal example: My paternal grandfather quit professional life at 60 to go home to Mississippi and farm. He worked hard and happily every day of the rest of his life and died at 82 of a heart attack while picking his beloved blueberries. My maternal grandmother, on the other hand, lives on at 92 in a north Alabama nursing home. For the past six years she's been unable to recall—within seconds after we depart—whether anyone has visited her. Grandpa won, hands down.

But isn't our fate simply in our genes? No. It's true that a strong genetic predisposition to, say, lung cancer can bring you down no matter how virtuous your habits, just as the reverse may permit you to puff three stogies a day until age 100. But much recent research, notably a study of Danish identical twins by American demographer James Vaupel, suggests that genetic factors account for no more than 30% of variance in life spans. What *you* do matters.

So what's the program? Rule No. 1: Don't smoke, or if you do, quit. A 40-year-old male with a pack-a-day cigarette habit can expect to die seven years before his nonsmoking peer. Anyone who still thinks this issue is debatable is smoking something, all right—but it's not tobacco.

Next, fasten that seat belt. Doing this regularly extends life expectancy by 69 days. That may not sound like a lot, but it's one of the most significant remaining ways to improve your odds on longevity. By comparison, a healthy man at 40 who lowers his cholesterol count from 280 to 240 adds, on average, just seven days to his life.

So if the prospect of too much virtue makes you sick, stick with the steak and hold the smokes. And while you're at it, have a glass of wine. Heck, have two! Heavy boozing is definitely not recommended, but various studies conclude that people who have one to two drinks daily live longer than those who never drink at all.

If you're over 40, you should also consider consuming a little extra vitamin E. Physicians have been reluctant to endorse nutrient supplements, fearing that Americans would assume they could pop a few pills and then keep pigging out on Cheetos and French fries. It *is* important to eat right. Your best guide is the bushman's diet now promoted by the U.S. government: loads of fruit (four servings daily) and vegetables (five), plus lots of whole grains and some lean meat. Even that, though, won't deliver the high levels of vitamin E that have been linked in epidemiological studies to lower risk of heart disease, and shown by scientists with the Department of Agriculture's research center on aging and nutrition at Tufts University to improve functioning of the immune system in older men and women.

How much E is enough? Official guidelines are still a few years away. But many experts interviewed by FORTUNE have, in the past year or so, begun taking a daily pill containing 400 international units—more than 12 times what's in the typical multivitamin. Some also take 15 to 25 milligrams of beta-carotene and 1,000 milligrams of vitamin C—though the consensus on their efficacy is less strong.

Finally, there's exercise. Yes, you need it, and, no, you don't have to train for a triathlon to reap large benefits. Half an hour of vigorous walking three times a week—shoot to cover a mile in under 15 minutes—can cut the risk of heart attack, stroke, diabetes, and even cancer by 55%. You might also consider a little twice-weekly weight-lifting. Aerobics has many virtues, but it doesn't fight the fall in bone density and rise in muscle weakness that accompany aging.

Most important, and contrary to received medical opinion until fairly recently, the case for working out strengthens as we grow older. One Stanford University study tracked the health of some 500 runners ages 50 and over against a comparable group of nonrunners. When the eight-year study began, the runners had a 2-to-1 advantage over the others in various measures of health. At the end, their edge had increased to five times. The gap was widest among 75- to 79-year olds. As Bob Butler of Mount Sinai Medical School says, "Two of the worst pieces of advice an older person can receive, we've learned, are: What do you expect at your age? and Take it easy."

That goes for mental exercise as well. Consultant Joseph Juran is one of the godfathers of the postwar quality movement and, at 89, a man with considerable standing on this subject as well. Says he: "My personal theory is that the key to aging successfully comes down to keeping your mind active." Indeed, the biochemistry of the brain, neurologists agree, supports the notion that it may well function better—and longer—when we keep those nerve cells firing.

Have we mentioned happiness? That's definitely one of the essentials too, as are friends, offspring, a spouse, and other reasons to live. Smile, hug your kids, be silly sometimes, and smell those darn roses whenever possible.

If all this leaves you thinking that a remarkable amount of the latest aging research seems aimed at elaborately and objectively verifying what most of us already thought we knew, well, you're right. "Our grandmother always said, 'People don't wear out, they rust out,'" recalls Don Feigenbaum, 67, who along with older brother Val, 73, runs a thriving systems engineering company that numbers Tenneco and Ford among its clients. Grandma Feigenbaum gets the last word: Use it or lose it.

—R.I.K.

HOW MUCH TIME IS LEFT?

Average life expectancy

Age	Female	Male
Birth	79.6	72.7
40	41.3	36.0
65	19.6	15.8
85	7.2	5.7

FORTUNE TABLE / SOURCE: CENSUS BUREAU

er the lowly roundworm. By manipulating the genes of a species of nematode, Thomas Johnson of the University of Colorado has already doubled its puny 30-day life span. Michael Rose's lab has successfully doubled the maximum and mean life spans of a species of fruit fly.

A series of fairly mundane experiments that seemingly do not involve genetics are helping scientists in their quest. So far, only one technique has consistently extended the life span of short-lived mammals, such as mice—and it requires practically starving them. Caloric restriction, as it's known, adds health as well as years. In the most important such experiment yet, the NIA in 1987 began testing it on primates, our closest relatives in the animal kingdom. Because these animals have a maximum life span of 40 years, vs. 2½ years for mice, the final results won't be in until many baby-boomers are wearing dentures. But already the animals on diets are reaching puberty a year or two later than their brethren who chow down as much as they please.

The goal isn't to persuade us all to go on truly draconian diets (though let's face it, it does seem one more reason to shed a few pounds). Explains Richard Sprott, head of the NIA's biology of aging program: "If we could understand how caloric restriction produces its effects, then we'd understand a great deal more about the basic biological mechanism of aging. And that would give us a way to intervene. It could provide that magic bullet we talk about."

Michael Rose draws a parallel with the success of the U.S. space program after World War II: "Sending men to the moon and back by the end of the 1960s seemed impossible too, until we decided to commit enough resources. Then the science developed. I know we can extend life span for a far smaller sum than the Apollo project cost. I'm doing it on a toy-model scale now." Consultant Kenneth Dychtwald, 43, whose firm Age Wave, in Emeryville, California, advises corporations like Johnson & Johnson, Kmart, and General Motors on what the graying of America means to their markets, believes such an investment is inevitable. Says he: "Breakthroughs that humans have dreamed about for thousands of years are right around the corner."

Exuberant prophecies like those, however, are still a minority. Most scientists, including the NIA's Sprott, suspect there may be hundreds of genes, rather than a handful, that interact to affect human longevity. That complexity, they argue, makes reaching into the genome and resetting the cellular clock a pretty remote possibility.

What we will see fairly soon is genetic repair of flaws that give rise to specific diseases. In the past year researchers—aided by the monumental Human Genome Project, which aims to map our genetic code by early next century—have identified a number of troublesome genes. Among the maladies they cause are Huntington's disease, amyotrophic lateral sclerosis (Lou Gehrig's disease), a form of colon cancer, and severe combined immunodeficiency, or SCID (a rare condition, better known as "the bubble boy disease," in which the immune system virtually ceases to function). By injecting several children suffering from SCID with a healthy copy of the defective gene that causes it, doctors have succeeded, for now, in revitalizing the immune system. More than 40 other trials are being conducted to test this sort of gene therapy's efficacy on cystic fibrosis, cancer, and AIDS.

EVEN WITH ALL THIS, lifting average life expectancy toward 90 and beyond will require solving some daunting arithmetic. Here's the problem: Because we've already conquered most of the infectious diseases that once killed large numbers of children and young adults, the gains we're making now come from adding a few extra years to an already long-in-the-tooth crowd's lives—and not six or seven decades to the lives of kids. As a result, future victories over disease—even major triumphs—will inevitably deliver small gains in life expectancy compared with those won earlier in this century.

Demographer Jay Olshansky of the University of Chicago Medical School calculates that completely wiping out cancer in the U.S. would add only 3.2 years to average life expectancy from birth. Eliminating heart disease would lift it by just three years for women and 3.6 years for men. "There's a large element of wish fulfillment in these optimistic projections about extending life expectancy," argues Dr. James Fries of Stanford University, who along with Olshansky is a leading proponent of the view that there's a

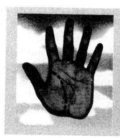

The paradox is that the longer we live, the more urgent it will become to learn how to die.

ceiling on average life expectancy of around 85. Indeed, the way Duke's Ken Manton gets life expectancy to 100 is by assuming that the entire U.S. population adopts and maintains optimum health habits throughout their lives. Wanna bet?

On the other hand, neither camp takes into account the enormous wild card of genetic engineering because its potential is impossible to model. And yet, most experts agree breakthroughs will happen—and have a sizable effect on longevity. Says the NIA's Dick Sprott: "Over the next 25 to 30 years, we're going to produce a tremendous change in the number of humans who will make it to something close to the species maximum."

The social and economic consequences of this acceleration in life span will be far greater than anything now contemplated by most American policymakers and institutions. Take inheritance. A few years ago, economists Lawrence Kotlikoff and Lawrence Summers calculated that 80% of the country's capital stock has been piled up through intergenerational bequests. What happens to capital formation if tomorrow's long-lived woopies (well-off older people) consume that seed corn and leave almost nothing behind?

Consider Social Security. As life expectancy rises toward 90, many Americans will spend almost as many years drawing a check from the government as they did working. This cannot stand—not when, even on a conservative demographic forecast, the number of workers per retiree shrinks from 3.3 to fewer than two after 2010. How will Social Security survive then except as a pared-down, straightforward welfare program for the poorest of the very old? But how and when will we transform it?

A society with more than 20% of its citizens over 65 will have to reengineer its physical as well as its fiscal landscape. Example: America's roadways—their signage, the distance to off ramps, and the like—seem optimally designed for 25-year-old males with excellent vision, quick reflexes, and high testosterone levels. But they can be deathtraps for the elderly. Since the mid-1970s, as the number of drivers over 70 rose sharply, deaths from car crashes among this group jumped 30% even though total fatalities among all drivers fell by 12%.

Finally, a paradox. The longer we live, the more urgent it will become to learn how to die. In Greek myth, Tithonus is the pitiful soul who won from the gods the gift of eternal life but, lacking eternal youth, was condemned to live—shrinking, shriveling, and longing for oblivion. Our nursing homes and hospital wards are filled with Tithonuses. There are many more who fear his fate. That grim fact is confirmed by brisk sales of books like *Final Exit*, the growing popularity of living wills, the record number of suicides among 65-and-olders, as well as the awkward career of Jack Kevorkian. Can't we as a society in the years ahead finally agree on better ways to decide—among families and physicians and not by government diktat—when it's worth fighting and when it's time to go?

Hard questions, easier to pose than to answer. One obvious answer, though, is to at least stop doing things that make matters worse. Right now, the Social Security system appears to treat the fraction of over-65s who still draw a paycheck the way America's welfare system treats low-income working mothers. It encourages dependency. If you're 65 to 69 and earn more than $11,160 a year, your monthly benefits get cut by one-third. Since interest and dividends don't count as earned income for this calculation, this disincentive is aimed not at the well-off but at those who could most benefit from a little extra money.

THE CULTURE still too often patronizes and stigmatizes its elderly citizens—a phenomenon for which Dr. Robert Butler, 67, the NIA's founding director, coined the word *ageism* back in the late 1960s. Many corporations continue to push older employees out the door as fast as you can say "early-retirement package." Few yet follow the exam-

ple of Travelers Insurance, which created a job bank of temporary employees from a pool of retirees and younger workers and found their higher productivity saved it $1.5 million a year, or the Days Inn hotel chain, which began a concerted drive to hire people over 55 as reservation agents when it found that, compared with younger employees, they cost 64% less to train and recruit.

The thumb rule offered by economist Larry Kotlikoff is that to keep the economy from slowing down, we should offset every 10% increase in life span with a 10% increase in the retirement age. Here's John Templeton's advice: "Don't retire until 75."

By all means, though, don't feel compelled to slog away at the same old grind unless you really love it. One large advantage of longer lives should be that they expand our opportunities for change. Such change may not involve highly paid work, unless you're self-employed. For some years yet, it will be difficult to find decent corporate jobs after age 65. But volunteerism can be personally rewarding and produce huge benefits for society. "The key is to have a real purpose to your life," says Bob Butler, now chairman of geriatrics at Mount Sinai Medical School. "Numerous studies confirm that when people have goals and a structure to their lives, they actually live longer and also enjoy better health." If you're not working or volunteering, take a course. Take a trip. Take a chance. Old men ought to be explorers, as the poet T.S. Eliot once observed. Old women too.

Perhaps the most critical question raised by the longevity revolution is how healthy tomorrow's outsize elderly population will be. About seven million Americans today require long-term care because they are too mentally or physically frail to fend for themselves. The annual cost is more than $54 billion. But that figure doesn't begin to reflect the cost of treating the disabling infirmities and diseases of old age. According to the most recent estimates, Americans over 65, though just 12% of the population, account for 36% of personal health care

spending. Unless we can shrink both the level of disability among older Americans and the time they spend in poor health during their final years—compress morbidity, in the jargon of gerontology—we may eventually have to choose between bankruptcy and health care rationing on a distressingly large scale.

IS THIS compression occurring? Various surveys confirm what our eyes tell us daily: The average 70-year-old today is considerably healthier than his or her counterpart 50 or even 20 years ago. In an important study last fall, Duke's Manton found that the rate of chronic disability among Americans over 65 may have declined by 5% between 1982 and 1989. But none of the evidence is conclusive. Says Laurence Branch, director of long-term-care research at Abt Associates, a Cambridge, Massachusetts, consulting firm: "We're increasing life expectancy, but it's still not clear if we're increasing most people's *active* life expectancy—the percentage of their lifetime they can expect to enjoy good health and independence. What is clear, however, is that we know we can do it."

That upbeat attitude is worth keeping in mind, since in some ways the biggest hurdle an aging America faces may be psychological. The U.S. has never stopped thinking of itself as a young country, a frontier country—a new world, not an old one. For such a people, growing up is hard to do. It's worth remembering, then, that alongside its many discomforts, long life has always been thought to bring with it large rewards—among them, perspective, maturity, insight. William Butler Yeats said it best in his poem "The Coming of Wisdom With Time":

Though the leaves are many, the root is one:
Through all the lying days of my youth,
I swayed my leaves and flowers in the sun:
Now I may wither into truth.

Maybe we will too.

OVER *WHAT* HILL?

A gallery of free spirits on the move, defying time and the once-common notions about growing old

Rae Corelli

If people are only as old as they feel, a lot of elderly Canadians are defying time. Here are the stories of men and women, some internationally famous, others prominent in their communities, who have taken the gloom out of growing old:

HUME CRONYN

Being old, says Canadian-born stage and film actor Hume Cronyn, doesn't get him down. "I like to think my reaction is healthier," he says. "I get mad. I mean I really get very angry. My eyesight's lousy. I have a degenerative disc in my back and immediately above it I have a broken vertebra, so I have a sore back most of the time. Bad eyesight and an aching back. I have lots to complain about." However, sighs the 82-year-old Cronyn, all that is only the inevitable accumulation of aging.

While his body may be somewhat worse for wear, the professional career that began in 1931—when Cronyn appeared in a Washington stock company production of *Up Pops the Devil*—shows little sign of infirmity. He and wife Jessica Tandy,* worked in three movies this year, which for him included a brief appearance as a Supreme Court justice targeted for assassination in the whodunit *The Pelican Brief.* "They told me I would have to look like an old man," he chuckled. "It took them five hours to apply the makeup." In mid-December, Cronyn and Tandy abandoned the wintry greyness of New York City for the Bahamas. "We're really staggering," Cronyn confessed. He has no outstanding film commitments and does not know what he will do when he returns from the sunshine. "I'm getting rather picky in my old age," he says.

Given his credentials, he can afford to be. Born in London, Ont., Cronyn was a student at St. Catharines' posh Ridley College and McGill University in Montreal, and during the succeeding 52 years appeared in dozens of stage plays, films and TV dramas, occasionally with Tandy, whom he met in New York City in 1940 and married two years later. He holds 22 awards

[*Jessica Tandy died in September 1994 at age 85.—ED.]

for distinguished performances, including two Tonys, two Emmys and the coveted U.S. National Medal of Arts award, bestowed on him by president George Bush in 1990. Some of his roles required only small shifts from reality, most notably the 1984 fantasy *Cocoon* in which a group of geriatrics are rejuvenated by a brush with travellers from outer space. But if *Cocoon* was supposed to awaken a yearning for immortality, it was lost on Cronyn.

"I just don't think about it," he says. "For example, I take great pleasure in going to church, any church, on occasion, but that has nothing to do with thoughts of an afterlife. If you live on to some degree in your children (they have three], that's about as close to immortality as we have a right to expect. I'm not afraid of death. There's a wonderful line in *Peter Pan* when Peter says, 'To die must be a wonderful adventure.' I subscribe to that. I mean, there may be no adventure at all, it may be nothing but an interminable sleep but I've always liked sleeping. I can think of worse endings." Of the Dec. 6 death of actor Don Ameche, who also appeared in *Cocoon*, Cronyn says: "Hell, every week now there's another one and my black suit gets too much usage. I think it was Bette Davis who said, 'Old age is not for sissies.'"

For now, says Cronyn, he will keep working because he dreads not being able to. "Some day I'll just have to stop and then what the hell will I do? I just can't sit and contemplate my navel hour after hour. I think actually if one could arrange one's parting as happily and easily as possible, it would be while holding the hand of someone you loved and in the middle of some real involvement with life." On a beach somewhere in the Bahamas, Hume Cronyn is enjoying that vision without the parting—still mad about his aching back.

ROBERTSON DAVIES

In 1991, author Robertson Davies told an interviewer that the widely acclaimed *Murther and Walking Spirits* would be his last novel. He evidently changed his mind because now, at age 80, he has nearly completed yet another. "That's a thing that makes writers live a long time," he says. "You give your book to a publisher in February and if he gets it out by the following October you're lucky, so you just have to hang on to see what he's going to do."

But for the bushy-bearded Davies, who has written 45 novels, plays and collections of essays during the past half-century, hanging on does not mean simply waiting around. He rises early at his rambling country home at Caledon East, north of Toronto, which he shares with his wife, Brenda. They have four grown children. Davies begins writing by 9 a.m. At 12:30, he breaks for lunch followed by a rest period and "some outdoor things, although I've never been a great one

for physical exercise. Hate it, as a matter of fact." Between 5 and 6 p.m., he returns to work, usually revising what he wrote in the morning. In the evening, he listens to music or watches television. "You've got to recognize your limitations," he says, "but not get silly and start coddling yourself."

Many of his contemporaries think the same way, Davies says, because the perception of aging has changed. "My grandmother, when she was in her early 60s, wore black skirts and a widow's veil and became as if she were a thousand. It was quite common then for an old person, even if they didn't have much wrong with them, to hobble around on a stick—'You go upstairs, your legs are younger than mine,' that sort of thing. People just got sick of that, both the young and the old."

He dislikes travel but does it frequently, giving lectures and readings and taking part in symposiums in the United States and Britain as well as in Canada. A onetime Shakespearean actor, stage director, magazine editor, newspaper editor, playwright and teacher, he is currently professor emeritus and founding master of the University of Toronto's Massey College. Continuing to work, he thinks, may have something to do with longevity. "If you really are serious about what you do, you always want to do it better than you did it before," he says. "I'm always hoping that before I die, I'll write one *really* good book and I don't feel I've done it yet. I think this perpetual looking into the future possibly is healthy."

At the same time, he says, he has confronted—and accepted—the fact of his own mortality. "You have to develop a measure of philosophy about it, which I find a lot of my contemporaries do not do. They allow a rather youthful dread of death to possess them and so they dash off to Florida, hoping that when death knocks at the door they won't be home. That kind of thing is just nonsense. Death is inevitable, it is not dreadful, and I am not one of those hopeless people who thinks that that's absolutely the end. The energy which has made you go for as long as you have, is never lost. It goes somewhere." Maybe eventually. For now, it drives Robertson Davies to finish his book—and contemplate the next one.

JEAN CLEATOR

In 1981, at age 55, Jean Cleator set a world record for 55-to-60-year-olds in the 5,000 m, but she quit running the following year because it was wrecking her knees. Now 67 and a widow, she restricts herself to competitive alpine skiing, camping, hiking and backpacking in summer, swimming in the Pacific Ocean and working an eight-hour day at the Vancouver ski service centre she owns with her son Barry. "It's a little harder to stay motivated when you get older," she says. "You have to force yourself a little bit more."

This winter, Cleator—skier for more than 40 years—competes in the 60-to-70 age category for downhill racers, mostly at B.C.'s Whistler Mountain and in the Rockies. She talks animatedly about life on the slopes, lacing her conversation with skiing terms—Nordic, bindings, alpine, slalom, ski faces, gates, moguls, snow conditions. When the snow disappears from the low ground later this year, Cleator will head for the wilderness regions of the province's Tweedsmuir park, pitch a tent and set up her propane stove. Then, she will spend a month as a parks department guide, noting where visitors come from, how long they plan to stay and what they want to see. "If anybody wants to know what it's like up ahead, I tell them," she says.

For Jean Cleator, life at home is no less active. Example: "Yesterday, I slept in and woke up at 7. Normally, I'm up at 6:30. I'm not a great early riser." Or. "I would love to have done it, but I have not taken up scuba diving or board-sailing. It came along a little bit late for me and besides, I'm a bit of a coward." In addition to swimming, she has also water skied but admits that "it took me a long time to get up on one ski."

Along with the lifestyle is a philosophy. "If you feel like doing it and you can do it, you do it. What's age got to do with it?"

AHAB SPENCE

A few months ago, Ahab Spence had open-heart surgery, which, at 82, slowed him down so much that he could walk only about a mile each day. But he had to get his strength back in anticipation of this month's return to work at Regina's federally supported Saskatchewan Indian Federated Colleges, where he is well into his second full-time career. "I felt like I could take on anything," he remembers, "but my wife wouldn't let me and the doctor backed her up."

For Ahab Spence of the Cree nation, the road out of the wilderness has been long and bumpy. He was born at Split Lake in north-central Manitoba in 1911 and got his first look at a classroom when his family sent him to school on a reserve near The Pas at age 10. He later graduated from high school in Moose Jaw, Sask., and went on to earn degrees in arts and theology from the University of Saskatchewan in Saskatoon.

"I'm an Anglican priest by trade," says Spence, who with his wife, Betty, raised six children. "I retired from the church when I was 70 but I've been working ever since. Various bureaucrats have tried to get rid of me. I've been told that I'm 80, I should quit teaching. They even gave me a title, professor emeritus. I thought that was a good hint but I didn't go. I notice when people retire and they have no hobby or anything, in two or three years they're gone. Being mixed up with young people, I think that keeps me young." The right atti-

tude helps, too—"keep your sense of humor, don't take life too seriously and get along with your wife."

Spence's "young people"—they range from 20 to 60—are mostly Cree wanting to know more about their language, heritage and legends. Spence teaches two classes, one a language course in advanced Cree, the other in Cree literature, which takes the form of storytelling. "What I try to do," says Spence, "is to translate the legends and ancient stories into English so the class can appreciate what good people they have come from." Many of the legends involve Wisakecahk, the cultural hero of the Cree nation. "He was a flatterer and a first-rate politician," says Spence. "He can do good or he can do bad. He was always hungry."

CHARLIE PIKE

When he was 12 years old, Charlie Pike developed a heart condition that twice nearly killed him. In his early 20s, he tried to buy life insurance but the companies he approached said he was an unacceptable risk. Now, at 79, Pike is a downhill skier and distance swimmer who works out regularly and last summer took up Rollerblading to help him stay in shape. He also sells insurance. "Life," says Charlie, "is full of surprises."

Pike owns Pike-Vezina Assurance and usually puts in a five-day week at his Boulevard René-Lévesque office in downtown Montreal. Three mornings a week, he alternates gym work with swimming, and most weekends he skis. He has a Montreal Amateur Athletic Association award for swimming 50 miles in the MAA pool during a recent winter. "I used to do 44 to 66 lengths but now I'm doing a little less," says Pike. Last March at B.C.'s Whistler resort, he won a gold medal in a seniors' alpine ski competition, negotiating the 46 gates in a mile-long slalom in 1:25. Then, in November at Alberta's Lake Louise, he finished three seconds behind 38-year-old former Olympic skier Ken Read in a 2,000-foot downhill race. "You want to get down there fast enough that all winter no one will beat you in your own age group," says Pike. "That's just sheer ego."

It is also—and perhaps more importantly—a reflection of his all-or-nothing challenge to the aging process. "Whenever I feel I've got too much to do, the pressure's too great at the office, I immediately start exercising," says Pike, married with no children. "Your attitude has become old when you say, 'I'm not going to do this or that because it's too much for me.' If you're starting to think that way, then you're really going to age." But fewer over-60s are falling victim to traditional thinking, Pike says. "I do think that a lot of people now believe they are 12 to 15 years younger than their chronological age. When I'm skiing, I go after the 50-year-olds—but the 40-year-olds can beat me."

Pike had some advice for 60-to-65-year-olds who sit around and don't do much of anything. "Get involved in an activity that's going to be a bit demanding," he says. "People are never depressed if they have an absorbing activity." Like Rollerblading. But wear protective padded clothing. Falling on concrete, says Charlie, is not a whole lot of fun.

ROSE OUELLET

She is liable to show up just about anywhere. In a TV commercial she sits vampishly on the hood of a pickup truck, the lights framing her red hair and flashing off the sequins in her dress as she moves. Another time, another channel and there she is, persuasively pushing beer. Or on a billboard high above a Montreal street, her image hustles cars. "I always wanted to do something outside the theatre and now I've done it," says comedian Rose Ouellet. "Now, I have done everything."

She probably has, for at age 90, La Poune—an affectionate—but untranslatable nickname picked by her agent decades ago—has been entertaining audiences longer than any other stage personality in French Canada. She entered professional vaudeville in 1917 when she was only 14 because she had become bored with amateur productions.

Ouellet lives by herself at Maison des Artistes, a retirement home for theatre people on Montreal's downtown St. Denis Street. She gets up anywhere from 7 a.m. to early afternoon and, when she's not working, sometimes visits old folks' homes. "Everyone laughs because they're all younger than me," she says. Her only visible concession to vanity is her hair; when it began to grey while she was still fairly young, she had it dyed red—and has kept it that way.

She walks a lot and smokes whenever she feels like it. "I listen to my body," she says. "If I eat something and it doesn't agree with me, I notice. If it happens a second time, I won't eat that food again. I think people can control their health. Mine is good. I don't even know what a headache feels like."

At the same time, says La Poune, "I never think about death. Why worry about it? I know someone who lives in my building and it's just terrible how she worries about death. I keep telling her, 'What's the point? You got yourself all worked up about it yesterday and you're still here! Are you going to worry all of today as well?' "When her time comes, adds Ouellet, "it will be an interesting voyage to a place I've never visited before."

PEARLEEN OLIVER

When Pearleen Oliver walked out of New Glasgow

High on that summer day in 1936, clutching her diploma, she became the first person among the impoverished blacks of Nova Scotia's Pictou County ever to graduate from Grade 12. "We simply had no money so I ran errands, I looked after sick people, washed windows and washed floors just to get the quarters which I saved to buy secondhand books," she recalls. If you were black in the Depression-ravaged Maritimes, she says, "it meant you were on your own."

She wasn't on her own for long: the same year she completed high school, she met and married William P. Oliver, a young black Baptist clergyman who had just graduated from Acadia University in Wolfville, N.S. For the next 53 years, until his death in 1989, husband and wife fought for the civil rights of Nova Scotia's blacks and made Oliver's Cornwallis Street Baptist Church in the slums of Halifax a symbol of hope—all while raising five sons. Now, at 76, Pearleen is once again on her own, living in the family home on 100 acres of land in the Halifax suburb of Sackville. She plays the church organ, conducts choirs and travels around the countryside adding to her lifetime total of more than 1,000 speeches. Both Saint Mary's and Mount Saint Vincent universities in Halifax have awarded her honorary doctorates.

The Second World War, says Oliver, meant jobs for blacks and the money to send their children to school. "Some went to Grade 10 and got certificates to go teach in the pitiful little black schools. Everything was pitiful. But to survive is the main thing. It was like being shipwrecked. The important thing was to have something to hang on to." But the war did more than provide pay cheques—"it gave us impetus and a new kind of thinking which opened more doors."

That new kind of thinking has influenced the way she looks at herself and the process of growing old. "Many people say when they get to be 65, 'I'm old. I've got to have somebody do my work, can't drive the car.' They start thinking like that and then they get that way. It's all in your mind. I don't think old. I don't look old. I don't act old. My hair is still black and I don't dye it. I don't dress like a little old lady. I walk snappy and if I want to wear heels, I wear heels." Oliver avoids seniors groups because "they do nothing but play cards and sit around and when they get in these groups, they're all alike, they have all the illnesses collectively."

As for herself, "if I get a little pain, I lie down and it goes away. If don't feel well, I examine myself and ask now what did I eat, why am I feeling this way? I believe in my body, I believe my body can heal itself." She claims not to fear death or even to think about it.

Which may be just as well—she already has her hands full, reading Dante's *Inferno*, the Roman poet Virgil and books about frontier science. "I get up at 6 or 6:30 in the morning and I thank God that I've awakened and I say to myself, 'Now, where am I going to go today, what shall I do first?'"

MORLEY SAFER

If senior citizenship begins somewhere between 60 and 65, then journalist Morley Safer, the 62-year-old co-host of CBS television's *60 Minutes,* has only reached the threshold. He has no irresistible desire to cross it but, rather, to pause and reflect. "I'm obviously aware of the passing decades and I'm also aware that after the age of 35, it's patch, patch, patch in terms of your body," says the Toronto-born Safer whose arrival at *60 Minutes* in 1971 followed seven years of covering the Vietnam War for CBS News. But in relation to work, growing older "never even crosses my mind."

Material things, he adds, have become much less important. "The only ones that count are the ones that make life a little bit easier," he says. "Like a fax machine. You don't *need* a Rolex." But he does need to work. "It takes on a special kind of importance, because around 60 you suddenly say, 'God damn, I can really do this work.' But God knows, I've not looked after myself. I still smoke three packs a day, I drink a bottle of wine a day and a couple of whiskies."

Meanwhile, he travels thousands of miles a year in pursuit of stories, leaving behind wife Jane, 51, and daughter Sarah. "Permanent adolescence is almost a job requirement," says Safer. "But it takes a fair whack of physical endurance because travel has become so bad, so wearing on the mind and body, that you have to pace yourself a lot better. I find that at 62 I can do more things at once than I could at 32. You just become more versatile as you grow older. It drives my wife crazy, but I can read a book and watch television at the same time."

For Morley Safer—and Charlie Pike, Jean Cleator and the rest—getting older, it turns out, really does mean getting better.

With JOHN DeMONT in Halifax and
NANCY WOOD in Ottawa

Undercover Among the Elderly

A young woman learns firsthand how older people are treated

Michael Ryan

As a young girl, Patricia Moore idolized her grandmother, who lived with her and her parents. "She was a wonderfully energetic, competent person," Patricia says of Margaret Mary Moore. "Sunday supper was her domain. I watched as she hand-cut homemade noodles." Nurtured by her tight-knit family, young Patricia entered the Rochester Institute of Technology. She dreamed of making her parents and grandmother proud of her, but fate intervened.

"After my first semester of college," she recalls, "I came home and found that my grandmother was no longer able to make our dinner because her arthritis was so bad. It was like ice water in the face to see this proud matriarch suddenly viewing herself as having no value because she could no longer manipulate the tools by which she could cook meals."

Margaret Mary Moore became depressed. No longer able to peel a potato or measure out flour for her noodles, she withdrew deeply into herself. "She lost the will to live," Patricia says. Within a year, at the age of 78, she was dead.

Patricia Moore did grow up to be the successful designer she dreamed of becoming. After college, in the mid-'70s, she landed a job with Raymond Loewy, the industrial designer known for everything from streamlined locomotives to shiny chrome toasters. But the memory of her grandmother stayed with her. She

was bothered that many of the designs she worked on would be difficult for people with arthritis to handle.

Soon after, she entered graduate school to study the needs of older people. However, Moore quickly realized that many older persons balk at talking about the difficulties they experience. "As a young designer, interviewing elders," she says, "the responses I was getting were, 'I'm fine, dear. Don't worry about me.' I knew why they were doing this—their independence and autonomy were threatened. They had a fear that if you let people know that you can't cook your own meals and you can't bathe yourself, they'll put you in a nursing home."

Moore consulted with her professors but found no good solutions. Then, at a party, she met a woman who handled makeup for TV's *Saturday Night Live,* transforming Dan Aykroyd and Jane Curtain into Coneheads. "I found myself blurting out, 'Can you turn me into an old woman?' And she said that she could," Moore recalls.

Her disguise—complete with prostheses that blurred her vision, dulled her hearing and made her joints stiff and slow—took weeks to perfect. Moore even gargled with salt to render her voice raspy and thin. When she first tried the disguise, she was stunned: "I saw this little old lady in the mirror. I looked like my grandmother."

Moore designed the disguise to make herself look and move like a woman in her 80s. She had three wardrobes—one

each for a poor, a middle-class and an affluent woman—to measure the responses she received. She was surprised that the appearance of money didn't make much difference.

In all three costumes, Moore moved slowly, needed to have things repeated, and fumbled for change in her purse. Many of the younger people she came in contact with saw her as a hindrance or a nuisance. People slammed doors in her face and verbally abused her as she struggled to board city buses, holding up impatient riders behind her. "I was knocked over in the Buffalo airport," Moore recalls. "Knocked to the ground like a turtle on its shell. This guy bumped into me while I was on the telephone and just kept going. I couldn't get up because I couldn't bend my knee. I eventually flipped to my side, and somebody helped me up."

Wouldn't such rudeness, while unforgivable, be experienced in any big city by people of any age? "But it wasn't in big cities," she says. "If anything, big cities are slightly more hospitable to elders [even though she was mugged twice in New York City]. In small towns, I felt the most vulnerable. There isn't the infrastructure of services for elders that you find in cities. I could walk for six blocks without being able to find a restroom. Rural elders are suffering. When I retire, it will be to a big city."

To make sure that her findings accurately reflected the reality of elder people's experience, Moore traveled to 116 big cities and small towns, from Florida to Canada, over a three-year period.

"I soon found out that people's reactions were very predictable," Moore recalls. "Some would be very sweet and kind. Usually, they had an elder in their lives. Another group was trying to be kind but often was patronizing. A cabdriver in New York hopped out to open the door for me, but he spoke so loud that, even wearing earplugs and nonworking hearing aids, I got a headache. He was making the assumption that all elders are deaf."

Overall, her disguise served its purpose: She was able to talk with elders openly about the small and large challenges they face. Two of the more common: the assumption that elders are less competent and that they grow depressed after retirement.

Today, Patricia Moore is 40, travels widely and lectures to students, designers and gerontologists. A TV movie based on her experience is in the works. She has become a leader in a movement called Universal Design, a school of architects and designers who create products and environments for *everybody*—including the elderly.

Moore displays a variety of designs she has worked on: One is a spatula with a special foam handle, from her "Good Grips" product line; another is a pill bottle with a timer built into the cap. "We have made the point, very subtly, in our society that when you age, somehow you're not as good as you were," she says. "We need to understand aging is a natural, evolutionary process. Why is younger necessarily better? We have to learn to age well in our hearts."

The Quality of Later Life

Although it is true that one ages from the moment of conception to the moment of death, children are usually considered to be "growing and developing" while adults are often thought of as "aging." Having accepted this assumption, most biologists concerned with the problems of aging focus their attention on what happens to individuals during the later part of the mature adult's life cycle. A common definition of senescence is "the changes that occur generally in the postreproductive period and that result in decreased survival capacity on the part of the individual organism" (B. L. Shrehler, *Time, Cells and Aging*, New York: Academic Press, 1977).

As a person ages, physiological changes take place. The skin loses its elasticity, becomes more pigmented, and bruises more easily. Joints stiffen, and the bone structure becomes less firm. Muscles lose their strength. The respiratory system becomes less efficient. The metabolism changes, resulting in different dietary demands. Bowel and bladder movements are more difficult to regulate. Visual acuity diminishes, hearing declines, and the entire system is less able to resist environmental stresses and strains.

Increases in life expectancy have resulted largely from decreased mortality rates among younger people, rather than from increased longevity after age 65. In 1900 the average life expectancy at birth was 47.3 years; in 1988 it was 74.9 years. Thus, in 88 years the average life expectancy rose by 27.6 years. However, those who now live to the age of 65 do not have an appreciably different life expectancy than did their 1900 cohorts. In 1900 65-year-olds could expect to live approximately 12 years longer, while in 1988 they could expect to live approximately 17 years longer, an increase of 5 years. Although more people survive to age 65 today, the chances of being afflicted by one of the major killers of older persons is still about as great for this generation as it was for their grandparents.

While medical science has had considerable success in controlling the acute diseases of the young—such as measles, chicken pox, and scarlet fever—it has not been as successful in controlling the chronic conditions of old age, such as heart trouble, cancer, and emphysema. Organ transplants, greater knowledge of the immune system, and undiscovered medical technologies will probably increase the life expectancy for the 65-and-over population, resulting in longer life for the next generation. Although persons 65 years of age today are living slightly longer than 65-year-olds did in 1900, the quality of their later years has greatly improved. Economically, Social Security and a multitude of private retirement programs have given most older persons a more secure retirement. Physically, many people remain active, mobile, and independent throughout their retirement years. Socially, most older persons are married, involved in community activities, and leading productive lives. While they may experience some chronic ailments, most are able to live in their own homes, direct their own lives, and involve themselves in activities they enjoy.

The articles in this section examine health, psychological, social, and spiritual factors that affect the quality of aging. All of us are faced with the process of aging, and by putting a strong emphasis on health, both mental and physical, a long, quality life is much more attainable.

The first unit essay, "A New Life for the Old: The Role of the Elderly in the Bahamas," examines a culture in which the old rarely retire and thus remain productive members of the community. "Sexuality and Aging: What It Means to Be Sixty or Seventy or Eighty in the '90s" examines ways of remaining sexually active throughout a person's life.

Emotional well-being has a direct effect on the "success" of aging, and marriage and religion are two very important factors in life satisfaction in the later years. In "Religiosity, Aging, and Life Satisfaction," the role that religion can play in providing social integration and a sense of community is examined.

Older persons experience a number of role losses and must adjust to a variety of new roles. Emerging recreational, leisure, educational, and volunteer roles are seen as enriching the lives of older people, and this thesis is examined in Harold Cox's article "Roles for Aged Individuals in Post-Industrial Societies." "Remarriage among the Elderly: Characteristics Relevant to Pastoral Counseling" explores the motivation to marry in later life and the obstacles that must be overcome for a successful marriage. The unique problems of older women are examined by Cynthia Taeuber in "Women in Our Aging Society: Golden Years or Increased Dependency?" In "Live and Learn: Patient Education for the Elderly Orthopaedic Client," Syble Oldaker encourages older persons regardless of their health problems to become more knowledgeable and actively involved in their own treatment. Finally, "Men and Women Aging Differently" illustrates how the timing of life course events differs between men and women and the different problems they are confronted with as a result of these factors.

Looking Ahead: Challenge Questions

While medical science has increased life expectancy at birth by controlling diseases of the young, there has been relatively little success in controlling the diseases of old age and increasing life expectancy after age 65. Can we expect new breakthroughs in medical technology that will increase the life expectancy of 65-year-olds? Defend your answer.

While many people expect they will live well into their eighties and nineties, very few imagine living to be 120 years old. Do many people really want to live beyond their 100th birthday? Why, or why not?

What changes in business, government, social services, and the economy will be produced by an increasing number of older people?

A New Life for the Old

The Role of the Elderly in the Bahamas

Joel Savishinsky

Joel Savishinsky is professor of anthropology at Ithaca College. He has done research and applied anthropology in Turkey, England, the Canadian Arctic, the Bahamas, and the United States. He is the author of The Trail of the Hare: Life and Stress in an Arctic Community *and* The Ends of Time: Life and Work in a Nursing Home.

Old age has sometimes been described as a foreign country, a place where we take on new identities, far removed from our former bodies and capabilities. One way to test this idea of old age as a foreign land is to look more closely at how the old live *in* a foreign land. By examining the lives of elderly people in other cultures, we can reassess our own society's assumptions about what is inevitable or natural in late life. That is, we can start separating what is "cultural" from what is "natural" in the human life cycle.

This kind of cross-cultural gerontology has attracted the attention of many anthropologists in recent years. They have found populations of active and long-living elderly people in areas as diverse as Soviet Georgia and highland Peru. I discovered some dramatic contrasts much closer to home when, in the late 1970s, I began to do fieldwork in the Bahamas, an English-speaking nation of seven hundred islands whose shores lie as close as seventy-five miles from the United States. While the places best known to Americans—Nassau, Freeport, Abaco, and Eleuthera—have been transformed by tourism, the more isolated communities on the "Out," or "Family," islands still retain a fairly traditional economy and social life. On Cat Island, for example, most inhabitants are the descendants of slaves freed by the British in 1834: Over a century later, they continue to support themselves through a combination of farming, goat herding, and fishing; and they still orient much of their lives around the extended family and religious values. When I settled in to live among a cluster of small villages at the south end of Cat Island, I soon realized how vital a role its elders played in the local culture.

The missing generation

With no industry and a subsistence base that provides little surplus, Cat Island's economy has seen a few periods of boom and bust over the centuries. Initially home to the native Arawak Indians and then to pirates, the island's first major European settlements were not established until the late 1700s. These centered on large cotton plantations and associated port facilities. Cat Island's estates, worked by African slave labor, were owned by wealthy English families, or by American Loyalists who had fled the United States after the Revolution. The plantation economy received a second wave of American émigrés when Southerners moved to the Bahamas after the Civil War in an attempt to reestablish some semblance of their antebellum lifestyle.

The cotton plantations, however, were only a modest success, and since the late nineteenth century, a number of other schemes for bolstering the island's economy have been attempted; these have focused on special crops, products, or services. There was a time of pineapple plantations; an era of sisal growing for sale to rope manufacturers; a profitable trade in salvaging wrecks off the treacherous coastline; and a period of banana exportation. Recently, a handful of tourist hotels have been built, and the island has been marginally involved in drug trafficking. During the 1930s, Cat Islanders also played a part in the lucrative Bahamian enterprise of rum-running to the Prohibition-bound shores of the United States.

But what Cat Island exports now is people. To get training, find work, and make money, many adults leave their home communities to go to Nassau, other islands, or the United States. (75 percent of the population lives on the islands of New Providence and Grand Bahama.) They send back some of their earnings in the form of remittances to help out their parents. And when they themselves become mothers and fathers, they also send back their children to be raised by the grandparents. The reasons for doing this are a combination of financial necessity and cultural sentiment. Child-free parents are able to work abroad and earn a double income, as well as have their offspring raised less expensively back on Cat Island.

Furthermore, in the view of both par-

Cat Island is one of the nearly seven hundred islands that make up the Bahamas.

ents and grandparents, the island is not only a cheaper but also a more wholesome environment to grow up in. Their view of Nassau, for example, is a somewhat expanded version of the proverbial midwesterner's feelings about New York City: It is a nice place to visit—or even work in for a while—but not a great place to live. The residents believe that it is better to have one's children raised on Cat Island, in a family environment, in a safer and cleaner world, and in the loving embrace of their elders.

Looking at who was living around me in Bramley*—a hamlet of some seventy people—is a first clue to what it means to be old on Cat Island. The most dramatic feature was not who *was* there but who was *absent*. The community has few young adult and middle-aged people, but there are an abundance of children and their grandparents. The very young are, in fact, frequently living with and being raised by the very old, a family pattern found elsewhere on the island.

To the people of Cat Island, the bond between young and old is not just affectionate but moral as well. Elders are a voice, not an echo, of those traditional values that younger generations still subscribe

_____
* The names of villages are pseudonyms.

to even when necessity compels them to leave the island. These values include a fundamental Christian faith, a stress on family ties, and a belief in the importance of community continuity. Motivated by some of the same concerns, unwed daughters with children often move in with their parents so that the latter can help rear their offspring. Whether the situation of young parents is one of single motherhood or off-island migration, when their children are raised by the grandparents, these youngsters are commonly encouraged to call their elders "Mommy" and "Daddy." Children are frequently allowed to believe that the older people are indeed their real parents. For immigrant adults feeling guilty about leaving *their* parents and for elders disappointed by the absence or marital status of their grown children, grandchildren fill the void left by the middle generation.

These positive emphases in grandparenting go hand in hand with a concern over the negative features of life beyond the island, particularly the seductions of the outside world, the erosion of faith and family that has occurred there, and the loss of intimacy that came when people moved from their homeland's small-scale communities. People cherish the forced but deeply felt togetherness of an island-

bound existence, the sense that Bahamian poet Susan Wallace once expressed in the words "when ocean fence ya in, all is kin." Cat Island's grandparents, caring for the young in a healthier place, not only articulate these values but model and put them into practice with their grandchildren each day. In essence, the young adults of Cat Island look to their parents, not just for child care, but for child rearing in the fullest sense of the word.

The productive years

The elders have their practical responsibilities, however, as they raise food as well as families. They cut and fire undergrowth, turn ash into the soil, and plant corn and other crops. Younger adults sometimes help them with the heavier work of slash-and-burn agriculture, but older people pride themselves on doing as much physical work as they can. They harvest their crops and carry them back home on horseback, grind their own corn, boil and bottle tomatoes, and put up preserves. Those whose advanced age limits their ability to raise food by arduous means keep small plots and vegetable gardens near their homes. Older people also keep herds of

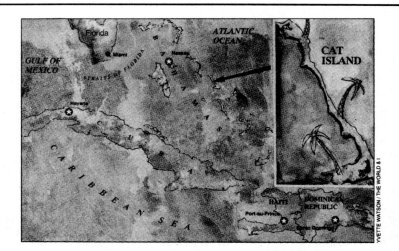

Cat Island

All of the Bahamian islands have a low topography. Cat Island actually boasts the country's highest point, Mount Alvernia, but with an elevation of only 206 feet above sea level, this "mountain" is really little more than a high hill. From its top a person can look out over the green carpet of thin forest and brush that covers the land. Visible around the island's edge is its one major road, which cuts through the mantle of trees and scrub to connect the shoreline villages.

Cat Island's low profile provides its 2,100 inhabitants little shelter from wind and storms. The necessity of locating communities close to the coast for fishing, communication, and boat travel only increases this vulnerability. Water and weather combine periodically when hurricanes sweep the island, wrecking the thatch-roofed houses that people build out of the local limestone and wood.

Cat Island's picturesque environment—the tourist's tropical paradise—is deceptive. Beneath the sunshine and palm trees, its thin soils lie in scattered pockets over a rocky limestone base. Agriculture is arduous and only modestly productive. Crops are planted by hand, using a simple, fire-hardened dibble stick to poke holes in the earth before dropping in the seeds. The fruits, sugarcane, corn, okra, pigeon peas, onions, tomatoes, and other vegetables raised in this way go mainly for household consumption, and only small amounts are sent off the island for sale.

Fishing in the offshore waters, done from locally made boats, is carried out primarily to feed the immediate family. Chickens roam in and around the homes, and small herds of goats, kept for meat and milk, are tethered in the abandoned fields outside the villages. The wild flora of the area helps meet other needs. With only one government nurse and no doctor on the southern part of the island, people continue to rely on local herbs and plants to make teas, bitters, and other forms of "bush" medicine to cure ailments that range from rashes and cuts to constipation and fevers.

—*J.S.*

goats in the vicinity of the village to supply their households with meat and milk.

At certain seasons of the year, it is not unusual for an older person of sixty-five or seventy to put in a full day's work at farming. In February, elderly couples get up early each morning to put in a few hours of labor before the noon heat becomes intense. They wake their grandchildren, feed them breakfast, and then pack lunches before heading out for the day. A man will often tend to his goats, bringing them water and moving them to new grazing areas.

If the grandchildren are of preschool age, his wife may take them with her on a half-hour walk to the plot she is cultivating. Such an older woman typically carries a machete, food, water, a light blanket to rest on, and string to tie up the taller plants. While her grandchildren play at the edge of the field, she walks from one pocket of soil to the next, stooping, weeding, mounding up the earth, and dropping in new seeds. Around her a few small trees are usually left standing to hold moisture and provide shade, while

Top: **It is not uncommon for a Bahamian man or woman of sixty-five or seventy to put in a full day of farming. Here, a woman pounds ears of corn in a cloth sack.** *Above:* **Older people take great pride in doing as much physical work as they can, like grinding corn into grits.**

A number of men in their seventies and eighties continue as the island's master boat builders.

that only certain kinds of leaves can be used, and that they have to be gathered at a particular stage in their growth. Still active in their seventies and eighties, these women gather fan-shaped palm leaves, or silvertops, at the new moon. Then, after sun drying the leaves for three to five days, they strip the outer edges off, leaving the long, thin slivers, or strings, from the center. These are then braided into long bands, which can be anywhere from five to twenty-one strings wide. It is these bands of plait that islanders eventually sew together to make the finished articles.

Each plaiter has certain products and patterns that she favors, and most women send off some of their more elaborate creations to be sold in Nassau's tourist markets. All their work is done by hand and is, quite literally, a cottage industry—the stripping, drying, and plaiting itself being carried out on the porches and front yards of people's homes. When the strings are ready for plaiting, each woman draws on a repertoire of designs and color schemes stored in her memory. They have names such as *Dip Through, Shark Gill, Fishpot, Feefors,* and *Hole-in-the-Wall.* Some patterns require alternating bands of light and dark fiber—what islanders call *Peas and Rice*—and a woman who likes to create such schemes has to know that silvertops and coconut leaves will yield the right shades for this when dried. The work is leisurely—done in the evening, between periods of active farming, or by people too old to engage in heavier labor—and it is social too: Small groups of women will sit together and talk, their hands moving in a fast, mechanical rhythm to strip the leaves clean or plait them into a work of art.

The late-life skills of men run in different channels. Few of the older males still fish actively, but a number of them in their seventies and eighties continue as the island's master boat builders—a role resting more on experience and expertise

elsewhere the stumps of others stand ready to support the vines of pole beans and the stalks of tomato plants. The boundaries between fields often go unmarked by fences or stone walls, being demarcated by large trees—such as the gomalimi—which tower above the scrub, giving shelter to workers and their grandchildren when they rest from the midday sun.

In some areas of economic life, the elderly on Cat Island use their skills in lieu of the strengths they once possessed. Women, for example, are particularly adept at *plaiting*—which is the manufacture of hats, baskets, mats, and carrying bags from long strips of palm, coconut, and sisal leaf. The process combines knowledge, dexterity, and a highly individualized sense of aesthetics. Older women know

JONATHAN LEVY

A seventy-five-year-old man rests with his granddaughters after making repairs to the thatched roof of his home. It is common for children to be raised by their grandparents while their parents work off Cat Island.

than muscle. The craftsmanship and art of their hands, like the whole plan of their vessels, are stored in their minds.

The process of construction begins not just with the woods a boatwright wants to use—madeira for the prow, dogwood for pegs, fir for planking, stern, and keel—but the knowledge of where on the island he can find them as standing trees, and the time required to season the timbers after cutting. The older men who practice this craft work entirely with hand tools, roughing out the wood and planing it to a thickness and pattern fixed in their memory. Most have no shop or shed but do all their labors outdoors.

The most skilled man from Three Rock Bay builds his boats in the shade of a grove of casuarina pines standing at the island edge of the beach near his home: The keel of his current project rests on an apron of sand, held in place with pegs,

with the ribs reaching up from it, braced on the outside by spare poles wedged into the earth. It takes him eight to ten months to complete a fishing vessel, and like his peers in this art, he confesses that now he never hurries. He says that "me and my boat are one, so why rush to be finished off." His work is slow, methodical, and thoughtful, but it is no less creative for the deliberate pace at which it is done.

Religion of reality

There is more passion than deliberation in one of the other major callings of the island's elders—that of the ministry. At the end of each week's practical responsibilities—children, grandchildren, goats, farming, and fishing—lies the Sabbath. And at the head of Sunday's celebration in most churches stands an

older man in the pulpit, backed by a phalanx of older women in the choir. Though the members of the senior generation are not alone in their sense of the spiritual, the active role of religious leadership does fall to them. They shepherd a flock that on other days they literally help to nurture.

One of the most respected and eloquent clergymen on the southern part of the island is the 73-year-old Baptist minister from Thrasher Creek. Both his outlook and his family life typify many of his generation. He is a father and grandparent, a man whose daughter and grandchildren live in his house, a straight-backed figure who often can be found weeding his garden or grinding corn in the hand-cranked machine that older islanders still use. The messages that come from his pulpit are less old-fashioned than the grinder, yet they express the perspective and leaven of age.

The evangelical sense of sin the minister feels is tempered by his Bahamian regard for human frailty, for the weakness of the flesh, for the power of social reality. He urges his congregation to seek out and honor the vows of marriage but does not condemn or hector those who have had "outside" children—the offspring born to unwed couples. The sons and daughters of such people, he sermonizes, deserve "our love, not our condemnation," their parents "the grace of understanding from those who know themselves well enough not to cast the first stone. Let God judge us, instead of us judging one another." Like his fellow clergy from nearby settlements, he is willing to look past personal failing if the greater love of family, community, and Jesus can bring redemption and salvation of the soul. Thrasher Creek's reverend calls his faith a "religion of reality," a passion tempered by time.

The beliefs that Cat Island elders sustain are, in turn, a source of sustenance for them. With the prospects of frailty and mortality before them, faith makes death less of a mystery, less of a lonely experience, than it commonly is in other places. When they part from kin or friends after a visit, voicing the hope of seeing them again soon, it is with the Bahamian caveat "if God spare life."

When God does not "spare life," people on Cat Island are likely to die at home, within the circle of family, rather than in a hospital or nursing home. And their final rituals, the funeral and burial, are dramas that bring together the whole community as a congregation of mourners. The faithful know not only that heaven will be their reward, but that their righteous example will be held up to others at their service: A funeral oration is a chance both to honor and to take lessons from the deceased.

Speaking to parishioners over the open casket of an 82-year-old man, a minister from Bramley once contrasted this individual's good deeds with his listeners' bad ones. His words alternated between reassurance and admonition. He first asked his audience: "Are you as good?! Be happy [for him that] he's dead; it was right!" He then went on to point out that the deceased would leave "our world" to "work in the land of the Lord," stressing that whereas the man being mourned was now "appointed," his listeners risked—through their misconduct—being "disappointed." The responsive mourners, caught up by then in loud wailing and singing, took the warning to heart: They echoed back the close, contrasting words antiphonally, rhythmically chanting "Appointed!" "Disappointed!" "Appointed!" "Disappointed!"

Death is made very real, very visible, and very audible on the island. People in church are expected to walk past the open coffin, to face the deceased, and then confront and comfort his family. At Bramley all will share the long walk from church to cemetery and take part in the burial by casting handfuls of dirt into the grave. Both the funeral and burial services are punctuated by passionately voiced cries and songs. A woman will shout out, in her grief, "O my mother! O my mother! I'll be there!" The hymns strike the most hopeful notes of all about aging and dying. "We'll all be there in heaven," prophesies one, and another proclaims "We never get old in the land of the Lord."

Elderly persons can even arrange to have the last word at their own funerals by requesting that their wills be read from the pulpit. This is common practice on Cat Island, and it gives the spirit of generosity a prominent place in the final ceremony. The reverend who spoke at one man's last rites talked about the Lord rewarding people who take nothing from this world: "You *enter* this world with your hands empty, and therefore you should *leave* this world with your hands

Funerals and burials are dramas that bring together the whole community as a congregation of mourners. At the graveside, hymns are sung with great intensity, striking hopeful notes about aging and dying.

empty." He pointed out that the deceased had done this: "That is why he has asked that no jewelry or anything else be placed inside his casket."

Finally, the minister told an anecdote to illustrate the moral that the way a person departs this life should reflect the way he lived it. It was the story of a recent funeral where, "to prove he would leave empty-handed, the dead man's will gave explicit instructions for burial. A hole was cut on either side of the coffin, one for each arm. Then, his two hands were slipped through each hole, outstretched. Well," he concluded, "this unique request was followed carefully at the time of his death, and when his coffin was carried to the place of burial, his hands could be viewed by all. They were

empty. He could hide nothing, take nothing. Just like Jesus on the cross, he died holding nothing. And the Lord could welcome him!"

Coming of age

The productive roles of Bahamian elders—in spiritual, in economic, and in family life—are built upon their desire and ability to remain active. Furthermore, none of their tasks are token ones, for the children, food, and spirits they help raise are all essential parts of life. But these varied roles are also made possible by the pace, scale, and layout of Cat Island's communities. With some support coming in from outside, older people are not burdened by the need for complete self-sufficiency, or the pressure to work at a speed and rate that exceed their capacity. The scope and size of their villages also make it feasible for the elderly to contribute what they can in these ways. Within a walk of their homes lie fields, friends, gardens, families, and herds. A comfortable place to sit—a seat, stump, or timeworn rock—from which to visit,

With the prospects of frailty and mortality before them, faith makes death less of a mystery.

plait, or simply watch community life and the sea, is within a few steps of their front doors. Work, leisure, and company are easy to reach, making each available with little effort and no expense.

Although the virtues of late life on Cat Island are real, they are accompanied by certain limitations. The island is neither a tropical paradise nor a faultless world in which to grow old. There is little in the way of medical care or government services. Making a living is hard and uncertain; and for those elders whose children have left to find work, years can go by without a chance to see their offspring.

Nor is Cat Island in any true sense a gerontocracy: Its older citizens do not wield much power or hold high office. Despite the respect that elders have earned, they are not to be counted among the island's legislators, its police, its government officials, or its major property owners and businesspeople. Their professions are more modest, their influence more subtle. Yet in the modest, subtle, and imperfect lives that they do lead, these elders offer some important lessons in how late life can be lived with meaning and dignity. Several elements of the picture they present stand out in sharp relief. On Cat Island, older people enjoy

● a strong sense of community;
● the presence of meaningful, accessible work;
● a pace to life and labor that they can accommodate themselves to;
● the chance to live and be around younger generations and other family members; and
● a physical layout for housing and communities that facilitates social and economic participation.

Contemplating these ingredients—elements that are commonly lacking in the lives of older people in more complex societies—might help us to rethink the expectations and conditions with which we surround our own elderly. Aged people on Cat Island benefit from high levels of regard, intimacy, involvement, and activity. In their culture there is no forced retirement, generation gap, nursing homes, or segregation of the aged.

In Western industrial societies, by contrast, the cultural disabilities that the elderly suffer from can be considerable. Contrary to Robert Browning's poetic call to

'Grow old along with me!
The best is yet to be …'

the negative images of old age often evolve into a self-fulfilling prophecy of decline and inactivity. The worst of the stereotypes—the older person as useless, senile, parasitic, and depressed—was once captured by Jonathan Swift: In *Gulliver's Travels*, he created the aged but immortal Struldbrugs, condemned by longevity to a melancholy, foolish, and envious eternity. Given the dubious gift of an endless but meaningless life, the Struldbrugs "must lie under the disadvantage of living like foreigners in their own country." The same plight, suggests Simone de Beauvoir in *The Coming of Age*, is shared by too many of today's elders: They must endure—in their own homelands—the special alienation which she calls "the loneliness of exile."

If old age is a foreign country, it is a land that we enter by passing through time rather than space. In this image, late life compels us to leave behind familiar roles and rewards, as well as our former bodies and capabilities. We take on a new, diminished identity as citizens of a place where we learn to do, and live with, less.

There are various metaphors that support this cultural concept of age. Growing older has been seen as a process of *stripping*, in which the aged person is divested of former powers and possessions. The body itself gets likened to a *run-down machine*. And in a seasonal figure of speech, people—like old plants and aging societies—enter the *autumn* of their years, perhaps to await the winter of their discontent.

On Cat Island, however, older people feel at home and are at home in their own country, even if their grown children must sometimes live a part of their own lives in exile. In the Bahamas, at least, the sons and daughters of this middle generation can still send their offspring back to the grandparents, while they live abroad with the assurance that the place which was once a home to them could be once again, in their own later years.

Additional Reading:

Simone de Beauvoir, *The Coming of Age*, translated by Patrick O'Brian, Putnam, New York, 1972.

Dean Collinwood and Steve Dodge, eds., *Modern Bahamian Society*, Caribbean Books, Parkersburg, Iowa, 1989.

Michael Craton, *A History of the Bahamas*, Collins, London, 1962.

Ashley Montague, *Growing Young*, third ed., Bergin and Garvey, Amherst, Mass., 1989.

Joel Savishinsky, ed., *Strangers No More: Anthropological Studies of Cat Island, the Bahamas*. Ithaca College, Ithaca, New York, 1978.

Jay Sokolovsky, ed., *The Cultural Context of Aging*, Bergin and Garvey, Amherst, Mass., 1990.

Sexuality and Aging

What it means to be sixty or seventy or eighty in the '90s

"It's the awfulness of it, " Harry said when asked how he was getting along after his wife died. It was the way he said the "awe"—with a stunned sound, as if he hadn't expected the blow to be so crushing.

Pounder of pianos, designer of great, black locomotives, father of five, this new fragility was a surprise. But it wasn't his last surprise.

After a year of bridge parties with old friends, Harry and his new fiancée turned up at a family dinner.

Their only worry was that the children would think Martha too young for him. She was 69. He was 78.

When they left for their honeymoon, the family still had questions. No one, including Harry and Martha, knew quite what to expect.

Three trends, longer life expectancy, early retirement and better health, are stretching the time between retirement and old age. These trends are redefining our image of aging for the 31 million Americans older than age 65. If you are in your 60s or 70s, you are probably more active and healthy than your parents were at a similar age. Many people are retiring earlier. This opens a whole new segment of your life.

Like everyone of every age, you probably want to continue sharing your life with others in fulfilling relationships. And, you may want to include sex in an intimate relationship with someone you love.

WHAT IS SEXUALITY?

The sexual drive draws humans together for biological reproduction, but it goes beyond this. Your sexuality influences your behavior, speech, appearance; indeed, many aspects of your life.

You might express your sexuality by buying an attractive blouse, playing a particular song or holding hands. Some people express their sexuality through shared interests and companionship. A more physical expression of sexuality is intimate contact, such as sexual intercourse.

Sexuality brings people together to give and receive physical affection. Although it's an important form of intimacy, sexual intimacy isn't the only one. For many people, sexual intimacy isn't an available or desired form of closeness. A close friendship or a loving grandparent-grandchild relationship, for example, can provide rewarding opportunities for non-sexual intimacy.

For some older people, though, sexual intimacy remains important. Despite this importance, sexuality in people after age 60 or 70 is not openly acknowledged.

MYTHS AND REALITIES

The widespread perception in America is that older people are not sexually active. Try to remember the last time the media portrayed two seniors in a passionate embrace. In America, sex is considered the exclusive territory of the young.

Comedian Sam Levinson expressed it well when he quipped, "My parents would never do such a thing; well, my father—maybe. But my mother—NEVER!"

This is a myth.

Realities

The reality is that many older people enjoy an active sex life that often is better than their sex life in early adulthood. The idea that your sexual drive dissolves sometime after middle age is nonsense. It's comparable to thinking your ability to enjoy good food or beautiful scenery would also disappear at a certain point.

In now famous studies, Dr. Alfred C. Kinsey collected information on sexual behavior in the 1940s. Drs. W. B. Masters and V. E. Johnson continued this research in the 1970s. Little of their research looked at people over 60. But in the last decade, a few telling studies show the stark difference between myth and reality.

In a 1992 University of Chicago study, Father Andrew Greeley, author and professor of sociology, released "Sex After Sixty: A Report." According to Greeley, "The happiest men and women in America are married people who continue to have sex frequently after they are 60. They are also most likely to report that they are living exciting lives."

Greeley's report, an analysis of two previous surveys involving 5,738 people, showed 37 percent of married people over 60 have sex once a week or more, and 16 percent have sex several times a week.

A survey of 4,245 seniors done by Consumers Union (*Love, Sex, and Aging,* 1984), concludes that, "The panorama of love, sex and aging is far richer and more diverse than the stereotype of life after 50. Both the quality and quantity of sexual activity reported can be properly defined as astonishing."

These surveys are helping today's seniors feel more comfortable acknowledging their sexuality. A 67-year-old consultant to the Consumers Union report wrote:

"Having successfully pretended for decades that we are nonsexual, my generation is now having second thoughts. We are increasingly realizing that denying our sexuality means denying an essential aspect of our common humanity. It cuts us off from communication with our children, our grandchildren and our peers on a subject of great interest to us all—sexuality."

From *Mayo Clinic Health Letter,* February 1993. Reprinted with permission of Mayo Foundation for Medical Education and Research, Rochester, Minnesota 55905.

Health and sexuality

Sex, like walking, doesn't require the stamina of a marathoner. It does require reasonably good health. Here are some guidelines:

■ *Use it or lose it* — Though the reason is unclear, prolonged abstinence from sex can cause impotence. Women who are sexually active after menopause have better vaginal lubrication and elasticity of vaginal tissues.

■ *Eat healthfully* — Follow a balanced, low-fat diet and exercise regularly. Fitness enhances your self-image.

■ *Don't smoke* — Men who smoke heavily are more likely to be impotent than men who don't smoke. Smokers are at an increased risk of hardening of the arteries, which can cause impotence (see page 47). Similar studies for women are needed.

■ *Control your weight* — Moderate weight loss can sometimes reverse impotence.

■ *Limit alcohol* — Chronic alcohol and drug abuse causes psychological and neurological problems related to impotence.

■ *Moderate coffee drinking may keep sex perking* — A recent study reported that elderly people who drank at least one cup of coffee a day were more likely to be sexually active than those who didn't. The reason for this association is unknown; further studies are needed.

■ *Protect against AIDS and other STDs* — The best protection against AIDS and other sexually transmitted diseases (STDs) is a long-standing, monogamous relationship. Next best: Use a condom.

SEX AFTER SIXTY: WHAT CAN YOU EXPECT?

Once you've reshaped your idea of what society should expect of you, you're faced with the sometimes more worrisome obstacle of what you can expect of yourself. Sex, something you've taken for granted most of your life, may suddenly be "iffy" at sixty.

Changes in women

Many women experience changes in sexual function in the years immediately before and after menopause. Contrary to myth, though, menopause does not mark the end of sexuality.

Generally, if you were interested in sex and enjoyed it as a younger woman, you probably will feel the same way after menopause. Yet menopause does bring changes:

• *Desire*—The effects of age on your sexual desire are the most variable of your sexual responses. Although your sex drive is largely determined by emotional and social factors, hormones like estrogen and testosterone do play a role.

Estrogen is made in your ovaries; testosterone, in your adrenal glands. Surprisingly, sexual desire is affected mainly by testosterone, not estrogen. At menopause, your ovaries stop producing estrogen, but most women produce enough testosterone to preserve their interest in sex.

• *Vaginal changes*—After menopause, estrogen deficiency may lead to changes in the appearance of your genitals and how you respond sexually.

The folds of skin that cover your genital region shrink and become thinner, exposing more of the clitoris. This increased exposure may reduce your sensitivity or cause an unpleasant tingling or prickling sensation when touched.

The opening to your vagina becomes narrower, particularly if you are not sexually active. Natural swelling and lubrication of your vagina occur more slowly during arousal. Even when you feel excited, your vagina may stay somewhat tight and dry. These factors can lead to difficult or painful intercourse (dyspareunia = DYS - pa - ROO - nee - ah).

• *Orgasm*—Because sexual arousal begins in your brain, you can have an orgasm during sexual stimulation throughout your life. You may have diminished or slower response. Women in their 60s and 70s have a greater incidence of painful uterine contractions during orgasm.

Changes in men

Physical changes in a middle-aged man's sexual response parallel those seen in a postmenopausal woman.

• *Desire*—Although feelings of desire originate in your brain, you need a minimum amount of the hormone testosterone to put these feelings into action. The great majority of aging men produce well above the minimum amount of testosterone needed to maintain interest in sex into advanced age.

• *Excitement*—By age 60, you may require more stimulation to get and maintain an erection, and the erection will be less firm. Yet a man with good blood circulation to the penis can attain erections adequate for intercourse until the end of life.

• *Orgasm*—Aging increases the length of time that must pass after an ejaculation and before stimulation to another climax. This interval may lengthen from just a few minutes at the age of 17, to as much as 48 hours by age 70.

Changes due to illness or disability

Whether you're healthy, ill or disabled, you have your own sexual identity and desires for sexual expression. Yet illness or disability can interfere with how you respond sexually to another person. Here's a closer look at how some medical problems can affect sexual expression:

• *Heart attack*—Chest pain, shortness of breath or the fear of a recurring heart attack can have an impact on your sexual behavior. But a heart attack will rarely turn you into a "cardiac cripple." If you were sexually active before your heart attack, you can probably be again. If you have symptoms of angina, your doctor may recommend nitroglycerine before intercourse. Most people who have heart disease are capable of a full, active sex life (see "Sex after a heart attack: Is it safe?").

Even though pulse rates, respiratory rates and blood pressure rise during intercourse, after intercourse they return to normal within minutes. Sudden death during sex is rare.

• *Prostate surgery*—For a benign condition, such as an enlarged prostate, surgery rarely causes impotence. Prostate surgery for cancer causes impotence 50 to 60 percent of the time. However, this type of impotence can be treated (see next page).

• *Hysterectomy*—This is surgery to remove the uterus and cervix, and in some cases, the fallopian tubes, ovaries and lymph nodes. A hysterectomy, by itself, doesn't interfere with your physical ability to have intercourse or experience orgasm once you've recovered from the surgery. Removing the ovaries, however, creates an instant menopause and accelerates the physical and emotional aspects of the natural condition.

When cancer is not involved, be sure you understand why you need a hysterectomy and how it will help your symptoms. Ask your doctor what you can expect after the operation. Reassure yourself that a hysterectomy generally doesn't affect sexual pleasure and that hormone therapy should prevent physical and emotional changes from interfering.

• *Drugs*—Some commonly used medicines can interfere with sexual function. Drugs that control high blood pressure, such as thiazide diuretics and beta blockers, can reduce desire and impair erection in men and lubrication in women. In contrast, calcium channel blockers and angiotensin converting enzyme (ACE) inhibitors have little known effect on sexual function.

Other drugs that affect sexual function include antihistamines, drugs used to treat depression and drugs that block secretion of stomach acid. If you take one of these drugs and are experiencing side effects, ask your doctor if there is an equally effective medication that doesn't cause the side effects. Alcohol also may adversely affect sexual function.

• *Hardening of the arteries and heart disease*—About half of all impotence in men past age 50 is caused by damage to nerves or blood vessels to the penis. Hardening of the arteries (atherosclerosis) can damage small vessels and restrict blood flow to the genitals. This can interfere with erection in men and swelling of vaginal tissues in women.

• *Diabetes*—Diabetes can increase the collection of fatty deposits (plaque) in blood vessels. Such deposits restrict the flow of blood to the penis. About half of men with diabetes become impotent. Their risk of impotence increases with age. Men who've had diabetes for many years and who also have nerve damage are more likely to become impotent.

If you are a woman with diabetes, you may suffer dryness and painful inter-

Sex and illness

Changes in your body due to illness or surgery can affect your physical response to sex. They also can affect your self-image and ultimately limit your interest in sex. Here are tips to help you maintain confidence in your sexuality:

■ *Know what to expect* — Talk to your doctor about the usual effects your treatment has on sexual function.

■ *Talk about sex* — If you feel weak or tired and want your partner to take a more active role, say so. If some part of your body is sore, guide your mate's caresses to create pleasure and avoid pain.

■ *Plan for sex* — Find a time when you're rested and relaxed. Taking a warm bath first or having sex in the morning may help. If you take a pain reliever, such as for arthritis, time the dose so that its effect will occur during sexual activity.

■ *Prepare with exercise* — If you have arthritis or another disability, ask your doctor or therapist for range-of-motion exercises to help relax your joints before sex.

■ *Find pleasure in touch* — It's a good alternative to sexual intercourse. Touching can simply mean holding each other. Men and women can sometimes reach orgasm with the right kind of touching.

If you have no partner, touching yourself for sexual pleasure may help you re-affirm your own sexuality. It can also help you make the transition to intercourse after an illness or surgery.

course that reduce the frequency of orgasm. You may have more frequent vaginal and urinary tract infections.

• *Arthritis*—Although arthritis does not affect your sex organs, the pain and stiffness of osteoarthritis or rheumatoid arthritis can make sex difficult to enjoy. If you have arthritis, discuss your capabilities and your desires openly with your partner. As long as you and your partner keep communications open, you can have a satisfying sexual relationship.

• *Cancer*—Some forms of cancer cause anemia, loss of appetite, muscle wasting or neurologic impairment that leads to weakness. Surgery can alter your physical appearance. These problems can decrease your sexual desire or pleasure.

Cancer may also cause direct damage to your sexual organs or to their nerve and blood supplies; treatment can produce side effects that may interfere with sexual function, desire or pleasure. Discuss possible effects of your treatment with your doctor. If cancer has disrupted your usual sexual activity, seek other ways of expression. Sometimes cuddling or self-stimulation can be enough.

TO REMAIN SEXUALLY ACTIVE, WHAT CAN A WOMAN DO?

Long-term estrogen replacement therapy (ERT) can not only prevent osteoporosis (bone thinning) and heart disease, it can help prevent changes in vaginal tissue, lubrication and desire as well.

Testosterone enhances sexual desire in women. But, it also can produce unwanted, sometimes irreversible side effects such as deepening of the voice and increased facial hair.

Your doctor may prescribe estrogen cream which, applied to your genital area, can prevent dryness and thinning of vaginal tissue. You can also use over-the-counter lubricants just before sexual activity. It's best to use a water-based lubricant, such as K-Y jelly, rather than oil-based mineral oil or petroleum jelly.

If you have problems reaching orgasm, talk to your physician. Your doctor might adjust your medications or offer other options, including counseling, if the problem is non-medical; or, your doctor may refer you to a specialist.

What can a man do?
Only a few years ago doctors generally thought that about 90 percent of

Sex after a heart attack: Is it safe?

If you can climb a flight of stairs without symptoms, you can usually resume sexual activity. Ask your doctor for specific advice. Here are some guidelines:

■ *Wait after eating* — Wait three or four hours after eating a large meal or drinking alcohol before intercourse. Digestion puts extra demands on your heart.

■ *Rest* — Make sure you are well rested before you have intercourse, and rest after.

■ *Find comfortable positions* — Positions such as side-by-side, or your partner on top, are less strenuous.

impotence was psychological. Now they realize that 50 to 75 percent of impotence is caused by physical problems. There is a wide range of treatments. Keep in mind that the success of any treatment depends, in part, on open communication between partners in a close, supportive relationship. Here are some treatment options:

• *Psychological therapy*—Many impotence problems can be solved simply by you and your partner understanding the normal changes of aging and adapting to them. For help in this process, your doctor may recommend counseling by a qualified psychiatrist, psychologist or therapist who specializes in the treatment of sexual problems.

• *Hormone adjustment*—Is testosterone a magic potion for impotence? No. Although testosterone supplementation is used in rare instances, its effectiveness for aging men experiencing a normal, gradual decline in testosterone is doubtful.

• *Vascular surgery*—Doctors sometimes can surgically correct impotence caused by an obstruction of blood flow to

the penis. However, this bypass procedure is appropriate in only a small number, less than 2 percent, of young men who have impotence problems. The long-term success of this surgery is too often disappointing.

• *Vacuum device*—Currently one of the most common treatments for impotence, this device consists of a hollow, plastic cylinder that fits over your flaccid penis. With the device in place, you attach a hand pump to draw air out of the cylinder. The vacuum created draws blood into your penis, creating an erection.

Once your penis erect, you slip an elastic ring over the cylinder onto the base of your penis. For intercourse, you remove the cylinder from your penis. The ring maintains your erection by reducing blood flow out of your penis. Because side effects of improper use can damage the penis, you should use this device under your doctor's care.

• *Self-injection*—Penile injection therapy is another option. It involves injecting a medication directly into your penis.

After age 60, intercourse may require some planning

Problems	Solutions	
Decreased desire	■ Use mood enhancers (candlelight, music, romantic thoughts). ■ Hormone replacement therapy (estrogen or testosterone).	■ Treatment for depression. ■ Treatment for drug abuse (alcohol). ■ Behavioral counseling.
Vaginal dryness; Vagina expands less in length and width	■ Use a lubricant. ■ Consider estrogen replacement therapy.	■ Have intercourse regularly. ■ Pelvic exercises prescribed by your doctor.
Softer erections; More physical and mental stimulation to get and maintain erection	■ Use a position that makes it easy to insert the penis into the vagina. ■ Accept softer erections as a normal part of aging.	■ Don't use a condom if disease transmission is not possible. ■ Tell your partner what is most stimulating to you.
Erection lost more quickly; Takes longer to get another	■ Have intercourse less frequently. ■ Emphasize quality, not quantity.	■ Emphasize comfortable sexual activities that don't require an erection.

One or more drugs (papaverine, phentolamine and prostaglandin-E1) are used. The injection is nearly painless and produces a more natural erection than a vacuum device or an implant.

• *Penile implants*—If other treatments fail or are unsatisfactory, a surgical implant is an alternative. Implants consist of one or two silicone or polyurethane cylinders that are surgically placed inside your penis. Implants are not the perfect solution. Mayo experts say there is a 10 to 15 percent chance an implant will malfunction within five years, but the problem almost always can be corrected. Many men still find the procedure worthwhile.

There are two major types of implants: one uses malleable rods and the other uses inflatable cylinders. Malleable rods remain erect, although they can be bent close to your body for concealment. Because there are no working parts, malfunctions are rare.

Inflatable devices consist of one or two inflatable cylinders, a finger-activated pump and an internal reservoir, which stores the fluid used to inflate the tubes. All components—the cylinders, pump and reservoir—are implanted within your penis, scrotum and lower abdomen. These devices produce more "natural" erections.

• *Medications*—Neurotransmitters are chemicals in your brain and nerves that help relay messages. Nitric oxide is now recognized as one of the most important of these chemicals for stimulating an erection. Unfortunately, there is as yet no practical way to administer nitric oxide for treatment of impotence. Other drugs have not proven effective.

SEX IN SYNC

You might wonder how sex can survive amidst tubes, pumps and lubes that can make you feel more like a mechanic than a romantic.

Actually, many people discover that late-life sexuality survives in an increased diversity of expression, sometimes slow, tender and affectionate, and sometimes more intense and spontaneous.

In some ways, middle- and late-life sex are better than the more frantic pace of your younger years. Biology finally puts sex in sync. As a young man, you were probably more driven by hormones and societal pressure . You may find that now desire, arousal and orgasm take longer and aren't always a sure thing. You may find setting and mood more important. Touch and extended foreplay may become as satisfying as more urgent needs for arousal and release.

As a woman, you were probably more dependent on setting and mood when you were younger. You may feel more relaxed and less inhibited in later life. You may be more confident to assert your sexual desires openly.

COMMUNICATION

It can be difficult to talk to another person about sex—doctor, counselor or even a lifetime lover. But, good communication is essential in adapting your sex life to changes caused by aging. Here are three cornerstones of good communication:

• *Be informed*—To start the process, know the facts. Gather as much reliable information as you can about sex and aging and share the facts with your partner.

• *Be open*—If there are unresolved problems in your relationship, sex won't solve them. Be sensitive to the views and feelings of your partner. Work out the differences that are inevitable - before you go to bed. Appropriate sexual counseling can help you and your partner work out problems and enhance your relationship.

• *Be warned*—Most likely, your physician will be willing to discuss questions concerning sexuality with you, but it would be unusual if he or she were a specialist in treating sexual problems. Ask your doctor to refer you to a specialist in this area.

ADAPTING TO CHANGES

As your sexual function changes, you may need to adapt not only to physical changes but to emotional changes as well, perhaps even to changes in your living arrangements.

Lovemaking can lose its spontaneity. Adapting may mean finding the courage to experiment with new styles of making love with the same partner. It may mean trying alternatives to intercourse. You may feel self-conscious about suggesting new ways to find pleasure. But, by changing the focus of sex, you minimize occasional erectile failures that occur.

And, adapting may mean having the flexibility to seek a new partner if you're single. Because women outlive men an average of seven years, women past 50 outnumber unmarried men almost three to one. Older women have less opportunity to remarry.

Families also need to be flexible. Children may need to deal with issues such as inheritance and acceptance of the new spouse.

Another factor that often limits sexual activity is the status of your living arrangements. If you live in a nursing home, you may face an additional problem. Although there are a few nursing homes that offer the privacy of apartment-style living, most do not. Fortunately, this problem is becoming more widely recognized. In the future, nursing homes may offer more privacy.

If you live independently, getting out and around may be a chore. Yet, many older men and women do find new partners. And, they report the rewards of sharing your life with someone you care for may be well-worth the extra effort.

THE NEED FOR INTIMACY IS AGELESS

It takes determination to resist the "over-the-hill" mentality espoused by society today. Age brings changes at 70 just as it does at 17. But you never outgrow your need for intimate love and affection. Whether you seek intimacy through non-sexual touching and companionship or through sexual activity, you and your partner can overcome obstacles. The keys are caring, adapting and communicating.

Religiosity, Aging, and Life Satisfaction

Harold Cox, PhD
André Hammonds, PhD

Harold Cox and André Hammonds are affiliated with the Department of Sociology and Social Work, Indiana State University, Terre Haute, IN 47809.

ABSTRACT. A review of the past studies of religiosity and aging indicates that a number of common patterns of church attendance, belief in God, life satisfaction and personal adjustment can be found. Past research indicates that church attendance hits a low point between 18 and 24, remains relatively stable between 25 and 54, rises slightly after 54 and drops slightly after 80. Thus for most of one's adult life up to age 80, church attendance is fairly stable with a slight rise in the later years. The data indicated that a majority of all age groups express a belief in God but that the older one becomes the more likely he/she is to express a belief in God. There is a tendency for a higher percentage of older age groups to believe that religion is important in one's life and to believe in immortality. All of the past studies that looked at religiosity and life satisfaction came to the same conclusion—those persons who attend church experience greater life satisfaction and are better adjusted than those who do not. A plausible explanation for the positive value that religious participation has on the lives of the elderly is that the church becomes a focal point of social integration and activity for the elderly, providing them with a sense of community and well-being. This concept of the positive functions the church serves in the lives of the elderly is analogous to Durkheim's discussion of the church as a moral community.

INTRODUCTION

When reviewing the past articles and research reports that address the subject of religion and aging, one cannot help but notice the dearth of materials that exist on this topic. On occasion, sociology of religion textbooks will refer to religious participation over the life cycle, to age and religious participation or to differences in religious participation by men and women. In examining research articles in the various gerontology journals, one will find a few articles dealing with religion and aging but this clearly is not a topic that has caught the imagination and attention of large numbers of gerontologists. Given the fact that the great majority of older persons profess some religious belief and when questioned will assert that religion is very important in their lives, the sparsity of scientific writing on this subject is surprising. Assuming that a knowledge of the relationship between religion and aging should provide us with greater insight into the beliefs, values, and attitudes of a very large percent of the older American population, this paper will attempt to review the past research on this topic, to summarize the more significant findings of these studies, and to suggest future directions for researchers interested in this field.

CHURCH ATTENDANCE

While researchers have devised a variety of methods to measure a person's religiosity, perhaps one of the quickest and best indicators of religious commitment is church attendance. Several studies have examined church attendance to determine what pattern was most prevalent over the life cycle. The early studies done in the 1950s and 1960s had indicated a slightly higher church attendance among older people than among younger people.[1] Later studies done in the 1970s did not indicate this pattern of church attendance.[2] The research findings on church attendance throughout the life cycle are inconclusive and subject to a variety of interpretations. One major problem of interpretation is that most of these were cross-sectional studies based on interviews and questionnaires given to younger and older persons at a single point in time. Thus, in the cross-sectional studies it is impossible to determine whether these differences show changes over time or whether the recent generations are simply less religious than earlier ones.

Bahr reviewed the earliest studies of church attendance and developed four different models based on the findings of these studies.[3] These models are:

1. The traditional model which reveals a steady drop in church attendance from ages 18-35 with the lowest point for most people being between 30 to 35 after which church attendance increases until old age.
2. The stability model asserts that there is no relationship between aging and church attendance and that the pattern of church attendance remains stable throughout one's lifetime.
3. The family cycle model indicates that church attendance is altered by stages of the family cycle. Families peak in church attendance when the children reach Sunday school age. As the children grow up and leave home, the church attendance of the parents begins to drop.
4. The disengagement model assumes that like many other areas of social participation after middle age, church attendance declines.

The pattern of religious belief and church attendance found by most of the more recent studies tends to indicate a stability of religious belief and church attendance over the life cycle, the only exception being a decline in church attendance among the very old. Blazer and Palmore report that religious beliefs and attitudes remain fairly stable over the life cycle with no significant increase or decrease.[4] They did however find a gradual decrease in religious activity during the later years. Similarly Riley and Foner, in their inventory of research on religion, observed that church attendance tends to decrease rather than increase in old age.[5] Moberg also observed a pattern of declining church attendance among older persons.[6]

The 1975 Harris poll (see Table 1) indicates a low in church attendance between ages 18-24 and a fairly stable attendance pattern over the life cycle with a slight increase after the age of 55 and a slight decrease after the age of 80.[7]

The Harris findings confirmed the earlier findings of Havighurst and Albreckt[8] that women attend church more frequently and maintain a higher degree of religious participation for a longer period of time than men do.

From *Journal of Religion and Aging*, Vol. 5, Nos. 1/2, 1988, pp. 1-21. © 1989 by The Haworth Press, Inc. Reprinted by permission.

TABLE 1

Attendance at a Church or Synagogue in Last Year or So

| | Attended in Last Year % | When Attended Last | | | | |
		Within Last Week or Two %	A Month Ago %	More Than 3 Months Ago %	Not Sure %	%
Total Public	75	71	13	7	9	*
18 to 64	74	70	14	7	9	*
65 and over	77	79	9	5	7	*
18 to 24	67	60	18	8	14	*
25 to 39	73	72	11	7	10	*
40 to 54	78	70	15	8	7	--
55 to 64	81	79	11	4	6	--
65 to 69	80	79	9	5	6	1
70 to 79	78	79	10	4	7	*
80 and over	68	76	10	6	8	*

*Less than 0.5 per cent.
Source: Louis Harris and Associates, The Myth and Reality of Aging in America, Washington, D.C.: National Council on the Aging, 1975, p. 181.

Lazerwitz found that among persons 65 and over, 66 percent of the Catholics, 46 percent of the Protestants, and 25 percent of the Jews attended church regularly.[9]

While the diverse research findings on age and church attendance do not entirely support any of Bahr's four models, there appear to be some common trends. Other than for 18-24 year olds, the pattern of church attendance over the life cycle is fairly stable with a slight increase after age 55 and a slight decrease after age 80. The low point in church attendance for 18-24 year olds can perhaps best be explained by the fact that this is a period of transition in their lives from teenage to adult status. They are frequently moving away from their home communities to go into the service, attend college or to take a job. It takes time to become established in the new community and reestablish the same religious ties and commitments they had in their home community. The drop in church attendance and activity noted in many of the studies among the very old was probably related to poor health and a lack of available transportation to attend church services.

BELIEF IN GOD

Crandall argues that a person's commitment to religious beliefs is important because it tends to shape his/her attitudes, beliefs, opinions and values.[10] Simultaneously it provides the individual a framework with which to see and interpret events in the world for himself/herself and others.

Riley and Foner indicated that the older the person was, the more likely he/she was to express a belief in God.[11] In every age category from the 18-24 to the 65 and over group, the proportion expressing a belief in God increases.

These results were obtained, however, from cross-sectional data and it is impossible to determine if this reflects an increase in religious belief as one ages or merely generational differences in belief. Some would argue that this is a reflection of the increasing secularization of society by which each succeeding age cohort is somewhat less religious than their predecessors.

Whether these differences are a result of generational differences in religious belief or of a gradual shift in religious belief over the life cycle, it does appear that the current group of older persons is more likely to believe in God and to consider religion more important than those persons under 65.

It is interesting to note a similar pattern of response by age when inquiring about the importance of religion in one's life.[12] According to Harris' data, only 34 percent of those persons 18-24 indicate that religion is "very important" but 73 percent of those 80+ do so (Table 2).

BELIEF IN IMMORTALITY

The belief in immortality may have special significance for older persons since they must recognize that at some point they will die. Moreover the older they become, the more they must realize and accept the fact that death for them will occur sometime in the not too distant future. Past studies have indicated that most older persons have come to accept the reality of their own death and are not unduly worried about the termination of their lives.

While one's degree of religious faith and commitment apparently remains fairly stable over the life cycle, Stark hypothesized that because of its special relevance for the elderly, belief in immortality would increase systematically with age.[13] The data clearly indicate that this is the case for Protestants whether liberal, moderate, or conservative, but not for Catholics for whom the data are ambiguous and difficult to interpret (Table 3).

In a study of the psychology of religion, Pratt had observed that in the modern secular world, religion had lost much of its sacred and supernatural status and the most important pragmatic value of religion was the belief in a personal future life.[14] In a similar view, Riley and Foner conclude after a review of the research on religion that belief in God and immortality is firmly ingrained in most older people and the public as well.[15]

ORTHODOX RELIGION

Stark attempted to determine if people were more orthodox in their religious belief as they aged.[16] Orthodox religious beliefs were presumed by Stark to be the most conservative beliefs and he felt that older persons might be more likely to hold these beliefs. The four measures of orthodox belief which Stark measured were a firm belief in a personal God, a belief in the divinity of Jesus Christ, a belief in the authenticity of biblical miracles and a belief in the existence of the devil. As Table 4 indicates, Stark did not find a gradual shift toward orthodox religious beliefs as one ages but rather a lower percentage of orthodox believers for those post-World War II generations. The meaningful shift for both moderate

TABLE 2

The Importance of Religion in Your Life

	18-64	65+	18-24	25-39	40-54	55-64	65-69	70-79	80+
Very important	49	71	34	45	58	65	69	71	73
Somewhat important	33	21	40	35	29	25	22	21	19
Hardly important at all	17	7	25	20 o	12	10 o	8	8 o	6
Not sure	1	1	1		1		1		

o Less than 0.5 percent.

SOURCE: Louis Harris and Associates, The Myths and Realities of Aging 1975.

TABLE 3

Age and Belief in Life after Death

Percentage who think it "completely true" that
"there is a life beyond death"

Age:	Liberal Protestants		Moderate Protestants		Conservative Protestants		Roman Catholics	
Under 20	38%	(21)	56%	(16)	87%	(15)	90%	(10) a
20-29	41	(95)	62	(99)	90	(89)	84	(93)
30-39	47	(249)	65	(205)	92	(105)	78	(145)
40-49	44	(278)	69	(251)	90	(103)	77	(122)
50-59	51	(169)	75	(149)	99	(68)	80	(87)
60-69	75	(91)	86	(92)	96	(45)	81	(47)
70 and over	70	(52)	87	(59)	100	(20)	78	(18)

aToo few cases for a stable percentage, presented for descriptive interest only.

Source: Rodney Stark, "Age and Faith: A Changing Outlook or an Old Process?" in Religion in Sociological Perspective: Essays in the Empirical Study of Religion, edited by Charles Y. Glock. Belmont, CA: Wadsworth.

and conservative Protestants came between the prewar generations who were above 50 in age and the 40-year olds who were considered by Stark to be the postwar generations. The postwar generations were less likely to hold orthodox religious beliefs. The Catholics remained fairly orthodox throughout the life cycle. The liberal Protestants were relatively nonorthodox in religious belief throughout the life cycle.

Stark concluded that post—World War II America was a more urban and a considerably more secular society and as a result less accepting of orthodox religious beliefs. Stark states:

World War II was a watershed between the new world and the older America of parochial small-town and rural society. While all the persons in this sample live today in this new America, those past fifty did not grow up in it. This data strongly suggests that in new America traditional Christian orthodoxy is less powerful.[17]

Wingrove and Alston noted a similar trend toward secularization of society when they concluded that all cohorts reached their peak in religious service attendance between 1950 and 1960.[18] They found that after 1965 all cohorts showed a decline in religious attendance.

RELIGIOUS RITUALISM AND PRIVATE DEVOTIONALISM

Stark examined the relationship between age and both religious ritual involvement and private devotionalism.[19] The relationship which Stark found between ritual involvement and private devotionalism can be seen in Table 5.

The only noticeable pattern for Protestants was for those persons 70 and over to be more inclined to ritual commitment than those under 70. There seems to be no distinct pattern for those under 70 except that those under 20 are a bit less likely to become involved in ritual than are those over 20. It should be noted, however, that there are so few respondents under 20 that one should be careful in drawing any conclusions. Other than the under 20 group being less involved in ritual than the rest, there appears to be no noticeable relationship between ritual involvement and age of Roman Catholics.

The most notable result of Stark's research can be seen in the bottom half of Table 5 where it seems apparent that private devotionalism increases noticeably with age. Only 34 percent of the liberal Protestants in their 20s scored high on private devotionalism, whereas 48 percent of those in their 50s and 68 percent of those 70 and over did so. For moderate Protestants, the figures indicate that private devotionalism was practiced by 35 percent for those in their

TABLE 4

Age and Orthodoxy

===

Percent High on Orthodoxy Index

Age:	Liberal Protestants	Moderate Protestants	Conservative Protestants	Roman Catholics
Under 20	5 (19)	29 (15)	a (12)	a (9)
20-29	10 (91)	26 (95)	75 (89)	64 (89)
30-39	10 (243)	27 (203)	79 (101)	66 (141)
40-49	9 (262)	28 (244)	78 (102)	48 (124)
Postwar generations				

Prewar generations				
50-59	11 (157)	40 (134)	94 (67)	61 (83)
60-69	14 (80)	49 (79)	89 (43)	73 (41)
70 and over	27 (40)	45 (51)	100 (19)	64 (15)

----

a Too few cases for stable percentages

SOURCE: Rodney Stark, "Age and Faith: A Changing Outlook or an Old Process?" in Religion in Sociological Perspective: Essays in the Empirical Study of Religion, edited by Charles Y. Glock. Belmont, CA: Wadsworth.

20s, 58 percent for those in their 50s and 81 percent for those 70 and over. The proportions of conservative Protestants who engaged in private devotionalism were 62 percent for those 70 and older. Among Roman Catholics the same pattern is found going from 56 percent for 20-year olds to 74 percent for 50-year olds to 75 percent for those 70 and above.

Moberg[20] and Hammond[21] both found a similar pattern of private devotionalism and age and concluded that although church attendance or "external" religious practices decline with increasing age, internal religious practices such as reading the Bible at home, praying, and listening or watching religious programs on radio and television all increase.

This turning inward to very private and personal religious practices as confirmed by several researchers would seem to be consistent with the psychological studies of personality changes in later life which indicate a closure of personality in old age and less need for group support and external sanctions for one's behavior.

RELIGIOSITY AND LIFE SATISFACTION

A number of scientists have observed the potentially positive value that religious faith and activities can have on the lives of older Americans. Barron notes some of the psychological supports that religion provides for older persons which include helping them: (1) face impending death; (2) find and maintain a sense of meaningfulness and significance in life; (3) accept the inevitable losses of old

age; and (4) discover and utilize the compensatory values that are potential in old age.[22] Socially the church provides a number of functions which can be particularly useful for older Americans. The church provides a variety of different social activities which bring people of all ages and backgrounds together. The social interaction that ensues tends to pull the individual into an active social involvement and to reduce social isolation. These activities can involve the older persons in community concerns and the current issues of the day, whatever they may be, since they will inevitably be discussed on such occasions. Moreover, the interest shown the individual by others involved in the activities becomes a source of social support. In addition, they draw the older person's attention away from himself/herself and to the problems and concerns of others. All of these things have positive consequences for the older person and are likely to improve the overall morale and outlook on life. Wolff observed that religious belief, prayer, and faith in God all helped the aged to overcome many of the common problems of old age such as loneliness, grief and unhappiness.[23]

A number of studies have attempted to determine if there was a positive relationship between religion and life satisfaction for older Americans. Moberg and Taves made a study of church participation and life adjustment in old age.[24] They questioned 5000 persons over 65 in four midwestern states. They found that church members had higher personal adjustment scores than nonmembers and that church leaders and officers had higher adjustment scores than the church members. They concluded that their evidence convincingly indicated church participation was related to good personal adjustment in later life. Moberg and Taves did observe that the direction of this relationship was difficult to determine. Do those who are

TABLE 5

Public Ritual Involvement, Private Devotionalism, and Age

Percent High on Index of Public Ritual Involvement

Age	Liberal Protestants		Moderate Protestants		Conservative Protestants		Roman Catholics	
						a		a
Under 20	19	(21)	38	(16)	36	(14)	30	(10)
20-29	23	(97)	40	(99)	73	(89)	46	(92)
30-39	38	(247)	45	(208)	73	(107)	47	(146)
40-49	28	(282)	46	(258)	75	(104)	46	(129)
50-59	24	(168)	41	(146)	83	(65)	43	(94)
60-69	24	(95)	47	(90)	75	(43)	54	(46)
70 and over	54	(54)	53	(60)	90	(21)	41	(22)

Percent High on Index of Private Devotionalism

Age	Liberal Protestants		Moderate Protestants		Conservative Protestants		Roman Catholics	
						a		a
Under 20	37	(19)	29	(14)a	64	(14)	56	(9)
20-29	34	(90)	35	(97)	62	(87)	58	(93)
30-39	41	(237)	43	(204)	75	(105)	63	(142)
40-49	35	(268)	46	(246)	79	(104)	62	(125)
50-59	48	(163)	58	(148)	88	(68)	74	(91)
60-69	51	(94)	71	(93)	93	(45)	77	(47)
70 and over	68	(53)	81	(57)	96	(21)	75	(20)

a Too few cases for stable percentages, presented for descriptive purposes only.

Source: Rodney Stark, "Age and Faith: A Changing Outlook or an Old Process?" in Religion in Sociological Perspective: Essays in the Empirical Study of Religion, edited by Charles Y. Glock. Belmont, CA:Wadsworth.

well adjusted choose to engage in many religious activities or does engaging in many religious activities lead one to be well adjusted?

Studies by both Edwards and Klemmeck[25] and Spreitzer and Snyder[26] came to the same conclusion regarding the positive value of religious participation for older persons. Their evidence indicated that religiosity was related to life satisfaction and other measures of well-being for older persons. Similarly, Blazer and Palmore found that happiness and a sense of usefulness and personal adjustment are significantly related to religious activity and attitudes.[27]

Guy, in a study of religion and life satisfaction, found that the group which scored highest on the measure of life satisfaction was the one which reported attending church more frequently today than fifteen years ago.[28] They were closely followed by the group whose church attendance pattern had remained relatively stable. Respondents attending church less today than fifteen years ago score lower than the other two groups (on life satisfaction) with the lowest (on life satisfaction) scores being made by those who never attended church. Similarly, Markides, in a study of church attendance, self-rated religiosity, and practice of private prayer and life satisfaction, found only church attendance was significantly related to life satisfaction.[29] Markides concluded that apparently the integrative function of religion was the crucial determinant of life satisfaction rather than the spiritual function.

Ortega, Crutchfield and Rushing's findings, in a study of race differences and personal well-being of the elderly, would tend to support Markides' argument with a respect to the integrative function of the church.[30] Ortega et al. found elderly blacks reporting higher life satisfaction scores than elderly whites. After introducing a multitude of control variables to explain the race differences in life satisfaction scores, they concluded:

that control with friends mediates the relationship only where friendships have the church as their locus. It appears that the

association between race and life satisfaction is due, at least in part, to greater church related friends among the black elderly.[31]

One possible explanation of their findings which they suggest is that the black church in the South forms a focal point of the community, serving as a pseudo-extended family, particularly for the aged. As noted, this argument is very similar to Markides' hypothesis of the integrative function of religion.

The past studies then overwhelmingly support the fact that there is a positive relationship between religious belief, religious participation and life satisfaction in later life. While as Moberg observed, it is not possible at this time to determine the direction of this relationship, it is clear that older church members score higher on tests of personal adjustment, maintain a healthier outlook on life and express a greater degree of life satisfaction. Markides and Ortega et al. argue that the church serves as a focal point for individual and community integration of the elderly and that this is crucial to their sense of personal well-being.[32]

CONCLUSION

The subject of religion and aging has not been one of the more widely researched areas of gerontology. Admittedly there may be a degree of scientific bias here since scientists are somewhat less likely to be religious than the general public and simultaneously may reflect the more secular attitudes of a society that is becoming more urbanized.

Regardless of the limited and sometimes dated nature of studies of religion and aging, some trends and patterns can be located. Church attendance hits a low point between 18 and 24, remains relatively stable between 25 and 54, rises slightly after 54 and drops slightly after the age of 80. Most researchers concluded that the drop in church after age 80 is a reflection of the declining health of older persons and the fact that many of them don't drive and frequently have no way of getting to church. For most of one's adult life up to age 80 then, church attendance is fairly stable with a slight rise in the later years. Stark has estimated that this pattern of church attendance may not remain true for future generations of old persons since he felt that the post-World War II generations were on the whole somewhat less likely to attend church than their elders had been. Blazer and Palmore, in one of the few longitudinal studies of religious attitudes and participation, found that religious attitudes are fairly constant over time but that religious activities do decline with age.

In terms of the individuals believing in God, past research had indicated that a majority of all age groups express a belief in God, but that the older one becomes, the more likely he/she is to express belief in God. Similar patterns were found with regard to the importance of religion in a person's life, and a belief in immortality. Once again, a majority of all age groups believe that religion is important in life and believe in immortality. There is a tendency for a higher percentage of the older age groups to believe that religion is important in one's life and to believe in immortality. Since these studies of church attendance and religious beliefs have, for the most part, been cross-sectional, the interpretation of the results and any conclusions drawn must be made with considerable caution.

Stark, in examining whether persons became more orthodox and conservative in their religious beliefs as they aged, did not find this to be the case. He felt that his most significant finding was that the post-World War II generations were less likely to be orthodox in their religious beliefs.

In terms of their involvement in private devotions several studies found that older persons were more likely to engage in private devotions than younger age groups. Apparently older persons compensate for some of their decline in religious activity which Blazer and Palmore found by engaging in private devotions. Perhaps the psychological studies which indicate a closure of personality and a turning inward on the part of older persons are true and can explain the increase in private devotionalism on the part of the older persons.

All of the past studies that looked at religion and life satisfaction came to the same conclusions: those persons who attend church experience greater life satisfaction and are better adjusted than the average church member. This relationship may, in part, be explained by Crandall's[33] observation that faith in religion provides the individual with a philosophy of life as well as a whole series of attitudes, values and beliefs which help him interpret and understand the world around him. Moreover, persons with strong religious beliefs are likely to attend church services and social functions which are comprised of others who share their beliefs and views of reality and thereby receive group support for their convictions. Markides'[34] and Ortega's[35] studies indicated that the church provides for individuals a sense of social and community integration which is highly correlated with their sense of personal wellbeing. This integrative function of the church described by Markides and Ortega is very similar to Durkheim's discussion of the church as a moral community.[36]

Religious activities tend to provide useful roles for older persons during the retirement years. They can become deacons, elders, or Sunday school teachers and thus assume leadership roles in religious activities which they may have been deprived of in work activities at the time of their retirement. Since the work of the church in ministering to the needs of the community is a never ending task, there are always a great variety of volunteer activities the older person can become involved in from visiting the homebound, to working with counseling services, to directing a recreational program for young people. The church does provide for its older members a wide range of social activities which tend to pull the older person into contact with other people and to reduce the possibility of social isolation and loneliness. Regardless of the reasons, older church members tend to be happier and better adjusted than nonmembers.

A critical unanswered question which researchers in this field should address is whether Stark is correct that post-World War II generations are less religious and less orthodox in their religious views than those born prior to this time.

ENDNOTES

1. Joseph H. Fichter, "The Profile of Catholic Religious Life," *American Journal of Sociology*, 1952, 58:145-149; Geoffry Gorer, *Exploring English Character* (London: Cresset, 1955); Charles Y. Glock, Benjamin Ringer, and Earl Babbie, *To Comfort and to Challenge* (Berkeley: University of California Press, 1967).

2. C. Ray Wingrove and Jon P. Alston, "Age and Church Attendance," *The Gerontologist*, 1971, 4:356-358.

3. Harvard M. Bahr, "Aging and Religious Disaffiliation," *Social Forces*, 1970, 49:57-71.

4. Dan Blazer and Erdman Palmore, "Religion and Aging in a Longitudinal Panel," *The Gerontologist*, 1976, 16:82-85.

5. Matilda White Riley and Ann Foner, *Aging and Society, Vol. 1: An Inventory of Research Findings* (New York: Russell Sage, 1968).

6. David O. Moberg, "Religiosity in Old Age," *The Gerontologist*, 1965, 5:80.

7. Louis Harris and Associates, *The Myth and Reality of Aging in America* (Washington, DC: National Council on the Aging, 1975).

8. Robert J. Havighurst and Ruth Albreckt, *Older People* (New York: Logmans Green, 1953), pp. 202-203.

9. Bernard Lazerwitz, "Some Factors Associated with Variations in Church Attendance," *Social Forces*, 1961, 39:301-309.

10. Richard C. Crandall, *Gerontology: A Behavioral Science Approach* (Reading, MA: Addison Wesley, 1980).

11. Op. cit.

12. Op. cit.

13. Rodney Stark, "Age and Faith: A Changing Outlook or an Old Process?" in *Religion in Sociological Perspective: Essays in the Empirical Study of Religion*, edited by Charles Y. Glock (Belmont, CA: Wadsworth, 1973), p. 4.

14. James B. Pratt, *The Religious Consciousness* (New York: Macmillan, 1928).

15. Op. cit.

16. Stark, p. 51.

17. Ibid.

18. Op. cit.

19. Stark, p. 55.

20. Op. cit.

21. Philip E. Hammond, "Aging and the Ministry," in *Aging and Society, Vol. 2, Aging and the Professions*, edited by Matilda White Riley, John W. Riley, Jr., and Marilyn E. Johnson (New York: Russell Sage, 1969) pp. 293-323.

22. Milton L. Barron, *The Aging: An Introduction to Social Gerontology and Geriatrics* (New York: Thomas Y. Crowell, 1961), p. 166.

23. Kurt Wolff, "Group Psychotherapy with Geriatric Patients in a State Hospital Setting: Results of a Three-Year Study," *Group Psychotherapy*, 1959, 12:218-222.

24. David Moberg and Marvin J. Taves, "Church Participation and Adjustment in Old Age," in *Older People and Their Social World*, edited by Arnold M. Rose and Warren A. Peterson (Philadelphia, PA: F. A. Davis, 1956).

25. J. N. Edwards and D. L. Klemmach, "Correlates of Life Satisfaction: A Reexamination," *Journal of Gerontology*, 1973, 28:497-502.

26. Elmer Spreitzer and Eddon E. Snyder, "Correlates of Life Satisfaction Among the Aged," *Journal of Gerontology*, 1974, 29:454-458.

27. Op. cit.

28. Rebecca Faith Guy, "Religion, Physical Disabilities, and Life Satisfaction in Older Age Cohorts," *International Journal of Aging and Human Development*, 1982, 15:225-232.

29. Kyriakos S. Markides, "Aging, Religiosity, and Adjustment: A Longitudinal Analysis," *Journal of Gerontology*, 1983, 38:621-625.

30. Suzanne T. Ortega, Robert D. Crutchfield, and William A. Rushing, "Race Differences in Elderly Personal Well Being, Friendship, Family and Church," *Research on Aging*, 1983, 5:101-118.

31. Ibid., pp. 110-111.

32. Op. cit.

33. Op. cit.

34. Op. cit.

35. Op. cit.

36. E. Durkheim, *The Elementary Forms of Religious Life*, translated by J. W. Swain (New York: The Free Press, 1915).

ROLES FOR AGED INDIVIDUALS IN POST-INDUSTRIAL SOCIETIES

Harold G. Cox

Department of Sociology and Social Work
Indiana State University

ABSTRACT

Cowgill and Holmes in their book *Aging and Modernization* predicted an inverse relationship between industrialization and status accorded older persons. They argued that the more industrialized a country becomes the lower the status accorded older persons. A more careful examination of historical and anthropological work suggests that if we look at the status of the old over the course of history and make projections into the future an S curve is a more realistic pattern. The pattern projected would be one in which the old were accorded a low status in early nomadic tribes, a high status in settled agricultural communities, a low status in industrialized society and ultimately will receive a somewhat higher status in the post-industrial period.

Historically we find a wide variety of patterns of treatment of the aged in different societies. Fischer traced the statements of Herodotus which indicated that at one extreme were the Issedones who gilded the heads of their aged parents and offered sacrifices before them [1]. They seemed to worship their oldest tribal members. At the opposite extreme were the Bactria who disposed of their old folk by feeding them to dogs. Similarly, the Sardinians hurled their elders from a high cliff and shouted with laughter when they fell on the rocks. In traditional China the old men were granted a privileged position. In politics and in family the aged men occupied the top positions of power in a hierarchical society that lasted for thousands of years. This was a value of the prevalent Confucian ideology. Thus we can find diverse patterns of how the aged were treated in different societies and in different historical eras.

An attempt will be made in this article to trace the changing status of aged individuals in different historical periods and to make some educated guesses about what roles aged persons will occupy in post-industrial society.

CRITICAL VARIABLES DETERMINING THE STATUS OF THE AGED

There are a number of variables, often interrelated, which either separately or in combination seem to relate to the status accorded older persons in various cultures. These include: family form, religion, knowledge base of the culture, harshness of the environment, the means of production, and the speed of social changes.

In the consideration of cultural type and status of the aged person, the general rule has been that in the nonindustrial, settled, agricultural societies aged individuals exercise considerable power and are granted a high status. In industrial societies, on the other hand, aged individuals exercise relatively little power and are granted less status. Cowgill and Holmes, in their work on aging and modernization, found an inverse relationship between the degree of modernization and the status accorded old persons [2]. In other words, the more industrialized the system became, the lower the status of the older person. While this is generally the case, a closer look reveals differential treatment of the elders even in the traditional societies. Sheehan, in a study of forty-seven traditional societies, found three different patterns of treatment of aged individuals [3]. Approximately one-fifth of the traditional societies were geographically unstable, as semipermanent bands of people periodically relocating their villages or, in some cases, perpetually mobile. The lowest esteem for seniors was often found in these small and nomadic societies. They have the fewest material resources for seniors to accumulate, thereby gaining respect in the eyes of the youngest person; they are usually located in harsh environments which favor youth and vigor. Food is often in short supply and individual existence is precarious. Elderly individuals may have to be sacrificed to insure the survival of the entire group. Among

From the *International Journal of Aging and Human Development*, Vol. 30, No. 1, 1990, pp. 55-62. © 1990 by Baywood Publishing Company, Inc. Reprinted by permission.

the societies studied, a plurality were comprised of various forms of tribes which were basically permanently settled, inhabiting fairly large villages, and governed according to a belief in their common ancestry or kinship. Another group of the traditional societies was comprised of small peasant communities whose economic base centered around agriculture or animal husbandry. The most highly developed social organizations were the ones with large landed peasantries; there, the highest esteem was enjoyed by older persons.

It appears that once traditional societies become located in a permanent place with stated residence and property rights, the old began to exercise considerable power over the young by the ownership of the property and the ability to pass it on to their children. Fisher pointed out that [1, p. 6]:

Nearly to our time, the story goes, western society remained nonliterate in its culture, agrarian in its economy, extended in its family structure, and rural in its residence. The old were few in number, but their authority was very great. Within the extended family the aged monopolized power: within our agrarian economy they controlled the land. A traditional culture surrounded them with an almost magical mystique of knowledge and authority.

Where property is the only means of production, by controlling property aged individuals are able to control younger generations. The future occupations and chances for success of the younger generation are tied to seeking the favor of their elders, who control all the resources. While one's parents are alive they are of critical importance because they provide employment and means of survival in the form of resources. After they die, the heirs inherit shares of their lands and control of these resources for themselves and their children. Therefore, in traditional societies that are permanently located, the individual is directly dependent upon his own senior generation for the acquisition of the means of production. The anticipated transfer of the property at the death of the parent provides the children with an incentive that encourages respect for their older family members. It is easy to see why the young defer to their elders and attempt to seek their special favor. Similarly, it is easy to understand how the old, by the development of stable institutions and the control of property, are able to maintain their power and privilege in the social system. This may also explain the higher value placed on the family in rural America where the transmission of land to the next generation may secure that generation a livelihood and a secure position in the social structure.

Thus, rather than Cowgill and Holmes's prediction of an inverse relationship between the degree of modernization and the status accorded old persons [2], we find a curvilinear one in which the old are accorded a low status in simple nomadic societies, a high status in settled agricultural communities, and a low status in modern industrial nations.

Sheehan equates what happens to older persons in the nomadic tribes to what happens to them in modern industrial societies [3]. Sheehan believes that with the development of modern technology, social and geographic mobility become goals and individual autonomy reemerges as a primary value. The young forfeit the security of the village or family to work in factories and offices. They attain financial and social separation from many traditional restraints. Lifestyles turn away from extended family ties. There is no special reason for younger family members to secure the favor of their parents and grandparents. The older family members lose their status, decision-making power, and the security they once had in earlier cultural settings. The result is that the old are considered much less valuable in modern contemporary states. In both the simple nomadic and modern industrial societies the old quickly become dependent on the young for their well-being and survival.

The form of the family is often related to the kind of culture and structural relations among institutions in a particular society. In traditional societies that are primarily agricultural in nature, the extended form of the family (most often comprised of mother, father, their sons and their wives and children) is the prevalent one. The extended family is most often patriarchical, which means that power and lineage are traced through the males of the family. The wife, upon marriage, moves in with the husband's family. When their children are old enough to marry, the parents arrange for their marriages; expect the wives of their sons to move into their household and their daughters to move into the households of their husbands. This family arrangement is one in which the oldest male member of the family exercises the greatest power, privilege, and authority. Individualism is discouraged. The individual is always subserviant to the demands of the group. The concept of romantic love (strong, intense emotional attachment between members of the opposite sex) is nonexistent. The criterion for the success of the marriage is the amount of family disruption caused by the entrance of the new bride. If she gets along well with her in-laws and does not cause difficulty it is considered a good marriage. The son's happiness is secondary to the good of the group. The extended family works best in stable cultures which are primarily agriculturally based. This culture is one in which the older members exercise the greatest power and maintain the highest status.

Industrialization leads to the breakup of the extended family. One no longer depends upon land as the principle means of production. New jobs, careers, resources, and opportunities become available. Modern industry requires mobile labor which can be moved from place to place as needed. Extended family ties are broken in order to move the labor force where it is most needed; if not, the industrial system itself would break down. The nuclear family—husband, wife, children—is dominant. The influence of the father and mother over adult children is weakened. The size of the family declines as children become units of consumption rather than production and thereby become less desirable.

The difference between extended and nuclear families for the status of the aged persons can best be seen in Israel. Weihl observed that the older people among the migrants from the Orient are given a relatively high status in comparison to the relatively low status accorded older immigrants from the Western countries [4]. The migrants from the Orient evidence considerable commitment to the extended family concept in contrast with the commitment to nuclear family evidenced by migrants from the West.

The religions of the Far East have generally supported the extended family and higher status of elder members by the moral and ethical codes that they espouse. The Confucian concept is one in which the aged are to be given tender loving care. They are to be exempt from certain responsibilities when they reach old age. Pre-World War II families in China and Japan were ones in which children cared for their elders, and older family members exercised the most authority. This meant also that the elders were the most respected members of the family.

While Christianity clearly admonishes the individual to honor his father and mother, this religious principle has probably had less impact in the Western world than one might expect. The pressure of industrialization results in the educational functions being gradually removed from the family socialization process to formal training outside the home. The nature of wealth changes from land to tangible property. The emphasis shifts to productivity. The young are always seen as more productive and the old as less productive. Degradation generally occurs for the older, and supposedly slower, workers.

Another aspect of modern industrial society is the location of knowledge. In traditional agricultural societies, the old are the reservoirs of knowledge—of past problems and their solutions, of old customs and the appropriate religious rituals. In industrial societies, books, libraries, universities, and current research enterprises are a base for the generation and transmittal of knowledge. The freshly trained college student is often more valuable in the business and industrial world than the older and more experienced employee whose knowledge and expertise may have become obsolete. The inability to maintain control of critical knowledge in modern society has been another factor that has contributed to the general loss of status of older persons.

American society has a well-developed and sophisticated educational system which prepares young people to enter an occupation, but it is ill equipped to retrain older workers when new technologies require additional schooling.

The harshness of the environment in which the culture is found and the amount of physical labor required for survival are also factors that can reduce the usefulness and thereby the status of the older members of a culture.

Holmberg noted that among the Sirono of the Bolivian rain forest, it is the general belief that [5, pp. 224–225]:

> Actually the aged are quite a burden; they eat but are unable to hunt, fish or collect food; they sometimes hoard a young spouse, but are unable to beget children; they move at a snail's pace and hinder the mobility of the group. When a person becomes too ill or infirm to follow the fortunes of the band, he is abandoned to shift for himself.

Cowgill and Holmes noted that there is some difficulty in adjusting to reduced activity in old age when a society is so strongly dedicated to hard physical labor [2]. Kibbutz society in Israel is one example; there, older persons may arrive at an ambiguous status because of their inability to physically keep up with younger counterparts.

Related to the changing knowledge base in modern society is the speed with which social change occurs within the system. Cowgill and Holmes believe that rapid social change in modern societies tends to undermine the status of older persons [2]. Change renders many of the skills of older Americans obsolete. Not only can they no longer ply their trade, there is also no reason for them to teach it to others. In a rapidly changing society younger people are nearly always better educated and possess more knowledge of recent technology than their elders; thus, the latter lose their utility and the basis of their authority.

Referring to both the speed of social change in modern society and the location of the knowledge base in the system, Watson and Maxwell hypothesized that societies can be arranged along a continuum whose basis is the amount of useful information controlled by the aged individuals [6]. They believe the greater the elders are in control of critical information, the greater is their participation in community affairs. Their participation is, in turn, directly related to the degree of esteem in which they are held by other members of the community. Watson and Maxwell believe this control of information and consequent social participation declines with industrialization and its rapid sociocultural change [6, pp. 26–29].

Watson and Maxwell argued that one of the most fruitful models developed for the investigation of human societies has relied heavily on the information storage and exchange model and is described as systems theory [6]. Goffman has demonstrated that groups which share secret information will tend to be more integrated and unified than those which do not [7]. All stored information, according to Goffman, involves a stated arrangement of elements in the sense that they are a record of past events [7, p. 70].

In traditional societies, one of the main functions of old people is to remember legends, myths, ethical principles, and the appropriate relations that should be arranged with the supernatural, and they are frequently asked about these matters.

Elliott described this pattern among the Aleuts in northern Russia [8, pp. 170-171]:

> Before the advent of Russian priests, every village had one or two old men at least, who considered it their special business to educate the children, thereupon, in the morning or evening when all were home these aged teachers would seat themselves in the center of one of the largest village courts or oolagumuh; the young folks surrounded them and listened attentively to what they said.

Watson and Maxwell believe that the printing press was to end this kind of arrangement in the social system [6, p. 20]. In industrialized societies the information that is important is written down, printed, and sold in bookstores.

Some historians have argued that economically, politically, and socially older people are more conservative than younger people and tend to have a stabilizing effect on any social system. The young, being much more changeable in their view, offer adaptability and in some ways may increase the changes for survival in the social system.

One final factor which may in some way explain the declining status of aged individuals in modern industrial countries is the relative proportion of the entire population that they comprise. In most of the ancient and traditional societies they comprised less than 3 percent of the total population. It is easy to reserve a special status for a group of people that comprise a very small percent of the total. In modern society the old have come to comprise between 8 to 15 percent of the total population. Cox observed that it may become increasingly difficult to preserve privileged status for a group that comprises such a large percentage of a total population [9]. Cowgill's book, *Aging Around the World* indicates how rapidly the older age populations are now expanding in even the underdeveloped countries [10]. This is a phenomenon that neither the anthropologists nor the gerontologists had earlier anticipated.

ROLES FOR THE ELDERLY IN POST-INDUSTRIAL SOCIETY

While historically we find a curvilinear relationship with the old being accorded a low status in nomadic tribes, a high status in settled agricultural communities and a low status in modern industrial societies one wonders what roles and status older persons will be granted in post-industrial society. An educated guess would be that there will be a wider variety of roles to choose from and a slight upturn in the status of older persons in post-industrial society. Thus the pattern would be one of an S curve in which the status of the older adults improves following the low that was experienced by them during the industrial period.

Everett Hughes, Daniel Bell, and other social scientists have speculated on what life will be like in post-industrial society [11, 12]. The consensus of the social scientists seems to be that the post-industrial period will see a shift away from expansion in manufacturing and industry to the expansion of social services, entertainment, athletics, recreation and leisure enterprises. The basic argument of the scientists is that as the industrial development of a nation peaks and as an ever efficient manufacturing technology emerges, less of the population will be required to produce the nation's goods. This will make a surplus of manpower available which will ultimately be employed by the expanding service occupations, the entertainment industry, and industries catering to recreation and leisure activities. The post-industrial period will also bring reduced working hours, the advent of a four-day work week which will result in larger amounts of free time for the average citizen. For both the younger and the older members of the society this will mean greater opportunity for entertainment, athletic events, recreation, and leisure pursuits as well as opportunity for education and cultural enrichment. The Protestant ethic which admonished the person to be totally committed to the work role and view recreation and leisure roles as at best a waste of one's time and at worst as sinful will undoubtedly be altered. Recreation, leisure, education and a variety of other emerging roles will be seen as legitimate means of enriching the quality of one's life. They should do two things for the older members of society; first, it will provide a wide range of nonwork roles in which they may choose to participate; and second, these roles will be more highly valued and provide them with a higher status and more respected position in society.

Older persons upon retirement will be deciding whether or not to invest greater time and energy in family roles, recreation and leisure roles, volunteer roles, educational roles, political roles, or perhaps a second career. Post-industrial society will undoubtedly offer a wider range of roles for the elderly to choose whether they will or will not participate.

In all probability they will not have had this much freedom to choose among the different roles they wish to enter at any other time in their lives. Moreover, changing values in post-industrial society will include less emphasis on the importance of productivity and greater emphasis on the quality of life. Volunteer and leisure roles will be more highly valued, giving older persons who occupy them greater respect. In short it would seem that older persons will have a wide variety of roles to choose from in their retirement years and that these roles will bring them greater status than retirees have been accorded in the past.

REFERENCES

1. D. H. Fischer, *Growing Old in America*, Oxford University Press, New York, 1978.

2. D. O. Cowgill and L. D. Holmes, *Aging and Modernization*, Appleton Century Crofts, New York, 1972.

3. T. Sheehan, Senior Esteem as a Factor of Socioeconomic Complexity, *The Gerontologist, 16:5*, pp. 433–444, 1976.

4. H. Weihl, Aging in Israel, in *Aging in Contemporary Society*, E. Shanas (ed.), Sage Publications, Inc., Beverly Hills, California, pp. 107–117, 1970.

5. A. R. Holmberg, *Nomads of the Long Bow*, Natural History Press, Garden City, New York, pp. 224–225, 1969.

6. W. H. Watson and R. T. Maxwell, *Human Aging and Dying: A Study in Sociocultural Gerontology*, St. Martin's Press, New York, pp. 2–32, 1977.

7. E. Goffman, *The Presentation of Self in Everyday Life*, Doubleday, Garden City, New York, 1959.

8. H. W. Elliott, *Our Arctic Province: Alaska and the Sea Islands*, Scribner's, New York, pp. 170–171, 1887.

9. H. Cox, *Later Life: The Realities of Aging*, Prentice-Hall, Inc., Englewood Cliffs, New Jersey, 1988.

10. D. O. Cowgill, *Aging Around the World*, Wadsworth Publishing Company, Belmont, California, 1986.

11. E. Hughes, *Men and Their Work*, Free Press, New York, 1964.

12. D. Bell, *The Coming of Post Industrial Society*, Basic Books, New York, 1973.

Remarriage Among the Elderly: Characteristics Relevant to Pastoral Counseling

Hanns G. Pieper, PhD
Ludwig A. Petkovsek

Hanns G. Pieper and Ludwig A. Petkovsek are affiliated with the University of Evansville.

ABSTRACT. Family counseling has long been an important aspect of pastoral counseling. With recent trends toward increasing remarriage among older persons, pastoral family counseling will take on an additional dimension. This study provides information concerning motivation and attitudes toward remarriage, behavior during the interim period, adjustment to remarriage and the impact of remarriage on family relationships.

INTRODUCTION

In their timely article in this journal, Bert Katschke-Jennings and David Healy[1] discussed remarriage among the elderly. It was suggested that this trend toward remarriage among the elderly would have implications for pastoral counseling in the areas of marital and pre-marital counseling. We agree that not only are there counseling ramifications for couples who are involved, but also for the adult children who will become indirectly involved. Little has been published concerning this topic, so pastoral counselors may have few resources to consult. This article focuses on factors related to remarriage among the elderly which would be of particular interest to individuals involved in pastoral counseling.

The remarriages of fifty elderly couples were examined in this study. It focused on a range of questions relating to previous marriages, the interim period between marriages, the marriage itself and relationships with family members before and after the remarriages.

STUDY DESIGN

The sample was drawn from public marriage records of a medium sized midwestern city. Potential couples had to meet the following three criteria to be included in the sample:

1. At least one person had to be 65 years old or older.
2. The couple had to be married at least one complete year.
3. Both the husband and the wife had to agree to participate in the study.

Based on the first two criteria a list of 116 couples was developed. Each couple was sent information about the study and asked if they wanted to participate. Fifty-two couples agreed to participate, but two couples had to be eliminated because of incompletely filled out questionnaires. The final sample consisted of 50 couples, or 43 percent of the population of remarried couples.

The data were gathered using a 17 page questionnaire. The presentation of the data in this paper is mainly descriptive since the size of the sample did not allow for elaborate crossclassifications.

SAMPLE PROFILE

Half of our subjects were over 69 years of age. One-fourth were over the age of 74 and one-fourth were under the age of 64. Most of the younger subjects were the wives.

For the most part the respondents were quite healthy. Forty-three percent rated their health as either excellent or good, and only fourteen percent said that bad health kept them from doing things they really needed to do.

Most subjects were financially secure. Three-fourths of the subjects were satisfied with their finances and none felt that they had to do without things that they really needed.

Widowhood had ended the previous marriage for seventy percent of the subjects. Most had been married to their previous spouse for a long time. The average duration of the previous marriage for husbands was forty years and thirty-one years for wives. They had been married to their present spouse for an average of almost two and a half years. German, English and "Old American" ethnic backgrounds were heavily represented in the sample.

How typical of the general older population were our subjects? To answer this question the background data for the present subjects were compared with the background data from a sample of an earlier study by Pieper.[2] In the earlier study a random sample of older persons was drawn from the same community that was utilized for the present study.

The two sample groups were quite similar regarding age and financial status. The major difference between the two groups was health. The present remarried sample was, as a group, much healthier than the general sample. While only 14 percent of the remarried sample stated that their health kept them from doing things they needed to do, 47 percent of the general sample of elderly persons claimed that to be the case.

The majority of the subjects (eighty percent) lived by themselves during the interim period. Only about ten percent of either husbands or wives were living with children. The proportion living by themselves was higher for the present remarriage sample than the general community sample.

FINDINGS

Attitude Toward Remarriage: Respondents were asked to recall how they had felt about getting remarried before contemplating their present marriage. In general, their attitudes at that time were not pro-remarriage. Only nine percent of the husbands and four percent of the wives said that they had been firm in their desire to remarry. In contrast, half of the wives and just over a third of the husbands stated that they believed that they definitely would not remarry. About a third of the husbands and just under a third of the wives said that they had never really thought about it. It would not appear that attitudes toward remarriage which are expressed earlier in life are good predictors of behavior later in life.

When did the subjects change their minds about getting remarried? Not surprisingly, half of the husbands and about a third of the wives noted that they changed their minds when they met their present spouse. This finding is consistent with recent social psychological research on attitudes which suggests that the actual social situations may influence attitudes more than previously thought. This is a departure from early studies which suggest that attitudes are primary motivators of behavior. The amount of time that had transpired since the end of the previous marriage was not related to changing attitudes.

Behavior During the Interim Period Between Marriages: For the husbands there was an average of five years between their previous marriage and their current marriage, while for the wives the interim period lasted an average of eight years. These averages are a bit misleading because the subjects tended to either remarry quite soon after their previous marriage ended or to wait an extended period of time.

The amount of time that they had known their present spouse before the marriage also took on a bimodal distribution, since they either knew their present spouse for a very short period of time or for a rather long period of time, in some cases 20 years or more. Those who had known their present spouse for a long period of time were often family friends while the previous marriages were still intact.

Half of the husbands and just over a third of the wives stated that they actively dated during the interim period. While husbands reported a higher degree of actual dating activity, wives generally reported higher overall general activity levels.

Children were the number one source of activity for both husbands and wives, but husbands depended on their children for activity far more than did the wives, who listed friends almost as often as children. The size of the social world of elderly females appears to be far greater than the social world of elderly males.

The end of the previous marriage appeared to precipitate a significant change (either increasing or decreasing) in the activity levels of about two-thirds of the subjects. Activity levels were more likely to increase for the wives, while activity levels were likely to decline for husbands. While there was over-all decline, it is interesting to note that activity levels between the husbands and their friends, children or other relatives remained fairly constant. This strongly suggests that for males the dominant activity resource was their wives and that the loss of the wife has much greater impact on the activity level of the husband than does the loss of the husband for the wife.

None of the respondents felt that their relationship with their children or friends changed dramatically. However, many did report some changes. Unfortunately, for the majority of these persons the changes were in the negative direction, and this was particularly true for women. Just over a third of the males and quarter of the females noted some changes in their relationships with their children. Only about 2 out of 10 males reported any changes in their relationships with friends but almost 4 out of 10 women reported such changes.

To what extent did the respondents feel it desirable to have the support of relatives and friends for their dating activity? In general, support needs were felt more where relatives were concerned. About a third of the men felt the need for approval as compared with just over half of the women and the majority of these were looking for support from their children. While approval was desirable, overall only about a fourth of respondents felt it was necessary. Less than a fourth of the respondents desired support from their friends. Interestingly, men thought support from friends was more important than did the women.

When asked which persons had been least supportive of their dating activities, children were reported most frequently. Over a third of the men and over half of the women listed children who had not been supportive of their dating. Four reasons were cited to explain the lack of support. Jealousy was the most frequently given reason (39%), followed by "others were worried about me" (15%), "people thought I was too old" (15%) and "others felt I had no respect for my former spouse" (15%).

Friends were generally perceived as being supportive. Half of both the husbands and wives said that a friend had been the most supportive person. This was somewhat unexpected since we thought the friends might be among the most likely to be threatened by an impending marriage. A child was listed as the most supportive person by about a third of both husbands and wives.

Where Did the Couples Meet? Four settings stood out from the rest. Most respondents met their second spouse through their memberships in organizations to which they belonged. Meeting people through mutual friends accounted for the second highest number of meetings. The third source was the blooming of a long standing relationship and the fourth most likely meeting place was at church.

Comparisons of Present and Former Spouse: As expected, there was a greater age difference between the present spouses. Age differences in the previous marriage averaged about four years, while age differences in the present marriages averaged about seven years. While spouses were more different in terms of age they were more alike in educational attainment, although the differences were not great (less than half a year). There was also greater religious homogeneity between the second spouses.

Respondents were asked to compare their present and former spouses regarding common interests and personality traits. Both husbands and wives perceived that they had more in common with their present spouse than they did with their previous spouse. Overall, both husbands and wives shared twice as many of their major interests with their present spouses.

For both husbands and wives the present spouse was also more likely to receive more favorable personality ratings on friendliness, being interesting, being active, being able to communicate, being considerate and being affectionate than did the previous spouse. However, husbands tended to remember their previous wives considerably more positively than the wives remembered their previous husbands.

Reasons for Remarriage: Why did our subjects get remarried? Both husbands and wives were remarkably candid in answering this question and there were a great many different reasons which were given for remarriage. Respondents were asked to give as many reasons as applied to them and over forty different specific reasons were given.

Without doubt, the number one reason was companionship or having someone to go to restaurants or movies with or just to talk with on a regular basis. This item was first or second on virtually everyone's list of reasons.

Emotional reasons made up the second largest category. Many of these reasons centered around falling in love, but other themes included needing to be loved or needing to love someone. Some just hoped to reestablish a normal home life.

Various reasons relating to the themes of loneliness and needs for security comprised the next highest category. Husbands were more likely to cite these reasons than were the wives. In particular, security reasons were more important for the husbands, who were much more likely to state that they needed someone to take care of them.

Appraisals of Second Marriages: All of the marriages studied in this sample were very positively appraised. In general, both husbands and wives had a more positive appraisal of their present marriage than they did of their former marriage. A number of reasons were given for this.

Personal maturity was the most frequently given reason by both husbands and wives. They simply felt that they were more prepared to deal with their marriages and any problems which might arise. Husbands in particular, stated that they were now much more settled down than they were in their previous marriage.

Experiencing fewer family related problems was also a major reason given for the positive attitude toward their present marriages. In particular, lack of problems with children and finances were singled out.

The third major reason was that their present relationship was more central to their lives. In short, they simply spent more time with each other. Perhaps because of the perceived limited time available they were more involved with each other and spent a great deal more time doing things together.

Acceptance by Spouse's Family: Wives seem to have a slightly easier time finding acceptance from their present spouse's children. Overall about six out of ten husbands felt that they had been accepted by their wives' children, while this was the case for seven out of ten of the wives. There was a very high level of agreement between the spouses concerning acceptance of their spouse by their own children.

Spouses had an easier time finding acceptance from relatives other than children. Eight out of ten husbands felt that their wives' other relatives had accepted them. The wives agreed with this perception. Nine out of ten wives thought that they had been accepted by their husband's other relatives. The husbands agreed with this perception.

DISCUSSION AND SUMMARY

The responses of the husbands and wives in this survey provided some interesting insights for those involved in pastoral counseling. Somewhat unexpectedly, the remarried elderly did not differ significantly from the general older population regarding basic demographic characteristics. The only real difference was that they appeared to be healthier than the general older person.

There appear to be few accurate predictors as to whether or not an older person will remarry. One's attitude earlier in life certainly is not a good predictor. Neither is age, since our sample included persons from under sixty to individuals well into their seventies and eighties. Perhaps some clues may be found in the reasons they gave for remarriage. In our society "love" is considered to be the dominant legitimate factor influencing marriage and certainly the romantic notion of love was involved in many of the remarriages. Particularly interesting was a response given by a number of persons that they needed not only to love but to be loved by someone. It may well be that remarriages, rather than showing "disrespect" for the former spouse, may be the ultimate testimonial to the former marriage in that persons are trying to reestablish a relationship which was sorely missed. There are other indications that this may be true. Almost three-fourths of the respondents had been widowed and a number stated that they wanted to reestablish a "normal" home life.

Aside from the marriage itself there are a number of things which may be discomforting to adult children. For about half of the elderly remarrieds the marriage occurred fairly soon after the death of the previous spouse. This would certainly be traumatic for adult children who may not have adjusted to the death of the parent themselves. Furthermore, there are strong indications that the elderly persons take the remarriages very seriously and seek very hard to please each other. This may unwittingly set up a rivalry between the adult children and the new spouse of the parent. The children may feel particularly threatened when they see the attention lavished on the new spouse and this may account for some of the perceived negative feedback from adult children. The fact that a sizable proportion of the respondents only knew their new spouse for a short period of time may lead to additional concerns about the wisdom of the choice. Husbands should be aware that they are likely to encounter greater resistance from the children of their spouse than are wives. Perhaps we simply see our older mothers as more vulnerable than our older fathers.

Overall, the marriages seemed to have had a very positive effect on the participants. In fact, while many of the respondents viewed their former marriages and spouses positively they had even more positive assessments of their present marriages. Both husbands and wives worked very hard at making their remarriages a success and felt that they were better prepared to make their remarriages positive relationships. Remarriage certainly appears to be a positive alternative to the loneliness of widowhood and old age for an increasingly large number of elderly persons.

NOTES

1. Bert Katschke-Jennings and David Healy, "Remarriage and the Elderly," *Journal of Religion and Aging*, Vol. 3 (3/4), Spring/Summer, 1987.
2. Hanns G. Pieper, "Church Membership and Participation in Church Activities Among the Elderly," *Activities, Adaptation and Aging*, Vol. 1, No. 3.

WOMEN IN OUR AGING SOCIETY:

Golden Years or Increased Dependency?

*As American women grow older, their future may be precarious
as budget squeezes force cuts in social services.*

Cynthia M. Taeuber

Ms. Taeuber is chief, Age & Sex Statistics Branch, Population Division, U.S. Bureau of the Census, Washington, D.C.

THE U.S. IS IN the midst of a demographic revolution that already has penetrating effects on the nation, families, and individuals. That revolution is the aging of the population, with a significantly higher proportion of Americans in the older age groups.

America's growing elderly population has varying levels of abilities, needs, and resources. Diversity and growth are two terms that describe it. The population aged 65 years and over commonly is grouped together under the label "the elderly," yet this is a heterogeneous population. Elderly women tend to have life circumstances quite different from elderly men. Some older people, especially single women, have significant financial and health problems and are most likely to be poor. Others, especially men and married couples, generally are more secure.

The implications of greater numbers of people 85 years and older affect women, young and old. Most care of the frail elderly is provided by females and is received by oldest women.

The lives of young women will affect their prospects in older age. Women of the baby boom generation have much higher levels of education than their mothers and grandmothers. Young women in the labor force are employed in occupations covered by Social Security and are more likely to have private pensions than is true of their

In 1993, about 60% of America's nearly 33,000,000 elderly are women.

mothers. Other considerations that greatly impact on women as they age include increases in divorce, the likelihood of never marrying, and single motherhood, as well as behaviors that affect health such as smoking.

For women in an aging society, their own health is not the only issue. The health of others and provisions made for care of the frail elderly affects quality of daily lives and women's choices and movements.

How these factors evolve among the elderly in the future greatly could modify the lives of women, especially those in their 50s and 60s, the age group most likely to have very old, frail relatives. Changes in women's participation in the labor force, for instance, could affect their ability to provide unpaid care. As a society and for women, the economic and psychological costs of providing this care is an issue. A nettlesome question is what young women need to do to prepare for their own old age and what kind of care they eventually will have.

In 1900, one in 25 Americans was elderly. In 1990, the proportion was one in eight. By 2030, it is likely to be one in five. Four-generation families will be common. In 1993, about 60% of America's nearly 33,-000,000 elderly are women.

Changes in age composition can have dramatic political, economic, and social effects on a nation. In the past, declines in the number of births have been the most important contributor to the long-term aging trend. Now, however, the improved chance of survival to the oldest ages, especially for females, is the most significant factor in the growth of the very old population.

Because of relatively low birth rates from the 1920s through World War II, growth in the size of the elderly population will be steady, but undramatic, until after 2011, when the baby boom generation (born 1946-64) begins to reach age 65. From 2011 through the middle of the 21st century, growth in the elderly population will be more dramatic as the baby boom becomes the grandparent boom. From 2011 to 2030, the baby boom generation will be the young old (65-74 years old) and the aged (75-84 years old).

It is the size of the oldest elderly population (most of whom are women) that will be noticed most after 2030 as the great-grandparent boom begins. Already, the size of the oldest elderly population is sufficient to have a major impact on the nation's health and social service systems. The population aged 85 and over is expected to grow from 3,000,000 in 1990 to more than 8,000,000 in 2030. This group would more than double in size again by 2050, to nearly 18,000,000, as the baby boom cohort reaches the oldest ages. These projections assume recent trends continue. If life expectancy increases at a faster rate, particularly among the oldest elderly, the numbers will be much higher.

Under current mortality conditions, 80% of newborns would live to see their 65th birthday. Life expectancy at birth is about 75 years. Women aged 65 can expect to need to finance an additional two decades of life on average. Most will outlive their husbands, which has economic implications for females.

As life expectancy continues to increase, the number of years of good health in relation to those of chronic illness is important. Without major improvements in health among the very old, it can be expected that there will be many more people with long-term dependency. It is highly likely that more people in their 50s and 60s will have very elderly family members who need the care and attention traditionally provided mostly by females.

Work and retirement

The aging of America and developments among the elderly population do not take place in a vacuum. The projected trends for women's work and education will affect the experience of women in an aging society.

Today, most females work continuously until retirement. Those in their 50s and early 60s are increasingly likely to be in the paid labor force. Such females are the ones who probably will be called on to provide care for the frail elderly.

The women of the baby boom generation, many of whom delayed marriage and

As men's chances of survival improve thanks to medical advances, women will face widowhood later than today's elderly females are experiencing it.

childbirth while establishing themselves in the labor force, are more likely to be working than their mothers were. The attachment of females under age 45 to the labor force is unprecedented. Women retiring in 1980 averaged 45% of their adult lives in the workforce. The Social Security Administration projects that those retiring in 2020 will have spent 71% of their adult lives in the labor force. That increased commitment has implications for women's lifetime

earnings, pension coverage, and ability to provide significant levels of care for frail elderly relatives.

The over-all labor pool remains sharply segregated by sex. Women have made some progress entering management and the professions. The majority, though, still are in traditional, low-paying occupations where more than half the workers are female. The number of women in high-paying jobs remains small relative to men. The most improvement in occupational mix has been among younger women.

Pension coverage. Men generally receive higher pension benefits than women. Elderly black women tend to have fewer resources for retirement than older white ones. They are less likely to receive a pension, have completed high school, own their homes or other valuable assets, or be married. These differences in resources exist even when educational level is the same, which could reflect the effects of past discrimination.

As a result of the greater likelihood of women working now than in the past, young and middle-aged females have a better chance of having been in the labor force long enough to have savings, pensions, and Social Security in their own names. This could make a significant difference in the economic status of more women as they age. Nevertheless, males aged 35-64 have higher pension coverage and vesting rates than females in that age group. The disparity in earnings between men and women is one factor in this difference.

It is difficult to predict whether, in the future, as large a proportion of people in their early 60s will be able to afford to retire early as do now. Some believe society is seeing the "golden age of the golden years." Baby boom retirees may be less well-off economically than today's retirees. Savings are down; pensions are becoming less generous; and workers are supporting an increasing portion of the cost of their retirement plans.

Income differences. Over all, the economic position of elderly men and women has improved significantly since the 1970s. Yet, not everyone within the elderly population has shared equally in the income gains. Elderly women who live alone, for example, have lower incomes on average than do married couples.

Elderly females generally are less secure economically than elderly males. There may be some improvement in a few decades as more women with higher education have a history of long-term employment. It is likely that unmarried elderly women, most of whom are widowed and relatively old, will continue to be at risk financially and have low pensions compared to men and married couples.

There has been a dramatic reduction in the last 30 years in the percentage of elderly who are poor. In 1959, 35% were; in 1990, 12%. Nevertheless, there are important differences among subgroups. The elderly poor are disproportionately female, black or Hispanic, 75 years and older, and living alone. The economic situation for elderly black women has been particularly intractable; their poverty rates did not improve over the decade of the 1980s. Among the elderly aged 75 and older, the 1990 poverty rate for black women (44%) was more than double that for white women

(17%) and over five times that for white men (eight percent).

The elderly who live alone are much more likely to be poor than aged married-couple family householders. In 1990, 24% of white elderly females who lived alone were poor, compared with 58% of black elderly women and 50% of Hispanic aged females. For elderly married couples, poverty rates were lower for whites (four percent) than blacks (22%) or Hispanics (16%).

Education is associated closely with lifetime economic status. This is especially important for the future because a greater proportion of females of the baby boom generation have completed high school and college than have today's elderly women.

Marital status, living arrangements, and educational attainment vary considerably within the older population and will change in future generations. Because of longevity factors, elderly men are much more likely than women to be married. Thus, most elderly males have a spouse for assistance when health fails, while most elderly females do not. Over 9,000,000 elderly live alone; 78% are women.

As men improve their chances of survival, women will face widowhood later than do today's elderly females. It also appears that a higher proportion of younger women never will marry. This and the much higher rates of divorce indicate long-term economic strains that could affect the eventual economic status of a large group of women as they age. The trend leads to expectations that females in their 50s will want to remain in the labor force.

The older population increasingly is more educated. Since the better educated tend to be better off economically and stay healthier longer, it is important that the proportion of elderly with at least a high school diploma is increasing.

Educational attainment generally is lower among blacks and Hispanics, compared with whites. More than 84% of whites aged 45-49 have a high school education, and about 25% have had four or more years of college. By comparison, 69% of blacks and 48% of Hispanics aged 45-49 have a high school diploma. Only one in seven blacks that age have completed four or more years of college, as have one in 10 Hispanics. This implies the likelihood of continued differences in health and economic status in old age.

Population aging and patterns of dependency

It is increasingly likely that more and more people in their 50s and 60s will have surviving parents, aunts, and uncles. Many will face the concern and expense of caring for very old, frail relatives.

Over 4,000,000 elderly persons need assistance with one or more everyday ac-

tivities. Chronic illnesses increase with age and are more common among women, who average more years of chronic illness than men. Among those aged 85 and over, almost 25% live in a nursing home because of serious health problems. Of the oldest elderly living at home, about 20% are unable to carry on a major activity and 40% have a condition that limits their activities. Functional limitations are highest among elderly black women and those with relatively low incomes.

It is possible to get a rough idea of the need for family support over time by looking at the relative sizes of the population 85 years and over, compared with the number aged 50-64 years. In 1950, there were three people 85 years and older per 100 aged 50-64. In 1990, there were nine. That ratio will at least triple again to 28 by 2050.

The experience and problems of the young old caring for the oldest old will become more and more familiar throughout society. The physical condition of the young old, especially women since they provide most care, may become a serious issue as they try to help frail elderly move from beds to baths and toilets. It is likely there will be increased demand for mechanical aids and changes in private homes as well as access to public buildings for the disabled.

As medical technology provides more ways to save and extend lives, the U.S. can expect to see the duration of chronic illness to lengthen and the need for help to increase. The strain of caring for frail elderly relatives could affect worker productivity. Women in particular face decisions about leaving the labor force or working part time to care for frail relatives at just the time when they want to work for retirement benefits for their own old age. Other women are responsible for frail relatives while adjusting to their own retirement, widowhood, physical limitations, and reduced incomes. If medical advances slow mortality rates among the elderly, but not disability rates, the number of elderly disabled would grow in the future just from the increased number of surviving oldest elderly.

In an increasingly interdependent and aging world, the U.S. is remarkable for the diversity of its female population. It never is easy to arrive at a shared vision when there are strong differences, but that is America's challenge. The pace and direction of demographic changes will create compelling social, economic, and ethical choices for individuals, families, and governments into the 21st century. The directions Americans choose and the decisions they make directly will affect the quality and vitality of their lives for many decades.

Individual women, and all of American society, face the challenge of anticipating and preparing for the changing needs and desires of a diverse, aging U.S.

Live and Learn: Patient Education for the Elderly Orthopaedic Client

Syble M. Oldaker

Syble M. Oldaker, PhD, RN, is Associate Professor in the Department of Nursing Science at the College of Nursing, Clemson University, Clemson, South Carolina.

Patient education is a critical component of nursing interventions for health maintenance and illness prevention in assisting older persons with orthopaedic problems to maintain optimum independence and quality of life. This article focuses on the needs of the adult learner with emphasis on the elderly. Theoretical considerations of learning and characteristics of the adult learner are briefly introduced. Changes attributed to aging and factors that affect learning for elders are discussed. The article closes with strategies for planning effective patient education.

Predictions about the growth of the aging population are well documented in the literature. During the 1980s, the U.S. population aged 65 and over grew by 24%, compared to just 10% for the overall U.S. growth rate (Denton, 1990). It is projected that in the 50-year period from 1980 to 2030, the 65+ age group will double, and will make up 21.7% of the population by 2050 (Guilford, 1988).

Steady rise in the aging population has important implications for nursing as do recent changes in the politics of health care. Increasing federal and state emphasis on cost containment together with new technologies for treatment of orthopaedic conditions have resulted in increasing numbers of hospitalized older adults being discharged early in the course of treatment or postoperatively.

Compounding this are increasing numbers of older adults living with chronic orthopaedic problems. A major goal of nursing and of elderly clients relates to remaining at home safely while maintaining independence. Nursing interventions for patient education are becoming more criti-

cal in view of these situations as public health, community, hospital, and home health nurses focus on health teaching, discharge planning, primary prevention, and health maintenance for elderly clients with orthopaedic problems.

There are no age limits to independence and enhancing the quality of one's life. Nurses are in a unique position to affect change in patient's lives to enhance the quality of life and increase optimum levels of health. Much of this depends on intervention strategies incorporating patient education.

This article focuses on the older adult as a learner. Factors important for nurses to consider for successful teaching/learning interventions with older adults are discussed, as well as strategies of educational interventions.

Aging

What constitutes "normal" aging is so wide and diverse that age change norms are difficult to determine. Paradoxically, this age group is most often characterized by age stereotypes. Many of the specific changes generally attributed to age are experienced within only a small percentage of the population. The majority of individuals do experience age-related changes, but in various patterns and to various degrees.

Many myths have persisted about the decline of intelligence with age because of views about aging that encourage expectations for disease and incorporate acceptance of chronic illness as "normal" to the aging process.

People change as they age, but age has biologic, psychologic, and sociocultural aspects. Biologic and psychologic aging can be shaped by social experience. The number and complexity of these variables has led to much diversity among older adults. In fact, chronologic age may be a meaningless descriptor of age!

Neugarten (1974) makes distinctions between the "young-old" (55 to 74 years) and the "old-old" (75 and older). There are other designations of "elderly" (those over 75) and the "very old" (those over 85). These age distinctions are reminders of the differences and diversity of those generally thought of as "older adults."

According to Kalish (1979) in an account of historical views of aging, the first model used to describe old age was the pathology model in which no distinctions were made between aging and the disease process. In this view, old age and the elderly are seen as sick, strange and falling apart.

From *Orthopaedic Nursing,* Vol. 11, No. 3, May/June 1992, pp. 51-56. © 1992 by the National Association of Orthopaedic Nursing. Reprinted by permission.

This view has been followed by the decrement model in which old age is represented as a decrease in function.

In the more positive "normal person model," older people are seen as any other age group: diverse and adaptive in their choices and responses. Kalish finds the contemporary "personal growth" model more reflective of humanistic values, with recognition that older people have unique abilities for personal growth fulfillment.

Adult Learning Styles

Learning is the formation of new associations as well as the acquisitions of general rules and knowledge about the world (Craik, 1977). A widely held belief is that learning ability in later years tends to diminish. To understand and appreciate learning ability of the older adult, distinctions between the internal processes of cognition and the external actions of performance are necessary. The ability to learn may be unchanged, but other factors may interfere with the ability to demonstrate learning. Older people may have more difficulty expressing what they know.

A variety of factors influencing performance include education, personality, kind and degree of chronic illness, fatigue, or motivation. The elderly may in fact choose not to perform in test situations because of lack of energy or interest in "proving themselves" (Kermis, 1984).

Craik's (1977) information processing view provides a structure for understanding age-related differences in learning. This model views three terms relevant to learning and memory: encoding, the symbolic representation of one thing by another; storage, the persistence of information over time; and retrieval, the recovery and utilization of stored information. In this model, information in the environment is first detected by the senses and placed in sensory stores for specific modalities (vision, hearing, touch, etc.). If the person attends to the information, it moves into short-term memory; if it is then rehearsed, it is displaced into longer-term storage.

Short-term memory includes both primary and secondary processes. Primary memory is generally a temporary holding and organizing process. Secondary memory involves the manipulation and organization of information. Tertiary memory is memory that has been processed through secondary memory and placed in long-term storage.

Understanding and assessment of decreases in the older person's capacity to remember newly acquired information may be enhanced using this model. Problems of learning may be attributed to either encoding (with vision or hearing deficits), inattention to stimuli (perhaps low motivation to attend) as well as with retrieval and recall, which most often are faulted.

If too few opportunities have been provided to rehearse new information with practice, handouts, or coaching, or if there has been insufficient time for rehearsals, then the information simply may not have reached secondary storage.

Lorsbash & Simpson (1984) found that older people remember, but it merely takes longer to occur (retrieve). Other study findings have shown that older people are actually more efficient than younger people in searching long-term memory (Fozard, 1980). It is important to note that while some studies show that processing operations do not change with normal aging, *the time needed for processing increases* (Schmidt & McCroldey, 1981; Johnson, Schmitt, & Peitrukowicz, 1989).

Babins (1987) proposes that older adults differ in the way information is processed. Three dimensions of processing style were described:

Content — a detail versus main idea learner
Initiative — an active versus passive learner
Tactical — an analytical/objective learner versus an intuitive/creative learner

Ideally, learners would be midpoint on learning continuum. Gardner, Greenwell, and Costich (1991) provide examples of learning style behaviors that could assist nurses in assessment and interventions using style dominance. Clients who are primarily detail learners would ask for a step-by-step explanation and may have difficulty understanding or comprehending the overall idea and implications. Main idea clients are more interested in the "big picture," but have difficulty (may be impatient) with specifics, details, or instructions.

Clients who are active aggressive learners ask many questions but may be impatient and jump to conclusions too rapidly. Passive learners would not initiate questions and must be encouraged and coaxed.

Analytical learners respond to logic, structure, and organization. Intuitive learners need open-ended and unstructured strategies, and are more likely to be receptive to shared decisions.

It is important to remember that learner-centered strategies are flexible and accommodate learning styles, while teacher-centered instruction accommodates the instructor's style and convenience without regard for patient learning and style (Gardner, Greenwell, & Costich, 1991).

Arenberg and Robertson-Tchabo (1977) believe that all adult learning is transfer of training or the effects of new learning on previous learning. This view proposes that the older person's new learning is a function of previous learning and experience. In this model, transfer effects may be positive or negative. They may enhance or hinder the acquisition of new information. Teaching should be planned with consideration of previous information and experience as well as what future learning needs might be.

Factors Affecting Learning and Specific Intervention

Memory

According to Samuel Johnson, the art of memory is the art of attention. Both attentiveness and vigilance are important to memory and learning. Selective attention and divided attention are two categories of attention that show age-related changes. These include decreases in perfor-

Learner-centered strategies are flexible and accommodate learning styles.

mance levels in the presence of competing stimuli when a person is asked to perform certain tasks simultaneously.

As stated earlier, the most accepted change of aging related to memory is the decreased capacity to remember newly acquired information. Application, practice, and rehearsal will facilitate the older adult's processing and retention of information in primary or short-term memory. Practice over time activates secondary memory (see Table 1).

These findings support brevity and simplicity in structured teaching. Keep sessions short and to the point to minimize fatigue. Keeping messages simple eliminates irrelevant, confusing information. Maintaining a single focus for each session eliminates need for the patient to divide attention. Redundancy is important. Remember that learning by doing, using multiple senses, is more effective. Given these findings, nurses should reconsider the use of pamphlets, visuals, and written instructions to older patients. Written information is more likely to be remembered if nurses also discuss this information (see Table 2).

Levy and Spelman (1967) suggested that teaching strategies might be more effective if the following information were considered. (1) The more older adults are told, the greater the proportion of that information will be forgotten. (2) Patients will remember best what is told first as well as what they consider important. (3) Instructions and advice are more likely to be forgotten than other information. This information is rarely given first and is generally regarded as less important by the learner.

Psychosocial

One of the assumptions of patient education is that the client does have a choice. There are factors which affect choice—the client's personal view of learning and education, as well as the relevance of the information presented.

According to Atchley (1980), previous level of formal education and past experiences with learning often shape attitudes to new information. People who have had greater opportunity for education tend to place more value on these activities. Those who have encountered earlier frustration or failure are more likely to discount or undervalue the need for learning.

Self-concept, self-esteem, and confidence also affect decisions to learn. Atchley (1980) points out that the personal view of self is related to a willingness to learn and to the individual's perceived ability to learn new information. Nurses must work to help patients overcome negative self-perceptions of their learning ability. Family encouragement and social supports are needed to encourage the feeling of capability of learning how to live with new situations.

Eysenck (1979) discusses the relationship between motivation to learn and emotional dimensions such as depression or anxiety. Emotional status is closely related with physical status so that in health care settings and in situations of altered health status, there is greater potential for emotional disturbance. Not only is motivation a factor, a person's ability to receive information and process information can be disrupted by emotional conflicts. A breakdown in processing sequence can make learning extremely difficult (Gardner, Greenwell & Costich, 1991).

High levels of anxiety, depression, adjustment reactions, and acute reversible confusion are frequently part of

Table 1
Age-Related Changes in Memory

- Short-term memory is higher when stimuli are presented auditorily rather than visually.
- There is significant decrease with age in recall of sequencing of nonsense syllables, words, and symbols.
- There is greater difficulty on recall performance than on recognition tasks. Speed of recall also decreases in older people.

(Kermis, 1984)

Table 2
People Remember

- 5% to 10% of what they read
- 10% to 20% of what they hear
- 30% to 50% of what they hear and verbalize
- 70% of what they verbalize and write
  and
- 90% of what they say as they perform a task

(Dale, 1969)

the clinical course of older clients hospitalized for orthopaedic problems of trauma and/or surgery. One of the most common responses to illness is anxiety (Lambert & Lambert, 1985), and depression is the most common psychiatric disorder of later life as many losses and challenges often exceed personal resources to adapt.

Compounding these problems are myths and stereotypes of older persons expressed through references to their being "childlike" or "cantankerous" or "confused and senile" often obscuring and interfering with accurate assessment (Eliopoulos, 1987). Many times, situational problems or adjustment reactions can mimic depression in patients and clients dealing with chronic pain or hospitalization, making assessment more difficult.

The experience of anxiety or depression in older persons interferes with functioning, increases feelings of helplessness and becomes self-perpetuating. "Helplessness anxiety" is most prevalent in the elderly and is related to threatened loss of emotional and social supports such as loss of spouse, other important persons, reduced income, and reduced personal mastery for competence and control (Verwoerdt, 1989). Learning capability is likely to be restricted in these instances. Indecisiveness, inattention, decreased concentration, as well as agitation can be encountered.

In these situations only the most important points should be covered. Feedback should be immediate, consistent, and factual. Patients in these situations often evaluate their performance negatively, so positive reinforcement and opportunities for patient success are important. Therapeutic strategies for avoidance of overstimulation, frustration, and agitation need to be included. Teaching sessions should be brief, to the point, quiet, and "low-key." The nurse will need to attend to patient behaviors and clues indicating decreased tolerance for continuation and modify accordingly.

Communicate respect to help build self-esteem and confidence.

Vision

About 20 percent of those over age 65 report some difficulty with vision. After heart disease and arthritis, visual impairment is the greatest handicap among the aged (Heckheimer, 1989).

Some elderly, believing that failing eyesight is normal and fearing that visual problems indicate decreased ability to take care of themselves, deny that problems exist. Several common changes in vision are associated with aging which have implications for learning if printed material is used. (See Table 3).

Recognizing these limitations, nurses can plan interventions which incorporate strategies that minimize vision deficits. Using large **bold** print and clear simple writing styles (instead of *fancy script*) will be easier reading for older adults. Nonglare surfaces and appropriate color contrast between words or symbols and background are helpful. Visual aids and posters should be developed with consideration for difficulty with discrimination between "cool" colors such as blues, greens, and violets.

It is important to assess environmental light sources to reduce reflective surfaces. It is important also to avoid standing in front of windows or bright light sources so that the face may be seen and not obscured by the bright background light. Lighting needs vary, but about twice as much illumination is needed at age 60 than age 20. The area of visual concentration should be brighter than the background by a ratio of 3:1 and no greater than 10:1 (Heckheimer, 1989).

Hearing

More than 50 percent of Americans over 65 are affected by hearing impairment. Presbycusis or decreased ability to hear higher pitch sounds, and the ability to discriminate between certain speech sounds are especially common hearing problems. Increasing volume may not improve the quality of sound and may in fact lead to greater sound distortion. People often are unaware of hearing deficits. Cerumen or the accumulation of wax in the ear is most often responsible for hearing loss. Assessment leading to removal of cerumen of the external canal by the nurse can often improve hearing noticeably.

Strategies for improving communication with hearing impaired people include the following:
1. Plan ahead to minimize environmental barriers that interfere with communication such as a quiet area with low background noise or "buzz" of other conversation, television or music.
2. Lower the voice pitch and maintain a good conversational quality, not necessarily increasing the volume.
3. Attend to the rate of speech as rapid speech results in decreased comprehension.

4. "Matching and pacing" is one way of increasing communication. The nurse listens and observes the client for rate and manner of speech and matches this style. Often this increases comprehension and can also broaden a shared field of experience between the patient and nurse (Daum, 1991).
5. Emphasize the visual, and face the person directly for a distance of about 3 to 6 feet maintaining eye contact.
6. Avoid chewing gum or covering the mouth while talking.
7. Use facial expressions and gestures to clue topics and changes of topics.

Communicate respect to help build self-esteem and confidence. Sometimes touch may be threatening to the elderly with hearing loss. Handshakes can be benign and provide an opportunity to signal acceptance or rejection (Heckheimer, 1989).

Addressing Patient Needs and Implementing Strategies

To effectively address the older patient's learning needs, the attitude that older people do not know what is best for them must be replaced with the attitude that older people can be assisted to decide what is best. In this role, the nurse becomes a facilitator working in collaboration with the patient, exploring and assessing needs. Often troubling to nurses and other health care providers is the fact that what is presumably in the older adult's best interest and what the older adult chooses to do are not always the same (Ayers & Wharton, 1991).

The goal of patient education is not only to gain the older adult's cooperation (compliance) but also to encourage the older adult to change behavior (adherence). Compliance means that the older adult follows medical or nursing orders and does what has been instructed. Adherence has connotations of willingness to participate rather than obedience to authority. The nurse assists the patient to identify problems, goals, and options. The patient's responsibility is to choose among the options available and to take action to implement the chosen option to achieve the goal (Esberger & Hughes, 1989).

After problems have been identified, the nurse's role is to help the patient turn problems into goals. The goals will

Table 3
Age-Related Changes in Vision

- Decreased acuity or sharpness of vision
- Decreased ability to discriminate color, especially blues, blue-greens, and violet
- Decreased depth perception
- Decreased peripheral vision
- Decreased adaptation to light change
- Decreased tolerance for glare
- Decreased accommodation of lens to focus
- Decreased convergence or ability to focus both eyes on an object
- Decreased ability to look up

(Heckheimer, 1989)

Table 4
Strategies for Effective Learning for Older Adults

A. Do not require that the learner infer important information. Be specific. Comprehending and "figuring out" are different things.
B. Sequence material so that most important and critical material is taught first. In this way, patient spends most time on most important content.
C. Negotiate goal and the statement of the goal in the patient's language. Using the patient's own words can enhance success.
D. Prerequisite skill or knowledge that is needed should be presented before subsequent tasks or information is presented.
E. Learning should proceed from simple to complex, concrete to abstract, and easier to more difficult. Sufficient time is needed to learn, and the process cannot be hurried.
F. Redundancy of information is important. This means repetition of information in various ways using a variety of modalities. Incorporate opportunities for the patient to restate, paraphrase, or demonstrate information or skills. Present information in a variety of formats: auditory, written, or graphic.
G. Limit the amount of information that patients are expected to learn, and clearly differentiate the necessary from the nonessential.
H. Use vocabulary that is meaningful to the patient. We cannot assume that patients of any age share the medical vocabulary that is second nature to practitioners. Even if patients and practitioners are using the same words, practitioners should clarify meaning before assuming shared understanding. A vocabulary that reflects common usage and is concrete and avoids abstract terminology is best.
I. Use advance organizers; tell how the information will proceed and "announce" information that is to follow.
J. Interpersonal communications are important in learning. Negative perceptions communicated by health care professionals will have a detrimental effect on older adult learning. Attitudes and misinformation about older people need confrontation, because these attitudes will be imparted to patients and more so if there is a lack of awareness by the nurse or health provider.

The goal of patient education is not only to gain the older adult's cooperation (compliance), but also to encourage the older adult to change behavior (adherence).

---

how these are uniquely expressed in the learner. Table 4 shows suggestions for designing strategies.

Patient Education as an Empowering Process

Patient education is usually rather specific in addressing specific needs with appropriate content, goals, and outcome. However, there is an additional, rather nonspecific consequence that can occur when patients participate in their recovery and assume more control over their lives with active participation in their healing process.

All people are enhanced when they make decisions about their health status, lifestyles, and health management. Control of one's environment and health is diminished as the older person advances in age. Empowering patients to maintain some measure of control by participating in choice of goals and how they are to be achieved and measured enhances feelings of self-worth and competence. Patient education can benefit the person in perhaps the most meaningful and significant way, by recognizing the person as the unique, valued individual that he or she is.

References

Arenberg, D., & Robertson-Tchabo, E. A. (1977). Learning and aging. In J. E. Birren, & K. W. Schaie (Eds.), *The handbook of the psychology of aging.* New York: Van Nostrand Reinhold.

Atchley, R. C. (1980). *The social forces in later life* (3rd ed.). Belmont, CA: Wadsworth.

Ayers, D., & Wharton, M. A. (1991). Improving exercise adherence: Instructional strategies. *Topics in Geriatric Rehabilitation, 6*(3).

Babins L. (1987). Cognitive processes in the elderly: General factors to consider. *Gerontology and Geriatric Education, 8* (1/2), 9-22.

Cattell, R. B. (1963). Theory of fluid and crystallized intelligence: Critical experiment. *Journal of Educational Psychology, 54,* 1-22.

Chin, R., & Benne, K. D. (1976). General strategies for effecting change in human systems. In W. Bennis, R. Chin, & D. Corey (Eds.), *The planning of change* (3rd ed.). (pp. 22-46). New York: Holt-Rinehart & Winston.

Craik, F. I. M. (1977). Age differences in human memory. In J. D. Birren & K. W. Shaie (Eds.), *Handbook of the psychology of aging.* New York: Van Nostrand Reinhold.

Dale, E. (1969). Cone of experience. In C. Wiman (Ed.), *Educational media.* Charles, E. Merrill.

Daum, S. G. (1991). Increasing communication effectiveness in rehabilitation programs. *Topics in Geriatric Rehabilitation.* 6(3), 17-25.

Denton, D. R. (1990). *Caring for an aging society: Issues and strategies for gerontology education.* Atlanta, GA: Southern Regional Education Board.

state what the patient would like to have happen, and are best stated in the patient's language and vocabulary. The nurse and patient and often family, significant other, or caregiver together will examine the goals and variables that may impede or enhance attainment of the goals. Focusing on goals, rather than problems, and abilities, rather than disabilities, is a key factor in successful interventions as well as assessments.

A teaching plan usually includes components of (1) assessing patient needs; (2) formulating patient goals and acceptable outcomes; (3) determining learning needs and appropriate outcomes; (4) designing individualized learning strategies; and (5) evaluating progress. In designing individualized learning strategies, needs of the learner can be addressed through considerations of the aging process and

Edwards, L. (1990). Health education. In C. L. Edelman & C. L. Mandle, *Health promotion throughout the lifespan* (pp. 173-191). St. Louis: Mosby.

Eliopoulos, C. (1987). *Gerontological nursing* (2nd ed.). Philadelphia: Lippincott.

Esberger, K. K., & Hughes, S. T. (1989). *Nursing care of the aged.* Norwalk, CT: Appleton and Lance.

Eysenck, M. W. (1979). Anxiety, learning and memory: A reconceptualization. *Journal of Research in Personality, 13,* 363-365.

Fozard, J. S. (1980). The time for remembering. In L. Poon (Ed.), *Aging in the 1980's: Psychological issues.* Washington, DC: American Psychological Association.

Gardener, M. A., Greenwell, S. C., & Costich, J. F. (1991). Effective teaching of the older adult. *Topics in Geriatric Rehabilitation, 6*(3), 1-14.

Gottsdanker, R. (1982). Age and simple reaction time. *Journal of Gerontology,* 342-348.

Guilford, D. (Ed.). (1988). *The aging population in the twenty-first century.* Washington, DC: National Academy Press.

Heckheimer, E. F. (1989). *Health promotion of the elderly in the community.* Philadelphia: Saunders.

Johnson, M. M., Schmitt F. A., & Peitrukowicz, M. (1989). The memory advantages of the generation effect: Age and process differences. *Journal of Gerontology, 44,* 91-94.

Kalish, R. A. (1979). The new ageism and the failure models: A polemic. *The Gerontologist, 19*(4), 398-402.

Kermis, M. D. (1984). *The psychology of human aging.* Boston, Allyn, and Bacon, Inc.

Lambert, V., & Lambert, C. E. (1985). *Psychosocial care of the physically ill: What every nurse should know.* Englewood Cliffs, NJ: Prentice-Hall.

Levy P., & Spelman, M. S. (1967). *Communicating with the patient.* St. Louis: Warren H. Green.

Lorsbash T. C., & Simpson, G. B. (1984). Age differences in the rate of processing in short-term memory. *Journal of Gerontology, 39*(3), 315-321.

Neugarten, B. (1974). Age groups in American society and the rise of the young-old. *Annals of American Academy of Political and Social Science, 415,* 189-198.

Orem, D. E. (1990). *Nursing: Concepts of practice* (4th ed.). New York: McGraw Hill.

Pender, N. J. (1987). *Health promotion in nursing practice* (2nd ed.). Norwalk, CT: Appleton & Lange.

Rogers, C. R., & Holm, M. B. Teaching older persons with depression. *Topics in Geriatric Rehabilitation, 6*(3), 27-44.

Schmidt, J. F., & McCroldey, R. L. (1981). Sentence comprehension in elderly listeners. The factor of rate. *Journal of Gerontology, 36,* 441-445.

Stabb, A. S., & Lyles, M. F. (1990). Intellectual function disorders. In A. Stabb, & B. Lyles (Eds.), *Manual of Geriatric Nursing.* (pp. 521-526). Glenville, IL: Foresman/Little, Brown Higher Education.

Verwoerdt, A. (1989). Anxiety, dissociative and personality disorders in the elderly. In E. W. Busse & D. Blazer (Eds.), *Handbook of geriatric psychiatry* (pp. 368-380). New York: Van Nostrand Reinhold.

Yurick, A. G., Spier, B. E., Robb, S. S., & Ebert, N. J. (1989). *The aged person and the nursing process.* Norwalk, CT: Appleton & Lange.

MEN AND WOMEN AGING DIFFERENTLY

Barbara M. Barer

University of California, San Francisco

ABSTRACT

Gender differences in health, socio-economic status, and social resources persist into advanced old age and result in variations in life trajectories and responses to the challenges of longevity. The implications of these differences are examined in a sample of 150 community-dwelling white men and women. The majority are women, a high proportion of whom are unmarried, living alone, functionally impaired, and have reduced financial resources. Men, in contrast, have fewer decrements, they are more independent, and they exercise more control over their environment. However, their well-being may be undermined by some unanticipated events such as widowhood, caregiving, and relocation. Case examples illustrate how the timing of life course events differs among men and women and results in differences in the problems they face in late-late life.

At the turn of the century, when the average life expectancy in the United States was forty-nine years of age, only 5 percent of white men and 7 percent of white women could expect to survive to eighty-five years old. Now life expectancy has increased to seventy-six years, with 18 percent of white men and 38 percent of white women projected to live to eighty-five years [1]. One striking change in the older population is the widening gender gap, as proportionately more women than men live longer. Among the population age sixty-five to sixty-nine there are eighty-one men for every 100 women, but the gender ratio drops to thirty-nine men for every 100 women over the age of eighty-five [2]. Today in our country, there are 841,000 men and 2.2 million women of that age or older [3].

This article will explore the implications of gender differences in the lives of men and women in advanced old age. Based on data from our initial sample of 150 white respondents, men and women will first be compared on their demographic characteristics, physical status, and social networks. Second, men and women will be compared by how they manage their daily activities and adapt to the typical problems encountered in advanced old age. Then case examples will illustrate how gender-specific events lead to differing responses among the oldest-old. These case studies will illustrate how such events as widowhood, caregiving, and relocation are timed at different periods over the life course, so that men and women face quite different kinds of problems in late-late life.

BACKGROUND

The New York Times [4] recently reported that the prospects for elderly men are brighter than those for elderly women. Men who survive beyond the age of eighty-five are more likely than women to be in better health and to have more remaining years of independent life. While men are prone to acute and fatal diseases, women are subject to the disabling effects of chronic conditions [3]. National surveys also find that more men than women, aged eighty-five and over, are still married, 48.7 percent of white men in comparison to only 10.3 percent of white women [1]. The tendency of women to marry men older than themselves compounds the likelihood of their being widowed at a younger age. As a consequence, more women live alone in late-late life, two-thirds compared to one-third of men [1].

A further disadvantage for women in this age group is their relatively poor economic status. Twenty-three percent of women aged eighty-five and over live at the poverty level, compared to 16 percent of men [5]. This cohort of women either did not work outside the home or had discontinuous work patterns that excluded them from pensions and related benefits in old age. Hence the nation's oldest and fastest growing population today is dominated by a disproportionately large number of unmarried women who not only suffer from increased functional impairment but also are most likely to live alone and to have economic problems.

While very old women are more impaired than men, they may be better equipped to handle the physical and social losses usually encountered with longevity. Some researchers [6, 7] suggest that widows are better able than widowers to develop and sustain intimate relationships. They tend to form confidante relationships with other widowed women, whereas widowed men, who had relied on their wives for their emotional needs, are left with no one [8, 9]. Moreover there is a great difference in the meaning of friendship to men and women. Women place more importance on friendships and engage in trusted relationships, while men usually have more superficial, less emotionally close relationships [10]. Furthermore when a man is widowed, other men his age are most likely to still be married [11].

From the *International Journal of Aging and Human Development*, Vol. 38, No. 1, 1994, pp. 29-40. © 1994 by Baywood Publishing Company, Inc. Reprinted by permission.

Gender differences over the life course also influence the daily lives of the very old. For example, women of this cohort were encouraged to be more passive and family oriented, an orientation that, along with unchanging domestic roles, results in continuities in late-late life [10]. In contrast, male roles throughout life place a premium on competency, activity, productivity, independence, and self-reliance, all characteristics that are difficult to sustain with the increased disability that occurs in late-late life [12]. As a consequence, very old men and women are likely to differ not only in how they manage their daily routine, but also how they adapt to continuities and discontinuities.

Help seeking behavior also varies by gender and is predictable among the oldest-old. Women are usually more willing to acknowledge their need for assistance and to seek or accept help from others [12]. Since men do not like to see themselves as dependent, they may actually accept less formal support than they need [13]. Therefore, as men's needs increase with age, current gender norms may inhibit their adaptation. These variations suggest that men and women who survive into advanced old age have quite different demands placed upon them as well as varied resources and competencies.

SAMPLE CHARACTERISTICS BY GENDER

The mean age of the sample is 88.1 for men and 89.2 for women (Table 1). Consistent with national surveys, one-half of the men in the *85+ Study* are currently married, in comparison to only 10 percent of the women. Household composition also replicates national data, with less than one-half of the men living alone in contrast to two-thirds of the women. Economically, most women report less financial security than men. Men's income tends to be more substantial since more of them receive a pension in addition to social security.

Men are further advantaged in their health status, with over one-fourth perceiving their health to be excellent. They have significantly fewer problems with functional limitations and are less restricted in their mobility. Significantly more women than men have some impairment in their basic activities involving personal care (ADL), and the difference is even greater for the activities of daily living (IADL).

Table 1. A Profile of the White Oldest Old by Gender
(Percentages (n + 150))

	Women n = 111 (73%)	Men n = 39 (27%)
Demographic Profile		
Mean age	89.2	88.1
Married	10	49
Living alone	62	46
Economic Status		
Income from pension	38	53
Income from social security	90	100
Income from SSI	9	3
Income from savings	75	85
Income from work	5	11
Income Adequacy		
Good	52	74**
Fair	42	23
Poor	6	3
Perceived Health Status		
Excellent	14	28*
Good	56	51
Fair	24	21
Poor	6	—
Activity Restriction		
None	28	47*
Some	41	23
A great deal	31	18
ADL		
No impairment	69	92*
Impaired 1–3 tasks	22	3
Impaired 4+ tasks	9	5
IADL		
No impairment	18	64***
Impaired 1–3 tasks	12	23
Impaired 4+ tasks	70	13

*p < .05
**p < .01
***p < .001

In contrast to men's advantages physically and economically, women have more extensive social networks (Table 2). While similar numbers have a child in proximity, twice as many women receive some instrumental support from children. Both men and women enjoy expressive or emotional support from children. Forty-seven percent of the women, but only 11 percent of the men had a child functioning as a caregiver. These significant differences could be related to women's greater needs, or to the fact that more men still have a spouse and do not have to turn to children for help [14].

Not only do women receive more support from children, but they also maintain more contact with them (Table 2). Although not statistically significant, over two-thirds of the women report weekly or more contact with a child, compared with less than one-half of the men. They also maintain closer ties with children and are more likely than men to name a child as a confidante. Men more typically respond, "I only share problems with my wife." The difference be-

Table 2. Social Supports by Gender
(Percentages)

	Women	Men
Family Structure		
Those with children	68	70
Child in proximity	58	46
Social Supports from Children		
Instrumental supports	60	30**
Expressive supports	80	74
Child as caregiver	47	11**
Weekly or more contact	69	48
Child as confidant	25	19
Friends		
Instrumental support	41	18
Expressive support	96	25
Friend as confidant	38	10
Formal Supports		
Choreworker	50	23*
Senior/community association	40	46
Transportation services	15	5
Unmet needs	24	10

*p < .05
** p < .01
***p < .001

tween men and women in their receipt of expressive support from friends is also significant. The greater propensity among women to name a friend as a confidante, also reflects women's continuing ability to maintain intimate relationships outside of the family.

These findings indicate that gender differences in social resources persist into late life, with women continuing to be better able than men to rally social supports to meet their greater needs. Furthermore, since women experience more disability in late life, they also use significantly more formal supports than men; twice as many women as men regularly use household assistance. Finally, one-fourth of the women, compared to only a few men, have unmet needs for social services.

Managing Daily Routines

Table 3 reports on how men and women differ in managing their daily activities in advanced old age. Global measures point to significant gender differences. Women do more socializing on a daily basis, but men rated significantly higher in all other categories. Specifically, men maintained a higher level of activity, they were more involved in hobbies and household maintenance, they participated more in organizational activities and they exercised more independence.

Three types of competencies required to adapt to community living (as described in the Introduction) were also coded into global measures that are reported in Table 3. These are competencies in exercising control over the physical environment, maintaining social integration, and sustaining a sense of well-being and motivations. Again men were significantly more able than women to exercise control over their environment and maintain their motivations (Table 3). Gender differences in maintaining social integration were not significant, however, nor was there significant variation in maintaining a sense of well-being.

In keeping with their better physical status, men in their advanced years are more apt to retain some characteristics as younger men. For example, eighty-six-year-old Mr. Bascomb maintains an active daily program. In describing his typical day as being "rather busy," he indicated his datebook was filled with daily entries. As a still productive member of several committees, he attends four or five luncheon meetings a week. In his own words, he elaborated, "I have a number of civic assignments. I keep up quite a correspondence, writing five to eight letters a day. I also have a number of projects going and spend time in my workshop repairing or making furniture. I play the piano after a fashion, jazzing it up in the evening." Keeping up an active correspondence was not unique to Mr. Bascomb. In fact, political activism in the form of letter-writing was a major

Table 3. Adaptation to Daily Living by Gender (Time 2)
(n = 111)

	Women (n = 85)		Men (n = 26)		Sig.
	M	S.D.	M	S.D.	
Daily Routine:					
Sociability	2.92	1.03	2.58	1.10	
Active	2.76	1.18	2.12	.864	*
Hobbies	3.23	1.35	2.31	1.19	**
Home maintenance	2.98	1.36	2.31	1.29	*
Organizations	3.37	1.50	2.62	1.29	*
Independence	2.46	.936	1.92	.796	*
Adaptive Responses					
Control of environment	1.93	.946	1.42	.578	*
Social integration	2.53	1.25	3.15	1.29	
Well-being	2.41	1.08	2.42	1.14	
Maintain motivation	2.12	1.12	1.58	.758	*
Mood					
Affect balance	17	5.00	16	4.18	

*p < .05
**p < .01

motivating force in the life of Mr. Atkins. "I sit down every day and write to big shots. What's keeping me alive is the pursuit of Reagan!"

With fewer physical restraints men are significantly more able to sustain their independence and devote time and energy to maintaining their hobbies and interests. These covered a wide range of activities, including stamp collecting, carpentry, gardening, and "playing my fiddle." Like eighty-eight-year-old Mr. Walsh, men also participated more in organizational activities outside the home. "I'm a member of two Mason lodges. That gives me things to do, luncheons, meetings, outings." As others summarized their days, "I look at my calendar to find out what to do today. I belong to organizations and I follow plans." "I don't have anything to do in a business way. Now it's all centered around senior activities."

Not surprisingly men with their better health are better able to exercise more control over their environment. A precisely timed day was outlined by an energetic eighty-seven-year-old musician who, unsolicited, gave a minute-by-minute account of his morning schedule. He was meticulous in describing not only what he ate, but when he ate, eating the same thing at the same hour every day— 6:45 a.m., 10 a.m., 12 p.m., 4:30 p.m., and 7:30 p.m. He was emphatic about the need for regularity in all activities. Similarly, Mr. Logan controlled his daily routine. "At 7 a.m. I listen to the news for an hour. At 8 a.m. I get up and have coffee and read the paper until 9 a.m. From 9 to 9:30 I take a shower and shave. At 10 o'clock we eat. At 10:30 I go to the office and stay until 1. After lunch I walk in Golden Gate Park for one or two hours."

Women usually described a more passive approach to their daily activities, most likely compatible to their current disabilities. "I'm very free to do what I want, but I just don't get out. When you get to my age, you're glad to rest more." "Mostly I stay home and just spend the day sitting around. I sleep a little. Unfortunately I can't do the things I used to do." "I'm more or less an observer of life now." Women were prone to talk about their limitations and the time and energy consumed in performing basic tasks. Specifically, a ninety-year-old woman explained, "What used to take me three hours to do, now takes me three days. And then I need a two hour nap in

the middle of the day, so I lose those hours." Continuities were also evident. "When the children were small, I never went out much. I was never a gadabout so it comes natural for me to stay home."

Life Course Trajectories

Because of marked differences in their life trajectories, men and women usually experience events at different ages and thus require differing types of adaptation. Not uncommonly, men who survive into advanced old age might have to adapt to widowhood, the caregiver role, and relocation, transitions that women experienced at younger ages. The shift in roles required of men is particularly challenging at the age of eighty-five, ninety, or ninety-five, at a time when disability and social losses are more likely. In contrast, the life course for women of this generation was traditionally timed to family events so there was greater role continuity as they aged.

Timing of Widowhood

Recently widowed very old men experience this loss at an age when they are most vulnerable. Although many more women are widowed, they have been widowed for a much longer time (a mean of 25 years in comparison to 10 years for men). As a consequence, they have had time to build networks that substitute for the sociability in marriage. Most men in advanced old age had not expected to outlive their wives, and thus they were not prepared for their bereavement. Many express feelings of inadequacy and abandonment. In the words of one eighty-eight-year-old widower, "We were like two peas in a pod. Now I'm just one man in this big house. I'm helpless here!" Others say, "I am alone with no support. I'm losing confidence in myself and my strength," "I've got nothing without my wife," or, "I have nobody and I am nobody!"

This cohort usually socialized in couples—the men relied on their wives to arrange social activities. Left on their own, few demonstrated resourcefulness in planning social get-togethers. Since these men were unaccustomed to establishing social relationships, they often resist forming new relationships to substitute for their loss. Widowers frequently remarked on their social isolation, "Since my wife passed away, I've drifted away from friends." "When my wife was alive we saw people jointly. She

arranged everything. Now I don't bother." "I'm not at an age where I can make friends again."

Eighty-five year old Mr. Long lamented that the death of his wife four years previously was the worst thing that had ever happened to him. "When my wife died, I didn't know what to do with myself—the aloneness, the empty apartment, everything. We had a good marriage and an ordinary life. Now I can't find any suitable companions. I don't visit anybody and nobody visits me. I'm not the least bit interested in sitting and listening to strangers tell me their life story, and they must feel the same way about me! This is the worst kind of life."

Mr. James, at ninety-five, was widowed two years before our first contact. Even though he is the father of four sons, he conveyed a profound sense of loss and desolation. "Before my wife passed away, I was feeling very, very good. Since she died, I've hated living alone. I miss Ginny so much that I almost cry. We had closeness, intimacy, and interest in each other. It was something to live for. Now I've got nothing. Even the last years of looking after Ginny were better than being alone. I haven't the will or mind to engage in anything. All I know is that I'm goddamn lonesome."

Among this generation of oldest-old, women who have been widowed for several years may be better adapted to independent living than widowers. Their prior involvement in domestic and community activities often continues in the absence of a spouse. Eighty-seven year old Mrs. Granger, who has been widowed for half of her life, still lives in the family home, a residence she has maintained for forty-nine years. In addition to her weekly volunteer work serving meals to the homeless, Mrs. Granger is involved in numerous church projects and social activities with her friends and neighbors. Her five children and eleven grandchildren further occupy her energies and time. She reports she never gets depressed or lonely, and she feels good about being able to accomplish so much on her own.

Generally women have had more years than men to adapt emotionally to their losses. For example, Mrs. Richards, now aged ninety, lost her husband when she was only forty-two years of age. Now she lives alone in a high rise apartment building with mostly other older residents. Her only complaint is, "I'm not able to go out as much as I used to." When asked about her marriage, Mrs. Richards responded, "It was a beautiful marriage. I miss him very much but I really don't remember too much about my married life. It was too long ago." Similarly, ninety-three-year-old Mrs. Scott lost her husband thirty-nine years ago. "He died suddenly of a cerebral hemorrhage. He was just found dead. It was horrible but people have had worse things happen. I had a good marriage. He was a lovely gentleman and a marvelous father. I can't imagine wanting anything else. I have no concerns."

Anticipatory socialization may serve to ease the burden of grief for women who, unlike men, had expected to be widowed. Ninety year old Mrs. Billings had outlived two husbands and viewed her status as being the norm. "We were a family of widows, three girls in my family. My mother buried three husbands, and my sisters buried two each. Maybe we all loved our men to death. Burying a husband is no fun, but what good does it do to let it get you down?"

Men as Caregivers

Elderly men who must assume a caregiving role are particularly vulnerable to stress. Typically these men, born at the turn of the century, had not been socialized to a more androgenous gender role, so that they are ill-prepared to tackle domestic chores. In addition, men in their late eighties and nineties may have to contend with their own disabilities that complicate the difficulties of caregiving. Mr. Watts, an eighty-seven-year-old retired banker, recounted his recent experience of caring for his impaired wife. "I took care of her for three years at home and went through Hell. I did it all myself, I did everything, bathed her, everything. I'd do it again, but it was rough. I had never done a darn thing around the house before. I did my own cooking, shopping, cleaned the best I could. Finally I ran out of strength."

Another eighty-seven-year-old retired executive confessed that his life had been much easier running a large corporation than managing his household. He said, "I didn't become a housewife until I was eighty. The hardest thing is taking care of my wife. I help her dress, undress, and take a bath. Although we have nurses, she won't let anyone help her but me. I wish I didn't have to do it. There's no explaining it, you just do it." A similar situation was described by Dr. Chalmers, aged eighty-nine and married fifty-eight years, who was coping with his wife's recent stroke. "I've become a full-time husband. I shop, cook, clean up. I'm a little housebound now. My life is much more lived around my wife these days. She is confused sometimes. I encourage her and read to her. I'm lucky it happened so late in life though. A year ago we still hiked for miles."

Relocation

A problem common to both men and women in advanced age is the potential "threat" of relocation, but the responses are quite divergent. Men, more than women, tend to be less accepting of relocation to senior or "retirement" housing. Their responses to such a move ranged from outright resistance to resignation. In the words of one eighty-eight-year-old widower, "I can't get enthusiastic about a retirement home. It would bother me to be cooped up in one room. It's confining and restrictive. You have to be on time for meals, be dressed, shaved, cleaned up. I plan to stay where I am." An eighty-seven-year-old former engineer described his reaction to life in a senior residence as follows. "I don't like living like this, but it's the lesser of two evils. Being here I don't have any problems. It's just a matter of getting up and going through the day and going to bed. It's like a jail. If you added bars and threw away the key, it would be the same. I'm stuck with it. No sense in getting upset about it." Another man expressed even greater discontentment. "Senior housing is the end of the line. Before I was busy all the time. Now I have nothing special to live for."

With longer life expectancy, earlier widowhood, and usually reduced financial resources, women more often leave their family dwelling at a younger age and move to an apartment or senior housing. Changes in living arrangements may also be related to women's increasing levels of impairment and their need for more instrumental supports. Like widowhood, relocation usually occurs at an earlier age for women than for men. Some respondents had resided in senior residences for a long time. Ninety-three-year-old Mrs. Dixon bought into a senior residence at the age of seventy-four. "As I think back, I've come to a happy conclusion here. We're well cared for. I came nineteen years ago when they didn't expect us to live this long. I still pay only $550 a month."

Mrs. Hall, aged ninety, is also a long-term resident of senior housing. In spite of her breathing difficulties and painful arthritis, she maintains active involvement in her building. "This is a lovely place to live. I've had four houses of my own, but when I was in my 70's, I had the chance to come in here. There's always something to do, visit someone, help someone, play cards. Whenever someone is ill, I help them. I enjoy every day. I like the activities, and I like to visit."

CONCLUSION

Among the oldest-old, gender-based disparities are evident in functional status, socioeconomic status, and social resources. While these differences favor men, other differences appear to favor women. Consistent with national data, one-half of the men in our sample are married and thus living with someone. Only 10 percent of the women are married, two-thirds live alone, and many experience economic problems. These women also have greater physical disability because of chronic health conditions. With depleted energy and limited mobility, women are less able to independently manage their activities of daily living. Most often they need help with household maintenance. Their physical limitations further restrict their ability to exercise control over their environment and to maintain motivations. Typically women in advanced old age demonstrate a more passive orientation.

An analysis of gender variations in life trajectories, however, illustrate some advantages for women. Many of them had experienced widowhood at a younger age, so they had time to adjust to their loss and form substitute relationships with other widows. Sex role socialization also benefits these women's adjustment to old age. Having been socialized to domesticity and family responsibilities, they experience greater role continuity in their late life activities and relationships. Although very old women, more than men, have gone from strength to frailty, from self-sufficiency to some degree of dependency, from marriage to widowhood, and from independent living to group living, their problems are in part counteracted by their increased social supports from children and friends.

As an aggregate, men are at an advantage physically and have less need for social supports. However, as their needs increase, cultural norms and the timing of events may threaten their well-being. Widowhood, caregiving, and relocation are off-time events and rarely anticipated in the lives of very old men, so they usually have difficulty in coping with them. These men have been ill-prepared to handle the domestic chores and emotional stresses of living alone or caring for an impaired spouse. Case studies also reveal that men are not particularly amenable to age-segregated living situations, a relocation that is increasingly likely in late life. Our findings also indicate that men in advanced old age have a high risk of social isolation when confronted with widowhood in late late life.

An examination of the daily lives of these men and women, as told in their own words, offers us a unique opportunity to enrich our understanding of the problems they face. These conclusions have implications for policy and further research. Women's ability to sustain community living in advanced old age would be enhanced by the greater availability of quality home care help. With the prolongation of life, more attention must also be given to gender differences and the potential risks faced by very old men.

REFERENCES

1. C. M. Taeuber and I. Rosenwaike, A Demographic Portrait of America's Oldest Old, in *The Oldest Old*, R. M. Suzman, D. P. Willis, and K. G. Manton (eds.), Oxford University Press, New York, 1992.
2. B. Hess, The Demographic Parameters, *Generations,* Summer, pp. 12–15, 1990.
3. C. M. Taeuber, *Sixty-Five Plus in America,* Current Population Reports, United States Department of Commerce, Bureau of the Census, P23-178, 1992.
4. *The New York Times,* November 10, 1992.
5. U.S. Bureau of the Census, *Money, Income and Poverty Status in the United States 1988* (Advance Data), Washington, D.C.: United States Department of Commerce, Current Population Reports, Series P-60, No. 166, U.S. Government Printing Office, 1989.
6. P. M. Keith, The Social Context and Resources of the Unmarried in Old Age, *International Journal of Aging and Human Development,* 23, pp. 81–96, 1986.
7. J. A. Kohen, Old but not Alone: Informal Social Supports among the Elderly by Marital Status and Sex, *The Gerontologist, 23,* pp. 57–63, 1983.
8. C. E. Depner and B. Ingersoll, Employment Status and Social Support: The Experience of the Mature Woman, in *Women's Retirement: Policy Implications for Recent Research,* M. Szinovacz (ed.), Sage, Beverly Hills, pp. 61–76, 1982.
9. G. Peters and M. Kaiser, The Role of Friends and Neighbors in Providing Social Support, in *Social Support Networks and the Care of the Elderly,* W. Sauer and R. Coward (eds.), Springer, New York, pp. 123–158, 1986.
10. J. A. Levy, Intersections of Gender and Aging, *The Sociological Quarterly, 29:4,* pp. 479–486, 1988.
11. R. A. Kalish, Death and Dying in a Social Context, in *Handbook of Aging and the Social Sciences,* R. H. Binstock and E. Shanas (eds.), Van Nostrand Reinhold, New York, pp. 483–510 1976. (publisher . . .) 1976.
12. P. A. McMullen and A. E. Gross, Sex Differences, Sex Roles, and Health-Related Help-Seeking, in *New Directions in Helping,* J. D. Fisher, A. Nadler, and B. M. Depaulo (eds.), vol. 2, Academic Press, Inc. 1983.
13. C. Longino and A. Lipman, Married and Spouseless Men and Women in Planned Retirement Communities: Support Network Differentials, *Journal of Marriage and Family, 43,* pp. 169–177, 1981.
14. C. L. Johnson and L. Troll, Family Functioning in Late Late Life, *Journal of Gerontology, 47:2,* pp. 566–572, 1992.

Societal Attitudes toward Old Age

There is a wide range of beliefs regarding the social position and status of the aged in American society today. Some people believe the best way to understand the problems of the elderly is to regard them as a minority group, faced with difficulties similar to those of other minority groups. Discrimination against older people, like racial discrimination, is believed to be based on a bias against visible physical traits. Since the aging process is viewed negatively, it is natural that the elderly try to appear and act younger. Some spend a tremendous amount of money trying to make themselves look and feel younger.

The theory that old people are a minority group is weak, however, because too many circumstances prove otherwise. The U.S. Congress, for example, favors senior members of Congress, and it delegates considerable prestige and power to them. The leadership roles in most religious organizations are held by older persons. Many older Americans are in good health, have comfortable incomes, and are treated with respect by friends and associates.

Perhaps the most realistic way to view the aged is as a status group, like other status groups in society. Every society has some method of "age grading," by which it groups together individuals of roughly similar age. ("Pre-teens" and "senior citizens" are some of the age grade labels in American society.) Because it is a labeling process, age grading causes members of the age grade, as well as others, to perceive themselves in terms of the connotations of the label. Unfortunately, the tag "old age" often has negative connotations in American society.

The readings included in this unit illustrate the wide range of stereotypical attitudes toward older Americans. Many of society's typical assumptions about the limitations of old age have been refuted. A major force behind this reassessment of the elderly has been the simple fact that there are so many people living longer and healthier lives, and in consequence playing more of a role in all aspects of our society. Older people can remain productive members of society for many more years than has been traditionally assumed.

Such standard stereotypes of the elderly as frail, senile, childish, and sexually inactive are topics discussed in this section. Jennifer McLerran, in "Saved by the Hand That Is Not Stretched Out: The Aged Poor in Hubert von Herkomer's *Eventide: A Scene in the Westminister Union*" illustrates how ostensibly harmless visual representation can function to propagate and reinforce ageist attitudes. In the article "In Search of a Discourse on Aging: The Elderly on Television," John Bell observes how current television shows have moved from the previous negative view of the elderly to more positive presentations of them. John Graham's essay, "Getting Older Is Getting Better," examines ways of getting past the traditional stereotypes and interacting with older persons on the basis of equality.

"What Doctors and Others Need to Know: Six Facts on Human Sexuality and Aging" examines the myths that deny the sexuality of older persons and makes suggestions on how to eradicate them. "Amazing Greys" indicates how well-known public figures who have remained active are improving the image of older persons.

Looking Ahead: Challenge Questions

Do most people see older persons as sexually inactive?

Do Americans generally look upon old age as a desirable or an undesirable status?

How do the attitudes of children toward older persons differ from those of adults?

How are attitudes toward old age likely to change as older persons become a larger segment of the total population?

Focusing on the work of the Victorian "old age painter," Hubert von Herkomer, this article explores how, through the production of "truth" effects, ostensibly harmless visual representations can function to propagate and reinforce ageist attitudes. Because it depicts the old seamstresses who are its subject as redeemed by the work they perform, Herkomer's painting is proved complicit with an ideology of labor which dooms its subjects to the conditions of squalor deemed necessary to the workhouse environment.
Key Words: Images of aging, Ageism, Workhouses, Victorian

Saved by the Hand That Is Not Stretched Out: The Aged Poor in Hubert von Herkomer's *Eventide: A Scene in the Westminster Union*

Jennifer McLerran, MFA

Department of Art History, University of Washington. Address correspondence to: Jennifer McLerran, Department of Art History, School of Art DM-10, University of Washington, Seattle, WA 98195.

These poor old bodies formed a most touching picture. Work they would, for industry was still in them, but it was of the most childish work — still, it was work. The agony of threading their needles was affecting indeed. (Hubert von Herkomer quoted in the Graphic, *April 7, 1877, regrading his wood engraving,* Old Age, *printed in the same issue)*

When Robert Butler coined the term "ageism" in 1969, he was primarily concerned with the deleterious effects of *negative* stereotypes upon the aged (Butler, 1989). More recently, Erdman Palmore has warned of the equal danger of *positive* stereotypes which, by imposing unrealistic positive expectations on the elderly, can result in an equally oppressive form of ageism (Palmore, 1990). Palmore observes a recent trend toward regard of the aged as better off financially, physically, and socially than may actually be the case. Viewing this as an instance of positive stereotyping, he sees this trend as evidence of a form of ageism which threatens to propagate public policies and institutional practices which ignore the specific needs of the elderly.

Examples of both positive and negative stereotypes can be found in visual culture past and present. When we survey Western cultural history, the Victorian era stands out as particularly rife with such images. An examination of the work of one highly popular European artist from that period, the painter Hubert von Herkomer (1849–1914), will serve to illustrate how visual art which ostensibly expresses sympathy for society's less fortunate elderly can actually function to justify and reinforce ageist attitudes that contribute to the neglect and oppression of the aged. Such an examination involves an exploration of the ways in which artistic representations function within cultural apparatuses of power. It is an approach that is based on the belief that representations are integral to the functioning of oppressive social practices (Owens, 1982). The ways in which the artist uses the technical and pictorial devices of the medium to produce "truth," to produce a seamless realistic image which does not reveal the artifice which produced it, are examined. The means by which the artist conveys "truth" and controls the truth of the subject depicted is revealed as complicit with culturally dominant ideologies. Representation — in the case of Hubert von Herkomer, representation which exhibits positive stereotypes which support an ageist bias — is thereby revealed as an apparatus of power.

Nineteenth-century England was beset by many social ills. The changes which industrialization and urbanization imposed on the family structure, combined with the increased life expectancy which medical science engendered, resulted in a crisis in public policy regarding the elderly (Wohl, 1983; Wood, 1991; Woods and Woodward, 1984). Within the new industrial context, the elderly were regarded as no longer productive and thus they were devalued. Nei-

The author wishes to thank the University of Washington Graduate Opportunity Program for the financial assistance which made work on this article possible, and Professor Constantine Christofides for his encouragement.

From *The Gerontologist*, Vol. 33, No. 6, December 1993, pp. 762-771. © 1993 by the Gerontological Society of America. Reprinted by permission.

ther the world of commerce nor that of the family, which in the agrarian context provided the aged a vital productive role, could, in the new urban industrial context, accommodate the elderly. The dependent elderly population saw a dramatic increase with which existing social policies and institutions were unprepared to deal. This crisis is reflected in the work of several Victorian artists who made elderly men and women their repeated subject. Most illustrative is the work of Herkomer.

Herkomer became highly popular in England for his production of works of social commentary that were believed to exhibit documentary truth as well as a high degree of humanitarian sensitivity and compassion. So highly regarded were Herkomer's abilities that he was honored with knighthood in 1907. Most fond of producing works in which the elderly were the central subject, especially those who occupied London homes for the indigent, Sir Herkomer was deemed by his contemporaries the "old age painter." Ostensibly sympathetic and well-intended, Herkomer's works, upon closer examination, demonstrate how seemingly positive depictions of the elderly can work at cross-purposes with efforts to improve the lot of the aged. By looking at Herkomer's work, we may find examples of how visual imagery which gives every appearance of humanitarian concern can simultaneously support an ideology which works to further the oppression of its subjects.

Herkomer's 1878 painting *Eventide: A Scene in the Westminster Union* (Figure 1) illustrates a Victorian belief in labor as a means to transcend the necessarily sinful condition of human existence. As Michel Foucault explains in *Madness and Civilization: A History of Insanity in the Age of Reason*, the dominant European view since the advent of the Age of Reason has been that humans are born sinful and are doomed to labor as a means to expiate that sin (Foucault, 1965). Those who do not work, whether by choice or by unfortunate circumstance, fail to expiate sin and are therefore sinful and godless. The system of public assistance devised by the Victorians, which depended upon the workhouse as the primary means of relief, reflects this ethic of labor. Those who would not or could not work, including the aged and/or infirm, were given public assistance only on the provision that they consent to confinement in the workhouse, an environment where they would be *forced* to work and thus to abandon their "unholy" way of life. I will attempt to show how Herkomer's *Eventide*, which has been interpreted as an indictment of the workhouse system, is complicit with the dominant Victorian ideology of which the workhouse is the most cogent expression.

"Poor Law Bastilles" and the Victorian Ideology of Labor

Reform of the British Poor Law in 1834 prompted a vehement attack by Friedrich Engels in his publication of 1845, *The Condition of the Working Class in England*. Calling the workhouses "Poor Law Bastilles," he claimed they were designed to scare away anyone who could possibly survive otherwise. He further noted that, in order to avert people from relying on relief, the workhouse environment was designed to be "as truly repulsive an abode as the perverted ingenuity of the Malthusians can devise" (Engels, 1845). Engels further criticized the Poor Law of 1834 as follows:

> That law was firmly based on the idea that since paupers were criminals it followed that workhouses must be prisons. It followed that the inmates of workhouses were people beyond the pale of the law — even beyond the pale of humanity. Workhouse paupers were regarded as objects of horror and disgust. No pious instructions to the contrary from the Poor Law Commissioners can avail against the spirit of the law itself. Workhouse paupers have discovered that in practice it is the *spirit* of the law — and not the *letter* of the law — that counts (Engels, 1845, p. 325).

Engels' caustic indictment of the Poor Law Commissioners' intent makes one wonder how anyone could treat the poor so harshly. One possible explanation is that such behavior and lack of regard had the force of religious ideology behind it. The authority of what was perceived as a higher law (God's law) was directing the thoughts and actions of those in power. They were doing what was righteous and good according to the Christian work ethic. Foucault's description in *Madness and Civilization* of the ethic of work and the expiation of sin illuminates this way of thinking. Foucault explains how, in Christian culture, the leper, through his isolation and abandonment, achieves salvation. He gives as an example the Biblical parable of the leper who "died before the gate of the rich man and was carried straight to paradise" (Foucault, 1965). Through suffering, the leper was granted entrance to the divine. The leper was, thereby, a constant reminder to others of both God's grace and God's anger. Foucault says of the leper:

> Hieratic witnesses of evil, they accomplish their salvation in and by their very exclusion: in a strange reversibility that is the opposite of good works and prayer, they are saved by the hand that is not stretched out. The sinner who abandons the leper at his door opens his way to heaven (Foucault, 1965, p. 7).

After the Crusades, leprosy subsided in Europe, leaving the housing of the lepers unoccupied. The lepers were gone, but the structures and systems whereby they were marginalized remained, fixed in what Foucault calls a position of "inverse exaltation" (Foucault, 1965). This vacant housing was soon filled with madmen, criminals, the indigent, and the aged poor. Foucault writes, "With an altogether new meaning and in a very different culture, the forms would remain — essentially that major form of a rigorous division which is social exclusion but spiritual reintegration" (Foucault, 1965, p. 7). These places of confinement became filled with a heterogeneous group, united by one common characteristic: the individuals occupying them were either unable to

Figure 1. Hubert von Herkomer *Eventide: A Scene in the Westminster Union*, 1878, oil on canvas, 43½" × 78¼" Walker Art Gallery, Liverpool. Courtesy of The Board of Trustees of the National Museums and Galleries on Merseyside (Walker Art Gallery, Liverpool).

Figure 2. Rowlandson, I. and Pugin, A. *St. James Workhouse Interior*, 1809, aquatint. From: *The Microcosm of London; or London in Miniature, Vol. III.* London: Methuen, 1904. Courtesy of Special Collections Division, University of Washington Libraries (negative no. UW 14845).

work due to infirmity and/or old age or were unwilling to work.

Confinement was no longer required to protect others from the contagious state of those incarcerated, as it had been in the case of lepers. It was now required to institute and reinforce an ethic of labor. Confinement was the eighteenth century's response to dire economic circumstances. It was now considered the government's responsibility to provide individuals with sustenance as a basic human right; however, such assistance came at a price. Foucault explains: "Between him [the recipient of relief] and society, an implicit system of obligation was established: he had the right to be fed, but he must accept the physical and moral constraint of confinement." (Foucault, 1965, p. 48). Under such conditions of constraint, the indigent individual could be forced to work and thereby to pay for his keep. Unfortunately, such cheap, forced labor constituted unfair competition for other manufacturers, thereby exacerbating the problem and creating more unemployment and poverty. However, at this point the problems created by such labor were overshadowed by a regard for labor as a general panacea. Labor could not be the source of economic problems since it was the one cure-all, the remedy to all economic and social problems. A basic opposition between poverty and labor was perceived as fundamental. Labor's power to abolish poverty derived, according to Foucault, not from its capacity for production but from "a certain force of moral enchantment." Labor's power as a cure-all was based on an "ethical transcendence" (Foucault, 1965). Since the Fall, man had been cursed to labor as a form of penance and a means of redemption. Foucault explains:

> It was not a law of nature which forced man to work, but the effect of a curse. The earth was innocent of that sterility in which it would slumber if man remained idle: "The land had not sinned, and if it is accursed, it is by the labor of the fallen man who cultivates it; from it no fruit is won, particularly the most necessary fruit, save by force and continual labor." (Foucault, 1965, p. 15; Foucault quoting Bousset, *Elevations sur les mysteres*, Sixth Week, Twelfth Elevation.)

According to the Christian work ethic, man's labor alone will not result in abundance. Such labor will not bear fruit without God's intervention. Though man's labor alone is not sufficient, such labor is obligatory. Idleness, according to Calvin, tries "beyond measure the power of God" (John Calvin, *Forty-ninth Sermon on Deuteronomy*, 1555, in Foucault, 1965, p. 56). If man does not "torment" the land, he cannot benefit from witness of God's miracle as the reward for his labor. Idleness is a second rebellion of man against God because "it waits for nature to be generous as in the innocence of Eden, and seeks to constrain a Goodness to which man cannot lay claim since Adam" (Foucault, 1965, p. 56). Idleness, "the absurd pride of poverty," displaces pride as man's supreme sin after the Fall (Foucault, 1965).

Consequently, forced labor in the workhouses assumed an ethical force. Meaningless, profitless work, such as that imposed in these places of confinement, was an appropriate punishment for the rebellious act of idleness. Confined and punished, forced into a marginalized existence, the workhouse poor replaced the leper. Foucault explains:

> It was in a certain experience of labor that the indissociably economic and moral demand for confinement was formulated. Between labor and idleness in the classical world ran a line of demarcation that replaced the exclusion of leprosy. . . . The old rites of excommunication were revived, but in the world of production and commerce (Foucault, 1965, p. 57).

In this view, to not work is to openly defy God. Consequently, those in Christian culture who do not work are sinful. Society, in refusing to support those who are idle, forces them to save themselves through labor or perish. As Foucault writes, such individuals are "saved by the hand that is not stretched out" (p. 7). The moral force of this ideology of labor was of such strength that it allowed no compromise. In order that their salvation be assured, all workhouse inmates were required to work, regardless of age. Herkomer, in his portrayal of the old women engaged in seamstress' work in *Eventide*, shows his compliance with this ideal. The artist's numerous visits to workhouses in search of subject matter made him well aware of the degradation which such habitations imposed on the aged poor. However, Herkomer does not seem to question the imposition of labor on the elderly. Instead, he seems to comply with this ideology, portraying his aged seamstresses as cosy and comfortable, enjoying the company of their fellow workers in a communal circle. They seem to transcend the physical degradation of workhouse life through the virtues of labor.

The Aged Poor in British Workhouses

British legislation providing for assistance to the poor originated in the Elizabethan codification of laws in 1597–1601. Elizabethan Poor Law provided for two forms of relief to the unemployed. The able-bodied (those who *could* work but could not find jobs) were to be provided with "outside relief" in the form of rent subsidies and employment by individual parishes through a tax levied for this purpose. Those who *could not* work (the very young and those infirm due to illness or advanced age) were to receive relief in almshouses. A distinction was drawn between workhouses, which were restrictive and punitive in character, and almshouses, which were intended to house the "deserving" poor. Those able-bodied individuals who *would not* work would not receive relief. Instead, they would be punished through incarceration.

Although enforcement of the Poor Laws was intended as uniform, treatment varied widely by individual parish, with central government authority often exercising little or no authority (Wood, 1991). Usually individual parishes, due to limited funds, combined the services of an almshouse for the dependent and infirm and the function of correctional facility for the able-bodied. Nineteenth-century Poor Law maintained the Elizabethan distinction between two groups eligible for indoor relief. As in the original Pool Laws, differentiation was made between the able-bodied and those incapable of work. However, advanced age was no longer interpreted as a qualification for the infirm classification (Longmate, 1974). Consequently, the elderly, regarded as able-bodied individuals, became subject to the same punitive measures as other adults, regardless of diminished capacity with age.

The aged poor always constituted the largest group of long-term workhouse inmates. Numerous justifications existed for incarceration of the elderly poor. Many regarded such individuals as of "bad character" because they had failed to adequately provide for their own old age. Others felt that aged inmates' relatives could be shamed into providing support by the prospect of the disgrace which accrued to the family of an individual so incarcerated. These arguments were used to justify the subjection of the aged poor to deplorable living conditions. The elderly in the workhouses were required to wear the same clothing (which resembled prison garb) as other inmates. They were also required to eat the same food (regardless of the fact that much of it was unsuitable for an aged digestive system) and sleep in the same crowded, dormitory-like rooms. There were often no chairs, so they were forced to sit on the ground or on their beds. Up until the 1850s the workhouses were not open to visitors, so their only contact with the outside world was through clergymen. Some workhouses even prohibited reading and/or needlework. The New Poor Law (1834) provided separation of husband and wife in the workhouse. This regulation, ostensibly intended to preclude the production of additional offspring by inmates, was, when applied to aged couples, revealed as simply a punitive measure. In 1847 the new Poor Law Board enacted a clause stipulating that all workhouses, when requested, provide accommodations allowing any married couple over age 60 a private bedroom. However, in most cases this clause was not honored (Longmate, 1974). In 1877 the provision for separate sleeping quarters was extended to couples of which one partner was either disabled or older than 60. However, as late as 1895, only 200 married couples housed in all of the workhouses of England and Wales had their own rooms. The dubious justification given was that communal sleeping arrangements were preferred by such individuals (Longmate, 1974).

It has been estimated that there were more than one million "paupers," or "undeserving poor," in London in the 1870s (Black, 1974). No official count of paupers by age was taken until 1890. In 1867, however, 37% of the inmates of 40 London workhouses (10,300 of 28,000) fell within the aged class, and by the middle of the 1890s the elderly reportedly formed half the population of many workhouses (Booth, 1894; Longmate, 1974; Wood, 1991). There was no established or generally recognized age of retire-

ment in 19th-century England — people generally kept working until too old and infirm. Aged manual laborers were forced to compete at diminished capacity in the labor market and were eventually thrown back on the resources of their families.

Charles Booth, author of two major studies on the social conditions of Victorian England, *Labour and Life of the People, London*, two volumes (1891), and *Life and Labour of the People in London*, 13 volumes (1902–1903), pointed to old age as the greatest cause of pauperism. In a third publication on the topic, *The Aged Poor in England and Wales*, Booth also explained that the rate of pauperism among the elderly did not decrease with an increase in generally favorable economic conditions:

> . . . a comparison between the rates of pauperism in old age and the general rate for all ages shows how intimately the two are connected, though that of old age shows naturally somewhat less variety. As a rule the rate in old age is four or five times as high, but when the general rate is very low the proportion tends to rise, and in some instances reaches ten to one (Booth, 1894, p. 104).

Booth reported that, as age increased, so did dependence on public assistance. His statistics showed that, in the 56–69 age group, 20% were paupers; and, of those over 75, 40% were recipients of poor relief. An increased life expectancy did not carry with it a corresponding likelihood of better health. Instead, it resulted in longer periods of infirmity and dependence. This caused major problems for the Victorian welfare system (Booth, 1894). With an increase in population, there was a corresponding increase in the number of workhouses throughout England. Two thousand were listed in a 1776 census and 3,765 in a census of 1802–1803.

The early years of Victoria's reign, 1837–1844, saw a great economic depression in England. Due to lack of employment, over one million people starved (Anstruther, 1973). Such general economic hardship placed a heavy burden on the social welfare system. The capacity of individual parishes to care for the poor who resided within their territories was severely overburdened. An 1843 report of the Poor Law Commission described conditions common to many parish workhouses:

> Many of the township poorhouses were merely converted farmhouses or cottages, in which every variety of pauper was thrown together in a squalid jumble. An investigation into the state of the Bolton workhouse in 1843 discovered "the aged and the young covered with vermin; infants, patients suffering from scarlet fever, or scaldhead, and children free from disease, all cooped up in the confined rooms of a series of cottages" (Boyson, 1960, pp. 256–266; Fraser, 1976, p. 139).

With worsening economic conditions, the Poor Law became the focus of much debate. Malthus' 1803 *Essay on the Principle of Population* (which became popularly known as his *Second Essay*) expressed the views of a highly conservative contingent which wished to abolish relief altogether (Malthus, 1803). In

1834 the Poor Law was reformed. Although not instituting reforms as severe as those suggested by Malthus and his followers, the Poor Law Commissioners instituted reforms which were widely criticized for their inhumanity. These reforms were based upon institution of the "workhouse test" and application of the principle of "less eligibility." Less eligibility was a concept essential to maintenance of a distinction between pauper and poor. It was necessary to establish that the able-bodied pauper in receipt of relief live under "less eligible," or less favorable, conditions than the poorest of independent laborers. The Poor Law Commission established the principle of less eligibility as the foundation of the reformed Poor Law. This led to formulation of what came to be known as the "workhouse test."

The workhouse test stipulated that those who applied for relief must receive it within the confines of the workhouse, an environment which could be controlled so as to assure that the recipients of relief subsisted under conditions of "less eligibility" than those under which they would have otherwise lived. This tested the true motivations of the applicant. If he or she were applying with the intent of merely escaping labor and thereby undeservedly benefiting from support of the state, the "less eligible" conditions of the workhouse would serve as a deterrent. This, along with severe economic restrictions imposed by a failing economy, produced the degrading conditions of the workhouse. Individuals were forced to work longer hours at harder labor and subsist on less nourishing, less palatable food than even the poorest of laborers. The relief itself was employed as the test of eligibility for relief. The elderly were not exempt from the workhouse test. Alfred Power, the first Assistant Poor Law Commissioner for West Riding and Lancashire, argued that in his district the workhouse test was necessary particularly for the elderly and the infirm "on account of the dissimulation and fraud constantly practised by the relatives of the paupers at the expense of the poor rates" (Fraser, 1976). Mott, Powers' successor, however, pointedly criticized this application of regulations intended for able-bodied paupers to the elderly poor (Fraser, 1976).

Reform of the Poor Law stipulated that the able-bodied poor could receive relief only in the workhouse. Outside relief was eliminated. The most important function of the workhouse was to provide supervised work. It was stipulated that this work should not be a form of work which the destitute would refuse to undertake, but it should be of a nature which would cause them to be averse to enduring it any longer than absolutely necessary. Work deemed of this nature included bone crushing, the breaking of untilled earth, and stone breaking. This work was not to be of an economically profitable nature, since it was not to compete with the work of laborers outside the workhouse.

The New Poor Law brought all workhouses under a central administration with the goal of establishing uniformity. Workhouse masters were recruited from former soldiers and police. Many were experienced as prison officers or had formerly worked in the workhouses which existed under the Old Poor Law. The comments of Reverend H. H. Milman to Edwin Chadwick, secretary to the Poor Law Commission in 1832 who later authored *Report to the Poor Law Commissioners on the Sanitary Condition of the Labouring Population of Great Britain* (1842), communicate the aversive quality which the reformers desired the workhouse to have: "The workhouse should be a place of hardship, of coarse fare, of degradation and humility; it should be administered with strictness — with severity; it should be as repulsive as is consistent with humanity" (Anstruther, 1973).

Early in the nineteenth century, poor relief was considered primarily a rural problem. However, with the advent of industrialization and the migration of people to the cities in search of jobs, the problem of poor relief became increasingly an urban concern. Edwin Chadwick exposed the deplorable sanitary conditions in urban areas in an effort to illuminate the connections between inadequate sanitary provisions and pauperism in his 1842 report to the Poor Law Commissioners (Chadwick, 1842; Flinn, 1965). Henry Mayhew reported on conditions in London in 1848 for the *Morning Chronicle*, which was covering the conditions of the working classes by sending reporters into the field. After leaving the paper in 1850, Mayhew wrote *London Labour and the London Poor* (Mayhew, 1861–1862). His work drew attention, previously focused on northern manufacturing areas, to London as a site of increasing poverty and of a growing division of wealthy and poor.

In the 1880s and 1890s, London increasingly became the focus of debate on issues of poverty and relief. In the 1890s the investigations of Charles Booth, among others, resulted in less punitive treatment of the aged poor in the workhouses. Booth's studies resulted in the conclusion that the condition of extreme poverty of such individuals was "involuntary" (Longmate, 1974). Showing that at least one-third of the population over age 70 were forced to seek government assistance, these studies led to greater sympathy and greater leniency in treatment of such individuals. By 1895 and 1896 the policy of equal treatment of all individuals, regardless of age, was abandoned. Uniforms were no longer required; additional rooms for married couples were provided; the elderly were not required to eat and sleep at specified times, and they were allowed to go on walks. Provision was made, as well, for separate day rooms for aged residents who had led more "respectable" lives in the past, so they would no longer be required to congregate with those of questionable character and background.

By 1900 other restrictions were eased. Earlier provided with no accommodations for personal possessions, the elderly were now provided with locked cupboards for their possessions. Separation of men and women was lifted, as well. Both sexes were allowed to mingle in day rooms previously segregated by sex (Longmate, 1974). When it was necessary to provide indoor relief, it was now seen as appropriate to grant certain privileges to the aged "deserving" poor, including segregation from the "undeserving." Such privileges included separate sitting rooms where meals could be served, separate sleeping cubicles, and less rigidly regulated times for sleeping and rising. The freedom to come and go and to receive visitors to the workhouse was to be widened, and the houses were now to be required to provide tea, sugar, and tobacco (Local Government Board, 1900–1901, App. A, No. 11). Although this showed a significant change in sentiment, the governing board's proviso was merely advisory. Also, it was up to local authorities to decide who were "deserving" and what freedoms and provisions served as "adequate."

Victorian Representations of the Elderly Poor: Truth Enhanced by Sentiment and Pathos

Studies by Booth and Mayhew contributed to the growing concern of the public regarding the plight of the poor. Novels such as Charles Dickens' *Oliver Twist* (1838) and Frances Trollope's *Jessie Phillips* (1844) provided the public with literary representations of the harsh realities of existence in the workhouse and in the London slums. Later documentary accounts such as James Greenwood's *A Night in a Workhouse* (which appeared in the *Pall Mall Gazette* in 1864) contributed to a growing public concern.

Newspapers such as *The Times* of London and the London publication for which Herkomer worked, the *Graphic*, provided reports and published documentary-style woodcuts in efforts to draw attention to such problems. *The Times* consistently ran editorials in the 1830s critical of the Poor Law Commission. John Walter, editor of *The Times*, included in every single issue from July, 1839, to July, 1842, reports, articles, and letters critical of the Commission (Anstruther, 1973).

Prominent newspapers of early nineteenth-century England, most notably the *Illustrated London News*, were limited in the accuracy of depiction of current events by a practice similar to the use of file footage in television news today. A file of standard engravings was kept which included depictions of various cities and towns. These were quickly revised to suit the specifics of events. For instance, the first issue of the *Illustrated London News*, published May 14, 1842, carried the story of a fire in Hamburg. An engraving of the city of Hamburg was already in the possession of the newspaper. An engraver added flames and groups of spectators to this already existing print to serve as an illustration for the story. It was also common practice to recaption illustrations from previous reports to accompany reports of current events (Edwards, 1984; Fox and Wolff, 1973).

In contrast, the *Graphic*, founded in 1870, published illustrations that were the result of direct observation. Editor William Thomas sent his artists into the field to observe London events and conditions directly. His artists did not work with standardized engravings altered to reflect specific events. Rather, they produced original works with a high degree of naturalistic detail intended to enhance the realism, and thus convey the "truth," of the scene depicted. Illustrators for the *Graphic* made social ills and problems of the poor the frequent subject of their work. They also depicted one of Victorian society's remedies for such conditions: care of the poor in religious institutions. Such a focus emphasized the Christian ethos of "good works" (or charity) as a means of alleviation of the suffering of the poor. So as to compel human interest and elicit sympathy from the readers, highly individualized portraits were emphasized in the *Graphic*. This type of depiction differed from the documentary photography which displaced it in the 1890s. Though the *Graphic* illustrations appeared in a journalistic context, they were regarded by their creators as not only conveying truth but as possessing qualities akin to poetry and literary narrative. They were intended to tell a story and evoke an emotional response, not simply document an event. As Julian Treuherz notes, and as the *Graphic* illustrations demonstrate: "For the Victorian artist, truth was to be enhanced by sentiment and pathos" (Treuherz, 1987).

Sir Hubert von Herkomer: The "Old Age Painter"

Herkomer's *Eventide* was based on the artist's wood engraving, *Old Age, A Study in Westminster Union*, published in the *Graphic* on April 7, 1877. As a result of one of his many sojourns through London in search of subject matter, Herkomer's engraving derived from first-hand observation (Herkomer, 1877). *Old Age* was regarded by both Herkomer and the critics as a feminine companion or counterpart to his widely popular painting of 1875, *The Last Muster: Sunday in the Royal Hospital, Chelsea* (Edwards, 1984). *The Last Muster* was based on another *Graphic* wood engraving, *Sunday at Chelsea Hospital*, published on February 18, 1871 (Mills, 1923).

Herkomer chose St. James's workhouse, which was administered by Westminster Union and located between Poland Street and Marshall Street in Soho, as the source for *Old Age*. He chose this particular workhouse, most likely, because it was located in central London and was easily accessible. In providing specifics of his subject's location in the title of the work, Herkomer showed his intention to produce an artwork of a documentary nature. However, as the description of the female workhouse residents which was published in an article accompanying *Old Age* shows, even such documentary descriptions tended to take on a remonstrative and didactic tone in the Victorian context: "Female paupers are often dragged down to pauperism by a bad husband.... Still, it must be admitted that a good many of the women who have to seek relief in their declining days have themselves to blame for it" (Herkomer, 1877).

Two earlier wood engravings by Herkomer with aged female workhouse residents as their subject appeared in the *Graphic*: *Low Lodging House at St. Giles* (August 3, 1873) and *Christmas in a Workhouse* (December 25, 1876). *Christmas in a Workhouse* reflects the Victorian ideal of "good works" through extension of charity to the poor (Himmelfarb, 1983, 1991). It also exhibits a theme common to Victorian art: the presentation of contrasting images of youth and old age. This theme, a highly popular one in Victorian painting, is seen in Herkomer's depiction of two youthful volunteers aiding and offering a gift to an aged workhouse resident. A plaque on the wall of the workhouse depicted reads: "God Bless our Master and Matron." This reflects the paternalistic attitude of the government toward workhouse residents expressed in the *Annual Report of the Poor Law Commissioners* (Great Britain, 1846). "The workhouse is a large household. . . . It resembles a private family on an enlarged scale" (Longmate, 1974, p. 98).

Herkomer seemed to make a practice of altering the paintings he derived from earlier woodcuts to present a more pleasant view. His wood engravings were intended as primarily documentary in nature; however, he regarded his paintings as "art" and felt compelled to compromise accuracy in favor of aesthetics. His painted version of *The Last Muster (Sunday at Chelsea Hospital)*, although it retained an emphasis on realistic detail so as to convey truth, was subtly altered so as not to offend the more reserved sensibilities of his Victorian audience (Edwards, 1984). Herkomer altered *Eventide* also, adding elements which softened the depressing quality of its precursor's more realistic depiction. The old women in *Eventide* possess more cheerful expressions than those in *Old Age*. One holds a Bible on her lap. A vase of flowers and a pot of tea with teacup are added to the foreground, although these amenities were rarely found in the workhouse. An optimistic note is added also in the helpful personage of a pretty, young volunteer.

An illustration in F. H. W. Sheppard's *Survey of London* (volume XXXII) depicts the day room of St. James workhouse as it appeared in 1809 (Figure 2). Showing a sprawling, factory-like interior with little furniture, bare walls and barred windows, it presents an image quite different from that portrayed by Herkomer (Sheppard, 1809, 1963, vol. XXXII, Part II, Plate 38B). Herkomer was interested not merely in documentary work. He wished to infuse his work with individual artistic interpretation, with a quality which he regarded as akin to poetry. He wrote: "The truth of a scene represented by mere mechanical skill without the spirit of interpretation would be *nil*; . . . the highest refinement of expression is but an interpreted representation of fact, the product of a mind capable of ascertaining truth" (Herkomer, 1882, p. 133).

Herkomer greatly admired and wished to emulate the British painter Frederick Walker (1840–1875). Herkomer's first oil painting exhibited in the Academy, *After the Toil of the Day* (1873), was so similar to Walker's work that it was mistaken as Walker's by viewers (Mills, 1923). Walker became a legend in English art after his early death. He chose typical realist subject matter, but portrayed his subjects in a highly romanticized fashion. Walker exhibited *The Harbour of Refuge* at the Royal Academy in 1872, the year before Herkomer exhibited his *Sunday at Chel-*

sea Hospital. Walker's painting, set in an almshouse garden bathed in a rosy glow where a symbolic reaper employs his scythe, presents a highly romanticized view of old age and institutionalization. Walker was called by his contemporaries the "Tennyson of painting." They admired, according to Mills, "the refined and poetic sentiment which was his chief characteristic" (Mills, 1923). The critic Sir Edward Cook said of Walker: "Walker's originality in art consists in the way he interpreted (as Millet has done in France) the grave beauty of rustic labour, showing its stern reality and yet endowing it . . . with something of the grace of antique sculpture" (Mills, 1923, p. 47). In the Royal Academy exhibit of 1873 Herkomer praised Walker for depicting "the truth that was in keeping with his love of the tender and graceful" (Edwards, 1984). The following statement by Herkomer regarding Walker (published in 1893 in *Magazine of Art*) shows Herkomer's blindness to Walker's romanticization of the conditions of the poor:

> In Walker, we have the creator of the English Renaissance, for it was he who saw the possibility of combining the grace of the antique with the realism of our everyday life in England. . . . True poet that he was, he felt all nature should be represented by a poem. The dirty nails of a peasant, such as I have seen painted by a modern realist, were invisible to him. . . . He started with some definite poetic notion, and nature came to his aid as the handmaid of the poet . . . (Mills, 1923, p. 47).

Two artworks appear on the walls of the workhouse depicted in *Eventide*: a portion of Herkomer's *The Last Muster* depicting the dead pensioner which was published in the *Graphic* (May 15, 1875), and a reproduction of Luke Fildes' painting of a young milkmaid, *Betty*, which was published in the *Illustrated London News* Christmas Supplement of 1875. Although paintings on the walls of the workhouse are an attractive fiction, such a situation is highly unrealistic. Herkomer was not averse to such poetic fictions. The image of Betty juxtaposed with the figures of the old women affords him the opportunity to present a poetic juxtaposition of youth and old age and thus provide Victorian audiences with a theme dear to them.

Eventide was exhibited in 1878 at the Royal Academy in London and in 1879 at the Salon in Paris. Writer Joris Huysmans praised it for its naturalism when he saw it in the Paris exhibition (Huysmans, 1883). Reviewers of the work's exhibition in London were less positive. The art writer for the *Illustrated London News* criticized its broad brushwork as "well-nigh to the verge of coarseness" (*Illustrated London News*, May 11, 1878, p. 435). They generally ignored the context of impoverishment, describing the inhabitants as "cosy and comfortable" (*The Art Journal*, 1878, p. 179). Blackburn's "Academy Notes" described Herkomer's painting as representing "happy and comfortable old age" and "the sunny side of life in a workhouse" (Blackburn, 1878, p. 67). Herkomer's *Eventide* contains another popular Victorian subject, the seamstress, or "sempstress."

3. SOCIETAL ATTITUDES TOWARD OLD AGE

Thomas Hood's highly popular poem *Song of the Shirt* (which appeared in the Christmas 1843 issue of *Punch*), described the impoverished conditions and hard labor of the seamstress, and Richard Redgrave's painting of 1843, *The Sempstress*, which shows a bleary-eyed seamstress working into the early morning hours in a lonely garret, provided heavily romanticized depictions of the seamstresses' squalor (Treuherz, 1987). Herkomer produced a number of other works with aged seamstresses as their subject. *Weary*, a watercolor of 1873, shows an aged woman asleep at her spinning wheel, and *The Spinners*, a wood engraving published in the *Graphic* (date unknown), shows three aged spinners in what may be a workhouse environment.

Because of their longer life expectancy and displacement by mechanization of the garment industry (which was traditionally the largest employer of female workers as handloom weavers, hand combers, knitters, lace makers, etc.), women usually formed the majority of workhouse occupants. Whether "spinster" or widow, they were required to subsist on a wage insufficient to cover even the most meager living expenses and were eventually forced to enter the workhouse (Longmate, 1974). The 1909 *Minority Report of the Royal Commission on the Poor Laws and Relief of Distress* provides a description of typical women's day rooms and sleeping quarters in workhouses of the time: "The servant out of place, the prostitute recovering from disease, the feeble-minded women of any age, the girl with her first baby, the unmarried mother coming in to be confined with her third or fourth bastard, the senile, the paralytic, the respectable deserted wife, the widow to whom Outdoor Relief has been refused, are all herded indiscriminately together" (Great Britain, 1909, pp. 739–744).

Herkomer stated in his memoirs, "My whole work can testify that it has been towards the pathetic side of life, towards a sympathy for the old, and for suffering mankind" (Herkomer, 1910). The effects of the harsh realities of workhouse existence on the aged poor must have been apparent to Herkomer through his visits to such places in search of subject matter. However, Herkomer, as a "good" Christian and a "respectable" member of Victorian society, was compliant with the ideology of transcendence through labor. This is evident in his artworks.

Conclusion

In Victorian England, a form of ageism which worked through positive stereotypes such as those seen in Herkomer's work furthered and produced ageist attitudes and supported institutionalized ageism. Culturally dominant ageist beliefs directed the formation and enactment of Victorian public policy regarding the aged poor. This policy, formulated in a period of dire economic straits, was predicated on a belief that the elderly were as able-bodied and capable of their own financial support as anyone else; consequently, when such individuals could not support themselves they were regarded as immoral and deserving of assistance only if they consented to incarceration and enforced labor. Herkomer participated in and served to propagate the ageist assumptions which directed this policy.

The popularity of Herkomer's work is evidence of the Victorians' failure to recognize that most individuals of advanced age experience a diminishment of physical capacity and are thus less capable than others of productive physical labor. Herkomer's intentions may have been honorable and sincere. However, in using positive stereotypes to depict the aged poor, he supported a Victorian ideology of labor which, when applied to the aged, constituted a form of ageism and furthered policies that resulted in institutionalized ageism. Thus, he complied with that which was the cause for the harsh treatment of those for whom he professed such heartfelt sympathy. Herkomer's old seamstresses are redeemed by the work they perform; however, they are, at the same time, doomed to conditions of squalor by an ideology of labor which allows no compromise. They are, in Victorian eyes, saved by the hand that is not stretched out.

References

Anstruther, I. (1973). *The scandal of the Andover workhouse.* London: Geoffrey Bles.

Black, E., ed. (1974). *Victorian culture and society.* New York: Walker.

Blackburn, H. (1878). *Academy Notes.* London: Royal Academy of Arts.

Booth, C. (1891). *Labour and life of the people, London,* 2 volumes. London: Williams and Northgate.

Booth, C. (1894). *The aged poor in England and Wales.* London: Macmillan and Company.

Booth, C. (1902–1903). *Life and labour of the people in London,* 13 vols. New York: Macmillan & Co.

Boyson, R. (1960). *The history of Poor Law administration in North-East Lancashire, 1834–1871.* Manchester University, M.A. thesis.

Butler, R. N. (1987). Ageism. *Encyclopedia of aging.* New York: Springer.

Carr, J. C. (1882–1884). Hubert Herkomer, A.R.A. In F. G. Dumas (Ed.), *Modern artists.* London: Chapman and Hall.

Chadwick, E. (1842; 1965). *Report to the Poor Law Commissioners on the sanitary condition of the labouring population of Great Britain,* reprinted with an introduction by M. W. Flinn. Edinburgh: Edinburgh University Press.

Edwards, L. M. (1984). *Hubert von Herkomer and the modern life subject.* Doctoral dissertation, Columbia University.

Engels, F. (1845; 1968). *The condition of the working class in England.* Stanford: Stanford University Press (reprint).

Flinn, M. W. (Ed.). (1965). *Report on the sanitary condition of the labouring population of Great Britain,* by Edwin Chadwick, 1842. Edinburgh: Edinburgh University Press.

Foucault, M. (1965). *Madness and civilization: A history of insanity in the Age of Reason.* New York: Random House.

Fox, C., & Wolff, M. (1973). Pictures from the magazines. In H. J. Dyos & M. Wolff (Eds.), *The Victorian city: Images and realities,* II. London: Routledge & Kegan Paul.

Fraser, D. (Ed.). (1976). *The new Poor Law in the 19th Century.* New York: St. Martin's.

Great Britain. Poor Law Commissioners. (1909). *Minority Report of the Royal Commission on the Poor Laws and Relief of Distress.* London.

Great Britain. Poor Law Commissioners. (1842; 1965). *Report on the sanitary conditions of the labouring population of Great Britain.* Edinburgh: Edinburgh University Press (reprint).

Great Britain. Poor Law Commissioners. (1846). *Annual Report of the Poor Law Commissioners.* London.

Herkomer, H. (1877). Letter to the editor of the *Graphic,* London, April 7, 1877, p. 326.

Herkomer, H. (1882). Drawing and engraving on wood. *Descriptive catalog of the portraits, etchings and engravings exhibited at M. Knoedler's Gallery.* New York: Knoedler's Gallery.

Herkomer, H. (1910). *The Herkomers,* 2 vols. London.

Himmelfarb, G. (1983). *The idea of poverty: England in the early Industrial Age.* New York: Random House.

Himmelfarb, G. (1991). *Poverty and compassion: The moral imagination of the Late Victorians.* New York: Alfred A. Knopf.

Huysmans, J.-K. (1883; 1908). *L'Art Moderne,* Paris: Plon-Nourrit.

Longmate, N. (1974). *The workhouse.* London: Temple Smith.

Malthus, T. R. (1803; 1817). *An essay on the principle of population, or a view of its past and present effects on human happiness, with an inquiry into our prospects respecting the future removal or mitigation of the evils which it occasions.* London: J. Murray.

Mayhew, H. (1861–1862). *London labour and the London poor; A cyclopedia of the condition and earnings of those that will work, those that cannot work, and those that will not work:* London: Griffin, Bohn & Co.

Mills, J. S. (1923). *Life and letters of Sir Hubert Herkomer . . . A study in struggle and success.* London: Hutchinson & Co.

Owens, C. (1982). Representation, appropriation, and power. *Art in America,* May, 9–21.

Palmore, E. B. (1990). *Ageism: negative and positive.* New York: Springer.

Sheppard, F. H. W., general editor. (1809; 1963). *Survey of London,* vol. XXXI, part II and vol. XXXII, part II, reprint. London.

Treuherz, J. (1987). *Hard times: Social realism in Victorian art.* London: Lund Humphries and Mt. Kisco, New York: Moyer Bell, in association with Manchester City Art Galleries.

Wohl, A. S. (1983). *Endangered lives: Public health in Victorian Britain.* Cambridge, MA: Harvard University Press.

Wood, P. (1991). *Poverty and the workhouse in Victorian Britain.* Wolfeboro Falls, NH: Alan Sutton.

Woods, R. W., & Woodward, J. (1984). *Urban disease and mortality in nineteenth century England.* London: Batsford Academic and Educational Ltd.; and New York: St. Martin's Press.

This article analyzes the images of aging presented in five of the prime-time television programs of 1989 most watched by the elderly: *Murder, She Wrote, The Golden Girls, Matlock, Jake and the Fatman,* and *In the Heat of the Night,* all of which have central elderly characters. An examination of the title sequences reveals that earlier television stereotypes of the elderly "as more comical, stubborn, eccentric, and foolish than other characters" have been replaced by more positive stereotypes of them as powerful, affluent, healthy, active, admired, and sexy.

Key Words: Character presentation, Mass media, Stereotypes, Gender, Title sequences

In Search of a Discourse on Aging: The Elderly on Television

John Bell, PhD

English Department, New York City TechnicalCollege, The City University of New York, 300 Jay St., Broklyn, NY 11201.

To a great extent I side with Neil Postman (1985) when he argues that television's technological bias is to entertain rather than to inform:

Entertainment is the supra-ideology of all discourse on television. No matter what is depicted or from what point of view, the overarching presumption is that it is there for our amusement and pleasure. (p. 87)

Television is primarily a visual medium. People watch it: "Sustained, complex talk does not play well on television" (Postman, 1985, p. 92). It is a medium that discourages reasoned discourse; it encourages argument "with good looks, celebrities and commercials," not "with propositions" (Postman, 1985, p. 93).

[Television] does everything possible to encourage us to watch continuously. But what we watch is a medium which presents information in a form that renders it simplistic, nonsubstantive, nonhistorical and noncontextual; that is to say information packaged as entertainment. (Postman, 1985, p. 141)

The elderly watch more television than any other audience segment, on the average over 40 hours a week. To many of them, television is a comfort, a companion, a window on the world. No one can deny these virtues, nor the pleasurable entertainment television brings to the elderly as well as to most other members of our culture. But just as surely, I believe, no one can deny that television, on the whole, and especially prime-time television programs, insulate us from the great concerns of our culture, and especially those concerns that are pressing to the elderly. Television, for example, makes us aware of the wonders of medicine. Medical technology, indeed, makes beautiful images and suggests marvelous cures that are often manifested on prime-time shows. But do such shows really center us on a

rational discourse about caring for the sick and the infirm (see Minkler, 1989), especially those who are elderly? Are all the elderly entitled to the care often witnessed on prime-time television — high-tech care without paper work or loneliness? Who is to pay for such care?

Television does touch on the major problems of our day, usually in prime-time dramas in which viewers can see their effects on particular characters. But television programs do not (and some would say cannot or are not meant to) encourage or facilitate extended, rational discourse on these problems, which might lead to positive social change. Many television critics, especially the so-called cultural studies critics, have argued that television simply supports the status quo, that television presents the ideology of those in power who have most to gain from keeping things the way they are, and that audiences buy in to the status quo, often to their own detriment, because they accept television and other media presentations as statements of a permanent real rather than as socially negotiable constructions (Fiske, 1987).

But although television's prime-time dramas and situation comedies for the most part do not encourage rational discourse on such important issues as health care for the elderly, they do participate in our society's overall discourse on aging by providing compelling, often unexaminedly accepted images of aging and the elderly, thereby fueling stereotypes about elderly persons and their lives.

Television and Aging

At the end of his article on mass communication and aging in the second volume of the comprehensive 1969 study *Aging and Society,* Schramm concluded:

It seems to us that enlightened self-interest as well as public responsibility recommend that the mass media devote some special attention, some of their very special imagination and talent, to the older audience. For . . . mass

An earlier version of this paper was presented at the 5th Annual Visual Communication Conference, Breckenridge, CO, June 27, 1991.

communication stands in a position of unique importance between millions of people who are trying to work out a new way of life for which there is no real precedent in history. . . . (p. 375)

Schramm was mindful that the mass media, driven by advertising's focus on younger people, had directed little attention to older people, but he believed that older people are far more active and important than the media stereotype handed down about them indicated and that appropriate assessments of the older audience could help us know "the kind of mass communication older people really want and need, [could] give them the kind of programming and publishing they need to remain engaged rather than isolated" (p. 374).

In the years since Schramm wrote these words, television has surely become the paramount means of mass communication in our society. Considering the vast impact of television on the formation of attitudes among our society's people, it is important to study the images of the elderly that are presented on television now and to ask whether these images are appropriate, accurate portrayals of the elderly in our society. For if these presentations are inappropriate, surely the presentations are contributing on some level to a perhaps undesirable discourse on aging in America.

Literature Review

The literature dealing with presentations of the elderly on television has been reviewed in a number of places, but most notably by Davis and Davis (1986) and by Powell and Williamson (1985). Virtually all of the studies cited represent scholarly work done in the 1970s, although a few studies in the early 1980s are also included. In general, as Davis and Davis put it, "the numbers of older people appearing on television do not correlate with the numbers of older people in society" (Davis & Davis, 1986, p. 45).

Of the few presentations of the elderly that do appear, many of them are sexist. Men are far more likely to appear, and they are also likely to be more powerful, active, and productive. Women, when they appear, are likely to be passive and, for the most part, "act as useful accoutrements to males" (Davis & Davis, 1986, p. 47). The elderly are likely to be well-off and in good health, except on public service specials where they are usually seen as deprived and suffering (Davis & Davis, 1986, pp. 46–49; see also Gerbner et al., 1980). Finally, especially on prime-time programs, "the elderly tend to be shown as more comical, stubborn, eccentric, and foolish than other characters. They are more likely to be treated with disrespect" (Davis & Davis, 1986, p. 46).

Television's image of the elderly, at least until the early 1980s, can hardly be said to have been very flattering. In truth, what Schramm generalized about mass communication and older people 10 years earlier still held true for television in the 1970s — the elderly just didn't seem to count for much.

In the mid-1980s, Americans began to get wind of our changing age climate. An article titled "A New Golden Age" (Waters & Huck, 1985), for example, asserts that in the past television was a medium for the young, and the old were "likely to be cast as either boorish foils or helpless fools. . . . These nights, however, prime-time entertainment has entered a true golden age. Suddenly the elderly are finding themselves portrayed as intelligent, attractive, vital — even, astonishingly enough, sexy and hip" (p. 107). Among the shows cited as proof are *The Golden Girls, The Equalizer, Murder, She Wrote, Crazy Like a Fox,* and *Mr. Belvedere.* Waters and Huck go on to say that presumably the networks are catching up to the one-fifth of the population that will be 55+ by the end of the century and TV advertisers are more aware of this new market, especially the baby boomers who are getting older. They see Angela Lansbury's Jessica Fletcher (on *Murder, She Wrote*) as a "potent role model for females of any socioeconomic strata" (Waters & Huck, 1985, p. 107). And they conclude with a prediction of more shows featuring older characters in the future.

Their prediction obviously has come true, but many of the earlier shows have folded as well. Still, more positive portrayals seem to be the norm, as Dail concludes in her study of portrayals of older Americans in the context of family life, although she is troubled by gender stereotypes that stress male dominance (Dail, 1988). She also notes: "The importance of the elderly population as a market group cannot be ignored and may account for the apparent emergence of a more positive image of them" (p. 705). Indeed, the presence of an increasingly larger elderly market does seem to influence some programming decisions, and TV does watch the aging baby boomers closely, but programmers still follow the 18 to 49 market in looking for good shows (Buck, 1989). And marketing executives who see the 50+ market as the next hot market are apparently ahead of creative departments (Diddlebock, 1989), a point that Swayne and Greco earlier implied in their study of television commercials (1987), which pointed out that elderly Americans were still underrepresented and not presented often enough as positive role models in situations of consumption.

The picture of the elderly on television, then, appears to be far more positive than it was 10 years ago, probably because of advertising's attempts to target older audiences. But the elderly are still an incomplete presence, and significant problems of role presentation, especially in terms of gender, persist.

Method

In order to determine how much the images of the elderly on television had changed, and in which directions they had changed, I examined presentations of elderly characters on five prime-time network shows — four dramas and one sitcom — that have been popular with elderly audiences over the past few years: *Murder, She Wrote* (1984–), *The Golden Girls* (1985–), *Matlock* (1986–), *Jake and the*

3. SOCIETAL ATTITUDES TOWARD OLD AGE

Table 1. Top 10 Prime-time Television Programs According to Adults Aged 55 +, 1989–1990 and 1990–1991, by Gender

| Rank | 1989–1990 | | 1990–1991 | |
	Women	Men	Women	Men
1.	Murder, She Wrote	60 Minutes[a]	Murder, She Wrote	60 Minutes[a]
2.	60 Minutes	Murder, She Wrote	60 Minutes[a]	Murder, She Wrote
3.	Golden Girls[a]	Matlock	Matlock	Matlock
4.	Matlock	In the Heat of the Night	In the Heat of the Night	Roseanne[a,b,c]
5.	In the Heat of the Night	Monday Night Football	Golden Girls	In the Heat of the Night
6.	Jake and the Fatman	Unsolved Mysteries	Empty Nest	Jake and the Fatman
7.	Unsolved Mysteries	Jake and the Fatman	Jake and the Fatman	Unsolved Mysteries (tied with 6)
8.	Dallas	Golden Girls[a]	Unsolved Mysteries	All in the Family
9.	CBS Sunday Movie	50 Years of Television	All in the Family	Golden Girls
10.	Barbara Walters Special	Empty Nest	Dallas	Law and Order

Note: These data were taken from Nielsen Media Research, 1989b, 1991a, 1991b.

[a]Also in the top five for all viewers of all ages during that year. The other top shows in 1989–1990 were *Bill Cosby, A Different World, Cheers,* and *Roseanne.* The other top shows in 1990–1991 were *Cheers, NFL Monday Night Football,* and *Designing Women* and *A Different World* (tied for 5th).

[b]Among the top five shows for teenagers, ages 12–17, during that year. In 1990–1991, teenagers also selected *Ferris Bueller, Fresh Prince of Bel Air, America's Funniest People,* and *Blossom.*

[c]Among the top five shows for women ages 18–49. In 1990–1991, these women also chose *Cheers, Coach, A Different World,* and *Designing Women.* The top five shows for men ages 18–49 for 1990–1991 were *NFL Monday Night Football, Cheers, America's Funniest People, America's Funniest Home Videos,* and *Married . . . With Children.*

Fatman (1987–), and *In the Heat of the Night* (1988–). As shown in Table 1, these were the five most popular television programs for the 55 + audience in 1989 (Nielsen Media Research, 1989a), and each features older characters portrayed by well-known elderly actors — Angela Lansbury (66 in October 1991), Bea Arthur (68 in May 1991), Betty White (68 in January 1992), Estelle Getty (67 in July 1991), Rue McClanahan (58 in February 1992), Andy Griffith (66 in June 1991), William Conrad (71 in September 1991), and Carroll O'Connor (69 in August 1991).

The Nielsen organization does not collect specific TV viewing data for audiences of 65 +. Their general categories are children 2–11, teens 12–17, and adults 18–34, 35–54, and 55 + (Nielsen Media Research, 1989a). It is worth noting that adults 55 + watch more television than any other audience segment, approximately 41 hours for women and 38 hours for men per week, roughly twice the time teenagers 12–17 watch (Nielsen Media Research, 1989a). Table 1 shows that women and men don't watch exactly the same programs, nor do they rank the top 10 programs in the same order, but of the 10 shows listed, seven appear on both lists for 1989–1990 and eight appear for 1990–1991. Six of the 10 shows listed appear on all lists: the five shows to be discussed here plus *60 Minutes.*

As measures of character presentation, I used the title sequences from the 1989–1990 season of each show. Each title sequence is essentially a 1-minute introduction to the characters, setting, and general ethos of each program. In a sense, title sequences, which remain the same show after show, often year after year, type the shows and their characters.

Properties of Title Sequences

Title sequences generally have two significant practical (as opposed to aesthetic) functions: to display the name of the show and to identify the actors who play the principal characters, what can be called naming and credit functions. In addition, the name

of the show's creator may also be displayed in the last shot, as in the case of *Matlock,* for example. This function does not operate in *The Golden Girls* or *Murder, She Wrote,* however.

In the five shows studied, the title sequences range from roughly 40 seconds for *The Golden Girls,* the only half-hour sitcom studied, to 45 seconds for *Murder, She Wrote,* an hour-long drama, to 60 seconds for the other three hour-long dramas. Average shot lengths were less than 2 seconds; *Matlock,* for example, averaged roughly 2 seconds a shot and *The Golden Girls,* 1.75. The longest shot recorded was 5.33 seconds (in *Murder, She Wrote*) and the shortest was .16 seconds (in *Jake and the Fatman*). Shots were timed with a stopwatch during playbacks of recordings of recent episodes of the shows.

Generally speaking, the significance of characters in a show can be measured by the number of times they appear, their total time of appearances in the title sequence, and especially by their personal credit shot, which displays the name of the actor as a graphic under the image of the character, usually in a bust shot. Andy Griffith's credit shot in *Matlock,* with a graphic underneath "STARRING/ andy griffith," to illustrate, lasts 5.08 seconds, while the credit shot of Julie Sommars (who plays a colleague of Matlock), with her name underneath, lasts only 3 seconds.

Title sequences only present visual images, usually of the characters and their show's setting; one does not hear the characters speak, although they may appear to be speaking. Instead, one hears the show's theme song or theme music on the audio track. For each of the five shows studied, the show's theme music or song characterizes an essential quality of the show. In the case of *Murder, She Wrote, The Golden Girls,* and *Matlock,* it is a sense of jauntiness, perhaps friendliness, that dominates, although there is also a touch of foreboding in the music of the shows that deal with crime. In the theme music of *In the Heat of the Night,* one hears steamy, troubled

Southern blues, and in the theme music of *Jake and the Fatman*, a driving, active rhythm dominates, though a touch of striptease can be heard. Insofar as essential qualities are captured, it is fair to say that a show's theme song or music and the images shown in the title sequence work together to create for viewers an impression of the show and its characters that is true to the portrayals in the show's episodes.

Today's Portrayals of the Elderly

Turning now to the images in the title sequences of the five shows selected as indexes of presentations of the elderly on today's television, what do we find? Eight significant, interrelated generalizations can be drawn from repeated viewing of the sequences.

First, the elderly characters are at the center of the shows. In two of the title sequences — *Murder, She Wrote* and *The Golden Girls* — they are the only characters we see; in the other title sequences they are most prominently featured, from the dominant manner of *Matlock*, where Matlock's face is frozen on the right or left in a large number of shots, to the shared billing with Jake in *Jake and the Fatman*, to the lead character billing in the more ensemble *In the Heat of the Night* sequence. The central nature of elderly characters means that the audience can identify these shows with the elderly and look forward to the active participation of characters they may empathize with or see as role models. Since all the actors who perform the elderly characters' roles have histories as performers, it is also likely that many viewers have followed them over time and feel a kinship with them, a sense that both actor and audience member carry on.

Along with being at the center goes the concept of being powerful. These elderly characters are presented as powerful members of their communities, and the most powerful character is Jessica Fletcher of *Murder, She Wrote*. The title sequence leads us not only to believe that she constructs the story that is bound in the red folder during the last shot, but also that she constructs her own life as well in the memory iris shots with faded and blurred white edges, which contrast with the sharp and full writing shots. Moreover, we are led to believe that she may be constructing our lives, too, as we can infer from the shot of the typewriter keys that seem to strike the TV screen, the paper of our eyes or mind, and thereby "type" us.

But all of the other elderly characters are powerful, too. *Matlock* opens with a shot of a white courthouse, which is then digitized to sweep us into a courtroom where a silvery-haired Matlock commands the attention of the confederate flag and a crowd. The last shots of the show display Matlock walking down the courthouse steps in front of an image of Justice, and we are led to believe that he is the very embodiment of that ideal. The women in *The Golden Girls* seem to live totally in a world of their own making in their communal home, the creators of an idyllic Miami. The Fatman (whose name is Jason McCabe) walks around Honolulu as if he com-

mands the island, and in the last shots, Jake, who has been busy with adventurous, active work, meets his fatherly boss at a statue that seems to confirm the Fatman's historical presence in Hawaii. Clearly the Fatman rules the world of *Jake and the Fatman*. Even in *In the Heat of the Night*, where each ensemble character is presented in a 4.20-second blue naming shot over a night scene, Carroll O'Connor's Chief Bill Gillespie comes first, and he wears the signs of a leader — a cowboy hat with a badge in its center, a pair of dark sunglasses, and a neat uniform and tie. We expect the characters who follow will report to him.

Third, the elderly characters are affluent, as can be inferred from the settings in which we meet the characters, their dress, their activities, and their roles. The Golden Girls, for example, live in a spacious, well-decorated house and seem to own endless outfits of fine clothing. Matlock, who in contrast to the well-clothed Golden Girls seems to have only one white-knightly suit, is clearly a lawyer with a staff and a comfortable office, and we see him in one shot drinking wine at a party. He may shine his own shoes, part of his good-country-boy persona, as he does in another shot, but there is also a shot of mysterious hands counting hundred dollar bills — a bribe, perhaps, or a fee. In either case the message is, there is lots of money about, and surely the good lawyer Matlock is more than comfortable.

Similarly, the various images of Jessica Fletcher and Fatman McCabe bear witness to affluent living, although Fletcher's is the quiet affluence of a fairly well-off New Englander who fishes and plants flowers in a quiet New England village, whereas the Fatman's affluence partakes more in the glitzy, active day- and nightlife of Honolulu. In essence, as we look at the title sequences, we say to ourselves that if the characters can live in the places shown and do what they are shown doing, then they must be well-off. Only Chief Bill Gillespie seems to live in modest circumstances. His modest town looks like the kind of place the train just passes through, and we infer that as a police chief, he probably lives better than many in the town, but he is not wealthy in the way Jessica Fletcher, Ben Matlock, and Jason McCabe are.

Fourth, the elderly characters are always healthy and physically and socially active. There are no signs of poor health, only active, robust people. In *The Golden Girls*, we see all the women together frequently, jumping up, touching, singing. Ben Matlock is in court standing up, waving his arms, or walking outside with reporters hounding him, or shaking hands with an associate and smiling. The well-rounded Jessica Fletcher rides a bicycle, jogs, fishes, waves at people, investigates, and writes. Jason McCabe is out in the city walking and looking around. Bill Gillespie is not shown in any active images, but police cars roam the streets of his town in shot after shot, and we imagine him participating in and coordinating all this activity.

Where physical activity is present, mental activity usually follows, and this is certainly the case for the characters under study. Fifth, then, the elderly are portrayed as mentally active and quick-witted. Jessica Fletcher's act of composition is a fine example of this, especially because her chosen genre, the mystery, has always been a genre for the mentally active and smart. Besides being a writer, she is also an amateur sleuth (who outsleuths the professionals), and the title sequence of *Murder, She Wrote* in a number of night shots invites us to watch her searching for clues. Interactions among the Golden Girls—a nudge, a look, a reaction—suggest lively intercourse and good humor, all indicators of quick-wittedness. The Fatman seems always to be observing; Matlock is listening to a witness or turning a green blackboard to display a diagram and make a point; Bill Gillespie is a policeman. The very nature of the jobs of most of the elderly characters and their normal activities, displayed in numerous shots, all suggest the characters are particularly bright and alert.

Sixth, the elderly characters are looked up to and admired. There is a comical shot in *Jake and the Fatman* where the Fatman looks down at his old pet bulldog, Max, who has a lei around his neck. The shot accents the similarity of the Fatman to his dog, both in size and nature, but it also shows the dog looking up to its owner. Appropriate "looking up to" is a measure of relationships in most of the shows, a common visual device for expressing admiration. Clearly Jake looks up to the Fatman as a kind of fatherly boss. The same holds for Matlock's staff. The press also follow Matlock, and witnesses and the public in the courtroom constantly eye him, as does the female district attorney who opposes him as well as toasts him, in separate shots. In *The Golden Girls,* the various group shots speak of friendship and group admiration; friends may sometimes get fed up with each other, but they look up to each other, too, and the same holds for mother and daughter, Sophia and Dorothy. Looking up to, in *In the Heat of the Night,* can only be inferred from the image of the chief and his coming first. *Murder, She Wrote* has no obvious internal means of conveying admiration, but its subtle juxtaposition of irised memory scenes and "present" typing scenes suggests the writer's admiration of memory, the stuff of writing in an important practical sense, and the activities and the presented self remembered become the admired.

In addition, we, the audience, are encouraged to offer admiration to the characters. The title sequence of *Murder, She Wrote,* more clearly than the other title sequences, actively positions the audience as admiring other, there being no "other" on the screen. A fine symbol of expected audience admiration can also be found in *Jake and the Fatman.* The title sequence opens with bubble shots of Jake and the Fatman positioned in the surrounding Hawaiian landscape. When Fatman appears, the surrounding scenery has the feel of mountains behind, and when the Fatman juts his jaw forward, one gets the sense of witnessing a sculpture on Mount Rushmore or the face of an important historical personage on a coin. In a subtle way, then, the audience is invited to watch an admired living ikon perform.

Seventh, sexuality is generally removed from the lives of elderly characters, and when the elderly display sexuality, they are likely to be sexy, that is, exciting, attractive, titillating, alluring, and perhaps flirtatious, but not sexual. Elderly erotics, when they exist, consequently, are the erotics of the gaze and desire and not the erotics of touch and the satisfied body. Sexiness is an important element in the manifestations of admiration found in *Matlock,* especially, and, in smaller measure, it is part of the Fatman's allure in *Jake and the Fatman.* Matlock appears in the presence of two pretty, and clearly much younger, women who both look at him with eyes that suggest desire as well as admiration. Each woman — Michelle Thomas, played by Nancy Stafford, and Julie March, played by Julie Sommars — is found in a number of shots with Ben, and in one shot he holds Michelle's hand as he leads her down the courthouse steps and in another he toasts Julie with a glass of wine. There is nothing aggressive or sexual about Matlock's behavior, however. If anything, he is romantic and gentlemanly — and capable of attracting at least two pretty younger women.

A slightly different kind of sexiness is displayed in the *Jake and the Fatman* title sequence, but the result, I believe, is similar. The Fatman, himself, is never shown directly with women. He is either alone or with Jake. In the other shots, however, Jake is displayed in muscle shirts, by the shore, in a car with a beautiful woman; there are shots of hula girls, a stripper, night clubs, the beach, swimming pools . . . in short, the activities of sensual day and night Honolulu, shot after shot, and all these images create a sexual ambience that Jake certainly is a part of but that only touches the Fatman insofar as he touches Jake. Our sense, then, is that Jake rubs off on the Fatman — the Fatman, therefore, is sexy, by association, but not sexual.

Sexuality is not an issue in the other title sequences, a point worth emphasizing. Jessica's life is absorbed in personal activities and work. Chief Gillespie's life appears to be summed up in his work. And the Golden Girls apparently structure their lives around themselves. Sexuality, thus, is an important absence in the lives of most elderly television characters, and especially in the lives of elderly women.

The eighth and last generalization flows from all the rest: what can be called the "old order" generally rules in all of the shows. Removed from the mythic centers of the problematic in modern life — cities like Chicago, Los Angeles, or New York — the title sequences present the old South of Atlanta in *Matlock,* with its assurances of fair play and justice, and the old South again in Sparta, Mississippi, in *In the Heat of the Night,* where some of Virgil Tibbs's North has reared its presence, but the police are still (literally, as the superimposed blue police images show) on top of things. In *The Golden Girls* we see the new South in Miami, but it is the romantic retirement Miami, the orange morning or evening of the opening airplane shot or the sparkling sunlit buildings, blue sky, and clear water of the shot that follows, not the drug world of *Miami Vice.* We see old

New England in *Murder, She Wrote,* with its sense of small-town America, individualism, and bounded stories. Only in the title sequence of *Jake and the Fatman* do we meet images of the problematic — the sizzling scene, so to speak — but these are countered by the tourist motif of the Fatman walking around, alone or with Jake, enjoying the fun of Honolulu, images asserting that the show's territory is safe because the great bulldog is watching, and he can always set Jake into protective motion. In short, the title sequences assert that crime is contained; there is excitement and pleasure to be had but within a context of civility; women can venture forth and be heroes, but the essential values of the old patriarchy hold.

Changing Stereotypes

What can we say has changed, then, in the last 10 years? Have we in fact reached a new golden age on prime-time television in regard to portrayals of the elderly?

If one recalls the literature review presented earlier, I think it can be said that this study upholds the notion that elderly characters have become more prominent on prime-time TV and that positive elderly characters most certainly have drawn significant audiences to the shows that feature them, especially older audiences. In addition, each of the shows studied has withstood, and continues to withstand, a television show's biggest adversary — ratings. Moreover, each of the shows, assuming the title sequences are adequate indexes, in various ways subverts or reverses the earlier negative stereotypes of the elderly, and each presents each elderly character as a respected person.

Elderly women appear to be presented a little better than they used to be, but their presentations are still troubling. Women are clearly featured in three of the shows, although it is young women with subsidiary roles who are found in *In the Heat of the Night* and *Jake and the Fatman,* traditional action cop shows. Where women dominate, in the two shows *The Golden Girls* and *Murder, She Wrote,* they are seen as commanding and powerful, yet they are also viewed as essentially separate from men. Where they work in conjunction with men, in *Matlock* and perhaps in *In the Heat of the Night,* they are seen as secondary. Finally, in *Jake and the Fatman,* women are viewed as the traditional accoutrements of men and the male gaze. Two universes, thus, seem to be depicted — a female universe of older women where there are no men, and a male universe of older men where there are women but no older women. We can conclude that women seem better treated than they have been, if only in sheer numbers presented, but when men appear with women, the old stereotypes of male prominence and dominance still operate. We can also conclude that prime-time television doesn't seem to know how (or wish) to handle a continuing intimate relationship between two elderly people of the opposite sex.

The stereotype of the elderly being extremely healthy and active physically and socially continues. True, most elderly are fit and active, but most also retire at younger ages than the elderly characters of the shows studied, and many elderly people are not as active or fit as the characters studied. Related to activity and fitness is income, and the continuing stereotype of the well-off elderly is more problematic than that of the healthy and active elderly, which at least serves as an ideal model for all. Many elderly persons, especially women, are poor, and the older the elderly are, the more likely they are to be poor. Stressing the elderly affluent in dramatic presentations may satisfy the fantasies of many older or younger viewers, but it hardly presents an accurate picture of American life. In fact, it may undercut positive portrayals of the elderly, for without a fairly substantial income who, in truth, could possibly participate in many of the various modeled activities depicted in the shows' title sequences?

Another way to evaluate the portrayals of the elderly on the five studied programs is to ask what the title sequences show in their attempts to conceal, and what the sequences actually leave out.

Family in the blood sense is almost totally left out. Only Dorothy and Sophia, daughter and mother on *The Golden Girls,* are blood family. Here, of course, we go beyond the title sequences because if we read them alone, we have to assume that each defines a family in its cast of characters. Indeed, for the most part, this is exactly what family means in most of the shows, for each show's working family is the featured family in the show. Even *Murder, She Wrote* has a kind of working family like the rest of the shows — not the people identified in the credit shots who constitute a living-together or working-together family, but a family of images that constitute a kind of story family. More and more Americans are certainly living within created families, groups at work or social groups, for example, but most Americans, the elderly included, still live in, struggle with, and enjoy a blood family context, a context that is missing from the shows studied.

Crime and other common social problems are not missing from the title sequences, but they are cleverly submerged. Even in *The Golden Girls* sequence there is a shot of the four women at night huddling together as they pass through a room where a picture on the wall is askew, suggesting they are fearful of a robber. But the shot passes by quickly amid many other happy shots . . . and theirs is a comedy show. All the other shows are directly involved with crime, yet one finishes watching the title sequences feeling secure — because there are enough police, as in *In the Heat of the Night,* or Jessica Fletcher will solve the mystery, as in *Murder, She Wrote,* or justice reigns, as in *Matlock.* In *Jake and the Fatman,* if there are problems, we are led to believe, surely Jake or the Fatman will protect us. The point here is that the title sequences say that we are safe, that the old mythic order will prevail, and the fact that the title sequences continue to say this year after year both stretches and compounds this illusion.

3. SOCIETAL ATTITUDES TOWARD OLD AGE

Have TV's portrayals of the elderly changed enough to support the idea of the present being a golden age? In some ways, yes. Reverse positive stereotypes — the flip side of earlier negative stereotypes — are prominent, an improvement of sorts. And older people are featured a little more, an improvement. The addition of some strong female characters is also an improvement. I tend to agree, then, with critics such as Waters and Huck (1985), Dail (1988), and Cassata (1985) that older people are being presented in a more positive light on television today than they have been in the past (see Television Information Office, 1985).

But portrayals of the elderly still have a long way to come. The patriarchy and the affluent still hold sway in the television world, along with the mythic old order — significant problems. Even more problematic is the continuing wide gap between TV demographics and the real demographics of the American population.

One implicit message in much content analysis scholarship, especially scholarship carried on by those who are concerned with cultivation theory and cultural indicators (Littlejohn, 1989, e.g.), is that television should mirror the demographics of the real world. They seem to argue that if television only presents the elderly as 4% of its total persons and the real figure in the population is 12%, then an increase in the number of presentations to equal the percentage of the elderly in the population will somehow solve the problem. It would help, but the networks would also have to address more subtle contents such as gender, race (all of the characters studied are white), class, marital status, and health status, to name a few, as well. And even if all the numbers were right, in some statistical sense, there would be no guarantee that television reflected the "real" of our society, for entertaining fantasies and stereotypical portrayals might still be television's common fare.

Nevertheless, if television viewers — both the young and the elderly — choose TV characters as role models and tend to accept the dramatically presented television world as real, all members of society would be better served if television mirrored demographic realities more closely. In the case of elderly television characters, we need to see more of them more often, and in richer, more diverse lights than they are now presented. We need to see them spread throughout our communities, interacting with people of all ages and all walks of life.

Future research on television and aging might explore the possibility that more accurate and diverse portrayals of the elderly on television could have a positive effect on the lives of viewers. In addition, it could examine whether, how, and to what extent young and middle-aged people's attitudes toward aging and the elderly are influenced by these TV portrayals.

References

Buck, J. (1989, December 10). TV's new golden agers. *Daily News*, pp. 32–33.

Cassata, M. (1985). Images in transition [Introduction]. In Television Information Office, *Television looks at aging*. New York: Television Information Office.

Dail, P. W. (1988). Prime-time television portrayals of older adults in the context of family life. *The Gerontologist, 28*, 700–706.

Davis, R. H., & Davis, J. A. (1986). *TV's image of the elderly: A practical guide for change*. Lexington, MA: Lexington.

Diddlebock, B. (1989, May 22). Creative departments slow to act. *Advertising Age*, 5–6.

Fiske, J. (1987). British cultural studies and television. In R. C. Allen (Ed.), *Channels of discourse: Television and contemporary criticism* (pp. 254–289). Chapel Hill, NC: University of North Carolina Press.

Gerbner, G., Gross, G., Morgan, M., & Signorielli N. (1980). Aging with television: Images on television drama and conceptions of social reality. *Journal of Communication, 30*, 37–47.

Littlejohn, S. W. (1989). *Theories of human communication*, 3rd ed. Belmont, CA: Wadsworth.

Minkler, M. (1989). Gold is gray: Reflections on business' discovery of the elderly market. *The Gerontologist, 29*, 17–23.

Nielsen Media Research. (1989a). *Nielsen report on television 1989*. New York: Nielsen Media Research News.

Nielsen Media Research. (1989b). *National audience demographics, vol. 1, Nov. 1989*. New York: Nielsen Media Research News.

Nielsen Media Research. (1991a). *Primetime 90–91 season, regularly scheduled programs Sept. 17, 1990 — Aug. 15, 1991*. New York: Nielsen Media Research News.

Nielsen Media Research. (1991b). *1990–1991 season in review: Program rankings by age*. New York: Nielsen Media Research News.

Postman, N. (1985). *Amusing ourselves to death: Public discourse in the age of show business*. New York: Viking.

Powell, L., & Williamson, J. B. (1985). The mass media and the aged. *Social Policy, Summer*, 38–49.

Schramm, W. (1969). Aging in mass communication. In M. W. Riley, J. W. Riley, Jr., & M. E. Johnson (Eds.), *Aging and the professions*, vol. 2 of *Aging in society* (pp. 352–375). New York: Russell Sage Foundation.

Swayne, L. E., & Greco, A. J. (1987). The portrayal of older Americans in television commercials. *Journal of Advertising, 16*(1), 47–54.

Television Information Office. (1985). *Television looks at aging*. New York: Author.

Waters, H. F., & Huck, J. I. (1985, November 18). A new golden age. *Newsweek*, pp. 107–108.

GETTING OLDER
Is Getting Better

In the years ahead, the growing presence of seniors in our midst means that we will come to regard age with honor.

John R. Graham

Mr. Graham is president of Graham Communications, Quincy, Mass.

FOR the past 50 years, Americans have worshipped at the altar of youth. Everything has been geared to acting, looking, and staying young. Much of consumers' dollars have gone—and continue to go—to being young or young at heart.

A change is on the way, however. By the year 2000, approximately 50,000,000 Americans will be 65 years of age or older, with about 5,000,000 over age 85. No longer can we "hide" older people in the U.S. Their sheer numbers are changing how senior adults feel about themselves.

Until now, getting old has been a curse. Once you pass 50, you're headed for the scrap heap. You're out of the loop—everything worthwhile has passed you by. This is how older people have been made to feel. Yet, as senior adults become omnipresent in American life by the turn of the century, our priorities and our view of age will be changing. It is already.

Much of what we observe about older people is quite accurate, except that what we *think* we are seeing is not what's happening at all. We misread the signals because we view them through our own eyes, rather than those of senior adults. The following are nine ways to understand how they think and behave.

As many people get older, they move with greater caution. Because it makes us feel somewhat uncomfortable when this happens, we're not really sure what we're supposed to do. We act as if they're going to crack or break if we touch them.

In reality, most of the deliberate movement on steps and unfamiliar territory comes from sight problems or concern about the possibility of falling. This is a major fear of the elderly because broken bones—particularly hips—mean a potential loss of independence, which, more than just about anything else, is a source of tremendous personal pride.

The point is simple: No one should make other people feel there is something wrong with them if they behave or act differently.

Some seniors may be quite suspicious of other people. There are legitimate reasons why the elderly are fearful. Physically vulnerable and often defenseless, they become easy prey for everything from purse snatching to housebreaking. There are people who take advantage of those who are the weakest—children, women, and the elderly.

Senior adults have another, quite different, concern—an overwhelming fear of rejection. Images of youth have been the dominant theme in American life. There is nothing more devastating—and depressing—than a sense of worthlessness. Being suspicious is how many seniors protect themselves from unnecessary hurt.

Senior adults often seem insecure. Having been conditioned to believe getting old is the worst thing that can happen to anyone, it is only natural for senior adults to demonstrate feelings of insecurity. The common view is clear: Old people, however we define them, are second-class citizens because they are non-productive, at least by society's prevailing standards. This view further is reinforced by the emphasis on the staggering Social Security

and medical costs as people live longer. The loss of personal dignity may be the senior's greatest fear. Therefore, it is normal to be sensitive or even insecure regarding one's identity.

Seniors may act as if they didn't understand what you said. They aren't stupid, although that's an all-too-common conclusion. First, hearing disorders are a problem. Often, a sense of pride keeps many older people from dealing with this impediment.

Second, there may be certain common ideas, trends, and situations that the elderly do not understand simply because they are not active within particular environments. If you are active in the field of computers, it is easy to confound people who don't work with them every day. On the other hand, if you're 35 and want to feel "out of it," just ask a 70-year-old about World War II.

Older adults tend to seek out situations, particularly at stores and restaurants, where there are people to give them personal assistance. This isn't because they are lazy or self-centered. Since older people tend to feel diminished and less secure, they feel most comfortable in situations where they can receive feedback from others. In short, they want to be noticed.

We can learn from the way senior adults behave in public. At church, for example, they will wait patiently to shake hands with the clergy. In the same way, seniors tend to hold office in voluntary organizations even beyond a time when they can perform the duties required. This is yet another way of saying, "I'm still important."

Senior adults may seem more picky than

others. They act that way concerning virtually everything. Food, clothes, heat, arrangements of just about any type, seating, accommodations—you name it, and an older person will find something wrong with it. At least this is the way it seems to many people.

Why does this happen? There can be legitimate medical considerations, of course, but there could be another factor. When a senior adult is cut off from the mainstream of life, from regular interaction with a cross section of people, a turning inward and a preoccupation with self develops. The individual, in other words, becomes the center of the universe. The important point is that this happens to anyone if the conditions are right. Age itself isn't the issue.

Seniors sometimes act as if they don't know what's going on. Because society has made them feel they have been sidelined permanently, it should not be surprising that they can be less aware than other people.

Yet, think about it. Once you have lived 70 or 80 years, haven't you developed such a broad perspective on life that your equilibrium isn't upset by what's going on at the moment? You can be less involved and better able to see things as part of a larger context. Many seniors simply see very few things as being of such utmost importance that it is necessary to get excited about them.

Many are exceptionally trusting, particularly with those who show an interest in them. At first, this seems to contradict the earlier contention that senior adults are more suspicious than many other people. While they may be suspicious, they also are trusting—at times, too much so. There are countless stories of an aged widow who gives her life savings to a stranger to invest for her, then never sees either the "investor" or her money again. Even more common are the home improvement scams where someone is charged thousands of dollars for minor repairs or work that does not need to be done.

Why are some senior adults seemingly so gullible? If you're lonely, you'll do almost anything—including paying—for friendship. "But he seemed like such a nice young man. Just like my grandson." How many times have we heard those words after the rip-off? Senior adults aren't more gullible than anyone else. Just as with all of us, the desire for friendship, recognition, and love is so strong that it can result in poor judgment.

Senior adults are just like the rest of us. They picture themselves as 10 to 15 years younger than their actual age. After about 35, we all tend to view ourselves through "young colored glasses." Most of us regard ourselves as years younger than our actual age. "Don't judge me by the date I was born," we're saying. "See me as I am."

We don't actually believe we're younger than we are. Rather, as human beings, we plead to be understood, accepted, and appreciated as we are—not in terms of being too young, middle-aged, or too old.

Dealing with senior adults

There are several implications in these nine issues that can be helpful in dealing appropriately with senior adults. The elderly are no different than anyone else, but, as with any segment of the population, certain values seem to be more important to them, so:

● Show your personal interest. For senior adults, personal relationships often take precedence over price, availability, speed, and just about everything else. They often are content with a lower savings account interest rate if they value the personal attention they receive from a financial institution.

● Don't be in a hurry. Take your time because there's no reason for most senior adults to rush. They've done all the rushing they intend to do. They want to enjoy. Don't be pushy and you'll get their appreciation.

● Be sensitive. Far too many of us seem to look at life from only our own perspective. Being sensitive to senior adults can increase our understanding and empathy.

● Senior adults' lifestyles are changing. In the years ahead, their growing presence in our midst means that we will come to regard age with honor. It is time to get ready mentally for this rapidly approaching time.

WHAT DOCTORS AND OTHERS NEED TO KNOW

Six Facts on Human Sexuality and Aging

Richard J. Cross, MD

Certified Specialist in Internal Medicine, Professor Emeritus at the Robert Wood Johnson Medical School, NJ

Most of us find that our definition of old age changes as we mature. To a child, anyone over forty seems ancient. Sixty-five and older is the common governmental definition of a senior citizen, and it is the definition that I will follow here, although the author (who is in his late 70s) long ago began to find it hard to accept. There is, of course, no specific turning point, but rather a series of gradual physical and emotional changes, some in response to societal rules about retirement and entitlement to particular benefits.

Demographically, the elderly are a rapidly growing segment of the population. In 1900, there were about three million older Americans; by the year 2000, there will be close to 31 million older Americans. Because of high male mortality rates, older women outnumber men 1.5 to 1, and since most are paired off, single women outnumber single men by about 4 to 1. By definition, the elderly were born in the pre-World War I era. Most were thoroughly indoctrinated in the restrictive attitudes toward sex that characterized these times.

In my opinion, the care of the elderly could be significantly improved if doctors and other health workers would remember the following six, simple facts.

Fact #1: All Older People Are Sexual

Older people are not all sexually active, as is also true of the young, but they all have sexual beliefs, values, memories, and feelings. To deny this sexuality is to exclude a significant part of the lives of older people. In recent decades, this simple truth has been repeatedly stated by almost every authority who has written about sexuality, but somehow the myth persists that the elderly have lost all competence, desire, and interest in sexuality, and that those who remain sexual, particularly if sexually active, are regarded as abnormal and, by some, even perverted. This myth would seem to have at least three components. First, it is a carryover of the Victorian belief that sex is dangerous and evil, though necessary for reproduction, and that sex for recreational purposes is improper and disgusting. Second is what Mary S. Calderone, SIECUS co-founder, has called a tendency for society to castrate its dependent members: to deny the sexuality of the disabled, of prisoners, and of the elderly. This perhaps reflects a subconscious desire to dehumanize those whom we believe to be less fortunate than ourselves in order to assuage our guilt feelings. Third, Freud and many others have pointed out that most of us have a hard time thinking of our parents as being sexually active, and we tend to identify all older people with our parents and grandparents.

For whatever reason, it is unfortunate that young people so often deny the sexuality of those who are older. It is even more tragic when older people themselves believe the myth and then are tortured by guilt when they experience normal, healthy sexual feelings. Doctors and other health workers need to identify and alleviate such feelings of guilt.

How many people are sexually active? It is generally agreed upon by experts that the proportion of both males and females who are sexually active declines, decade by decade, ranging according to one study from 98% of married men in their 50s to 50% for unmarried women aged 70 and over.[1] At each decade, there are also some people who are inactive. It is important to accept abstinence as a valid lifestyle as well—at any age—as long as it is freely chosen.

Fact #2: Many Older People Have a Need for a Good Sexual Relationship

To a varying extent, the elderly experience and must adapt to gradual physical and mental changes. They may find themselves no longer easily able to do the enjoyable things they used to do; their future may seem fearful; retirement and an "empty nest" may leave many with reduced incomes and no clear goals in life; friends and/or a lifetime partner may move away, become ill, or die; and the threat of loneliness may be a major concern. Fortunately, many older people are not infirm, frustrated, fearful, bored, or lonely; nonetheless, some of these elements may be affecting their lives. An excellent antidote for all this is the

Research Note

Andrew Greeley, priest, author, and sociologist at the University of Chicago analyzed national-poll data of 6,000 respondents and found that sexual activity is plentiful, even after the age of 60. He reported in 1992 that 37 percent of married people over 60 have sexual relations at least once a week—and one in six respondents had sexual relations more often. Greeley concluded that sexually active married men are happier with their spouses at 60 than 20-year-old single males who have many sexual partners. His report, "Sex After Sixty: A Report," based on surveys by the Gallup Organization and the National Opinion Research Center included the following results:

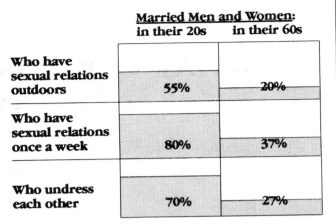

| | Married Men and Women: | |
	in their 20s	in their 60s
Who have sexual relations outdoors	55%	20%
Who have sexual relations once a week	80%	37%
Who undress each other	70%	27%

warmth, intimacy, and security of a good sexual relationship.

Fact #3: Sexual Physiology Changes with Age

In general, physiological changes are gradual and are easily compensated for, if one knows how. But when they sneak up on an unsuspecting, unknowledgeable individual, they can be disastrous. Health workers need to be familiar with these changes and with how they can help patients adapt to them.

Older men commonly find that their erections are less frequent, take longer to achieve, are less firm, and are more easily lost. Ejaculation takes longer, is less forceful, and produces a smaller amount of semen. The refractory period (the interval between ejaculation and another erection) is often prolonged to many hours or even days. The slowing down of the sexual response cycle can be compensated for simply by taking more time, a step usually gratifying to one's partner, especially if he or she is elderly. But in our society many men grow up believing that their manliness, their power, and their competence depend on their ability to "get it up, keep it up, and get it off." For such an individual, slowing of the cycle may induce performance anxiety, complete impotence, and panic. Good counseling about the many advantages of a leisurely approach can make a world of difference for such an individual.

The prolonged refractory period may prevent a man from having sexual relations as often as he formerly did, but only if he requires that the sexual act build up to his ejaculation. If he can learn that good, soul-satisfying sexual activity is possible without male ejaculation, then he can participate as often as he and his partner wish. Finally, men (and sometimes their partners) need to learn that wonderful sex is possible without an erect penis. Tongues, fingers, vibrators, and many other gadgets can make wonderful stimulators and can alleviate performance anxiety.

Some women find the arrival of menopause disturbing; others feel liberated. If one has grown up in a society that believes that the major role for women is bearing children, then the loss of that ability may make one feel no longer a "real woman." The most common sexual problem of older women, however, is vaginal dryness, which can make sexual intercourse painful, particularly if her partner is wearing an unlubricated condom. The obvious solution is to use one of the many water-soluble lubricants available in drug stores. Saliva is a fairly good lubricant and it does have four advantages over commercial products: 1) it is readily available where one may be; 2) it is free; 3) it is at the right temperature; and 4) its application is more intimate than something from a tube.

An alternative approach attacks the root of the problem. Vaginal drying results from a decrease in estrogen and can be reversed with estrogen replacement which also prevents other consequences of menopause like hot flashes and loss of calcium from the skeleton. But estrogen administration may increase the risk of uterine cancer; therefore, each woman and her doctor will need to balance out the risks and benefits in her particular situation.

Aging inevitably changes physical appearance and, in our youth-oriented culture, this can have a profound impact on sexuality. It is not easy to reverse the influence of many decades of advertisements for cosmetics and clothes, but doctors can at least try to avoid adding to the problem. Many medical procedures—particularly mastectomy, amputations, chemotherapy, and ostomies—have a profound impact on body image. It is of utmost importance to discuss this impact before surgery and to be fully aware of the patient's need to readjust during the post-operative period. When possible, involvement of the patient's sexual partner in these discussions can be very helpful.

Fact #4: Social Attitudes Are Often Frustrating

As indicated above, society tends to deny the sexuality of the aged, and in so doing creates complications in their already difficult lives. Laws and customs restrict the sexual behavior of older people in many ways. This is particularly true for women, since they have traditionally enjoyed less freedom and because, demographically, there are fewer potential partners for heterosexual, single women, and many of the few men that are available are pursuing women half their age.

Some professionals have suggested that women explore sexual behaviors with other women. However, we know that sexual orientation, although potentially fluid throughout a life-span, is more complicated than the suggestion implies. While some women discover lesbian sexuality at an older age, it is rarely the result of a decrease in the availability of male partners. When doctors see an older woman as a patient, they can, at least, inquire into sexual satisfaction. If sexual frustration is expressed, they can be understanding. Some women can be encouraged to try masturbating, and some will find a vibrator a delightful way to achieve orgasm.

Older people are living in a variety of retirement communities and nursing homes. This brings potential sexual partners together, but tends to exaggerate the gender imbalance. In retirement homes, single women often outnumber single men, eight or ten to one. Furthermore, rules, customs, and lack of privacy severely inhibit the establishment of intimate relationships at these sites. Administrators of such homes are often blamed for this phenomenon. Some are, indeed, unsympathetic, but we must also consider the attitudes of the trustees, the neighbors, and the legislators who oversee the operation, and particularly the attitudes of the family members. If two residents establish a sexual relationship, it is often followed by a son or daughter pounding the administrator's desk and angrily shouting, "That's not what I put Mom (Dad) here for!"

Fact #5: Use It Or Lose It
Sexual activity is not a commodity that can be stored and saved for a rainy day. Rather, it is a physiologic function that tends to deteriorate if not exercised, and it is particularly fragile in the elderly. If interrupted, it may be difficult (though not impossible) to reinvigorate. Doctors should work with the patient and partner on reestablishing the ability if desired.

Fact #6: Older Folks Do It Better
This may seem like an arrogant statement to some, but much depends on what is meant by "better." If the basis is how hard the penis is, how moist the vagina, how many strokes per minute, then the young will win out, but if the measure is satisfaction achieved, the elderly can enjoy several advantages. First, they have usually had considerable experience, not necessarily with many different partners. One can become very experienced with a single partner. Second, they often have more time, and a good sexual relationship takes a lot of time. The young are often pressured by studies, jobs, hobbies, etc., and squeeze their sexual activities into a very full schedule. Older folks can be more leisurely and relaxed. Finally, attitudes often improve with aging. The young are frequently insecure, playing games, and acting out traditional roles because they have not explored other options. Some older folks have mellowed and learned to roll with the punches. They no longer need to prove themselves and can settle down to relating with their partner and meeting his or her needs. Obviously one does not have to be old to gain experience, to set aside time, or to develop sound attitudes. Perhaps the next generation of Americans will discover how to learn these simple things without wasting thirty or forty years of their lives playing silly games. One hopes so.

Conclusion
In summary, older people are sexual, often urgently need sexual contact, and yet encounter many obstacles to enjoying its pleasures, some medical, most societal. Doctors and other healthcare providers need to be aware of these problems and need to help those who are aging cope with them.

Dr. Richard J. Cross originally wrote this article for the SIECUS Report in 1988.

Author's References
1 Brecher EM. *Love, Sex, and Aging.* New York: Little, Brown and Company, 1984.

AMAZING GREYS

Old images of aging are changing in an era when seniors are living longer, healthier, wealthier and more independently than they ever have before

Mary Nemeth

In his office across from Parliament Hill hang framed newspaper cartoons spoofing Mitchell Sharp at various points in his long career. Once a high-profile civil servant, a successful businessman and a cabinet minister, and now–for $1 a year–Prime Minister Jean Chrétien's special adviser, the 82-year-old Sharp remembers a time when society's entire focus was on youth. "People in their 70s and 80s," he says, "were considered incapable of having a reasonable opinion about current events." The fact that the Prime Minister has turned to Sharp for assistance–not *in spite* of his age but because of his seniority–is evidence of a dramatic shift in popular images of aging. "People pay more attention to what I say now than perhaps they should," laughs Sharp. "I think there is quite a significant change in attitude going on. Somehow, once again, experience counts."

North Americans, raised on evil old crones like the one in *Hansel and Gretel* and bombarded by Hollywood images of youthful beauty, have long ignored, even feared, old age. Blanket stereotypes afflicted anyone over 65: sickly, feebleminded, confined to nursing homes, a burden on their children, haggard and bitter–or, at best, cute and childlike. True, many seniors *are* very ill, some are impoverished, some are physically abused. And some who live with their grown children require more care than younger families can provide. But those troubled seniors are in a minority, often at the top end of an aging scale that can last into the 80s, 90s and beyond. "Old age is not all frailty," notes Neena Chappell, director of the University of Victoria's Centre on Aging. "Without minimizing the difficulties of those who are really suffering, in truth the majority of seniors are doing very well, thank you."

Canadian seniors, in fact, are living longer, healthier, wealthier and more independently than ever before. And old stereotypes are under assault. American author Betty Friedan, whose 1963 book, *The Feminine Mystique,* inspired modern feminism, has turned to the myths surrounding the elderly. In her latest book, *The Fountain of Age,* the 72-year-old Friedan refutes the "image of age as inevitable decline." She argues that gerontologists concentrate too much "on the victims of the most extreme ravages of senility, the sick, helpless old." That focus, she writes, may have blinded not only the profession but older people themselves to the possibilities of life after 60. But Friedan is only at the thin edge of a demographic wedge: the number of Canadians over 65 is expected to grow from 3.2 million now to 8.7 million within four decades. The first of the baby boomers–the group that used to distrust anyone over 30–will start turning 65 in the year 2011. That generation, through force of numbers, has dictated trends in everything from hairstyles to consumer spending, and is certain to demand an end to negative stereotypes of aging, as well.

Already, Hollywood seems to sense a shifting wind. Among a spate of recent movies featuring older characters, Billy Crystal was slathered with wrinkle and liver-spot makeup for his role as a fading comic in the 1992 *Mr. Saturday Night,* and an equally made-up Bette Midler played a past-her-prime siren in the 1991 *For the Boys.* But Robin Williams said that in his latest movie, *Mrs. Doubtfire*–after first making him up to look like a haggard old crone–film-makers settled on a more attractive older woman character.

And advertisers now poke fun at the aged only at their peril. In response to public outrage over a recent Doritos tortilla chip commercial–which showed a befuddled old woman getting steamrolled into wet cement–the contrite manufacturer delivered cases of free chips to a food bank. "I do think some sensitivity is developing," says Ethel Meade, 74, co-chairman of the Older Women's Network, a Toronto advocacy group. "Of course, lots of older women are busy and active. They are breaking stereotypes by showing what older women can do."

Senior men and women volunteer or work part time. They travel to exotic locations and take study vacations at home. A Kingston, Ont.-based group called

From *Maclean's* magazine, January 10, 1994, pp. 26-29. © 1994 by Maclean Hunter, Ltd. Reprinted by permission.

Elderhostel Canada offers courses in subjects ranging from cross-country skiing to watercolor painting. And the Raging Grannies, who caricature aging stereotypes by dressing up in floppy hats and frilly dresses, campaign against everything from nuclear arms to the GST. Another grandmother, 73-year-old Lenore Wedlake from Halifax, teaches a weekly class in t'ai chi, a Chinese martial art that focuses on relaxation and meditation. "I guess, because of my age, they thought I would be a good role model," says Wedlake, who maintains that "old" is a concept "perpetuated by younger people." She adds: "When you get to be older, you just don't feel that much older inside. I don't have quite as much energy as I once did. But generally, I've been blessed with good health."

Even as seniors swing into action, however, some people argue that the anti-ageism movement has missed its mark. Tracy Kidder, a Pulitzer Prize–winning author, just published *Old Friends,* based on patients in a Massachusetts nursing home. In a recent interview, he argued that the increasingly common images of seniors in tennis shoes implies that the only way to age "successfully" is to be in good health. That, he says, ignores the real problems of the disabled and the weak. "There are people who are very sick," says Kidder, "who manage against the odds to lead meaningful lives." Among them, he says, is an arthritic elderly man at the nursing home who insisted on dressing himself, even though it took him 1½ hours each morning. "When it takes 1½ hours," says Kidder, "the fact that you do it for your own dignity is a kind of routine heroism."

Of course, physical health does decline with age. According to the University of Victoria's Chappell, studies have shown that anywhere from 13 to 20 per cent of all seniors endure disabilities severe enough to hamper independent living—the inability to get dressed, go to the bathroom, get around the house—that can be caused by anything from arthritis to a stroke. But health may vary vastly depending on how old a senior is. According to Statistics Canada, 82 per cent of people aged 85 and over report some level of disability, compared with only 37 per cent of those aged 65 to 74. For most people, says Chappell, deteriorating health "tends to be gradual and things we can cope with."

Nils Hoas is among the golden oldies. A 66-year-old retired railway worker, he plays golf and slow-pitch baseball in the summer. And he was curling recently at the Peace Arch Curling Club in White Rock, B.C., at a bonspiel for those aged 60 and over. Hoas argues that inactivity can be demoralizing. When many of his co workers retired, he says, "they just stopped, they didn't do anything—they just sort of vegetated and seemed to give up on life."

Elsie McKenzie skipped the masters bonspiel—she travelled about 100 km from Vancouver to Chilliwack for an over-80s tournament instead. McKenzie talks gleefully of the time when, as a 67-year-old, she and three friends won a bonspiel in Scotland—even beating a squad of fit young Canadian airmen visiting from a base in Germany. That was in 1969. Now 91, McKenzie still curls at least once a week. "I think I would have been dead years ago, she says, "If I hadn't been curling."

As it happens, there has been some debate over whether seniors, as a group, are healthier than ever. In the past century, the life expectancy of Canadians has approximately doubled to 73 years for men, 80 for women. But some researchers say that as average life span continues to grow, healthy life does not. Even as heart diseases decrease, the argument goes, some cancers are increasing. But Statistics Canada senior analyst Russell Wilkins found that in 1986 Canadians' average life span was 76.4 years, up 7.8 years from 1951. Wilkins calculated that 2.8 of those extra years were lived with some disability. But most of the increase—five of the extra eight years of life—was disability-free.

When life expectancy was shorter, the few people who did live into their senior years had likely lost their spouses. Only in this century, writes Andrew Greeley, 65, an American priest and sociologist, have large numbers of men and women "survived into the 'senior' category in good health and with sexual desire still very much alive." But attitudes lag behind. Greeley published a study last year to counter perceptions that passionate love is non-existent among seniors. He found that about 37 per cent of married men and women over 60 have sex at least once a week; 20 per cent of those in their 60s report making love outdoors. Such data, he writes, is ignored amid "the snide snicker of the prevailing culture."

Al Bennett, a retired Toronto accountant, knows firsthand about late-blooming love. A widower, he met his match through an introduction agency. "I was just looking for companionship," says Bennett, 66. "But then the lights went on and the whistles blew." He and Margaret, a 59-year-old widow, plan to marry next year. "There's a whole new world in front of us, he says, adding that their families—seven children and eight grandchildren between them—have been supportive. "But I think some children throw roadblocks," he says. "They think someone else will get the inheritance, or they think daddy or mommy shouldn't be doing these things."

As for sex, Bennett allows that some seniors may not require it. "But it shouldn't be taken for granted that because you're 65, you're dead from the waist down." While sex "may not be as frequent in many cases," he says, "it is far more satisfying. We are who we are, we're not trying to demonstrate that we are Michelle Pfeiffer or whoever."

Grey may not only be beautiful—it can be bountiful. According to Andrew Wister, associate professor of gerontology at Simon Fraser University in Burnaby, B.C., "wealth and health work together." Health-promotion programs, which push nutrition and more vigorous exercise, seem to reach higher-educated, and usually wealthier, people. The good news is that the overall financial picture for seniors is also improving. Unattached senior women are the poorest group. According to the National Advisory Council on Aging, 38 per cent of them were below the low-income cutoff, or poverty line, in 1990, but that was a marked improvement over 1980, when 60 per cent were below the poverty line. Only 26 per cent of unattached senior men were in that category in 1990, compared with 53 per cent in 1980. And among senior couples, only 4 per cent, down from 13 per cent, were that poor. Improved financial circumstances have helped ever

greater numbers of seniors live independently. Stats-Can reports that even among seniors aged 75 and over, 59 per cent of women and 75 per cent of men were either living with a spouse or alone in 1991—an increase of more than 10 percentage points in the past two decades.

Independent seniors are making important contributions. A renowned trapper in the Yukon, 77-year-old Alex Van Bibber was awarded the Order of Canada last year for teaching younger generations about the wilderness. Among other skills, he now teaches other trappers about the proper care of fur and about the new quick-kill traps favored by animal-rights activists. At the same time, the Yukon's native elders—once a significant force in maintaining native culture—are getting more involved again in guiding their commu-

RETIREMENT: WHO PAYS?

Canada has been greying since Confederation. But with increasing longevity and lower fertility, the pace has accelerated since the 1970s. And when the baby boomers start to turn 65 just 17 years from now, the bulge in the senior population will be enormous. There is mounting alarm that the generation born after the mid-1960s will be unable—or unwilling—to bear the cost of social security for retiring baby boomers. But that potential crisis, experts say, can be contained—if only Canadians take steps now to prepare for the senior surge. "There has been a horrendous exaggeration of the magnitude of the problem," maintains Robert Brown, a professor of actuarial science at Ontario's University of Waterloo. "Yes, there are some concerns, but if we start to deal with them sooner, they will be manageable."

Most of those concerns surround the Canada Pension Plan, which now siphons off 5.2 per cent of earnings, split evenly between employees and employers. The CPP uses a pay-as-you-go system that will work only if future generations keep up their obligations—which are certain to grow. According to Sta-

tistics Canada, over the next four decades the number of seniors will increase 168 per cent to 8.7 million from 3.2 million. At the same time, the working-age population will grow by only 28 per cent. As a result, the CPP schedule calls for the rate of contributions to rise to as high as 13 per cent of earnings by the year 2030. "If the economy stays on line," says Jean Dumas, head of current demographic analysis at StatsCan, "the demographic burden will be heavy on the shoulders of wage earners. If the economy booms, there will be no problem."

The economy, of course, is notoriously unco-operative. But some experts say that, even without an economic turnaround, the government can help alleviate potential pension problems. It could marginally reduce CPP payments. Or it could follow the American example. In the year 2002, the United States will begin increasing the age of eligibility for pensions by an average of one month a year for 25 years, ultimately raising the age to 67 from 65. For Canada, says Brown, "the time to do something is now so we have a gradual transition, rather than walking to the edge of the cliff." According to the

Canadian Institute of Actuaries, based in Ottawa, the government could reduce future CPP contributions—to 10 per cent from 13 per cent—by raising the age of eligibility for retirement from 65 to 70.

Such measures would require major adjustments—including, perhaps, working longer. Seven provinces allow employers to impose mandatory retirement. The exceptions are Manitoba, Quebec and New Brunswick, plus the federal civil service. "Employers will have to stop saying, 'At 65, you're out,'" says Ellen Gee, a demographer at Simon Fraser University in Burnaby, B.C. "And employees will have to realize that they can't go fishing for the next 30 years." With baby boomers not getting any younger, the debate over how to finance future pensions is sure to heat up. But that debate, advises Ann Robertson, a University of Toronto social scientist, should focus on "who we are as a society, and not pit one generation against another. We don't have to buy the apocalyptic scenario that the elderly will bankrupt us."

SHARON DOYLE DRIEDGER

nities. "The elders can see what our young people have lost, there are so many problems with identity, self-esteem," says Pearl Keenan, 73, a Tlingit elder living in Whitehorse. "They are pulling us off our rocking chairs and crying for help." last fall, she says, elders representing each of the 14 Yukon First Nations held their second annual conference, passing recommendations on alcohol and drug abuse, gambling, education, language and culture.

Elsewhere, as well, seniors are doing good works. Blake Caldwell, a pastor at the Moncton Wesleyan Church in New Brunswick, argues that they have not only a right, but a responsibility, to grow spiritually. "It's not enough to get over the line, to say, 'I've become a Christian, I've arrived,'" says Caldwell, who runs the church's Golden Years Fellowship. As many as 100 seniors participate in the interdenominational program each week, doing Bible study, babysitting or visiting other seniors in nursing homes. "We're trying," adds Caldwell, "to defeat that rocking-chair mentality that it's time for me to sit back and let the younger people do things." Not that there is anything wrong with rocking chairs. But as a symbol of the lifestyles of all Canadians over the age of 65, they seem increasingly outdated.

With WARREN CARAGATA in Ottawa, CHRIS WOOD in Vancouver, JOHN DeMONT in Halifax and CHUCK TOBIN in Whitehorse

Problems and Potentials of Aging

Viewed as part of the life cycle, aging might be considered a period of decline, poor health, increasing dependence, social isolation, and—ultimately—death. It often means retirement, decreased income, chronic health problems, and the death of a spouse. In contrast, the first 50 years of life are a period of growth and development.

For a young child, life centers around the home and then the neighborhood. Later, the community and state become a part of the young person's environment. Finally, as an adult, the person is prepared to consider national and international issues—wars, alliances, changing economic cycles, and world problems.

During the later years, however, life space narrows. Retirement may distance the individual from national and international concerns, although he or she may remain actively involved in community affairs. Later, even community involvement may decrease, and the person may begin to stay close to home and the neighborhood. For some, the final years of life may once again focus on the confines of home, be it an apartment or a nursing home.

Many older Americans try to remain masters of their own destinies for as long as possible. They fear dependence and try to avoid it. Many are successful at maintaining independence and the right to make their own decisions. Others are less successful and must depend on their families for care and to make critical decisions.

Most older persons are able to overcome the difficulties of aging and lead comfortable and enjoyable lives. The article "How to Take Care of Aging Parents" gives sound advice to children who must begin assuming responsibilities for aging parents.

In "Older Problem Drinkers—Long-Term and Late-Life Onset Abusers: What Triggers Their Drinking?" the authors distinguish different patterns of alcohol abuse in later life. According to "American Maturity," the young elderly (65–74) and the old elderly (75 and older) are viewed as distinct groups with quite different problems and interests.

This thesis continues in "Older Persons and the Abuse and Misuse of Alcohol and Drugs." Anthony Traxler contrasts the different patterns of abuse of drugs and alcohol among older persons compared to the general population.

"Silent Saviors" delineates the ever-increasing number of children being raised by their grandparents. Linda Creighton suggests a liberalization of child custody laws that nearly always grant custody to parents even when parents are incapable of this responsibility.

Looking Ahead: Challenge Questions

Which aspects of life after 65 are desirable and should be anticipated with pleasure?

Which aspects of life after 65 are undesirable and should be a cause of concern to people of all ages?

What significant steps might be taken by both business and the local community to assist the elderly in overcoming the problems of aging?

How does drug abuse among young people differ from drug abuse among the elderly?

How to Take Care of Aging Parents

Elder care is a lot easier if you talk to your parents early on, plan way ahead, and get help from a big and growing network of resources.

Brian O'Reilly

It's Sunday night. Time to make the weekly how're-you-doing phone call to your mother living alone back in Omaha. But when she finally answers, something is wrong. Her speech is labored and slurred, and she is talking about things that make no sense.

You, friend, won't be at the office tomorrow; you'll be on the first plane to Omaha. Your mother—the exuberant *bon vivant* who was going to outlive you all—has suddenly gotten old. And you have just landed a second career: caregiver to an elderly parent.

What will it be like? Don't even try to predict. A thousand variables will determine what burdens elder care has in store for you, including the illnesses that befall your parents, how far away they live, and how much money you and they have. Nothing can make the decline of a proud patriarch or a once lively mother the least bit pleasant. But ignoring the inevitable and refusing to think about it could vastly increase the emotional, medical, and financial problems you and your parents will face. If you can pull your family together, talk frankly about options before a crisis develops, and get in touch early with the network of service and information providers designed to assist the elderly, you can make your job easier.

A few common misunderstandings about elder care are best dispelled early. First, it is not child care—treating an ailing adult like a child is demeaning and unnecessary. Second, do not assume that moving your parents permanently into your home is the best solution; they may not want to live with you, either. Third, you probably don't need to put them in a nursing home, but if you do, you may be stunned to discover that Medicare, which spares no expense to cure every medical problem, will *not* pay for extended nursing home care.

Reporter Associate Rosalind Klein Berlin

Chances are, your parents won't need much outside help before they are in their late 70s or early 80s. But the odds that you will wind up taking care of an older relative are good and growing. A 65-year-old male can expect to live to be 80, a female to 84. The fastest-growing segment of the population is the over-85 crowd. Relatively few of them—only about one in four—can live alone without difficulty, says Eileen Crimmins, a demographer at the University of Southern California. According to a Conference Board study, about 25% of the working-age population describe themselves as responsible for the care of an elder. They spend an average of ten hours a week at the task. Unlike child care, elder care isn't necessarily "women's work." One employee counseling service reports that males make only 10% of the calls concerning child care problems, but 40% of the calls about problems with elderly parents.

Executives are as likely as blue-collar workers to wind up responsible for the care of aging parents. When Eric Mayer's mother had a stroke that left her partially paralyzed, Mayer, managing director of a Beverly Hills firm that oversees a $6.5 billion real estate portfolio, spent most of the next six weeks arranging her care. "It completely changes your life," says Mayer. "Taking care of someone is not the kind of thing you delegate to your staff."

About half the time, an elderly person becomes incapacitated suddenly, going from independent to infirm because of an event such as a stroke or a broken hip, says Michael Creedon, a gerontologist in Vienna, Virginia. Even when parents decline slowly, their transition from frail-but-independent to needing help often comes as a jolt: A cop lifts Dad's driver's license after some confusion on the highway; now he can't shop for food anymore. Mom's arthritis becomes so uncomfortable she can no longer button her blouse. They get depressed or confused and fail to pay utility bills, and a neighbor calls you to say their lights have been off all week.

Raising the subject of old age with your parents is often exquisitely difficult. But J. B. Hancock, head of a video production company in Arlington, Virginia, discovered a good opening line: "I just went over my will and estate plan with my attorney," she told her elderly parents, who live in Florida. "It made me wonder if you folks need any help with your plans or want to talk things over." The hope is that your parents will be relieved if you bring up the subject—it indicates you don't plan to abandon them when they get old. If they balk at the topic, back off and try again in a few months. The consequences of not planning can be severe. When a crisis hits, you won't have the information you need or the authority to act on your parent's behalf. As a result, you could spend weeks or months lining up the services you need.

It is best to involve your whole family in any discussion of care—not just your brothers and sisters, but their spouses as well. And don't load everything onto the eldest daughter who happens to live nearby. Michael Creedon tells of one woman who announced her plans to retire, only to discover that her brothers and sisters then decided she should spend the rest of her life taking care of their parents. Says Creedon: "She went right on working." If you have a family that cannot discuss the weather without fighting, bring in a minister or other trusty outsider to act as referee.

A family meeting is a good time to learn some important basics, such as your parents' Social Security and Medicare identification numbers, their doctors' names, and as much of their medical history as they think you need to make intelligent decisions with them. Ask if you might meet their neighbors and exchange phone numbers for use in emergencies. Inquire, very gently, about their income, insurance, and other financial resources. Under which rhododendron have they buried their safe deposit box keys, wills, and other papers?

Parents should give power of attorney to someone to make legal, financial, and medical decisions if they are incapacitated and cannot decide for themselves; a will, which disperses assets *after* death, does not accomplish that. Afraid your parents will think you plan to fleece them if they put you in charge? Point out that most states forbid self-serving asset transfers by caretakers. Also find out what kind of medical heroics they want and encourage them to fill out a living will.

Now to the big question: Where should they live? While they are healthy and can afford it, staying in their own home is usually best. Anne Brophy Putney, community affairs director for WOGL, a CBS-owned radio station in Philadelphia, realized during a visit earlier this year that her 87-year-old mother in Palo Alto, California, was growing more fragile. Through a company-sponsored elder care program, she learned of a Palo Alto firm, Older Adults Care Management, that could evaluate her mother's needs and provide help. "We decided not to move her now," says Putney. "She's lived in her home for 40 years. The camellias are blooming, the freesias are out, and the fruit trees are laden with oranges. And she's the neighborhood candy lady who's been giving treats to the neighborhood children for more than 20 years. We decided she'd be happiest at home." The firm helped Putney find two women who take turns as her mother's live-in caregivers.

If either parent is likely to want or need an alternative form of housing, start planning early. Attractive places are hard to find, and waiting lists may be long. In Memphis, where the Methodist Church sponsors several well-run, federally subsidized apartment buildings for seniors, Jerry Corlew, one of the directors, says there is a waiting list of 1,400 for the 400 apartments. Depending on the location, the wait ranges from three months to three years. The lesson: Get on several lists early.

Parents should also know that if they wait until they are sick to move to new housing, they will limit their options significantly. King's Row, an apartment complex that provides meals, housekeeping, and social activities for the elderly in Middletown, New Jersey, requires residents to be—and to remain—"continent, mobile, and oriented to time and space," says manager Bonnie Coffino. An oldster who remembers $90 mortgage payments will be stunned at the cost too. King's Row, though neat and pleasant, isn't much fancier than a good motel, but studio apartments cost $1,864 a month. "You can't live here on Social Security alone," Coffino warns.

Elders whose medical or family history makes them worry about a stroke, Alzheimer's, or any long period of incapacity might want to look at a so-called continuing-care facility. This is one of the fastest-growing new forms of senior housing. It combines apartments for those able to live independently, an "assisted care" section for people who have trouble dressing or using the bathroom, and a nursing home for those needing full-time care.

Continuing-care facilities vary in important ways. Some, like Applewood Estates in Freehold, New Jersey, require a big entry fee up front—between $90,000 and $140,000, depending on the size and type of apartment. Monthly rent and fees for a couple come to another $1,700. However, the rent does not go up if one of them needs to move to the nursing home. The facilities appear similar at Bedford Court, a continuing-care facility run by Marriott in Silver Spring, Maryland. But the finances are much different. Bedford's up-front fee of $7,000 is refundable, with interest, if a tenant leaves; the nursing home, on the other hand, costs $40,000 a year.

Last year Jack Whitwell, a retired Princeton professor, and his wife, Blanche, moved to Applewood. She had fully recovered from a serious illness, but both feared a recurrence might mean moving her to a nursing home. "We were paying a lot for our house and for nursing

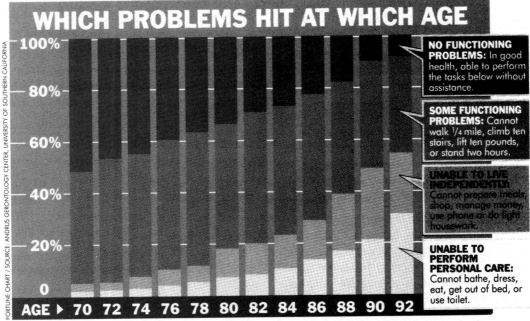

WHICH PROBLEMS HIT AT WHICH AGE

NO FUNCTIONING PROBLEMS: In good health, able to perform the tasks below without assistance.

SOME FUNCTIONING PROBLEMS: Cannot walk ¼ mile, climb ten stairs, lift ten pounds, or stand two hours.

UNABLE TO LIVE INDEPENDENTLY: Cannot prepare meals, shop, manage money, use phone or do light housework.

UNABLE TO PERFORM PERSONAL CARE: Cannot bathe, dress, eat, get out of bed, or use toilet.

AGE ▶ 70 72 74 76 78 80 82 84 86 88 90 92

FORTUNE CHART / SOURCE: ANDRUS GERONTOLOGY CENTER, UNIVERSITY OF SOUTHERN CALIFORNIA

Most people in their 70s are healthy enough to live independently; by their 80s, however, many need help. About 42% of 70-year-olds live to be 85. But only one-quarter of 85-year-olds are in good health.

home insurance, and determined that a continuing-care facility would cost about the same," says Whitwell.

Your parents must be in good health to enter a continuing-care home. Applewood asks to see their medical records and reviews their finances to make sure they can afford the place, says marketing director Jack Titus. Study the track record of the operator of any home you're considering, and have a lawyer familiar with elder care issues review any contracts. Some homes have gone bankrupt, often meaning that residents lost their up-front fee.

Should you plan to move your parents into your own home? Most expert opinion counsels against it. They get cut off from their friends, lose autonomy, and often bicker with their children. "There is no kitchen big enough for two women," argues Rose Dobrof, head of the Brookdale Center on Aging at Hunter College in New York City. Dobrof says her father-in-law made her promise, on her wedding day, that she would never put him in a nursing home. When he could no longer live independently, she felt obliged to move him into her house. He missed his home and friends of 50 years, and his last years were difficult for everyone. "I should never have been pressured to make that promise," she says.

Elder care is not welfare. Many services are available regardless of how affluent the recipient is.

"Get help early. Often it's the people who try to do too much who wind up abusing parents."

Parents sometimes won't admit they can no longer manage by themselves. A mother may hide from the children that her husband has Alzheimer's, or that an expensive new prescription means they can't afford groceries. The result: When the kids go home to visit, they are often aghast at the problems they discover. Agencies that work with caregivers report a spike in the number of desperate phone calls right after Christmas, when all those offspring returning to the family homestead have discovered their parents' lives in disarray.

Suddenly or gradually, ready or probably not, you understand just how hard a time your parents are having as they try to cope unassisted. Diane Piktialis, who heads the elder care referral program for Work/Family Directions, a Boston firm that advises employees at dozens of large corporations, identifies the following signs of trouble: forgetfulness, mood swings, weight loss, lack of grooming, and unpaid bills. Your job is to help your parents keep safe and independent for as long as possible. A surprising number of services are designed to assist you.

If an accident or illness already has your parent in the hospital, contact the social services director there. Virtually every hospital has one, though your doctor may not think to tell you. A good social service person will evaluate a patient's needs for assistance after discharge and arrange his care—even place him in a nursing home. The hospital should not pressure you into taking home a relative you can't handle.

If, after discharge, your parent still needs help from medical professionals, doctors can prescribe an array of services. Cedars Sinai Hospital in Los Angeles, for example, has a small mock village, complete with shops, curbs, kitchens, and teller machines, to help stroke and accident victims regain skills. Occupational therapists can teach an impaired person how to brush his teeth again or cook, and devise solutions to other problems by using such props as oversize buttons and grab bars for bathtubs. Medicare will sometimes pay for such services—but usually only for a few weeks.

If your parent's problems develop more gradually, there are other avenues of assistance. Large corporations often have elder care resources for employees that include literature, videotapes, and seminars on topics ranging from guilt to finances. You can also call on your local government for help. The department responsible is often listed under the Area Agency on Aging. Don't worry, it's not welfare; many elder care services are available regardless of how affluent the recipient is. One man in Santa Monica, California, uses the town's elder care ambulance to get his mother to the doctor because her stretcher won't fit in his limousine.

In most cases the town or county contracts with local nonprofit groups to provide care. A confederation of 350 churches handles virtually all the organized elder care in Memphis. Sister Mary Simon, a Catholic nun, runs the Monmouth County, New Jersey, office on aging. "Call us early," she suggests. "Ninety percent of the time, people wait until they are exhausted from elder care before they seek help. Often it's the people who tried to do too much and get to the end of their rope who wind up abusing their parents."

Nearly all area agencies will send a trained social worker to evaluate your parent's problems and to help arrange services. Most agencies provide transportation for shopping and medical visits, day care centers where otherwise isolated seniors can socialize with peers, and daily home delivery of a hot meal. The last is particularly useful, because the volunteers are trained to look for signs of trouble and report back if the person fails to answer the door. For frail elderly who cannot afford to pay, some agencies will provide homemakers to help with grooming and housekeeping a few hours a week. Waiting lists for free services are often long, but sometimes just a little money will go a long way: Memphis oldsters who pay $3.75 a day can be put on the "upscale" Meals on Wheels route without delay.

For families who can afford it, one of the most useful new services for elder care is the private geriatric care manager. These are typically social workers and nurses who arrange and supervise most of the help an elderly person needs. They are particularly useful if parents live far away from children, or if relations between the generations are strained. New York City case manager Edith Bayme hires, inspects, and fires in-home care aides for clients; pays bills; arranges placement in nursing homes; and even made daily visits to a dying woman whose kids couldn't get to her bedside.

Robert Giese, chief executive of a computer sales and service company in Rochester, New York, hired geriatric care manager Marianne Ewig three years ago after his mother in Milwaukee was found unconscious in a diabetic coma. When she recovered, Ewig noticed a hearing problem and had it diagnosed and treated. Giese says Ewig then realized that his mother was depressed. She arranged for Louise Giese to see a psychiatrist and set up visits between her and other lonely seniors. Once the depression was controlled, Mrs. Giese was emotionally prepared to move to an apartment complex for the elderly that Ewig found.

Private care managers aren't cheap. Ewig charges $65 an hour. Mary-Ellen Siegel, a private geriatric social worker, says the going rate in New York City is $75 to $100 an hour; the bill for a typical case requiring two visits monthly and phone calls to the parent and children could be $250. How do you find the right person? The National Association of Private Geriatric Care Managers in Tucson, Arizona, offers lists of experienced professionals by region. Local organizations that work with the elderly can also make suggestions. Keep in mind that states don't license elder care managers.

Are you a failure as a son or daughter if you have to send Mom to a nursing home? No. For many older people, especially those requiring 24-hour care, a home eventually becomes the best choice. Alzheimer's victims may start wandering the streets at night or leave the stove burning for hours. In other cases a caregiver may be unable to lift the still-at-home parent out of bed.

If your parents pressure you to promise never to send them to a nursing home, don't humor them or lie. Assure them that they will be involved in the decision, that it will happen only if it is absolutely necessary, and that it won't be a surprise.

Evaluate nursing homes carefully. The lady at the front desk will have a big smile, but the care your mother really gets comes down to the low-wage aide, often an immigrant, who hoists her out of bed and changes her diaper. Inquire about staff turnover, training and wages, the ratio of nurses to patients, and the visiting hours, which should be almost unlimited. Many states perform regular inspections of nursing homes; you can get copies of the evaluations from local agencies for the aging.

There are several kinds of nursing home care, and the differences are important. Medicare, "Medigap," and most private health insurance policies pay a limited amount for "skilled nursing home care," which requires the services of doctors, nurses, and rehabilitation experts. They do *not* cover nursing home costs if the patient there can get by with relatively unskilled custodial care. The probability that a woman will enter a nursing home at some point in her life is 1 in 2; for men it is 1 in 3. Many patients stay only a few weeks to recover following hospitalization. But the risk of a long stay—one year or more—is 1 in 7 for men and 1 in 3 for women. The homes cost a bundle—an average of $30,000 a year in 1990, and as much as $50,000 in large cities. Since the median household net worth for people over 65 is $73,500, and the average annual income for senior males is $14,000, according to the American Association of Retired Persons, a long stay will bankrupt many families.

Daniel Fish, a New York attorney specializing in law for the elderly, sees the problem up close. "The phone call I get a lost is from the spouse or children of an elderly person about to be released from the hospital. They've just been told he has to go to a nursing home and that Medicare won't pay. They are hysterical and desperate."

What happens? When the family gets poor enough, a welfare program, Medicaid, will pick up the cost. Rules vary by state, but a single or widowed person can have only about $2,000 in assets to qualify for Medicaid. Depending on the state, a spouse can retain between $13,700 and $68,700 in assets—hardly enough to live off the income.

There is an escape: A person anticipating a long nursing home stay can transfer all his assets to his children or to an irrevocable trust, and thus qualify for Medicaid. The hitch is that the transfer must usually be made 2½ years before Medicaid begins. It is perfectly legal, says Fish, who arranges many asset transfers.

Proponents of transfers view them as ethically akin to shrewd tax-avoidance maneuvers. Opponents say transfers, especially when orchestrated by greedy relatives who don't want to "waste" their inheritance on Dad's nursing home care, take money away from the truly needy.

Once the money has been given away, the parents cannot get it back even if the children are spending it on themselves. Also, good nursing homes usually charge

---

Are you a failure as a son or daughter if you have to send Mom to a nursing home? No.

---

more than Medicaid pays. A person relying solely on Medicaid may have to settle for a shabbier setting. Many good homes, however, will let people who came in paying the full private rate remain once they must use Medicaid.

For families who have made some advance preparations, elder care should not be a crushing burden. It may be a disruptive surprise, but professionals in the field have observed that most children—even harried baby-boomers struggling with young children and midlife crises—assume their responsibilities willingly and without resentment. The caregivers who suffer most are those who try to do too much alone. They should realize they will do themselves and their parents a greater service by seeking help. When your turn comes, be conscientious. Remember, your own children will be watching. And someday you may be on the receiving end of elder care.

Older Problem Drinkers— Long-Term and Late-Life Onset Abusers:

What Triggers Their Drinking?

U. of South Fla. Treatment Program Focuses on Age-Related Problems

**Lawrence Schonfeld, Ph.D.
and Larry W. Dupree, Ph.D.**

Lawrence Schonfeld is Chair, and Larry W. Dupree is former Chair and currently a research faculty member, of the Department of Aging and Mental Health of the Florida Mental Health Institute at the University of South Florida in Tampa.

Growing older exposes an individual to many forms of stress uncommon to younger individuals. While the majority of older people may be relatively healthy and living independently, others experience difficulties in coping with the changes associated with aging. One such indication may be excessive or problem drinking.

About 20 years ago, researchers began to investigate the problem of the elderly alcohol abuser. In the late 1960's and early 1970's, surveys and descriptive studies began to differentiate two major categories of older problem drinkers (Gaitz and Baer, 1971; Rosin and Glatt, 1971; Simon et al., 1968; Zimberg, 1974). The "Early Onset" elderly alcohol abuser was described as an aging alcoholic who has demonstrated significant alcohol-related problems for many years, often beginning abusive drinking by his or her 30's or 40's. This individual is often well known to the medical profession, social services, and the community. According to Zimberg (1984), early onset alcohol abusers have similar personality characteristics to younger alcoholics.

In contrast, the "Late-Life Onset" elderly alcohol abuser may begin abusing alcohol in his or her 50's or 60's. This person is often viewed as a reactive drinker, i.e., one whose problem began after the occurrence of such events as the death of a spouse, retirement, moving away from their original home or state, reduction in income, and impaired health. It is less likely that this individual will be seen as a public inebriate, and more likely that he or she will drink at home and alone.

Early investigations often produced estimates or projections related to the prevalence of the problem, a problem in itself since relatively few elderly utilize mental health or substance abuse treatment services. Previous estimates of elderly living in the community who abuse alcohol range from 2 to 15 percent.

Current literature often adds little to the implications for treatment and simply cites the early researchers in the field. Brody (1982) called for an end to simply repeating these original estimates and stressed the need for new investigations. In the last few years there has been increased interest in the study of the older alcohol abuser.

Problems with Screening

One problem that may cause the older drinker to be overlooked is that many of the instruments used to investigate potential alcohol or drug abuse have been based on younger populations, relying on indicators that may not be relevant for the older individual (Graham, 1986). Brief screening instruments often inquire about a potential alcohol abuser's problems at work, difficulties with the family or marriage, problems with the law (driving while intoxicated), or drinking in the morning.

However, for many of the older problem drinkers, these items would not apply. Despite age of onset (early or late-life) of the drinking problem, most elderly who have been admitted to our treatment programs drank at home, alone, and in response to depressive states. Few were employed, few were active drivers, and many were widowed or divorced, and socially isolated. Thus, there appears to be a need for items on screening assessments which relate to more later-life issues.

Even if we were able to accurately predict or identify alcohol-related problems through a screening instrument, few older individuals enter treatment for alcohol abuse. There are numerous reasons for this underutilization. Substance abuse treatment programs, especially those that are publicly funded, are inundated with young people who abuse illegal drugs. Private substance abuse treatment is expensive, especially for those on limited incomes, with limited insurance coverage.

In addition, we must consider the person's reluctance to enter treatment and difficulty in "navigating" through social services for the first time, as well as service providers' difficulty in identifying older problem drinkers. Dementia or other cognitive impairment may be identified as problems, when in fact alcohol abuse may be responsible for changes in mood, physical functioning, or cognition.

From 1979 to 1981, the Gerontology Alcohol Project (Dupree, Broskowski, and Schonfeld, 1984), admitted late-life onset elderly alcohol abusers into a treatment program using cognitive/behavioral, skills building techniques within a Relapse Prevention framework

(Marlatt and Gordon, 1980, 1985). Each individual was assessed for the events and emotional states that preceded the consumption of the *first* drink on a "typical" day of drinking, e.i., high-risk situations. In most cases, loneliness and depression preceded the first drink. Treatment often focused on rebuilding the social support network, self-management approaches for overcoming negative emotional states, and general problem solving.

Almost three quarters of the individuals who completed the program and a subsequent one-year follow-up maintained their drinking goals (in most cases abstinence). From this program, additional questions were raised, primarily: Would the program be as effective with early onset individuals? What differences would be observed between the two categories of elderly alcohol abusers? And, would there be a need for separate treatment modalities based on age of onset, just as there may be differences in treatment needs for young and elderly alcohol abusers?

A newer program, the Substance Abuse Program for the Elderly, began in 1986. This program is aimed at elderly alcohol abusers (regardless of age of onset) and individuals who abuse or misuse medications. Because of the program's wider admission criteria, comparisons of the antecedent conditions to recent drinking for early onset and late-life onset alcohol abusers were possible (Schonfeld, Dupree, and Merritt, 1987).

Schonfeld and Dupree (in press) compared the admission data from 23 early and 23 late-life onset alcohol abusers over age 60, matching pairs of individuals for age and sex. Results indicate that the early onset elderly alcohol abuser had significantly higher depression scores (Mean = 17.1) on the Beck Depression Inventory (Beck, 1972) than did their late-life counterparts (Mean = 6.6). Similarly, as indicated by life satisfaction scores (Neugarten, Havighurst, and Tobin, 1961) and trait anxiety scores (Patterson, O'Sullivan, and Spielberger, 1980), more severe psychological problems were present in the early onset group.

All 46 people had been asked to focus on their drinking in the 30 days before their last drink prior to admission. Both

groups consumed alcoholic beverages on an average of about 22 of those 30 days. Both groups consumed substantial quantities on a "typical day" of drinking. Alcohol consumption was measured in terms of Standard Ethanol Content units or SECs. One SEC is the equivalent of one ounce of 100 proof liquor. On a typical day of drinking, the early onset group consumed 17.5 SECs and the late-life onset group consumed 12.4 SECs. Although the difference in quantity consumed was not statistically significant, frequency of intoxication was. The early onset group reported that they were intoxicated an average of 16 days out of the 30-day period as opposed to 8 days for the late-life onset group. Finally, the individuals in the early onset group were more likely to drop out of treatment (56 percent dropped out) than late-life onset individuals (only 26 percent dropped out).

Previous literature suggested similarities in personality between the early onset individual and young alcohol abusers (Zimberg, 1984). If this were true, perhaps they would use alcohol in a similar manner, i.e., in response to interpersonal problems, peer pressure, conflicts with spouse, etc., rather than depression or isolation. Because such findings would have implications for treatment, the determinants of drinking on a "typical day" of drinking for the early and late onset older alcohol abusers were investigated as derived from a structured interview (the GAP Drinking Profile; Dupree, et al., 1984).

What the interviews revealed were many similarities—not between early onset older drinkers and young drinkers—but between the early onset and late onset older drinkers. Most were steady (daily) drinkers, who drank at home and alone, and in response to such negative emotional states as sadness, loneliness, depression, and boredom. Many were widowed, divorced, and retired. Social support networks were minimal. If such similarities hold true for elderly alcohol abusers as a general population, it may indicate that while the etiology and duration may differ, the antecedents to current drinking behavior are similar.

The similarity of current drinking behavior in the two groups of elderly individuals may be due to the age-related problems (increased losses, death of a loved one, retirement, etc.) predominating in their lives. A second possibility is that the two groups experience alcohol abuse and the diminution of social support through different avenues. The late-life onset individual may begin to abuse alcohol in response to the losses, whereas, the early onset individual may have caused some of the losses or alienation of family and friends by continued alcohol abuse over many years.

Age-Specific Treatment?

As indicated by our 1-year follow-up data, cognitive behavioral approaches seem to be effective with older individuals, but similar results have been found with younger treatment groups (Chaney, O'Leary, and Marlatt, 1978). Some have suggested, without supportive data, that we "mainstream" the older person with the younger individual, rather than develop age-specific programs (Brown, 1986). However, many of the treatment plans developed in our program through identification of each individual's personal antecedents to drinking were aimed at increasing socialization, decreasing negative self-statements, and improving self-esteem, rather than dealing with interpersonal conflicts and peer pressure. If we were to combine different age populations into group therapy, the older, less vocal and perhaps less self-disclosing individual might not have an opportunity to express his or her needs and learn skills for overcoming losses and coping with problems.

The issue of age-specific programs has been addressed in several studies. Janik and Dunham (1983), using data gathered by the National Institute on Alcohol Abuse and Alcoholism, indicated that elderly alcoholics were just as successful as younger individuals in treatment programs, implying that age-specific programs were unnecessary. However, this finding only indicates the relative effectiveness of treatment for the two age groups. To further investigate the potential benefits of specific programs, Atkinson, et al., (1985) and Kofoed, et al.,

(1984, 1987) compared elderly alcoholics who were entered into a mixed-age group treatment with a group of elderly subjects in age-specific treatment. They found that those in the age-specific group treatment remained in treatment longer and completed treatment more often.

Age-specific treatment has some advantages. The approach should promote more cohesiveness in group treatment. Whereas confrontational approaches have been used with younger populations, less confrontive and more supportive approaches would serve to focus on the needs of the older individual. The needs and issues of younger individuals often relate to peer pressure, interpersonal conflicts, work-related problems, marital difficulties, and parental responsibilities. For the older individual, drinking appears to be a reaction to losses. Treatment would emphasize rebuilding of the social support network (Dupree, et al., 1984; Zimberg, 1984) and coping with problems common to later life. For instance, group treatment could discuss adjustment to retirement, loss of income, widowhood, and coping skills to handle feelings of loneliness and boredom when finances and transportation are limited.

Few of the elderly we have treated were working, many were widowed or divorced, and lived at a considerable distance from their adult children. If the elderly were entered into mixed-age group treatment or support groups, the common denominator of discussion would most likely become the consumption of alcohol. The potential danger is that while abstinence might be stressed, the high-risk situations that led to alcohol abuse prior to treatment. if not attended to, would result in relapse after treatment. These high risk situations seem to be different for the elderly population.

The disadvantages for the specific programs for the elderly alcohol abuser are largely in terms of cost. The elderly as a population underutilize substance abuse services (Kola, Kosberg, and Joyce, 1984; Kosberg and McCarthy, 1985) making it difficult to justify the cost of personnel, time, and money, when client census is low. Low utilization rates might be due to an inability of the "sys-

tem" to identify alcohol problems; the reluctance of social service workers to label someone as an alcohol abuser; or to the amount of resources which need to be devoted to younger populations of substance abusers. Whatever the reason, given the low admission rate and the reality of budgets, specific programs for the elderly may be a low priority.

It would be repetitious with other researchers if we were to say the problem of elderly alcohol abuse needs further verification of its extent and treatment implications. The problem may continue to be overlooked due to the older problem drinker's lack of visibility. However, as the number and proportion of older people increases, alcohol abuse in the elderly is likely to become less hidden.

REFERENCES

Atkinson, R.M., Turner, J.A., Kofoed, L.L. and Tolson, R.L. (1985) Early versus late onset alcoholism in older persons: Preliminary findings. *Alcoholism*, 9, 513-515.

Beck, A.T. (1972) *Depression: Causes and treatment.* Philadelphia: University of Pennsylvania Press.

Brody, J.A. (1982) Aging and alcohol abuse. *Journal of the American Geriatric Society*, 30, 123-126.

Brown, N. (1986) Mainstreaming reduces elderly isolation. *Alcoholism and Addiction*, 7 (1), p. 41-42.

Chaney, E.F., O'Leary, M.R., and Marlatt, G.A. (1978) Skill training with alcoholics. *Journal of Consulting and Clinical Psychology*, 48, 305-316.

Dupree, L.W., Broskowski, H., and Schonfeld, L. (1984) The Gerontology Alcohol Project: A behavioral treatment program for elderly alcohol abusers. *The Gerontologist*, 24, 510-516.

Gaitz, C.M. and Baer, P.E. (1971) Characteristics of elderly patients with alcoholism. *Archives of General Psychiatry*, 24, 372-378.

Graham, K. (1986) Identifying and measuring alcohol abuse among the elderly: Serious problems with existing instrumentation. *Journal of Studies on Alcohol*, 47 (4), 322-326.

Janik, S.W. and Dunham, R.G. (1983) A nationwide examination of the need for specific alcoholism treatment programs for the elderly. *Journal of Studies on Alcohol*, 44, 307-317.

Kofoed, L., Tolson, R., Atkinson, R., Toth, R., & Turner, J. (1984) Elderly groups in alcoholism clinic. In R.M. Atkinson (Ed.) *Alcohol and drug abuse in old age.* Washington D.C: American Psychiatric Press, Monograph Series, 35-48.

Kofoed, L., Tolson, R., Atkinson, R., Toth, R., Turner, J. (1987) Treatment compliance of older alcoholics: An elder-specific approach is superior to "mainstreaming". *Journal of Studies on Alcohol*, 48 (1), 47-51.

Kola, L.A., Kosberg, J.I. and Joyce, K. (1984) Assessment of policies and practices of local programs for the aged toward the problem drinker, *The Gerontologist*, 24 (5), 517-521.

Kosberg, J.I. and McCarthy, E.J. (1985) Problem drinking participants in programs for the elderly: Programmatic considerations. *Journal of Applied Gerontology*, 4 (2), 20-29.

Marlatt, G.A. Gordon, J.R. (1980) Determinants of relapse: Implications for the maintenance of behavior change. In P.O. Davidson & E.O. Davidson (Eds.) *Behavior therapy assessment: Diagnosis, design, and evaluation.* N.Y.: Springer.

Marlatt, G.,A. & Gordon, J.R. (1985) *Relapse Prevention: Maintenance strategies in the treatment of addictive behaviors.* N.Y.: Guilford Press.

Neugarten, B., Havighurst, R., and Tobin, S. (1961) The measurement of life satisfaction. *Journal of Gerontology*, 16, 134-143.

Patterson, R.L., O'Sullivan, M.J., and Spielberger, C.O. (1980) Measurement of state trait anxiety in elderly mental health clients. *Journal of Behavioral Assessment*, 2, 89-97.

Rosin, A.J. and Glatt, M.M. (1971) Alcohol excess in the elderly. *Quarterly Journal of Studies on Alcohol*, 32, 53-59.

Schonfeld, L., Dupree, L.W., & Merritt, S. (1987) Alcohol abuse and the elderly: Comparison of early and late-life onset. Presented at the 95th Annual Convention of the American Psychological Association, New York.

Schonfeld, L. and Dupree, L.W. (in press) Determinants of drinking for early and late-life onset elderly alcohol abusers. *Journal of Studies on Alcohol.*

Simon, A., Epstein, L.J., and Reynolds, L. (1968) Alcoholism in the geriatric mentally ill. *Geriatrics*, 23, 125-131.

Zimberg, S. (1974) The elderly alcoholic. *The Gerontologist*, 14, 221-224.

Zimberg, S. (1984) Diagnosis and the management of the elderly alcoholic. In R.M. Atkinson (Ed.) *Alcohol and drug abuse in old age.* Washington D.C: American Psychiatric Press, Monograph Series, 23-34.

American Maturity

SUMMARY *Americans aged 65 and older are a fast-growing and formidable market. Some older people move to be closer to their family, and some move to a better climate, but most stay put. The "young" elderly, aged 65 to 74, are a relatively affluent and healthy group. The "older" elderly, aged 75 and older, are far more likely to be disabled. Elderly people with disabilities cluster in the fast-growing Southeast, while the Midwest has a slow-growing but healthy elderly population.*

Diane Crispell and William H. Frey

Diane Crispell is executive editor of American Demographics *and editorial director of* The Numbers News *and* American Demographics Books. *William H. Frey is research scientist and associate director for training at the Population Studies Center, University of Michigan, Ann Arbor.*

As your car speeds down Interstate 95, pine trees and scrub palms blur into a wash of green and brown. You could be anywhere in central Florida—until you reach The Watertower. A huge blue inverted waterdrop marks the entrance to "Palm Coast," America's newest population oasis. Stop the car at the edge of Palm Coast. Get out, and you can almost hear the town creaking under the weight of rapid growth and demographic change. This is Flagler County, the place with the fastest-growing elderly population in the country.

In the 1980s, an explosion of Americans aged 65 and older added a new dimension to demographic change. Because of increased longevity and the aging of larger generations, most U.S. counties saw their elderly populations grow rapidly. The 1990 census counted 31.2 million Americans aged 65 or older, a 22 percent increase since 1980. Elderly people are now 13 percent of the U.S. adult population, up from 11 percent in 1980.

Growth in the mature market presents a new set of opportunities for businesses. But to reach mature Americans effectively, businesses must understand this market's considerable diversity. One aspect of this diversity is geographic. America's elderly populations are growing in different places for different reasons.

CLOSER TO FAMILY

Willie Tomlinson, a 74-year-old retired teacher, lived in the same house in Falls Church, Virginia, for 47 years. Then she moved to Peachtree City, Georgia, a small but rapidly growing town in Fayette County. She moved to be closer to her son, a colonel stationed at nearby Fort McPherson.

Tomlinson's story is a common one among older residents of Peachtree City. Retirees move to the planned developments southwest of Atlanta because of their low crime rates, unhurried and friendly atmosphere, temperate climate, and other amenities. But the main reason, many willingly concede, is to be near their children and grandchildren.

At first glance, elderly people may seem isolated. The 1990 census found that fewer than two-thirds of the elderly live in family households, compared with 83 percent of adults aged 18 to 64. More than one in four people aged 65 or older lives alone, compared with 9 percent of younger adults. But at least one demographic trend keeps older people from getting too lonely. Life expectancy has risen for both men and

women. Consequently, couples who don't divorce may live together well past the age of 65.

Today's elderly people are nearly as likely as younger adults to be married (in each group, about half are married). About 56 percent of people aged 65 or older either head a family or are married to a family householder. Their numbers have grown 25 percent since 1980, when the proportion stood at 55 percent.

Even so, women live an average of seven years longer than men. Moreover, most women marry older men. As a result, nearly half of elderly women are widowed, compared with just 14 percent of elderly men. The number of elderly people who live alone grew 27 percent during the 1980s, and the proportion who live alone rose from 28 percent to 30 percent. Nearly 80 percent of elderly Americans who live alone are women, and elderly people make up 40 percent of all single-person households, according to the census.

But living alone and being lonely are two different things. Other research shows that the share of elderly parents who live within 25 miles of adult children has hovered around 75 percent for the past 30 years. A 1992 *Modern Maturity/Roper Organization* study finds that 58 percent of grandparents see their grandchildren quite often. Grown children and their offspring often remain within drop-in distance of grandma and grandpa. And sometimes older people relocate to be near the kids and grandkids, especially if the kids have moved to a southern clime.

A BETTER CLIMATE

Migrants young and old accounted for virtually all of the growth in Flagler County during the 1980s. Thirty years ago, the Palm Coast region was a rural area known best for growing telephone poles. Then International Telephone and Telegraph (ITT) changed its focus from tree farming to city building. Flagler's population grew 163 percent during the 1980s, making it the fastest-growing county in the U.S. Its elderly population grew even faster, by 267 percent. But in seven of the years between 1967 and 1987, the number of deaths in Flagler exceeded the number of births.

Flagler County lies on the Atlantic coast midway between St. Augustine and Daytona Beach, at the eastern fringes of the Orlando and Jacksonville metropolitan areas. In this way, it is similar to many other counties that have fast-growing elderly populations. Magnets of elderly growth cluster in the coastal regions, the Southwest, and the Rocky Mountains. Some are large, economically prosperous areas. Others are rural counties where the climate and scenery attract younger and older people alike.

Four of the top-ten growth counties for the elderly are also among the fastest-growing counties for all ages. These are Flagler and Hernando in Florida; Fayette, Georgia; and Matanuska-Susitna Borough, Alaska. In contrast, a broad swath of counties in the nation's heartland—including the farmbelt, rustbelt, and oil-patch states—saw slow growth or

even declines in both their younger and older populations during the 1980s. These places had struggling economies that could do little to attract or retain people.

As a result, places with fast-growing elderly populations are often better-off and healthier markets than those with slow-growing elderly populations. Many are retirement areas that attract long-distance migrants, both seasonal and permanent. Long-distance moves are especially popular among "sixtysomething" couples who have both the financial resources and wanderlust to relocate during their early elderly years. Retirement migrants of the 1980s favored Hernando, St. Lucie, Collier, and Marion counties in Florida. They also chose newly popular retirement areas in South Atlantic coastal states (Beaufort County, South Carolina) and the Rocky Mountains (Summit County, Colorado).

Retirees may not be employed, but their presence creates jobs and consumer demand. "The average retirement migrant household's overall impact on the local economy is $71,600 a year," according to a 1992 analysis prepared for the Appalachian Regional Commission. Estimates of the number of jobs retirees create range from one-third to one full job for each new migrant.

The longer a retirement migrant stays put, the better for the magnet area. "Major durable expenditures are not so much a function of age as . . . the length of time a household resides in an area," says the commission report.

Retirement migrants like Willie Tomlinson are one reason for Fayette County's fast-growing elderly population, which ranked fourth in the U.S. during the 1980s. But the main reason is a phenomenon called "aging in place."

In the 1970s, thousands of people moved to rural Fayette County in search of roomy homes in tranquil subdivisions, good schools, and a quick commute to Atlanta. "It's not so much that a lot of older people have moved into the county, but that a lot of middle-aged people moved

in a while ago. Now they have gotten old," says Bart Lewis of the Atlanta Regional Commission.

Most counties with fast-growing elderly populations have also experienced aging in place. Many of these are affluent suburbs or exurbs of small metropolitan areas. These areas have spent the past few decades building up a sizable working-age population, and now those migrants are getting older. Nevada, Alaska, Colorado, New Mexico, Utah, California, and Texas have many such communities.

Suburban areas all over the country are becoming havens for retirees who choose not to move. They include Fayette and Gwinnett counties in suburban Atlanta, Virginia's Fairfax and Prince William counties in suburban Washington, D.C., and Howard County in suburban Baltimore. Many other counties with fast-growing suburban elderly populations don't appear on the top-50 list: these include St. Charles County in suburban St. Louis, Anoka County in suburban Minneapolis-St. Paul, Macomb County in suburban Detroit, and Bucks County in suburban Philadelphia.

THE "YOUNG" ELDERLY

The scattering of counties with large shares of elderly people are tempting targets for businesses that market to mature Americans. But a focus on total elderly share can be misleading. Some counties with high elderly shares have fast-growing older populations, while in many others, elderly populations have declined.

A good way to understand elderly growth is to divide the elderly into two age groups: 65 to 74, and 75 and older. In 1990, the U.S. had 18 million 65-to-74-year-olds. Most people in this group live with a spouse, are in good health, and are financially comfortable. They are a prime target for leisure markets such as travel and recreation. But most of the 13 million Americans aged 75 or older are women. "Older" elderly people have poorer health, and they are more likely to live alone, with relatives, or in institutions. They are a different market than the "younger" elderly, and they also concentrate in different places.

Younger elderly are more likely than their older counterparts to move, and they are also the ones who age into "elderhood" by staying put. As a result, counties with high shares of young elderly are the best

places to find fast-growing elderly populations. Seven of the top-ten counties for share of 65-to-74-year-olds are also among the 50 fastest-growing elderly counties. All are in Florida: Hernando, Charlotte, Highlands, Citrus, Flagler, Indian River, and Martin. But only two of the top-ten counties for share of people aged 75 or older are also on the top-50 growth list (Highlands and Charlotte).

Many counties with large shares of very old people have lost younger people. As a result, the aged-in-place in these counties make up a bigger piece of a diminishing pie. They cluster in rural regions and in cities with sustained economic declines. The exceptions are older retirement communities that have seen their younger elderly age in place. Florida counties such as Sarasota, Pasco, and Pinellas have high concentrations of both younger old and older old people.

Despite its concentration of affluent older people, Fayette, Georgia, is not a true retirement county. Only 7 percent of its population is aged 65 or older, lower than the average for Atlanta or the U.S. But James Price, executive director of Fayette Senior Services, believes that most of the county's middle-aged residents will stay put. He wants to expand his operations by opening a new senior center. Peachtree City grew from about 2,000 residents in 1975 to 22,000 in 1990 and is planning for about 45,000 residents by 2000. The area should draw active retirees with its abundant parks, two golf courses and lakes, an amphitheater, and numerous pools and tennis courts.

Many independent elderly move to retirement communities while they are still physically and financially able to enjoy recreational and social activities. Retirement meccas like Peachtree City have sprouted up in many areas of the South and West. Not all of these meccas have the kind of family ties that Peachtree City residents commonly mention, but they make up for it in other ways. Retirement migrants value companionship with peers, and they insist on access to high-quality health services.

DISABLED IN THE SOUTHEAST

Even the healthiest elderly must face the future possibility of long-term disability. This is an especially crucial concern for those who don't have family nearby. The number of elderly people living in group quarters, mostly in nursing homes, grew 17 percent during the 1980s. The share of the population in group quarters remained stable, at about 6 percent.

Although the share of elderly in nursing homes is small at a given point in time, a person's risk of being institutionalized later in life is high. Almost half (43 percent) of people who turned 65 in 1990 may end up in a nursing home at some time in their lives, according to Peter Kemper and Christopher Murtaugh. Even vigorous states like Alaska, which had the smallest number and share of people in nursing homes in 1990, have a fast-growing older population at risk of becoming institutionalized. Three of the top-ten counties for growth of the elderly population in the 1980s were Alaskan boroughs.

Younger people take their good health for granted, but older people cannot. Chronic conditions begin to accumulate after age 45. Twenty-four percent of people aged 65 to 74 have hearing impairments, 38 percent have high blood pressure, and

> **Almost two-thirds of elderly Americans are free of serious chronic health problems.**

44 percent have arthritis, according to the National Center for Health Statistics' 1989 National Health Interview Survey. The share with cataracts rises from 11 percent of those aged 65 to 74 to 23 percent of those aged 75 or older. Reflexes also slow with age, and activities like shopping and driving become difficult and unsafe.

The 1990 census asked people about three kinds of limitations that affect their daily lives. In the census definition, people with disabilities have a physical or mental condition lasting six months or more. A work disability prevents them from working or limits the work they can do. People with "mobility limitations" have difficulty getting out of the house on their own, and those with "self-care limitations" have trouble doing things like dressing, bathing, and feeding themselves. Some people have all three types of limitations; others have just one or two.

All told, 62 percent of noninstitutionalized elderly Americans have no limitations that interfere with their daily lives. But 33 percent are unable to work as much as they want to, 16 percent have a mobility limitation, and 12 percent have a self-care limitation. Seven percent have both mobility and self-care limitations.

Elderly men are less likely than elderly women to have mobility or self-care limitations. One reason is that more elderly men are in the 65-to-74 age group, but this doesn't explain all of the difference. Even among 65-to-74-year-olds, 15 percent of women have trouble getting around or taking care of themselves, compared with 12 percent of men. Among those aged 75 or older, 34 percent of women have mobility or self-care limitations, compared with 24 percent of men. Women of all ages are more likely than men to suffer from chronic conditions such as arthritis, bursitis, and osteoporosis.

> **Elderly men are less likely than elderly women to have mobility or self-care limitations.**

SLOW-GROWING BUT HEALTHY

It could be that mountain air is good for elderly circulation systems. Perhaps only sturdy lungs can endure the high altitudes. Whatever the reason, six of the top-ten counties for elderly people who suffer from no mobility or self-care limitations are in the Mountain states of Colorado, Wyoming, and Utah. Most of the 50 best counties for physically fit elderly are scattered throughout the North and West, with five each in Colorado, Minnesota, and

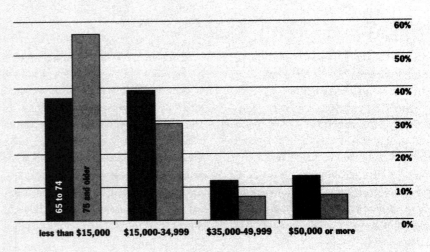

Mature Money

The majority of older elderly householders have low household incomes, while younger elderly fall in the low- to middle-income range.

(percent of households headed by people aged 65 to 74 and 75 and older by 1989 household income)

Source: 1990 census

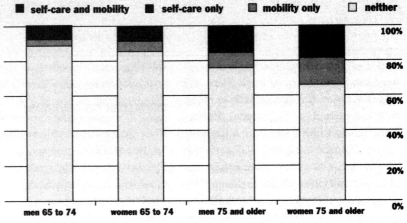

Reaching Limits

Even among older elderly women, two-thirds have no mobility or self-care limitations that interfere with their daily lives.

(percent of men and women aged 65 to 74 and 75 and older by type of limitation, 1990)

■ self-care and mobility   ■ self-care only   ■ mobility only   □ neither

Source: 1990 census

Wisconsin; four each in Idaho and Nebraska; three each in Washington and Alaska; two each in Montana, Kansas, North Dakota, Utah, and Wyoming; and one each in Oregon, South Dakota, Vermont, Nevada, Pennsylvania, Maine, New Hampshire, and California. But only two counties on this list are in the South, both in Florida. Altogether, there are 621 U.S. counties where at least 85 percent of the elderly population are free of mobility or self-care limitations.

Maturing Rapidly

Florida is not the only state experiencing rapid growth among its elderly population. Counties in Nevada, Georgia, and even Alaska rank high on the top-50 list for elderly growth.

(counties ranked by percent increase in number aged 65 and older, 1980-90, and total aged 65 and older, 1990)

rank	county (metropolitan area)	number aged 65 and older	percent increase 1980-90
1	Flagler, FL	7,345	266.7%
2	Hernando, FL (Tampa-St. Petersburg-Clearwater)	31,048	186.1
3	Nye, NV	2,179	166.4
4	Fayette, GA (Atlanta)	4,468	159.5
5	Matanuska-Susitna, AK	1,866	155.6
6	Summit, CO	300	145.9
7	Kenai Peninsula, AK	2,015	143.7
8	Anchorage, AK (Anchorage)	8,258	134.6
9	Los Alamos, NM (Santa Fe)	1,668	131.0
10	Washington, UT	7,898	127.0
11	Mohave, AZ	19,273	125.5
12	Clark, NV (Las Vegas)	77,678	121.2
13	Douglas, NV	3,352	116.3
14	Douglas, CO (Denver PMSA)	2,524	115.7
15	St. Lucie, FL (Fort Pierce)	31,534	113.1
16	Collier, FL (Naples)	34,583	111.0
17	Okaloosa, FL (Fort Walton Beach)	13,319	109.0
18	Marion, FL (Ocala)	43,189	106.7
19	Indian River, FL	24,592	101.9
20	Beaufort, SC	10,664	101.1
21	Pitkin, CO	557	100.4
22	Fairbanks North Star, AK	2,540	99.1
23	Okeechobee, FL	4,807	96.1
24	Gwinnett, GA (Atlanta)	16,776	95.9
25	Virginia Beach city, VA Norfolk-Virginia Beach-Newport News	23,214	94.9
26	Brunswick, NC	7,494	94.8
27	Fairfax, Fairfax,* Falls Church,* VA (Washington)	57,118	94.4%
28	Arapahoe, CO (Denver)	29,171	94.3
29	Horry, SC	18,229	94.0
30	Lyon, NV	3,019	93.7
31	Yavapai, AZ	25,613	92.0
32	Columbia, GA (Augusta)	3,872	91.5
33	Brevard, FL (Melbourne-Titusville-Palm Beach)	66,382	91.5
34	Chesterfield, Colonial Heights,* VA (Richmond-Petersburg)	15,305	91.1
35	Santa Rosa, FL (Pensacola)	7,759	90.6
36	Charlotte, FL	37,489	88.8
37	Howard, MD (Baltimore)	11,399	87.5
38	Sandoval, NM	6,385	86.6
39	Citrus, FL	29,283	84.5
40	St. Johns, FL (Jacksonville)	13,791	83.9
41	Hood, TX	4,668	83.1
42	Highlands, FL	22,897	82.8
43	Carson City, NV	6,041	82.3
44	Clay, FL (Jacksonville)	8,984	82.2
45	Lee, FL (Fort Myers-Cape Coral)	83,003	81.0
46	Nevada, CA	14,251	81.0
47	Davis, UT (Salt Lake City-Ogden)	11,567	77.8
48	Prince William, Manassas,* Manassas Park,* VA (Washington)	8,167	77.5
49	Juneau, AK	1,364	76.9
50	Martin, FL (Fort Pierce)	27,690	76.9

U.S. average equals 22.3 percent.
* Independent city.
Note: Includes only counties with 10,000 or more people in 1990. Metro areas defined before December 1992.

Source: 1990 and 1980 censuses

Because physical condition deteriorates with age, it seems contradictory that regions with high concentrations of relatively fit elderly people are the same places that have high shares of people aged 75 or older. But if you insist on living in Minnesota at the age of 80, you should be able to shovel your driveway. Those who can't take the cold move south, whatever their age.

One of the biggest unknowns older people face is whether they will become disabled and how much it will cost.

Elderly people who are plagued with arthritis and other disabling conditions are clustered in milder climates. They are also found in regions where the jobs are dangerous (such as coal mining) and poverty is common. Kentucky has six of the top-ten counties for share of elderly with mobility or self-care limitations: Knox, Breathitt, Lawrence, Leslie, Letcher, and Clay. All but one of the top-50 counties for

Younger Old

Nine of the top-ten counties with the highest share of population aged 65 to 74 are in Florida.

(counties ranked by percent aged 65 to 74, and number aged 65 to 74, 1990)

rank	county (metropolitan area)	number aged 65 to 74	percent aged 65 to 74
1	Hernando, FL (Tampa-St. Petersburg-Clearwater)	21,312	21.1%
2	Charlotte, FL	23,195	20.9
3	Highlands, FL	14,081	20.6
4	Citrus, FL	18,525	19.8
5	Llano, TX	2,273	19.5
6	Flagler, FL	5,496	19.2
7	Pasco, FL (Tampa-St. Petersburg-Clearwater)	53,270	19.0
8	Sarasota, FL (Sarasota)	49,857	18.0
9	Indian River, FL	15,444	17.1
10	Martin, FL (Fort Pierce)	16,828	16.7
11	Baxter, AR	5,137	16.5
12	Lake, FL	24,641	16.2
13	Roscommon, MI	3,189	16.1
14	Curry, OR	3,033	15.7
15	Manatee, FL (Bradenton)	33,028	15.6
16	Northumberland, VA	1,638	15.6
17	Sharp, AR	2,191	15.5
18	Lee, FL (Fort Myers-Cape Coral)	51,424	15.4
19	Yavapai, AZ	16,351	15.2
20	Van Buren, AR	2,112	15.1

U.S. average equals 7.3 percent.
Note: Includes only counties with 10,000 or more people. Metro areas defined before December 1992.

Source: 1990 census

Older Old

Just 5.3 percent of the U.S. population is aged 75 and older, but 15 percent are this old in Llano County, Texas.

(counties ranked by percent aged 75 and older, and number aged 75 and older, 1990)

rank	county (metropolitan area)	number aged 75 and older	percent aged 65 to 74
1	Llano, TX	1,692	14.6%
2	Sarasota, FL (Sarasota)	39,551	14.2
3	Cloud, KS	1,500	13.6
4	Pasco, FL (Tampa-St. Petersburg-Clearwater)	37,553	13.4
5	Highlands, FL	8,816	12.9
6	Charlotte, FL	14,294	12.9
7	Baxter, AR	3,970	12.7
8	Pinellas, FL (Tampa-St. Petersburg-Clearwater)	106,792	12.5
9	Manatee, FL (Bradenton)	26,380	12.5
10	Monona, IA	1,231	12.3
11	Marion, KS	1,578	12.2
12	Marshall, KS	1,425	12.2
13	Iron, MI	1,599	12.1
14	Bosque, TX	1,831	12.1
15	Comanche, TX	1,615	12.1
16	Kiowa, OK	1,363	12.0
17	Linn, MO	1,641	11.8
18	Cottonwood, MN	1,494	11.8
19	Sharp, AR	1,643	11.7
20	Montgomery, IA	1,405	11.6

U.S. average equals 5.3 percent.
Note: Includes only counties with 10,000 or more people. Metro areas defined before December 1992.

Source: 1990 census

share of elderly with limitations are in the South—13 in Kentucky, 12 in Mississippi, 7 in Alabama, 4 each in West Virginia and Georgia, 2 each in Virginia and Oklahoma, and 1 each in Arkansas, Louisiana, South Carolina, Tennessee, and Florida. Apache County, Arizona, is the only nonsouthern county on the top-50 list, and it also happens to rank number 1 in its share of elderly with mobility or self-care limitations.

Apache is the northeasternmost county in Arizona, bordering on both New Mexico and Utah. Thirty-eight percent of its elderly residents are restricted by mobility or self-care limitations. The county is rural and poor, and two-thirds of its residents live on the Navajo Reservation. Native Americans, particularly elders, are known to suffer from poor health. But the high limitation rate may be due to both the phys-

ical condition of older Indians and the lack of public transportation, according to Joe Weidman of the Northern Arizona Council of Governments. "The older people on the reservations have a hard time getting out of the house. They are quite isolated," says Weidman. On the other hand, there's no place they really have to go. "The young people often live and work off-reservation," says Weidman. "But they come back on weekends to be with their families."

THE ECONOMICS OF OLD AGE

One of the biggest unknowns older people face is whether they will become disabled and how much it will cost. In the 1980s, Social Security payments kept up with the cost of living better than salaries did. Many of today's elderly also enjoy substantial pensions. Yet advancing age usually brings

declining income and increasing health costs. Forty-five percent of households headed by someone aged 65 or older had a 1989 annual income below $15,000, according to the census. Many householders aged 75 or older are widowed women without substantial survivor or retirement benefits, and 56 percent of householders this old had 1989 household incomes below $15,000.

The share of affluent elderly households is not insignificant, however. Eleven percent of households headed by someone aged 65 or older had 1989 incomes of $50,000 or more, and 4 percent had incomes of $75,000 or more. These people often hoard considerable assets and savings. Except for health care, older people often spend less than younger adults do; their homes are paid off, and they are no longer supporting children.

The Healthiest Elderly

The most physically fit older bodies are in nonmetro areas of the West and Midwest.

(counties ranked by percent of population aged 65 and older with no mobility or self-care limitations, and number aged 65 and older, 1990)

rank	county (metropolitan area)	number aged 65 and older	percent without limitations
1	Pitkin, CO	549	94.0%
2	Gunnison, CO	615	93.7
3	Union, SD	1,592	93.0
4	McLean, ND	1,869	92.9
5	Lincoln, WY	1,265	92.7
6	Summit, CO	283	92.2
7	Curry, OR	4,669	92.1
8	Summit, UT	892	91.9
9	Jefferson, WA	4,089	91.6
10	Routt, CO	772	91.6
11	Holt, NE	2,011	91.5
12	Whitman, WA	3,527	91.4
13	Gooding, ID	1,926	91.3
14	Blaine, ID	871	91.2
15	Lamoille, VT	2,018	91.1
16	Seward, KS	1,701	91.1
17	San Juan, WA	2,064	91.1
18	Douglas, NV	3,295	90.9
19	Swift, MN	2,365	90.8
20	Marshall, MN	1,921	90.6

U.S. average equals 79.9 percent.
Note: Includes only counties with 10,000 or more people. For definitions of limitations, see text.

Source: 1990 census

The Sickest Elderly

Elderly people who have trouble getting around concentrate in the poorer southern states.

(counties ranked by percent of population aged 65 and older with mobility or self-care limitations, and number aged 65 and older, 1990)

rank	county (metropolitan area)	number aged 65 and older	percent with limitations
1	Apache, AZ	3,863	38.2%
2	Lowndes, AL	1,605	37.4
3	Knox, KY	3,640	37.2
4	Breathitt, KY	1,609	37.2
5	Lawrence, KY	1,732	37.0
6	Leslie, KY	1,198	36.2
7	Clarke, AL	3,457	36.1
8	Montgomery, MS	1,964	36.1
9	Letcher, KY	3,080	36.0
10	Clay, KY	2,201	35.9
11	Dickenson, VA	2,085	35.8
12	Jefferson Davis, MS	1,950	35.7
13	Smith, MS	2,028	35.7
14	Greene, MS	1,145	35.6
15	Floyd, KY	4,923	35.5
16	Wayne, MS	2,238	35.4
17	George, MS	1,827	35.4
18	Noxubee, MS	1,668	35.4
19	Mingo, WV	3,394	35.3
20	Simpson, MS	2,931	35.1

U.S. average equals 20.1 percent.
Includes only counties with 10,000 or more people.

Source: 1990 census

The treasure troves guarded by elderly Americans may empty a bit in the future. Baby boomers got a late start buying homes and raising families, and growing shares of adults will have children and mortgages to support even after they reach "retirement age." If life expectancy continues to rise, more and more boomers will also have to support their own elderly parents. But the news isn't all bad: many retired boomer couples will collect two Social Security and pension checks.

Things will be different for older people in the 21st century. Today's elderly Americans come from a different era. When they were younger, women were half as likely as men to have a college education,

> **As boomers age, the educational equality and ethnic diversity of elderly people will increase.**

and minorities were not as numerous or visible as they are today. As boomers age, the educational equality and ethnic diversity of elderly people will increase.

Some things may never change, however. Retired boomers of the 21st century may resemble Adele Carson, a spunky 84-year-old who maneuvers her golf cart around a 60-mile network of paved paths that winds through the forested neighborhoods, golf courses, and shopping centers of Peachtree City. Life is good for Mrs. Carson, despite her failing eyesight. "It's one reason I came here," she says. "I knew I could drive a golf cart."

But the biggest reason for Mrs. Carson's move had nothing to do with golf-cart paths. "Who are we kidding? Nobody would come from Montana or wherever just because we have a senior citizens' center," she says. "If it were a desert, we would live here—just to be near the family." —*Additional reporting by John Hoeffel and Ron Cossman Maps prepared by Linda Jacobsen*

Older Persons and the Abuse and Misuse of Alcohol and Drugs

Anthony Traxler, Ph.D.

Anthony Traxler, Ph.D., is Professor of Psychology and Director of the Gerontology Program, Southern Illinois University at Edwardsville. He is a teacher, researcher, consultant, and speaker who has conducted numerous workshops on various aspects of aging and development across the life-span. He has authored over 40 articles and papers on the psychological aspects of aging. He is a board member for the Illinois Alliance for Aging, past president of the Mid-America Congress on Aging, and the 1989 winner of that organization's Outstanding Achievement in the Field of Aging award.

In his introduction to a thin little book published almost 20 years ago entitled "Drug Issues in Geropsychiatry," Professor George L. Maddox of Duke University wrote:

> "We live in a society which desperately wants to believe that better living can be achieved through chemistry. Informed individuals are now less confident than they once were that their faith is well placed, but the will to believe is still there. Although reliable comparative evidence is limited, Americans have earned a reputation for consuming large quantities of a variety of drugs, some prescribed, some not. Members of the younger generation have inherited a culture which generally accepts drugs so casually that we now have a new category of drugs— the recreational ones. And when

adults remonstrate with the young about the dangers of drugs, the young are quick to point out who has set a national example of excessive drug use. Physicians sometimes wonder aloud about the questionable example they themselves set as tutors of public understanding and taste regarding drugs." (Maddox, 1974, p. 3)

Although we have learned much since 1974, I was struck by how apropos Maddox's comments are to the substance abuse scene in 1991. Certainly drugs and alcohol have become firmly established facets in contemporary American society. When used appropriately, drug therapy can increase both the quality and length of life of individuals for all ages. When they are misused and abused, however, they can wreak havoc on the lives of older persons.

Due to space limitations, this article will only address alcohol use and abuse in older persons and the misuse of prescription and over-the-counter medicinal drugs. The problem of over-medication with medicinal drugs prescribed either by the physician or the older patient is especially acute and relevant to today's older population. It might also be pointed out that most of the substance use disorders of the elderly do not involve illegal drugs and that surveys of elderly substance abusers have shown that the use of certain classes of drugs such as hallucinogens, amphetamines, and inhalants is extremely rare (Whanger, 1984). A brief discussion of aging and risk factors and the demo-

graphic changes which have to do with the "graying of America" is also covered.

Demographics — The Graying of America

In 1989, persons 65 years or older numbered 31 million, representing 12.5% of the total population, or about one in every eight Americans. The number of older persons increased by 5.3 million, or 21%, since 1980, compared to an increase of 8% for the under-65 population. During the 1990s, the older population growth will slow somewhat because of the small number of babies born during the Great Depression of the 1930s. However, a rapid increase is expected between the years 2010 and 2030, when the "baby boom" generation

---

Most of the substance use disorders of the elderly do not involve illegal drugs

---

reaches age 65. By 2030 there will be 66 million persons 65+, representing 21.8% of the population. A closer look at the 65+ population reveals an older population itself getting older. For example, in 1989, the 65-74 age group (18.2 million) was eight times larger than in 1900, but the 75-84 group (9.8 million) was 13 times larger and the 85+ group (1 million) was 24 times larger (American Association of Retired Persons [AARP], 1990).

With more people reaching an older age than ever before, gerontologists have come to view older persons as consisting of several groups: the young-old who are 55-74, the middle-old, 75-84, and the old-old, 85 and over. As would be expected, the young-old have better health than the middle- and old-old, are better educated, and are more active. Certainly there are important differences between the average 55-year-old and the average 75- or 85-year old, and thus finer age categorizations are useful in describing the aging population more carefully and planning for its needs (Traxler, 1980).

Citing these demographic figures underscores the need to plan now to deal with the potentially serious social, economic, health, and personal consequences of this increase in the number of older persons in our population. Our challenge as practitioners, planners, service providers, and legislators is to guarantee that this population does more than just survive. We need to continue our efforts to insure that the "quality of life" will make surviving into old age, without the felt need to turn to alcohol and drugs, worthwhile for each individual.

Aging and Risk Factors

In a nutshell, the biological changes that occur with aging and that have impact on alcohol and drug use and abuse in later life are as follows: there is a general slowing of biological processes; decreased reserve of energy; breakdown in the function of various body systems; and changes in the structure of body parts such as cells, tissue, and organs. Peter P. Lamy of the University of Maryland at Baltimore discusses primary age changes (normal physical changes with age), secondary age changes (those resulting from diseases in old age), and tertiary age changes (those associated with social, behavioral, or environmental change with age) (Lamy, 1988). These three areas of aging alter older persons' response to alcohol and the many prescription and over-the-counter drugs they take. Loss of physiologic reserve capacity in the older person is related to decreased capacity to respond to stress and stress-induced problems.

Changes in critical organs such as the liver and kidneys and in body composition (with advancing age there is a decrease in muscle tissue and an increase in fatty tissue) result in decreased ability of the older person's body to absorb and dispose of alcohol and other drugs.

Social, psychological, and cultural changes and pressures can also be a significant source of stress for the older person (Hawkins and Traxler, 1988). Negative societal attitudes toward aging expressed as ageism prevent older persons from developing and realizing their full potential. Successful aging requires the older person to continue to adapt to his or her biological, psychological, and social needs under recurrently changing circumstances. Many of these changing circumstances in later life involve losses. Losses occur across the life-span but are ubiquitous in old age (see Figure 1). The bunching up of significant losses (i.e., work and social roles, spouse and friends, health, income, social status, etc.) in later life creates stress and a resultant climate for potential misuse and abuse of alcohol and drugs by the older person if he or she does not have skills for coping and managing stress.

Our challenge as practitioners, planners, service providers, and legislators is to guarantee that this population does more than just survive

It should be pointed out, however, that in spite of older persons' aforementioned risk factors, most older persons cope and adapt to changes and losses without resorting to the use of alcohol and other drugs. This fact points to the remarkable resilience and psychological strength of the majority of older persons (Traxler, 1988). Nevertheless, there is a subset of the older population that attempts to cope with stress by turning to alcohol and other drugs.

Alcohol use and abuse

Maddox (1988) reported that older adults are more likely to abstain from the use of alcohol than their younger counterparts, and females of all ages are more likely than men to be abstainers. The older the age, the more likely the person is to abstain from alcohol. Maddox (1988) points out that longitudinal research indicates that after about age 60, both alcohol use and abuse declines due to changes in health and patterns of sociability related to retirement. There is a group of older persons, however, that begins to drink excessively and abuse alcohol for the first time after age 65. These "late onset" alcohol abusers represent only a small fraction of older persons that abuse alcohol. Most older persons with drinking problems have had a history of alcohol abuse that began in their early adult life. Epidemiological surveys and studies of institutional psychiatric elderly patient populations show tremendous variability in the number of older alcohol abusers ranging from 2-10% of the older population. Applying this percentage range to our current over-65 population yields numerical estimates of between 600,000 and 3 million older alcoholics. (Whittington, 1988). Quite obviously, we need to do additional research to resolve this discrepant percentage-range in order to establish the appropriate public policy approach to alcohol prevention and intervention for older persons.

Older men are about four times as likely to have alcohol problems than their female counterparts and drinking problems tend to be the highest among older persons of lower socio-economic status. Data on alcohol abuse by older minority populations is too sparse and incomplete to make any generalizations at this time (Maddox, 1988). Research on the relationship between alcohol use and abuse and socioeconomic status among older adults is also inadequate. Maddox (1988) states that the best current evidence on this relationship is provided by the National Institute of Mental Health (NIMH) Epidemiologic Catchment Area research. This research fails to show any consistent pattern between alcohol abuse and social or economic status among older persons. There is, however, enough information on older clients and patients seen by clinics, health and welfare agencies, psychiatric hospitals, and nursing homes to indicate that they constitute a special subgroup of older adults that exhibits high rates of alcohol problems.

Intervention and Prevention Strategies

Reaching the older person with an alcohol problem can be difficult since their moral orientation toward drinking may be different. Having grown up with prohibition, the older person is more likely to view his drinking problem as a moral issue and find it hard to accept the concept of alcoholism as a disease that is treatable. Older people also fear losing control of their life circumstances and want and need to be independent. Older persons with drinking problems feel they should be able to handle the problem themselves and often resent someone suggesting they need professional services.

Denial — the hallmark of alcoholism — can be especially difficult to deal with in the older alcoholic since he is often isolated and cut off from family and community support systems. This makes intervention more difficult due to problems in gathering reliable background information and getting support from significant others to help motivate the older alcoholic to accept treatment. Once in treatment, however, recovery rates for older alcoholics are at least as good as for other age groups.

I would like to conclude this section on alcohol use and abuse by listing six myths on alcohol and aging reported in the Fall 1983 Newsletter of the Kansas City National Council on Alcoholism:

Myths: Alcohol and Aging

Wrong: Older people have acquired a tolerance for alcohol. *Right:* Physically, the human body develops less tolerance for alcohol with aging.

Wrong: Older alcoholics are happy that way! *Right:* Like others who are addicted to alcohol, older people are desperate, alienated, physically and mentally sick.

Wrong: If they've been drinking for 40 years, they're not going to stop now. *Right:* With proper treatment and aftercare, recovery rates for older alcoholics are at least as good as for others.

Wrong: "Oh, he has always drunk like that; he's just old and getting senile." *Right:* Senility is often misdiagnosed; if incorrectly diagnosed, the elderly problem drinker may be subjected to inappropriate treatment, or alcoholism may not be diagnosed at all.

Wrong: Older problem drinkers often lack financial resources to pay for treatment. *Right:* They may be unaware that alcoholism treatment is reimbursable under Medicare and Medicaid and that publicly supported

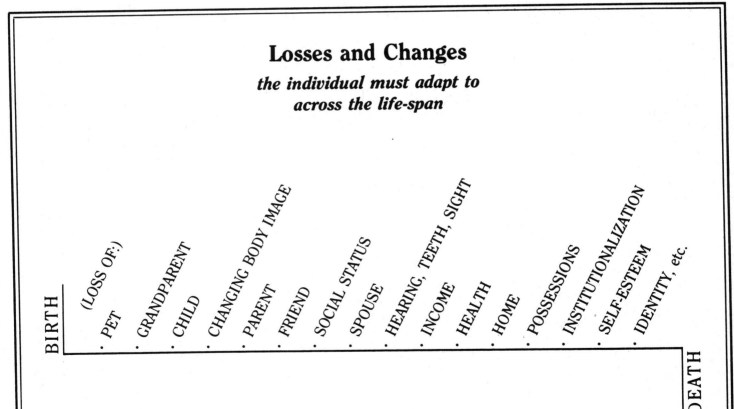

Losses and Changes
the individual must adapt to across the life-span

BIRTH

(LOSS OF:)
PET · GRANDPARENT · CHILD · CHANGING BODY IMAGE · PARENT · FRIEND · SOCIAL STATUS · SPOUSE · HEARING, TEETH, SIGHT · INCOME · HEALTH · HOME · POSSESSIONS · INSTITUTIONALIZATION · SELF-ESTEEM · IDENTITY, etc.

DEATH

Note: Many elderly people experience numerous losses over a short period of time.

Figure 1

treatment facilities exist in many communities.

Wrong: "We've always dealt with our own family problems; we don't need outsiders to help." *Right:* Alcoholism is a disease and responds best to educated trained professionals in that field and the self-help group of Alcoholics Anonymous.

Prescription and Over-the-Counter Drugs (OTC)

Most older persons take medication, usually for chronic illnesses such as arthritis, hypertension, diabetes, digestive problems, heart disease, and mental and nervous disorders. As indicated earlier, people over 65 represent 12.5% of the U.S. population. However, they account for 36% of total personal health care expenditures and 30% of all prescription drugs sold in this country. Since older persons often have a number of chronic conditions or disabilities, they typically take many different drugs, some prescription and some over-the-counter (OTC). Substances such as

---

We need to continue our efforts to insure that the "quality of life" will make surviving into old age worthwhile for each individual

---

vitamins, laxatives, cold remedies, antihistamines, analgesics (aspirin, acetaminophin, ibuprofen), and antacids used in combination with prescription drugs or alcohol may lead to serious problems.

Drug therapy has certainly added a great deal to the quality of life of many older persons; however, medication misuse has also resulted in many older persons becoming sicker and more dysfunctional. For example, a recent study conducted by Col, Fanale, and Kronholm (1990) on the role of medication noncompliance and adverse drug reactions in hospitalizations of the elderly, found that 10% of all elderly medical admissions were related to noncompliance with therapeutic drug recommendations. Older patients can

be noncompliant either intentionally or unintentionally. The most common reason for unintentional noncompliance in the elderly is forgetting to take doses of medication.

Successful aging requires the older person to continue to adapt to his or her biological, psychological, and social needs under recurrently changing circumstances

---

Also, the drug may be taken incorrectly — too much, too little, or with other substances that may cause an adverse reaction, due to nonspecific or confusing instructions (Shimp and Ascione, 1988). The most common reasons for intentional noncompliance among older persons (which refers to the patient knowingly deviating from the prescribed recommended regimen) are not filling the prescription and discontinuing the medication if they feel it is not working (Stewart, 1988).

Additional reasons besides noncompliance for drug misuse by older persons include inappropriate selection of non-prescription medication and misjudgment in physician prescribing (Shimp and Ascione, 1988). The wide range of OTC drugs available to older consumers, many of questionable efficacy but highly advertised, makes the appropriate selection quite complicated.

Misjudgments in physician prescribing and the emphasis on drug therapy as the panacea for all the problems of America's older adults is an especially serious problem impacting on the health and welfare of today's older population.

There is a pressing need to carefully evaluate the quantity of medications being prescribed for today's elderly patients. It is not uncommon for community-dwelling older persons to be on numerous prescription drugs at the same time. Elderly residents in nursing homes and other institutional settings are also prescribed too many drugs, and understaffing patterns can

lead to the use of drugs as chemical restraints in lieu of more appropriate behavioral interventions.

In addition to the cost of unnecessary prescription and non-prescription drugs, older persons are at a greater risk for adverse drug reactions. Research and clinical studies show that the number of drugs being used correlates with the rate of adverse reactions, and thus it is imperative that older adults use only needed drugs.

Risk Factors in Misuse Of Prescription and OTC Drugs

Several factors place the older person at greater risk for adverse drug reactions. Shimp and Ascione (1988) single out the following factors as being especially relevant:

1) Number and types of prescription and OTC drugs used. This factor was discussed earlier.

2) Complex medication regimens. The more drugs a person takes, the more complicated the regimen. The management of multiple medications can be a major challenge for patients of any age and lead to significant miuse and errors.

3) Multiple diseases and symptoms. Shimp and Ascione (1988) point out that the combination of aging, multiple medical problems, and multiple medications creates a complex clinical picture that makes diagnosis and appropriate intervention strategies difficult for the health professional.

4) Multiple prescribers. Since older persons often have multiple health problems, they are more likely to consult a larger number of medical specialists and receive more prescriptions.

Most older people cope and adapt to changes and losses without resorting to the use of alcohol and other drugs

---

5) Inadequate and ambiguous instructions. Older patients tend to depend on their physicians more than younger persons for most of their prescription drug information, and

they are more passive in their dependence upon their physicians for advice. They are inclined to believe that their doctor alone should make the decision about their medication, and they often fail to tell one physician about medication prescribed by another (Shimp and Acione, 1988). To make matters worse, they rarely ask their physicians questions (AARP, 1984).

6) Sensory and cognitive impairments. Impaired hearing and vision are common sensory impairments of older persons. Hearing is important when verbal instructions and comments are given regarding drugs to be taken. Older persons may also find it more difficult to differentiate drug tablets by color, especially in the blue-green range, due to age-related changes in vision. As discussed earlier, they are often prescribed multiple drugs which results in more complicated regimens. Older persons with cognitive impairments become confused and forgetful and have considerable

difficulty managing their own medications.

Intervention and Prevention Strategies

Prevention of the misuse of prescription and OTC drugs by older persons will require the dissemination and utilization of the large body of research and clinical knowledge on aging and the older adult population. Health care professionals (especially physicians, pharmacists, and nurses), social service and aging network professionals, family members, and older persons need to learn about the role of drugs and aging in their lives. Currently, few medical students and residents receive adequate training in drug therapy and pharmacology with respect to aging. Prevention programs need to target this glaring deficiency in medical education.

Prevention programs focusing on *information* about aging and older persons and drugs, both prescription and OTC, need to be implemented at all levels of society including schools,

colleges and universities, churches, and, of course, for those professionals and paraprofessionals who work directly with the older population.

Older persons must increasingly learn to take charge of their lives

---

Few medical students and residents receive adequate training in drug therapy and pharmacology with respect to aging

---

which includes their health and the role of drugs in their lives. More programs such as "Healthy Older People," sponsored by the Office of Disease Prevention and Health Promotion, Public Health Service, U.S. Department of Health and Human Services, need to be developed and implemented. The "Healthy Older

People" program is a national public campaign to educate older persons about health practices which can reduce risks of disabling illness and increase their prospects for more productive, active lives.

The following anecdote reported by Joan Baker, Staff Writer, in the March, 1984 (Vol. 5, No. 4) issue of *Active Aging*, nicely summarizes the type of "take charge" older person that is needed to help prevent drug misuse in the older population.

An 81-year-old Wichita gentleman had been feeling bad for about two years. He went in several times to see his physician. Each time he came home with a new prescription. Each time he felt progressively worse. He made yet another appointment.

"You have to realize you're just getting older," the doctor told him.

"I just didn't buy that," the man reported. Later, he was talking about his health with a friend, who asked how many medications he was taking. He went directly to the medicine chest and counted. He had 14 prescriptions. First thing next morning, he made an appointment with the doctor. He told the doctor that he wanted to talk, and expected to pay for an office call.

The doctor was seated behind his desk when the man walked in, carrying a paper sack filled with the 14 prescription containers. The patient emptied them onto the desk.

"Did you know I was taking all these?" he demanded.

"Of course I know; I prescribed them," the physician replied.

"Are all of these drugs safe?" the man asked.

"Of course they're safe — I wouldn't have prescribed them for you if they weren't," the doctor replied, obviously offended.

"That's good news," the man replied, "because I want you to open every bottle on this desk and take one of each — right now."

"I'm not going to do it," the doctor responded, indignantly.

"Why not?" the man shot back. "You're the one that said they were safe."

The doctor said, "I might be allergic to some of those drugs."

"How did you know that I was not allergic to them?" the man asked.

The doctor considered, then reached for the man's file and opened it. Together, they reviewed all the medications. They discovered many prescriptions had been made without discontinuing the old ones.

The patient was reduced from 14 prescriptions to four — and almost immediately began to feel better.

"I asked this man whether he was going to change doctors or go back to the same guy," said a health professional who talked with him about the experience.

"I wouldn't think of changing doctors now," the man replied emphatically. "I've almost got this one trained."

References

American Association of Retired Persons (1984). *Prescription drugs: A survey of consumer use, attitudes, and behavior.* Washington, DC.

American Association of Retired Persons. *A Profile of Older Americans 1990.* Program Resources Department [P.F. 3049 (1290.D996)], Washington, DC.

Col, N., Fanale, J.E., and Kronholm, P. (1990). The role of medication noncompliance and adverse drug reactions in hospitalizations of the elderly. *Archives of Internal Medicine,* (April) 841-845.

Hawkins, R. and Traxler, A. (1988). Elder abuse and communication. In C.W. Carmichael, C.H. Botan and R. Hawkins (eds.), *Human communication and the aging process* (pp. 221-234). Prospect Heights, IL: Waveland Press.

Lamy, P.L. (1988). Actions of alcohol and drugs in older people. *Generations, 12* (4), 9-13.

Maddox, G.L. (1988). Aging, drinking, and alcohol abuse. *Generations, 12* (4), 14-16.

Maddox, G.L. (1974). Drugs, physicians, and patients. In W.E. Fann and G.L. Maddox (eds.), *Drug issues in geropsychiatry* (pp. 3-6). Baltimore: Williams & Wilkins.

Maddox, G.L., Robbins, L., and Rosenberg, N. (1985). *Nature and extent of alcohol problems among the elderly.* New York: Springer.

Mishara, B.L. and Kastenbaum, R. (1980). *Alcohol and old age.* New York: Grune & Stratton.

Shimp, L.A. and Ascione, F.J. (1988). Causes of medication misuse and error. *Generations, 12* (4), 17-21.

Stewart, R.B. (1988). Drug use in the elderly. In J.C. Delafuente and R.B. Stewart (eds.), *Therapeutics in the elderly.* Baltimore: Williams & Wilkins.

Traxler, A.J. (1980). Let's get gerontologized: Developing a sensitivity to aging. In the *Multipurpose senior center concept: A training manual for practitioners working with the aging* (pp. 1-19). Springfield, IL: Illinois Department on Aging.

Traxler, A. (1988). Issues and theories of adult development: The middle years. In W.B. Scott (ed.), *Generations in the middle: Issues and insights* (pp. 7-44). Kansas City, KS: Mid-America Congress on Aging.

Whanger, A.D. (1984). Substance use disorders. In A.D. Whanger and A.C. Meyers (eds.), *Mental health assessment and therapeutic intervention with older adults,* (pp. 157-188). Rockville, MD: Aspen.

Whittington, F.J. (1988). Making it better: Drinking and drugging in old age. *Generations, 12,* (4), 5-7.

Silent saviors

Millions of grandparents have stepped into the breach to rescue children from faltering families, drugs, abuse and violent crime

Linda L. Creighton

On a raw, wintry night, Georgie Simmons waited at a hospital in Richmond, Va., for the birth of her first grandson. Nervously pacing the tiled halls, she watched the clock stretch to 4 a.m. Finally a doctor appeared, putting a gentle hand on Georgie's shoulder to guide her to a nursery. There, in an incubator, lay a baby boy, eyes open. Georgie leaned down and whispered, "Welcome to the world, my beautiful grandson." Crying softly, she turned to the doctor and said. "Now I need to say goodbye to my own baby."

Together, they walked down the hall to a darkened room where her 30-year-old daughter, Deborah, shot in the head hours before by a jealous boyfriend, lay comatose, breathing only with the help of a respirator. "You gave him to me," Georgie whispered to her youngest child, "and I'll take care of him." Then the machines that had sustained life long enough for the baby to be born were shut down, and Simmons was left alone with her grief and her grandson.

On that night, DeDongio Simmons became one of the 3.2 million children in the United States who live with their grandparents—an increase of almost 40 percent in the past decade, according to the U.S. Census Bureau. Those, at least, are the known figures; many who are now coming to grips with the trend fear that it could be three to four times worse than that. There is hardly a more frightening leading indicator of the devastation wrought by the nation's manifold social ills, and no class or race is immune. Some 4 percent of all white children in the United States and 12 percent of black children now live with grandparents. Of these, half the families have both grandparents and most of the rest live only with the grandmother. Beyond them are the

millions of grandparents who have assumed important part-time child-rearing responsibilities because of the growth of single-parent households and the number of families where both parents work.

The elaborate system of child protection and support agencies throughout the land is more of a hindrance than a help to these beleaguered families. It is very difficult for grandparents to gain unchallenged permanent custody of threatened children. And the financial support they get is less than one third that available to foster families: The national average is $109 per child per month for grandparents who are sole care givers, compared with $371 per child per month for foster parents.

But nothing can really ease the unique burdens these grandparents bear. Many of them are racked by shame and guilt at the fact that their own children have failed as parents—and many blame themselves, wondering where they went wrong as parents. In order to provide safe and loving homes to their grandchildren, some must emotionally abandon their own abusive or drug-addicted children. The stresses are compounded by the fact that some of the children they inherit are among the most needy, most emotionally damaged and most angry in the nation.

There is not a town in America untouched by this version of the extended family. Richmond, capital of the Old Confederacy, is now a very typical home of the nation's new civil wars. It is just like many communities where drugs, crime and financial and emotional distress are splitting families apart and reorganizing them. In the first six months of this year, the city's Juvenile Court handled almost 700 custody cases involving children under 18—many of whom were eventually placed with grandparents.

Richmond's ad hoc way of coping with these problems is fairly typical of other communities. It is the diligence of Wanda Cooper, a resource coordinator at the Richmond Capital Area Agency on Aging, that has begun to convince city officials that special attention must be paid to these new grandparent-led families. In her work visiting homes of senior citizens on fixed incomes, Cooper began to notice more and more small children. She later learned that more than 600 people over 65 were receiving aid to dependent children—the basic welfare program. Now she sees her mission as helping grandparents become parents again and comforting them that they are not alone. It is a message many yearn to hear.

FOGLE FAMILY

Fighting the effects of the drug epidemic is heartbreaking work

Nothing devastated many American families in the 1980s with quite the same malign swiftness as the cocaine epidemic. Katherine Fogle and her two granddaughters are three of its victims. Ask Katherine why she is rearing the girls and she squares off and says, "Drugs." A life rooted in poverty and inner-city hardship has made this 55-year-old strong and unbending. But three of her five children have been stolen from her by drugs, AIDS and hard living, and she is determined her granddaughters will not also be claimed.

That is why, five years ago, Katherine made sure that Melba, then 9, and 2-year-old Katherine, or Kat, were taken

"I knew I had to take the girls when my daughter looked at me and said, 'Just let me be a junkie.'"

from their cocaine-addicted mother, Penny. For years, Katherine lived across the hall from Penny in a run-down apartment building in New York City and watched her daughter slide into the drug world. Katherine says she had repeatedly tried to intervene, reporting neglect to the child-protection agency, feeding the little girls, washing them and listening for their cries when their mother left them alone. "Melba used to go to school with her clothes turned inside out," says Katherine. "I found out it was because her clothes were so filthy, she was ashamed to wear them right." The animosity between mother and daughter grew until Katherine decided to move home — to Richmond.

But the nightmare only got worse. "I got a phone call from the babies' paternal grandmother, saying Melba was in the hospital. When I asked for what, she broke down and told me Melba, my 9-year-old grandbaby, had gonorrhea. She had been raped." Left by her mother with friends, Melba had been repeatedly assaulted by a young boy. Notified of the rape, the New York Child Welfare Administration placed the girls in protective custody and agreed to let Katherine take them back to Richmond. After nearly five years of extending probationary periods for Penny, authorities finally granted Katherine legal custody of the girls.

In the meantime, Penny had more children, at least two of whom were born drug-influenced. The Sheltering Arms Childrens Service, a private agency that places children throughout the city of New York, contacted Katherine and asked if she would take more of the children to raise. Suffering from diabetes and other health problems, Katherine had to say no. "I'm not physically or mentally capable of taking care of more children," says Katherine. "I held one in my arms and I was tempted. It rode my mind for a long time."

Katherine has refused contact with her daughter for almost five years. And Penny could not be reached for comment for this story. "I'd love to see her get things together, come and take the girls back, but it's just not going to happen," she says. Her eyes soften. "She was my baby, after

all." Straightening, she puts her hands together in a firm clasp. "But I just can't think about it that way anymore. I feel like she's just someone I knew." Katherine has come to terms with her own feelings by comforting herself that she did her best as a parent under difficult circumstances: "I never neglected my children, I kept them together. How can I blame myself for what's happened to them?"

In their three-room apartment in a modest, quiet part of Richmond, Katherine holds tight rein on her granddaughters. The girls share a bunk-bedded room. Rising in 6 a.m. darkness, they are on the school bus by 6:45. After-school time and evenings are carefully monitored by Katherine; Melba chafes a bit at not being able to go with friends to places with which Katherine is unfamiliar or to hang out after school talking with friends. "Straight home," says Katherine firmly.

To supplement the $231 a month she receives in ADC benefits, Katherine takes care of a baby during the week. Money for anything extra is tight, and she worries that the girls are being deprived of little extras that give teenagers confidence. On Sundays the three dress in their very best and take a church bus across town to their Baptist church, where they greet everyone by first name and spend the better part of the service waving to friends.

Kat's dark beauty is accentuated by a dazzling grin. At 7, she says she would like to be a teacher when she grows up. She has little memory of her mother, but she listens carefully as Melba speaks of Penny, and it is clear she is curious. "All I know is she's using drugs and she won't take care of us," Kat asserts.

Melba, 14, has inherited her grandmother's grace, but she is a bit uncertain of herself, glancing down as she speaks quietly about her mother: "I love her, but I don't like the things she does. I wish we could be together all in a big house, but I know that probably won't be. I love my grandmother, but I love my mother still, too." Melba talks about the bad things in her life with a steady voice and gaze. "I talked once with a counselor about the rape. But it's just something I need to put behind me." Recently, Melba found letters she had written to her grandmother in Richmond from New York and said: "Mama, I had forgotten what I felt then. It makes me cry now."

Recently, as early evening light began to paint the Richmond streets, Melba walked with her grandmother and sister and giggled self-consciously as a car filled with friends beeped its horn. Safely home, she told her grandmother that night, as she does every night: "Thank you, Mama, for loving me."

Some of the worst wounds are the emotional ones that take forever to heal

At 9, Brandy talks a good game. Chin thrust high and eyes narrowed, she does not hold conversations; she challenges. "Yeah, I've got two mothers," she declares. "It's called extra family." Shifting in her seat to face a visitor, she jumps ahead to unasked questions, always ready with a tough reason.

Brandy has had to be strong. She is one of the millions of emotionally scarred and struggling children who must face the fact that their parents couldn't — or wouldn't — care for them. At birth, her mother turned her over to 59-year-old Mary, Brandy's grandmother, and Brandy has lived with her since. Until last year, she thought she had an older sister who lived down the street. Then a neighbor told Brandy the "sister" was her mother. Brandy demanded to know the truth. "I called my daughter and we told her together," says Mary. "I told Brandy, your mother gave birth to you but I raised you. Brandy just sat there and said, 'Now I know.'"

The news had a devastating effect, one Brandy tried desperately to minimize but could not hide. At the William Byrd Community House, where Brandy had been in after-school programs, Elizabeth Moreau says Brandy began to show such hostility toward adults that she felt counseling was in order: "If asked to put away toys, for instance, she would yell, 'You can't make me do anything!' and run out of the room." Her grandmother says Brandy began for the first time to challenge her. "I needed help," says Mary. Finally, this fall, Brandy has begun counseling. "These kids need lots of special care," Mary notes.

This year, for the first time, Brandy gave out two cards on Mother's Day. But her contact with her mother is sporadic and her love and loyalties are defiantly with her grandmother. They asked that their last name not be used here, as Mary has not been able to adopt Brandy.

Bright and a good student, Brandy roller-skates with a hard passion that she hopes will land her in the professionals. But she has more hard roads to travel before she gets to the pros. Mary was diagnosed with emphysema four years ago, and has so far beaten the odds for survival. But she is increasingly tired, and Brandy senses this. "She's talked to me and said she's going to be all right," she says in clipped tones. "She's going to be here to see me get big." Roughly shoving back the bangs that are always in her eyes, she fixes a smile and looks away.

Then the girl with the perfect skin and long black lashes sums up her own soldierly view of life. "There is no such thing as a perfect family," she says. "The only thing I can tell you that's really perfect is heaven." But her time with her grandmother has enabled Brandy to survive and, now, to thrive, and that is a gift that even at 9 she understands. "There are probably some kids who don't feel special living with their grandparents," says Brandy. "I don't have to worry about that because I have a reputation for being very tough. I can beat up anyone in my class who doesn't believe me."

TAYLOR FAMILY

Violent crime turns the world upside down in every way

Until three years ago, Bertha Taylor and her husband, Robert, were living what they felt were their golden years. A respected schoolteacher recently remarried to a successful postal-service truck driver, Bertha was a grandparent for the first time. She and Robert got the usual thrills from visiting her son's 6-month-old baby, Evetta. Then, one night of violence turned their world upside down. Evetta's mother, on her way back from the grocery store, was raped and murdered. Devastated and unable to cope, Bertha's son asked his parents to take Evetta. "Our lives changed completely," says Bertha. "We got her on Saturday, and I thought, 'Lord, what am I going to do? I've got to go to work on Monday.'"

The Taylors became one of the hundreds of thousands of families whose lives were riven by violent crime that year in America. They were financially comfortable and did not have to struggle for the basic needs. "There were a lot of expenses, expenses you never plan for, and I don't know how people making less than our income manage," says Bertha. But there were other things precious to the Taylors—lingering dinners and evenings with friends—that were lost as a baby's schedule took over their lives. "I didn't even have time to go to the bathroom," says Bertha. "Your freedom is gone, your privacy is gone, and you're used to having it." Day care had to be found, and Bertha's work dealing with scores of children all day became exhausting when the end of the day meant a baby waiting for more attention. The marriage underwent stresses neither Bertha nor Robert had expected to con-

BERTHA TAYLOR AND EVETTA

"I believe the death of my daughter-in-law happened for a reason. I thank God for putting little Evetta into our lives. If she left us now, there would be a huge void."

front. "Hey, let me tell you, our sex life changed," she says. "You're tired and you've got no time."

With time, the Taylors adjusted and worked out ways of dealing with Evetta's needs. Robert rises early to dress and feed Evetta while Bertha organizes for her day of work at an elementary school. At night, Bertha prepares dinner, Robert does Evetta's bath and together they read stories to her.

Now 3, Evetta could be a star on a family sitcom, her affection and self-confidence bubbling irrepressibly. Though Bertha says she is not spoiling her, Evetta obviously thrives on her grandparents' doting. She is an addition to their relationship, they say, that they could not have foreseen. "If she left us now," says Bertha, "there would be a huge void."

Bertha's son has maintained close contact with the child, and he plans to marry again next year. Bertha says she wants whatever would make him happy, but she and her husband would like to adopt Evetta. As Bertha braids Evetta's hair, she talks of hoping to see "how this little child grows up and turns out." When night falls, a light comes on beside Evetta's bed in her pink satin and toy-filled bedroom. Her tiny voice chimes in with Bertha's schoolteacher singsong of night prayers, and she adds: "God bless all my mommies, and God bless all my daddies."

TOMAN FAMILY

The burden of poverty is worse when it has to be shared with the young

When the Richmond weather turns cold and bitter, 59-year-old May Toman and her two granddaughters pile blankets onto the worn living-room couch and chairs in their rundown row house. There, around an ancient gas burner, they sleep at night. The upstairs is without heat or electricity—and the leaky kitchen ceiling has already fallen in once. But May is afraid to complain for fear the landlord will raise her $110-a-month rent—a development that could leave them homeless.

The girls—Shelly, 8 and Tabatha, 9—make do with thrift-shop clothing, and a steak dinner is a treat remembered for weeks.

Shelly's mother was only 17 when Shelly was born, and soon afterward she and Shelly's father began leaving the baby with friends or near friends, sometimes for long periods without contact. For May, the final straw came when Shelly was 2. May found her alone in the yard one evening. She took Shelly home and called the Richmond Department of Social Services. After an investigation, May got legal custody.

Several years later, May's son, Wayne, ran into marriage problems. When his wife left, he gave his daughter Tabatha, then 7, to his mother and his infant son to his mother-in-law. Tabatha's health had been neglected; her teeth were abscessed. May applied for custody and got it.

The small, frail-looking woman the girls call "Nanny" became their mother, making ends meet by taking in sewing and cutting corners. Up at 7, she walks the girls to school, then cleans house and grocery shops with food stamps. At 3, she meets the girls outside their brick school eight blocks away "so they know there's someone waiting." Together they walk home and do homework until dinner.

One of Shelly's favorite pastimes is studying her baby album, staring intently at the pictures of herself and her mother smiling from behind plastic pages. The album ends abruptly when she is 2, and Shelly turns back to the first page to begin again. She speaks of her Nanny with affection but longs for a reunion with her mother. "I want to live with my mama in a big house," says Shelly, "but I don't really think I'll ever get that." Shelly's mother lives across town and sees Shelly fairly often. But she has another child now, a year old, and says she does not have plans to take Shelly back soon.

Tabatha readily lays her feelings out for inspection: "Well, my daddy lives in the neighborhood, but he can't take me right now. My mama used to call, which made me cry terribly, but she hasn't called now in a long time. She said she was going to send me a birthday card but she never did." Small and polish-chipped fingernails tap determinedly on the table. "I want to stay right here with my Nanny. See, I love my Nanny."

Her father, Wayne, lives next door with two new children and their mother, and though in many ways he and Tabatha are close, he says, "I feel like Tabatha's better off with Nanny."

But Nanny, a high-school dropout with a good deal of worldly wisdom to dispense, is bone weary from trying to make it on $291 a month while solving the typical childhood squabbles and problems of two kids. Her grandchildren are among the 13.4 million American children who live in poverty—1 out of every 5 children.

May is weary, too, of trying to figure out why she and other grandmothers have ended up raising another generation. "Sometimes I feel like I really failed showing my children what kids mean. I raised mine by myself, and I hung on to them hard. Kids don't have a choice about coming into the world, but adults have choices."

May puts a fragile hand to her forehead. "I put my life on hold for 39 years, raising my own children," she says. "Now it's still on hold, but how much life do I have left? Sometimes I feel like I'm just cracking into sharp little pieces that fall to the ground." Then, running a hand through graying hair, she shrugs a smile and says, "Then I just pick up and go on out to do what I have to do."

FOGG FAMILY

Sometimes, the government child-protection system is no friend of kids

Three winters ago, Brian and Stella Fogg left their warm colonial home in Richmond to drive in a dangerous ice storm to South Carolina. Every half-hour they stopped to scrape the windshield, then slid back onto the interstate. Late in the afternoon they pulled into the parking lot of a K mart store in Beaufort. A 2-year-old boy and a 5-year-old girl climbed hesitantly from a waiting car, each clutching a small trash bag filled with personal possessions. They watched as Brian and Stella came to them with arms outstretched and said, "Now you can come home with Grandpa and Granny."

With that, Brian and Stella saved two of their grandchildren, Justine and Brian, from the system meant to protect them. After their parents' separation and inability to care for them, the children were taken into custody by authorities in South Carolina. Unknown to the grandparents, the children were

then bounced from foster home to foster home for months, finally landing in a shelter for homeless children.

When the Foggs learned of the children's plight from their son, they immediately tracked down South Carolina child-care workers and asked for the grandchildren. Stella still flushes with anger when she remembers the months of futile pleading. Beaufort County officials have refused to comment on the case.

The Foggs were allowed to visit Justine and little Brian once, with a social worker present in a cramped office. Not having seen them in years, the children at first kept their distance from their grandparents. Finally, Justine walked over, put her hand on her grandmother's knee and said quietly, "I think I remember you now. You took me to see Santa once."

Within two weeks of the Foggs' visit, the South Carolina Department of Social Services, Beaufort County, without notifying Brian and Stella, had moved the children to yet another foster home, where Justine and Brian shared a bed with at least three other children. "I understand that the social services are swamped," says Stella. "But with us ready to take them, there was no reason for those kids to suffer any more."

Weeks passed, though, as the Foggs fought to get custody of the children. They thought they had reached a breakthrough four months into the process when they were told they could pick the children up. But they went before a judge who came to their hearing unprepared. He refused to recognize the Foggs' status and made a decision based on faulty information, granting custody to the Commonwealth of Virginia instead of the grandparents. "There is no continuity in the system, no one really looking out for these kids," says Brian. "We were the only ones trying to save them."

The Foggs thought they were prepared to deal with the kids' problems, but they were surprised at their own resentments. After rearing their four sons, they had settled into a new home, made good friends and were savoring each other's company. Now, with two small children, no financial help and no emotional support, they were not happy. They were angry at their son and his wife, and initially argued about whether taking the children was possible. Brian had suffered a bout with cancer, their home had to be remortgaged to support the children and their social life evaporated. "We asked ourselves, is this going to break up our 30-year marriage?" Stella notes. "But we felt we had no choice."

Their income was cut by a third because Brian reduced his business travel schedule as an equipment specialist for

the postal service. They had to pay for extra medical insurance because no local doctor would accept Medicaid patients, and they struggled with the children's emotional scars. Justine's cries for help came when she threatened to burn down the house or rip down the curtains. "There were lots of good days," says Stella. "But never a day when we said we're happy to be doing this."

Three years later, the Foggs say it is never an easy life but they have come to terms with the sacrifices they've had to make and now feel their lives are richer. "Some of our friends say we're crazy, that they would never do this," says Stella. "But if we hadn't done this, in 15 years there might have been a knock on our front door and a young man standing there saying, 'I'm your grandson. Where were you when I needed you, when I lay in bed at night crying for someone to help me?'" The Foggs say that if their son and daughter-in-law's situation does not change soon, they want to adopt Brian and Justine.

On a recent Sunday afternoon, the fireplace in the Foggs' living room snapped with dry logs. Stella brought in a tray filled with tea and hot chocolate, and in her still strong Scottish burr called the kids in from the yard. Racing each other through the leaves, Justine and Brian bounded up the stairs. With small, dirt-dusted hands, they lifted mugs to their lips and stuffed cookies in their mouths. But when Justine talked about what family means and what it is like to live with grandparents, her childishness fell away. "The foster homes were really bad. Mostly the people weren't mean but they didn't like me. And I didn't understand that my parents didn't take care of me. I just thought I got taken away."

Staring at a place on the table, she rested her head in her hand for a moment, then looked up and with an intensity beyond her 8 years said: "At first when I came here to live, I felt kind of sad. I didn't know them. But they act like another kind of parent. They're like they had me out of their own stomachs."

SEXTON FAMILY

After a child has been neglected, the best kind of love is the simple kind

Several weeks ago, 4-year-old James came home from kindergarten crying hysterically. A boy in his class had been given a BB gun, and in a moment of childish bravado told James that he was coming to his house to shoot his parents. Perhaps another 4-year-old boy might have met the challenge with a "Yeah? I'll shoot yours back." But for James, the idea of losing parents is no empty threat. He was taken from his biological parents after he was physically abused. Now James's grandparents, Charlotte and Eddie Sexton, are his parents, and he is afraid of losing them.

From the beginning, say the Sextons, they were worried about the care of James. Neighbors had complained about the baby's treatment. After James's parents showed up at the Sextons' house one afternoon with year-old baby James, asking to leave him, the Sextons readily consented. Desperate to protect the child, Charlotte and Eddie called the Richmond Department of Social Services and, eventually, James was awarded to them on a finding of neglect.

James lived with the Sextons for a year, and then his parents petitioned the court, showing proof of a job and a

CHARLOTTE AND EDDIE SEXTON WITH JAMES

"You have to earn the right to be called Mommy or Daddy. We're trying to. James knows when he's with us, we won't let anyone else hurt him."

new apartment. This time the judge ordered James returned to his parents. "It really looked like they had turned around, so how can you keep James from them?" says Charlotte now. "But we felt like our hearts had been ripped out."

Within a short period, the daughter's husband was jailed for four months in the Richmond City Jail for petit larceny. Almost a year to the day that James was returned to his parents, a social worker called the Sextons to say that he was in a hospital emergency room, with head injuries from a belt buckle. Could they please come to get James?

James has been with the Sextons now for over a year, and they want very much to keep him. "Every child has the birthright to be with his mother and father," says Charlotte. "But sometimes, with some parents, someone has to say 'Enough.' We have reached that point."

"Nobody hands you a pamphlet and says, 'Here, this is what you do when your kid dumps his child,' " says Charlotte. But that didn't stop the Sextons from becoming attached to James. "At first you build a wall," she says. "The longer he's with you, the wall starts to fall." They found free counseling to help deal with James's tantrums and chair throwing, in the process refining their parenting style. "I never felt I had to tell my kids I loved them, I thought they knew," says Charlotte. "With James, we had to start over, like with a baby, nurturing and showing him how much we cared." Now, their parenting combines some pretty tough old-fashioned strictness with newly learned techniques like "time out" to cope with his outbursts.

Charlotte is only 45, and her homespun temperament seems perfect for raising children. Her husband, Eddie, is partial to plaid shirts that do not quite conceal a burly physique kept strong by his work in a tractor-trailer-tire shop, and though his speech is rare, it is sharp and funny. On an annual income of just over $20,000 they feel financially lucky, treating James to burgers or subs occasionally and making Christmas special. "There are times we rob Peter to pay Paul," says Eddie. "But we're OK. Sometimes at the end of the month we actually have 30 or 40 dollars left in the account."

Although James has not yet spoken about his past, he talked for the first time this month about his little brother and sister, a 9-month-old and a 2-year-old still living with his parents. Perhaps he wishes they could be with him.

WHAT GRANDPARENTS WANT

Surer ways to save kids

If grandparents who have become parents again could wave a magic wand, at the top of their wish list would be a liberalization of the laws regulating child custody. Most feel that parental rights are given too much weight in clear-cut cases when custody should be changed. The number of times parents can appeal to get children back should be limited, they say, and it should be possible for grandparents to apply for adoption earlier.

Financially, grandparents suffer an enormous burden, one that might be relieved if resources available to them were more in line with those offered to foster parents. Some states have created "kinship care" programs under which relatives caring for children receive the same amounts as foster parents. Under current rules, though, grandparents are only eligible for such benefits if they give custody of the children to the state. In effect, this makes the grandparents "foster parents" of their own grandchildren, and most grandparents are reluctant to cede their authority to the government. In Los Angeles this month, a child whose aunt was forced to return him to the foster-care system because of financial difficulties was beaten to death in a foster home.

Nationally, there are more than 150 support groups for grandparents. If you want help organizing such a group or finding out what your rights are, here are some organizations that can help:

■ GAP: Grandparents as Parents. Sylvie de Toledo, Psychiatric Clinic for Youth, 2801 Atlantic Avenue, Long Beach, CA 90801, (213) 595-3151.

■ Grandparents Raising Grandchildren. Barbara Kirkland, P.O. Box 104, Colleyville, TX 76034, (817) 577-0435.

■ Second Time Around Parents. Michele Daly, Family and Community Services of Delaware County, 100 W. Front Street, Media, PA 19063, (215) 566-7540.

EPILOGUE

It has been nearly a year since the murder of Georgie Simmons's daughter Deborah. For Georgie and her grandson, life has gone on. These days, DeDongio is a curly-topped smiler who lights up at the sound of his grandmother's voice. He will be walking soon. There is not much chance he will ever get to know his father, who has been convicted and sentenced to life plus 36 years for killing Deborah. Georgie says justice was done, but not for DeDongio.

This season is excruciating because for Georgie it brings back memories of last year's celebrations with her pregnant daughter, especially how Deborah enjoyed eating extra pie at Thanksgiving. And Georgie remembers how excited Deborah was at Christmas when she got a new sweater. This year, Georgie has not yet decorated her house the way she has just after Thanksgivings in times past. But she says she will soon, for DeDongio.

In the meantime, they make regular pilgrimages to Mount Calvary Cemetery in Richmond, where Deborah is buried. Last month, as darkness fell, Georgie wrapped her grandson tightly in a blanket to fight the wind and they made their way across the rows of modest headstones. They stopped at a spot marked by wilted flowers and, as she shifted the blanket, DeDongio's tiny face peeked into the cold. "This is your mama's place," Georgie said softly as the boy gazed up at her. Reaching into her pocket, she took out a small pair of booties and bent to lay them on the grave. "I'm sorry I haven't got you a stone yet, my baby, but I needed the money for DeDongio." For a moment she stood quite still. Then the baby began to cry, and Georgie bundled him up thoroughly again. With one last glance back, she turned into the wind to carry her grandson home.

Retirement: American Dream or Dilemma?

Since 1900 the number of persons in America aged 65 and over has been increasing steadily, but a decreasing proportion of that age group remains in the workforce. In 1900 nearly two-thirds of those over 65 worked outside the home. Frank Sammarlino (1979) reports that by 1947 this figure had declined to 47.8 percent (less than half), and by 1975, only 21.7 percent of men 65 and older were still in the workforce. The long-range trend indicates that fewer and fewer persons are being employed beyond age 65. Some people choose to retire at age 65 or earlier; for others retirement is mandatory. A recent change in the law, however, allows individuals to work to age 70 before retiring.

Gordon Strieb and Clement Schneider (*Retirement in American Society*, 1971) observed that for retirement to become an institutionalized social pattern in any society, certain conditions must be present. A large group of people must live long enough to retire; the economy must be productive enough to support people who are not in the workforce; and there must be pensions or insurance programs to support retirees.

Retirement is a rite of passage. People can consider it as either the culmination of the American Dream or as a serious problem. Those who have ample incomes, interesting things to do, and friends to associate with often find the freedom of time and choice that retirement offers very rewarding. For others, however, retirement brings problems and personal losses. Often, these individuals find their incomes decreased, and they miss the status, privilege, and power associated with holding a position in the occupational hierarchy. They may feel socially isolated if they do not find new activities to replace their previous work-related ones. Additionally, they must sometimes cope with the death of a spouse and/or their own failing health.

The articles in this unit provide a clearer picture of the factors in the retirement decision. When a person elects to retire, a number of options are available—one being a life-care community. These communities can, however, fail. In "Retirement Prospects of the Baby Boom Generation: A Different Perspective," the authors point out the advantages that the baby boomers will have at the time of retirement over previous cohorts. "School Days for Seniors" examines why such large numbers of older Americans are returning to college. Finally, "Rethinking Retirement" addresses the different reasons that workers choose to retire early.

Looking Ahead: Challenge Questions

If given the choice of retiring or continuing to work, some people would choose to continue working. How would you explain a person's decision not to retire?

Why do you believe many older persons decide to retire early? What factors are crucial to this decision?

In your opinion, what are the major advantages of retirement? What are its major disadvantages?

From an economic point of view, should people be encouraged to retire earlier or later? Defend your answer.

Retirement Prospects of the Baby Boom Generation: A Different Perspective

Richard A. Easterlin, PhD,

Christine Macdonald, BA, and

Diane J. Macunovich, PhD

Richard A. Easterlin, Ph.D. and Christine Macdonald, BA, University of Southern California, University Park, Los Angeles, CA. Diane J. Macunovich, Ph.D., Williams College, Williamstown, MA.

We examine the average economic status of baby boom cohorts as they approach retirement chiefly using data on their life cycle income experience to date. Contrary to popular impression, baby boomers are likely to enter old age in an even better economic position than pre-boom cohorts. Economic and demographic adjustments that they made, such as deferred marriages, reduced childbearing, and increased labor force participation of wives, have compensated for their relatively low wage rates. Potential downside effects of reduced childbearing regarding Social Security and health care prospects are discussed. **Key Words:** Economic status, Baby boomers, Demographic adjustments.

This paper assesses, on the basis of experience to date, the economic status of the baby boom cohorts as they approach retirement in the next century. Recent improvement in the economic status of the elderly has received much attention since brought to the fore by Preston (1984). At least part of this improvement has been attributed to the greater accumulated assets and pension rights that have been carried into retirement by recent retirement cohorts (Duncan, Hill, & Rodgers, 1986).

These findings, however, refer only to pre-baby boom cohorts. The question remains: What will be the economic prospects of the baby boom cohorts as they enter old age? A common assumption is that the retirement outlook of baby boom cohorts is poor, because of their Social Security benefit prospects. Longman (1985), addressing the possible future insolvency of the Social Security system, suggests that "unless a number of fundamental trends are soon reversed, the Baby Boomers are headed for a disastrous retirement." In addition to prospective Social Security problems, baby boomers are known to have experienced difficulties in the labor market (Welch, 1979; Lillard & Macunovich, 1989), which seemingly forebode a reduction in personal sources of support compared with their predecessors. Levy and Michel (1986) note that a male born in 1935 gained 118% in average real income passing from age 25 to 35, whereas a male baby boomer born in 1948 gained only 16% during the same 10 years of the life cycle.

The present analysis shows that, contrary to popular impression, the baby boom cohorts, on average, are likely to enter old age in an even better economic position than pre-boom cohorts. This is because economic and demographic adjustments that they have made, such as deferred marriage, reduced childbearing, and increased labor force participation of wives, have compensated for their relatively low wage rates.

Concepts, Data, and Methods

The definition of economic status employed here is designed to take account of the demographic adjustments that people make to influence their economic status. For example, if a cohort is experiencing adverse labor market conditions, more of its members will opt for single status and some of these will turn up in the Bureau of the Census' sample survey as unrelated individuals, a group completely omitted in most comparisons of economic status. (In 1988 among males aged 20–39, over one in five was classified as an unrelated individual; in 1965 only 6% were so classified.) Also, members of such a cohort who form families are likely to decide to have fewer children. In both cases decisions are being made (to postpone or forgo marriage or to have fewer children) with a view to maintaining or improving economic status. If one were to focus only on the family as the unit of study, disregarding size of family and (by definition) excluding unrelated individuals, the role of these decisions in affecting the economic status of a cohort is lost from view.

In the present analysis, the economic status of an individual is defined as the total money income per adult equivalent (adjusted for price level change over time) in the household in which the individual resides. The definition of income is that of the Bureau of Census' Current Population Survey: pretax, post-

We are grateful to Donna Hokoda for excellent assistance, and to Eileen M. Crimmins and Mark Hayward for comments. John Goodman and Nancy McArdle provided helpful information on home ownership rates. Financial support was provided by a Guggenheim fellowship, 1988–89, and the University of Southern California. Address correspondence to: Richard A. Easterlin, Department of Economics, University of Southern California, University Park, Los Angeles, CA 90089-0253.

From *The Gerontologist*, Vol. 30, No. 6, December 1990, pp. 776-783. © 1990 by the Gerontological Society of America.
Reprinted by permission.

transfer money income, including public and private pension income, public assistance, other welfare payments, and alimony and child support payments. Income in kind is excluded. To adjust for price level change over time, the CPI-X1 index is used (for discussion of this index, see U.S. Congressional Budget Office, 1988). The definition of household is also the same as that of the Current Population Survey, except that here, unmarried couple households have been identified whenever possible, and differentiated from other types of households. Unmarried couple households are identified according to the Bureau of Census definition: two unrelated adults 15 years of age or over of the opposite sex living together in a household in which no other adults are present.

Income per adult equivalent (IAE) is computed for each household by dividing the household's total money income by the number of adult equivalents in the household, derived according to Fuchs' scale (1986). The aim of the conversion to a per adult equivalent basis is to obtain a better measure of individual differences in economic status by allowing for variations in household size and adult-child composition, and for economies of scale in consumption. There is evidence that international income comparisons are somewhat sensitive to the equivalence scale adopted (Burkhauser et al., in press). However, we find little effect on inferences about trends based on our adjustment to a per adult equivalent basis compared with the most common alternative, that based on equivalence scales derived from poverty thresholds (Macunovich & Easterlin, 1990, appendix A).

The economic status of an individual is assumed to correspond to the average economic status of the household in which the individual resides. This is similar to the assumption in governmental estimates of the poverty rates of persons, that an individual is in poverty if the family of which one is a member is so classified.

A birth cohort is a group of individuals born in a given year or period. Baby boomers are commonly defined as those born in the period 1946–64. The present analysis includes four 5-year baby boom cohorts, ranging from the leading edge cohort (born 1945–49), to that born at the baby boom peak (1955–59), to the trailing edge cohort (1960–64).

The average economic status of a cohort is measured as the mean value of the IAEs of all of the persons composing that cohort, excluding only those in group quarters. Although this procedure for determining the average status of a cohort may seem obvious, it is not the way that inferences are commonly made about differences by age (or cohort) in the population. This is because age of *head* of household (or family) is typically used as the basis for inferring such variations. It goes almost without saying that an individual of a given age may be living in a household or family headed by a person of a much different age.

The data used here are from the March Current Population Survey (CPS) tapes for quinquennial years 1965 through 1985 plus 1988. Demographic status is measured as of March of the survey year, but income refers to the previous calendar year. The life cycle income profile of a cohort is obtained by linking income averages for appropriate age groups from successive surveys (Table 1). For example, the birth cohort of 1935–39 was 26–30 years old in 1965 (the first survey date), 31–35 years old in 1970, 36–40 years old in 1975, and so on. By linking the income averages for these age groups it is possible to trace the average economic status of the 1935–39 birth cohort as it aged from 26–30 years to 49–53 years in the period of 1965–1988.

The six dates studied here are chosen to span as fully as possible the period for which data are available, and to provide observations at approximately 5-year intervals on each birth cohort. Observations at this frequency should give a representative picture of a cohort's underlying life cycle income trend, with one exception. Fluctuations in the economywide unemployment rate cause deviations from the basic trend. Moreover, these fluctuations, although they affect all age groups, impinge most severely on persons under age 35, the ages for which most of our observations on baby boomers are available. Fortunately, in 4 of the 6 years included here (1964, 1974, 1979, and 1987), the economywide unemployment rate was quite similar, between 5.2% and 6.2%. It was an unusually low 3.5% in 1969 and a relatively high 7.5% in 1984. In the subsequent analysis, we present income profiles both for all six dates and for the four

Table 1. Mean Income Per Adult Equivalent, in 1987 Dollars, by Birth Cohort, 1964–1987

Cohort	Year					
	1964	1969	1974	1979	1984	1987
1915–19	11,398 (45–49)	14,773 (50–54)	15,266 (55–59)	—	—	—
1920–24	10,566 (40–44)	13,935 (45–49)	15,584 (50–54)	16,725 (55–59)	—	—
1925–29	10,297 (35–39)	12,756 (40–44)	14,805 (45–49)	17,028 (50–54)	17,673 (55–59)	—
1930–34	10,173 (30–34)	12,303 (35–39)	13,700 (40–44)	15,863 (45–49)	17,768 (50–54)	18,726 (53–57)
1935–39	9,736 (25–29)	12,315 (30–34)	13,123 (35–39)	14,953 (40–44)	16,955 (45–49)	19,248 (48–52)
1940–44	9,443 (20–24)	12,794 (25–29)	13,977 (30–34)	15,134 (35–39)	16,224 (40–44)	18,525 (43–47)
1945–49	8,246 (15–19)	11,914 (20–24)	13,965 (25–29)	15,643 (30–34)	16,462 (35–39)	17,931 (38–42)
1950–54	—	10,145 (15–19)	12,507 (20–24)	15,346 (25–29)	15,686 (30–34)	17,108 (33–37)
1955–59	—	—	10,775 (15–19)	13,682 (20–24)	15,244 (25–29)	16,533 (28–32)
1960–64	—	—	—	11,487 (15–19)	13,170 (20–24)	15,481 (23–27)

Note. Age of birth cohort shown in parentheses.

5. RETIREMENT: AMERICAN DREAM OR DILEMMA?

dates with similar unemployment rates. Because we are interested in comparing preretirement income status, the profiles are terminated at ages 55–59.

Economic Status and Prospects of the Baby Boomers

Figure 1, based on data for all six dates, presents the life cycle pattern of real mean income per adult equivalent for successive birth cohorts from 1915–19 to 1960–64. For example, the birth cohort of 1935–39 is observed from the point when its average age was 27 and its average income was approximately $10,000 to when it was 50 with an income averaging over $19,000. (All income figures here are expressed in terms of the purchasing power of a dollar in 1987.) Because data are limited, only segments of the experience of each cohort can be observed.

Although the life cycle income trend of each cohort is reasonably apparent in the figure, fluctuations in the economywide unemployment rate, as noted, create fluctuations in the income profiles. These impinge on the various cohorts at different ages, making comparison more difficult.

A clearer picture of the basic income profiles emerges if the 2 years with disparate unemployment rates are omitted (Figure 2). We feel that this figure presents a better representation of each cohort's basic life cycle income trend, and accordingly, base our discussion on it, but the generalizations below would be essentially the same if Figure 1 were used.

The vertical distance between curves can be used to compare the mean income of cohorts at a given age. Thus, vertical comparison of the cohorts at ages 45–49 through 55–59 establishes what is commonly accepted — that those currently retiring, the cohorts of 1925–29 and 1930–34, are better off than their predecessor cohorts. For example, at ages 45–49, real

income per adult equivalent of the birth cohort of 1930–34 averaged 28% higher than that of the birth cohort of 1915–19.

What may come as a surprise to many, however, is that this upward march of economic status continues with the baby boom cohorts. This is shown by the four curves at the left side of the diagram depicting the income profiles of the 1945–49 through 1960–64 birth cohorts. Vertical comparisons of these cohorts with their predecessors reveals that the baby boomers have higher income levels at given ages than pre-boom cohorts. For example, at ages 25–29, the first baby boom cohort (that of 1945–49) averaged an adult equivalent income 44% higher than the pre-boom birth cohort of 1935–39; the peak baby boom cohort, that of 1955–59, averaged 56% higher. A comparison of the magnitude of the upward income shift of the later baby boom cohorts with the earlier ones suggests that the rate of improvement slowed between the leading and trailing edge of the baby boom, but it is still somewhat early in the observation of the youngest cohorts to be sure of this.

The general pattern is that each younger cohort — including the baby boomers — starts out better off than its predecessor, and that this advantage is maintained throughout the life cycle. Assuming that this pattern holds in the future, the implication is that the baby boomers will approach retirement age with higher income per adult equivalent than any prior cohorts. As noted, the improvement of the trailing edge over the leading edge of the baby boom generation is moderate, but taking all four cohorts together, the baby boomers seem well on their way to higher income levels than their predecessors. It is noteworthy that by 1987 the baby boomers, ranging in age from 23 to 42, had reached income levels of $16,000 to $18,000, about the same as those achieved

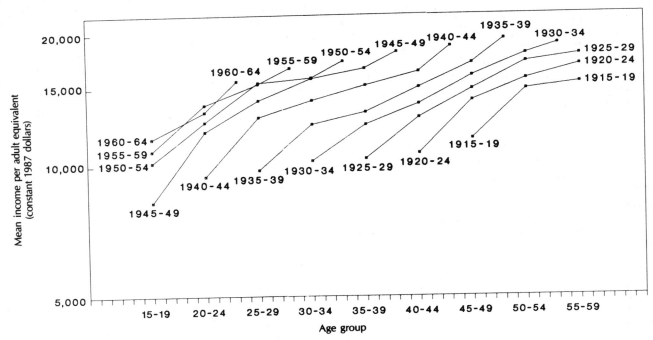

Figure 1. Mean income per adult equivalent: Life cycle profiles for 5-year birth cohorts 1915–19 to 1960–64.

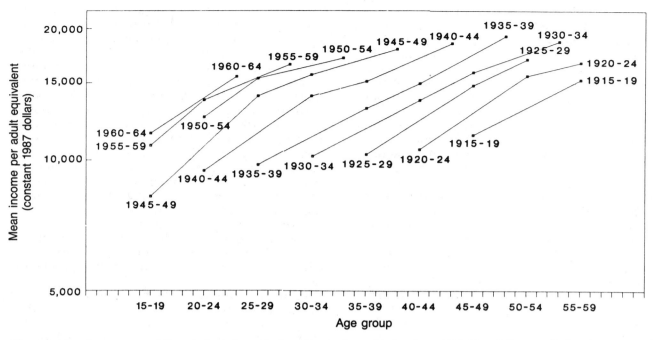

Figure 2. Mean income per adult equivalent: Smoothed profiles for 5-year birth cohorts 1915–19 to 1960–64 (excludes observations for 1969, 1984).

in their middle and late fifties by the currently retiring cohorts of 1920–24 through 1930–34 (Table 1).

The present analysis deals only with average economic status, and does not discuss income distribution. It is possible that the baby boom generation might reach retirement with a higher average income than its predecessors, but also greater inequality, and consequently a more severe problem of supporting the elderly poor. We can at present only note this possibility. Although there have been valuable general studies of income distribution (Danziger & Gottschalk, 1987; Levy, 1987) and cross-sectional analyses of age groups (Crystal, 1986; Crystal & Shea, 1990; Radner, 1987; Smeeding, Torrey, & Rein, 1987), the measurement and projection of income inequality as cohorts move through the life cycle is a virtually untouched topic of research. Studies based on panel data come closest to doing this, but these are typically confined to fairly short periods, provide less than comprehensive coverage of the population, and do not use overall measures of income inequality (see Burkhauser et al., 1985; Burkhauser & Duncan, 1988). We hope to say more on this at some future time.

Returning to the subject of average economic status, we cannot be sure, of course, that the better average income status of the baby boomers will translate into a better economic position at retirement. But one indication that this will be so is the substantial private and public employee pension coverage of baby boomers. In 1984 among wage and salary workers, pension coverage of the leading edge of the baby boom generation was virtually the same as that of older cohorts — somewhat over 70% — and coverage of the later baby boom cohorts was only 5–10 percentage points less, despite the comparative recency of their entry into the labor force (Table 2, column 3).

Table 2. Pension Coverage and Vesting Rate of Wage and Salary Workers Aged 25 + Years, by Age, 1984

Age	Period of birth	% of workers covered by a pension plan	% of covered workers that are vested
All workers, 25 +		67.1	67.3
25–29	1955–59	60.4	47.4
30–34	1950–54	65.9	61.4
35–39	1945–49	70.8	67.2
40–44	1940–44	72.1	72.4
45–49	1935–39	72.0	78.4
50–54	1930–34	70.1	81.7
55–59	1925–29	72.3	81.8
60–64	1920–24	63.4	79.5

Source. U.S. Bureau of the Census (1987).

Although vesting rates for the baby boom cohorts were somewhat less than for older cohorts, this was due to their shorter tenure in the labor force and hence their lessened opportunity to satisfy the usual vesting requirement of 10 years with one's current employer (column 4). (Similar differentials by age to those in columns 3 and 4 are shown in Andrews, 1985, though at slightly lower levels.) It is reasonable to assume that the vesting rates for the baby boomers will rise as they age. Indeed, given the substantially greater labor force participation of females among the baby boom generation, it is quite possible that as the baby boomers approach retirement age, both their coverage and vesting rates will be higher than for those currently approaching retirement. This assumes, of course, that major changes in employer policies regarding provision of pension benefits are not in store. (Predicting such changes and their effects would be a project in itself. Ongoing developments are working in opposing directions — e.g., vesting after 5 rather than 10 years versus the shift from defined benefit to defined contribution plans.) It is also pertinent to note that a recent study (Ferraro, 1990) found an unexpectedly high increase between 1974 and 1981 in retirement preparation activities of the baby boom cohort of 1950–56 compared with pre-baby boom cohorts.

Turning to other assets, it is widely believed that the baby boomers have suffered in terms of home ownership as a result of high interest rates and rising home prices. It is true that home ownership rates fell noticeably between 1977 and 1983, the period when interest rates soared to new post-World War II highs, although the impact of this was felt by all age groups, both baby boom and pre-boom (Avery, Elliehausen, & Canner, 1984). Even so, the baby boomers' home ownership percentage is not much less than that of their predecessors. The following compares the home ownership rate among persons aged 25–34 in 1986 (the baby boom cohort born 1952–61) with that of the corresponding age group 16 and 21 years earlier (the pre-boom cohorts born 1936–45 and 1931–40):

	Date of observation	Percentage owning own home
Baby boomers	1986	42.9
Pre-boomers	1970	48.0
	1965	47.0

(The figures for the pre-boomers are from Durkin & Elliehausen, 1978; for the baby boomers, the figure was supplied by Nancy McArdle, Harvard University Joint Center for Housing Studies, from the 1986 Federal Reserve data tape.) Moreover, the lower figure for the baby boomers is at least partly due to their different demographic mix. As shown in the next section, there is a markedly smaller proportion of married couples with children among baby boomers, and home ownership rates for this group average about twice as high as for others (Avery, Elliehausen, & Canner, 1984). In the absence of a return to the extremely high interest rates of the early 1980s, it seems reasonable to suppose that given their relatively favorable income per adult equivalent, baby boomers' home ownership rates will in time equal or exceed those of their predecessors.

Our data also provide a hint that baby boomers have, to some extent, accumulated more financial assets than their predecessors. Although we do not have information on the CPS tapes on assets as such, we do have data on the income generated by such assets — interest, dividends, and rents — commonly termed property income. The following compares the percentage reporting more than $1,000 property income (in 1987 prices) among persons aged 30–34 in 1987 (the baby boom cohort born 1953–57) with that of the corresponding age group 18 years earlier (the pre-boom birth cohort of 1935–39):

	Date of observation	Percentage with property income
Baby boomers	1987	7.9
Pre-boomers	1969	3.6

For both cohorts the percentages shown are certainly too low (only about 45% of property income is reported in the CPS), but the higher percentage of baby boomers with property income does not reflect a trend toward better reporting. Estimates of underreporting for 1972 and 1983 yield virtually identical figures (U.S. Bureau of the Census, 1973, 1989a). However, the higher percentage for the baby boomers does partly reflect a higher return on assets (for the baby boomers, long-term interest rates were about 30% higher, although short-term money market rates were moderately lower). If, to adjust for this, we raise (generously) the property income cutoff for the baby boomers from $1,000 to $1,300, the figure for the baby boomers falls from 7.9% to 6.9% still considerably higher than the 3.6% figure of the pre-boom group. This differential is probably a reasonable indication of the greater extent of substantial financial asset ownership among the baby boomers.

Although more needs to be done to clarify the comparative picture of baby boomers versus their predecessors with regard to asset acquisition, the figures above on pensions, home ownership, and property income seem reasonably consistent with the inferences from the income data drawn here. The prospect is that in comparison with those currently retiring, baby boomers approaching retirement age will have higher incomes and as good or better private and public pension coverage, home ownership rates, and financial asset holdings.

In a recent study of the prospective cost of caring for the disabled elderly, the underlying projections of income and assets, based on an elaborate simulation technique, yield conclusions very similar to ours. Comparing persons 65–74 in 2016–20 (the leading edge of the baby boom) with those 65–74 in 1986–90, median family income and median family assets (adjusted for changing prices) are projected, respectively, to be 115% and 39% higher (Rivlin & Wiener 1988). The estimates here of IAE put the 10-year birth cohort at the leading edge of the baby boom roughly 85% ahead of their predecessors 30 years ago. (This estimate is obtained from Table 1 by combining the average difference between the baby boom cohort and its predecessor 20 years earlier with the average difference between the latter and its predecessor 10 years earlier.) If this differential were to persist, our figures would thus yield a somewhat more conservative estimate than Rivlin and Wiener's (1988) of the improvement in real income for the baby boomers: 85% versus 115%.

How Baby Boomers Have Done It

How have the baby boom cohorts been able to improve their economic position, despite their comparatively adverse labor market conditions? The answer is primarily by a variety of demographic and economic adjustments that have compensated for their adverse wage and unemployment rates.

Although we cannot enter into a detailed analysis here, the contrasts between the baby boomers and pre-boom cohorts can be easily demonstrated (see also Easterlin, 1987). To illustrate, we take for comparison the baby boom cohort of 1950–54 and the pre-boom cohort of 1935–39 at the time when each was 26–30 years old; these two cohorts provide a fairly representative contrast between the baby boomers and their predecessors.

The first point of note is the marked decline in the proportion of baby boomers that are members of married couple, two-parent families, from 73% to 48% (Table 3, columns 1 and 2). Of this 25 percentage point decline, four-fifths is accounted for by a shift to childless living arrangements; the remainder, by a rise of those in single-parent situations.

The implications of this demographic shift for the economic status of the baby boomers is apparent when one considers how income per adult equivalent varies by demographic status (Table 3, columns 3 through 6). In both cohorts, childless persons' income averaged about 55% higher than that of persons in married couple, two-parent families, whereas that of single parents averaged about one-quarter lower (columns 5 and 6). Although the demographic shifts of baby boomers involve movements toward both higher and lower income situations, the shift toward the higher income situation (that of childless persons) has been dominant in affecting the baby boomers' average income. There are two reasons for this. First, the magnitude of the demographic shift to the higher income situation is much greater. Second, the income gap between the higher income and traditional married couple, two-parent situation is

greater than that on the lower income side. Thus, the baby boomers have, on balance, improved their economic status by avoiding parenthood, and opting for childless living arrangements. These childless situations embrace a variety of circumstances, all of which have increased in relative importance: forming a single-person household, living with one's parents or with others, or forming a childless marital or nonmarital union.

Two other devices may be noted by which the baby boomers have improved their economic status compared with their predecessors. First, among families with children, the average number of children has been reduced by 0.5 children, from 2.4 to 1.9 (Table 4, columns 1 and 2). This means that there are fewer claimants among whom a given family income needs to be shared. Second, in married couple, two-parent families, there has been a rise in the number of earners per household (Table 4, columns 3 and 4). (In single-parent families, earners per household declined, but a disproportionately large decline in children per household tended to offset this.) Thus, aside from the changes in Table 3, baby boomers have improved their economic status by reducing household size and, to some extent, by increasing earners per household.

Because demographic factors have played an important role to date in the economic advance of the baby boom generation, it is important to consider their likely impact in the future. Although baby boomers have had unusually low fertility before age 30, childbearing rates for women over 30 have been

Table 3. Cohorts of 1935–39 and 1950–54 at Ages 26–30: Percentage Distribution and Income Per Adult Equivalent by Presence of Children, Type of Union, and Living Arrangements

| Persons | % distribution | | Income per adult equivalent | | | |
| | | | Amount (1987 dollars) | | Index[a] | |
	1935–39 cohort	1950–54 cohort	1935–39 cohort	1950–54 cohort	1935–39 cohort	1950–54 cohort
All persons	100	100	9,736	15,346	110	119
Childless persons	20	40	14,070	19,999	159	155
Not in union						
Single-person household	3	9	14,923	20,205	168	157
Living in parents' household	5	6	11,545	16,776	130	130
Living with others	3	6	13,967	19,292	158	150
In union						
Married	10[b]	16	14,990	21,507	169[b]	167
Unmarried	—[c]	3	—[c]	18,980	—[c]	171
Persons in married couple, two-parent families	73	48	8,862	12,888	100	100
Persons in single-parent families	7	11	6,497	9,343	73	73
Male single parent in own or other household	—[c]	3	—[c]	11,484	—[c]	89
Male or female single parent in unmarried couple	—[c] } 4	1	—[c] } 7,883	12,006	—[c] } 89	93
Female single parent in parents' or other household	—[c]	2	—[c]	10,420	—[c]	81
Female single parent in own household	3	5	4,277	7,246	48	56

Note. Detail may not add to total because of rounding.

[a]Married couple, two-parent families = 100.

[b]Includes a small number of unmarried couples.

[c]Sample size less than 100.

Table 4. Cohorts of 1935–39 and 1950–54 at Ages 26–30: Mean Number of Children under 18 Years Old Per Household and Mean Number of Earners Per Household by Presence of Children and Type of Union

Persons	Children per household		Earners per household	
	1935–39 cohort	1950–54 cohort	1935–39 cohort	1950–54 cohort
All persons	1.94	1.14	1.54	1.74
Childless persons	0.00	0.00	1.82	1.82
Persons in married couple, two-parent families	2.40	1.90	1.43	1.68
Persons in single-parent families	2.64	1.91	1.90	1.66

rising in recent years. If this catching up were to push the baby boomers to an average completed family size as great as that of their predecessors, then the prior advantageous economic effect of their low fertility would, in time, be negated. In fact, however, survey evidence on fertility expectations indicates that the completed fertility of baby boomers will fall far short of their predecessors. For the baby boom cohorts, expectation of completed family size averages in the neighborhood of two children, compared with three for their predecessors (U.S. Bureau of the Census, 1981, 1988). Similarly, a reversal in female labor force participation rates that would adversely affect the economic status of the baby boomers seems unlikely. Projections to the year 2000 foresee rates for the baby boomers above those of their predecessors (U.S. Bureau of the Census, 1989b). The lower fertility expectations of the baby boomers, and hence reduced child care burden, is, of course, consistent with higher female labor force participation.

One demographic change in prospect, however, will work against the baby boomers. The lower fertility of the baby boomers means that as they approach retirement they will receive less of a boost to their personal economic status than their predecessors did as a result of children moving out of the family household. Although in itself this would somewhat flatten the income profiles of baby boomers relative to their predecessors as they move toward retirement ages, it is likely to be countered in part by a comparatively favorable effect relative to prior cohorts from the trend in female labor force participation.

Discussion and Conclusions

Most analysts, in addressing the retirement prospects of the baby boom generation, focus on the Social Security system and its role in dictating the baby boomers' future economic situation. This perspective, though important and relevant, disregards the potential contribution of the baby boomers' personal income experience to their retirement status. This paper seeks to complement the usual analysis by filling this void.

The present analysis shows that, on the basis of experience to date, the baby boom cohorts, on average, are likely to enter old age in substantially better economic position than pre-boom cohorts. Despite relatively adverse labor market conditions, baby boomers have improved their economic status rela-

tive to pre-boom cohorts by economic and demographic adjustments that have more than compensated for labor market difficulties. Relative to pre-boom cohorts, more baby boomers have remained single, they have reduced childbearing, and females in this cohort have higher rates of labor force participation. These developments have substantially outweighed the one adverse demographic change, the relative growth of single-parent families, and had a sizable net beneficial impact on the economic status of the baby boom cohorts as a whole.

Several caveats are in order. First, the demographic adjustments just mentioned — particularly childlessness and low fertility — might be argued to have a potential downside effect. Concerns about the Social Security and health care prospects of the baby boomers derive directly from the fact that their low fertility implies that when they retire there will be a relatively low ratio of the working age to older dependent population. Moreover, fewer children means less opportunity for informal family care of the elderly and hence greater need for formal care.

Our intention is not to dismiss such concerns, but to provide a corrective by pointing to the positive effects of low fertility on the personal economic status of the baby boomers. However, it is worth pointing out that if one credits the present demographic projections, they imply not only greater old age dependency, but also a historic low in youth dependency when the baby boomers retire. If one considers the *total* dependency rate, taking account of both young and old, the prospect is that this rate will be below its historic high when the baby boomers retire. Thus it is possible that the ability of the working age population to shoulder the burden of higher taxes to support programs for older dependents will be greater than is often assumed, because of reduced needs to support younger dependents. A continued uptrend in female labor force participation may also help offset the projected rise in old age dependency (see Easterlin, 1988; United Nations, 1988, for further discussion of these points).

Second, our analysis has focused on the average economic status of baby boomers, poor and non-poor alike. As mentioned, it is possible that the baby boom generation might reach retirement with higher average income than its predecessors, but also with greater income inequality. Moreover, if those in the lower end of the income distribution were differentially affected by high housing prices and high interest rates, the problem of the elderly poor would be exacerbated by disproportionately low home ownership. Clearly for policy purposes, one needs to attend not only to averages, but to distributional considerations as well.

Finally, the present analysis has addressed only the prospective economic status of the baby boomers. Economic status does not, of course, measure total welfare, though it is one component of welfare. As suggested, family considerations — the formation of a union or having a child — may be sacrificed in the interest of economic status, but such sacrifices certainly affect an individual's sense of total well-being. Moreover, such sacrifices carry over into retirement in that there will be fewer (or no) children to provide companionship and similar types of support for elderly persons. Concern about this is certainly relevant to assessing the overall well-being of baby boomers in retirement. This paper, however, is directed toward the concern foremost in the literature, the economic prospects of the baby boomers, and, on this score, the outlook seems more favorable than is commonly assumed.

References

Andrews, E. S. (1985). *The changing profile of pensions in America,* Washington, DC: Employee Benefit Research Institute.

Avery, R. B., Elliehausen, G. E., & Canner, G. B. (1984, September). Survey of consumer finances, 1983. *Federal Reserve Bulletin.*

Burkhauser, R. V., Butler, J. S., & Wilkinson, J. T. (1985). Estimating changes in well-being across life: A realized versus comprehensive income approach. In M. David & T. Smeeding (Eds.), *Horizontal equity, uncertainty, and economic well-being* (pp. 69–87). Chicago: University of Chicago Press.

Burkhauser, R. V., & Duncan, G. J. (1988). Life events, public policy, and the economic vulnerability of children and the elderly. In J. L. Palmer, T. Smeeding, & B. Boyle Torrey (Eds.), *The vulnerable* (pp. 55–88). Washington, DC: Urban Institute Press.

Burkhauser, R. V., Duncan, G. J., Hauser, R., & Berntsen, R. (in press). Economic burdens of marital disruptions: A comparison of the United States and the Federal Republic of Germany. *Review of Income and Wealth.*

Crystal, S. (1986). Measuring income and inequality among the elderly. *The Gerontologist, 26,* 56–59.

Crystal, S., & Shea, D. (1990). Cumulative advantage, cumulative disadvantage, and inequality among elderly people. *The Gerontologist, 30,* 437–443.

Danziger, S., & Gottschalk, P. (1987). Earnings inequality, the spatial concentration of poverty, and the underclass. *American Economic Review, 77,* 211–215.

Duncan, G. J., Hill, M., & Rodgers, W. (1986). The changing fortunes of young and old. *American Demographics,* August, 26–33.

Durkin, T. A., & Elliehausen, G. E. (1978). *1977 Consumer Credit Survey.* Washington, DC: Board of Governors of the Federal Reserve System.

Easterlin, R. A. (1987). *Birth and fortune* (2nd ed.). Chicago: University of Chicago Press.

Easterlin, R. A. (1988, December). Population and the European economy: Making mountains out of molehills? Paper presented at the Symposium on Population and European Society at the European University Institute, Florence, Italy.

Ferraro, K. F. (1990). Cohort analysis of retirement preparation, 1974–1981. *Journal of Gerontology, 45,* 521–531.

Fuchs, V. (1986). Sex differences in economic well-being. *Science, 232,* 459–464.

Kingson, E. R. (1988). Generational equity: An unexpected opportunity to broaden the politics of aging. *The Gerontologist, 28,* 765–772.

Levy, F. S. (1987). *Dollars and dreams: The changing American income distribution.* New York: Russell Sage Foundation.

Levy, F. S., & Michel, R. C. (1986). An economic bust for the baby boom. *Challenge,* March–April, 33–39.

Lillard, L. A., & Macunovich, D. J. (1989). Why the baby bust cohorts haven't boomed yet: A reconsideration of cohort variables in labor market analyses. Paper presented at the annual meeting of the Population Association of America, Baltimore.

Longman, P. (1985). Justice between generations. *The Atlantic Monthly,* June, 73–81.

Macunovich, D. J., & Easterlin, R. A. (1990). How parents have coped: The effect of life cycle demographic decisions on the economic status of pre-school age children, 1964–1987. *Population and Development Review, 16*(2), 299–323.

Preston, S. (1984). Children and the elderly: Divergent paths for America's dependents. *Demography, 21*(4), 435–457.

Radner, D. B. (1987). Money incomes of aged and nonaged family units, 1967–84. *Social Security Bulletin, 50*(8), 9–28.

Rivlin, A. M., & Wiener, J. M. (1988). *Caring for the disabled elderly: Who will pay?* Washington, DC: The Brookings Institution.

Smeeding, T., Torrey, B. B., & Rein, M. (1987). Comparative well-being of children and elderly. *Contemporary Policy Issues,* April, 57–72.

United Nations (1988). *Economic and social implications of population aging.* New York: Author.

U.S. Bureau of the Census (1973). *Current population reports,* Series P-60, No. 90, December. Washington, DC: U.S. Government Printing Office.

U.S. Bureau of the Census (1981). *Fertility of American women, June 1981, Current Population Reports,* Series P-20, No. 378. Washington, DC: U.S. Government Printing Office.

U.S. Bureau of the Census (1987). *Pensions: Worker coverage and retirement benefits. Current Population Reports,* Series P-70, No. 12. Washington, DC: U.S. Government Printing Office.

U.S. Bureau of the Census (1988). *Fertility of American women, June 1988. Current Population Reports,* Series P-20, No. 436. Washington, DC: U.S. Government Printing Office.

U.S. Bureau of the Census (1989a). *Current Population Reports,* Series P-60, No. 166, October. Washington, DC: U.S. Government Printing Office.

U.S. Bureau of the Census (1989b). *Statistical Abstract of the United States, 1989.* Washington, DC: U.S. Government Printing Office.

U.S. Congressional Budget Office (1988). *Trends in family income, 1970–1986.* Washington, DC: U.S. Government Printing Office.

Welch, F. (1979). Effects of cohort size on earnings: The baby boom babies' financial bust. *Journal of Political Economy, 87*(5), 565–596.

School Days for Seniors

Retirees are flocking to college, eager to learn

Even before he retired from his job as a securities broker in 1984, Mac Gibbons knew he wanted to learn more history. "I had traveled all my adult life, and everywhere I went, I was amazed by how little I knew," he says. Gibbons knew he wouldn't have the discipline to read history books on his own, so when he heard about a Yale program allowing alumni to attend classes, he headed back to his alma mater. At 67, Gibbons is now in his fifth fall term of his second Yale career, auditing art-history classes and taking history courses for credit. He has studied Tudor England, the Age of Augustus and Periclean Athens, driving to New Haven once a week from his home in Greenwich. "I take notes like mad. I work my tail off. And I've made more friends than in any period of my life, all of them about 20 years old," he says. This time around, he has earned straight A's.

More and more retirees like Gibbons are going back to college, hitting the books instead of the golf links. In 1989, the Census Bureau's latest count, some 320,000 Americans age 50 and over were enrolled in college courses—including more than 65,000 at the graduate and professional levels. Thousands more are auditing classes, forming retiree study groups, attending university lectures and joining study-travel programs. The back-to-school boom has even turned some college towns into new retirement meccas. "My name for Oberlin is Shangri-La in the fast lane," says Betty Gabrielli, a spokeswoman for the college where a continuing-care retirement community may be built next spring (see box).

A few older learners are preparing for late-life career changes; some are earning college degrees for the first time. But the vast majority are drawn back to school for the sheer joy of learning. "I've never had so much fun," says Daniel Wynkoop, 86, who finally received his Yale degree last year—65 years after he was expelled for getting married in 1925. He lived on campus and was a bit taken aback by the coed bathrooms, though he says, "At my age, these things become less important. You're more concerned about standing up."

Growth market: Attending classes can also help fill the void left by a deceased spouse, grown children or retiring from the working world. "If you've been running all your life, you don't just suddenly stop," says Roxana Arsht, 76, a former judge who has been a major benefactor of the University of Delaware. "I live alone with a small dog and he talks only dog language. So much is happening in the world that I'm dying to talk to someone about it," says 89-year-old Madeline Rubin, who began auditing courses at the University of Massachusetts at Amherst in her 70s. Once they begin taking classes, many older students find they want to keep going. Midori Arima was a bored California homemaker dabbling in community-college courses when she began to study anthropology. Last June, at 66, she received her Ph.D. from Stanford.

For colleges and universities, older students represent a new growth market when the pool of younger students is shrinking. Many have opened undergraduate classes to older people on a space-available basis. Boston University's Evergreen Program allows any intellectually curious senior to audit courses—for $15 each—regardless of his or her educational background. A record 500 are taking part this fall. Some states require public universities and colleges to waive tuition and fees for elderly residents who want to take courses.

Increasingly, universities are designing whole divisions for adult learners. Stanford's three-year-old Continuing Studies program is theoretically open to anyone with a high-school degree or equivalent. But many of its 700 students are elderly college grads, lured by the rich offering of 60 night courses—from the History of Jazz to Genetics and Disease—taught by Stanford faculty members. They find teaching older learners refreshing. "I don't mean to denigrate Stanford students, but it *is* a joy to look out at an audience and see them hanging on every word," biological-sciences professor Craig

Heller told the Stanford News. This fall, Stanford began offering a five-year Master of Liberal Arts degree to part-time adult students. More than 85 applicants, many of them elderly, competed for the first 20 spaces. "A few people wrote about how they couldn't wait for their grandchildren to see them march down the aisle to get their diploma," says associate dean of Continuing Studies Jeff Wechtal.

Some of the fastest-growing programs are "Learning in Retirement" study groups tailored specifically to older students. Members pay an annual fee and design their own courses, recruiting instructors from among their ranks. The concept was pioneered by the New School for Social Research in New York in 1962. Some 161 LIR programs are now offered nationwide, mostly under university auspices. Harvard's Institute for Learning in Retirement, for example, has 430 members in 49 study groups. The chance to learn with fellow retirees is a key attraction. "They may be interested in World War II, but they want to discuss it with other people who lived through it, not with some 18-year-olds for whom it is ancient history," says University of Delaware associate provost Richard Fischer.

Delaware's "Academy of Lifelong Learning" is one of the largest LIR programs. This year, some 1,400 students 55 and over are participating in 110 courses. The academy has its own plush new $6 million building on the Wilmington campus; classrooms are wheelchair accessible and feature enhanced lighting and PA systems. Many of the member/instructors are retired professionals, but they often teach their avocations instead. A retired chemical engineer leads the class on mythologies of the Middle East; a jewelry-store owner teaches a survey of Broadway musicals. There are no grades or exams, yet the courses are demanding and discussions can be electric. "Here we're searching for understanding, not to please some professor," says Roberta Brown, 56.

Some LIR programs are highly selective. UCLA's 375-member PLATO Society (for Perpetual Learning And Teaching Organization) has a waiting list; members must have at least 20 years' work experience and are expected to give dissertation-style presentations in classes of graduate-level quality. The 152 members of the Academy of Senior Professionals at Eckerd College in St. Petersburg, Fla., include former governors, congressmen and ambassadors, as well as retired physicians, lawyers and business leaders. They serve as mentors to Eckerd undergraduates and assist in teaching two required undergraduate courses. Mostly, though, the lively retirees relish each other's company as they pursue eclectic interests. A former periodontist leads the study group on opera. "For years he looked into people's mouths—but his heart was in opera," says ASPEC's executive director, Art Peterson. Last year five members—none with construction experience—built an ultra-light plane from a kit. Flying the one-seater doesn't require a license—just the ticket for amateur pilots who have had heart attacks and can't qualify to ferry passengers. "It's the first plane in our silver-hair force," says Peterson.

No grades: Still another option for intellectually curious older people is Elderhostel. The Boston-based, nonprofit education network, founded in 1975, offers one-to-four-week study programs at more than 1,600

A New Breed of Retirement Community

It's just after lunch and the Green Hills bus is filling up with riders. Vilas Morford, 91, sits near the front, Margaret Davidson, 84, takes a seat across the aisle. Then come Waldo and Katie Wegner, both 78, Bill Thompson, 82, Ruth Hamilton, 77, and Virjama Hamilton, 75. You might assume they were bound for a geriatric clinic, but you'd be wrong. It's a fall Saturday at a Big Eight university and that can only mean football. The Green Hills delegation is heading to watch their beloved Iowa State Cyclones take on the Oklahoma Sooners—and it's only the first campus-related activity of the day. Tonight, many of these folks will be back on the bus to take in an opera—Mozart's "Magic Flute"—at Iowa State's C.Y. Stephens auditorium.

Green Hills is one of a new breed of retirement communities being built on or near college campuses. Last month, the Marriott Corp. dedicated the Colonnades at the University of Virginia in Charlottesville. The nonprofit Kendal Corp. opened Kendal at Hanover near Dartmouth in July, and hopes to break ground for Kendal at Oberlin next year. Plans are in the works for more Kendal facilities near Lehigh and Cornell. Some such communities were initiated by university officials; others have no formal link to the schools beyond attracting alumni and retired faculty as residents. Even so, universities generally welcome their presence. "It can have a positive impact on alumni giving," says Bob Wheeler, president of the firm that runs Meadowood, near the University of Indiana at Bloomington. And for residents, "it's like an ongoing college reunion."

The relationships have other advantages, too. U. Va. medical and nursing students can train at the Colonnades's nursing-care center, and the new Center on Aging will have a source of volunteers for research projects. In turn residents have access to classes, concerts, libraries and research facilities. The bustle of campus activities is helping the Colonnades attract a far younger clientele than ordinary life-care communities.

At Green Hills, 76-year-old Kenneth Carlander often walks by the house he and his wife once owned on his way to the office the former zoology and fishery professor still maintains at ISU. "Many of our friends thought we were giving up too early to move into a place like this," he says. "But we know too many people who waited too long."

PATRICK HOUSTON *at Green Hill and bureau reports*

colleges and other educational institutions in the United States and 43 foreign countries. Elderhostelers live on campus and attend classes provided by the host school. "It's a concentrated dose of what it's like to be a college student"—without homework or grades, says spokeswoman Cady Goldfield. Elderhostel expects an enrollment of some 235,000 this year in courses such as "History and Culture of the Shenandoah Valley" at Mary Baldwin College in Virginia and "Humans and the Sea" at the University of Southern California at Santa Catalina Island. More adventurous learners can go trekking in Nepal while studying the culture of the Sherpas.

Studies have repeatedly shown that the more education people have, the more they want. Even further opportunities for extended learning will soon be needed. The first baby boomers will begin to retire by the end of this decade, and with longer life expectancy, many will have 25 or more years in which to pursue studies. Some may one day attend classes via video and computer links—continuing to learn even from their hospital beds, savoring new fields that keep their minds young.

MELINDA BECK *with* DANIEL GLICK *in Wilmington,* JEANNE GORDON *in Los Angeles and* LAUREN PICKER *in Boston*

Rethinking Retirement

SUMMARY   Since 1950, the average retirement age has declined from 67 to 63. Baby boomers want to retire even sooner, but can they afford it? One-third of retirees now return to work within a year. Retirement decisions depend on many factors, including pensions, savings, disability, job satisfaction, and social attitudes. All these and more will affect the boomers' ultimate quitting time.

Paula Mergenhagen

Paula Mergenhagen is a sociologist and researcher in Nashville, Tennessee. This article is adapted from her book, Targeting Transitions: Marketing to Consumers During Life Changes *(American Demographics Books, 1994).*

Before he retired in 1985, Gleason Pebley searched the Southeast for the perfect spot. At age 55, after 30 years in management positions with AT&T, Pebley and his wife left Basking Ridge, New Jersey, for Cookeville, Tennessee, population 24,000 in 1992.

Pebley isn't like most retirees for two reasons: 83 percent of 55-year-olds are still in the labor force, and only a small proportion of adults relocate when they retire. But he represents the well-established trends of early retirement and affluence in the mature market. Between the periods 1950-55 and 1985-90, the median retirement age dropped from 67 to 63.

Can baby boomers continue these trends? Although the majority of boomers say they would like to retire by age 60, many of them won't be able to afford it. Others will rejoin the labor force after they find that retirement isn't as enjoyable or as inexpensive as they had imagined.

At the turn of the century, the average American's life expectancy wasn't quite 50 years. As a result, most people never retired. Now, retirement can last 20 years or more, and a number of factors influence a person's decision to leave work. The most important are economic factors, such as the availability of pensions and Social Security benefits. Yet health, occupation, and social conventions also play important roles.

Men have traditionally been the breadwinners, so the husband's resources have steered most retirement decisions. But women will be a greater factor in the future, because many baby-boom women will enjoy full-fledged pensions of their own.

Trends in retirement age are important for several reasons. Retirees are a prime market for many products and services, including travel, health care, and new homes. People on the verge of retirement also buy services that can help prepare them financially and emotionally for this important transition. As baby boomers decide to retire, they will create huge markets for financial planners and retirement counselors.

ONE-THIRD RETURN

About 14 million men and 22 million women aged 55 and older are not in the labor force, according to 1993 data from the Bureau of Labor Statistics (BLS). Among those under age 60, 22 percent of men and 43 percent of women are not in the labor force. At ages 60 to 64, the shares increase to 49 percent of men and 63 percent of women. And among those

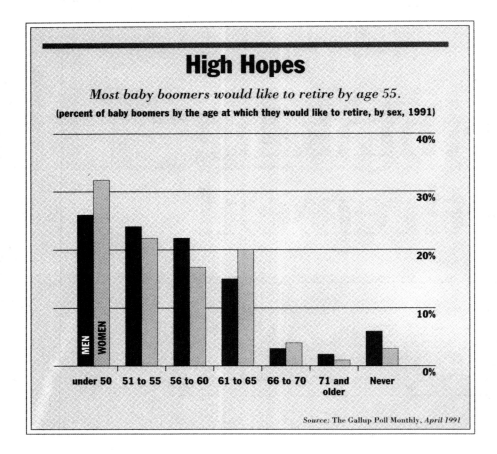

High Hopes

Most baby boomers would like to retire by age 55.

(percent of baby boomers by the age at which they would like to retire, by sex, 1991)

Source: The Gallup Poll Monthly, *April 1991*

income receive some of their income from a company, union, or government pension, according to the 1992 Current Population Survey. So do 13 percent of men and 5 percent of women aged 45 to 64.

Starting in the 1970s, employers began providing incentives for early retirement by making pensions and other benefits available before age 65. In 1974, about one-half of individuals participating in employer pension plans could receive some benefits prior to age 65. By 1989, this proportion had reached three-fifths, according to the BLS. One analysis suggests that men who are eligible for full pension benefits before age 65 are nearly twice as likely as other men to retire early.

The retirement-buyout trend became pervasive during the recent recession. In 1992, 38 percent of early retirements from large companies were the result of early-retirement incentive offers. This proportion was 26 percent only two years earlier, according to a survey of primarily

aged 65 to 69, 75 percent of men and 84 percent of women aren't part of the labor force. At age 70 and older, the share reaches 90 percent of men and 95 percent of women.

> **Retirees are a prime market for many products and services, including travel, health care, and new homes.**

These labor force participation rates are not a perfect measure of permanent withdrawal from the labor force. Many older adults who don't work will eventually return to other full- or part-time jobs. Some find that their retirement benefits do not sustain their lifestyle. Others miss the structure and social interaction that a job provides.

Mark Hayward, a sociologist at Pennsylvania State University, and his colleagues tracked a group of retired men over 17 years. They found that almost one-

third of the men returned to work at some point, and most returnees came back in the first year after retirement. Professionals, salesworkers, farm laborers, and self-employed individuals were most likely to return to work, as were younger retirees. Over two-thirds of returnees took full-time jobs.

If retirement is defined as permanent withdrawal from the labor force, then an average of 1.3 million individuals retired each year between 1985 and 1990, according to Georgetown University senior research scholar Jacob Siegel. Today, the median age of retirement is about 63 for both men and women, according to research by Siegel and colleague Murray Gendell. During the early 1950s, the retirement age was about 67 for men and 68 for women.

"A person's readiness to retire is prompted by the receipt of a private pension," says Siegel. Such pensions have become more widespread over the years. About 49 percent of men and 22 percent of women aged 65 and older who have

> **Advances in pensions and Social Security account for about half of the decrease in retirement age.**

large employers by Charles D. Spencer and Associates of Chicago. Corporations seeking to cut their payrolls are pushing early retirement as a more humane alternative to mass layoffs. So far, workers seem eager to accept.

Almost 6 percent of retirement-age employees receive special early-retirement "window" offers, and 36 percent accept them, according to a 1992 random survey of retirement-age adults analyzed by University of Michigan economist Charles Brown. Employees who receive such offers are most likely to be managers and to work for large firms in high-wage industries. "Age 51 is clearly not 'too young' to get such an offer," writes Brown, "and 61 is not near enough to normal retirement to discourage special efforts by employers."

Early retirement got another boost when Social Security benefits were substantially increased in the 1970s. Moreover, these benefits were protected from inflation because future increases were automatically linked to the Consumer Price Index. "Older workers who had planned retirement based on real benefits prevailing during the 1960s must have been surprised by their new wealth. Given their nearness to retirement, the realization that substantially higher benefits awaited them than they had counted on may have influenced many to retire early," writes Richard Ippolito, chief economist with Pensions Benefit Guaranty Corporation in Washington, D.C.

Over 90 percent of the labor force is covered by the Social Security retirement system, with partial benefits available at age 62 and full benefits at age 65. In 1993, 14 million men and 20 million women aged 62 and older were receiving Social Security benefits.

PENSIONS AND SAVINGS

Advances in pensions and Social Security account for about half of the decrease in retirement age between 1970 and the mid-1980s, according to Ippolito. But the trend toward earlier retirement is leveling off. Between the periods 1980-85 and 1990-95, the median age of retirement is expected to hover around 63. Based on BLS employment projections, Gendell and Siegel say that retirement age will then resume its decline and dip below 62 between 2000 and 2005.

Not all researchers agree with them. "The retirement age is constant now. If anything, it will go up a bit because there has been a major change in government policy," says Syracuse University economist Richard Burkhauser. The age at which Social Security recipients can receive full benefits will increase to 67 in a phased-in process that will start after 2000. Some of the financial penalties that recipients face by continuing to work are being removed as well. And in many work-

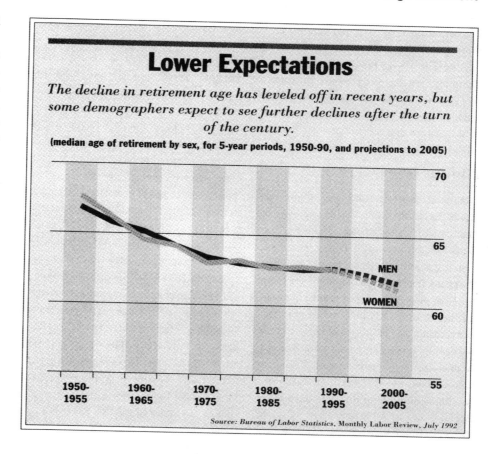

Lower Expectations

The decline in retirement age has leveled off in recent years, but some demographers expect to see further declines after the turn of the century.

(median age of retirement by sex, for 5-year periods, 1950-90, and projections to 2005)

Source: Bureau of Labor Statistics, Monthly Labor Review, July 1992

places, mandatory retirement ages have been eliminated.

The burden of retirement planning is shifting from the employer to the employee. As a result, how well employees plan for their retirement will have a major impact on the age at which they retire. Few individuals stay with one employer for their entire careers. And the employees most likely to have pension

> **Professionals, managers, and salesworkers are least likely to retire early; blue-collar workers are most likely.**

plans—unionized workers in goods-producing industries—are a declining presence in the labor force. In 1945, 36 percent of employees were unionized. In 1992, 16 percent were. In 1920, goods-producing industries accounted for half of all U.S.

jobs. By 1990, the share was one in four.

In the old days, employer-provided pensions almost always guaranteed specific benefits to employees upon retirement, and it was up to the employer to invest pension money wisely. But today, about one-quarter of those with employer-provided coverage are enrolled in defined contribution plans. Employees make contributions to these plans and control how their money is invested. They also assume the risk for bad investments. "To the extent that employees don't accept this responsibility and don't save or invest in an effective way, we will have a large segment of our population that can't afford to retire," says Susan Velleman, managing director of William M. Mercer, Inc., a benefits consultant in Boston.

Enrollment in the most popular type of defined contribution plan—the 401(k)—tripled between 1984 and 1991. About 19 percent of all U.S. workers—more than 17 million people—are enrolled in 401(k) plans, according to the Census Bureau's

5. RETIREMENT: AMERICAN DREAM OR DILEMMA?

1991 Survey of Income and Program Participation (SIPP). Participants' median monthly earnings that year were $2,495. The 401(k) plan is usually a big-company benefit; 69 percent of enrolled workers are employed by companies with 1,000 or more employees, and just 3 percent work for employers with fewer than 25 employees.

ATTITUDES AND DISABILITY

Financial considerations are only part of the retirement decision, according to economist Charles Brown. Social conventions also guide many decisions to retire. When workers see their peers retiring, they may feel that it may be time for them to leave also. "The retirement spikes at 62 and 64 are partly incentive and partly convention," he says.

Disability is an important contributor to early retirement. In a study of people who retired at least six months before becoming eligible for Social Security, the Social Security Administration found 35 percent of men who left their last job before age 55 said health was the primary reason. That compared with 30 percent of those who left between ages 55 and 61½, 26 percent between age 61½ and 62, and 21 percent after age 62. As the health of older adults improves, they will probably decide to stay in the labor force longer.

Professionals, managers, and sales-workers are least likely to retire early; blue-collar workers are most likely, according to sociologist Mark Hayward and his colleagues. "If the nature of work remains attractive and the demand for their labor continues, workers may be more likely to delay retirement," they write. Blue-collar workers are a declining share of the work force, while professionals and managers are an increasing share. These trends should work against early retirement.

The emerging influence of women on retirement is still a wild card, as few researchers have considered its effects. Some studies suggest that single women are affected by the same factors that men are when considering retirement. Married women may be different, however.

"The retirement decision of [married] women seems to be closely tied to the retirement decision of their husbands, but not vice-versa," says Syracuse's Burkhauser. "You find a correlation between when he retires and when she retires."

Many women reaching retirement age today did not participate in the labor force, or did so only sporadically. In 1992, 39 percent of women Social Security recipients aged 62 and older were receiving benefits based on their husbands' employment, not their own. This proportion is decreasing—it was 43 percent in 1980 and 57 percent in 1960—and it will continue to decline in the future.

The career histories and earnings of baby-boom women more closely resemble those of men. In 1960, just 40 percent of women aged 25 to 44 were in the labor force, compared with 98 percent of men. In 1993, 75 percent were working, compared with 94 percent of men.

Employed women are now almost as likely as employed men to be covered by pension plans; 67 percent of women wage-and-salary workers aged 25 and older are covered by pension plans, compared with 69 percent of men, according to the 1991 SIPP. Yet men are still slightly ahead of women when it comes to pension benefits. Just 44 percent of women workers are vested in pension plans and will receive full benefits, compared with 50 percent of men.

Changes in Social Security and pensions have been important factors in dropping the retirement age of men. They have only begun to enter into the retirement decision for women.

QUITTING TIME

Some workers who don't want to retire in their mid- or late-50s may do so because of corporate downsizings and early-retirement packages. Some of these reluctant retirees are ill-equipped to handle such a sudden and unexpected change. This has created a market niche for outplacement companies that advise organizations on how to implement layoffs and then offer assistance to laid-off employees.

Right Associates, an outplacement firm headquartered in Philadelphia, began an enhanced retirement counseling program in 1993. "I see a big market for it," says Graham Smith, the Right consultant in Canada who developed the program. Most of Smith's clients for retirement outplacement services are in their early 60s. "But the age is dropping," he says.

Some companies even provide retirement preparation for employees who aren't being pushed out the door. In fact, more than seven in ten benefits managers offer employees some type of retirement preparation, according to a 1993 Merrill Lynch survey. Small businesses are just as likely as large employers to offer this kind of service. And the eligible employees in companies offering these services do take advantage of them, according to benefits managers. Seventy-six percent of eligible employees read retirement brochures, 67 percent participate in seminars, 53 percent use multimedia resources like video- or audio-tapes, and 49 percent take part in counseling.

Kirk Brenner and Chris Brooke, financial consultants at Merrill Lynch's Indianapolis office, spend the majority of their time producing seminars for a wide variety of companies—from hospitals to factories. Some of their seminars are totally focused on retirement issues; others offer retirement planning as a major component. Speakers include financial experts, gerontologists, nurses, and attorneys. Estate planning is one of the most popular topics, says Brenner. The consultants do not make sales pitches during the presentations, but the Merrill Lynch name receives favorable exposure—and many participants ultimately become clients.

Many people who are on the verge of retirement want help and don't want to wait for their company to provide it. They go to see financial planners on their own. Eight in ten certified financial planners offer a specialty in retirement planning, according to a 1993 survey by the College for Financial Planning in Denver. "People will come to me with a retirement account or a 401(k) plan and say, 'I'm 55 and I want to retire at 65. Tell me how I need to invest my money,'" says

Jane King, president of Fairfield Financial Advisors in Wellesley, Massachusetts.

As baby boomers edge closer to retirement age, they will be more likely to want this type of help. About 64 percent of women and 50 percent of men aged 25 to 44 say they could use some help from a financial advisor or planner, according to the Merrill Lynch survey. "[Baby boomers] are concerned about getting guidance about taking [investment] risks," says King. "They know they have to take risks because no one else is going to take care of them."

Retirement is one of the most difficult transitions in life, according to a 1993 survey from Roper Starch Worldwide in New York City. Forty-one percent of people who have retired say the adjustment was difficult. In contrast, adjustment is seen as difficult by only 12 percent of newlyweds and 23 percent of new parents. The younger the retiree, the

> As baby boomers edge closer to retirement age, they will be more likely to want help with financial planning.

harder the transition: 36 percent of retirees aged 60 and older say the transition is difficult, compared with 45 percent of those aged 45 to 59.

Today, baby boomers are fearful that they'll make the wrong retirement decisions. A 1991 Gallup Poll found that 61 percent of boomers would like to retire by age 60. But a 1993 Gallup Poll found that 59 percent of 30-to-49-year-olds are afraid they won't be able to afford retirement at a reasonable age. Soothing those fears will create loyal, affluent customers for financial-services firms.

TAKING IT FURTHER

Labor force participation data are available from the Bureau of Labor Statistics, Division of Labor Force Statistics; telephone (202) 606-6378. The Current Population Survey (CPS) and the Survey of Income and Program Participation (SIPP) are conducted by the Census Bureau and contain information on receipt of pensions, pension coverage, and participation in 401(k) plans. More information can be obtained by contacting the bureau's Housing and Household Economic Statistics Division; telephone (301) 763-8576.

The *Annual Statistical Supplement* to the *Social Security Bulletin* contains information on numbers of Social Security beneficiaries, types of benefits, and levels of awards. It can be ordered from the U.S. Government Printing Office at (202) 783-3238 and costs $18. The cost of a yearly subscription to the *Social Security Bulletin*, including four quarterly issues and the *Annual Statistical Supplement*, is $13.

The Experience of Dying

Modern science has allowed individuals to have some control over the conception of their children, and it has provided people with the ability to prolong life. But life and death still defy scientific explanation or reason. The world can be divided into two categories: sacred and secular. The sacred (that which is usually embodied in the religion of a culture) is used to explain all the forces of nature and the environment that can neither be understood nor controlled. On the other hand, the secular (defined as "of or relating to the world") is used to explain all the aspects of the world that *can* be understood or controlled. Through scientific invention, more and more of the natural world can be controlled. It still seems highly doubtful, however, that science will ever be able to provide an acceptable explanation of the meaning of death. In this domain, religion may always prevail.

Death is universally feared. Sometimes it is more bearable for those who believe in a life after death. Here, religion offers a solution to this dilemma. In the words of anthropologist Bronislaw Malinowski (1884–1942):

> Religion steps in, selecting the positive creed, the comforting view, the culturally valuable belief in immortality, in the spirit of the body, and in the continuance of life after death. (Bronislaw Malinowski, *Magic, Science, and Religion and Other Essays*, Glencoe, Illinois: Free Press, 1948)

The fear of death leads people to develop defense mechanisms in order to insulate themselves psychologically from its reality. The individual knows that someday he or she must die, but this event is expected to occur in the far distant future. The individual does not think of himself or herself as dying tomorrow or the next day, but rather years from now. In this way people are able to control their anxiety about death.

Losing a close friend or relative brings people dangerously close to the reality of death. Individuals come face to face with the fact that there is always an end to life. Latent fears surface. During times of mourning, people grieve not only for the dead, but for themselves, and for the finiteness of life.

The readings in this unit address bereavement, grief, the arguments for and against euthanasia, and adjustments to the stages of dying. In "Coping with Dying: Lessons That We Should and Should Not Learn from the Work of Elisabeth Kübler-Ross," the author offers a critique of Kübler-Ross's stage-based model of coping with dying and suggests an alternative approach. "The Right Way To Die," by Vicki Brower, points out many of the problems of the current hospice program and how they could be improved.

"Is Dying Young Worse Than Dying Old?" examines why dying young is considered more tragic than dying old. The authors question whether these attitudes are backed by ethical considerations that are reasonable and easily defended. "Physician-assisted Dying: Contemporary Twists to an Ancient Dilemma" questions whether it is ever appropriate for the physician to intervene and ease the dying process. The usefulness of family support groups for the bereaved is examined in "A Comparative Study of Family Bereavement Groups."

Looking Ahead: Challenge Questions

Is the fear of dying really universal? Do all people share it equally?

What are the techniques by which people alleviate their anxieties about dying?

Should dying patients be told the truth about their impending deaths, or should this information be withheld? Defend your answer.

Are the elderly more afraid of death than the young?

Unit 6

Coping With Dying: Lessons That We Should and Should Not Learn From the Work of Elisabeth Kübler-Ross

Charles A. Corr

Southern Illinois University at Edwardsville

This article begins from an appraisal of the work of Elisabeth Kübler-Ross in the area of coping with dying. In that appraisal, some reasons are noted as to why we should not consider her stage-based model to be the heart of the useful lessons that she taught. Instead, three lessons are suggested that we can and should learn from the work of Kübler-Ross on coping with dying. Three further elements round out this exposition: 1) some broader conclusions are drawn about the processes involved in coping with dying; 2) an argument is offered on behalf of our need to develop better theoretical models to explicate what is involved in coping with dying; and 3) some requirements are suggested that should be satisfied by any adequate model in this field.

"Your heroes will help you find good in yourself; Your friends won't forsake you for somebody else."
Randy Travis, "Heroes and Friends"

In 1969, Dr. Elisabeth Kübler-Ross published *On Death and Dying*. In that book, she set forth a stage-based model for understanding coping with dying. The five stages which she postulated in this process of coping were: denial, anger, bargaining, depression (reactive or preparatory), and acceptance. In addition, hope was said to be possible throughout the entire process. Readers did not always give much attention to the books' brief remarks about hope, but the stage-based model for coping with dying attracted wide attention among professional care providers and the general public alike.

However, the early research literature (e.g., Metzger, 1979; Schulz & Aderman, 1974) did not provide much support for this stage-based model. In addition, more than 20 years later there still is no confirmation of its validity or reliability. In fact, some of the most knowledgeable and sophisticated clinicians who work with those who are coping with dying have made clear their view that the stage-based model put forth by Kübler-Ross is inadequate, superficial, and misleading (e.g., Feigenberg, 1980; Pattison, 1977; Shneidman, 1980; Weisman, 1977). Also, it has been argued that the stage-based model for coping with dying was widely accepted for reasons other than its own intrinsic strengths (Klass, 1982; Klass & Hutch, 1985).

Kastenbaum (1986) has raised the following points in his evaluation of the Kübler-Ross stage-based model: 1) the existence of these stages as such has not been demonstrated; 2) no evidence has been presented that people actually do move from stage 1 through stage 5; 3) the limitations of the method have not been acknowledged; 4) there is insufficient distinction between description and prescription; 5) the totality of the person's life is neglected in favor of the supposed stages of dying; and 6) the resources, pressures, and characteristics of the immediate environment can also make a tremendous difference.

Kübler-Ross has not responded to criticisms of this sort. Nor has she offered any evidence or additional arguments to support her stage-based model. Perhaps no such evidence or argumentation is available. In this article, I want to summarize the present position by: 1) offering some general comments about the work of Kübler-Ross in the area of coping with dying; 2) noting some reasons why we should not want to consider her stage-based model to be the heart of the useful lessons that she taught us; 3) suggesting three lessons that we can and should learn from the work of Elisabeth Kübler-Ross on coping with dying; 4) drawing some broader conclusions about the processes involved in coping with dying; and 5) arguing on behalf of our need to develop better theoretical models to understand what is involved in coping with dying and suggesting some requirements that should be satisfied by any adequate model in this field.

KÜBLER-ROSS ON COPING WITH DYING

Elisabeth Kübler-Ross (Gill, 1980) drew the attention of professional caregivers and the general public to the situation and needs of dying persons and of others who are coping with dying. Her book appeared at a time when there had been so much distancing of dying from the mainstream of living that many had begun to sense that something was wrong. As Jocelyn Evans (1971, p. 83), a British widow, wrote just two years later: "We have created systems which protect us in the aggregate from facing up to the very things that as individuals we most need to know." Evans was exactly right. Our understanding of the dying, of those who are coping with dying, and of their needs had become so distorted that it did not serve those very vulnerable individuals. I would add that, in the end, efforts to protect the society at the expense of its individual members also did not serve very well the needs of the aggregate community.

Kübler-Ross helped to bring about significant changes in the ways in which many people think about dying. As a psychiatrist, she was sensitive to some of the most basic ways in which human beings react to the challenges of dying. Naturally enough, the emphasis in the work of Kübler-Ross was on psychological or psychosocial dimensions and on the perspectives of psychotherapy. Her work was based on the investigative and teaching techniques of psychiatry, and on her own often heterodox point of view. She had much to offer to the emerging hospice movement, but her insights and interpretations did not originate within that movement and did not immediately reflect its holistic perspectives on care.

When Kübler-Ross spoke about coping mechanisms and different reactions in responding to dying, she said: "I am

From *Death Studies*, Vol. 17, No. 1, January/February 1993, pp. 69-83. © 1993 by Taylor and Francis, Inc., 1101 Vermont Avenue, NW, Suite 200, Washington, DC 20005. All rights reserved. Reprinted by permission.

simply telling the stories of my patients who shared their agonies, their expectations, and their frustrations with us" (Kübler-Ross, 1969, p. xi). That was humble and attractive, but it is also disingenuous. No one simply tells the stories of others. All of us select and interpret in some degree or other whatever it is that we relate.

A careful examination of *On Death and Dying* reveals that its emphasis, not surprisingly, is on defense mechanisms. At the outset of Chapter 8, one reads: "We have discussed so far the different stages that people go through when they are faced with tragic news—defense mechanisms in psychiatric terms, coping mechanisms to deal with extremely difficult situations. These means will last for different periods of time and will replace each other or exist at times side by side" (p. 138). Later, the author speaks of "patients who are fortunate enough to have time to work through some of their conflicts while they are sick and who can come to a deeper understanding and perhaps appreciation of the things they still have to enjoy" (p. 273).

It is important here to observe that dying is not a psychiatric illness. Dying is a normal process in human life, even if it seems in our society to have become an unusual and unfamiliar one. Thus, there is an important acknowledgment in *On Death and Dying*: "Simple people with less education, sophistication, social ties, and professional obligations seem in general to have somewhat less difficulty in facing this final crisis than people of affluence who lose a great deal more in terms of material luxuries, comfort, and number of interpersonal relationships" (p. 265). That is why speculations about the value of group therapy to assist those who are coping with dying are confined to a "selected" and "small" group of the author's patients.

Most people who are dying do not need psychotherapy. As Craven and Wald (1975) noted, "What people need most when they are dying is relief from distressing symptoms of disease, the security of a caring environment, sustained expert care, and assurance that they and their families will not be abandoned" (p. 1816). Helping those who are coping with dying emphasizes befriending, a caring community, and expert skills that are relevant to the needs at hand.

THE STAGE-BASED MODEL: LESSONS THAT WE SHOULD NOT LEARN

The model that is set forth in *On Death and Dying* is one that is limited in many ways. It is drawn from a particular social population dying in particular ways and in a particular time and location. It is organized around one author's clinical impressions, not around empirical data. Thus, this model depends very much upon the validity of a single author's interpretations.

Kübler-Ross's stage-based model focused on psychosocial dynamics, and to a lesser extent, the spiritual, almost to the exclusion of physical dimensions. It sees these dynamics mainly as involving defensive responses to threat and conflict. In classic psychotherapeutic terms, its aim is to work through conflict so that the protagonists need not be burdened with morbid, unhealthy, or even neurotic feelings. As Kübler-Ross has written: "If a patient has had enough time (i.e., not a sudden, unexpected death) and has been given some help in working through the previously described stages, he will reach a stage during which he is neither depressed nor angry about his 'fate' " (p. 112). This is "acceptance."

I think most readers of *On Death and Dying* ignored the perspectives within which it is grounded. Many were not sensitive to the limitations of the theoretical model which it presented. Some misused that model so as to stereotype dying

persons in new ways that are not consistent with the aims of its author. That is why she struggled against the implications of "staging" dying throughout the book, even though she did not take the obvious step of moving on to other language and perhaps an improved theoretical formulation.

In the end, there are three central reasons why we should not focus on the stage-based model as the central legacy that should be drawn from the work of Elisabeth Kübler-Ross in the area of coping with dying. First, there is no reason to think that there are in fact only five ways in which human beings cope with anything as fundamental as dying. People cope with living and with dying in far richer, more variegated, and more individualistic ways than that.

Second, even if there were compelling evidence to confine coping to just five basic forms, there is no reason to think that those five ways should be or somehow are interlinked as stages in a larger process. Actually, one should not speak of "stages" unless one intends to speak about elements in a linear standard of measurement (e.g., a thermometer or depth gauge). One can move forward or backward along the line that is measured by a set of stages. But one cannot really employ a stage-based model as an effective framework within which to characterize a process of jumping from one disconnected reaction to another (as Kübler-Ross seems to want to do; pp 263–264). If "anger" and "bargaining," for example, are no more than different aspects or dimensions in coping (as they surely can be), then they are not stages but discriminable coping strategies.

Third, and above all, there is no reason to think that the five "stages" or types of coping strategies that were identified by Kübler-Ross are somehow obligatory or prescriptive ways in which individuals must or should cope with dying. No one has to die in any particular way. To insist that individuals must cope with dying in what others regard as the "right" or "correct" way is simply to impose the additional burdens of an external agenda upon vulnerable persons. The transformation in this way of the stage-based model from a descriptive narration into a set of normative guidelines is perhaps more characteristic of some followers of Kübler-Ross, but it is greatly facilitated by suggestions implicit in the language of *On Death and Dying*. In any event, we might note that a symposium at the 1991 meeting of the Association for Death Education and Counseling addressed the topic of "Getting 'Stuck' During the Process of Dying." How can one speak in that way unless one has in mind a model and an agenda within which one can measure adequate or inadequate progress in coping with dying? Is there a unified process in coping with dying? Is it correct to speak of progress within that process? Have we lost sight here of the individuals who are coping with dying and become mesmerized by an inadequate theoretical model?

THREE LESSONS THAT WE SHOULD LEARN FROM THE WORK OF KÜBLER-ROSS

Informed and thoughtful criticism is a kind of recognition and tribute, not a devaluation or mistreatment. I am not primarily concerned here to quarrel with Elisabeth Kübler-Ross nor even with the rather obvious limits of her stage-based, theoretical model. Instead, I want to chastise many of the rest of us, at least all of those who settled for the simplistic surface of *On Death and Dying* and did not take the trouble to learn and put into practice the very real and important lessons of this little book.

Those who read *On Death and Dying* (or who have merely heard summaries of its contents) and who came away mainly with the ability to memorize and tick off on each finger the five stages of coping with dying missed the point of this work and its true value. How much did we settle for relying upon the interpretations of Kübler-Ross because they were simple and easy to recognize in our own behaviors? What would those of us who are not ambidextrous have done if Kübler-Ross had proposed six or more stages in her model of coping with dying?

Kübler-Ross herself drew attention to the central points of her work in her one-page preface (p. xi). As I understand them, the lessons that we should have learned and can still learn from this book are threefold:

1. Those who are coping with dying are still alive and often have unfinished needs which they want to address. This is fundamental and paramount. Dying patients are living human beings. Coping with dying is a humane and vital process. As his wife, Linda, said of her husband, Willie Loman—a man still alive, but from whom vitality is rapidly ebbing—"He's a human being, and a terrible thing is happening to him. So attention must be paid" (Miller, 1948, p. 40). This is the lesson about all who are dying and coping with dying.

2. We cannot be or become effective providers of care unless we listen actively to those who are coping with dying and identify with them their own needs. This is so basic as to be almost obvious, if one did not know that it is practiced far less frequently than it is preached. How can one ever presume to care for another human being if one does not actively listen to the needs and priorities of that person? How can one be an effective care provider if one is content to act on the basis of generalizations about people? How can one dare to approach another human being in order to act as a provider of care without entering into a relationship with them within which they play at least a part (if not *the* main role) in defining their own coping tasks? This is the lesson about becoming and being a provider of care.

3. We need to learn from those who are dying and coping with dying in order to come to know ourselves better (as limited, vulnerable, finite, and mortal; but also as resilient, adaptable, interdependent, and lovable). Here, the advice is to draw upon the experiences of those who are coping with dying for our own benefit and instruction. Kübler-Ross would have us regard dying persons and those who are coping with dying as our teachers. One cannot help but notice that this is reminiscent of Socrates, who constantly asked those whom he encountered to examine their own lives, who suggested that true wisdom is nothing but a preparation for death (Plato, 1961), and who regarded the role of teacher as one of assisting others to draw out of themselves their full potential for living. This is the lesson for all of us.

The language and the interpretations of these three lessons are my own. Kübler-Ross (1969) puts these lessons in the following way when she says that her book

> is not meant to be a textbook on how to manage dying patients, nor is it intended as a complete study of the psychology of the dying. It is simply an account of a new and challenging opportunity to refocus on the patient as a human being, to include him in dialogues, to learn from him the strengths and weaknesses of our hospital management of the patient. We have asked him to be our teacher so that we may learn more about the final stages of life with all its anxieties, fears, and hopes. (p. xi)

COPING WITH DYING: ACKNOWLEDGING A RICHER AND MORE COMPLEX PROCESS

Coping with dying should be understood in terms of a set of responses to a situational crisis. Those responses occur within a larger context defined by developmental and other challenges and processes. That larger context is always relevant to the individual who is coping and to a full explication of coping behaviors. For our purposes here, however, the important thing is to focus upon coping as a behavioral process.

This is consistent with the basic outlook identified by Kübler-Ross (1975) when she spoke of death as "the final stage of growth." By this, she meant that coping with dying in our society can often be an opportunity to develop as a person and as a member of a human community. Our responses to this opportunity are expressed in the ways in which we cope.

When we cope or attempt to cope, a number of elements come into play. The complexity and interplay of these elements is recognized in the following definition of coping as "constantly changing cognitive and behavioral efforts to manage specific external and/or internal demands that are appraised as taxing or exceeding the resources of the person" (Lazarus & Folkman, 1984, p. 141). Coping goes beyond automatized adaptive behavior. It involves efforts to manage, i.e., acting or doing (or a decision not to act, not to do).

Much of what we do or do not do depends upon how we feel, what we know or believe to be true, and what we value as significant in life. Part of what we do is simply a reaction and can often correctly be conceived as a defense against life's challenges. But the larger context for coping is "adaptation," not just "reaction," "response," or "defense" (White, 1974; see also Monat & Lazarus, 1991). That is, coping is an effort to adapt, or not to adapt, or at least to try to adapt. This is why Weisman (1984, p. 36) has observed that coping "is positive in approach; defending is negative." He meant that defending attempts merely to ward off problems or challenges, while coping seeks to resolve problems or to manage challenges.

The use of a stage-based model to describe coping processes—especially processes of coping with dying—is doomed to failure because the model is inherently inadequate. Stages are too rigid, too linear, and, above all, too passive a metaphor for the rich, supple, and active processes that are involved in coping with dying.

An adequate model for coping with dying will need to be as agile, malleable, and dynamic as is the behavior of each individual who is involved in coping with dying. Such a model should depict coping behaviors as available to be taken up or temporarily set aside, pursued with great vigor or renounced with equal determination. Such a model must understand that several coping behaviors may be pursued simultaneously, whether or not they are compatible. Also it should not confuse coping processes with their outcome, which may or may not be very successful. A model of this sort recognizes that decisions about coping with dying are or can be at the control of the individual who selects his or her coping tasks.

Few individuals who are coping with dying are simply "in" denial. Most of us are more complex and less monolithic than that. The goal for most individuals who are coping with dying is not merely to "get through" anger or bargaining. Short of acting in ways that are directly harmful to ourselves or to others, in coping with dying we do not really have to "get" anywhere. We merely have opportunities to live as well as we can and in accordance with our definitions of what constitutes quality in living. Being angry may be the best that I can do or it may be all that I want to do. After all, it is my life and my story that I am living out in this coping process, not some predefined or ideal plan developed by someone else (Brady, 1979).

More to the point, coping with dying is not just a matter of dealing with feelings. It involves the full range of the dimensions or behaviors that have been identified in good hospice care: physical, psychological, social, and spiritual (Corr & Corr, 1983; Kastenbaum, 1989; National Hospice Organization, 1987). These must be the basic dimensions in any model that purports to offer an adequate explication of that which is involved in coping with dying.

A good model for coping with dying should emphasize both that which is universal and that which is individual. That is, it should describe features that apply to all human beings who are coping with dying, and it should direct our attention to the unique and distinctive ways in which those features are implicated in the life of each particular individual who is coping with dying. Here, it is the universal features of coping with dying that are emphasized. In applying the lessons of this analysis, one must enter as an attentive listener and fellow coper into the world of each particular individual who is coping with dying. That is, when we presume to approach individuals who are coping with dying, we must undertake to view their experiences in terms of their perspectives and their coping tasks (Stedeford, 1984).

To say this another way, a stage-based model risks stereotyping vulnerable individuals who are coping with dying because it is founded neither on individuality nor on universality. In fact, the stages in the model are generalizations. The plausibility of those generalizations makes a stage-based model both attractive and dangerous. It is attractive because the so-called "stages" are some of the ways in which some (many?) human beings respond to the experience of dying; it is dangerous, because they are no more than some of the responses of some of these people. In other words, a stage-based model for coping with dying is prone to erect obstacles to individualization. As Ted Rosenthal (1973) said, "being invisible I invite only generalizations" (p. 39).

In view of the emphasis which Kübler-Ross placed upon "unfinished business," it is important to add that the work which any individual undertakes in coping with dying is never fully completed as long as he or she is alive. Such an individual might return once or often to business that remains unfinished. He or she might make progress in working with or through such business. Perhaps sometimes one can even be so fortunate as to complete very specific pieces of business. But coping with dying is part of the ongoing business of living. It is never really completed; it merely ends with the individual's death.

It is not enough merely to criticize flawed theoretical models. We must learn from their inadequacies, overcome their limitations, and work to devise constructive alternatives to guide improved understanding and practice.

REQUIREMENTS FOR AN ADEQUATE MODEL FOR COPING WITH DYING

Any acceptable model for coping with dying should meet four requirements: 1) it should provide an improved basis for understanding all of the dimensions and all of the individuals that are involved in coping with dying; 2) it should foster empowerment for those who are coping with dying by emphasizing the options that are available to them as they live out what is often a difficult time in life; 3) it should emphasize participation or the shared aspects of coping with dying, those aspects whereby people draw together in small communities and assist each other in interpersonal networks; and 4) it should provide guidance for

care providers and helpers, whether they are professionals, volunteers, or family members.

Kübler-Ross's stage-based model for coping with dying did contribute in some degree to helping us understand such coping. It reminded us that dying patients are still living human beings. Coping is an activity of the living, not of the dead. This may seem to be only a modest contribution, but it is in fact of fundamental importance.

Nevertheless, Kübler-Ross's stage-based model for coping with dying did not give equal attention to all of the dimensions of human living. By limiting itself primarily to feelings and psychosocial reactions, it attended mainly to selected segments or aspects of the coping person's life and did not offer a holistic perspective on this most human of all processes.

In coping with dying, much is or seems to be out of control. An adequate model for coping with dying should empower individuals who are engaged in such coping by emphasizing their opportunities to influence or take charge of that process. In some small measure, Kübler-Ross's stage-based model did contribute to empowerment by drawing attention to the feelings, reactions, and activities of those who are coping with dying. In so doing, it tended to free individuals to experience the reactions that it recognized and sanctioned. In the end, however, a stage-based model for coping with dying is not to be preferred because its breadth is inadequate, it accentuates passivity by focusing upon defensive reactions to threat, and it fails to explain how one passes from one stage or coping strategy to another.

An adequate model for coping with dying should enhance participation or sharing in the life that remains to be lived. It should do this by delineating coping processes that are undertaken by three broad groups of people: individuals who are dying or who have a life-threatening illness; their friends and family members (whatever "family" may mean for the individuals in question); and their caregivers, whether professional or lay. This gives express attention to all of the people who actually take part in coping with dying and explicit acknowledgement to the fact that each individual is not only engaged in his or her own coping processes, but also is implicated or entangled in the coping work of others who are sharing in the same dying experience. The model set forth by Kübler-Ross was not confined solely to the dying person, but it is essentially limited to the unique psychological process of each individual coping person.

Finally, an adequate model for coping with dying should provide direction or guidance for helpers by enabling them to relate their efforts to the coping work undertaken by the individual whom they are helping in what he or she is doing in relationship to dying. Too much of the stage-based model set forth by Kübler-Ross is content merely to identify or give a name to coping processes. A richer and more helpful model would undertake to describe coping with dying in ways that can also serve as benchmarks for organizing the work of helpers. Active participation by potential helpers deserves this sort of guidance and encouragement.

As we develop our alternative model, we might turn Kastenbaum's (1986) criticisms of Kübler-Ross into positive guidelines for our work. That is, we should: 1) set aside stages; 2) refrain from suggestions of linear directedness; 3) try to be clear about our method; 4) emphasize description and refrain from prescription; 5) take into account the totality of the coping person's life; and 6) attend to influences from the person's immediate environment.

CONCLUSION: HEROES AND FRIENDS

When Randy Travis sang about "Heroes and Friends," he advised us that true friends do not forsake their comrades. That is relevant to our argument here in two senses: 1) we must devise models for understanding coping with dying which enable us to recognize the human processes and dimensions in such coping and which encourage us not to forsake any of our comrades who are engaged in such coping; and 2) we must also not forsake our colleague, Elisabeth Kübler-Ross, who helped us at an early point to pursue our investigation of coping with dying and who encouraged us to walk alongside and learn from those of our fellow human beings who are coping with dying. Kübler-Ross was not the earliest pioneer in this field. To mention just one other important contributor, Herman Feifel's work (1959) antedated Kübler-Ross's book by at least ten years. But Kübler-Ross was an early leader and an important publicist for efforts to understand coping with dying. She did not contribute the first or the last word to this important conversation, but she was and is an instructive participant.

Randy Travis's song "Heroes and Friends" described our heroes (and heroines) as those who help us to find good in ourselves. Certainly, Elisabeth Kübler-Ross is a person who helped many of us—those who are dying, those who are family members or friends of the dying, those who are caring for the dying, and those who seek to understand and explicate what is involved in coping with dying—to find good in ourselves. But we cannot permit that process to stop with the publication of *On Death and Dying* in 1969. Although we all benefited from the work of Kübler-Ross, we cannot simply lean upon her work for the rest of time. Instead, we must continually strive to find additional good and further riches within ourselves. In particular, we must look within ourselves to go beyond the inadequacies of the stage-based model for coping with dying that Kübler-Ross set forth so many years ago.

I believe that it is now time to develop new and improved models for understanding coping with dying. There are important lessons that we should have learned and still can learn from the work of Elisabeth Kübler-Ross. I believe that the stage-based model that she set forth in *On Death and Dying* is not at the heart of these constructive lessons.

It is my conviction that our new models for coping with dying should emphasize improved understanding of coping with dying, empowerment, and participation for those who are coping with dying, and guidance for helpers. Elsewhere, I have attempted to describe a new task-based model for coping with dying that seems to satisfy these requirements (Corr, in press). In this article, it is sufficient to describe some of the challenges that face us in this area and to attempt to build a bridge between the past (which is represented here by the work of Elisabeth Kübler-Ross on coping with dying, but which is certainly not confined to that single source) and the future that lies ahead of us.

No matter how hard we strive to develop new models for coping with dying, they will inevitably be limited in one or more ways. In addition, very real problems are always involved in applying any theoretical model to vulnerable persons who are coping with dying. Thus, we will do well in these efforts to keep our limitations in mind and to recall a caution from Carl Jung (1954, p. 7) who wrote in 1938 that "theories in psychology are the very devil. It is true that we need certain points of view for their orienting and heuristic value; but they should always be regarded as mere auxiliary concepts that can be laid aside at any time."

REFERENCES

Brady, E. M. (1979). Telling the story: Ethics and dying. *Hospital Progress, 60*, 57–62.

Corr, C. A. (1992). A task-based approach to coping with dying, *Omega, 24*, 81–84.

Corr, C. A., & Corr, D. M. (Eds.). (1983). *Hospice care: Principles and practice*. New York: Springer Publishing Co.

Craven, J., & Wald, F. S. (1975). Hospice care for dying patients. *American Journal of Nursing, 75*, 1816–1822.

Evans, J. (1971). *Living with a man who is dying*. New York: Taplinger.

Feifel, H. (Ed.). (1959). *The meaning of death*. New York: McGraw-Hill.

Feigenberg, L. (1980). *Terminal care: Friendship contracts with dying cancer patients*. New York: Brunner/Mazel.

Gill, D. L. (1980). *Quest: The life of Elisabeth Kübler-Ross*. New York: Harper & Row.

Jung, C. G. (1954). *The development of personality* (Vol. 17). In H. Read, M. Fordham, & G. Adler (Eds.), *The collected works of C. G. Jung* (20 vols.). New York: Pantheon.

Kastenbaum, R. (1986). *Death, society, and human experience* (3rd ed.). Columbus, OH: Charles E. Merrill.

Kastenbaum, R. (1989). Hospice: Philosophy and practice. In R. Kastenbaum and B. Kastenbaum (Eds.), *Encyclopedia of death* (pp. 143–146). Phoenix, AZ: Oryx Press.

Klass, D. (1982). Elisabeth Kübler-Ross and the tradition of the private sphere: An analysis of symbols. *Omega, 12*, 241–261.

Klass, D., & Hutch, R. A. (1985). Elisabeth Kübler-Ross as a religious leader. *Omega, 16*, 89–109.

Kübler-Ross, E. (1969). *On death and dying*. New York: Macmillan.

Kübler-Ross, E. (1975). *Death: The final stage of growth*. Englewood Cliffs, NJ: Prentice-Hall.

Lazarus, R. S., & Folkman, S. (1984). *Stress, appraisal, and coping*. New York: Springer Publishing Co.

Metzger, A. M. (1979). A Q-methodological study of the Kübler-Ross stage theory. *Omega, 10*, 291–302.

Miller, A. (1948). *Death of a salesman*. New York: Dramatists Play Service.

Monat, A., & Lazarus, R. S. (Eds.) (1991). *Stress and coping: An anthology* (3rd ed.). New York: Columbia University Press.

National Hospice Organization. (1987). *Standards of a hospice program of care*. Arlington, VA: Author.

Pattison, E. M. (1977). *The experience of dying*. Englewood Cliffs, NJ: Prentice-Hall.

Plato (1961). Phaedo. In E. Hamilton & H. Cairns (Eds.), *The collected dialogues of Plato, including the letters* (pp. 40–98). New York: Pantheon Books.

Rosenthal, T. (1973). *How could I not be among you?* New York: George Braziller.

Schulz, R., & Aderman, D. (1974). Clinical research and the stages of dying. *Omega, 5*, 137–144.

Schneidman, E. (1980). *Voices of death*. New York: Harper & Row.

Stedeford, A. (1984). *Facing death: Patients, families and professionals*. London: William Heinemann.

Weisman, A. (1977). The psychiatrist and the inexorable. In H. Feifel (Ed.), *New meanings of death* (pp. 107–122). New York: McGraw-Hill.

Weisman, A. (1984). *The coping capacity: On the nature of being mortal*. New York: Human Sciences Press.

White, R. W. (1974). Strategies of adaptation: An attempt at systematic description. In G. V. Coelho, D. A. Hamburg, & J. E. Adams (Eds.), *Coping and adaptation* (pp. 47–68). New York: Basic Books.

The Right Way to Die

Despite good intentions, some hospices end up bullying patients who won't pass away gracefully.

Vicki Brower

VICKI BROWER *is a free-lance writer based in New York City.*

ach year, thousands of Americans choose hospice care for themselves or for those they love, believing it to be the most compassionate way of tending to the terminally ill. Small wonder, since experts say the chief goal of a hospice is to make the transition from life to death as peaceful as possible for both the patient and family.

But as I discovered in 1989 during my mother's battle with terminal lung cancer, hospices can sometimes be a mixed blessing. In the difficult last days of a patient's life, the good intentions of these institutions may go awry for many reasons, including financial considerations, severe Medicare restrictions, poor medical supervision and poorly trained personnel who interpret hospice philosophy too rigidly.

Part of the problem is that policies and guidelines to guarantee quality have evolved only recently, so services are inconsistent. Some hospices are far better than others. "We have learned a lot since hospices began, and we are always learning," says Sarah Gorodezky, director of the Alive Hospice of Nashville in Tennessee. "But there is still plenty to do as far as quality assurance goes."

MOM AND I CONFRONT MORTALITY

During my mother's second hospitalization for lung cancer in April 1989, we learned that nothing more could be done to stop the disease. Mom was going to have to be discharged to free up a bed. I was her closest child, so I took on the responsibility of investigating her options. Because Mom wanted to be home, and because of recommendations by doctors and friends, we opted for at-home hospice care. I learned that *most* hospice patients actually remain in their own residences. They have 24-hour access to help by phone and, when necessary, can be brought to an in-hospice unit for emergency medical or respite care (short-term residence).

From the literature I read, I understood that "hospice" represents a concept of care rather than a place. According to hospice philosophy, curative at-tempts and "heroic" life-saving measures, such as placing a patient on a respirator, are shunned once death is seen as inevitable. Instead, all efforts are devoted to helping the patient live as fully and comfortably as possible up to the moment of death. For example, the hospice health-care team has special training in pain management and a relatively free hand in dispensing palliative drugs. Many hospitals and nursing homes, in fact, have adapted hospice's advanced pain control techniques. "The point is to improve the patient's quality of life, not to extend life," says Ira J. Bates, Ph.D., consultant to the National Hospice Organization in Arlington, Virginia.

Hospice care started as an alternative movement in the mid-'70s but has evolved into a part of the mainstream health industry. In 1983, Congress voted to accept hospice care as a Medicare benefit, and according to the 1990 National Hospice Census, today some 1,500 hospice programs in the United States serve about 200,000 patients. Such programs are now administered not only by free-standing hospice facilities, but also by certain hospitals and other health-care agencies. Unlike traditional approaches such as nursing home care, hospices

Reprinted from *Health*, June 1991, pp. 39-43. *Health*, published by Family Media, Inc.

163

assign each patient a coordinated, interdisciplinary team—not just a doctor and nurse, but also a social worker and a volunteer (part counselor, part gofer), as well as a religious advisor if the patient wants one. In most cases, these team members make regular house calls to at-home patients. Generally, everyone on the team is trained to work with the dying. "The hospital model gets turned upside down," explains Bates. "A hospital is designed to work around the needs of employees; patients have to eat, sleep and wake up according to a schedule. But in a hospice, care is specifically designed to meet the physical and emotional needs of the patient and family."

Based on my research, I felt confident that hospice care was the best choice for my mother. I contacted a highly recommended New York–area program by phone, and spoke with the nurse who served as intake coordinator. After I described Mom's terminal condition, she said, "Your mother sounds like a perfect candidate for the program." But during our face-to-face interview a few days later the nurse changed her tune. She asked me about my mother's attitude toward her illness and impending death. "Mom's fighting. She still loves life, and she's not ready to die," I told her. The nurse slowly shook her head and said, "That's too bad. Her attitude isn't realistic or appropriate."

Although small and frail in appearance, Mom had long ago earned the family nickname "Moose" for her feistiness and tenacity. Thirty-five years earlier, she had developed paralysis in her legs because of a tumor. After a maze of tests, surgery and radiation, she began to recover, only to learn she was pregnant. Fearing the baby would be damaged by all she'd been through, the physicians advised her to have an abortion. She refused, relying on her gut feeling that she and the baby would be fine. If she had listened to the doctors, I never would have been born. So now, if she wanted to battle for her life in the same way she'd battled for mine, I was certainly going to stand by her. "What right have you to decide what's 'appropriate' for my mother or anyone else?" I snapped at the nurse. She seemed taken aback but didn't say a word.

I worried that if this woman's rigidity toward patients was typical of hospice workers, it might affect medical choices, hastening Mom's death or adding to her misery. "If my mother had trouble breathing because of fluid around the lung, would the doctor tap [drain] it?" I asked in trepidation. Mom had had three surgical taps in the past, and they had given her almost instant relief. The procedure was commonly used to give lung cancer patients comfort, and not considered curative or heroic.

The nurse looked at me quizzically and asked, "Why would you want to put your mother through that?" Incredulous, I explained the obvious—that the tap would make Mom more comfortable and might even allow her to live a little longer. "Why would you want her to live longer in her condition?" she pressed. "It sounds as though she may not be right for our program after all."

HARD CHOICES, HARD RESULTS

In retrospect, the nurse may have been right—maybe we weren't ideal hospice candidates. But for many reasons, the hospice still seemed the best option open to us, so we entered the program. In the three months leading up to my mother's death, I questioned my decision many times. My mother and I repeatedly faced criticism, indifference and even negligence, stemming from the same attitude the intake nurse had shown—the idea that Mom should just embrace death quietly and peacefully. It wasn't until later that I found out that other hospice patients and their families are sometimes treated this way, because of problems rooted in the hospice system itself. Here are some of our low points:

■ Medicare rules stated that before Mom could be accepted for hospice coverage, she had to give her signed "informed consent" to forgo any curative treatment. The hospice program also had her sign a "do not resuscitate" order and other stipulations that no mechanical life supports would be used. If that wasn't rubbing her nose in death enough, she was also shown a pamphlet which noted that patients who enter hospices must have a very limited life expectancy. Under federal law, Medicare-funded hospices must get a physician's signed statement that a prospective patient is not expected to live longer than six months. (This is part of Medicare's attempt to keep costs down.) Though not a legal requirement, many hospices advise the patient of this time frame as part of the preparation for death. My mother and I expressed displeasure at all the emphasis on death, and my mother announced bluntly, "No one's going to tell me when to die." A hospice worker later admitted that we were labeled "difficult" from then on.

"Most hospice patients understand and accept that their condition is terminal," says Jill Rhymes, M.D., hospice medical director at the VNA Hospice of Chicago. "If not, they don't belong in a hospice."

■ Being branded as we were seemed to slow the response to our phone calls and requests. It took weeks of urging on our part before the head social worker, who saw us only once every two weeks, assigned us a counselor who could come more often to help Mom with her panic and depression. A staffer finally informed us that we'd been stalled for so long out of fear that we were "too hard for anyone but the head social worker to handle." According to Gorodezky, patients who question hospice policy or fail to adhere to certain core hospice beliefs risk being labelled in this way. A woman called Joan* told me the same thing happened to her and her friend Laurie*, who received care from another hospice in the months leading up to her death from metastatic cancer. The nurses labeled Laurie "difficult" because she didn't want to see a social worker at all, and because she occasionally balked at taking her pain medication.

■ Medical care for my mother was abysmal. In the three months before her death, the hospice doctor visited just once despite a number of urgent requests. The hospice home-care attendants who did come twice a week were often poorly trained; and since they changed from week to week, I constantly had to brief them on Mom's medication and oxygen. Also, on two occasions when Mom had extreme difficulty breathing, I frantically called the hospice, but neither an ambulance nor a nurse was sent, nor was I given medical instructions. One nurse told me outright, "There's nothing we can do." And once, when I called in the middle of the night, the nurse merely told me to wait until morning, then hung up on me when I asked to speak to her supervisor.

Again, Joan and Laurie had a similar experience. Three times in the first week and a half of care, the home-care aides didn't show up or even call. "I was at work once when I found out Laurie was home alone, and I had to rush back," Joan

*These names have been changed.

told me. "The hospice should have made a greater effort to provide reliable help."

"Many hospice programs are nurse– and volunteer-dominated, with marginal physician involvement," explains Balfour M. Mount, M.D., director of palliative care at McGill University Faculty of Medicine in Montreal, Canada. "Consequently, they're medically impoverished. It's a form of neglect throughout the hospice system."

QUESTIONABLE QUALITY

Obviously, this wasn't how hospice care was meant to be. Nearly 25 years ago, Cicely Saunders founded the hospice movement in Great Britain on the ideal of "humane and compassionate care" for the terminally ill. In 1969, psychiatrist Elisabeth Kübler-Ross, M. D., published the seminal book *On Death and Dying* (Macmillan), which became the unofficial manifesto of the hospice movement. Kübler-Ross suggested that dying is a "journey," a complex process which encompasses specific emotional steps: disbelief, denial, bargaining, anger, grief, and finally acceptance. This process "requires assistance," Gorodezky points out. "Not all patients arrive at acceptance—there's not a 'right' or 'wrong' way to die in true hospice philosophy," she says. "But by helping to alleviate pain and discomfort and offering psychosocial support, the hospice reduces the patient's and family's fear of abandonment and makes them closer and more secure."

Some medical professionals, like Porter Storey, M.D., believe that hospices are "ushering in a new age in medical care." Affiliated with The Hospice at the Texas Medical Center in Houston since its start eight years ago, Storey values the integrated, holistic teamwork of varied professionals. "Working in hospice care has shown me there's much that we can give beyond just medicine," he says. Other proponents say hospice care is a vast improvement for many patients over the old bleak possibilities: being sent home to fend for oneself; being allowed to remain in a hospital only if submitting to experimental procedures; or dying in terrible pain in a nursing home.

Some studies, however, have raised questions about how well hospices perform their mission. For example, the National Hospice Study, conducted by Brown University from 1981 to 1983, followed 1,754 terminal cancer patients in 20 in-hospice settings, 20 home-care hospices and 14 conventional-care situations. Based on the patients' own judgments, the study showed that while the "quality of death"—the last three days of life—was significantly better for hospice patients, the "quality of life" throughout the period of care was not.

This and other studies have also shown that, contrary to what I had been told by some experts, in-hospice may be in some ways better than home-hospice care: Because of the more comprehensive, more immediate support patients can receive in-hospice, pain and symptom control may be better, and both family members and caregivers are under less stress.

Hospice advocates such as Bates insist that because the National Hospice Study was completed several years ago, and because hospices have improved since then, the study's results mean little today; but the findings certainly reflect my mother's experience just two years ago. Patrice O'Connor, former director of St. Luke's-Roosevelt Hospital's Palliative Care Center in New York City, believes that quality of life for hospice patients can sometimes be far lower than it should be. And patients such as my Mom and Laurie may find that a gap indeed still exists between in-hospice care and at-home hospice care.

If my mother had been in-hospice, for example, or at least had more access to a hospice doctor, getting a lung tap to increase her comfort might have aroused less resistance. In general, help might have been more readily available during her breathing crises and depression, and I might have been spared the necessity of fighting to get her the care she needed. Unfortunately, most hospice programs in the United States are home-based, because of Medicare incentives to keep spending down, according to Rhymes.

THE MEDICARE MESS

Many experts agree, in fact, that Medicare rules contribute significantly to the problems hospice patients face. Hospices were born out of an altruistic ideal, but the Medicare hospice option was mainly created to save Medicare money by reducing hospitalizations and expensive life-saving attempts. According to Paul R. Torrens, a professor of public health at the University of California at Los Angeles, Medicare changed everything for hospice workers because they are now caught between helping the patient on the one hand and keeping costs down on the other. So when deciding not to give palliative surgical procedures, for example, hospice personnel may sometimes be guided more by economic pressures than by hospice philosophy. "Since the Medicare hospice benefit began, almost everything about hospice programs has had an economic flavor," says Torrens. "There are always economic pressures, though most hospice workers try to resist them."

Because of finances, some patients don't get complete care. "Hospice philosophy says the needs of each individual must dictate treatment, but many patients may not receive the best treatments due to financial restrictions," laments O'Connor. "Medicare limits a patient's options." For example, she notes, Medicare requires hospice patients to be treated at home at least 80 percent of the time and restricts how much hospices are allowed to spend on them. "Why should caregivers be allowed to spend only a fixed amount on care?" she asks. "Why should patients be required to sign a paper saying that their life expectancy is less than six months? Why should some hospice patients have to sign a 'do not resuscitate' order? These are invasions of privacy. To care effectively for the dying, we need flexibility, not all these rules and regulations."

COLD SHOULDERS

Of all the "rules" that can impinge on hospice patients, the most insidious may be the prescriptions about peaceful death. Some of Kübler-Ross's modern disciples have over-interpreted their mentor's theories about the "process" of dying to mean that there is one and only one right way to die. In my mother's case, for example, it was apparently "right" for her to calmly accept the news that she was supposed to die within six months, and to gasp for breath without expecting medical treatment because she was going to die soon anyway.

Judy A. Donovan, director of Jansen Memorial Hospice in Tuckahoe, New York, believes that if any hospice workers hold to such rigid prescriptions, it may be the by-product of increasing institutionalization. "Compassion has always been the essence of hospices," she says. "Their challenge is to remain compassionate despite continued growth. Most programs, I believe, are achieving that goal, but it isn't inconceivable that some may lose sight of it."

Gorodezky believes that rigid attitudes are seen too often. "They're the result of oversimplified thinking," she says. "Kübler-Ross gave us a framework to understand the complexity of dying, but not a recipe. Patients have a right to die in their own way, and our only job as caregivers is to make them as comfortable as possible."

While admitting that he has heard of cases like my mother's "more than once," Bates emphasizes that hospices have improved tremendously in the past several years and keep getting better. And Rhymes insists that, whatever the flaws remaining in hospices, most experts believe they represent the best form of care available for the dying. The workers, she says, are generally warmer, more understanding and better trained than those who care for the dying in more traditional situations. But she admits that the training still needs to get considerably better. "There's still a lot we don't know about caring for the dying," she says. "There are still some things we need to learn about pain management, and still some symptoms we can't treat well."

For Mount at McGill University, what's needed above all is stronger medical direction in both physician training and treatment. "Hospice patients are among the sickest in the health-care system, with the most complex and demanding needs. We need a caliber of medical involvement equal to the commitment and competence we display with those who are earlier in the disease process. The problem now lies in caregivers' overly narrow perception that our function is just to cure disease and prolong life," he says. "Study after study has shown that quality of life for patients, along with frequency and intensity of involvement from physicians, immediately drops off when curative interventions are no longer appropriate. We have to broaden our perspective, so we see that *alleviating suffering* is really what we're here for."

In contemporary Western society, people experience the deaths of older and younger persons differently. We are disposed to feel that the death of a small child is a greater injustice than the death of an older adult, and we experience correspondingly greater sorrow, anger, regret or bitterness when a very young person dies. This article examines these responses critically to determine whether they are backed by ethical considerations that reason can discern and defend. We contrast contemporary attitudes with those of ancient Greece and show the relevance that different attitudes toward death have for health care decision making.
Key Words: Attitudes toward death; Elderly; Children; Medical futility; Age-based rationing

Is Dying Young Worse Than Dying Old?

Nancy S. Jecker, PhD,[1]
and Lawrence J. Schneiderman, MD[2]

[1]University of Washington, Department of Medical History and Ethics and Department of Philosophy, Seattle, Washington 98195.

[2]University of California, San Diego, Department of Community and Family Medicine and Department of Medicine, La Jolla, California 92093.

Often we experience the death of a very young person differently than the death of an older individual. We may be disposed to feel not only greater sorrow, anger, despair or bitterness, but also a greater sense of injustice when death strikes a very young child. Is there any ethical justification for these divergent feelings? Or are such tendencies prompted by false stereotypes that should be shed? Furthermore, what practical difference might our responses to death make? If we are warranted in feeling comparatively worse in response to the death of a very young person, does this mean that we are also warranted in recognizing a greater duty to avert such a death? For example, should we measure the call upon medicine to preserve the life of people in different age groups as different? Should scarce medical resources be used first to save the life of younger patients even when this entails letting elderly patients die? Should health professionals exert a greater effort to defeat the odds and apply futile treatments when the patient is very young, while avoiding "heroics" on behalf of older patients?

Giving Feelings Their Due

To begin to answer these questions, we first consider the weight that ethical argument should give to ordinary moral feelings. Ethical argument is more than a description of moral feelings or beliefs, but instead involves reflecting critically on competing moral claims in order to clarify their nature and underlying basis of support. Thus we ask: Is there anything that is uniquely of *ethical* importance about responding differently to different deaths? One line of thinking is that our feelings surrounding death are more amenable to psychological, than to ethical or philosophical, justification. According to some views, reasoners should not assign special weight to ordinary moral sentiments, but should strive to be wholly impartial. Feelings cloud judgment, it is said, and render ethical reasoning suspect if not spurious.

Should we then resist the pull of emotion and sentiment? Does ethical reasoning demand this? Against this approach we note that the different psychological reactions to death we observe often present themselves not simply as feelings, but as *normative* truths. That is, we not only feel sharper regret when a small child dies, but feel that sharper regret is *merited* because such a death constitutes a greater injustice. Likewise, we sometimes sense that a lesser injustice takes place when an older person dies and so feel that a lesser degree of anger or bitterness is appropriate. Understood in this light, our different reactions to death may prove helpful to ethical reasoning because they may point to underlying ethical reasons.

Yet some might challenge the assumption that having certain moral feelings automatically shows that those feelings are backed by valid ethical norms. Perhaps our moral feelings are instead instincts that we are innately programmed to feel. Or perhaps they are the product of crude indoctrination by our parents and teachers. These suggestions await empirical analyses, and are more properly the domain of the social sciences (psychology) than the humanities (philosophy). However, ethical reasoning might take as its starting point what the philosopher Thomas Nagel (1986; see also Gibbard, 1990) has described as a middle ground view. Rather than either automatically debunking common moral sentiments as coarse and unfounded, or trusting them blindly and uncritically, Nagel suggests that we place enough faith in moral feelings to inquire what more precisely they involve and whether or not they are ethically

The authors appreciate the valuable assistance provided by two anonymous reviewers of *The Gerontologist*. The paper was presented in Washington, D.C. at the 1993 annual meeting of the Society for Health and Human Values.

justified. In support of this approach it can be said that ethical inquiry is not infrequently rewarded by tentatively trusting moral sentiments and letting them navigate inquiry in the direction of underlying norms. For instance, when moral feelings and critical ethical analysis are at odds, letting feelings guide reason may induce us "to continue looking beyond the proposed arguments, to keep searching and broaden the review. Later we may ... feel profoundly grateful that we were not carried away by abstractions" (Callahan, 1988, p. 12).

Let us consider our response to death's timing in light of Nagel's model. We will attempt to clarify the content of our response, lay bare the underlying reasons that might support it, and explore alternative responses. Throughout, our inquiry will be limited to specific Western attitudes toward death and to current and ancient time frames; a more complete analysis of attitudes toward death must address a fuller range of cultural and historical perspectives.

Our Response to Death's Timing

In characterizing our response to death's timing, Daniel Callahan (1987, 1993) has written that when we view people's deaths in distant retrospect, we tend to regard the deaths of very young persons with sharp regret, while seeing the deaths of older individuals as sad, but relatively acceptable, events. For example, recalling the death of a young child who could not raise the money needed to pay for a bone marrow transplant may still arouse in us bitter disappointment and the feeling that death was cruel and unnecessary. But we may feel comparatively less regret upon learning of the death of a 70-year-old who failed to obtain kidney dialysis due to age-based rationing of this technology. Extending this point, we may also find that the *anticipation* that death is imminent, and that there is nothing medicine can do to forestall it, is frequently met with deeper resistance in those treating small children as opposed to those treating elderly patients. Thus, a medical team may be more inclined to press for aggressive interventions, despite low odds of success, when the dying one is a child, rather than someone age 80. Extending this point still further, we may discover that many people find the actual *event* of death harder to witness in patients whose lives have barely begun to unfold than in those with many years behind them. Death in an elderly patient may be deemed "peaceful," implying "free from strife or commotion," "undisturbed, untroubled, calm, tranquil, quiet" (*Compact Oxford English Dictionary*, 1971). By contrast, a child's death may be called "senseless," which indicates it is "without sense or meaning ... purposeless" (*Compact Oxford English Dictionary*, 1971).

Suppose, for the purpose of this article, that such observations are roughly true. That is, suppose that we as a matter of fact feel worse when we recall, anticipate, or witness the deaths of very young persons than when we recall, anticipate, or witness the deaths of elderly persons. (Actually validating this assumption would require collecting empirical evidence which we do not attempt, although others

have done so [Reynolds, 1979]). These divergent feelings and attitudes toward death would not yet suffice to show that dying at a very young age is genuinely worse than dying late in life. After all, our psychological responses may be underlaid by illusions and false stereotypes about old age and youth. Or they may be backed by nothing more than an arbitrary cultural bias of Western industrialized societies that favors youthfulness and disparages old age. Should the death of a very young person truly merit the deeper resistance we apparently feel, we should be able to produce the reasons that support our feelings and attitudes.

One consideration that lends credence to the view that death is more acceptable when it occurs in old age is that "the elderly have lived a full life, have done what they could, and thus are not victims of the malevolence of the forces either of divinity or of nature" (Callahan, 1987, p. 72). By contrast, the death of a very young person may strike us as evidence that cruel forces govern the universe, and that responsible adults have failed to shield defenseless children against these forces.

Yet even when we assign no one responsibility for a person's death, we may still undergo more profound or bitter regret when the dying person is quite young. For example, the fact that the instrument of a small child's death is seen as an accident or fluke, rather than the product of divine will, does not necessarily make it seem less senseless or cruel. Even when God and nature are exculpated, we may continue to hold that death occurring early in the lifespan is particularly unfair.

A different justification for thinking death worse when it befalls a young child is simply that such a person has more potential years ahead to lose. What's more, when many future years are forgone, the individual is likely to miss major stages of life in their entirety. Thus, unlike the 65-year-old, the 5-year-old will never grow up to become an adult, or experience the events typically associated with this, such as falling in love, becoming a parent, developing and fulfilling life ambitions, and sustaining and deepening close relationships over time.

A related point holds that losing very young persons is a greater blow because younger persons have more potential contributions to make to society. Older persons, by contrast, have fewer years remaining to contribute. Moreover, beyond a certain age, older persons as a group may have contributed most of what they will contribute in areas such as economically productive labor, science and technology, or art and culture.

A further reason why the loss of a very young person may be harder to bear is that to lose such a person is tantamount to losing the future. Not infrequently, we refer to children as "our country's future." In contemporary American society the ideal of perpetual progress for each new generation continues to inspire us. This inclines us to invest special meaning in the welfare of our children: children stand for the improved life toward which our present labors are leading. By contrast, our nation's elderly may symbolize a past that will inevitably be improved upon and surpassed.

On a more personal level, the death of one's own child may convey what psychiatrist Irvin Yalom (1989, p. 132), has called "project loss": the loss of "what one lives for, how one projects oneself into the future, how one may hope to transcend death." By contrast, the death of an aging parent is not the loss of a life project but of an "object" or figure who has played an instrumental role in the constitution of one's personal past. Thus, with the loss of a parent one's personal future remains viable, even enlivened. Robert Jay Lifton and Eric Olson (1974) convey a similar thought, noting that offspring can represent a kind of "symbolic immortality" for parents. Lifton and Olson describe "symbolic immortality" as a psychological process of creating meaningful concepts, imagery, and symbols that fulfill the human need for a sense of historical connection beyond the individual life. Offspring afford parents symbolic immortality not only through continuing their physical/genetic material, but also by virtue of showing the imprint of parents' values and attitudes in the way they lead their lives. Parents may feel that their influence on children connects them to humankind as it enters "into a general human flow beyond the self" (Lifton & Olson, 1974, p. 77).

Finally, our attitudes toward death's timing may reflect our underlying attitudes toward time and temporal passage (Mellor, 1981). Although an individual's personal past grows more distant with the death of those (i.e., the elderly) who store its memory, the loss of the past may already be perceived as inevitable. Thus, the forward march of time makes the past appear increasingly temporally distant, further and further away from present reality. By contrast, we perceive the future as perpetually approaching, rather than slipping away. Parents fully expect their children to be represented in the future, even if they themselves are not. Thus, when death befalls children, parents feel deprived of something they did not expect to lose. The future that they imagined, and that seemed to be moving closer and closer to fruition, is now gone forever.

An Alternative Response

Are the above considerations compelling? Are our different responses to death in children and the elderly indeed warranted? It is instructive to juxtapose the response to death elaborated above with an alternative response. This approach features the aging process from youth to maturity as *adding* to the individual's capacity to appreciate life, and so *heightening* one's capacity to experience loss and deprivation of tragic dimension.

The response that treats the death of a mature adult as a greater hardship is particularly salient in the philosophy and literature of ancient Greece. Greek tragedies, for example, often take as their subject great men brought low. A great man's fall aroused compassion by leading the audience to put themselves in his place and feel empathy for his tremendous suffering. Thus, Sophocles takes Oedipus, a good man and king, as his subject and depicts Oedipus' downfall; the audience is drawn into Oedipus' despair and led to feel his upheaval and horror upon learning that he has killed his father and slept with his mother. Similarly, Aeschylus tells the tale of an eminent and morally blameless man, Orestes, who is ordered by Apollo to kill his mother. The audience is made to experience Orestes' torment as the Eumenides (which symbolically represent the fury of Orestes' mother) pursue him relentlessly.

Whereas Greek playwrights expected the losses of great men to excite compassion, they did not consider compassion equally applicable when similar harms were visited upon children. In contrast to our contemporary ethos, the ancient Greeks apparently regarded the death of small children as beneath tragic dimensions. This was perhaps because the infant or very small child lacks the adult's capacity to appreciate what is happening. An infant whose death is imminent may coo and wiggle; a toddler, not comprehending the import of a terminal diagnosis, may appear bored or listless. When Greek literature portrayed a child's death, the implications that the child's death carried for others received greatest emphasis. Thus, in *Medea*, Jason's wife seeks revenge against Jason by maliciously killing the children she bore him. Euripides treats the tragedy as befalling King Jason, rather than his murdered children, and makes the climactic moment the moment when Jason's fury erupts in the aftermath of his children's murders:

> [T]hou hast broken me! . . . Thou wife in every age abhorred . . . who didst kill my sons, and make me as the dead . . . Out from my road . . . And let me weep alone the bitter tide that sweepeth Jason's days, no gentle bride to speak with more, no child to look upon whom once I reared. All, all forever gone! (Euripides, 1943, pp. 491–492).

The point of view described here places our contemporary perspective in sharper focus. To begin with, whereas our forebears regarded maturing as heightening tragic potential, our contemporary ethos treats maturing as limiting tragic possibility. Contemporary attitudes tend to regard the death of young children as representing a greater injustice because the younger one is, the more innocent and blameless one is thought to be. According to contemporary thinking, maturing spoils purity and innocence, so it inevitably lessens the tragedy of death by inviting the possibility that one is somehow responsible for one's own downfall. The mature man is considered "worldly" and accountable, in contrast to the babe in arms who is considered naive and good.

A second contrast concerns the distinct emotions that ancient and modern attitudes call forth. Whereas the ancients underscored the adult's travails to summon empathic concern, contemporary views highlight the child's defenselessness and vulnerability to awaken a sense of *responsibility* that triggers protective impulses. We view a mature man as strong and self-reliant in the face of danger, but feel disposed to nurture and protect an imperiled child from harm.

Finally, our modern thinking envisions aging as *consuming* and *reducing* a person's entitlement to a finite resource, namely, the lifespan. The older people become the more they have "had their share" and depleted their entitlement to further existence. Whereas a newborn possesses the greatest entitlement to life, an aged person, like a gentle but lame horse, has already "drunk from the trough," and now it is time for her to let the next horse drink. Switching metaphors, some invoke a "fair innings" concept to convey that early in life people have not yet played the game, but once they have had their turn at bat playing further innings is no longer a strict entitlement (Somerville, 1986).

Notwithstanding these differences, certain affinities exist between ourselves and ancient Greeks. Thus, both we and our predecessors may anticipate with excitement the birth of a healthy baby, take special care in choosing names, feel pride in our children's development, and enjoy nursing and caring for our young. Despite notable differences then, the Greeks' intuitions are not exactly in counterpoint to our own. For all that is said here, the Greeks may well *support* the claims of children over very old persons, even if they subordinated the claims of both to the mature man. Or they may regard the death of a mature person of base character as less significant than the loss of a very young child from a good family who promises well.

Yet why should we even take Greek views about children seriously? Perhaps the Greeks simply became inured to child death because the survival of children was so precarious. Rates of childhood mortality were high, and in contrast to our society the survival of infants and small children was unpredictable. What's more, for all their vaunted tragedies, the Greeks had less than admirable views about women and non-native Greeks. Why should we expect their attitudes toward children to be any better? The answer here, as before, is that even if Greek views about children turn out to be unfounded, we cannot dismiss them outright. Instead, we ought to examine their views critically, and learn whether or not they are supported by ethical considerations that reason can come to discern and defend.

The response that treats the death of a small child as a more catastrophic event might gain an initial foothold from the observation that as one becomes a mature adult, the greater becomes one's capacity to comprehend the nature and import of catastrophe and so to experience and feel wounded by misfortune. Recognizing this, onlookers rightly perceive a mature adult's death as more potently tragic than the death of a young child.

In reply, however, it can be said that we recognize misfortunes as befalling persons who do not experience suffering and who are even wholly unaware of their condition. Thus, we count betrayal and deception as evils even when those betrayed or deceived remain ignorant of their situation. And we consider a disease process that results in gross mental deterioration as a tragic misfortune to its victim, even when the victim does not understand or mind the condition (Nagel, 1979). These reflections seem to indicate that tragedy can also befall an infant or small child who cannot comprehend tragedy's dimensions.

Yet the viewpoint that takes death as worse when it befalls a mature adult might spring from an alternative set of premises. A mature adult's death may be thought more tragic because mature persons are in the prime of life: they are at the height of their physical strength, and many of the life goals they have set may, for the first time, appear within reach. Hence, there is more reason to shake one's fist at the world when death takes a mature adult, since it brings to an end a more fully realized perfection.

The conviction that death qualifies as a greater evil for the mature person also may be accounted for on the ground that the death of an adult cancels the realization of goals and projects already underway. As the philosopher Ronald Dworkin observes, the frustration of desires and aspirations that death produces "is greater if it takes place after rather than before the person has made a significant personal investment in his own life. . ." (1993, p. 88). Thus the mature adult, unlike the infant or small child, has dreams for the future and death deprives such a person of the chance to realize hoped-for possibilities.

A further reason for regarding the death of a mature person as worse than the death of an infant or small child is that by maturity a person has entered into more relationships with others, and these relationships have grown more meaningful over time. For example, the Akamba people of Kenya treat the death of a mature person as worse for this reason. According to their view, "the more personally interwoven a person becomes with others through time, the greater the damage done to the social fabric when that person is torn away by death" (Kilner, 1990, p. 88).

Finally, persons may feel greater aversion to the death of mature adults because more than children, mature persons have earned our respect and honor. As a group, they merit respect merely by virtue of having lived through life. According to Jonsen, "Living a life is an achievement. Some persons do it with great vigor and style; others barely make it; yet everyone who survives accomplishes it. The accomplishment deserves acknowledgement" (1991, p. 346).

Implications for Health Care Decision Making

So far we have provided some basis for questioning our contemporary response to death by setting it alongside an alternative view gleaned from our own historical past. To summarize what has been said, the contemporary conception that a youthful death is a more tragic event may stem from a variety of sources. When a very young person dies we may feel that that individual has not yet lived a full lifespan or has not yet had an opportunity to make lasting contributions to society. Further, contemporary observers may find the loss of a young child less acceptable because the young stand for the future and seem to afford us the opportunity for progress and for exerting an enduring influence on humankind.

An alternative response toward death's timing is provided by the ancient Greeks, who portrayed tragedy in terms of a mature man brought low through death or personal devastation. Unlike the child, the mature individual understood his predicament and experienced the anguish it occasioned. He felt the loss of a hoped-for future as he found his plans and desires disappointed. To the extent that ancient Greeks considered a mature man to be an exemplar of the human species, the mature man's death or ruin was a greater loss than the death or devastation of a small child.

With this background, we now proceed to show that even if we continue to find contemporary attitudes compelling, their scope of practical application is limited. It might at first glance be thought that how we regard death carries immediate practical implications in many areas, including health care. Thus, ancient Greek attitudes toward death are apparently reflected in that society's treatment of newborns. The Greeks routinely "exposed" infants to the threat of death by abandoning them when they were born with deformities or were healthy but unwanted. Reflecting the ethos of ancient Greek society, caring for sick or defective newborns "was not a medical concern in classical antiquity"; moreover, no laws existed to prohibit either the killing of defective newborns or the exposing of healthy ones (Amundsen, 1987, p. 15). Philosophers, including both Plato and Aristotle, generally accepted the morality of exposing infants for the purposes of selective breeding or on purely economic grounds (Rist, 1982). Nor does Greek civilization stand alone in permitting the active or passive killing of infants. According to Post, "the Netsiliks, an Eskimo society that placed importance on having enough sons as hunters to ensure food for its members, practiced female infanticide because suckling a female infant for several years would prevent the mother from having a son" (Post, 1988, pp. 14–17). Other societies, including the !Kung of the Kalahari and the Tikopia of Polynesia, apparently practiced infanticide due to the difficulty of providing food for children.

If contemporary responses to death are justified, does it follow that our society should take an opposite tack? Should we, for example, devote great resources in medicine to saving the lives of children while investing comparatively few resources to saving the lives of older persons? Should we engage in heroic efforts to beat the odds on behalf of the tiniest babies, while refraining from exerting extraordinary efforts to benefit older patients? To address such questions we explore several possible claims one might be led to make on the basis of the view that death is worse when it happens to a very young person. Although we continue to focus on attitudes toward death at different ages, it is important to note that age is but one of several factors that informs our contemporary conception of "valuable-person-we-want-to-keep-alive." A more complete analysis would place attitudes toward age in the broader context of attitudes toward race and ethnicity, gender, economic status, and other factors.

Resource Allocation. — In considering possible ramifications of contemporary attitudes toward death, one set of issues relates to how we should distribute finite lifesaving resources among different age groups in society. It might be assumed that if the death of very young persons is worse than the death of very old persons, for example, then the young merit comparatively more lifesaving resources than the old. Callahan has argued for rationing publicly financed lifesaving resources on the basis of old age (as well as other criteria). He claims that by old age, people have passed the marker of a natural life span and their death may then be viewed as a sad, but relatively tolerable event (Callahan, 1987).

However, even assuming that our attitudes concerning death in old age are warranted, there are other reasons that tell against old age-based rationing. First, it might be argued that the young and old alike deserve equal access to basic health care because unequal access signals unequal respect for persons. Persons treated with lesser respect doubt their own value as persons and find their sense of self-worth and self-respect undermined (Gutmann, 1983).

Second, old age-based limits on medical care might be opposed because they violate the moral thrust of Judaic and Christian religions. Both traditions emphasize the equal worth and dignity of human beings. Both regard human dignity as age-transcendent rather than age-influenced (Post, 1991).

Special duties to the old might also follow from the fact that older persons as a group have made substantial contributions to society. Society therefore owes the elderly a debt of gratitude, and this debt cannot be paid unless the elderly have access to basic forms of medical care, including lifesaving care. Old age-based rationing represents, in this view, an ungrateful response to all that the elderly have given us.

Finally, old age-based rationing may be challenged on the ground that it affects women disproportionately. Women live longer than men, and so would be affected by ageist policies in greater numbers. Moreover, the deprivation of life-saving medical care in old age would be a greater deprivation for women because they have on average more years ahead to live (Jecker, 1991).

In light of these remarks, we conclude that it is wrong to suppose that old age-based rationing is justified just because death in old age is less tragic than death early in life. Even assuming it is correct to feel that an older person's death is relatively acceptable, it does not follow that the old can be ethically deprived of scarce life-saving medical resources so that such resources may be distributed to young age groups. Instead, a host of other considerations emerge as relevant.

Medical Futility. — A different set of issues is at stake when the tragedy associated with the loss of a small child disposes health care providers to pursue medical interventions against all odds in order to rescue a small child from death. Whereas rationing has to do with treating different groups fairly in the allocation of scarce resources, futility concerns the likelihood and quality of benefit that medical treatment affords for a single individual (Jecker & Schneiderman, 1992). By calling a life-saving treatment futile, we mean that the likelihood that it will in fact prolong life is exceedingly low or the quality of life thereby gained would be exceedingly poor (Schneiderman, Jecker, & Jonsen, 1990). Under such circumstances, some may insist that even when the chance of a successful outcome is slim, health professionals have a stronger duty to attempt beating the odds on behalf of very young patients. The reasoning here may be that the death of a small child is a more terrible thing, and so more effort must be expended to prevent it from occurring.

Yet this reasoning breaks down once the odds of success approach a very low threshold. When the odds of success become exceedingly slim, attempting to defy them is not in the patient's best interest, but instead functions as a means for health professionals, patients, and family to evade hard choices and flirt with fantasies of omnipotence. Clinging relentlessly to the life of a very small child by pursuing aggressive medical treatments may even add to the patient's or parents' misery by creating an emotional roller coaster of raised, then dashed, hopes. In addition, efforts to beat the odds through medical means may only increase suffering by prolonging the dying process; entailing the use of painful and invasive methods; and leading the medical team to dwell on pointless therapies rather than focusing their attention on truly beneficial measures, such as palliative and comfort treatments (Jecker & Schneiderman, 1993). In light of this, we urge health professionals who care for very young patients to move beyond the relentless pursuit of futile technologies to an ethic of care (Schneiderman, Faber-Langdeon, Jecker, in press).

There is a slightly different objection one might raise in defense of making a greater effort to forestall death in the young. It might be claimed that even if health professionals have no ordinary duty to provide an intervention that is very unlikely to succeed, they should be more inclined to make an exception on behalf of the very young patient on the basis of compassion. In other words, empathizing with the very small child should prompt health professionals to exceed their ordinary duty and do everything possible to ward off death.

Yet this reasoning does not withstand careful scrutiny. Compassion involves an attempt to "be in" the patient's persona and experience the suffering the patient does. As suggested already, a very small child may feel immediate pain or fear, yet lacks the deeper understanding and capacity for suffering we attribute to an adult. Thus, when the physician "steps into" a very young patient's shoes, the physician is unlikely to find there a stronger basis for compassion. When compassion is stirred in response to some harm that befalls a small child, it is often more properly directed toward the child's parents than the child. For example, when a small child's life is in peril, the child's parents are more likely to grasp the moment's finality and recognize an incalculable loss. The life

that is lost may even be perceived as *theirs* (the parents'), as much as the child's. The parents, like the protagonist in Euripides' *Medea*, may sense that they have been "broken" and are "as the dead."

Conclusion

We submit that the response of deeper anger, despair and bitterness in the face of a youthful death is not universal. Following Nagel's model, we have placed enough faith in these sentiments to inquire what more precisely they involve, and the reasons that can be advanced to support them. The juxtaposition of ancient and contemporary attitudes has made evident that the various norms that underlie contemporary attitudes are subject to alternative interpretations. Thus, the impending death of an infant or very small child will seem less cruel when it is emphasized that the infant or child does not comprehend the magnitude of the situation. On the other hand, the imminent death of a mature adult will appear more tragic when the mature adult is portrayed as innocent of wrongdoing, e.g., when death is attributed to the malign acts of others, or to genetic causes beyond the person's power to control or influence.

Finally, even assuming that contemporary responses to death's timing are justified, it does not immediately follow that the ethical obligations of physicians toward very young patients are more stringent. Nor does it follow that a tendency to "write off" elderly patients more readily, or feel absolved sooner of responsibility toward them, is warranted. Instead, justice standards are far too complex to reduce to a single rationing criterion, such as age. With regard to medical futility, it is clear that the boundaries of medicine apply to young and old alike, and even death's specter cannot undo medicine's ineluctable limits.

References

Amundsen, D. (1987). Medicine and the birth of defective children: approaches of the ancient world. In R. McMillan, H. T. Engelhardt, & S. F. Spicker (Eds.), *Euthanasia and the newborn* (pp. 3–22). Dordrecht: D. Reidel.

Callahan, D. (1987). *Setting limits.* New York: Simon and Schuster.

Callahan, D. (1993). *The troubled dream of life: Living with mortality.* New York: Simon and Schuster.

Callahan, S. (1988). The role of emotions in ethical decision making. *Hastings Center Report, 18,* 9–14.

Compact edition of the Oxford English dictionary. (1971). New York: Oxford University Press.

Dworkin, R. (1993). *Life's dominion.* New York: Alfred A. Knopf.

Euripides (1943). *The Medea.* In L. Cooper (Ed.), *Fifteen Greek plays* (pp. 447–494). New York: Oxford University Press.

Gibbard, A. (1990). *Wise choices, apt feelings.* Cambridge, MA: Harvard University Press.

Gutmann, A. (1983). For and against equal access to health care. In President's Commission for the Study of Ethical Problems in Medicine and Biomedical and Behavioral Research, *Securing access to health care, vol. 2* (pp. 51–66). Washington, DC: U.S. Government Printing Office.

Jecker, N. S. (1991). Age-based rationing and women. *Journal of the American Medical Association, 266,* 3012–3015.

Jecker, N. S., & Schneiderman, L. J. (1992). Futility and rationing. *American Journal of Medicine, 92,* 189–196.

Jecker, N. S., & Schneiderman, L. J. (1993). Medical futility: the duty not to treat. *Cambridge Quarterly of Healthcare Ethics, 2,* 149–157.

Jonsen, A. R. (1991). Resentment and the rights of the elderly. In N. S. Jecker (Ed.), *Aging and ethics* (pp. 341–352). Clifton, NJ: Humana Press.

Kilner, J. (1990). *Who lives? Who dies?* New Haven, CT: Yale University Press.

Lifton, R. J., & Olson, E. (1974). *Living and dying*. New York: Praeger Publishers.

Mellor, D. H. (1981). *Real time*. New York: Cambridge University Press.

Nagel, T. (1979). Death. In T. Nagel, *Mortal questions* (pp. 1–10). New York: Cambridge University Press.

Nagel, T. (1986). *The view from nowhere*. New York: Oxford University Press.

Post, S. G. (1988). History, infanticide and imperiled newborns. *Hastings Center Report, 18,* 14–17.

Post, S. G. (1991). Justice for elderly people in Jewish and Christian thought. In R. H. Binstock & S. G. Post (Eds.), *Too old for health care?* (pp. 120–137). Baltimore: Johns Hopkins University Press.

Reynolds, F. (1979). Natural death: A history of religious perspectives. In R. M. Veatch (Ed.), *Life span: Values and life-extending technologies*. San Francisco: Harper and Row.

Rist, J. M. (1982). *Human value: A study in ancient philosophical ethics.* Leiden, The Netherlands: E. J. Brill.

Schneiderman, L. J., Faber-Langdeon, K., & Jecker, N. S. (In press). Beyond futility to an ethic of care. *American Journal of Medicine.*

Schneiderman, L. J., Jecker, N. S., & Jonsen, A. R. (1990). Medical futility: Its meaning and ethical implications. *Annals of Internal Medicine, 112,* 949–954.

Sommerville, M. A. (1986). "Should the grandparents die?": Allocation of medical resources with an aging population. *Law, Medicine and Health Care, 14,* 158–163.

Yalom, I. D. (1989). *Love's executioner and other tales of psychotherapy.* New York: Harper Collins.

Received April 15, 1993
Accepted August 9, 1993

Physician-Assisted Dying:
Contemporary Twists to an Ancient Dilemma

Russell L. McIntyre, Th.D.

When a patient is dying, or has a terminal prognosis with only a limited time to live, would it ever be appropriate for a physician to intervene and ease the dying process or directly cause death? Would it make any difference if that person were in excruciating, intractable pain? Would it make any difference if that person had specifically made such a request to the physician while he/she was competent or left such instructions in a "living will?"

In the last two decades, primarily because of the development of life-prolonging/death-delaying artificial life-support systems, the debate over a physician's responsibility to the dying patient has intensified. How long should life be prolonged if there is no hope for meaningful recovery? How should expensive, perhaps scarce, medical technologies be used in the support of the critically ill in a way that is morally responsible to the needs of other patients and society at large? Does a doctor have a responsibility to insure that his or her patient not die a horrible death? If so, what exactly does this mean?

Primarily because of the introduction of high-tech life-support systems, choices today are different than they were even a single decade ago. Some people, including some physicians, seem to believe that medical science can keep a person's body alive, especially at the biological level, almost indefinitely. But, if we can, should we? And, if so, under what circumstances should this be allowed? Would it be justified if the patient were brain dead but pregnant, and there was significant opinion that the "dead" woman could be kept on total life supports until her fetus had developed to the point of viability outside the womb? This, of course, is already happening. But, what if the brain dead person could be kept alive to test new drugs or perfect surgery techniques that we would never contemplate trying on those who had any possibility for recovery? Are any of these arguments compelling enough to justify a change in the moral perceptions of society about what is acceptable, and what is inhumane and anathema to our individual or collective conscience?

The debate over a physician's responsibility to the dying patient is not new. Even before the introduction of new technological options, doctors wondered what their responsibility was to ease the suffering of the dying. The debate is as old as medicine itself, for, even in ancient Greece, physicians knew recipes for "potions" to terminate life or to ease the dying process.

In more recent times, however, several events have called our attention to this debate. And, while many might feel that this is an acceptable position under certain circumstances, we find considerable disagreement on the question of what ought to be public policy in the United States on this dilemma. One must also add that, since 1984, euthanasia has been openly practiced in the Netherlands on terminally ill but competent patients who specifically request assistance in dying. While not technically legal, the government is not interested in prosecuting physicians who follow guidelines established by that country's medical association.

This issue of *TRENDS IN HEALTH CARE, LAW & ETHICS* will tackle this debate head-on. . . . in this article, we will describe five major recent events that have focused national attention on this question. . . .

I. IT'S OVER, DEBBIE

In the January 8, 1988 issue of the *Journal of the American Medical Association*, an un-named physician described an incident that he had participated in during his training as a hospital resident in the field of obstetrics and gynecology. No specific details are given as to when or where this event took place.

The resident was "on call" in the hospital and toward the middle of the night a nurse paged him to see a 20 year old patient named "Debbie" who was dying of ovarian cancer and was experiencing "unrelenting vomiting apparently as the result of an alcohol drip administered for sedation." As he approached the room he heard her loud, labored breathing. When he entered the room he saw:

. . . an emaciated, dark-haired woman who appeared much older than 20. She was receiving nasal oxygen, had an IV, and was sitting in bed suffering from what was obviously severe air hunger. The chart noted her weight at 80 pounds. A second woman, also dark-haired but of middle age, stood at her right, holding her hand. Both looked up as I entered. The room seemed filled with the patient's desperate effort to survive. Her eyes were hollow, and she had suprasternal and intercostal reactions with her rapid inspirations. She had not eaten or slept in two days. She had not responded to chemotherapy and was being given supportive care only. It was a gallows' scene, a cruel mockery of her youth and unfulfilled potential. Her only words to me were, "Let's get this over with."[1]

The physician returned to the nurses' station, obviously moved by her desperate plight. He comments that she "was tired and needed rest." He could not give her health but he "could give her rest." Whereupon, he asked the nurse to fill a syringe with 20mg of morphine sulfate and returned to the patient's room. He comments:

I took the syringe into the room and told the two women I was going to give Debbie something that would let her rest and to say good-bye. Debbie looked at the syringe, then laid her head on the pillow with her eyes open, watching what was left of the world. I injected the morphine intravenously and watched to see if my calculations on its effects would be correct. Within seconds her breathing slowed to a normal rate, her eyes closed, and her features softened as she seemed restful at last. The older woman stroked the hair of the now sleeping patient. I waited for the inevitable next effect of depressing the respiratory drive. With clocklike certainty, within four minutes the breathing rate slowed even more, then became irregular, then ceased. The dark-haired woman stood erect and seemed relieved. "It's over, Debbie."

The JOURNAL encouraged reactions to the piece and, several weeks later, published an editorial, two articles and many of the letters they had received in a special section.[2] Needless to say, the reactions were intense, ranging from horror and disbelief (and a suggestion that perhaps the article was fiction) to sympathy for the patient who was caught in the most horrible stages of dying and some toleration—if not total acceptance—of what the doctor did as being humane. One of the major criticisms, however, was that "it was not his patient." The implication being that if it had been "his" patient,

he would have had a longer relationship with her and would have understood her statement, "Let's get this over with," as an expression of her own legitimately held values. The primary criticism, aside from those who felt it to be an outright violation of the ethics of medicine and everything sacred to the doctor-patient relationship, was that he acted in haste, in the middle of the night, perhaps as an "angel of mercy," but, in reality, as an "executioner." In the words of one critic, "we should never conceive of our physicians as our executioners."

II. DEATH AND DIGNITY: A CASE OF INDIVIDUALIZED DECISION MAKING

In March of 1991, a physician on the staff at Genesee Hospital in Rochester, New York, Timothy E. Quill, M.D., published a signed article in the New England Journal of Medicine, in which he described how he had facilitated the suicide of a woman in the final stages of dying from acute myelomonocytic leukemia. Unlike the previous unsigned article, Dr. Quill describes the intensity of his long-term relationship with Diane and how, over time, he came to believe that her decision to end her life when the time came, was "the right decision for her" given that it was "extraordinarily important to [her] to maintain control of herself and her own dignity during the time remaining to her."[3]

Diane had had a hard life, overcoming the lasting effects of being raised in an alcoholic family, overcoming vaginal cancer as a young woman, and struggles which eventually overcame alcoholism and depression in her own life. Dr. Quill writes:

I had come to know, respect, and admire her over the previous eight years as she confronted these problems and gradually overcame them. She was an incredibly clear, at times brutally honest, thinker and communicator.

With only a 25 percent chance of survival after a long arduous battle

of chemotherapy and bone marrow transplantation, Diane weighed the impact of treatment on her life, her lifestyle and her own deeply held personal values of independence and control. She decided for no treatment, although room was left for her to change her mind at any time.

Diane, however, wanted more than simply the assurances from Dr. Quill that he would keep her as comfortable as possible; she wanted the ability to be able to take her own life when she decided she had had enough.

In our discussion, it became clear that preoccupation with her fear of lingering death would interfere with Diane's getting the most out of the time she had left until she found a safe way to ensure her death. I feared the effects of a violent death on her family, the consequences of an ineffective suicide that would leave her lingering in precisely the state she dreaded so much, and the possibility that a family member would be forced to assist her, with all the legal and personal repercussions that would follow. She discussed this at length with her family. They believed that they should respect her choice. With this in mind, I told Diane that information was available from the Hemlock Society that might be helpful to her.

A week later she phoned me with a request for barbiturates for sleep. Since I know that this was an essential ingredient in a Hemlock Society suicide, I asked her to come to the office to talk things over. She was more than willing to protect me by participating in a superficial conversation about her insomnia, but it was important to me to know how she planned to use the drugs and to be sure that she was not in despair or overwhelmed in a way that might color her judgment. . . . It was clear that she was not despondent and that in fact she was making deep, personal connections with her family and close friends. I made sure that she knew how to use the barbiturates for sleep, and also that she knew the amount needed to commit suicide. We agreed to meet regularly, and she promised to meet with me before taking her life, to ensure that all other avenues had been exhausted. I wrote the prescription with an uneasy feeling about the boundaries I was exploring—spiritual, legal, professional, and personal. Yet I also felt strongly that I was setting her free to get the most out of the time she had left, and to maintain dignity and control on her own terms until her death.

During the next several months, her son and husband were able to spend significant amounts of time with her. Dr. Quill even had her come in to the hospital for a conference with the residents, "at which time she illustrated in a most profound and personal way the importance of informed decision making, the right to refuse treatment, and the extraordinarily personal effects of illness and interaction with the medical system." Diane's disease progressed and she became weaker.

It was clear that the end was approaching. Diane's immediate future held what she feared the most—increasing discomfort, dependence, and hard choices between pain and sedation. She called up her closest friends and asked them to come over to say goodbye, telling them that she would be leaving soon. As we had agreed, she let me know as well. When we met, it was clear that she knew what she was doing, that she was said and frightened to be leaving, but that she would be even more terrified to stay and suffer. In our tearful goodbye, she promised a reunion in the future at her favorite spot on the edge of Lake Geneva, with dragons swimming in the sunset.

Two days later her husband called to say that Diane had died. She had said her final goodbyes to her husband and son that morning, and asked them to leave her alone for an hour. After an hour, which must have seemed an eternity, they found her on the couch, lying very still and covered by her favorite shawl. There was no sign of struggle. She seemed to be at peace. They called me for advice about how to proceed. When I arrived at their house, Diane indeed seemed peaceful. Her husband and son were quiet. We talked about what a remarkable person she had been. They seemed to have no doubts about the course she had chosen or about their cooperation, although the unfairness of her illness and the finality of her death were overwhelming to us all.

Diane had died at a time of her own choosing; but what now to do about her death? Dr. Quill then called the medical examiner and reported that a hospice patient had died of "acute leukemia." The fact that she had ended her own life in the face of death by her disease was deliberately withheld. Dr. Quill remarks:

Although acute leukemia was the truth, it was not the whole story. Yet any mention of suicide would have given rise to a police investigation and probably brought the arrival of an ambulance crew for resuscitation. Diane would have become a 'coroner's case,' and the decision to perform an autopsy would have been made at the discretion of the medical examiner.

Following the publication of Dr. Quill's article, his fears about an investigation did come true. Investigations were conducted by the prosecuting attorney for the City of Rochester and by the New York State Department of Health. While it initially proved to be difficult to link an actual patient—and body—with the case as described by Dr. Quill, no one doubted that it was not a true story. Finally, after more than six months of investigations, New York announced that it would no longer be seeking either a criminal indictment against Dr. Quill for his actions nor any licensing action by the state medical licensing board. The debate over what Dr. Quill did, however, continues.

III. DR. JACK KEVORKIAN'S SUICIDE MACHINE

In July of 1990, Dr. Jack Kevorkian, a Michigan pathologist, rigged up a home-made suicide device in the back of his Volkswagen van and instructed Janet Adkins, a patient from Portland, Oregon, who suffered from Alzheimer's disease, how to activate the machine to end her own life. Mrs. Adkins pushed a button that administered a sedative into her veins which was followed by the drug sodium pentothal to stop her heart. Dr. Kevorkian was charged with first-degree murder but that indictment was dismissed by a Michigan District Judge because that state does not have an accessory statute making it a crime to assist someone in committing suicide.

Dr. Kevorkian was ordered by the Michigan court not to use the machine again, but on October 23, 1991, he assisted in the suicide-deaths of two more patients, one by using a more sophisticated version of his "machine"; the other by administering carbon monoxide gas through a mask placed over her nose and mouth. The patients were Sherry Miller, a 43 year old woman who had been suffering from multiple sclerosis for twelve years, and Marjorie Wantz, a 58 year old woman with an "unspecified pelvic disorder." The deaths, however, were classified as "homicides" by the county coroner and Dr. Kevorkian has now been charged with first-degree murder. The controversy that Dr. Kevorkian created was heightened by the judge who dismissed the first charges against him when the judge was recently quoted as saying, "There is a place for this in society," and suggested that "assisted suicide could be a viable alternative for the terminally ill if laws were drafted to regulate it."[4]

IV. DEREK HUMPHRY, FINAL EXIT

Derek Humphry first organized The Hemlock Society in 1980 "to campaign for the right of a terminally ill person to choose voluntary euthanasia."[5] His book, Final Exit, was on the New York Times Best-Seller list for over a dozen weeks in 1991. The book is a treatise on the advantages of planning one's death when one decides that meaningful life is over. Billed as "the ultimate how-to book," specific instructions are provided on using various drugs and methods to accomplish one's "self-deliverance." Instructions are provided on how to use sleeping pills, drugs, plastic bags, self-starvation, "and other means"; and suggestions are made on how to deal with questions of insurance and the law.

Part I of the book is for patients who are thinking about taking their own lives and who want to know how to accomplish this without making mistakes or being left to survive in a worse state than before attempting the act of self-destruction. Chapters are devoted to: Shopping For The Right Doctor; Beware Of The Law; The Hospice Option; The Cyanide Enigma; Death—Hollywood Style?; Bizarre Ways To Die; The Dilemma Of Quadriplegics; Storing Drugs; How Do You Get The Magic Pills?; Self-Deliverance Via The Plastic Bag; The Final Act. Part II of the book is prepared for those who are able to get a physician to assist them in dying. Chapters here are devoted to: Justifiable Euthanasia; A Doctor's Suicide Machine; Euthanasia By Physicians; Nurses On The Frontline; and Methods Reviewed.

V. WASHINGTON STATE INITIATIVE 119, THE "DEATH WITH DIGNITY" PROPOSAL

In November, 1991, voters in Washington, by a margin of only 8 percent, rejected a proposal that would have encouraged the state legislature to make physician-assisted dying, or euthanasia, a legal reality in that state. The proposal made its way to the ballot after obtaining more than 223,000 signatures from people who were ready to affirm that "the timing of one's death is a basic right."[6] Similar proposals several years ago in California and Oregon failed to get the needed number of signatures. The Washington vote was the first time in U.S. history that such an issue became the subject of a statewide referendum. If the measure had passed, terminally ill patients would have been allowed to commit suicide with the assistance of their physician. The measure would have also permitted doctors to use active euthanasia on patients who had less than six months to live and who had made a written request to die.

The measure was extremely controversial and had been vigorously opposed by the Catholic Church and by a wide margin of the House of Delegates of the Washington State Medical Association; but the entire membership of the state association, polled last spring, was about evenly split on support/opposition.

Each of the above events has served to force not only the attention of the medical community to these issues, but the public as well. That the public is entering this debate with significant force, is new. The debate, prior to this particular time in history, has largely been within the private realm of doctor and patient or doctor and family. Virtually no one wants to see a patient suffer as they are dying. But, the polarizing roles of the doctor as "angel of mercy" or as "executioner" has forced the debate to adversarial sides. . . .

ENDNOTES

1. *Journal of the American Medical Association,* Vol. 259, No. 2. Jan. 8, 1988; p. 272.

2. *Journal of the American Medical Association,* Vol. 259, No. 14, April 8, 1988; p. 2094–98; 2139–42.

3. *New England Journal of Medicine,* Vol. 324, No. 10, March 7, 1991.

4. *The New York Times,* October 27, 1991, p. 21.

5. Derek Humphry, *Final Exit: The Practicalities of Self-Deliverance and Assisted Suicide for the Dying* (Eugene, Oregon. The Hemlock Society, 1991), p. 180.

6. *The New York Times,* October 14, 1991, p. 1.

A Comparative Study of Family Bereavement Groups

Estelle Hopmeyer and Annette Werk

School of Social Work, McGill University, Montreal, Quebec, Canada

Although many authors have advocated the use of bereavement support groups, little research has been done comparing groups that differ in their structure and membership. We conducted such research on five bereavement support groups offered in the Montreal area and report preliminary findings from three of them. These three groups serve widows, family survivors of suicide, and family survivors (other than parents) of the death of a family member by cancer. Although members of all groups tended to report strong satisfaction with their group experience, both the reasons for joining a group and the most valuable aspects of the group experience varied as a function of group setting and objectives.

In this article, we report some preliminary data from a comparative study of five bereavement groups currently meeting in Montreal. The groups serve five different populations who have experienced the death of a family member. The populations are those bereaved through death by adult cancer, AIDS, suicide, childhood cancer, and loss of a husband. Family members include those related by blood, legal or common-law marriage, or homosexual relationship.

Because bereavement (the state of having suffered a loss) is a natural part of life, it is important to understand what it is and how it affects people. Rando (1988) has very succinctly described the multidimensional experience of grief. She has divided grief reactions into three groups: the psychological, the social, and the physical. The psychological reactions, or thoughts and emotions, can vary in terms of range and intensity and can include anxiety, anger, fear, guilt, relief, sadness, depression, yearning, and a search for meaning. The social or behavioral reactions can be experienced as a

lack of concentration, lack of energy, and an inability to sustain relationships or to nurture. The physical reactions can also vary a great deal but can include eating or sleeping disorders; heart palpitations; sickness; or death, possibly by suicide.

Writers such as Rando (1988), Schiff (1977), and Worden (1991) have pointed out that losses are both physical and symbolic. Symbolic losses include the loss of hopes and dreams, as well as unfulfilled expectations. The death of a child clearly activates all levels of loss.

In addition to being personal and unique, losses through death encompass the past, present, and future. In terms of the past, a loss might entail unresolved or unfinished business with the person, may be part of a history of other unresolved losses, may raise intergenerational issues, and may trigger feelings such as "never had and never will have." In terms of the present, the loss affects roles, tasks, and responsibilities, and in terms of the future, the death means the loss of dreams and hopes and yearning for what might have been.

The special circumstances of a death can affect the grief process as well. A sudden, violent death, as in the case of suicide, accident, or murder, has significant impact. Feeling that the death was preventable is another critical variable. The "what if"s and "if only"s are often part of the aftermath of a suicide, the death of a child, or the death of a lover through AIDS. The stage of the family life cycle at which the death occurs is also very significant to the bereavement process. When the death occurs out of the natural order, as in the case of a child's death, it has significance for the resolution of grief. The death of a family member also has to be considered in terms of a family perspective. Other stresses on the family, such as unemployment, mental or physical illness, and intergenerational issues (e.g., suicide in an earlier generation) need to be understood. Finally, social factors and social recognition of the death need to be considered. A stigma is attached to suicide or death from AIDS that has created a group of disenfranchised mourners (Doka, 1989). Support systems are not readily available to these populations.

A revised version of this article was published in *Groupwork*, Fall 1993.

Address correspondence to Estelle Hopmeyer, School of Social Work, McGill University, 3506 University Street, Montreal, Quebec, Canada H3A 2A7.

Lindemann (1944), Rando (1988), Schwartz-Borden (1986), and Worden (1991) have written on the normalcy of grief reactions and the need to do grief work. Parkes (1972) identified three forms of service that could be beneficial to those experiencing uncomplicated or normal grief: professional, volunteer (trained by the professional), and peer (bereaved people helping others) support.

The forms of help selected for the present project were peer support and peer self-help groups. The literature (e.g., Gottlieb, 1985, and 1988; Videka-Sherman & Lieberman, 1985) suggests that these forms of groups can

1. Help participants develop and strengthen informal support networks.
2. Help participants gain hope, receive new ideas for solutions to problems, receive information regarding other sources of help, improve skills in developing social relationships, and become less lonely and isolated.
3. Give participants a sense of belonging as well as feelings of fellowship and solidarity.

These benefits can be summarized as commonality, normalization, solidarity, reciprocity, and control.

Although this literature suggests that participation in self-help or support groups can be an effective way to reduce the trauma of coping with the death of a significant person, there has been an absence of a family focus on loss. The extent of this oversight is appreciated when one realizes that the definition of family now includes not only the traditional family, but also families of choice. Only recently has the literature addressed the special needs of disenfranchised mourners (Doka, 1989, Winiarski, 1991). Moreover, there has been limited systematic comparison of specific groups and no comparative research that could offer insight into the effectiveness of groups based on their structural elements (e.g., setting, leadership, membership, content, and duration). Gottlieb (1988) maintained that if the beneficial impact of groups is to be maximized, comparative studies that systematically vary the structural components are needed.

The present research, then, had several purposes. The first was to evaluate and improve the group service offered to these five populations. The second was to use the comparative data to develop a training manual for professional and peer facilitators. Finally, we wished to accumulate data for theory building for classroom teaching in two major curriculum areas: social work practice with groups and life-threatening illness and bereavement.

THE GROUPS

The five bereavement groups (see the Appendix for descriptions) differ from one another in structure, for-

mat, and leadership. As can be seen in Table 1, the Family Survivors of Suicide (FSOS) is the only one of the self-help groups that is open ended and continuous. It is led by a peer facilitator without professional assistance. A professional attends most meetings as a consultant/ resource person. The HIV/AIDS Bereavement Support Group, which is led by a professional, does not have a peer cofacilitator and discusses preselected themes. The other three groups, Hope & Cope (adult cancer), Bereaved Parents Support Group (childhood cancer), and Widow-to-Widow, are alike in terms of leadership (cofacilitation by a peer, and professional), structure (closed membership and predetermined number of meetings), and format (themes and open discussions).

SURVEY INSTRUMENT

Members who had attended one of the five groups over a period of several years were mailed an adapted version of the Social Support Project Questionnaire (Taylor, 1990). The respondents were asked to describe their social network, to identify their reasons for attending the group, to indicate their satisfaction/dissatisfaction with their group experience, and to identify their ideal group format. The questionnaire also provided space for comments and an overall evaluation of the group experience.

RESULTS FROM THREE OF THE GROUPS

Although five groups were included in this study, because the questionnaires were distributed at different times, the preliminary results presented herein are limited to the Widow-to-Widow, Hope & Cope, FSOS groups. These results suggest that all members who completed the questionnaire felt very satisfied with their bereavement groups. In their qualitative comments at the end of the questionnaire, they frequently mentioned the excellent quality of group leadership, describing their leaders as empathic, knowledgeable, and helpful. Their responses to the series of questions asking what they believed an ideal group would be indicated that they thought their groups were ideal.

However, there were some specific interesting items that we would like to focus on.

Contributions to the group. Sixty-one percent of the members of all three groups believed they received more from the group than they contributed, 37% believed they gave and received equally, and 2% indicated that they received less from their group than they contributed. This finding suggests that members may not realize when they are being helpful to other members and thus perceive themselves as getting more than they are giving.

Involvement in the group. In response to the question regarding their involvement in the group, it was interesting to note that a much higher percentage of the members of Widow-to-Widow than of the members of FSOS and Hope & Cope indicated great involvement. Hope & Cope members indicated moderate involvement, and less than 50% of FSOS members indicated great or moderate group involvement. This finding may well have been related to the open-ended, ongoing nature of FSOS as compared with the closed, specific number of sessions of both other groups. We would like to see whether this hypothesis is true in further analysis of our data and of other studies.

Reasons for joining the group. Other interesting findings related to the reasons for joining a bereavement group. As shown in Table 2, we ranked the reasons for joining from 1 to 13 for each of the three groups. Table 3 indicates the three most important reasons for each group. The similarity in the responses may be observed. Both FSOS and Hope & Cope members gave the same three reasons as most important although in different rank order. The widows included two of these three items, but their third most important reason was to make new friends. This was consistent with their responses to many of the other questions. Companionship appeared to be very important to members of Widow-to-Widow and was less so to members of the other two groups. As shown in Table 4, the three least important reasons for joining the group were also similar for members of all three groups, except for the reason of making new friends, which was cited by FSOS members, but not Widow-to-Widow and Hope &

Cope members, as are of the three least important reasons for participating in a group.

Most valuable things gained from joining the group. The reasons for joining the groups were fairly consistent with the most valuable things gained from participation in the bereavement groups. The question regarding the most valuable things gained from group participation was a write-in question, but we tabulated the qualitative responses into the categories listed in Table 5. Each response was repeated a number of times. It is interesting to note that although all members believed they benefited from the opportunity to share with others, the FSOS members repeatedly responded "Important not to be alone," whereas Hope & Cope members and Widows worded this as "Sharing and supporting others." This finding could have been related to the fact that family survivors of suicide are a stigmatized group in our society. The widows' most frequent responses, one again, related to friendship and companionship.

Degree to which other members' behaviors were upsetting. The question regarding how uncomfortable or annoyed members felt when other members talked too much, were extremely negative, were too dependent, gave advice, or kept bringing up the same issues showed that respondents were very accepting of each other, in that none of these issues seemed very upsetting to any of the group members. The items that were mentioned most frequently as being upsetting were when members talked too much or were extremely negative. Yet even these two items were mentioned by only a small minority of women. The male group

TABLE 1   Profiles of Family Bereavement Support Groups Compared

Structural element	Widow-to-Widow	Family Survivors of Suicide	Hope & Cope[a]	HIV/AIDS Bereavement Support Group	Bereaved Parents Support Group[b]
Location	Community agency	University	Secondary building of hospital	University initially; now community	Hospital
Structure	Closed membership; predetermined number of meetings	Open-ended membership; continual meetings	Closed membership; predetermined number of meetings	Closed membership; predetermined number of meetings	Originally open membership and now closed; predetermined number of meetings
Format	Thematic open discussion	Open discussion	Thematic open discussion	Thematic	Open discussion
Leadership	Peer/professional cofacilitation	Peer facilitator	Peer facilitator and professional	Professional leadership	Professional/peer facilitator
Membership	Women who have lost husbands	Any family member	Family members (except parents)	Lovers of AIDS victims	Parents
Other information	Group is part of a comprehensive program for widows.	Professional attends meetings as consultant/resource person.	Part of a comprehensive program for cancer patients and their families	New group in its first session—no peer facilitator	Group used to be led by professional.

[a]Survivors of loss of adult family member to cancer.
[b]Survivors of loss of child to cancer.

TABLE 2   Importance of Various Reasons for Attending Bereavement Groups

Reason for joining	Widow-to-Widow		Family Survivors of Suicide		Hope & Cope[a]	
	% Very important	Rank	% Very Important	Rank	% Very Important	Rank
Share what I learned	80	1	45	4	50	5
Share similar experience	70	2	85	1	70	3
Make new friends	67	3	10	11	30	8
Gain comfort and reassurance	60	4	76	2	90	1
Get advice	53	5	41	7	50	4
Get information	50	6	30	9	30	7
I was depressed	47	7	41	5	40	6
Learn new skills for coping	47	8	76	3	80	2
Help others	40	9	31	8	30	9
I was desperate	33	10	20	10	10	12
Was something to do	27	11	0	13	10	10
Curiosity	20	12	7	12	10	13
There was no one else	7	13	41	6	10	11

[a]Survivors of loss of adult family member to cancer.

members were not at all upset by any of these issues.

Amount of time devoted to specific items. Interestingly, when members were asked how much time should be devoted to specific items, their responses fell along gender lines. The female respondents gave first place to "Sharing feelings and emotions," while this ranked tenth among male respondents, who ranked "Learning how others solve problems like mine" as first. This suggests that professionals need to be sensitive to how men and women perceive their needs and need to use this knowledge in the pregroup phase of group publicity and member recruitment.

IMPLICATIONS FOR PRACTICE

These preliminary data strongly suggest that self-help groups offer their members the opportunity to complete the tasks of bereavement (Worden, 1991) in an atmosphere that is both supportive and encouraging. The groups create an informal support network that is available on an ongoing basis. Family and friends, the traditional source of support, are often unwilling or unable to remain accepting over a lengthy time period. They tend to expect the bereaved to get over their loss and get on with their lives. This can be particularly true for widows. Disenfranchised mourners (e.g., lovers of AIDS victims and, to a less but still significant extent, survivors of suicide) and parents who have lost a child need the validation and acceptance they receive from other group members.

This need was expressed by several of the respondents in their qualitative comments. For example, one participant stated, "My parents and my brother don't know that my son died by suicide. They all live in the U.S." The strength gained by attending a group with others who have had the same experience was pointed out by another member, who said she "liked the sense

TABLE 3   Reasons for Joining Bereavement Groups That Were Considered Very Important by Participants

Rank	Widow-to-Widow	Family Survivors of Suicide	Hope & Cope[a]
1	Share what I learned	Share similar experience	Gain comfort and reassurance
2	Share similar experience	Gain comfort and reassurance	Learn new skills for coping
3	Make new friends	Learn new skills for coping	Share similar experience

[a]Survivors of loss of adult family member to cancer.

of being with others in the same situation—the all-in-the-same-boat feeling."

A Hope & Cope respondent explained, that "You are not alone in your grief. You can share the pain, discuss, cry, help each other. This releases the guilt. You can ask questions and realize there are no answers." A FSOS group member added, "The contact with another person in the group who had experienced things very similar to me gave me the feeling that I am not alone."

Normalization is an important process for bereaved people. Seeing others with similar grief reactions helps members to recognize that their responses are neither crazy nor unnatural. One person indicated that the group demystified the bereavement process and helped her to feel normal. A family survivor of suicide explained,

In the group I felt a sense of acceptance, of being more among others who understand and therefore don't expect more of me than I can do. Especially the reassurance that I am part of a very diverse and normal group of people who have in common the loss of a loved one by suicide. The reassurance that I am still a good—o.k.—person, not a pariah. Our common experience of helplessness before another suicide allows me to believe that I am not to blame—none of us are—and that I can go on with my life.

TABLE 4   Reasons for Joining Bereavement Groups That Participants Considered Not Very Important

Rank	Widow-to-Widow	Family Survivors of Suicide	Hope & Cope[a]
13	There was no one else	Was something to do	Was something to do
12	Curiosity	Curiosity	Curiosity
11	Was something to do	Make new friends	There was no one else

[a]Survivors of loss of adult family members to cancer.

Although our findings indicate that many group members believed they received more help from other members than they gave, their qualitative comments indicated that many of them did get an increased sense of self-worth by reaching out to each other. "I myself feel better when I think I'm helping someone else—usually a person whose bereavement is more recent than mine," said a family survivor of suicide.

Another significant aspect of self-help groups is to assist their members to gain a sense of control over their lives by developing coping strategies. One respondent pointed out, "The group has helped me a lot. It's not easy to make the decision to go to that room, face other people and face the awful event of my husband's suicide. It is hard—it is painful. But when I make a commitment to go there, it helps."

Another agreed: "I make a commitment to myself to get better, to learn more; I make a commitment to living a fuller life. If I didn't have this group, where would I go? I would be stumbling around in the dark; isolated."

TABLE 5   Six Most Valuable Things Gained from Group

Widow-to-Widow	Family Survivors of Suicide	Hope & Cope[a]
Made new friends	Not alone	Place to vent my feelings
Gained confidence	Not the only one	Chance to talk
Shared with others	Someone understands	Opportunity to share my grief
Gained hope	Shared my grief	Comforting not to be alone
Gained strength and purpose	Not alone in my pain	Sharing, support
Learned I can have a normal life	Others have similar tragedies	Similar to others

[a]Survivors of loss of adult family member to cancer.

SUMMARY

The present research supports the theoretical position taken by many authors (e.g., Gottleib, 1985, 1988; Videka-Sherman & Lieberman, 1985) that self-help groups can be a useful tool in assisting bereaved per-

sons to come to terms with their grief and to move ahead with their lives. The group members appeared to benefit from the shared experience with others who were similarly bereaved and often could be helped to regain hope for their own futures when they saw how others had survived. It is important to keep in mind, however, that although there were many similarities across the three groups, there were also some differences. It will be interesting to see whether the data generated from the other two groups will be consistent with the preliminary results for these three groups. We believe that the statistical analysis of the data from all five groups will be helpful to professionals attempting to develop effective group programs for the bereaved population.

REFERENCES

Doka, K. (Ed.). (1989). *Disenfranchised grief: Recognizing hidden survivors.* Lexington, MA: Lexington Books.
Gottleib, B. H. (Ed.). (1985). Social support and the study of personal relationships. *Journal of Social and Personal Relationships, 2,* 351–375.
Gottleib, B. H. (Ed.). (1988). *Marshaling social support: Formats, processes and effects.* Newbury Park, CA: Sage.
Irizarry, C. (1981). Group services: A primary mode of hospital social service delivery. In N. Goroff (Ed.), *Reaping from the field: From practice to principle* Itebrun: Practitioner's Press.
Lindemann, E. (1944). Symptomatology and management of acute grief. *American Journal of Psychiatry 101,* 141–148.
Parkes, M. (1972). *Bereavement studies of grief in adult life.* London: Tavistock Press.
Rando, T. A. (Ed.). (1986). *Parental loss of a child.* Champaign, IL: Research Press.
Rando, T. A. (1988). *Grieving: How to go on living when someone you love dies.* Lexington, MA: Lexington Books.
Schiff, H. S. (1977). *The bereaved parent.* New York: Crown.
Schwartz-Borden, G. (1986). Grief work: Prevention and intervention. *Social Casework: The Journal of Contemporary Social Work, 65,* 499–505.
Taylor, S. E. (1990). *The Social Support Project Questionnaire.* Los Angeles: Franz Hall/University of California, Los Angeles.
Videka-Sherman, L., & Lieberman, M. (1985). Effects of self-help groups and psycho-therapy after a child dies: The limits of recovery. *American Journal of Orthopsychiatry, 55,* 70–82.
Worden, J. W. (1991). *Grief counseling and grief therapy: A handbook for the mental health practitioner* (2nd ed.). New York: Springer Publishing Company.
Walsh, F., & McGoldrick, M. (1991). *Living beyond loss: Death in the family.* New York: W. W. Norton.
Winiarski, M. G. (1991). *AIDS related psychotherapy.* New York: Pergamon Press.

APPENDIX: BEREAVEMENT SUPPORT GROUPS COMPARED IN THE PRESENT STUDY

Hope & Cope Bereavement Support Group

Hope & Cope is a support group based on the self-help model for family members (excluding parents) who have been bereaved by cancer. Members are screened by a social worker. The group is close-ended and meets biweekly for six to eight sessions. Group size varies (4–13); age limit is approximately 20–75. Leadership is by two peer facilitators, with a professional social worker in attendance. Educational material is presented regularly and is discussed according to the wishes of the group.

Bereaved Parents Support Group

Bereaved Parents is a support group based on the mutual-aid model for bereaved parents whose children have died of cancer at the Montreal Children's Hospital. The group is open-ended, meeting every 3 weeks in the hematology clinic of the hospital. There are separate group meetings for English- and French-speaking parents. Group size varies (6–12); age range is approximately 25–50. Members are screened by a social worker who also sponsors the support group and regularly attends the 2-hr meetings. The group is led by a professional, with the assistance of a peer facilitator.

Family Survivors of Suicide

Family Survivors of Suicide is a mutual-aid group for family survivors of suicide. The group is open-ended, meeting twice a month at the McGill University School of Social Work. Notices placed in the local newspaper before each meeting prompt self-referrals, and other members are referred by social agencies or the clergy. Members are not prescreened. Group size varies (5–12), and family members have included parents, siblings, children, and partners. Group management is by group members who have formed an executive committee that meets before each meeting. A professional social worker serves as consultant to the group and attends the majority of meetings by members' request.

Widow-to-Widow Program

Widow-to-Widow is a support group designed to help newly widowed women obtain ongoing support from peers who have resolved their grief, as well as to provide pragmatic input regarding economic, social, career, and education issues. The group is close-ended, meeting weekly for 8 to 10 sessions. Group size varies (8–12), and the age limit is 40–65 or 20–40. Each group is coled by a widow (peer facilitator) and a professional.

HIV/AIDS Bereavement Support Group

This support/mutual-aid group is for individuals surviving a loss due to HIV/AIDS. Although it was originally intended to include family members, significant others, as well as care givers (both informal volunteer and professional), it is predominantly gay male lovers of deceased AIDS patients who attend. The group size varies (two to six), and the age range is 20–60. The leadership is assumed by a professional social worker, who acts more as a facilitator. This group is a closed-membership group after initial intake interviews. It has weekly meetings for 9 consecutive weeks. Each session has a predetermined, specific topic or objective.

Living Environments in Later Life

Unit 4 noted that old age is often a period of shrinking life space. This concept is crucial to an understanding of the living environments of older Americans. When older people retire, they may find that they travel less frequently and over shorter distances because they no longer work and most neighborhoods have stores, gas stations, and churches in close proximity. As the retirement years roll by, older people may feel less in control of their environments due to a decline in their hearing and vision as well as other health problems. As the aging process continues, the elderly are likely to restrict their mobility to the areas where they feel most secure. This usually means that an increasing amount of time is spent at home. It has been estimated that individuals 65 and over spend 80 to 90 percent of their lives in their home environments. Of all other age groups, only small children are as house- and neighborhood-bound.

The house, neighborhood, and community environments are, therefore, more crucial to the elderly than to any other adult age group. The interaction with others that they experience within their homes and neighborhoods can be either stimulating or foreboding, pleasant or threatening. Across the country, older Americans find themselves living in a variety of circumstances, ranging from desirable to undesirable.

Approximately 70 percent of the elderly live in a family setting, usually a husband-wife household; 20 percent live alone or with nonrelatives; and the rest live in institutions such as nursing homes. Although only about 5 percent of the elderly live in nursing homes at any one time, a total of 25 percent of persons 65 and over will spend some time in a nursing home setting. The longer one lives, the more likely he or she is eventually to live in a total care institution. Since most older Americans would prefer to live independently in their own homes for as long as possible, their relocation—to other houses, apartments, or nursing homes—is often accompanied by considerable trauma and unrest. The fact that the aged tend to be less mobile and more neighborhood-bound than any other age group makes their living environment most crucial to their sense of well-being.

Articles in this unit focus on some of the alternatives available to the aged: institutionalization, the provision of adequate health care, and the dynamics of family care. The first unit article, "The Story of a Nursing Home Refugee," addresses the advantages and disadvantages of nursing home living. Traditionally the family was the main support for elderly relatives, but the family's capacity to provide care has been eroded by economic pressures.

Living independently with various levels of support is the topic of the next article. Mary Kalymun's article, "Board and Care Versus Assisted Living: Ascertaining the Similarities and Differences," points out that board and care and assisted living are similar in concept with sharp differences in practice.

Various living arrangements of older persons are examined in the next three articles. "From 'Our Town' to 'Ghost Town'?: The Changing Context of Home for Rural Elders" describes the plight of many small rural communities that are dying. The lifestyle of single-room occupants located in major metropolitan areas is examined in "A Room of One's Own: The SRO and the Single Elderly." Group homes were developed to minimize behavioral disturbances associated with dementia while supporting functional competencies. Bo Malmberg and Steven Zarit examine this issue in "Group Homes for People with Dementia: A Swedish Example."

Looking Ahead: Challenge Questions

As medical technology increases the life expectancy of the average American, will it be more or less likely that individuals will spend some of their later years living in a nursing home setting? What are some positive and negative aspects of nursing home life?

As both the number and percentage of older Americans in the total population increases, will neighborhoods become more age segregated? Why, or why not?

What new kinds of living arrangements will become more common for older Americans in the future?

Is relocating sick or feeble older persons a threat to their health and survival?

The story of a nursing home refugee

KATHARINE M. BUTTERWORTH
WHOLE EARTH REVIEW

Taking care of the elderly is not something we do very well in our society. Most older people prefer to live out their last years on their own or with loved ones rather than in a nursing home, so the burden of caring for them falls squarely on their family and friends. But because there is little public support—either in financial help or in tangible services—for those caretakers, sometimes that burden becomes too great and a nursing home becomes the only option. That's what happened to 91-year-old Katharine Butterworth, and this is her spirited account of that time. Dollars & Sense *magazine describes the mixed-up financial picture of aging policy in the United States and reminds us that with our rapidly growing population, the problem is only going to get worse.*

Young families who have the responsibility of caring for old people find it hard to tuck them in the chimney corner, mainly because there is no longer a chimney corner in which to tuck them.

A bulletin from my college proudly lists 10 graduates who lived to be 100, but every one of them is in a nursing home. A nursing home used to be a halfway house between hospital and going home. Now too often it is the permanent home, the last resort for a family desperate to handle an elderly invalid. Nursing homes are expensive and to receive any financial aid from the government, such as Medicaid, one must be destitute, but that is another story.

I know about three nursing homes, two for my husband, one for myself. My husband and I had had a good and healthy life when in our mid-80s he became ill, a bladder operation leaving him in need of a permanent catheter, the infection sometimes affecting his mind. I became ill and had to enter a hospital myself, so our children insisted he go into a nursing home.

When I recovered and returned home, I visited him. He had been given a small room opposite a noisy laundry room, and a woman patient next door was moaning all night. He said he was going to jump out the window, and I told him he was on the ground floor and could walk out. I sat with him in the dining room with three men who didn't talk; they had Alzheimer's disease. The trays were metal, and noisy when handed out. He was served a huge sausage, the kind he particularly disliked, no knife, and a little dish of stewed fruit with a limp piece of cake on top. No fruit juice or water, liquids he was supposed to have plenty of. In addition he was tied in a wheelchair, making it difficult for him to reach the table. It depressed both of us.

At a meeting with the head nurses and an accountant, in which I was asked to sign many papers to make my husband's acceptance in the nursing home permanent, plus pay a $3,000 deposit in case we got behind in our payments, I burst out, "He's coming home." The nursing home had started out as a solution to a problem but it had turned into a nightmare. We would both be home in our apartment, would manage some way and die together.

Our help at home was erratic and our children again insisted my husband be placed in a nursing home. He needed more care and often wandered at night, waking me up. Once he fell out of bed at 2 a.m., which entailed my calling the police because I could not lift him or help him to climb back in.

This second "home" was much more elegant, with Georgian-style architecture, trees, garden, the room itself large and pleasant, but help here was short and he was often left in bed most of the morning. The dining room had none of the clatter of metal trays and the varied food was attractively served, each person seated at an individual table or in a wheelchair with a tray. It seemed quietly civilized until one patient shoved his tray with everything from soup to dessert and it shot with a crash across the floor, requiring that some poor soul clean up the mess. The patients looked normal but, one could guess, often were not.

Then we found Sandy and a nursing home was no longer necessary. Sandy was with us part time for

From *Utne Reader,* January/February 1991, pp. 42-49. Excerpted from *Whole Earth Review,* Fall 1990. © 1990 by Katharine M. Butterworth. Reprinted by permission of the author.

over a year until my husband died. She was going to college, wanted to earn extra money, and we paid her above the minimum wage. Never have I known a more dedicated, hard-working, cheerful, intelligent young girl. She likes old people, and plans to run her own nursing home some day. May her dream come true. She was ideal for us, permitting my husband to stay home where he was happiest. She was strong enough to give him a tub bath, for example, and because she was cheerfully persuasive there was little friction, and I began to relax. He died at home, which in itself was a comforting end.

Six months after my husband died I came down with pneumonia, and my son and daughter-in-law took me to the emergency room in the nearby hospital. Slowly I recovered physically. There were many complications, X-rays, medicines, a speech therapist and psychologist (which confused me, but apparently I had had a slight stroke that I didn't realize until later). The best medicine was my roommate, Ruth, a rollicking, cheerful woman who was seriously ill, but made everyone who came to our room—cleaning woman, nurse, or doctor—smile.

Eventually a physical therapist got me out of bed and walking, leaning on a walker. I was shocked at how wobbly I had become. I had been in the hospital two weeks and it was time for me to move out. My son, ever helpful and concerned, phoned, "Be ready, Ma, at nine, packed and dressed. The nursing home has a room for you." We decided that this was necessary because my son and daughter-in-law were away all day, and I could never manage alone.

This home was brand new, elegant and very expensive. The girl at the entrance desk was attractively dressed and gave the impression that we were being welcomed to some country estate although the two checks my son made out, one for a large deposit, the other for a week's stay in a double room, provided hard reality.

My first impression was that a great deal had been spent on decor—charming wallpaper, heavy pink bedspread, modern lamp at the bedside table, and a modern picture on the wall. All I wanted was to get undressed and into bed, and I promptly went to sleep.

Looking back I can see why I have been critical of my elegant surroundings. One loss was not having a telephone. In the hospital I could lie in bed and gossip with all my friends. My son usually called every day. Eventually I could use the nurses' phone down the hall, but I had to have the phone handed to me across the desk, stand up, and naturally the call had to be short.

I shared a room with Rose, a woman who had been there for some time and who was a favorite with all the nurses. Her dressing often needed changing at 2 a.m., a process that involved a great deal of nurse chatter, lights, and curtain noisily pulled for "privacy." That I was awoken was unimportant to everyone but me.

Rose had a telephone that her son had had installed. I asked Rose if I could use hers and would

pay her and she agreed. I used her phone just once, when she was taken for some test and I thought my conversation would not bother her. With my address book in hand I went to her bedside table to make the call. As I was dialing, a tall head nurse stalked in, accused me of using Rose's property when she was out, and snatched my address book, saying that I must have taken it from Rose's drawer. I was startled by this false accusation and angry that this woman could think I would use the phone without Rose's permission. Later I made a scene with a superintendent but nothing came of it. Rose laughed when she returned, and all that really happened was I couldn't sleep that night and was given a sleeping pill. It was a good example of the old and the weak versus the young and the strong.

Was I doomed to spend the rest of my life in this nursing home? For one thing I felt it was too expensive. How long would my money last, spent in this ridiculously extravagant fashion? It was up to me to get up and return to normal life. Weak, I got dressed and with my walker managed to make it to a big living room, where I had breakfast off a tray. There I found a dozen other more active people doing the same. The next day I carried in the portable radio my son had brought me and I came back to the world and listened to the news and my favorite classical music station. At lunch, again with my walker, I went to the dining room despite the 20 minutes it took me to travel the short distance down the hall. I began to feel that with determination I could grow strong.

The staff of this particular home worked hard to make things easy and pleasant for the patients—one could say they ought to for the price. There was an exercise class every morning, and I joined this. We sat in a big circle, some in wheelchairs, others in regular chairs. A young, peppy woman led us. She brought a huge lightweight ball that she would roll to each in turn and we would kick it back with right then left foot. Many of us were weak but one could see an improvement. There were exercises with arms, "pick the apple out of the tree, then put it down in the basket"; silly, but it got one's muscles moving.

The staff organized movies and an ice-cream party for those of us who could walk or get someone to push our wheelchairs to the parlor. I began to walk the corridors for exercise, and to explore different areas. There was one much more expensive-looking area that had a living room arranged with couches and easy chairs as in a private home. Here the public library had installed a wide choice of books in large print and this attracted me. Just by signing my name and room number I could help myself. I realized for the first time that my illness had been severe enough for me to give up reading. I took out a novel that looked lightweight and easy to follow, and this room became my favorite.

In my own area there was a music room that was not used much, and I would take my book here, pretending there were no hospital beds around the corner. This room had an expensive grand piano made in China. Here on Sunday afternoon there was a concert for piano and harp. A young lady brought in her harp, an undertaking that took more time than the concert itself. Unfortunately there were barely more than a dozen people who attended.

As I walked around more I became acquainted with more patients. There was one pleasant woman with one arm paralyzed, who was always in a wheelchair. She explained to me that when she and her husband found they had physical problems they could not solve, they sold their house and both entered this nursing home with the idea of ending their lives here. They had enough money to pay for the most expensive suite, brought their own furniture, and often had special meals ordered. I never met her husband, but she was such a cheerful realist she was a pleasure to talk to.

There was another alert old gentleman whose son visited him every Sunday, and he was eager to talk. He knew the area, had been in business all his life, and would have preferred to stay home. His wife had died, and he needed too much care for his daughter-in-law to handle. Again there was enough money for him not to worry.

Many of these old people grumbled and complained and were dull to talk to. The patients whose minds were affected I found depressing. One attractive woman beautifully dressed in different outfits was like a flitting bird. She explained that her children had left her here, and she wanted to escape but she didn't know how to get out. Then she would jump up and run down the hall. There was one man with Parkinson's disease who would walk endlessly up and down the hall never meeting one's eye, looking vaguely for someone, something, perhaps his own identity.

There was a dumpy little woman with Alzheimer's disease, and she too was a wanderer with fluttering hands. She liked my room and once tried to get into my bed, to my horror. Another time

Who cares for our elders?

"Why should a woman in her 60s feel she must use up her life savings—even sell her home—to keep her mother in a nursing home for less than two years?" asked American Association of Retired Persons vice president Robert Maxwell. "Why should a couple married for 30 years be forced to get a divorce in order to protect the wife's income and assets, while the husband impoverishes himself to qualify for Medicaid-funded nursing home care?"

They shouldn't, of course. These are consequences of government inaction on an issue that affects nearly all people at some time in their lives. Mention long-term care of older citizens to most Americans, and the first image that comes to mind is the nursing home. While nursing homes constitute a thriving industry in the United States, they are not where most care for elders takes place.

For elders who can no longer fully care for themselves, most care is provided at home by family members and friends. An estimated seven million older Americans require some sort of assistance—from once-a-week shopping help, to once-a-day meal preparation, to round-the-clock nursing care.

For incapacitated elders and their families, the choices are hard. Nursing home care is costly and of poor quality. Home care services are virtually non-existent in many states, and where they are available they are expensive. For most who quit their jobs to care for their parents, there is little income support. The lack of long-term care is indeed a national crisis.

Though most surveys of elders indicate they would rather not be institutionalized in nursing homes, institutionalization is precisely what our present system of long-term elderly care encourages.

Given the demographics of the United States, nursing homes are a growth industry. Roughly 1.6 million nursing home beds were in use in 1986. Because the number of elders in the U.S. population is projected to rise through the year 2030, the demand for nursing home beds is expected to increase to over two million in 2000, and to nearly three million by 2030.

Nursing homes are now a $38 billion industry with more than 19,000 homes. Once dominated by "mom-and-pop" operators and charitable organizations, the industry is increasingly composed of large, for-profit chains.

For nursing home residents, absentee ownership brings negative consequences. The Massachusetts Department of Public Health, charged with monitoring nursing home care, reports that absentee-owned homes have significantly more code violations than locally owned and non-profit homes.

For the patient or the patient's family, nursing home care is extremely costly. Average costs per day run as high as $100. Annual costs range from $25,000 to $40,000. Unless residents are extremely poor—or until they reach that point—most of the cost of nursing home care is borne by elders and their families. Medicare will pay only up to 100 days of acute medical and rehabilitative services in a nursing home, leaving people needing long-term care completely uncovered. Medicare pays only 2 percent of the nation's nursing home bill.

she stole a book I had carelessly left on my bed. I had a nurse search her room, but we never found it, and I wrote the public library apologizing, hoping someone would return it.

Unlike the pleasant woman and her husband who planned to make this their permanent home, my attitude from the beginning had been to get strong and to leave the nursing home as soon as possible. I was lucky that I had no debilitating disease, that I could walk, and that my mind was normal. My finances were not great enough to pay for this "hotel" (for a bed and meals were what it amounted to, with little mental stimulation). In a little over three weeks I persuaded my son and daughter-in-law to take me in.

When I got to their rather cold house (the nursing home had been overheated), and had to get my own breakfast and lunch, and be alone all day, I realized I had been too impatient. I was not as tough as I had thought I was. I often would crawl back in bed and sleep an uneasy sleep, but soon I would force myself, warmly dressed, to walk around the back yard or go out for the mail. There was plenty to read, too much, but the most endearing feature was the family cat, Brandy. She too was lonely during the day, and she and I would lie down together on my bed, or she'd sit in my lap, and we'd talk and purr and were close company. Evenings and weekends were wonderful, with the stimulating company of my son and daughter-in-law, and delicious meals where all I did was set the table. The nursing home seemed far away. The next jump was to my own apartment, but this was cushioned by the arrival of my daughter, who cooked for me and spoiled me. Without the help of my children could I have recovered so quickly?

Now, two years later, at 91, I live alone. How long can I hope to keep moving about with family and friends, to take walks around the pond in the neighboring park? Can I hope to escape the permanent nursing home?

Medicaid, known as the long-term care insurance policy that requires impoverishment for a premium, is the major public payer for long-term care services. For the poor and those older Americans impoverished by the high costs of long-term care, Medicaid covers nearly all nursing home expenses. Medicaid pays nearly half the nation's nursing home bill, making it—by default rather than by design—the country's long-term care insurance policy.

Once on Medicaid, older people needing care are hardly free of worry. Medicaid sets a fixed payment rate for nursing home care that is on the average 15 to 20 percent lower than the rates charged private payers. This gives nursing home operators a strong incentive to discriminate against those on public assistance. Medicaid-supported elders seeking nursing home care typically wait four times as long for a bed in a nursing home as privately paying elders.

With all of the problems associated with nursing home care, it is perhaps not surprising that older people overwhelmingly prefer to be cared for in their own homes. Yet government spending for long-term care is heavily biased in favor of nursing homes. Neither Medicare nor Medicaid covers any significant part of home care services. As a result, 85 percent of home care is provided by friends and family members without institutional support. Of the 15 percent who receive care from paid providers, 60 percent pay the entire bill themselves. High turnover among home care workers, who are overworked and underpaid, further hampers the availability of adequate home care.

Not surprisingly, most of the caregivers—paid and unpaid—are women. Women frequently care for their infirm husbands, whom they outlive by six years on average. The burden of care also falls on adult children, usually daughters and daughters-in-law, who give up paid work to care for frail family members. The vast majority of paid home care workers are also women.

Ironically, although home care tends to be much cheaper than nursing home care, cost containment is one of the major reasons for the government's bias toward institutional care. Public officials, recognizing that the number of elders currently going without publicly supported services far exceeds the number receiving support, fear a surge in demand for home care if the government were to provide it.

According to a recent survey commissioned by senior advocates, the U.S. public is greatly concerned about the inadequacy of long-term care. Sixty percent of respondents said they had direct experience with family members or friends needing long-term care, and more than 80 percent said nursing home costs would be a major hardship on their families. Most significant, over 70 percent said they wanted a government program providing universal long-term care and would be willing to pay higher taxes to support it.

—*Dollars & Sense*

Excerpted with permission from Dollars & Sense *(Jan./Feb. 1988). Subscriptions: $19.50/yr. (10 issues) from Economic Affairs Bureau, 1 Summer St., Somerville, MA 02143. Back issues: $3 from same address.*

Board and Care Versus Assisted Living: Ascertaining the Similarities and Differences

Mary Kalymun, Ph.D.

An environmental gerontologist, the author serves as Assistant Professor, Department of Human Developments, Counseling, and Family Studies, University of Rhode Island, Kingston, R.I. 02881.

ABSTRACT: Terminology used to describe living arrangements in the retirement and long-term care industry represents a semantic tangle. A pressing need currently exists for a clear distinction between board and care (B&C) and the contemporary assisted living (AL) units emerging across the country. The purpose of this paper is to identify the general attributes of each of these facilities and to ascertain their similarities and differences from the existing literature. There is strong evidence to suggest that B&C and AL are similar in concept with sharp differences in practice.

Terminology used to describe living arrangements associated with meeting the needs of frail elders is endless. Results of a national survey verified the existence of a semantic tangle (Palmer, 1983). A congressional report provided an extensive list of titles representing such facilities nationwide (House Select Committee on Aging, 1989). It is noted that facilities for frail elders are more effectively identified by the services they provide as opposed to titles associated with them (Haske, 1988). In general, they are referred to as residential care.

Variation in terminology for residential care facilities has created much confusion in the retirement and long-term care industries. For example, questions arise concerning similarities and differences between board and care (B&C) and assisted living (AL). In concept, they are similar in that they attend to the needs of frail elders in a community-based residential setting (Kalymun, 1990). Both are associated with low to moderate degrees of service when all levels of care are represented in a continuum of care topology (see Figure 1) (Morton, 1981), and are classified with homes for the aged and personal

care homes (Kalymun, 1990). In practice, however, B&C and AL are very different. One of the most pressing needs of the long-term care industry is for a clear distinction between B&C and "the contemporary assisted living environments emerging in the many communities across the country. Most states have no legal mechanism to distinguish the profound differences between the two" (Seip, 1990a, p. 33). The purpose of this paper is to identify general attributes of B&C facilities and contemporary AL environments and to ascertain their similarities and differences.

BOARD AND CARE

B&C traditionally represents an industry dominated by small "mom and pop" operations and by larger homes operated by charitable nonprofit organizations (Dobkin, 1989). B&C provides room, board, personal care, and protective oversight (McCoy & Conley, 1990). Rooms are rented to individuals unrelated to the owner, and meals are provided on a regular basis. Cleaning of the resident room, laundry, transportation, supervision of medications, and limited help with activities of daily living (i.e., eating, bathing, grooming) constitute personal care and services. Owners of B&C facilities oversee residents on a 24 hour basis whereby they are aware of residents' functioning, know their whereabouts, and are able to intervene if a crisis arises (Conley, 1989).

There is a long tradition of boarding home care in the United States. It developed as a private sector approach to an existing need that later was indirectly funded by the federal government through Supplemental Security Income. Boarding home care is traced to . . . "the colonial community practice of boarding out the indigent elderly, for a fee, in private households—a practice that the growth of almshouses never entirely replaced" (Vladeck, 1980, p. 38). Boarding homes were firmly established during the depression of the 1930's and World War II.

Figure 1

Continuum of Care; Typical Patterns of Movement When all Levels of Care are Available.

	SERVICES*	TYPE OF INSTITUTION	BRIEF DESCRIPTION
Dependence	High	Acute Care Hospital Rehabilitation Hospital	Diagnosis, Medical Supervision, Surgery
	Moderately High	Hospice	Care for Terminally Ill Cancer Patient
		Skilled Nursing Facility (also: SNF, Convalescent Home, Rest Home)	Registered Nurse 24 hours/days; about 2.5 hrs/patient day of nursing care; all meals; housekeeping; activities.
	Moderate	Intermediate Care (also: Nursing Home, Rest Home, ICF)	Licensed Practical Nurse (requirements vary) supervises; about 1.5 hrs/patient day of nursing care.
	Moderate-Low	Homes for the Aged (also: Adult Homes; Personal Care Homes)	Meals, housekeeping; personal assistance, may be a nursing staff available (not generally required.)
		Congregate Care Apartments	Apartment residences with central meals available or accessible; may be emergency or coordinating staff available.
		Apartments for Disabled	Like Congregate Care Apartments; typically more architecturally accessible.
	Very Low	Group Homes	Smaller residences for adults and/or children; emphasis on minimal staff intervention in adult residences.
		Shared Housing/Small Group Cooperative Housing/Self-help housing	Clusters of 8 - older people in residential style community-based housing; tasks may be shared by occupants and/or supplemented by community agencies.
Independence		Specially Built Apartments (also: Apartments for Elderly; High Rise for Elderly; Garden Retirement Housing)	Apartment residences, typically age and often income prerequisites; may include government rent support for some or all apartments; may be no meal service.

*Number and variety of services.

NOTE: The data in figure 1 comes from "The age of the aging" by D. Morton, 1981, *Progressive Architecture*, 8, p. 63. Copyright 1981 by *Progressive Architecture*. Reprinted with permission of *Progressive Architecture*, Penton Publishing.

They represented a private business involving an informal agreement between a caregiver and resident without public regulations. In the early 1980's, efforts were made to tie boarding homes into the adult foster care concept (McCoin, 1983). Adult foster homes are considered the antecedent of the modern nursing home and noninstitutional adult residential care.

During the 1970's, reports of scandals prompted the federal government to become involved in regulating B&C homes. The Key's Amendment of 1976 attempted to standardize these facilities nationally by withholding federal subsidies to individuals who resided in unlicensed homes. This legislation proved to be ineffective because it penalized the resident rather than the institution. In 1989, the National Board and Care Reform Act required that every B&C facility in the country with two or more recipients of Social Security or Supplemental Security Income meet minimum national standards related to resident rights, admission requirements, adequate staff, physical structure and fire safety, sanitation, proper diet, access to needed health care, and resident activities (U.S. House of Representatives, 1989), allowing states to control the specifics thereof.

States establish their own requirement for minimum size, the most frequent being one to three unrelated individuals (Morgan, Eckert & Lyon, in press). They identify requirements for functional status and specify types of services necessary to assist residents. Administering medications and providing nursing home care are commonly prohibited. Residents are expected to be sufficiently mobile to leave the building during a fire or other emergency. This regulation places restrictions on serving wheelchair bound or confused residents.

Rules governing a license for B&C vary from state to state (Haske, 1988). Some are relatively strict while others are limited. Licensing involves inspection of the facility and the on-going supervision of residents and caregivers by a state agency. The State Department of Health typically inspects large facilities. Small ones are inspected by a mix of programs administered by various state agencies (Mor, Sherwood & Gutkin, 1986). Some B&C homes operate without a license.

States encourage the use of B&C homes for isolated elderly persons and deinstitutionalized mental patients. B&C facilities are a primary vehicle for reducing the numbers of elderly residents in skilled and intermediate care settings and mental institutions. B&C has become an alternative to institutionalization and an acceptable option within a continuum of long-term care. In 1982, the U.S. Department of Health and Human Services estimated that there were 30,000 B&C facilities nationally (Haske, 1988), serving approximately one million elderly persons (McCoy & Conley, 1990).

Low cost housing with support services for the poor and middle class is a distinguishing characteristic of B&C (Haske, 1988). Even though cost is considered quite modest, prospective residents who are poor typically lack sufficient funds to afford B&C. Consequently, federal (Supplemental Security Income) and state support (State Supplemental Payment, where applicable) function as the source of payment. Whereas federal reimbursement rates are the same throughout the country, there are differences in payment among states. This distinction shapes the variation in cost of facilities and services available to residents (Dittmar, 1989; House Select Committee on Aging, 1989). In 1987, combined federal and state monthly payments ranged from $450–$600 per person (Newcomer & Grant, 1989). Since B&C homes are not considered medical facilities, they ordinarily do not qualify for Medicare or private insurance. Medicaid waivers can be obtained in some instances, however. In 1988, the average monthly fee of B&C ranged from $240–$1151 per month (Haske, 1988).

Rental agreements are commonly negotiated between the resident and the management. Month to month arrangements give the resident and operator more flexibility while longer ones (6–12 months) protect the resident from eviction. However, longer rental agreements make it more difficult to leave prematurely and may create complications for family members should the resident die (Haske, 1988).

Operators of B&C facilities are typically middle-aged women (Morgan et al., in press; Namazi, Eckert, Rosner & Lyon, 1991), who live in the home with their spouses and/or children and clients. Two-thirds worked previously in health care settings as nurses or nurses aides. Relationships between homeowners and residents often become quasi-familial. After having lived together for several years, operators are viewed by residents as family members and conversely, residents are considered by operators as part of their family in all but legal ways.

Motivation for ownership of B&C facilities is commonly altruistic as compared to aspirations for monetary reward (Sherman & Newman, 1988). Mor et al. (1986) found that 57% of the owners had revenues that did not defray their cost of operation. Turnover rate of operators is highest in small private homes where owners do most of the work without staff and in the absence of formal services (Dittmar, 1989). Larger facilities consistently hire staff to provide such necessities.

The public's perceptions of B&C conjure up negative images from the past. A governmental report concluded:

> . . . that the nation's over 1 million elderly, disabled and mentally ill currently residing in board and care homes in America—and the more than 3.2 million more at risk of placement in such homes—are frequently the victims of fraud, neglect and abuse. Warehoused, and drugged, this vulnerable population is usually unaware that their rights to board, care, and protection can easily be circumscribed by unscrupulous home owners or greedy and uncaring home managers. (House Select Committee on Aging, 1989, p. viii)

Mismanagement of the resident's money is the most frequently reported abuse (Haske, 1988). The news media reported the incident of Dorothea Perente in Sacramento, California, who was "accused of killing and burying in her yard a number of impaired residents, while continuing to receive and cash their checks" (Morgan et al., in press). Opponents of board and care view it as "another form of institutionalization, one that is underfunded, poorly regulated, and likely to expose the public to questionable care" (Newcomer & Grant, 1989, p. 102).

ASSISTED LIVING

In the 1980's AL emerged as a new term associated with a special kind of community-based residential care facility. It is considered a recent trend involving for-profit developers in the retirement and long-term care industry. AL aims to delay institutionalization among frail elders through residential housing with supportive services that assist in achieving activities of daily living, by providing medical assistance as opposed to care (Senior living news, 1988), and by making options available for leisure activities. Laventhol and Howarth defined AL as a "transition level of care between independent living and the lowest level of nursing care" (Sherman, 1988, p. 2).

Paul Klaassen, a leading developer of AL in the United States (Real estate hybrid, 1989), maintains that versions of AL existed prior to the 1980's. Variations date back centuries in European countries, particularly in the Netherlands. Members of the retirement and long-term care industry trace the development of AL to the time when B&C became a housing option for the poor and homeless. Developers affirm that AL evolved as something distinctively different from B&C and therefore it could no longer, by definition, be associated with it (Seip, 1990b). Others report that AL is the brain child of the '80's responsive to trends associated with consumer attitudes focusing on "aging in place" and a demand for "in-home" service. It emerged in response to a softening of the traditional housing market for seniors who are governmentally subsidized, causing developers to reconfigure the market for private-pay consumers. A concern for the projected costs of long-term care added to setting the stage for AL (Wilson, 1990).

The expanding popularity of AL is causing developers to include it in future projects and incorporate it in a continuum of care plan. Through AL developers aim to respond to the needs of the fastest growing segment of the elderly population, those who are 75 years of age and older. It is expected that this population will reach 17 million by the year 2000 (Hendrickson, 1988) with an anticipated need for 125,000 units of AL between now and the turn of the century (A little help, 1988). Current estimates of elderly people receiving support services to achieve activities of daily living ranges from 1 million to 1.5 million in facilities that number from 50,000 to 90,000 (Pristic, 1991).

There is evidence to suggest that current regulations for AL are a modified version of those originally established for B&C in the 1970's (Wilson, 1990). Licensing requirements vary from state to state and typically focus on the functional status of residents, the intensity of services required and environmental features of the facility. Implications for new regulations, separate and distinct from B&C, are on the horizon with the passage of the Frail Elderly Act. Through it, $580 million of Medicaid funds will be used for support services that include: homemaker home health aid services, chore services, personal care services, nursing care services provided by, or under the supervision of, a registered nurse, respite care, training for family members in managing the individual, and adult day care (Pristic, 1991).

The Assisted Living Facilities Association of America (ALFAA) plans to work with Congress and the Health Care Finance Administration to establish guidelines for AL facilities that qualify for Medicaid funds through the Frail Elderly Act. Eligibility for funding will be dependent upon meeting the criterion established for a license and for certification of AL facilities, to be approved by the United States Department of Health.

AL facilities will be required to have case managers to conduct in person interviews with participants of the program every 90 days. This measure is intended to keep the focus of the program on the individual as opposed to the facility. Additionally, facilities will be expected to meet applicable state and local requirements for being licensed and certified; uphold zoning, building and housing codes; and meet fire and safety regulations.

With federal approval, states became eligible to implement this Medicaid program as of July 1, 1991. Although they are not required to participate in it, ALFAA's involvement is perceived as a means of homogenizing AL across the country (Pristic, 1991).

AL facilities are built with the private-pay resident in mind. The cost varies depending upon the floor plan, extensiveness of the space provided, and number of people living in the unit. In some facilities, all services are included in the cost; and in others, cost reflects only those services being used. Cost is also subject to the rental of furnished versus unfurnished units. The average monthly range in cost per person for a single room is from $1154–$1462 and from $864–$1027 for double occupancy (Seip, 1990b).

Owners of AL facilities are known to provide a variety in types of living arrangements for elderly people. For some, their principal business is that of AL whereas the emphasis for others is on retirement facilities and nursing homes. More recently, the hotel and hospital industries became involved with developing AL facilities. Results of a national survey (Seip, 1990b) show that owners of AL have from two to seven of these arrangements and plan to build more of the same. Relationships with residents are of a business contractual nature and motivation for ownership is dominated by economic gain.

It is premature to ascertain the general public's view of the contemporary version of AL. Founders aim to create an image that acknowledges AL as a residential environment with paid services to sustain independence with dignity among the frail elderly. Perceptions of AL by the middle-aged offspring of prospective residents are especially important (Moore, 1991), since they are the ones who most often assist their parents in locating suitable living arrangements. Therefore, developers are known to market to the values of middle-aged people (Kalymun, 1990) who select facilities that they themselves would like to live in and ones that make them feel proud that their parents are residents thereof. Emphasis is placed on securing a lifestyle that would not be possible if their parents were living on their own. Owners want prospective residents to think of AL as a place to live that looks and feels much like a home as the normal aging process advances.

ASSISTED LIVING VERSUS BOARD AND CARE

Comparisons made here between B&C and AL are based on the following perceptions. B&C is associated with the old "mom and pop" operation conducted in a large and usually old family home with a number of unoccupied bedrooms available to boarders. This for-profit version represents the traditional and outnumbers the larger non-profit run facility (Mor et al., 1986). The for-profit contemporary AL facility emerging in many communities across the country is represented by new construction with a limited number of units (not usually more than 60), designed to resemble a homelike setting. Structurally, it represents an entity within itself and is often coupled with another level of care on the same premises. The tendency to use these terms interchangeably suggests conceptual overlap. Owners in the long-term care industry often describe AL as an old "mom and pop" operation, meaning B&C, while Namazi et al. (1991) refer to B&C as "an assisted living arrangement" or "an assisted care setting." Nevertheless, all facilities at this level of care are characterized by limited numbers of residents who share a homelike environment, and are in need of services short of skilled medical care.

B&C and AL provide room, board, supportive services, and protective oversight. However, distinct aspects of their identities emerge upon closer examination of these attributes. B&C facilities provide the resident with a bedroom in a private home, whereas AL facilities offer self-contained units represented by various types of floor plans for single or double occupancy. Units may consist of a studio or one and two bedroom apartments. State of the art designs for AL facilities are featured as large Victorian homes with suites and well appointed common spaces to facilitate a sense of community and by structures that resemble apartment complexes (Kalymun, 1990). There is currently no evidence of an existing prototype for the design of contemporary AL facilities.

Meals are included in the rental agreement and are provided regularly in both instances. However, characteristics surrounding them in the different settings deserve some mention. Residents in both instances eat all of their meals together and are given assistance when necessary. AL facilities make a special effort to limit the number of people at one seating to sustain a more personal atmosphere. Meals are provided with significant variance in scheduling. One study on B&C revealed that in more than half of the instances, three meals were served in a ten hour period or less (Dittmar, 1989). Spacing of meals was used as an economic measure that failed to consider the nutritional needs of elderly people unable to consume a sufficient amount of food in three closely spaced servings. Special diets and snacks between meals were offered by B&C in nearly three fourths of the facilities. Although AL typically offers a choice in the selection of an entree, there is little evidence of attention given to special diets for chronic illness like obesity, high blood pressure, and diabetes (Kalymun, 1990). Amenities attached to meal service in B&C and AL facilities include room service in instances of convalescent care. After a given period of time, this service represents an additional charge for AL residents. Guest dining and catering services are also available to them.

Owners of B&C homes commonly represent a one person operation drawing upon outside agencies to provide services for disabled residents. AL facilities hire trained staff to provide services that accentuate resident abilities as opposed to disabilities. Services are based on choice and changing needs of residents. They are provided when needed as compared to following a routine format. While B&C facilities are limited in making available planned social activities (Dittmar, 1989), AL facilities prosper through full time activity directors, which owners believe are a key to promoting resident independence.

A shared characteristic between B&C and AL is that of protective oversight. Although this term is associated with B&C, both types of facilities claim to implement the concept as part of their service delivery system. Administrators and staff are expected to observe changes in any physical and/or psychological function that may affect the well-being of residents, and intervene when necessary. Continuous responsibility for the well-being of residents is considered common practice.

B&C is associated with meeting the needs of indigent elders and adults with mental illness and retardation who typically have no access to traditional forms of housing. In contrast, AL responds to an expanding population of frail elders who are unable to remain in their own homes, but with assistance, can sustain their independence in a homelike setting. Current trends focus on expanding the availability of AL facilities as opposed to B&C.

Both types of living arrangements shelter elders from being institutionalized. B&C traditionally provides housing to individuals who lived previously in an institutional setting (i.e., nursing home, mental institution) whereas AL aims to delay the onset of institutionalization. The length of stay for residents in a B&C home ranges from three to five years (Newcomer & Grant, 1989). It typically exceeds that of AL which is about 2.7 years on the average (Sherman, 1988). This difference in length of stay may be attributed to the way each facility responds to the advancing needs of residents. B&C facilities tend to step up services as functional status declines whereas AL facilities identify definite cut off points that require the need for relocation. Factors that precipitate relocation include incontinence, reliance on the use of a wheelchair, and mental confusion that exceeds the mild state. Criterion for physical and psychological function are used to determine the suitability of placement at this level of care.

Most B&C facilities represent small business operations generated by philanthropic interests whereas AL facilities are represented by entrepreneurs and the corporate world. The public image of B&C is negative, and perceptions of AL are currently in process. The former serves the poor who qualify for governmental subsidies whereas the latter caters to the upper middle class and wealthy (Kalymun, 1990). However, AL units are occasionally being set aside for those who are less financially endowed (Senior living news, 1988).

In spite of the evidence that B&C and AL are similar in concept, the ways in which they present themselves are distinctively different. Central factors that seem to account for their distinctiveness in identity appear to be related to the nature of residents in terms of income, wealth and functional ability, the characteristics of the physical environment, and the philosophy that guides the presentation of services. What we clearly have is a heavily subsidized industry (B&C), run on a small scale, taking care of deinstitutionalized mentally ill persons and frail, at-risk elderly persons and a second system (AL), under corporate for-profit auspices, serving those elderly who are not quite at risk for financial and social reasons.

Two major issues prevail relative to meeting the needs of clientele in B&C and AL. They focus on the reputability of B&C and the affordability of AL. B&C is faced with freeing itself from the negative stigma of the past, associated with inferior care by greedy and unscrupulous owners. AL appears affordable to only those who are financially well-endowed, as opposed to being available to a broader spectrum of frail elders. Resolutions to these issues are imperative and need to be addressed for the continued viability of B&C and AL, and their success in meeting the special needs of adult populations.

REFERENCES

A little help: Housing for the aging. (1988, April). *Architectural Record,*, 98–107.

Conley, R. (1989). Federal policies in board and care homes. In M. Moon, G. Gaberlavage & S. J. Newman (Eds.), *Preserving independence, supporting needs: The role of board and care homes* (pp. 41–59). Washington, DC: Public Policy Institute, American Association of Retired Persons.

Dittmar, N. (1989). Facility and resident characteristics of board and care homes for the elderly. In M. Moon, G. Gaberlavage & S. Newman (Eds.), *Preserving independence, supporting needs: The role of board and care homes* (pp. 1–26). Washington, DC: Public Policy Institute, American Association of Retired Persons.

Dobkin, L. (1989). *The board and care system: A regulatory jungle.* Washington, DC: American Association of Retired persons.

Haske, M. (1988). *A home away from home: Consumer information on board and care homes* (2nd ed.). Washington, DC: American Association of Retired Persons.

Hendrickson, M. (1988, July). Assisted living: An emerging focus in an expanding market. *Contemporary Long-Term Care,* pp. 20, 22.

House Select Committee on Aging, Subcommittee on Health and Long-Term Care (1989), *Board and Care Homes in America: A National Tragedy.* Washington, DC: U.S. Government Printing Office.

Kalymun, M. (1990). Toward a definition of assisted living. *Journal of Housing for the Elderly, 7,* 97–132.

McCoin, J. M. (1983). *Adult foster homes: Their managers and residents.* New York: Human Sciences Press, Inc.

McCoy, J. L. & Conley, R. W. (1990). Surveying board and care homes: Issues and data collection problems. *The Gerontologist, 30,* 147–153.

Moore, J. (1991, August). Sandwich generation carries plenty of clout. *Contemporary Long-Term Care,* pp. 22, 62.

Mor, V., Sherwood, S. & Gutkin, C. (1986). A national study of residential care for the aged. *The Gerontologist, 26,* 405, 417.

Morgan, L. A., Eckert, J. K. & Lyon, S. M. (in press). Housing at the margin: Small unlicensed board and care homes. *The Gerontologist*.

Morton, D. (1981, August). The age of the aging. *Progressive Architecture*, 59–63.

Namazi, K. H., Eckert, J. K., Rosner, T. T. & Lyon, S. M. (1991). The meaning of home for the elderly in pseudo-familial environments *Adult Residential Care Journal*, 5, 81–96.

Newcomer, R. J. & Grant, L. (1989). Residential care facilities: Understanding their role and improving their effectiveness. In D. Tilson (Ed.), *Aging in place: Supporting the frail elderly in residential environments*. (pp. 101–124). Glenview, IL: Scott, Foresman and Co.

Palmer, H. C. (1983). Domiciliary care: A semantic tangle. In R. J. Vogel & H. C. Palmer (Eds.), *Long-term care: Perspectives from research and demonstrations* (pp. 437–461). Washington, DC: Health Care Financing Administration.

Pristic, S. (1991, February). Assisted living in the spotlight: New association eyes expanding Medicaid funding. *Contemporary Long-Term Care*, pp. 40, 42.

Real estate hybrid, 'assisted living', a boon for elderly. (1989, February). *The Providence Journal*, pp. G1, G2.

Seip, D. (1990a, July). Piecing together the fragments. Contemporary Long-Term Care, pp. 30, 32–33.

Seip, D. E. (1990b). *Survival handbook for developers of assisted living*. Boca Raton, FL: The Seip Group, Inc.

Senior living news. (1988). *Multi-Housing News*, pp. 13, 21.

Sherman, F. J. (1988). *Overview: Retirement housing industry*. Philadelphia, PA: Laventhol and Horwath Publications Dept.

Sherman, S. R. & Newman, E. S. (1988). *Foster families for adults*. New York: Columbia University Press.

U. S. House of Representatives. (1989). National Board and Care Reform Act of 1989: H.R. 2219.

Vladeck, B. C. (1980). *Unloving care: The nursing home tragedy*. New York: Basic Books.

Wilson, K. B. (1990). The merger of housing and long term care services. *Long term care advances: Topics in research training, service & policy*. Duke University Center for the Study of Aging and Human Development, Durham, NC, 1(4), 1–8.

FROM 'OUR TOWN' TO 'GHOST TOWN'?: THE CHANGING CONTEXT OF HOME FOR RURAL ELDERS*†

Carolyn Norris-Baker, Ph.D.
Rick J. Scheidt, Ph.D.

Kansas State University, Manhattan

ABSTRACT

This research, grounded in a contextual view of environmental stress, employed an experiential field approach to explore outcomes of the continuing rural crisis of the past decade for elderly residents of four small Kansas towns. These rural changes threaten the survival of many towns, and affect their elderly residents, who often have enduring economic, social, and psychological investments in their homes and communities. At the same time, changes associated with aging may lead to transitions in the experience of home and community for these elderly individuals, regardless of the town's health. The two sources of change may have multi-faceted impacts on the well-being of the elderly individuals who experience them. Aspects of the research described here focus on environmental stressors related to housing and the meaning of attachment to home within economically-threatened communities. Some findings presented support previous research, while others reflect the region's unique socio-historical environment as a part of the Western Frontier.

*This research was supported in part by grants from the Ford Foundation through the Kansas Center for Rural Initiatives and from the Kansas State University Bureau of General Research and President's Fund for Faculty Development.
†Portions of this manuscript were presented at the Symposium on Housing Research and Design Education, conducted by the International Association for People-Environment Studies and the South Bank Polytechnic, London, in July 1991.

Implications for policy alternatives and the well-being of rural elderly are discussed.

Thornton Wilder, the American playwright, wrote of his play *Our Town,* that it did not offer a portrait of life in a New England village, but rather "set the village against the largest dimensions of time and place" [1, p. xii]. He wrote,

> Every action which has ever taken place—every thought, every emotion—has taken place only once, at one moment in time and place. Yet the more one is aware of this individuality in experience . . . the more one becomes attentive to what these disparate moments have in common, to repetitive patterns [1,p.x].

When *Our Town* was first performed in 1938, the elderly individuals who live in small rural towns today were young adults whose experience of the village milieu, of home and community, probably resembled the description of the Stage Manager as the play opens: that of a "very ordinary town" [1, p. 24].

> Well, I'd better tell you how our town lies. Up here . . . is Main Street.
> Way back there is the railway station; tracks go that way . . .
> Over there is the Congregational Church; across the street's the Presbyterian.
> Methodist and Unitarian are over there.
> Baptist is down in the holla' by the river.
> Catholic Church is over beyond the tracks.
> Here's the Town Hall and Post Office combined; jail's in the basement.
> Bryan once made a speech from these very steps here.
> Along here's a row of stores. . . .
> Here's the grocery store and here's Mr. Morgan's drugstore.
> Most everybody in town manages to look into those two stores once a day.
> Public School's over yonder. High School's still farther over.
> Quarter of nine morning, noontimes, and three o'clock afternoons,
> the hull town can hear the yelling and screaming from those schoolyards . . . [1, p. 6].

From the *International Journal of Aging and Human Development*, Vol. 38, No. 3, 1994, pp. 181-202. © 1994 by Baywood Publishing Company, Inc. Reprinted by permission.

THE CHANGING CONTEXT OF HOME

Today, many of those 'Our Towns' of the first half of the twentieth century are in danger of becoming 'Ghost Towns.' The appearance of one of these towns in rural Kansas inspired the rock band *Kansas* to compose the song "Ghosts," and a local poet to write the following lines:

> dawn eyes the apparition, a townsite on the flat bottom
> beside the river that pledged unlimited future
> time has stripped flesh from the living . . .
> socketed storefronts always staring at each other
> mindless as the placid river, murmuring its victory . . .
> the bombed out look on the ruin of the school
> occupied by a battery of pigeons
> their only enemy now themselves and the vines
> ever so plenty prying away stone after stone . . . [2, p. 67].

Figure 1 contrasts the images of the small town portrayed in these words as it appeared in the earlier part of the century and today.

The Plight of Our Towns

While some small towns have thrived, others risk or have experienced the fate described in the lines of this poem and illustrated in Figure 1. Yet, many of the same people whose lives, values, and homes were reflected in *Our Town* still live in these endangered towns, survivors of a different culture. Now, they are elderly individuals. Residents over age sixty-five comprise a greater proportion of the population than any other age group among rural villages of 1,000 to 2,500 [3]. They make up as much as 25 percent of the total county population in some Midwestern states, and up to 40 percent of the population of the Kansas towns discussed here. In recent years, many of these older residents have experienced environmental stressors associated with persistent economic and population decline, rather than the enduring milieu of Wilder's village. Data on rural poverty indicate that the decimation of small rural communities is widespread [3, 4], and economic stress will continue and perhaps increase in many rural communities in the foreseeable future [5]. Many small communities have struggled for decades to remain viable, leading one regional planner to remark that the demise of the small American town is the "longest deathbed scene in American history" [6]. Towns more than thirty miles from a large community that can provide the range of goods and services judged necessary for a decent quality of life are losing or have lost their mainstreets, their health services, their schools, and much of their tax base [7]. In some towns, the transformation of older homes into low-income rental housing for younger poor has led to stigmatization of place [8], that may divide or eventually engulf the entire community. Likewise, in rural Kansas, elderly individuals retiring from farm to town may leave a house empty rather than allow the deterioration associated with renting it [9].

Housing as a Source of Environmental Stress

Housing can be defined to encompass not only the physical structures, but also the surrounding physical and social environment and its functions, including neighborhood characteristics and services such as shopping, recreation, health care, and transportation [cf. 10]. If housing is defined in this way, then housing is a major source of stress for many older residents in endangered small towns. A disproportionate number of rural elders live in single family detached dwellings, including mobile homes; over 90 percent of rural elders live in this type of home, and over 80 percent of them are owner-occupied [10]. Thus, few residential options are available, especially in tiny, declining towns; apartments or more supportive housing environments needed by frail elderly individuals must be sought in other, larger communities. Moving from one home to another, especially if such a move is perceived as involuntary, can have great costs in terms of physical and mental health [11–13]. On the other hand, rural elderly who age in place typically experience a gradual deterioration in the physical quality of their housing, much of which is attributable to aging of the structure, limited

Figure 1. From Our Town[1] to Ghost Town.
[1]Photograph from the collection of the Kansas State Historical Society.

income, and the elderly person's own health and mobility limitations that may preclude their completing many maintenance chores they once did themselves [10, 14, 15]. When an elderly individual has become too frail, the dwelling may deteriorate to the point where it is only marginally habitable.

Much research has suggested that physical and subjective evaluations of the quality of these dwellings are relatively independent judgments. When housing quality is measured using physical standards, a number of studies suggest that rural elders live in substandard or low quality housing when compared to either their urban counterparts or younger residents of rural areas [10]. In a recent study, Fitchen concludes that substandard housing in open country, in small towns (particularly rental units) and mobile homes continue to be problems for elderly residents [8]. If the neighborhood and service characteristics of the housing context are considered, very small towns are likely to offer major deficits when compared even with larger rural towns [16]. Yet, even for physically substandard housing, elderly individuals tend to express satisfaction [12, 15], that may in turn be related to place meaning. Satisfaction with dwelling also is linked to greater psychological well-being for rural small-town elderly [17]. These subjective responses may be influenced by income, differing personal definitions of quality, and aging and cohort effects that foster remaining in one's own home and not accepting assistance [10].

Attachment to Home

Satisfaction with home is distinct from, but related to attachment to place—the way in which "lives and environmental features are subjectively intertwined" [18, p. 52]. Extensive research has begun to identify the complex dimensions and processes which form attachments to home and neighborhood [cf. 15, 18–20]. Shumaker and Taylor have suggested five factors influencing the relation of people and places: local social ties, physical amenities, individual and household characteristics, perceived choice of residential location, and perceived costs/benefits of relocation [21]. They hypothesized that people's failure to develop attachment to place may threaten their health and well-being. Rivlin added symbolic connections and feelings to this list, and suggested four neighborhood domains that may combine to create strong attachments: the ways in which personal needs (ranging from shopping to religious activities) are met, the degree to which those services are concentrated in the neighborhood, the strength of affiliation and shared values with residents of the neighborhood, and the extension of these patterns over time [22]. Although the recent review completed by Després [20] suggested ten general categories of the meaning of home, the dimensions that have been identified specifically for elderly residents include: embodiment or sustenance of identity, traditional family orientation or creation of a legacy, optimization of personal competence that can be related to the perception of home as refuge and protection, a symbol of status or achievement, and tradeoffs of costs and comforts [15, 23]. Rowles also proposed that the relationships between the home and its immediate surroundings and ambiance of the neighborhood contribute to the meaning of home for elderly individuals [15].

Against this background, the attachment to home experienced by older residents of economically-threatened small towns must be considered as a source of stress as well as a source of identity, refuge, and comfort. Many older residents have life-long economic, social, and psychological investments in their homes and communities. At the same time, Rowles suggests that, at least for declining towns in rural Appalachia, the diversification of elderly persons, their increasing mobility, changing values, and acceptance of formal services have led to multiple images and styles of attachment to place [24]. In addition to the old-old, who may represent residents who are the survivors of Wilder's image, towns are now populated by indigenous young-old who have greater mobility and experience with a larger world and whose attachment to place may be less intense; return migrants whose attachment may be mediated by selective images of a childhood past; aging back-to-the-landers whose attachments may vary in strength; and amenity retirees whose attachments may be more tenuous [24].

At the same time, as Sixsmith and Sixsmith have stated, we must recognize that the experience of home is a developmental one, and that "later life is commonly accompanied by a number of changes and transitions that can in turn lead to transitions in home experience: body aging; social aging; life events; remembering and place; and an awareness of death" [25, p. 181]. In a similar vein, Rubinstein's research suggests many elderly individuals in mainstream American culture may give meaning to home environments through three types of psychosocial processes related to the sociocultural order, the person's life course, and the body [18]. Thus, socio-historical changes, such as the rural economic crisis, are interwoven together with individual life course changes in each resident's experience, transforming attachment to home across the lifespan. There also is a need to preserve a sense of enduring place or continuity in the face of life transitions [25]. Since identity of person and place may be intertwined or fused for many older individuals, changes in the physical environment, especially abrupt changes beyond one's control, may place elderly individuals at psychological risk [26]. Likewise, Tuan suggests that people who actively engage in changing their environment and have a sense of control have little cause for nostalgia, while those who perceive too little control and too rapid change will yearn for an idealized past [27]. Thus, changes in elderly individuals' attachments to home, and perhaps their well-being, may be outcomes of rural restructuring.

CASE STUDY METHODOLOGY

To explore these issues among older residents of endangered communities, our research strategy is grounded in a framework for understanding the impacts of rural change [28] that is derived from the contextual view of environmental stress recently forwarded by Aldwin and Stokols [29], and from extensions of behavior setting theory [30, 31]. This transactional approach is appropriate for issues related to the concept of home. A central theme of current theories is that home is a person-environment transaction with "different meanings, such as privacy, security and comfort, reflecting the intentions of the dweller within their specific environmental context" [25, p. 182]. Within this approach, the physical environment affords constraints and opportunities to the person.

We conducted an exploratory study of four small towns in Kansas using an experiential field approach [32]. This research represents the first step in a larger research project examining a broad range of communities experiencing different types of change. The methodology is convergent with recommendations by Fitchen [33] and Barlett [34] for the use of qualitative methods in rural communities, and with the use of multiple methods recommended for the study of transitions in the experience of home [35]. Our case studies of these four towns were based largely on observations gathered through open-ended interviews with twenty-four older residents, some who had lived in the towns all their lives, and some who had moved in from surrounding farms, married a town resident many years before, or had returned as retirees after absences of many years. These interviews were tape-recorded and later transcribed. Additional information was obtained through 1) more informal structured conversations, 2) archival research to trace the history of each town's behavior settings and its responses to economic threats, 3) participant observation in selected behavior settings, 4) tours with residents of the community and its surroundings, and 5) photography.

The data that we have gathered reflect adaptive processes which, for most older residents, evolved over time. This chronology distinguishes these residents from older persons living in communities that have only recently begun to cope with environmental stressors. In addition, our data pertain to individuals who have decided to remain in these communities; hence, the sample itself reflects the effects of selective attrition. It also remains unclear whether some of the experiences we have recounted are unique to a few individuals in very small towns of the Plains, or whether some are more universally shared by older residents of endangered communities in other regions.

HOME TOWN: FOUR COMMUNITIES

"Home" has many meanings, some extend beyond the locus of the dwelling. It may incorporate the neighborhood of the dwelling [15] or the even larger context of hometown and region [27, 36]. The four communities in this study all developed as agricultural service centers [37], and the strength of the enduring connections to surrounding farmland is evident. These connections can be seen in a male resident's description of his father: "He's 87 and he just bought a farm . . . He's a farmer, you bet he's a farmer." The communities also share a heritage as former frontier communities, and this history has shaped their physical and social milieus [38]. Older residents include indigenous young-old and old-old, as well as a substantial number of return migrants, but not back-to-the-landers or amenity retirees whom Rowles identified in Appalachian towns [24]. The four towns are geographically dispersed in the eastern

Figure 2. The context of home town.

third of Kansas, but they all are similar in size (100–250 residents) and chronological age (100–130 years), remote from large communities, experiencing varied degrees of economic decline, and have high and increasing proportions of elderly residents. When viewed within the context of what traditionally has been included in the definition of rural small towns, these communities fall at the smallest and most endangered end of the spectrum.

Small rural communities have been characterized as simple, comprehensible environments that are aesthetically as well as socially pleasing to many people, but now combine "pleasant small-town living tarnished by . . . decay" [39, p. 455]. Major contributors to the visual organization of small towns in the Midwest are the dominance of the grid pattern, the single highway or street that is a spine for commercial development and bisects the town, the commercial district one block deep along this street, the railroad in proximity to this axis, and the grain elevator as a prominent focal point in terms of both activity and form [39]. Each of the four communities we selected reflects this visual organization, although only traces of some of these elements remain in some towns. Broadly-spaced, predominantly single family homes are located along side streets and at the ends of the main street, with homes at the edges of town forming a link between town and farms. Figure 2 illustrates the kinds of homes located in the communities. Most homes are of modest size, one or two-story frame buildings with porches and pitched roofs. The great majority were constructed during the first half of this century. A few newer homes are interspersed with the older housing near the perimeter. The scale of these tiny towns is reminiscent of a neighborhood; the circumference of the vicinity [32] circumscribes the entire community.

The first community, Kaw Rapids, is described in the poem [at the beginning of this article]. Founded in 1857 and labeled in the early part of this century as *The Biggest Little City in the World,* Kaw Rapids now has the reputation of a 'ghost town.' In addition to experiencing the slow economic decline common to many agricultural communities, Kaw Rapids suffered a series of natural disasters about forty years ago. A flood struck what some residents feel were terminal blows to the town's economic base and to the morale of many residents. After this flood, many residents moved away, abandoning homes and businesses. Today, the town's mainstreet consists of a post office/community building, senior center, church, tavern, a recently opened antique shop, and the ghostly remains of what was once a thriving business community. Away from the mainstreet, about sixty-five houses remain—some in great disrepair, but many that are well-maintained. Despite severe and persistent threats, Kaw Rapids continues to exist, and many older residents continue to call it home.

Like Kaw Rapids, Plainsville was a bustling town in earlier years. It was founded just over 100 years ago as a railroad town along the route of the Santa Fe Trail. Although its population is smaller, it has more businesses than Kaw Rapids: a grocery, gas station, bank branch office, two cafes, a grain elevator open at harvest, and a small manufacturing plant in addition to the church, post office, and senior center. The town has been spared natural disasters, but it has experienced the gradual decline, including the losses of schools and railroads, that has occurred in many farming communities during the past fifty years as the size of farms increased and the population base decreased. Both Plainsville and Kaw Rapids can be reached only via gravel roads.

The third town, Bluestem, is one of a cluster of small towns in a remote area of a county with low population. Founded in 1871, Bluestem shares many of the characteristics and a pattern of agricultural decline with Plainsville, although it is accessible by paved road. Bluestem is a slightly larger town, and still has its post office, a craft shop, grain elevator, clothing store, a combination hardware and grocery, tavern, beauty shop, town hall/library, senior center, branch bank, churches, gas station,

an elementary school, and a high school shared with another town.

The fourth town, Centerville, is part of the same cluster of towns as Bluestem, and is the location of the remaining school shared with Bluestem. It was founded in the same year as Plainsville, and it, too, was a railroad town. In the earlier half of the century, Centerville, *The Prairie Pearl,* identified itself as the county's most 'progressive' and 'energetic' town. Fires and tornados have wreaked periodic havoc on the town (including the loss of a school and cafe within the past year), but the response of residents has been resilient, with many buildings replaced. As one older resident commented ironically, "We didn't have to plan what to do with our old buildings—they never seemed to last that long!" Today, it has the school, several churches, a bank with branch offices in other towns, grocery, gas station, a new cafe, senior center, post office, tavern, grain elevator, and several other businesses.

HOUSING AND HOME: SOURCES OF ENVIRONMENTAL STRESS

The differing situations of these four towns, and the responses of their older residents to community decline, provide support for some of the stressors mentioned above. We will discuss briefly those observations that support findings from previous research in order to focus in more depth on those that suggest more contextual aspects of the stressors experienced in these Kansas towns. Stressors involving housing and home appear intertwined for the elderly residents of these four towns. The elders interviewed provided support for the perceptions of stress associated with the lack of housing options, involuntary relocation, high maintenance costs and declining property values of their homes, quality of housing, and in the town located closest to an employment center, in-migration of poor. Their concerns also highlighted themes of identity, personal competence, and cost/comfort tradeoffs in attachment to home.

Despite the threatened business areas, each town still includes many owner-occupied single family homes, and in some towns, a few rental properties and mobile homes. Most residents interviewed in all four towns perceive that relatively few habitable houses were unoccupied. However, we observed a number of uninhabitable houses in each town, often located in close proximity to well-tended homes. Figure 3 illustrates two such houses, located across the street from one another. Even in Kaw Rapids, where the shells of some flood-damaged houses still stand as reminders after over forty years, a sixty-nine-year-old man said: "There's some beautiful old houses there. They're well kept, all kept up. That's really a lot of places that we can be proud of as far as the houses are concerned."

Some residents believe the best solution to the problem of empty, substandard houses is demolition, and they have strong feelings about the people who do not maintain their homes, especially if they are newcomers to the town. As one older man in Kaw Rapids said of the deteriorated houses in general, " . . . there's not very many. Most of them have been going down. There's not many empty houses." But when referring to the one next door (beyond a row of trees), he was vehement.

A widow woman lived there. She finally died. . . . [a person from another town] finally bought that and it's just a mess. If it wasn't for those trees, I wouldn't care if it burns down. It's just a mess . . . I'll be glad to be rid of [the people living there].

Aging-in-place is a common experience for residents of all four towns. Like their counterparts in previous studies, the elderly individuals in this study typically reported satisfaction with their housing and little desire to move. Perceptions about relative costs and comforts of home were linked to maintenance, property value, and quality. Maintenance of aging houses was a continuing problem for many, especially widows and those who traditionally had been self-sufficient in home repairs. One resident of Centerville captured the essence of the problem when, shaking his head sadly, he said of his neighbor in her nineties, "She's old. The old house is old . . ." However, at times aging-in-place may become involuntary. As a recent widow in Plainsville said about several neighbors: "They couldn't sell the house . . . I don't know if they will ever get out of it what they have in it. Unless there's somebody that wants to retire and move into town."

The majority of older residents, even the frail and old-old, appear unwilling to relocate voluntarily, even to an apartment in a neighboring community. As a man from Kaw Rapids summarized the situation:

A lot of older people have still got their little home that they've had many years ago and still living there. If they get too bad off, they end up over in [larger town/county seat] in the nursing home or . . . a place like that.

This response may reflect an intensity of attachment to home and community strengthened by length of residence, the high value placed on personal competence and independence, and lack of housing alternatives. These interwoven feelings are expressed clearly in two statements by an eighty-five-year-old bachelor in Plainsville. The first highlights the importance of competence and independence:

People rushing off to the old folks home . . . Ah, that's no good if you don't hav' to. . . . But it's nice they're there if you have to. You got a place to go [rather than impose oneself on relatives].

The second, discussing another couple's decision not to move, reflects the intensity of attachment to home.

They don't want to . . . They were thinkin' . . . about going to, ah, one of these low-income housing deals. In [a town about 10 miles away]. But he said, "No, no, I'll never leave Plainsville. Been here that long, I'm gonna stay right here!" There you go . . . you know. Of course, he's lived here all his life. I feel the same way about it.

A couple in Kaw Rapids is even considering converting their home into a group home for frail elders after they no longer live there. Their motivations reflect the probable difficulty in selling their home, but also a desire to perpetuate the town by providing a housing option that might enable more residents to remain "at home."

ATTACHMENT AND ADAPTIVE RESILIENCE: DECISIONS TO REMAIN OR RETURN

Residents of two towns in particular, Kaw Rapids and Centerville, exhibit a history of remarkable adaptive resilience in handling stressors. Over fifty years ago, a newspaper article commented that the residents of Kaw Rapids were not the type that surrender even to an accumulation of misfortunes. Indeed, through a process of selective attrition, we believe that many of the current older residents exhibit a stronger sense of attachment as well as personal responsibility for dealing with the devastating consequences of acute and chronic stressors. They have aged-in-place while those unable or unwilling to deal with these events have moved elsewhere. A life-long female resident and a male return-migrant in Kaw Rapids commented:

I think some of them had stronger constitutions, like that's my home. I am not going to let that flood take my home . . . I'm going to fix it up. I'm going to stay here. The others thought that's it. That's the last straw. That's the last flood I'm going to clean up after.

When they looked at their house or where they lived and saw

Figure 3. Environmental stress: housing variety.

what kind of shape it was in, they just kind of threw up their hands. Other people said, well, we're here. Just like you can't get old timers away from their house when the bulldozer operators come in. It's home to them.

Figure 4 illustrates a painting of a home in Kaw Rapids before the floods, and as it looks today. Thus, it is possible that residents who coped most effectively with acute and chronic environmental stressors are those who perceived negative events as arising from the external environment, but maintained a sense of personal control and competence in handling the consequences of those events [40].

A similar resilience may exist in the former residents who return to these towns to retire. They offer a wide range of reasons for returning "home," but all come by choice, knowing the lack of housing options and services in the town. Young-old couples come back to care for old-old parents. A family homestead or vacant house in the town may offer affordable housing combined with a return to roots. Life-long residents of the larger community often follow the tradition of moving from farm into town when they retire, strengthening their ties to the town. The sixty-nine-year-old mayor of Kaw Rapids, a return migrant, put it this way:

> We could settle anyplace in these United States . . . We come home. Anyway, this is what happens to a lot of people that's out there, that's retired. They come back home . . . Some of them will never come back. But they're [living in larger towns] within a few miles of Kaw Rapids . . . where really they're close enough to be, in their own minds, home.

The frontier heritage that is evident in the physical patterns of these communities may also help to explain residents' adaptive resilience. Roger Barker suggested that the milieu of the American frontier, including the lack of many physical-social structures deemed necessary for community life, demanded such resiliency and compromise [38]. Pioneer residents who did not give up or leave the town "developed a workable congruence between the envisioned and real psychological environments through modification of the envisioned environment toward the real environment and alteration of the real environment toward the envisioned environment" [38, p. 90]. He proposed that the ecological environments of many small towns today perpetuate the values and satisfactions of the early pioneers who settled these towns, and that adaptive resiliency still means "goals [are] set in accordance with the compromise" [38, p. 90]. We believe this milieu helps shape older residents' attachments to home and community, and their abilities to compromise between real and envisioned environments as threats to their communities persist. Such resilience may not be common among elders in rural small towns, but where it predominates through selection over time, attachment to home appears intense.

THE LEGACY OF HOMEPLACE AND COMMUNITY

As indicated in previous research on attachment to homes in Kansas and other regions [9, 15, 23], the continuity of family heritage is a dominant theme in many elderly individuals' accounts. However, this theme has new variations among the

Figure 4. One home before the floods[2] and in 1990.
[2]Photograph from the collection of O. L. and T. H. Henderson.

residents of these small Kansas towns where characteristics of the frontier/agricultural milieu pervade. Although elderly persons express appreciation for continuity brought by residing in a home in the town for several generations, this experience is not the norm. Many have faced the loss of one or more homes, victims of natural disasters, deterioration, or export to a different town. Thus, older residents more often point to the place where a home once stood and describe their feelings about it. The oldest resident of Kaw Rapids took us to the site of his birthplace, where trees and weeds covered an empty field. He reminisced, "Ya. I was born right here. Right in there . . ." Later, he visited the sites of the first house he built, the in-law's house where he had lived, and his farmhouse. All are gone, leaving only the land as a source of attachment. Even in Bluestem, which escaped disasters, responses to these losses are equivocal. An older woman in Bluestem remembered her childhood home, which she owns but lets stand vacant and neglected:

> I was born on a farm about three miles out of town. My father was born in the same house I was . . . My kids grew up out

Figure 5. The Homeplace.

there in the country. And they went 'cross the bridge, up to Grandma's house . . . I suppose I could become nostalgic over it, but it would be wasted effort.

Yet, when asked about the landscape that hangs on her living room wall, her face suffused with pride and pleasure. "That's my pasture . . . it was my mother's."

Attachment to the land which outweighs that to physical structures of home, is a common theme. An older farmer living at the edge of Centerville told us about the land he now farms, accumulated over many years: "I can remember seven people, seven places . . . [wife interjects] Seven homes. [he resumes] . . . and there's nothing there. God . . . I tore up one, two, three, about four homes . . . we tore the buildings out. Figure 5 illustrates an abandoned stone farmhouse, surrounded by the wheatfields near Centerville.

The name given to the family's original farm is the "homeplace," no matter what structures presently exist there, or where the elderly person presently lives. It is the continuity of this home that seems most important to some. Said the older farmer in Centerville, who was concerned about his son's future,

This outfit just won't keep two people, two families . . . God, do you know how badly I feel to see this just fold up. . . . I don't know, I can't figure it out . . . how to make it work.

A woman who retired from a farm into Plainsville expressed her feelings this way:

We have a farm yet . . . [her children] say don't sell it, keep it. We still want it in the family.

Perhaps an eighty-five-year-old man in Plainsville, who moved from the family farm to town over forty years ago, but still goes out to the farm frequently, put it most succinctly when he stated why he had stayed in the community: "Well . . . I've got the farm to hold me here."

Again, the milieu of the frontier with its limited resources, and perhaps the Jeffersonian ideal of an agrarian culture of independent farmers, seem to color attachment. The scarcity of wood for building and lack of structures on the frontier meant

that houses often were moved, adapted to other uses, or torn down for materials. Rural schoolhouses that had been closed were frequently moved into town and converted into homes. In one case many years ago, the frame buildings from an entire town located a few miles away were moved into Centerville when the other town died. This new meaning of "mobile home" can be found today in these communities. One resident of Plainsville reported that homes frequently are moved, citing this example, which reflects the social as well as economic circumstances in the community:

This old fella who has a new [house] right up the block here, he wants to move it out of town . . . I guess if he's unhappy here, he'd better move out . . . He wants to sell it. He can't get what he wants for it, so he's going to move it out . . . It'll cost him to get it out of town, though.

At the same time, because of the problems of declining property values and the many vacant lots, residents of mobile homes may experience less stigma, especially if they have long-term ties to the town. Said a Kaw Rapids resident:

People who buy mobile homes and put them on lots in many cases own the lots. There had been a house there that they may have been raised in. And the house was destroyed by the flood. So they've bought a mobile home and brought it in and I think it's just as permanent as a house.

Thus, attachment to a piece of land, rather than a house, has been fostered in many ways.

In the same vein, attachment to the wider community may have been enhanced if immediate structures associated with the home disappeared. In all four towns, residents identified places within the community, such as churches, schools, and civic buildings, to which they showed strong attachment [41]. While the legacy of home clearly is important to older residents of these towns, the particular form of this legacy varies. For some, the home they wish to pass on is as much a community as a house or land. While some elderly persons see a town's future as problematic, a number are committed to preserving its existence as well as valued images of its past. Asked about the future of the town, the oldest resident of one town said, "Well, it's home to me."

IMPLICATIONS

It is clear that attachment to home remains strong for indigenous elders and return migrants, whether the meaning of home is found in house, land, or community. The implications of these attachments pertain to resettlement policies, to housing policies and needs assessments, and to ways in which individual elderly individuals experience the transitions associated with home. The themes of home we identified suggest that rural resettlement policies proposed in the U.S.—the "Buffalo Commons" that would intentionally abandon the Great Plains as an area for settlement [42], or the triage model that would direct resources only to larger towns most likely to survive, allowing others to die [43]—are untenable in terms of the human costs to the predominantly elderly residents. Although triage might include home equity buyouts to enable elders to move to "salvageable" communities, the strategy ignores attachment to place, the importance of tradition, and health and mental health costs of relocation. Furthermore, such policies may be age discriminatory, exacting the highest toll from elderly individuals, especially the old-old.

At the same time, it is important to recognize that small towns do die. In Kansas, there is a "dead town" list containing names of 6,000 towns that were either planned or were born, flourished, and died since 1854. More will join the list before the turn of the century. Yet, we know little about how to help towns "die with grace and aforethought" [44, p. A-5]. What should such a hospice model include? How could we sustain themes important to home within this model? How would this model guide housing policy? For example, should the catchment areas for housing needs assessments in rural areas be defined in terms of community clusters? In this way, larger and smaller towns in the same vicinity might mutually benefit from shared housing resources, making residing in the smaller towns more attractive to younger workers.

Could we expand the kinds of factors now considered in housing policy decisions in order to identify and consider personal and shared meanings of home, as well as places that signify psychological continuity and possible future, so that we might assist planners, designers, and housing experts in their decisions? For example, should greater emphasis be placed on residential facilities, such as granny flats and factory-built homes, that can be relocated when a town no longer needs them? Such options might reduce the frequency of involuntary relocation, while limiting the investments in the infrastructure of declining towns. At a more individual level, what are the implications of residents' transitions in the experience of home? How can we better understand these experiences? Are there important differences in transitions between elderly individuals of different age cohorts, length of residence, or geographic region or nationality? Could we empower older residents of dying towns to cope with negative outcomes of environmental stress, including loss of home or dramatic changes in the way it is experienced? What are the health and mental health consequences of such losses? The agenda of research and policy issues is full, and we must begin considering responses to these questions.

ACKNOWLEDGMENTS

We are deeply grateful to the residents of small towns who shared with us so many valuable insights about their lives and their homes. In addition, we would like to thank Jeanne Moore, University of Surrey, for her comments on the manuscript.

The authors wish to express their appreciation to Harper Collins Publishers for permission to reprint portions of *Our Town* by Thornton Wilder; we also express our appreciation to *The Little Balkans Review* (Mr. Gene DeGruson, Editor) for permission to reprint portions of the poem, "Neosho Falls KS (1859–1937)" by Jimmy Aubert. Full citations for both works are provided in the references for this article.

REFERENCES

1. T. Wilder, *Three Plays: Our Town, The Skin of Our Teeth, The Matchmaker,* Harper and Row, New York, 1957.

2. J. Aubert, Neosho Falls, KS (1859–1937), *The Little Balkans Review: Southeast Kansas Literary and Graphics Quarterly, 3:*1, p. 67, 1982.

3. R. Coward, Poverty and Aging in Rural America, *Human Services in the Rural Environment, 10–11,* pp. 41–47, 1987.

4. J. Fitchen, When Communities Collapse: Implications for Rural America, *Human Services in the Rural Environment, 10–11,* pp. 48–57, 1987.

5. H. Johansen and G. Fuguitt, The Changing Rural Village, *Rural Development Perspectives, 6:*2, pp. 2–6, 1990.

6. J. Keller, personal communication, 1989.

7. I. Jacobsen and B. Albertson, Social and Economic Change in Rural Iowa: The Development of Rural Ghettos, *Human Services in the Rural Environment, 11:*1, pp. 58–65, 1987.

8. J. Fitchen, Poverty as Context for Old Age in Rural America, *Journal of Rural Community Psychology, 11:*1, pp. 31–50, 1990.

9. M. Boschetti, Continuity and Change in Century-Old Farm Homes, in *Coming of Age,* R. Selby, K. Anthony, J. Choi, and B. Orland (eds.), Environmental Design Research Association, Oklahoma City, Oklahoma, pp. 139–146, 1990.

10. R. Bylund, Rural Housing: Perspectives for the Aged, in *The Elderly in Rural Society: Every Fourth Elder,* R. Coward and G. Lee (eds.), Springer, New York, pp. 129–150, 1985.

11. J. Archer and J. Howes, Grief and Rehousing, *British Journal of Medical Psychology, 61:*4, pp. 377–379, 1988.

12. S. Golant, The Effects of Residential and Activity Behaviors on Older People's Environmental Experiences, in *Elderly People and the Environment,* I. Altman, M. P. Lawton, and J. Wohlwill (eds.), Plenum, New York, pp. 239–278, 1984.

13. L. Pastalan, Environmental Displacement: A Literature Reflecting Old Person Environment Transactions, in *Aging and Milieu: Environmental Perspectives on Growing Old,* G. Rowles and R. Ohta (eds.), Academic, New York, pp. 189–203, 1983.

14. S. Newman, J. Zais, and R. Struyk, Housing Older America, in *Elderly People and the Environment,* I. Altman, M. P. Lawton, and J. Wohlwill (eds.), Plenum, New York, pp. 17–56, 1984.

15. G. Rowles, A Place to Call Home, in *The Handbook of Clinical Gerontology,* L. Carstensen and B. Edelstein (eds.), Pergamon, New York, pp. 335–353, 1987.

16. P. Windley, Community Services in Small Rural Towns: Patterns of Use by Older Residents, *The Gerontologist, 23:*2, pp. 180–184, 1983.

17. P. Windley and R. Scheidt, An Ecological Model of Mental Health among Small Town Rural Elderly, *Journal of Gerontology, 37,* pp. 235–242, 1982.

18. R. Rubinstein, The Home Environments of Older People: A Description of the Psychological Processes Linking Person to Place, *Journal of Gerontology, 44,* pp. 545–553, 1989.

19. I. Altman and C. Werner (eds.), *Home Environments,* New York: Plenum, 1985.

20. C. Després, The Meaning of Home: Literature Review and Directions for Future Research and Theoretical Development, *Journal of Architectural and Planning Research, 8:*2, pp. 96–115.

21. S. Shumaker and R. Taylor, Toward a Clarification of People-Place Relationships: A Model of Attachment to Place, in *Environmental Psychology: Directions and Perspectives,* N. Feimer and S. Geller (eds.), Praeger, New York, pp. 219–251, 1983.

22. L. Rivlin, The Neighborhood, Personal Identity, and Group Affiliation, in *Neighborhood and Community Environments,* I. Altman and A. Wandersman (eds.), Plenum, New York, pp. 1–34, 1987.

23. S. O'Bryant, The Subjective Value of "Home" to Older Homeowners, *Journal of Housing for the Elderly, 1,* pp. 29–43, 1983.

24. G. Rowles, Place Attachment among the Small Town Elderly, *Journal of Rural Community Psychology, 11:*1, pp. 103–120, 1990.

25. A. Sixsmith and J. Sixsmith, Transitions in Home Experience in Later Life, *Journal of Architectural and Planning Research, 8:*3, pp. 181–191, 1991.

26. S. Howell, The Meaning of Place in Old Age, in *Aging and Milieu: Environmental Perspectives on Growing Old,* G. Rowles and R. Ohta (eds.), Academic, New York, pp. 97–107, 1983.

27. Y. Tuan, *Space and Place: The Perspective of Experience,* University of Minnesota Press, Minneapolis, 1977.

28. R. Scheidt and C. Norris-Baker, A Transactional Approach to Environmental Stress among Older Residents of Rural Communities, *Journal of Rural Community Psychology, 11*:1, pp. 5–30, 1990.

29. C. Aldwin and D. Stokols, The Effects of Environmental Change on Individuals and Groups: Some Neglected Issues in Stress Research, *Journal of Environmental Psychology, 8,* pp. 57–75, 1988.

30. P. Schoggen, *Behavior Settings: A Revision and Extension of Roger G. Barker's Ecological Psychology,* Stanford University Press, Stanford, California, 1989.

31. A. Wicker, Behavior Settings Reconsidered: Temporal Stages, Resources, Internal Dynamics, Context, in *Handbook of Environmental Psychology,* D. Stokols and I. Altman (eds.), Wiley and Sons, New York, pp. 613–653, 1987.

32. G. Rowles, Aging in Rural Environments, in *Elderly People and the Environment,* I. Altman, M. P. Lawton, and J. Wohlwill (eds.), Plenum, New York, pp. 129–157, 1984.

33. J. Fitchen, How Do You Know What to Ask if You Haven't Listened First?: Using Anthropological Methods to Prepare for Survey Research, *The Rural Sociologist, 10,* pp. 15–22, 1990.

34. P. Barlett, Qualitative Methods in Rural Studies: Basic Principles, *The Rural Sociologist, 10,* pp. 3–14, 1990.

35. R. Lawrence, The Meaning and Use of Home, *Journal of Architectural and Planning Research, 8*:2, pp. 91–95, 1991.

36. D. Hummon, House, Home, and Identity in Contemporary American Culture, in *Housing, Culture and Design,* S. Low and E. Chambers (eds.), University of Pennsylvania Press, Philadelphia, pp. 267–288, 1989.

37. F. Schroeder, Types of American Small Towns and How to Read Them, *Southern Quarterly, 19,* pp. 104–135, 1980.

38. R. Barker, The Influence of Frontier Environments on Behavior, in *The American West,* J. Steffen (ed.), University of Oklahoma Press, Norman, Oklahoma, pp. 61–92, 1979.

39. F. Hurland, Coping with Aesthetics and Community Design in Rural Communities, in *Environmental Aesthetics,* J. Nasar (ed.), Praeger, New York, pp. 449–458, 1988.

40. C. Norris-Baker and R. Scheidt, A Contextual Approach to Serving Older Residents of Economically-Threatened Small Towns, *Journal of Aging Studies, 5*:4, pp. 333–346, 1991.

41. C. Norris-Baker and R. Scheidt, Place Attachment among Older Residents of a Ghost Town: A Transactional Approach, in *Coming of Age,* R. Selby, K. Anthony, J. Choi, and B. Orland (eds.), Environmental Design Research Association, Oklahoma City, Oklahoma, pp. 333–342, 1990.

42. D. Popper and F. Popper, Great Plains from Dust to Dust, *Planning, 53 (December),* pp. 12–18, 1987.

43. T. Daniels and M. Lapping, Small Town Triage: A Rural Resettlement Policy, *Journal of Rural Studies, 9,* pp. 29–40, 1987.

44. J. Patrico, Too Small To Die?, *Farm Journal,* December, pp. A4–A5, 1990.

A survey of 485 single-room occupancy housing (SRO) residents in New York City found elderly residents strongly preferred to remain in centrally located neighborhoods where apartment housing was beyond their means; did not wish to share a housing unit; and had little confidence that they could find acceptable housing if they lost their present unit. For many elderly residents, SROs meet needs not easily met by available alternatives. Results suggest the need to maintain this housing option for older persons and replace losses that have accompanied gentrification in many central city areas.
Key Words: Housing, Homelessness, Social support

A Room of One's Own:
The SRO and the Single Elderly

Stephen Crystal, PhD and Pearl Beck, PhD

Institute for Health, Health Care Policy, and Aging Research, Rutgers University, 30 College Ave., Box 5070, New Brunswick, NJ 08903-5070.

Single-room occupancy buildings (SROs) have long served as an important source of affordable housing for poor single people, elderly and nonelderly. These buildings are often in central city locations. By a 1987 estimate, 400,000 elderly individuals lived in SROs nationwide (Eckert & Murrey, 1987). SRO units help to meet a housing need for nonmarried older urban individuals that has grown as part of the shift to independent living arrangements by this population, 68% of whom lived alone in 1989 as compared with 39% in 1960 (Crystal, 1984; Saluter, 1991). Such shifts led to increased demand in urban areas for housing units suitable to, and affordable by, lower-income single elderly (Kobrin, 1976), an increase that coincided with a decline in availability of SRO units. Concurrently, access to affordable apartment units by this population also declined in many "gentrifying" urban neighborhoods (Henig, 1981).

Single elderly often face housing problems more difficult than those faced by the elderly in families. They are likely to live in rental housing, and a disproportionate number are poor. They face a risk of social isolation after the roles and responsibilities of the workplace are no longer part of their lives. Their lower incomes are more often compounded by lack of an assets "cushion" in the form of home equity, and they have no spouse helper available if they become impaired (Commonwealth Fund Commission, 1988).

Single elderly also do not benefit from the "economies of scale" of shared housing. Although requirements for square footage are less, it costs practically as much to provide such amenities as a bathroom, kitchen, and refrigerator. Many single urban elderly have strong preferences for independence and reject "roommate" arrangements, yet cannot afford available, conventional independent apartments. For such individuals, especially those who would

also have some difficulty keeping up their own apartment, single-room occupancy is one alternative.

SROs lack amenities and provide very limited living space. Nevertheless, they offer affordability and a kind of independence that is valued by many single elderly, particularly as compared with congregate facilities such as domiciliary homes for adults (board and care). As a "substandard" housing type, SRO housing has been the object of considerable ambivalence on the part of planners, regulators, and housing researchers. Particularly when the supply was taken for granted and the needs that it met were not fully understood, SRO housing was often condemned as a relic to be phased out in favor of "standard" apartment housing as quickly as possible. According to a New York City Deputy Mayor in 1965:

The SRO should not be accepted as lawful housing for any segment of our citizenry. No community should equate such housing with the acceptable living standards of the 1960s. We should seriously consider the possibility of phasing the SRO out of existence by compelling its restoration to apartment use. . . . The SRO is a vestigial remnant of a past generation. Its history and use demonstrate that the time has come for the SRO to be regarded as extinct. (Blackburn, 1986)

Such views were accompanied by public policies in many cities that discouraged the SRO. In New York City, for example, during the 1960s and 1970s, subdivision of apartments to create new SROs was effectively illegalized and licensure for new SRO hotels was essentially unavailable, so SROs lost by conversion to apartments were not replaced.

During the 1970s and early 1980s, SRO rooms disappeared at a rapid rate nationally. Between 1970 and 1982, an estimated 1,116,000 units, representing half of all SRO units, were lost (Hopper & Hamburg, 1986), making SRO rooms a scarce commodity and inflating rents in remaining units. Housing that replaced the SRO units was typically out of the price range of the displaced residents (Finder, 1987). Several studies have found that aged, single-person

From *The Gerontologist*, Vol. 32, No. 5, October 1992, pp. 684-692. © 1992 by the Gerontological Society of America. Reprinted by permission.

households have been overrepresented among those displaced by gentrification (Goldfield, 1980; LeGates & Hartman, 1986).

The function served by SROs became fully apparent only as the effects of displacement became obvious; ironically, their importance was widely accepted only after there were, in some cities, relatively few left to save. The increasing visibility of the problem of homelessness contributed to a distinct change in attitudes in the late 1970s and the 1980s. Emergency moratoria in New York (Oser, 1986), San Diego ("Downtown hotel," 1986), and other cities were put in place as temporary measures, and efforts were initiated to preserve the remaining stock and to replace some of the lost SRO units.

New York City's SRO Moratorium and SRO Study

In New York City, the loss of SRO housing began in the 1960s and accelerated as the city recovered from the 1975 fiscal crisis. The Census Bureau's housing surveys found that the supply of SRO-type housing in New York City declined by 81% between 1960 and 1978 (Blackburn, 1986). A New York City Human Resources Administration study (1979) reported that the number of lower-priced residential hotel rooms declined by 35% between 1975 and 1979. In response to this decline, New York City's Local Law 59, enacted by the City Council in 1985, stated that:

A serious public emergency exists in the housing of a considerable number of persons, which emergency has been created by the loss of single-room occupancy dwelling units housing lower income persons . . . many of such occupants are elderly and infirm persons of low-income who are incapable of finding alternative housing accommodations . . . a considerable number of such persons have become part of a growing homeless population . . . the intervention of the City government is necessary to protect such housing stock by imposing a moratorium on conversions, alterations and demolitions of single-room occupancy multiple dwellings . . . during such moratorium the Department of Housing Preservation and Development [HPD] . . . shall arrange for the preparation of a study to determine the best means of making available single-room occupancy dwelling units and other housing for low-income persons.

The study was carried out in two parts. A consultant report was commissioned on the existing stock of buildings, their operations, and ways to preserve or replace the stock (Blackburn, 1986). A resident survey was also conducted and is the data source for this article.

This research provided a unique opportunity to examine the role of SRO housing for the elderly, using a systematic random sample of New York City SRO buildings. Although some data are available from other surveys in single buildings or clusters of buildings and from ethnographic studies of SRO lifestyles, the findings of such studies often depend heavily on chance factors of building selection (Shapiro, 1966; Eckert, 1980; Cohen & Sokolovsky, 1980). More systematic samples of SRO buildings and residents are scarce since fielding such surveys is costly,

and changes in housing uses are often undocumented in public records, making a complete current listing of SRO units difficult to obtain. In the present case, because of the legal, political, and financial significance of the study, it was possible to use a substantial workforce of city building inspectors to check the accuracy of the housing records prior to undertaking the actual survey. To evaluate the role of SRO housing for the elderly, we use a portion of the survey data to determine residents' socioeconomic characteristics; the formal and informal supports they receive; and the degree to which their housing needs are met in the settings they live in.

Methods

Findings are based on interviews with 485 residents of three types of SRO buildings between November 1985 and March 1986 — 122 residents over age 60 and 363 who were younger. The building types were hotels used for long-term occupancy; rooming houses; and apartment buildings converted to single-room use (referred to as Section 248 SROs). Buildings currently used as dormitories by universities or other institutions, hotels with room rates for transients of more than $55 per night, and facilities not available to the general public were excluded, as were units found to have both a private bath and a kitchen (some eligible units did have one of these two amenities).

The sampling methodology is described in detail elsewhere (New York City Human Resources Administration, 1988). A sampling frame for SRO buildings citywide was constructed from city building records, which reported a total of 130,433 SRO units. The sample, drawn from this total, was "cleaned" by site visits by city building inspectors, who verified the building usage and the number of dwelling unit doors. As a result of these inspections and subsequent information gained during the resident survey itself, additional buildings and units were found to be ineligible. Many of the rooms had been converted into non-SRO housing without a corresponding change in the housing records. In addition to these exclusions, we excluded vacant units and units in buildings found to be vacant, since it was believed these units were likely to be currently unavailable for rental. With these exclusions, the revised estimate of occupied supply was 52,000 SRO units (New York City Human Resources Administration, 1988).

Interviews were conducted by more than 100 city employees, most of whom were social service workers and had experience with this resident population. Interviews averaged about 45 minutes; residents were paid $5 per interview. Building visits were made at a combination of daytime, evening, and weekend hours to minimize underrepresentation of employed residents.

Using the "cleaned" building file, a sample of 1,554 units was established. Of these units, 637, or 41%, were determined during the interviewing process to be ineligible, leaving 917 eligible or undetermined

Table 1. Demographic Characteristics of Elderly and Nonelderly SRO Residents

Characteristic	Nonelderly %	Elderly %
Gender	(n = 356)	(n = 120)
Male	60.9	57.0
Female	39.1	43.0
Marital status	(n = 358)	(n = 119)
Married	10.9	5.9
Widowed	3.3	16.8
Divorced/separated	26.0	27.7
Never married	59.8	49.8
Have children	(n = 360)	(n = 119)
	47.2	28.6
Ethnic background	(n = 356)	(n = 120)
White	26.4	60.0
Black	44.9	23.3
Hispanic	23.9	15.0
Other	4.8	1.7
Education	(n = 362)	(n = 120)
< 9th grade	17.6	31.7
Some high school	27.6	16.7
High school graduate	26.8	28.3
Some college/college graduate	28.0	23.3

Table 2. Employment, Income, and Rent of SRO Residents

	Nonelderly	Elderly
Employed	(n = 351) 52%	(n = 120) 10%
Median rent	(n = 354) $246	(n = 118) $216
Mean rent	$317	$251
Median income[a]	(n = 140) $12,500	(n = 48) $9,700
Income/rent ratio	25%	44%

[a]Includes benefits.

units. Among the 917 not determined ineligible, contact with residents was unsuccessful in 272 cases (30%) because they were not home or management refused access to the building, leaving 645 units whose occupants could be contacted. Of these, interviews were successfully completed in 505 cases (78%); the remaining 140 (22%) represented refusals or, in a few instances, language problems. Twenty of the 505 respondents declined to indicate their age, so that the final sample used in the present paper was 485.

As a follow-up to the resident survey, interviews were conducted in 1991 with 10 administrators involved in the management of nonprofit SRO housing. They included the director of social services for one of the city's largest nonprofit SROs, whose residents are primarily elderly; the director of a large nonprofit senior housing organization; and the deputy director of a municipal office dealing with SRO issues.

Age 60 is used to demarcate the older population, since this is the criterion age used for admission to many of New York City's nonprofit senior residences and is also a commonly accepted cut-off for the young old (Soldo & Brotman, 1981).

Findings

Demographic Characteristics

Of the 485 respondents, 122, or 25%, were over 60, representing a projected 13,000 elderly SRO residents citywide. Most elderly residents lived alone in their rooms, but 8% shared the room, typically with a relative or spouse. Forty-three percent of those over 60 were women; the majority (56%) of these were in their 70s, and 47% were over 75, whereas only 39% of

men over 60 were in their 70s. Fifty percent of the elderly SRO population were never married, as were 60% of nonelderly residents. Seventeen percent were widowed, and most of the remainder were divorced or separated. Twenty-nine percent had children (Table 1).

Ethnically, elderly SRO dwellers were a diverse group. Sixty percent were white, 23% black, and 15% Hispanic. As in the city's population generally, the proportion of whites was higher among the elderly than among the nonelderly; whites accounted for only 26% of the nonelderly SRO residents. Educationally, too, elderly SRO residents were diverse: 32% had only a grade school education while 23% had at least some college.

Employment, Income, and Rent

As expected, relatively few older residents (10%) were employed, most often in unskilled, semiskilled, or service occupations. By contrast, 52% of respondents under 60 were employed, with a mean income of $14,000. Typically, older residents were dependent on Social Security benefits; 72% received Social Security with a mean monthly check amount of $392. Twenty-eight percent received Supplemental Security Income, some in combination with a small Social Security check. Only 40% of the interviewed sample provided information on their income; among these, median income of elderly respondents for the previous year (1984) was $9,700, compared with $12,500 for the nonelderly (Table 2).

Table 2 also compares the rent levels and (among those providing income information) the rent-to-income ratios of the elderly and nonelderly populations. The rents the elderly paid (median $216) were lower than those paid by the nonelderly ($246), partly because they had occupied their units for twice as long on average. (The means were more divergent, $251 vs. $317.) Nevertheless, the elderly's housing was less easily affordable to them, at least among those who reported their income. Although the income data were incomplete, they appear consistent with information on employment, benefit receipt and amounts, and other economic data collected in the survey, and suggest that elderly SRO residents paid higher proportions of their income for rent. Older residents' median rent required 44% of their median income, leaving a "median" older resident less than $65 per week for food and all other nonrent expenses; by contrast, a "median" nonelderly resident was spending only 25% of income for rent. This finding is also consistent with the results of the 1987 Housing and Vacancy Report, which found that elderly renters in New York had a higher rent-to-income ratio than nonelderly (Stegman, 1988).

Elderly residents who became displaced appeared to face substantially more difficulty in finding a replacement than the nonelderly. Few rooms were available at prices they could afford: only 31% of rooms rented for under $200, and only 12% for under $150.

Individuals who had moved into SROs during the previous 3 years had higher yearly incomes (median of $10,511) than those who had lived in these buildings 3 years or more (median of $7,067). Long-term elderly residents faced competition for rooms with increasing numbers of less poor, employed, nonelderly residents. Almost half the younger residents were employed, substantially raising their average income compared with that of the elderly. The growing employed population could compete for scarce rooms with resources that most of the elderly could not match.

Housing Conditions, Needs, and Attitudes

Elderly respondents lived disproportionately in SRO hotels as opposed to rooming houses or converted apartments (Section 248 SROs). Fifty-seven percent of elderly respondents versus 42% of the nonelderly were in hotels. Rooming houses accounted for only 24%, as compared with 35% of nonelderly. SRO hotels tend to be located in center city areas, and New York City is no exception; 97% of SRO hotel units in the sample were in Manhattan. Eighty-nine percent of the elderly in all types of SRO units (versus 77% of the nonelderly) were in Manhattan (Table 3).

Table 3 also provides data on housing conditions experienced by SRO residents. Both populations reported problems related to the physical condition of their housing. Eighteen percent of the elderly SRO residents experienced problems related to inadequate heat during the preceding winter, and 27% had holes in the walls of their rooms. Nevertheless, the elderly reported fewer such problems than the nonelderly residents. When the housing conditions reported by the surveyed SRO residents were compared with the conditions of multiple dwellings citywide, using New York City's 1984 Housing and Vacancy Survey (Stegman, 1985), the two settings were quite comparable.

Some elderly residents faced housing needs or constraints related to their health problems. Many were afflicted with chronic conditions common among older people: 37% suffered from arthritis, 9% from diabetes, and 19% from cardiac conditions. Health conditions limited activity for many: 22% said their health prevented their getting around a great deal, another 33% said it interfered with their mobility somewhat, and 19% used ambulation aids, usually a cane. However, only 9% rated their overall health

poor, with 44% fair and 46% good. Although 50% of the elderly reported that they could not do heavy housework, most said they could do light housework, prepare meals, do laundry, manage money, get around outside, bathe themselves, and dress themselves. Twelve percent received some help with one or more of these tasks, often from a home care worker: dressing, housework, and shopping were most often mentioned.

Overall, 81% of the elderly said they could live in an apartment on their own without help. Others felt they would need help, typically in housekeeping, cooking, or getting around; personal care tasks such as bathing and dressing were not mentioned as needs in order to live in an apartment. Elderly respondents were less likely than others ever to have been psychiatrically hospitalized, with 6% of the elderly and 12% of others reporting past hospitalizations. Fewer than 5% of the elderly considered that they had ever had a drinking problem, compared with much higher percentages among the nonelderly, and none admitted to hard drug use.

The relatively independent attitudes and life-styles of the elderly respondents were reflected in their housing preferences and their likes and dislikes concerning their current housing. These responses, summarized in Table 4, often reflected strong attachment to particular parts of the city. Elderly respondents had lived in their neighborhoods an average of 20 years and were much less likely than the nonelderly to consider moving to other boroughs, even though low-cost apartment housing is available primarily in the outer boroughs.

When respondents were asked what factors mattered most to them in considering where to live, a high priority for "a room of one's own" was virtually unanimous (98%), with the desire for safety in the neighborhood and building following closely. One's own apartment was considered as mattering a lot by

Table 3. Housing Characteristics and Conditions of SRO Residents

	Nonelderly %	Elderly %
Type of current SRO residence	(n = 353)	(n = 122)
SRO	23.0	19.0
Hotel	42.0	57.0
Rooming house	35.0	24.0
Type of previous housing	(n = 357)	(n = 119)
SRO	28.9	41.2
Non-SRO	71.1	58.8
Location of current housing	(n = 355)	(n = 122)
Manhattan	77.0	89.0
Other boroughs	23.0	11.0
Housing conditions	(n = 351)	(n = 117)
Heating problems in past winter	27.0	18.2
Rodents; last 3 months	41.9	33.3
Holes in wall	33.6	27.0
Holes in floor	16.6	9.0
Hot water out in past few months	18.6	11.9
Feel safe in building	78.3	84.7
Phone in room	42.5	46.7

Table 4. Neighborhood Ties and Housing Preferences
of SRO Residents

	Nonelderly[a] %	Elderly[b] %
Mean years lived in neighborhood	6.8	20.3
Mean years lived in building	2.3	4.5
"Never" uses public transportation	7.0	22.5
Housing preferences: "matters a lot"		
Own room	95.0	98.3
Own apartment	87.5	71.1
Own kitchen	86.6	68.1
Own bath	85.3	78.2
Safe building	96.9	97.4
Prepared meals	11.5	22.4
Social services	15.9	16.1
Near public transport	79.1	74.2
Near family or friends	50.3	49.6
Most liked feature of current housing		
Location	25.6	33.6
Nothing	16.1	10.9
Security	11.2	10.9
Ambiance	14.1	10.1
Cheap rent	8.0	6.7
Least liked feature of current housing		
Nothing	22.6	36.8
Building maintenance	9.5	14.2
Bad atmosphere	17.4	13.2
No private bath	11.3	6.6
Others in building	6.4	4.7
Would share to afford apartment	10.4	5.8
If had to, would live in:		
Brooklyn	39.8	22.3
Manhattan	82.1	89.6
Bronx	30.8	13.9
Queens	37.0	21.2
Staten Island	13.5	7.8
Housing expectations: If had to move		
Don't know	16.2	33.3
Another SRO	21.1	23.1
Apartment	32.5	14.5
Shared housing	16.8	12.0
Homeless/shelter/streets	13.1	6.8
Other	0.3	10.3

[a]Base N's for nonelderly range = 326–375.
[b]Base N's for elderly range = 99–121.

70%. Having a private bath was important for 85% of the nonelderly and 78% of the elderly. Services such as counseling or congregate meals were not considered important by most respondents.

Residents were asked what they liked most about their current housing. Overwhelmingly (more than 3 times as often as any other factor), location in a preferred neighborhood was cited as the most liked factor. Few older residents (only 6%) were willing to consider sharing an apartment in order to make it affordable. In combination with limited incomes and preference for particular, often higher-rent locations, this would virtually preclude a large proportion from affording available apartment housing.

Older respondents, by a strong majority (85%), stated that they felt safe in their buildings; they were actually slightly more likely to feel safe than younger respondents. Strikingly, fewer older respondents reported feeling unsafe (14%) than reported having been a victim of a crime in the building (18%). They overwhelmingly considered safety an important housing characteristic, but apparently most felt that their buildings provided it, despite some adverse personal experiences.

When asked where they thought they would end up if they lost their present housing, older respondents reflected higher levels of uncertainty than did the younger residents. Thirty-three percent, as compared with 16% of the nonelderly, replied that they didn't know what they would do if they lost their housing; for them, indeed, "don't know" was the modal response. Only 38% thought they would be able to find either another SRO room or an apartment (Table 4).

The elderly reported higher satisfaction with their housing than did the nonelderly. Sixty-eight percent would prefer remaining in their buildings to moving elsewhere, whereas a majority of nonelderly residents (58%) would prefer to move. Asked what they disliked about their housing, 37% of the elderly and 23% of nonelderly responded "nothing." Sixty percent, compared with 46% of the nonelderly, said they were satisfied with their current housing, and only 17% (compared with 29% of the nonelderly) stated they were dissatisfied.

The expressed degree of satisfaction with respondents' rather minimal housing does not necessarily demonstrate the adequacy of these accommodations. Respondents, particularly when somewhat insecure about the future of their living arrangements, may express overall satisfaction even when particular aspects of these arrangements are in fact troublesome to them. For example, most respondents valued having both a private bath and kitchen, though none had both these amenities. However, the responses to satisfaction items should be considered in the light of the priorities most often expressed by respondents, which may not match the scale of values implicitly applied by some housing planners. For example, social services and congregate meals were not a priority for the majority, though a significant subgroup could undoubtedly make good use of such services. The privacy and independence of SRO living, as opposed to the less independent life-style of residential options like board and care with a higher level of service, was important to many respondents, as was their attachment to centrally located neighborhoods.

Previous housing history and perceived alternatives should also be considered in interpreting these responses. Whereas 89% of elderly respondents were in rooms in Manhattan at the time of the survey, 39% had lived in other boroughs immediately prior to their present housing; for many their current housing represented a step up in terms of location. Only 46% had occupied their own apartment, more than 40% had been in a different SRO, and 14% had been in other accommodations ranging from friends' or relatives' homes to a public shelter. They

Table 5. Social Interaction and Support Among SRO Residents

	Nonelderly %	Elderly %
Percentage who "never":		
Visit with family	20.7	41.7
Visit with friends in building	33.5	44.6
Visit with friends outside building	17.6	28.3
Talk to family on phone	17.7	37.5
Talk to friends on phone	21.8	28.1
If sick, someone to help:		
In building	58.3	71.3
Outside building	69.7	72.1

had left their previous homes for a range of reasons, mostly involuntary; however, 31% said they left for a better place, in order to live on their own, or for lower rent. Thus, it was not uncommon for present housing to be perceived as an improvement over previous arrangements. In addition, the housing conditions of elderly SRO residents are somewhat superior to those of the nonelderly residents and are comparable to citywide housing conditions as reflected in the Housing and Vacancy Survey (Stegman, 1985, 1988).

Informal Social Supports

Socially, the elderly SRO residents were a strongly independent group (Table 5). Forty-two percent reported they never visit with family, 45% that they never visit with friends in the building, and 28% that they never visit with friends outside the building. Even among the 29% with children, 64% reported seeing their children several times a year or less, and 28% said they "never" saw their children. Fewer than one in seven acknowledged receiving any emotional, financial, or other help from family or friends, though most felt that someone would be available to help if they got sick.

Discussion

Survey results suggest that elderly SRO residents tend to have strong preferences for independence and weak family ties. Most had long-standing attachments to central city neighborhoods where the bulk of the units were located, and many considered their housing much preferable to available alternatives. The resident's room may be small and without amenities, but it is his or her own, with the freedom to come and go free of constraint from family, roommate, or facility management. Although not untroubled by poor building maintenance, lack of security, or building problems, many found the SRO an acceptable solution to their housing needs, could not afford "standard" accommodations in desired neighborhoods, and did not desire a more heavily serviced, less independent residential alternative or a shared apartment.

The estimated 13,000 persons over 60 in New York City SROs represent about 1% of the city's older population. The single poor elderly were dispropor-

tionately represented, with an estimated 3,500 from the ranks of the poorest elderly, those dependent on SSI. For many elderly SRO residents, given their low incomes, achieving independent housing of any kind in preferred neighborhoods was an important accomplishment. Not a few perceived themselves as being at risk of homelessness, a perception consistent with other available data. In a study of individuals entering New York City shelters for the homeless who were interviewed during a 1982–1983 study period, elderly residents (25%) were more likely than other homeless (13%) to have been living in SROs before coming to the shelter (New York City Human Resources Administration, 1985a).

According to a 1984 estimate, 343,000 single New Yorkers had incomes below 125% of the poverty level and were living alone (New York City Human Resources Administration, 1985b); the number of such individuals over age 60 can be estimated at 130,000, about 10 times the number of elderly SRO dwellers (New York City Human Resources Administration, 1985c). Thus, the SRO option was available to only a small proportion of the poor single elderly, who faced increasing competition with other, better-heeled populations for a diminished supply of rooms. These findings suggest the need not simply to preserve remaining stock and replace further losses, but to replace some of the losses of the last 2 decades. Losses similar to those in New York City have occurred in many U.S. cities during this period, as reflected in reports from San Francisco (Hartman, Keating, & LeGates, 1981), San Diego (Eckert, 1979), and Seattle (National Urban Coalition, 1981), as well as in reports from national data sources (Haley, Pearson, & Hull, 1981). The picture of undermet need for affordable SRO-type housing for the low-income single elderly characteristic of New York City likely also characterizes many other urban areas.

Even if the physical stock of SROs were stabilized and lost units replaced, would the availability of this housing to poor single persons, elderly and nonelderly, be maintained? Survey results indicate that SRO housing has become attractive to many individuals considerably more "upscale" than traditional SRO tenants. Of the nonelderly SRO residents, 46% were employed, most full-time, with median income 44% higher than that of elderly residents. As apartment housing in central city areas becomes scarcer, displacement of the poor by those of modest, and even by a few with relatively comfortable, incomes takes place. As a city official commented, in view of the study results: "Even if the number of single rooms remains the same, occupancy by the vulnerable and dependent group will decline" (Oser, 1986). The elderly as a group, and especially the poor elderly, are likely to be particular victims of such displacement.

Furthermore, elderly SRO residents face several disincentives when they consider moving either to an apartment or to another SRO. First, rents have increased faster for rental apartments than for rooms in hotels and SROs. According to data from annual apartment and hotel orders (A. McLaughlin, New York City Rent Guidelines Board, personal communication, May 18, 1992), hotel and SRO rents increased only 19.5% from 1982 to 1992, while apartment rents increased 49% for holders of 1-year leases. Second, even with development and conversion activity at a near standstill, SRO owners can severely limit the availability of permanent hotel rooms through the deregulation of vacant rooms by having them reclassified as "transient units." Charging nightly rates makes these units unaffordable to the elderly and to other needy populations and thereby seriously limits the availability for re-rental of vacated residential hotel rooms for long-term residents.

The Role of Nonprofit Management

If the SRO is to be an important resource for low-income single elderly and other special-need groups, and access maintained and improved for these groups, more is needed than simply maintaining the physical building stock. The policy study carried out in conjunction with the Resident Survey concluded that:

"Even if it were possible, which it is not, to require owners to rent only to low-income or otherwise deserving tenants, it is certain that the buildings would mostly be operated in the deplorable manner that has characterized their operations in the recent past. . . . If the City elects to retain at least some of these properties to deal with its low-income housing crisis, the City must therefore move to bring them into nonprofit ownership." (Blackburn, 1986)

Since the SRO survey was conducted, the city has taken steps to bring some of the large SROs under nonprofit management, despite a major legal setback in 1989. After years of court challenges, the New York State Court of Appeals ruled that the moratorium on the alteration or demolition of SROs was unconstitutional because it deprived owners of the right to determine how their properties would be used. The potentially adverse consequences of this ruling were cushioned by the overall economic downturn that began in the late 1980s. Because the real estate industry has been particularly hard hit by the recession, funding was scarce for both development and conversion projects. As a result, the pace of SRO conversions was significantly reduced. These difficult economic conditions were propitious for the acquisition of SROs by the city, which was able to purchase and renovate several SRO hotels and turn them over to nonprofit groups to manage (Finder, 1990).

In general, elderly residents have benefited from residing in nonprofit managed SROs, which provide access to increased on-site services. However, because much of the funding available in the late 1980s for the acquisition and renovation of SRO buildings was tied to homelessness prevention, previously homeless individuals, including the mentally ill, were increasingly housed in SROs. Although elderly SRO residents have often shared their housing with the mentally disabled — and some have themselves suffered from psychiatric problems — the newest wave of residents with histories of homelessness seems to have presented problems for older residents. In the 1991 follow-up interviews with administrators, several noted the concern of elderly residents about concentrations of previously homeless individuals, some of whom may overtly engage in drug use, drug dealing, or prostitution.

To date, there exists scant information on what constitutes an optimal population mix for SRO housing. An "age-dense" model may facilitate the emergence of sociability and helping networks among older residents (Hochschild, 1978). On the other hand, both practical considerations and an interest in avoiding age segregation have often led to highly heterogenous building populations. Placement practices by nonprofit SROs have varied. Although a few of the new nonprofit managed SROs have been limited to "elderly" (the cut-off age is sometimes as low as 50), more typically this funding stream has resulted in a "population-mixed" building.

Meeting the Needs of "Aging-in-Place" SRO Residents

The preference for independence and the somewhat isolated life-style of many SRO residents can result in difficulties for that subpopulation of residents who become, over time, increasingly frail and less able to meet all their own needs. Though most elderly respondents perceived that at least some support was available if needed, many maintained few social ties either inside or outside the buildings; fewer than one in seven acknowledged receiving any help from family and friends. These observations are consonant with Stephens's (1975) findings concerning the socialization patterns of SRO residents in a midwestern city. She found that hotel residents often limited their social encounters to instrumental exchanges, in a strategy that enabled them to create a structure for mutual help while maintaining their autonomy and avoiding more intimate relationships.

In the 1991 interviews of New York SRO administrators, several reported that the insularity of SRO residents becomes more problematic as they age. They were concerned that "aging-in-place" could create a level of need that could not be met by existing instrumental helping relationships and networks. SRO administrators also reported that assistance with the emotional problems of aging remains an unmet need for many elderly SRO residents.

Several strategies are used by nonprofit SROs to address their residents' varied needs. Buildings with large numbers of residents usually contain on-site social services that provide individual casework, counseling on financial benefits, and some socialization opportunities for interested residents. On-site professionals often make referrals to outside mental health, medical, and social service agencies, when needed. Smaller nonprofit managed SROs have a combination of on-site staffs and part-time specialists, such as psychiatrists and nurses, who are usually affiliated with a neighborhood medical institution. Privately owned SROs are least likely to have on-site social and health services or to have communal space for residents interested in socializing. Because all space is viewed as possibly income generating, SRO owners are usually averse to forfeiting any of it for non-income-producing activities. This strategy can be counterproductive since without support services, some residents can become disruptive, thereby destabilizing the entire building (Felton, Lehmann, & Adler, 1981). SRO administrators interviewed generally reported that the most practical strategy for helping elderly residents of private SROs is to link them to established community services, such as senior centers, lunch programs, and health clinics.

Physical deterioration with advancing age is particularly problematic for aging SRO residents. Because of their disaffiliated social interaction patterns, many elderly SRO residents lack access to the types of unpaid informal support that enable three-quarters of the nation's infirm elderly to reside in the community rather than in institutions (Manton & Liu, 1984). SRO residents who become increasingly impaired face difficult alternatives. Home care is more difficult to provide on an extensive basis in single-room housing units. Congregate housing, which typically offers a minimum service package consisting of on-site meals in addition to housekeeping, can provide a satisfactory alternative for those with mild to moderate impairment, but demand greatly exceeds supply (Eckert & Murrey, 1987). Domiciliary or board and care facilities provide a more institutional atmosphere than congregate care facilities, tending to serve an older, frailer, more dependent population of elderly who are receptive to accepting care from others. Such facilities have been criticized for inadequate provision of medical and social services and also for safety and sanitary code violations (Eckert & Murrey, 1987). For many SRO-dwelling elderly, congregate and domiciliary care facilities are not desired alternatives. Typically, such facilities require sharing a room; most are also located outside the active central city neighborhoods strongly preferred by most SRO dwellers. They involve a loss of independence and a level of social interaction that can be difficult for some clients; Lowenthal and Chiriboga (1973) find that higher levels of social involvement in later life can be stressful for people who had previously been near-isolates.

The survey results in combination with the follow-up interviews indicate the diversity of needs among the elderly SRO population and the need for a range of residential alternatives to meet these needs. For higher-functioning older residents, SROs provide affordable independent housing arrangements in preferred neighborhoods. Access to in-house social or other services is not a priority for most of these residents, for whom the "traditional" SRO meets an important need. Another group, aging in place and more frail, needs access to supportive services as well as respect for their independence and privacy needs. Housing models appropriate to this population can suitably be provided by serviced SROs under voluntary sponsorship, provided funds are available for the needed services. Such models, providing privacy along with such protective services as emergency call systems and housekeeping, might resemble the British "assisted independent living" model described by Heumann and Boldy (1982). Another alternative involves the more creative provision of supportive services within existing settings. In some "conventional" SRO buildings, for example, Medicaid-funded home care services are being provided on a "cluster" basis in which one aide provides services throughout the day to two or more individuals. Supported housing for the elderly was endorsed by New York City's federally mandated report titled "Comprehensive Housing Affordability Strategy" (CHAS). The report states: "In addition to affordable housing, elderly New Yorkers need housing that offers supportive services such as meals and housekeeping. This alternative allows seniors to remain in the community" (New York City Department of City Planning, 1992). Other supportive services mentioned in the report are case management, security, and a program supervisor.

Despite improvements in the elderly's income, a substantial group within the elderly population lives near the poverty line (Smeeding, 1986) and a large proportion of this population are single (Commonwealth Fund Commission, 1988). Increasingly, unmarried elderly live alone, apparently due largely to their own preferences for independence (Crystal, 1984). Plans to meet the future housing needs of the elderly must take account of the combined effects of increased numbers of elderly, aging within the elderly population, and increased probability of living alone within age groups of the elderly. These factors are likely to generate a sharp increase in the number of single-person elderly households.

The SRO survey results suggest that this type of housing provides a valuable and badly needed alternative to a significant segment of the single elderly population. Although housing programs for the elderly have concentrated overwhelmingly on conventional apartment housing, the special needs of low-income single elderly require increased attention. Initiatives are required to maintain the availability of SRO housing and to provide older SRO residents with the appropriate levels of support as they age. Allowing the disappearance of the remaining SROs — or permitting the elderly, or poorer residents in general, to be squeezed out of them — would entail the displacement of a population who often perceive that they have nowhere else to go that is acceptable to them.

References

Blackburn, A. (1986). *Single occupancy in New York City*. Prepared for the City of New York Department of Housing Preservation and Development. Cambridge, MA: Urban Systems Research and Engineering, Inc.

Cohen, C., & Sokolovsky, J. (1980). Social engagement versus isolation: The case of the aged in SRO hotels. *The Gerontologist, 20,* 6–44.

Commonwealth Fund Commission. (1988). *Aging alone: Profiles and projections*. A report of the Commonwealth Fund Commission on elderly people living alone. Baltimore: Author.

Crystal, S. (1984). *America's old age crisis: Public policy and the two worlds of aging*. Rev. ed. New York: Basic.

Downtown hotel evictions stir questions on SRO law. (1986, July 24). *San Diego Tribune*, p. B1.

Eckert, J. (1979). Urban renewal and redevelopment: High risk for the marginally subsistent elderly. *The Gerontologist, 19*, 496–502.

Eckert, J. (1980). *The unseen elderly. A study of marginally subsistent hotel dwellers*. San Diego: Campanile.

Eckert, J., & Murrey, M. (1987). Alternative housing modes. In J. Hancock (Ed.), *Housing the elderly*. New Brunswick, NJ: Transaction.

Felton, B., Lehmann, S., & Adler, A. (1981). SRO hotels: Their viability as housing options for older citizens. In P. Lawton & S. Hoover (Eds.), *Community housing choices for older Americans*. New York: Springer.

Finder, A. (1987, January 23). Council passes bill on SRO hotel conversions. *The New York Times*, p. B5.

Finder, A. (1990, February 9). Experts on homeless push for an old idea: SROs in New York. *The New York Times*, p. B1.

Goldfield, D. (1980). Private neighborhood redevelopment and displacement: The case of Washington, D.C. *Urban Affairs Quarterly, 15*, 453–468.

Haley, B., Pearson, M., & Hull, D. (1981). *Urban elderly residents of single-room occupancy housing (SROs), 1976–1980*. Paper presented at the 24th annual meeting of the Gerontological Society of America, Toronto, Canada.

Hartman, C., Keating, D., & LeGates, R. (1981). *Displacement: How to fight it*. Berkeley: National Housing Law Project.

Henig, J. (1981). Gentrification and displacement of the elderly: An empirical analysis. *The Gerontologist, 21*, 67–75.

Heumann, C., & Boldy, D. (1982). *Housing for the elderly: Planning and policy formulation in Western Europe and North America*. New York: St. Martin's.

Hochschild, A. (1978). *The unexpected community: Portrait of an old age subculture*. Rev. ed. Berkeley: University of California Press.

Hopper, K., & Hamberg, J. (1986). The making of America's homeless: From skid row to new poor, 1945–1984. In R. Bratt, C. Hartman, & A. Meyerson (Eds.), *Critical perspectives on housing*. Philadelphia: Temple University Press.

Kobrin, F. (1976). The fall of household size and the rise of the primary individual in the United States. *Demography, 13* (1), 127–138.

LeGates, R., & Hartman, C. (1986). The anatomy of displacement in the United States. In N. Smith & P. Williams (Eds.), *Gentrification of the city*. Boston: Allen and Unwin.

Lowenthal, M., & Chiriboga, D. (1973). Social stress and adaptation: Toward a lifecourse perspective. In C. Eisdorfer & M. P. Lawton (Eds.), *The psychology of adult development and aging*. Washington, DC: American Psychological Association.

Manton, K. G., & Liu, K. (1984, March 7–9). *The future of the long-term care population: Projections based on the 1977 National Nursing Home Survey and the 1982 Long-Term Care Survey*. Paper presented at the Hillhaven Third National Leadership Conference on Long-Term Care Issues, The Future World of Long-Term Care, Washington, DC.

National Urban Coalition. (1981). *Neighborhood transition without displacement*. Washington, DC: Author.

New York City Department of City Planning. (1992). *Comprehensive housing affordability strategy*. New York: Author.

New York City Human Resources Administration. (1979). *The diminishing resource: Lower priced hotels in New York City*. New York: Author.

New York City Human Resources Administration. (1985a). *The homeless mentally ill. substance abusers, youth, elderly, and employables in New York City shelters*. New York: Author.

New York City Human Resources Administration. (1985b). *Dependency: Economic and social data for New York City*. New York: Author.

New York City Human Resources Administration. (1985c). *The new SROs*. New York: Author.

New York City Human Resources Administration. (1988). *The changing face of New York City's SROs: A profile of single room occupancy residents and housing*. New York: Author.

Oser, A. (1986, May 4). The ripple effect produced by the SRO moratorium: It alters projects and derails plans for rehabilitation. *The New York Times*, pp. 7, 30.

Saluter, A. (1991). Marital status and living arrangements: March 1990. *Current Population Reports, Series P-20, No. 450*. Washington: Bureau of the Census.

Shapiro, J. (1966). Single-room occupancy: Community of the alone. *Social Work, 11*(4), 24–33.

Smeeding, T. (1986). Nonmoney income and the elderly: The case of the tweeners. *Journal of Policy Analysis and Management, 5*, 707–724.

Soldo, B., & Brotman, H. (1981). Housing where? In P. Lawton & S. Hoover (Eds.), *Community housing choices for older Americans*. New York: Springer.

Stegman, M. (1985). *Housing in New York: Study of a City, 1984*. New York: Department of Housing Preservation and Development.

Stegman, M. (1988). *Housing and Vacancy Report, New York City, 1987*. New York: Department of Housing Preservation and Development.

Stephens, J. (1975). Society of the alone: Freedom, privacy and utilitarianism as dominant norms in the SRO. *Journal of Gerontology, 30*, 230–235.

We describe the development and evaluation of group homes for dementia patients in Sweden. Group homes have been established on a social model of care to provide a better quality of life than in institutional settings, while making a small savings on cost. An enriched program of activities uses familiar, everyday household tasks, with staff trained to model appropriate behaviors. An evaluation of four homes indicated that residents could be well accommodated in the setting, even as their disabilities increased. Although there were some initial problems, staff satisfaction was high and turnover low.
Key Words: Personal care, Dementia, Long-term care, Community care

Group Homes for People With Dementia: A Swedish Example

Bo Malmberg, PhD.,[1]
and Steven H. Zarit, PhD[2]

[1]Institute of Gerontology, University College of Health Science, Box 1038, 551 11 Jönköping, Sweden.

[2]Department of Human Development and Family Studies, Pennsylvania State University, Henderson S-110, University Park, PA 16802.

We report on the development of group homes (Gruppboenden) for people with dementia in Sweden, examining in-depth four homes in the municipality of Jönköping. Developed as an alternative to traditional institutional care, group homes use a social model in which residents participate in everyday activities in a home-like setting. These facilities have no North American equivalent, differing from nursing homes in their emphasis on a social model and from personal care homes in the professionalization and training of staff.

As in the United States, Sweden is grappling with the problems of an aging population and high costs of care for disabled elders. Currently, the population of Sweden is one of the oldest in the world, with 17% over the age of 65 and almost 4% over 80. Until the 1980s, institutional care was emphasized. Recognition of the limitations of quality of life in institutional settings, however, has led to efforts to maintain people in the community. Home help services are available through municipalities to assist elders in their homes. Service apartments, which provide meals and other assistance (supplemented by home help, if needed) are an alternative living arrangement for elderly with functional limitations. Day care, including for dementia patients, is also available in many areas. Consistent with Swedish welfare poli-

cies, the costs of these programs to the individual are nominal and affordable.

While providing a comprehensive service net, these programs have not consistently been able to accommodate people with dementing illnesses. Personnel are often uncertain how to handle people with dementia, and, as a result, they have not been welcome in many settings. When their behavior or need for supervision can no longer be accommodated in ordinary housing or service apartments, they have been relocated to nursing homes or geropsychiatric hospitals.

Group homes have been developed as an alternative setting for people with dementia who can no longer be maintained in other community settings. The number of group homes has been increasing rapidly. In 1987 there were 60 group homes serving approximately 500 people. By 1992, there were 5,300 residents of group homes, with plans to develop facilities for another 6,400 people. Costs of the program are shared between the resident and the welfare system. While care in a group home is somewhat less expensive than in a nursing home, concern for quality of care has been a more important factor in their development than cost.

Group homes are organized on a social rather than medical model. The social model emphasizes maintaining personal autonomy and competencies through a combination of environmental features, programming, and the facilitative relationships staff develop with residents. Programs are organized around concerns for the quality of life and environment, rather than on management of symptoms or disease. Among the key features of this model are: (a) creation of a familiar, home-like setting; (b) combining privacy of single apartments with the security of around-the-clock staff; (c) use of familiar household chores as activities for residents; and (d) staff serving as role models to engage residents in activities. These aspects of the program are described in more detail below.

An Evaluation of Four Group Homes

We now turn to an examination of four group homes in Jönköping, a city of 110,000 inhabitants in south central Sweden. While regional variation in old age programs can be found in Sweden, the homes in Jönköping appear similar to facilities we have examined in other regions. Two of the group homes in this report were opened in the fall of 1988 and were investigated once, one year later. The other two group homes opened in the fall of 1989, and were evaluated at that time and again one year later. The evaluation included observations of the facilities and staff-resident interactions, and interviews with staff residents, and family members. Informal contacts, including visits and phone calls, have been maintained with staff since that time.

Facilities and Staff

The typical group home has 6 to 8 single apartments grouped around a common living room and a shared kitchen. In Jönköping, however, a different arrangement was made, placing two sets of 5 apartments each in close proximity, so that there could be some sharing of staff. Three of the group homes examined here follow this pattern, while the fourth group home has all 10 apartments on one corridor of an old age home. The apartments open onto hallways, which lead to kitchens and living areas that are shared by the residents and used for activities. Each apartment complex is locked, but residents who can walk around by themselves outdoors without getting lost are allowed to do so (see Figure 1).

Each resident has her own apartment, consisting of one or two rooms, toilet, shower, and a small kitchen area with a stove, refrigerator, and sink. Residents bring their own furniture, including pictures for the wall. They have keys to their apartments and can go inside and lock their doors. Staff can enter with their own keys if needed.

While there was initially some concern that having 10 residents in a group home would be too much for the staff to manage, the 5 plus 5 arrangement has given personnel more flexibility in covering for one another in the event of illness or for handling problems that might arise. This structure may also reduce staff's feelings of isolation that have been noted in smaller units.

During the day, the staff consists of from 4 to 6 people for the 10 residents. At 7 a.m., 4 people come on duty and receive a report from the single night person. They are joined later in the morning by 2 additional staff persons. Four staff are present in the evening. The lone night staff member monitors resi-

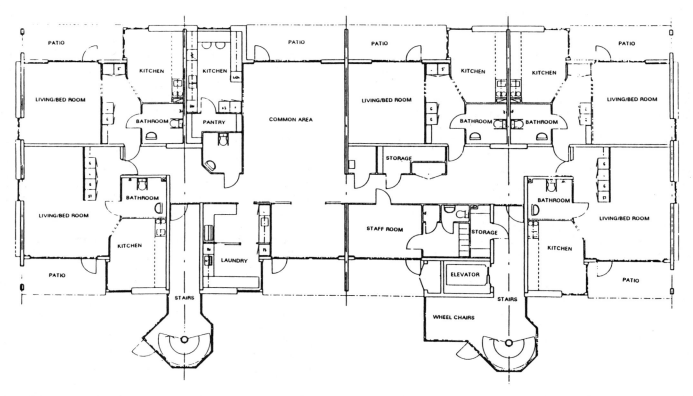

Figure 1. Drawing of a 5-unit group home. Five apartments consisting of a bedroom, kitchen, toilet and bathroom (with shower and toilet) and patio are arrayed around a common area. The common area includes a living area, reading and conversation room, kitchen and staff room. There is a locked entrance at one stairway and an elevator leading to an identical 5-unit group home on the second floor.

dents in both sets of apartments. Night staff indicated that it can be very challenging when residents need attention simultaneously in both units, but reported that this situation does not occur frequently. As a way of supplementing the night staff, the community's night patrol, which assists elders living alone, has its coffee breaks in the group homes each night between 1 and 2 a.m., and can provide assistance if necessary. Staffing during weekends is done by as few people as possible, so that personnel only have to work every third Saturday and Sunday.

Most of the staff had previous training and experience working with older people, though not with dementia. Of the 48 staff of the four group homes, 12 were trained as mental health technicians, 21 were old age home helpers, 9 were nurses aides, 3 had other health training, and 3 had no previous formal education for this role. The mental health technicians and old age home helpers had completed formal, post-high school training programs of 3 semesters at a health college. Nurses aides take a 4-semester training program which they can enroll in after ordinary school (9th grade). All but two of the staff were women.

At the opening of a facility, staff participated in a training program that lasted from 2 to 4 weeks. Training emphasized understanding aging and dementia, what kinds of activities to arrange, and how to be a model to stimulate participation in activities. Staff also received instruction in small group psychology, including how to work together, hold discussions, and solve problems. When staff were subsequently replaced, new personnel received briefer training.

A major feature of the social model is staff's use of ordinary daily activities with residents. They eat and have coffee with residents. The residents participate to the extent possible in meal preparation and cleanup. Staff also engage residents in housekeeping activities such as laundry, housecleaning, and ironing. Staff will take residents out for a variety of activities, for instance, grocery or clothing shopping, church, picking flowers, or visiting their relatives. It has been possible to engage male as well as female residents in these activities, and no special programming for men has been necessary.

One staff member is designated as each resident's contact person. This person is responsible for liaison with the resident's family, bank, physician, district nurse, or any other contacts.

Residents

Residents are referred to the group homes by community health teams, which coordinate care to elderly living in the community. When someone is identified as a possible resident for an available apartment, a staff person from the group home contacts that person's family, and goes to visit the potential resident. The home helper who worked with that person usually goes along. This initial screening determines the appropriateness of placement. Very aggressive or agitated people will be directed to nursing homes or geropsychiatric hospitals, instead of the group homes.

Forty people were living in the four group homes at their outset. Nearly all residents were women and were either widowed or never married. The nearest relative was typically a daughter or daughter-in-law.

Although the group homes were originally designed for people with mild to moderate dementia, the typical resident has been more impaired, especially over time. Functioning of residents was assessed in three ways. First, a Swedish language version of the Mini-Mental State Examination (MMSE) was administered to residents (Folstein, Folstein, & McHugh, 1975; Johansson & Zarit, 1991). Second, staff rated residents on a 6-point scale for severity of dementia, the Berger Scale (Berger, 1980). Finally, staff rated performance of 5 activities of daily living (ADL). Results are shown in Table 1.

Residents had moderate to severe dementia on the MMSE and the Berger Scale, both at baseline (for the two homes on which that data were available) and after one year. The most common kinds of ADL assistance were for dressing and hygiene.

Of note is the effort to keep use of psychotropic medications to a minimum. The modal pattern is for residents either to be maintained on low dosages or to have drugs administered only if needed. Staff administer medications under the direction of the physician and district nurse.

Outcomes

The group homes provide a very calm, noninstitutional environment. Residents' apartments are filled with their furniture and memorabilia. The common areas have been tastefully furnished with ordinary furniture, making the settings strikingly distinct from an institutional environment. While there are occasional problems, residents are generally calm, indeed, more so than comparable dementia patients in other settings. Residents' tranquility may reflect, in part, initial selection. Nonetheless, it is worth exploring more systematically if this combination of familiar setting and activities along with providing a measure of autonomy and the judicious use of medications may reduce behavior problems associated with dementia.

After one year, 36 of the initial 40 residents of the four group homes were still residing there; two had died, and two had to be moved to other facilities because of behavior problems that could not be managed in the home. The staff rated the remaining patients as having stable or declining cognitive function, as indicated by the Berger Scale (Table 1), but improved behavior and mood.

We also conducted a follow-up on the original residents after 4 years for two of the homes and 5 years for the other two. Of the original 40 residents, 12 still resided in the group homes, 10 died in the group homes, and 18 were moved to another facility. Retrospective accounts suggested that most relocations were due to declining health and mobility,

Table 1. Functional Performance of Group Home Residents

| | Homes 3 & 4 | | Homes 1 & 2 |
	Baseline	1 Year	1 Year Only
MMSE			
Mean Correct	12.2	10.1	6.3
Range (0–30)	0–23	0–21	0–19
Berger Dementia Scale			
Mean	3.0	4.2	4.1
Range (1 = mild, 6 = severe)	1–5	2–5	3–6
ADLs			
1. Dressing			
No Impairment	47%	27%	33%
Minor Help	21%	13%	17%
Major Help	26%	40%	39%
Completely Dependent	5%	20%	11%
2. Eating			
No Impairment	79%	73%	72%
Minor Help	11%	27%	11%
Major Help	11%	—	17%
Completely Dependent	—	—	—
3. Physical Activity			
No Impairment	79%	93%	83%
Minor Help	21%	—	11%
Major Help	—	7%	—
Completely Dependent	—	—	6%
4. Hygiene			
No Impairment	—	16%	20%
Minor Help	22%	42%	20%
Major Help	56%	37%	33%
Completely Dependent	22%	5%	27%
5. Toileting			
No Impairment	44%	63%	53%
Minor Help	6%	16%	27%
Major Help	22%	16%	13%
Completely Dependent	28%	5%	7%

Note: All percentages may not add to 100 due to rounding.

while a smaller number were because of difficulties managing the resident in the group home.

Interviews with a family member after 1 year indicate that they were very satisfied with the group homes. They hoped their relatives could remain in the group homes, and their main concern was how well staff could manage the workload in the long run.

Staff were interviewed after 1 year, and completed measures of work satisfaction (Rubenowitz, 1975) and work tedium (Pines, Aronson, & Kafry, 1981). In general, group home personnel were very positive about their work, with mean ratings of about 2 on most work satisfaction items (on a scale of 1 to 5, with 1 as positive and 5 as negative). Compared to ratings of nursing aides at geriatric hospitals and in home care (see Berg, Dahl, Dehlin, & Hedenrud, 1976; Berg & Holmgren, 1984), group home personnel were somewhat more positive in their ratings of coworkers but also reported more stress. Similarly, most staff reported low levels of tedium ($\bar{X} = 1.90$, $SD = 0.60$), although two people had high scores which suggest the possibility of physical and/or emotional exhaustion (Pines et al., 1981). The major issue reported by staff was that residents were somewhat more impaired than they had anticipated. They found it more difficult than expected to motivate residents to participate in activities. Because of considerable heterogeneity in functioning among residents, staff also did more one-on-one, rather than small group activities. As a result, staff had to modify their expectations about the kind of programming that was possible and the gains that residents could make.

In retrospect, the staff's initial training may have been too optimistic about what could be accomplished with residents. As a result, they went through a period of readjustment, trying to figure out what was actually possible. These problems were reduced somewhat for the two homes started a year later, with training emphasizing more realistic expectations about the ability of residents to respond to activities, for instance, indicating that they cannot be expected to achieve independent or near-independent functioning in ADLs, and that small group activities are difficult to sustain. Training for programs such as these must strike a balance between idealism, which is often needed to break the mold of conventional approaches to care, and practicality for responding to the exigencies of everyday demands.

Despite these problems, turnover has been low. During the first year, almost all staff remained with the programs. By the 4- and 5-year follow-up, 33 of the original 48 staff were still with the programs.

Conclusions

The overall implementation of group homes should be considered as successful, and the number of programs has been expanded in Jönköping, as well as other parts of Sweden. Group homes provide a safe and familiar environment, which appears to minimize behavioral disturbances associated with dementia while supporting remaining functional competencies. These settings appear a viable alternative for a majority of people with dementia until very late in the disease.

References

Berg, S., Dahl, L., Dehlin, O., & Hedenrud, B. (1976). Psychological perception of nursing aides work: An attitude study in a geriatric hospital. *Scandinavian Journal of Rehabilitation Medicine, 8,* 79–84.

Berg, S., & Holmgren, A. L. (1984). Sjukvård i hemmet: En studie bland patienter, anhöriga och personal [Nursing care in the home: A study of patients, family members, and personnel]. Jönköping: Institutet för gerontologi, Report no. 56.

Berger, E. Y. (1980). A system for rating the severity of senility. *Journal of the American Geriatrics Society, 28,* 234–236.

Folstein, M. F., Folstein, S. E., & McHugh, P. R. (1975). "Mini-mental state" — A practical method for grading the cognitive state of patients for the clinician. *Journal of Psychiatric Research, 12,* 189–198.

Johansson, B., & Zarit, S. H. (1991). Dementia and cognitive impairment in the oldest-old. A comparison of two rating methods. *International Psychogeriatrics, 3,* 29–38.

Pines, A., Aronson, E., & Kafry, D. (1981). *Burnout: From tedium to personal growth.* New York: The Free Press.

Rubenowitz, S. (1975). SKF-rapporten [SFK report]. Göteborg: Göteborgs Universitet, Psykologiska Institutionen.

Social Policies, Programs, and Services for Older Americans

It is a political reality that older Americans will be able to obtain needed assistance from governmental programs only to the degree that they are perceived as politically powerful. Political involvement can include holding and expressing political opinions, voting in elections, participating in voluntary associations to help elect a candidate or party, and holding political office.

Research has indicated that older people are just as likely as any other age group to hold political opinions, are more likely than younger people to vote in an election, are about equally divided between Democrats and Republicans, and are more likely than young people to hold political office. Older people, however, have shown little inclination to vote as a bloc on issues affecting their welfare. Activists, such as Maggie Kuhn and the leaders of the "Gray Panthers," have encouraged senior citizens to vote as a bloc, but so far they have not convinced them to do so.

Gerontologists have observed that a major factor contributing to the increased push for government services for the elderly has been the publicity on their plight generated by such groups as the National Council of Senior Citizens and the American Association of Retired Persons. The desire of adult children to shift the financial burden of aged parents from themselves onto the government has further contributed to the demand for services for the elderly. The resulting widespread support for such programs has almost guaranteed their passage in Congress.

Now, for the first time, there are groups emerging that oppose increases in spending for services for older Americans. Requesting generational equity, some politically active groups argue that the federal government is spending so much on older Americans that it is depriving younger age groups of needed services.

The articles in this unit discuss the rising cost of health care and senior services for older Americans. The first unit article, "Canada's Health Insurance and Ours: Real Lessons, Big Choices," compares Canada's health care program with the United States' to determine which is best.

Issues of poverty and economic hardship are the focus of the next two articles in this unit. "Can We Afford Old Age?" raises critical questions regarding the cost of the current programs assisting older Americans and what the taxpayers will be willing to pay for in the future. The authors of "Heading for Hardship: The Future of Older Women in America" assert that women continue to pour into the paid workforce but retirement income does not reflect their growing contributions.

The final unit article, "The Unquiet Future of Intergenerational Politics," examines communities with very large elderly populations to determine whether this factor increases or decreases generational conflict.

Looking Ahead: Challenge Questions

What new programs should the federal government institute in the next five years to assist older Americans?

What service programs for senior citizens could be more efficiently handled by state and local governments than by Washington? Give some examples.

Do you think that the elderly are often abused in the name of protection? Explain why or why not.

Do you believe the federal government is investing too much in social services for older Americans? Defend your answer.

Canada's Health Insurance & Ours:

Real Lessons, Big Choices

Theodore R. Marmor and
Jerry L. Mashaw

(Theodore R. Marmor is professor of public management at the Yale University School of Organization and Management. Jerry L. Mashaw is Gordon Bradford Tweedy Professor Law and Organization at Yale University Law School.)

As medical costs escalate and more Americans find themselves without insurance, Canada's approach to financing health care has taken center stage in the debate in the United States. Congressional committees have invited Canadian experts to testify. Political organizations have sent parades of representatives on crash study tours to Canada. Television networks, National Public Radio, major national newspapers and *Consumer Reports* have done stories on Canadian national health insurance.

Canada's health system raises three separable issues for the United States: Does Canada really have an exemplary medical care system worth importing? Is Canada's program politically feasible in the United States? Can we successfully adapt it?

Canada's National Health Insurance

Canada's ten provinces provide health insurance. The federal government conditionally promises to repay each province a substantial portion of the costs of all necessary medical care, roughly 40 percent. The federal grant is available as long as the province's health insurance program covers all citizens, has conventional hospital and medical care and has no limits on services or extra charges to patients. Each province must recognize the others' coverage and be under control of a public, nonprofit organization.

Annual negotiations between provincial governments and providers of care determine hospital budgets and physicians' fees. As in the United States, most hospitals are nonprofit community institutions.

Unlike U.S. hospitals, they never worry about itemized billings; they receive their budget in monthly installments. Budgets are adjusted each year for inflation, new programs and changes in their volume of services.

As in the United States, physicians practice in diverse individual and group settings, and most are paid on a fee-for-service basis rather than salary. Provincial medical associations determine the structure of a binding fee schedule and negotiate with governments, usually on an annual basis, a percentage increase in the total pool of money budgeted for physicians.

In most provinces, if the fees billed to the provincial insurance fund exceed the budget ceiling, the government grants less than it otherwise would at the next round of negotiations. Escalating physician costs —largely because of increases in procedures per patient—have led most Canadian provinces to explore more explicit limits on total payments to physicians.

As Figure 1 shows, growth patterns of Canadian and U.S. health care expenditures were nearly identical until 1971, when Canada implemented its national insurance plan. Then U.S. health expenditures rose considerably faster, to increase health-care spending from 9 percent of the total goods and services in the economy to 12 percent.

A good system should provide high quality care, timely treatment, good working conditions for health care professionals and other workers, and ultimately a satisfied and healthy citizenry. On these questions, it is time to separate myth from fact.

Myth 1. *National Health Insurance leads to bureaucratic red tape and high administrative costs.*

Canada's national health insurance is a federal plan that the pronvinces administer. Canada's doctors and hospitals receive all payments from a provincial ministry. They don't have to keep track of eligibility requirements or definitions of insured services in hundreds of insurance plans. Canadian patients never have to file claims. Americans, by contrast, file multiple, complicated claims.

Because of the simplicity of the Canadian system, administrative costs are negligible by American standards. The gap between U.S. and Canadian administrative costs has been widening steadily since Canada completed its program. (See figure 2.)

Myth 2. *NHI interferes with the doctor-patient relationship.*

An increasing number of companies trim health care costs by adopting alternatives such as health maintenance organizations or preferred provider organization. In Canada, citizens have no restrictions on their choice of physicians; physicians do not have to obtain approval from administrators for treatment they recommend. If freedom of choice is the deciding criterion for many people, it actually works in favor of the Candadian model.

Myth 3. *NHI leads to long treatment queues.*

Every country has waiting lists for elective procedures, sometimes even essential ones. Americans treated in hospital emergency rooms, particularly in big cities, often have to wait hours for critical care.

Overall rates of hospital use per capita are considerably higher in Canada than in the United States. Yet there have developed long waiting lists for some services, particularly for open-heart surgery, and magnetic resonance imaging—the newest radiological procedure for diagnosis.

Myth 4. *NHI lowers the quality of medical care.*

As Table 1 shows, some expensive, high-technology items are less available in Canada than in the United States. It is unclear, however, whether the rates of investment in such technologies in the United States represent a standard for judging other countries.

From *The National Voter*, Vol. 40, No. 5, April/May 1991, pp. 10-11. Adapted from *The American Prospect*, Fall 1990. © 1990 by Theodore R. Marmor. Reprinted by permission.

Analysts believe the United States has overinvested and overused some technologies. Canada has a full range of high technology facilities, but there is considerably less abundance and little competition for market share.

If we define quality by some measure that reflects effectiveness of treatment and respect and consideration shown to all patients—not just the affluent and insured—America ranks lower than other countries in the West, including Canada, that have national health insurance.

According to a ten-nation survey published in *Health Affairs*, Canadians are the most satisfied and Americans the least satisfied with their country's health care system. While only 10 percent of Americans surveyed say their health system functions "pretty well," 56 percent of Canadians thought their health care system works well. Eighty-nine percent of Americans say their system needs "fundamental changes" or "complete rebuilding."

Figure 1. Health Expenditures in the United States and Canada as Percent of Gross National Product. Vertical dotted line indicates 1971 when Canada enacted its National Health Insurance.

Myth 5. *NHI leads to rationing.*
Critics warn that Canada "rations" medical care. If by rationing they simply mean limiting services, every country in the world rations health care.

The United States limits services by ability to pay and shows significant differences in access to health care by race, class, and employment circumstances. By contrast, Canada and most other developed coun-

tries attempt to provide more uniform access to the entire population. Medical care depends more on a professional assessment of need than on insurance status.

Because Canadians have free choice of physician, they do not have to worry about rationing. While the rationing choices of an American HMO are private, Canada's choices about spending on hospitals and other health services are publicly debated and democratically decided.

Myth 6. *NHI causes an exodus of physicians.*
Canadian physicians were coming to the United States long before Canada introduced national health insurance. Emigration did not increase significantly afterwards. The ratio of physicians to population has steadily increased and actually grown closer to the U.S. level. In 1987 we had 234 doctors per 1,000 people, while Canada had 216.

Is It Politically Feasible Here?
The public wants broadened, simplified and stable coverage at reasonable out-of-pocket cost. Firms want to reduce their costs of insuring employees and, at the very least, to avoid paying for the health insurance of the unemployed and uninsured.

Although movement toward something

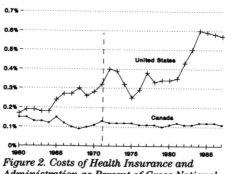

Figure 2. Costs of Health Insurance and Administration as Percent of Gross National Product.

like Canadian national health insurance may appear a large step, most pieces needed for a state insurance program already

are in place. What would it take to make the Canadian model work in the United States? We see two elements:

● Canadians in each providence are insured on the "same terms and conditions."
● Canadians lodge financing responsibility in a ministry of health or its equivalent. It creates more leverage in bargaining with providers.

Modified Universalism
Every Canadian belongs to the same provincial health insurance plan as his neighbor and enjoys the same coverage under the plan. To maintain "equal terms" of access, Canadian doctors have been barred since 1984 from charging patients anything above the government's fee schedule. In these respects, Canada is probably more egalitarian than any other comparable industrial democracy.

Great Britain concentrates financial responsibility in the national ministry of health. Sweden does so in each of its county councils. The lesson for the United States is that there are options.

The more difficult question is whether Canada's public financing and direct government administration are required for political accountability. Public financing makes Canadian outlays for health care highly visible.

Call for Challenge of Status Quo
In the United States of the 1990s, the crucial political problem facing national health insurance advocates may not be the clout of the health insurance industry but the public's hostility toward increased taxes.

Financing medical care out of general tax revenues, as in Great Britain and Canada, seems to reinforce constraints on medical inflation.

The message conveyed to the American public since 1975—that less reliance on government is the key to controlling medical costs—needs to be challenged. That is partly why the Canadian example has become so important.

Can We Afford OLD AGE?

"In America today, we see . . . a large group of people who have little retirement income other than Social Security, and who, because of a limited earnings record, may find even that benefit to be minimal or nonexistent."

Jack Meyer

Mr. Meyer is an economist and president of New Directions for Policy, Washington, D.C. This article is based on policy recommendations to the Ford Foundation Project on Social Welfare and the American Future.

PUBLIC ATTITUDES toward old age in America reflect two contradictory stereotypes. One portrays the elderly as needy, feeble, and dependent. A more recent caricature presents them as affluent, self-absorbed, and overindulged by taxpayers. The realities of old age are more complex, and the prevailing stereotypes serve mainly to distract attention from the real problems. Older citizens once were among the most destitute of Americans. Today, their improved economic status—resulting from a combination of public and private efforts (Social Security, Medicare, tax laws, personal savings, home ownership, etc.)—is a major success of U.S. social welfare policy.

Average per capita income for those older than 65 now is on a par with that per person in younger families, and the aggregate poverty rate for the elderly is below that of younger Americans. Nevertheless, there are huge disparities in resources and protection among them.

Social Security reforms in the past were designed to produce reserves that would help ease the burden of paying for the large number of retiring baby boomers in the 21st century. However, these have not been treated as a form of national savings and investment to enhance economic growth—and thus to increase the resources needed in the coming retirement

bulge. Instead, the Social Security surplus is being used to offset deficits elsewhere in the Federal budget. Meanwhile, Medicare, the national health insurance for the elderly, faces a mounting financial crisis. Current projections indicate that Medicare's Hospital Insurance trust fund will not be able to pay for current services shortly after the turn of the century. The day of reckoning could come even sooner if the experts' rather rosy assumptions about economic growth in the 1990s and the costs of catastrophic illness legislation are not borne out. As our population ages in the years ahead, the situation is going to get worse. Yet, we have not developed a workable public or private insurance approach to cope with the problem of long-term care.

The present system represents a paradoxical mixture of generosity and stinginess, huge spending and equally large gaps. Few realize that the inequality of wealth is greater among the elderly than among other age groups. Moreover, the disparities in old age between the haves and the have-nots likely will grow in the years ahead. This is because of the emerging difference between those depending almost exclusively on the Social Security benefits that will increase more slowly than in the past and those who will have profited from the escalating values of home ownership, tax-favored savings initiated in the 1970s, and expansions in private pension coverage that are most extensive for workers in higher-paying jobs.

There is a burgeoning mismatch between the vulnerability of old people and our social institutions that were designed to assuage it. Those elderly who can contribute more should do so—to help those who have been left behind and ensure a

solvent Medicare system and humane means of long-term care for themselves and others. New policies must not undermine the economic security and opportunity that already have been achieved for older citizens. Still, there are fair, progressive ways for the affluent elderly to help fill the gaps that exist in our social protection system, and we should not shrink from asking them to do so.

Older Americans have three lines of defense against economic hardship. First, almost all have access to Social Security and Medicare, two public social insurance programs to which individuals contribute throughout their working years. The poorest may claim income-tested benefits, mainly in the form of the Supplemental Security Income program, Medicaid, and Food Stamps. As a second line of defense, a significant number have private pensions and health insurance to complement Social Security and Medicare, although these "private" provisions also are subsidized publicly by favorable tax treatment. Finally, a much smaller minority have financial assets that generate significant income to help meet expenses. This combination of supports meets the income needs of most older Americans quite well, but still leaves too many in poverty.

Discussions of Social Security have a habit of concentrating on what will be happening 10, 20, and even 50 years into the future. It also is important to remember income needs that currently are going unmet. Today, Social Security is the single most important source of retirement income for older Americans. If it were not for Social Security benefits, nearly half of our aged, rather than the current 12%, would live in poverty. In general, the

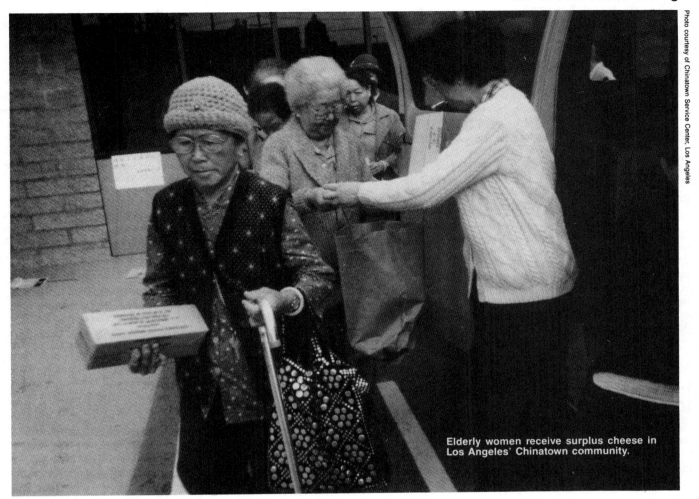

Elderly women receive surplus cheese in Los Angeles' Chinatown community.

lower one's income level, the more important Social Security becomes as a component of the household budget.

About one-third of retirees also have private pension income. Compared with those who are dependent solely on Social Security, they are in a much better position to cover their expenses and stay within reach of their pre-retirement living standard. Those without a private pension are about four times as likely to live below the Federal poverty line as those with such pensions. In the years ahead, the number of retirees with private pensions gradually will increase, a trend reflecting the growth of employer-based pension coverage from the 1940s through the 1970s. Since the late 1970s, however, private pension coverage has declined moderately, and projections show employer-provided pensions will not be available to more than about one-half of the workforce in the foreseeable future. For instance, of the unmarried women who will retire during the next five to 15 years, almost two-thirds will lack private pensions. Over all, nearly half of today's workers receive employer contributions to a private pension, but a smaller proportion actually will see those pensions, in part because some workers still lose pen-

sion protection when they change jobs. Nevertheless, the proportion of people who will benefit from them is higher today than it used to be.

Although many older people possess some assets, few are able to derive significant income from them. Net wealth is distributed much less evenly than either income or private pension coverage, so that the richest five percent of the elderly account for well over half of all the net wealth of older Americans. About one-quarter have no home equity, and many older citizens who are homeowners understandably are reluctant to re-mortgage their houses to generate income through reverse annuity mortgages.

In America today, we see—or, rather, we too often fail to see—a large group of people who have little retirement income other than Social Security, and who, because of a limited earnings record, may find even that benefit to be minimal or nonexistent. They lack private pensions and are in no position to gain either the current tax advantages or long-range protection that's produced by salary-reduction plans, individual retirement accounts (IRAs), Keogh plans, etc. These destitute people are most likely to be living alone, to

be very old, of minority race, and female. Single women represent almost two-thirds of the 3,500,000 elderly persons living in poverty. Despite the rising living standards and economic security of the elderly in the aggregate, this large subgroup lacks adequate resources to meet basic housing, food, and health-care needs.

Many measures might have a long-term impact in helping the poorest of older Americans. An expansion of private pensions could be encouraged through tax breaks, for example, and reverse annuity mortgages could be made more accessible. Many poor also would benefit eventually from changes in long-term care. However, there is one program that can help destitute old people now. Supplemental Security Income (SSI) offers Federally financed cash benefits representing 77% of the poverty level for individuals and 91% for couples. Somewhat fewer than half of SSI beneficiaries receive a very modest state supplement and the real value of these supplements has declined by half since their initiation in the mid 1970s. About one-half of those eligible for SSI benefits do not even participate in the program. Moreover, more than half of the elderly poor can not get financial help with the unreimbursed costs of Medicare treatment because they are not on the SSI rolls and thus have trouble meeting Medicaid eligibility rules.

To improve basic income support for the impoverished aged, it is recommended that there should be an increase in Federal SSI benefits to assure minimum poverty-line incomes for those without other sources of income; an easing of restrictive limits on liquid assets in order to qualify for SSI; and a more effective outreach program to increase participation among those eligible for SSI.

Protection for tomorrow

Social Security is likely to provide a basic minimum income for most Americans who retire in the future. Contrary to some popular impressions, the main danger in the years to come is not that the system will go broke. It is that the Federal government will consume the financial surplus that should be accumulating toward the day when the unusually large baby-boom generation begins to retire.

The Social Security amendments of 1983 averted a crisis in the program and also were designed to set it on a sustainable long-term path. The reforms reflected a roughly even division between tax and benefit changes. Scheduled payroll tax increases were accelerated, a portion of benefits above certain income levels was taxed for the first time, and the normal retirement age was raised starting in the early part of the 21st century and reaching age 67 in the year 2022.

With these changes—and with moderate assumptions about economic growth, mortality, and fertility—the Social Security system should be healthy for the next 50 years. Of course, it is possible that weaker economic growth and smaller increases in productivity and real wages could produce trouble in the 21st century. Even should these possibilities occur, however, solvency could be maintained without Draconian measures. It is difficult to imagine a future in which a payroll tax increase of about one to one and one-half points would fail to remedy any revenue shortfall. Such an increase probably would have some adverse effects on employment, but its impact certainly would be no greater than that of the payroll tax increases we have weathered in the last several decades.

The real problem to be faced in Social Security financing is not actuarial, but political. The balance in the Old Age, Survivors' and Disability Insurance (OASDI) trust fund, which is the source of benefit payments to eligible retirees, must grow now to avert a deficit later. The balance in the OASDI trust fund, totaling $109,000,000,000 in 1988, likely will triple to $352,000,000,000 in 1997, and could grow to trillions of dollars during the next two or three decades. These surpluses represent the

necessary accumulations for the long-range solvency of the system.

The more immediate danger is that the growing balance in the trust fund will be diverted in ways that remove these accumulations from the pool of savings and put them into current consumption. Every politician can develop a laundry list of new spending initiatives, or bailouts for old programs, that could be funded from the surplus.

Although Social Security has achieved a delicate financial balance over the long term, Medicare is headed for financial trouble in the near future. Current projections indicate that the Hospital Insurance trust fund will be exhausted in the early part of the 21st century. A weaker-than-expected economic performance would hasten the day of reckoning, as would health-care costs that grow more rapidly than anticipated. The Hospital Insurance trust fund that covers Part A, or the hospital part, of Medicare gradually will build a somewhat large balance in the next several years, and then quickly become exhausted about 15 years from now. By contrast, the OASDI fund will accumulate huge positive balances that dwarf the size of the very temporary positive balances in the Medicare fund.

The Medicare health insurance system, a vital source of protection for tens of millions of older Americans, must be kept solvent. In 1989, legislation enacted by Congress added to Medicare by providing protection against catastrophic acute-care expenses. That coverage will be financed through a combination of monthly premium increases and a tax liability surcharge on senior citizens. This is a worthwhile improvement that will help safeguard older Americans from some devastatingly large health bills. However, we should realize that the premium increases that finance this new coverage will do almost nothing to remedy the underlying financial imbalances in the existing Medicare system. If those added premiums fail to keep pace with the cost of the extra coverage, the imbalances will loom even larger.

The central challenge in Medicare is to devise ways of bringing expected outlays and revenues into line with each other through a combination of cost-control measures, premium increases, and higher taxes. Health-cost management techniques put in place in recent years, such as the payment system for hospital reimbursement, will continue to help. However, most experts do not expect that such cost-control measures will avoid the painful choices between raising taxes and increasing the financial contributions that the elderly make to Medicare. The situation is made more difficult by the fact that the program is headed for trouble even though it hardly addresses one of the most important and rapidly growing needs—long-term care for chronic illness. Consequently, it seems

likely that Medicare is going to require both new cost-control measures and new money so the program can assure actuarial soundness in the Hospital Insurance trust fund and extend a greater measure of government protection for long-term care.

Although cost-containment policies are in place for hospitals, Medicare needs a new system of paying individual physicians to help bring their spending under control. The current system underwrites cost escalation and fails to create incentives for physicians to economize on the use of health services. Other measures might include a greater emphasis on alternative health-care delivery systems and more government efforts to steer Medicare patients toward those "preferred providers" who charge reasonable fees and have demonstrated their cost-effectiveness. These reforms are easier to outline than to implement. One should not underestimate the difficulty of decelerating Medicare expenditures without jeopardizing the quality of health care or access to it.

Even though our society spends about $100,000,000,000 per year on Medicare and approximately $50,000,000,000 on Medicaid, the elderly remain vulnerable to the costs of lingering illnesses and disabilities. These can be huge ($20-30,000 annually for nursing home care), and they remain largely outside the social-insurance model of protection.

The U.S. health-care system drastically is imbalanced in dealing with long-term care. Many of the long-term needs of older people are more social than medical in nature. They involve lingering disability, rather than disease; are enduring or degenerative, rather than episodic or traumatic; and are largely outside the purview of doctors and hospitals. Yet, health care financing for the elderly still is designed for the traditional physician-directed, medical model of hospital care and short-term episodes of acute illness.

The insurance system also is quite fragmented. Care of the elderly calls for an integrated approach to acute and chronic needs. In some cases, a properly managed acute care system can help avoid the need for long-term care to the extent that it emphasizes prevention, recovery, and independence for patients who have had acute care episodes. At present, however, reimbursement systems for hospitals and doctors are separate from and poorly coordinated with those for home-care attendants, medical-equipment suppliers, and nursing homes. The public system of reimbursement is not coordinated well with the private voluntary network that provides services such as meals-on-wheels, companionship, and transportation for the elderly.

The result is a regrettable mismatch between needs and services. The most complex, heroic, and often hopeless medical procedures to prolong life routinely are covered, while preventive care, long-term help for chronic disability, rehabilitation, and health education often are neglected. Expensive institutional care is reimbursed heavily, but many home- and community-based services are not covered well. Some middle- and upper-middle-income people with minor medical needs pay little for their care, since they are covered for these routine problems by the combination of Medicare and private "Medigap" insurance. Others who are financially comfortable suddenly may be reduced to poverty should they require long-term care that falls outside the public and private insurance systems. Although the very rich can afford these services and the very poor are covered by Medicaid, all others in need of long-term care are thrown back on their own resources. Once they have "spent down" and become completely destitute, a welfare program in the form of Medicaid comes to the rescue on condition that they enter or remain in a nursing home.

The gap between changing needs and the traditional insurance system will become even larger as our population ages. Today, about 3,000,000 people, slightly more than one percent of the population, are 85 years of age or older. In the coming decades, this figure is projected to continue growing to at least 16,000,000 people, or five percent of the population, by the middle of the 21st century. Since we know that the need for assistance with the activities of daily living rises sharply with advancing age, demographics demand that we find ways to finance long-term care efficiently and fairly.

There is something fundamentally wrong with a system in which people must impoverish themselves to find even minimally decent care in their final years. People disagree about how much the government, as opposed to the private sector, should be involved in a new insurance-based approach to financing long-term care. This question is important, but, in our view, the critical issue is to move toward an insurance-based model—whatever the combination of public and private insurance—instead of the present system that relies so heavily on asset depletion and welfare.

The three major sectors of social protection—the private insurance industry, government insurance programs, and the voluntary sector—must participate actively in solving the long-term-care problem. We recommend the use of public subsidies to encourage the spread of private long-term-care insurance, recognizing that, without government participation, many people will be left uncovered and in jeopardy. These subsidies should be national in scope, although this expanded role for the Federal government does not rule out state government involvement.

Government's role could take the form of Medicare coverage for long-term-care expenses after the elderly have incurred a certain amount of out-of-pocket costs. This approach should be supplemented by government subsidies for the purchase of private long-term-care insurance by lower-income households. In this way, government would help people insure themselves against the front-end expenses associated with long-term-care and would provide public coverage for the bigger costs of extended care.

Although some might prefer that the government provide full insurance coverage for long-term care through Part C of Medicare, such a program appears beyond our Federal budget constraints at this time. A more targeted approach to government involvement is appropriate. In particular, the following are needed:

● Encouraging private insurance for long-term care, by means of labor-management efforts to integrate such insurance into a flexible benefit package, as well as targeted subsidies to help lower-income people purchase private insurance.
● Educating the public about the need for long-term-care protection.
● Greater coordination of acute- and long-term-care benefits, using savings from a better-managed acute-care system—with less unnecessary care—to help finance an extension of long-term-care coverage.
● Greater public and private insurance coverage for home care.
● Better organization and use of the private nonprofit sector to provide coordinated services to the elderly, since many of the types of services they need (transportation, delivered meals, counseling) are not provided normally by an insurance-based system.
● Respite care sponsored by community organizations to relieve the spouses and children who care for disabled people. Business can help by arranging for counseling and some flexibility in work time for employees who also are care givers.

The price tag

These cash-assistance reforms would cost about $2,600,000,000 in new spending during the first year. This total is dominated heavily by the proposed increase in SSI benefits. The estimate of $2,500,000,000 for this new step represents the cost of closing about one-half of the gap between the Federal poverty line and the current level of SSI benefits. It would be possible to recommend a larger increase that would close the gap completely. However, it is important to recognize fiscal constraints and the need to meet long-term goals in stages. It is worth noting that the additional $100,000,000 recommended for easing the SSI asset test would permit more than a doubling of the very low asset limits that now screen many low-income senior citizens out of SSI.

Estimates of the cost of greater government involvement in long-term care for the elderly are highly sensitive to assumptions about several program parameters. For example, adding long-term-care coverage to Medicare will cost much more if it becomes available immediately, considerably less if the elderly must spend their own resources for a substantial period of time before qualifying. Obviously, the greater the degree of asset protection under a public program, the greater the government outlay. The estimate provided here—about $7,000,000,000—is that of a program with a three-year waiting period. This estimate also includes a small amount of funding to begin a program that helps lower-income people purchase private long-term-care insurance. If the waiting period were reduced to two years, the expense would rise to about $15,000,000,000. A program with a rather short waiting period of a few months would run $30-40,000,000,000.

Other factors that affect the estimates include whether home care is included in the benefit package, the co-insurance rate (the proportion of bills paid by patients and their families), and the provider payment rates (nursing home reimbursement rates). Costs can be held down, for example, by raising the co-insurance rate or lowering payments to providers. However, such steps, if carried too far, could defeat the program's goals. A universal entitlement program for long-term-care with a short or no waiting period, low co-insurance rates, and full coverage for home and institutional care might cost the government $30-40,000,000,000 during the first year. New government spending on that scale isn't likely, given the existing deficit.

A more realistic solution would involve either a two- or three-year waiting period for Federal coverage, co-insurance rates on the order of 30%, and a standard that specifies the degree of disability that is required for eligibility. People would be expected to obtain private insurance to help them cover expenses during the waiting period, but the government would subsidize a portion of the premium on a sliding-scale basis for those who can not afford it. Under such an arrangement, Medicare benefits would begin where the private coverage ends. The difficulty of setting and maintaining a standard of disability for coverage, however, should not be underestimated.

In addition to the net increase of about $7,000,000,000 in government outlays, there also would be a big change in the mix of government spending, from the Federal-state sharing of costs that occurs today under Medicaid to a largely Federal-only spending approach under the new program. This would open up some interesting possibilities of tradeoffs. States could take over some of the funding from the Federal government in areas such as economic development in return for the Federal government's expanded role in long-term-care.

HEADING FOR HARDSHIP:
The Future of Older Women in America

Fran Leonard and Laura Loeb

Ms. Leonard, a California-based attorney, is an expert on legal and economic issues of older women. Ms. Loeb, an attorney, is former director of public policy, the Older Woman's League, Washington, D.C.

"Women will need to rely more on private savings to supplement their retirement income, given their lower Social Security and pension benefits."

WHEN today's 25-year-old woman retires, after having been employed for as long as 35 years, she can expect the same retirement benefits—adjusted only for inflation—that her mother received. For most women, decades of Social Security contributions will translate into virtually the same retirement benefits as those paid to their mothers, who may never have earned wages or paid Social Security taxes.

Women continue to pour into the paid workforce, but retirement income does not reflect their growing contributions. In 1970, women received 70% of the Social Security benefits men received; by 1989, that percentage had grown to just 73%. In 1974, women's average private pension income was 73% of men's; by 1987, that ratio had plummeted to 58%.

By the year 2020, Social Security and pension systems practically will have ended poverty among older men and couples, but it will remain widespread among older women living alone—those who are divorced, widowed, or never married.

Social Security and pension systems benefit male work patterns. Designed when lifestyles were dramatically different, the system best serves "traditional" families consisting of a lifelong breadwinner, a lifelong homemaker, and two children. Less than 10% of American families fit that definition today; even fewer will do so in the future.

Despite significant legislative reforms, fundamental biases against women persist in retirement income programs. Social Security discriminates against females by penalizing dual-earner families, caregivers, divorced spouses, and people who retire early and live long. Wives who are entitled both to benefits on their own work record and benefits from their husband may collect only one. With women's wages remaining low, most collect from their husbands' contribution. Since 1960, the percentage of women receiving a dependent's benefit has remained at 62%, despite more females in the workforce.

As long as women continue to assume greater child and elder parent care responsibilities, are paid less than men, and live longer, these biases will take an enormous toll on their retirement income. Unless Social Security and pension systems are revised radically, older women will remain significantly poorer than older men. With the baby boom generation only 20 years from retirement, escalating distortions in retirement incomes for men and women will become a political hot potato of immense proportions.

The future will not get any brighter for women unless fundamental changes are made in our nation's Social Security and pension programs. Contrary to the notion shared by most younger women that the equal rights battles already have been fought and won, there is no indication that they will face a retirement future any different from that of their grandmothers. Demographic and sociological factors will make the so-called golden years "beholdin' years" for many.

Almost three-quarters of the elderly living below poverty levels are female, approximately 2,500,000 over age 65. More than two out of every five older women are poor or near poor.

When today's 25-year-old retires, fewer women still will be married and, therefore, have access to a husband's retirement income. Seven of 10 baby boom females will outlive their husbands and can expect a widowhood of at least 15 years. In the year 2030, one of every three women over 65 will be married, compared to 40% today; more than one of every five will be divorced, a 400% increase.

Despite many more females being in the workplace, a young woman continues to face a future of significantly lower wages. Women now are earning 66 cents for every dollar men do. Employment discrimination and women's work patterns have kept and will continue to keep their wages far below men's.

Caregiving responsibilities continue to fall predominantly on women. Men may be changing more diapers and balancing more accounts for their aging parents, but most are not taking significantly more time away from work for caregiving. Females average 11.5 years away from the labor force; males, 1.3. Instead of more men remaining at home for caregiving, women are assuming the roles of breadwinner and caregiver.

Social insecurity

The Social Security Act was enacted in 1935 as the cornerstone of the New Deal. The program was designed to provide Americans with protection against the loss of wages due to retirement, disability, or death. Although the language of the act is gender-neutral, the program was designed to best meet the needs of a typical American family that is no longer typical. As long as the underlying false premises of the program remain unchanged, future generations of women will continue to receive Social Security benefits significantly lower than men's.

Social Security is a system of "worker" and "dependent" benefits. A woman receives benefits either by working the requisite number of years in covered employment or by being married to a man who qualifies for a worker benefit and receiving half of his benefit. A woman who qualifies for benefits on her own work record and also qualifies as a spouse is said to be dually entitled, but receives only the higher of the two benefits.

A lifetime homemaker does not receive Social Security protection in her own right. She only receives a spouse benefit equal to half of what her husband receives.

For the homemaker who divorces, half a benefit is not enough on which to live. A divorced woman is eligible to receive a spouse benefit if she had been married at least 10 years. However, half of her former husband's benefit is not half of what they would receive as a couple. Together, they were receiving 150% of his worker's Social Security. Apart, she only gets 50%—not 75%—leaving many divorced lifetime homemakers with benefits way below the poverty line. The average spouse benefit for a woman in 1989 was $294 a month.

Among retired workers receiving Social Security benefits on their own employment records, the average male gets nearly 25% more than the average female ($639 to $488). Because Social Security benefits are wage-based, women's continuing lower earnings translate into lower retirement benefits.

Women's work patterns are penalized strongly under Social Security. All Americans born in 1929 or later will have their Social Security benefit calculated as their average earnings over a 35-year period. Since 1950, the length of the com-

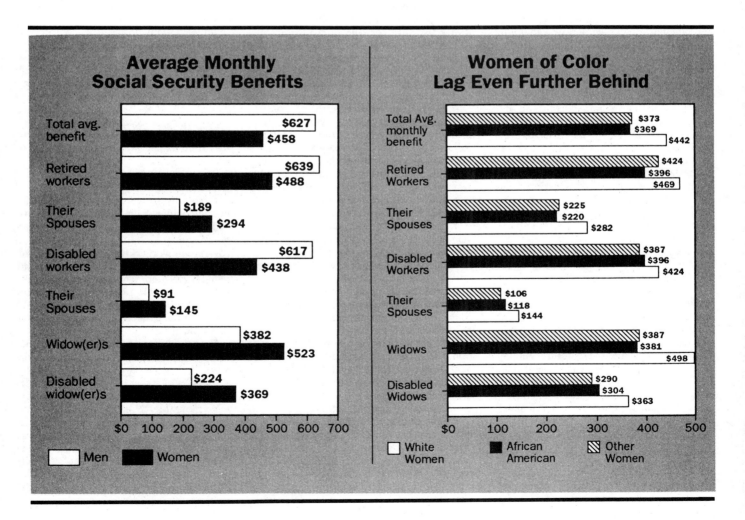

putation period has increased by a year each year. The computation period will reach its maximum of 35 years for those who reach age 62 in 1991 or later.

Persons with fewer years of covered income within the computation period have a zero averaged into their earnings record for each missing year. Men generally work 35 years or more, but women do not. Even by the year 2030, fewer than four in 10 females will have worked 35 years or more. The remaining 60% thus will have zeroes averaged into their earnings records.

Under current law, persons can drop five "zero years," but women average 11.5 years out of the workforce, compared to 1.3 for men. Additionally, average earnings of a working woman drop $3,000 the year a child is born and about $5,000 to $6,000 annually over the next two years. These periods of lower earnings are used to compute an average amount upon which Social Security benefits are based.

Women who are both homemakers and wage earners are particularly disadvantaged. A woman dually entitled to both a worker benefit on her earnings and a spouse benefit on her husband's can receive only the greater of the two—often the spouse benefit. If the latter is higher, those years a woman worked and paid into the system through payroll taxes will not be reflected in an increased benefit. She will receive the same spouse benefit as if she never worked outside the home.

Since 1960, the percentage of women drawing a benefit based on their own work record has remained constant, despite more women working today. Thirty-eight percent of female beneficiaries drew benefits on their work record in 1960 as well as in 1988. The number dually entitled on both their record and that of their husband increased over this period from five to 22%, but for these women, their dependent benefit on their husband's record was greater.

Two-earner married couples also are penalized under the current system. Because a spouse only receives the higher of benefits based on her work record or her spouse benefits based on her husband's record, dual-income couples with similar incomes can receive lower Social Security benefits than a couple with only one earner.

Women today and in the future will pay more into the Social Security system than their mothers and grandmothers. Rising payroll taxes, higher wages, and increased labor force participation mean that females are paying more into the system, but not necessarily getting more out. The payroll tax increased from 7.15 to 7.65% on the first $53,400 of income—for a maximum tax of $4,085 a year. In 1970, the tax rate was 4.8% on a wage base of $7,800—for a maximum tax of $374 a year. Given that so few females will qualify for benefits on their own employment record even by the year 2030, these higher taxes will not lead to proportionate increases in benefits.

Penny pensions

Pension law and practices, such as the lack of mandatory coverage and portability, heavily disfavor women's work patterns. Policymakers like to describe an adequate retirement income as a three-legged stool, supported by Social Security, a pension, and individual savings. Unfortunately for women, the pension leg is often missing, producing a shaky future far too often.

Improvements in pension coverage on the job will not translate to gender parity when benefits are paid in the next century. Today, more than twice as many men over age 65 receive pension income on their own work record as do women (46% to 23.5%). While the percentage of female beneficiaries should improve somewhat in the coming decades, the dollar gap between men's and women's pension income will remain high. In 1987, the mean pension income for males over 65 was $659 a month, compared to $394 for females. Currently, a mere three percent of women are receiving a surviving spouse pension benefit, because most couples waive survivor's benefits in order to receive higher benefits while both are living.

Job mobility penalizes women heavily in pension coverage because most plans require five years on the job before pension rights become vested. Half of all males have been on their current job less than 5.1 years; half of all females, 3.7. Women's job mobility is due to family responsibilities, following transferred husbands, and leaving dead-end jobs. Because benefits typically are calculated on final earnings, women's pensions often are based on outdated wages, with no indexing for inflation. A recent Labor Department study showed that, if a man and woman each worked 40 years—he in the same job and she in four different jobs with the same pension plan at all times—his pension would be twice hers.

Women are more likely to work in small businesses and for lower pay, neither of which are associated with pension coverage. Fewer than half of workers who earn less than $1,000 a month are covered by a pension plan, while more than three out of four paid more than that are covered. Only 25% of employers with less than 25 employees offer pension coverage, while 89% with more than 1,000 workers do.

Many flexible job arrangements made to accommodate working women's family responsibilities greatly will diminish their future retirement income. Consultancies, part-time and shared jobs, seasonal employment, and home-based self-employment are virtually unprotected by pension coverage.

Two of three part-time workers are female. Federal law allows employers to exclude employees working less than 20 hours a week or 1,000 hours a year from pension coverage.

State and local government workers are not protected by Federal pension law. State and local pensions are creatures of their own legislatures, and chaos reigns. In some states, public pensions are organized by political subdivision; in others, by occupational class. Some 17,000,000 full- and part-time government workers and their spouses are caught in this maze.

Federal law does not require states to consider private pensions as property subject to division upon divorce. A change in 1985 only required pension plan administrators to abide by court orders in states that consider a pension marital property. Among states that divide interests in pensions, many recognize only a vested one that is presently payable—meaning the worker must be of retirement age before it is divided at divorce.

Women will need to rely more on private savings to supplement their retirement income, given their lower Social Security and pension benefits. Unfortunately for many women, they have a diminished ability to save. In addition, tax reform laws make it more difficult for them to have private individual retirement accounts (IRAs).

Fewer women participate in Individual Retirement Accounts than men do. Over $200,000,000,000 in American retirement savings are in IRAs. Among full-time workers, 20% more males participate in IRAs than females. However, among part-time workers, twice as many women as men contribute to an IRA, suggesting that more part-time female workers view their status as a significant part of their career and prepare for retirement accordingly.

Married working women are penalized substantially by current IRA laws. Both husband and wife are disqualified from tax-deductible IRA contributions above a certain income level if either has pension coverage at work. Since men are more likely than women to have this coverage, females are more likely to be disqualified from a deductible IRA, even though they have no pension benefit in their own right and would need an IRA in case of divorce or widowhood.

Homemakers also are penalized. Under Federal law, if one spouse works outside the home, the couple only can contribute up to a total of $2,250 per year to IRAs, split between them however they would like, so long as no more than $2,000 per year is put into any one account. Normally, each individual wage earner can put up to $2,000 per year into an IRA. Therefore, in effect, the value of a homemaker's work is set at $250. The Federal law has demeaned her status and jeopardized her financial security in the event of divorce or widowhood.

Empirical studies of political opinion and behavior about national issues affecting the aging
have not revealed the intergenerational conflicts often predicted in recent decades. Using
public opinion studies of attitudes about the aging at the community level in Florida, this study
does identify significant cleavages in attitude and belief between generations, suggesting
intergenerational political conflict may be likely in the future. The research implies the most
important source of this conflict may be the community level and the "image" of the aging
that is developing among younger community residents.
Key Words: Retirement politics, Community politics, Aging and politics, Aging and voting,
Political gerontology, Generational conflict, Generational politics

The Unquiet Future of Intergenerational Politics

Walter A. Rosenbaum, PhD,
and James W. Button, PhD

Department of Political Science, 3324 Turlington Hall, University of
Florida, Gainesville, FL 32611. Correspondence should be addressed to
Walter A. Rosenbaum, PhD, at the above address.

For almost two decades, social commentators have been predicting a political confrontation between old and young Americans that has not materialized. Now, many observers cite empirical studies to demonstrate that a generational conflict is unlikely. This revisionist interpretation seems premature. Evidence of generational tension has been elusive, we think, in part because investigators have often looked in the wrong place for the wrong thing. If one turns to intergenerational stereotypes and attitudes — to the mutual images that contemporary generations hold of one another — social, economic and political dissonance does appear. And it appears at the community level, within the context of local government and politics.

We have found the data suggestive of these conclusions largely in the contemporary images and attitudes that old and young elicit from each other in Florida, an especially advantageous setting for an intergenerational study. In the Sunshine State, where almost 1 in 5 residents has reached retirement age (the highest proportion in the nation), generational relationships and their social consequences are thrown into particularly sharp relief and continually examined through politics, the media and daily civic life. With this large retirement population, moreover, Florida is frequently presumed to be an augury of graying America, the state where political and economic transformations implicit in the demographic aging of the U.S. population will be foreshadowed.

The perceptual foundations of generational political relationships have been relatively unexplored. Instead, public policy preferences and issue concerns have been the customary social barometers for generational conflict. Attitudes and stereotypes, however, should be especially important when intergenerational politics is discussed because, as many commentators have observed, it is the social image of the aging as much as any other social attribute that has fortified the elderly's political status. America's aging, as Roger Cobb and Charles Elder have aptly observed, have enjoyed a "peculiar potency" and "a special legitimacy" as claimants for budgetary priority in the political struggle for governmental resources (Elder & Cobb, 1984). To many observers, like gerontologist Eric Kingson, a deterioration in the public image upon which the political privilege of the aging is grounded is a bellwether of generational tension. "The budgetary politics of recent years," he has warned, "have placed the elderly interest-groups and elder advocates on the defensive, threatening . . . to reduce their legitimacy and [to] change the perception of the elderly population as a group deserving of government support" (Kingson, 1988, p. 771). The contemporary literature on generational conflict, in fact, is rich in assumptions about the social perceptions and attitudes that incite or perpetuate generational tensions. Since our survey protocols are largely derived from these studies, it will be helpful to review briefly those aspects most important in shaping the substance and administration of the survey questionnaire.

Age, Social Imagery and Generational Conflict

Generational amity has prevailed during the last several decades in defiance of the many jeremiads predicting its collapse as far back as 1951 (Longman, 1987). These predictions, increasing notably in the last 20 years, have awakened substantial concern among public advocates and organizational representatives for the elderly. Throughout the 1970s a

From *The Gerontologist*, Vol. 33, No. 4, August 1993, pp. 481-490. © 1993 by the Gerontological Society of America.
Reprinted by permission.

variety of observers, from academic gerontologists to political advocates of the aging, began to warn about a real, or potential, rise in resentment toward the aging as a result of their growing entitlements and political power (Longman, 1987; Schuck, 1979).

Dark prophecies of generational discontent, feeding on assumptions about the deteriorating social image of the aging, multiplied through the 1980s. The aging population was growing bigger and, said many critics, much greedier (Barnes, 1991; Huddy, 1989; Reeves, 1988; Tolchin, 1988). It seemed to many observers that older Americans had truncated Reaganomics to a single political principle — me first! — which they celebrated for a decade in their ferocious determination to expand already generous entitlements. The 1980s were also years of large, inflating federal deficits and diminishing federal spending for youth — the politically volatile ingredients perhaps sufficient to ignite a generational confrontation.

From Needy to Greedy Old

The new imagery of the aging was a composite of several qualities that suggested the design of this study's survey questionnaire. Many commentators saw in an expanding older population the foreshadow of a political gerontocracy forged from the aging's political power. "You're going to have [a society] ruled by old people," warned one business consultant in a major metropolitan newspaper, popularizing an idea already gaining public attention elsewhere (Philadelphia Inquirer, 1989; see also Grubb & Lazerson, 1982; Oberhofer, 1989; Petersen, 1991; Walker, 1990). In a more scholarly manner, Alan Pifer alerted readers of the *Annals of the American Academy* a few years earlier about the potential political problem in an enlarging older population: ". . . public officials, because of the voting strength of the elderly, may direct too much money in their direction, and too little towards other groups that lack voting strength" (Pifer, 1986; see also Hudson, 1980; and Hudson, 1978).

The provocative contrast between the aging's steadily enlarging share of the federal budget and the diminishing entitlements of the young also caused many commentators to warn of a political backlash. The entitlement gap emerged as a national issue in 1984 when Samuel Preston's *Scientific American* article reported a decline in health and education levels of American children and noted that the proportion of children in poverty was vastly greater than the proportion of the elderly poor and federal expenditures for the aging vastly exceeded that for children (Preston, 1984a). The media repeated and amplified this theme (Preston, 1984b). By 1991, a *Business Week* article posed the provocative question "Is Uncle Sam Shortchanging Young Americans?" and answered in the affirmative (Bernstein, 1991).

The decade's apotheosis in scholarly polemics against the federal budget's generational inequities was Phillip Longman's 1987 book *Born To Pay*, a longer version of his earlier, widely discussed *Atlantic Magazine* article. "So long as the wealthy elderly demand, in addition to return on their capital, to be provided with across-the-board old age subsidies," warned Longman, "the resentment of the young in general can only increase. . ." (Longman, 1987, p. 32). Despite evidence that social welfare during the 1980s was no zero-sum game in which the young were losing to the elderly (Jencks & Torrey, 1988), and Social Security would not necessarily discriminate against future generations (Aaron, 1989), arguments to the contrary continued to receive considerable media attention.

With increasing frequency during the 1980s, the aging were also portrayed in the media as self-indulgent and self-absorbed, as in a 1988 *Fortune* article on the American Association of Retired Persons (AARP): "Think of the American Association of Retired Persons as grandfather, very big and very rich . . . When grandfather taps his knife on the water glass, as he is doing now, everyone at the table pays attention. It could be the start of an expensive new project, and everyone else might have to give up at least a second helping of dinner" (Smith, 1988, p. 96). Apparently, grandfather (and grandmother) were quite comfortable with their newly affluent aspect. Phillips quotes an AARP media kit of the mid-1980s: "50 & Over people . . . They've got clout! Affluent . . . Aware . . . Active Buyers with over $500 billion to spend . . . They're spending on self-fulfillment *now* . . . rather than leaving sums behind."

Will There Be A Backlash?

The generational equity issue continues to worry many advocates and representatives for the aging. In 1986, The Gerontological Society of America published a major study, *Ties That Bind: The Interdependence of Generations*, intended to refute the growing literature on generational inequities while emphasizing the mutual dependence of American generations (Kingson, Hirshorn & Harootyan, 1986; see also Kingson, 1988).

Belatedly, the AARP initiated publicity and programs to defuse the generational equity issue and to refute the notion of generational conflict. Many advocates for the aging, like Ron Pollack, the Executive Director of Families United for Senior Action Foundation, believe the aging have already sustained significant political damage from their new stereotype (Skinner & Kinney, 1991). Reviewing the politics of the 1980s, gerontologist Fernando Torres-Gil recently concluded that the causes and consequences of generational conflict might be exaggerated, but "Despite the efforts of gerontologists to discount the generational conflict thesis . . . tensions are increasing between generations. . ." (Torres-Gil, 1992, p. 87).

The Elusive Evidence of Generational Conflict

Apprehension about generational antagonisms would seem ill-founded if one examined only the generational policy preferences upon which most empirical studies of generational conflict currently depend. Generally, these studies gauge the intensity of generational conflict by examining: (a) public policy preferences or attitudes about public policy which are widely shared within age groupings and, especially, that create significant cleavages between older and younger age cohorts; or, (b) voting patterns among the aging which distinguish them from younger voters or suggest significant issue cleavages across generations. These studies usually focus upon age-related policies such as Social Security, entitlement formulas, the generational equity of federal budget allocations and, less frequently, the degree of issue preference and consensus among the aging.

Policy Studies

Studies of policy preferences among generations, with few exceptions, provide scant evidence of intergenerational conflict, even over policies most likely to incite tension. Cook and Barret's 1986 study of public attitudes toward Social Security, for instance, found "few differences in supportiveness across age groups" and "little evidence" of diminishing support among younger Americans (Cook and Barret, 1988, p. 354). Other policy studies generally support the conclusions reported by Michael Ponza and his co-authors in their review of the University of Michigan's 1973 and 1986 General Social Surveys. "Taken as a whole," they conclude, "the results provide no support whatsoever for the 'cohort' view . . . that the elderly favor redistributive transfers away from low-income families with children and toward low-income families of their own age group." Moreover, ". . . lobbying efforts for programs that benefit the elderly are successful because they are consistent with the willingness of individuals in *all* age groups to support the elderly" (Ponza, Duncan, Corcoran, & Groskind, 1989, pp. 6–7; see also Day, 1990, p. 61; and Campos, 1986).

Studies focused on attitudes among the aging concerning almost all age-related policy issues generally uncover no mind-set common to the aging. Political scientists Laurie Rhodebeck and Roy Fitzgerald, for instance, examined political attitudes among the aging reported in seven National Election Studies conducted by the University of Michigan's Survey Research Center between 1972 and 1986. "The cumulative evidence," they conclude, "still points toward lack of unambiguous group-oriented interests among older Americans..." (Rhodeback & Fitzgerald, 1989, pp. 6–7; see also Beck & Dye, 1982).

Voting Studies

Studies of candidate and party preference among the aging, like policy studies, seldom reveal significant associations between age and voting choice that cannot be explained by other socioeconomic factors such as income, occupation or race. Even when an age-based voting pattern has been identified, it is apparently transient (Freiman & Grasso, 1982; see also Day, 1990; Foner, 1972; Rhodebeck & Fitzgerald, 1989; Schmidhauser, 1970).

But what about local education? Here, the elderly bear a distinctive stigma. The aging, so runs a common indictment, incite generational animosities by their pervasive hostility to local school bond referenda, tax increases or other pocketbook measures to support the schools. The elderly's "anti-education" bias, in fact, is a verity to many local public officials. The evidence supporting this "anti-education" assumption, however, is meager and inconclusive. Recent studies by Mullins and Rosentraub, and by Haas and Preston, for example, suggest that an increase in the size of retirement populations may have a positive effect on local government spending for education (Mullins & Rosentraub, 1990; see also Haas, 1989; and Haas & Serow, 1991). In contrast, Button's recent study of voting by the elderly in Florida local school bond elections suggests that the aging often — but not always — vote against local school bonds (Button, 1992). The pervasive "anti-education" bias among aging has yet to be persuasively demonstrated (Button & Rosenbaum, 1989).

Beyond Issues and Voting: Exploring Images and Stereotypes

Studies of issue preferences and voting patterns within or between generations provide little insight concerning development and change in the social and political image of the aging. Moreover, issue and voting studies have given little attention to the quality of generational relationships evolving at the local level, especially within communities where the young and old are daily, intimately brought into contact through the most ordinary civic rituals.

Sociopolitical image, however, is explicitly and implicitly a matter of enormous concern to scholars and social commentators writing about current intergenerational tensions. A sensitivity to stereotype and image as a potential source of generational tension is sensible, even essential. It reflects an awareness, well established in sociology and social psychology, that group attitudes and group beliefs about social reality are often the grounding and inspiration for social action. Equally important, attitude, belief or stereotype are often the *precursors* to action, the early warnings of imminent social events, the barometers of social change that may tell us that change is possible, or probable, even though the character and import of such change may be unclear. As sociologist Peter Berger observes, the transformation of social image foreshadows the fact of social change: ". . . when we look at revolutions, we find that the outward acts against the old order are invariably preceded by the disintegration of inward allegiance and loyalties. The images of kings topple before their thrones do" (Berger, 1963, p. 51). In short, the quality of intergenerational attitudes and stereotypes manifest today may open a window upon the future or, at the very least, alert us that social change may be imminent even before — perhaps long before — it becomes manifest.

An interest in social image and stereotype as a precursor of generational conflict led to our 1990–1991 Florida public opinion study which explored differences in generational perceptions about the character of the aging and their impact upon communities in which they reside. This study also replicates portions of our 1986 survey concerning attitudes toward the aging among Florida's local government officials and includes, as well, several questions addressed to the Florida public by another survey more than a decade ago (Burton & Rosenbaum, 1990). Thus, we can compare, at least tentatively, generational stereotypes among the public and its local officials and also examine the congruity between this recent study and earlier measures of generational relationships in Florida.

The Florida Survey

In November of 1990 and 1991, 9 items concerning community images and activities associated with the aging were included in the Florida public opinion poll, conducted monthly by the University of Florida's Bureau of Economic and Business Research (BEBR). The BEBR telephone poll, involving a variety of political or economic issues, is periodically taken among a random sample of the Florida public and includes standard information about the socioeconomic characteristics of respondents. The sample populations interviewed in November of 1990 and 1991 were representative of Florida citizens along basic demographic dimensions (age, gender and race) and the sample sizes (535 in 1990 and 556 in 1991) provided an acceptable confidence interval for all estimates ($\pm$ 4%). We were primarily concerned with the extent of agreement *within* age categories and disagreement *between* age categories on the items intended to probe generational differences.

The Questions

Five of the survey questions concerned the respondents' beliefs about the political behavior of the aging and their impact upon the local community. Two of these questions in 1990 related to the impact the aging might have on the local community (abbreviations for all variables are in brackets). Respondents were asked the extent to which they agreed with these statements:

The economic benefits brought to my community by older residents do not compensate for the burden they place upon local government. [GOVBURDEN]

Older residents generally help to improve the quality of life in my community. [QUALIFE]

A third item, used only in the 1991 survey, replicated a question used by Douglas St. Angelo in his 1980 survey of attitudes toward the aging in Florida (St. Angelo, 1981):

Do senior citizens in your area have too little political power, too much political power, or about the right amount of political power? [SENPOWER]

Two additional items in the 1990 survey concerned agreement with statements about the political behavior of the aging and its generational impact:

Older persons in my community tend to oppose paying for local public services which do not directly benefit them. [OPPGOVSV]

When older residents in my community advocate government policies that benefit themselves, this often creates political opposition from younger residents. [YOUNGOLD]

Two other questions, the first (originally a Gallup Poll item) used in both surveys and the second in 1990 only, concerned support for the local schools and for local economic growth (Gallup, 1978):

Suppose the local public schools said they needed much more money. As you feel at this time, would you vote to raise taxes for this purpose, or would you vote against raising taxes for this purpose? [EDVOTE]

I think continued economic growth is good for my community. [ECOGROW]

The final two questions in the first survey, adapted from an Eagleton Institute Poll, involved the amount of time spent by the respondents in voluntary local activities — a community service often attributed especially to the aging (Eagleton Institute of Politics, 1987):

Some people get involved in local affairs through donating their time to voluntary organizations — that is, working for no pay for non-profit groups or charity. In the last 12 months, have you volunteered time to any non-profit groups or charities? [CHARITY]

[If 'Yes'] About how many hours in an average month do you do volunteer work for these kinds of organizations? [HOURS]

Generational Consensus and Cleavages

Responses to each of these items concerning the local impact of the aging are presented in Table 1.

The responses to several of these items reveal important, and possibly contentious, differences between age cohorts in their evaluation of the aging. While a substantial majority of each age group believed the aging were generally an economic benefit to their community, about 42% of the younger respondents (those less than 55 years old) did agree with the contrary statement that the aging did not bring benefits to their community that compensate "for the burdens they place on local government." Moreover, about 25% of the older respondents concurred in this negative verdict. (That fully one-fourth of the older respondents may thus be stigmatizing themselves as a community burden is a remarkable statistic worth further study.) Although a clear majority of the age groups also agreed that older residents "generally help to improve the quality of life in my community," slightly more than a third (35%) of younger respondents did not agree that older residents improved their community's quality of life, compared with only 10% of the older respondents. Even on the issue of the aging's political power, where only a small minority of each age group believed that seniors had too much political power, the difference in responses between young and old was notable. Thus, on these items, the response patterns

Table 1. Beliefs About the Local Community Impact of the Aging

Item		Percent of respondents		
		All	<55	55 +
"The economic benefits brought to my community by older residents do not compensate for the burden they place upon local government." [GOVBURDEN]	Strongly disagree	4	4	6
	Disagree	51	47	59
	Don't know	9	7	10
	Agree	32	38	23
	Strongly agree	4	4	2
	(n =)	(491)	(306)	(146)
	T-value = .38, df = 450, p = .71			
"Older residents generally help to improve the quality of life in my community." [QUALIFE]	Strongly disagree	1	1	—
	Disagree	26	34	10
	Don't know	6	4	9
	Agree	62	57	70
	Strongly agree	6	4	11
	(n =)	(497)	(310)	(150)
	T-value = 3.46, df = 458, p = .00			
"Older persons in my community tend to oppose paying for local public services which do not directly benefit them." [OPPGOVSV]	Strongly disagree	1	1	2
	Disagree	36	33	42
	Don't know	12	12	10
	Agree	47	48	46
	Strongly agree	4	6	1
	(n =)	(495)	(311)	(148)
	T-value = −1.15, df = 457, p = .25			
"When older residents in my community advocate government policies that benefit themselves, this often creates political opposition from younger residents." [YOUNGOLD]	Strongly disagree	—	—	—
	Disagree	34	34	30
	Don't know	10	8	15
	Agree	51	52	55
	Strongly agree	4	6	1
	(n =)	(492)	(309)	(148)
	T-value = 2.23, df = 455, p = .03			
"Do senior citizens in your area have too little political power, too much political power, or about the right amount of political power?" [SENPOWER]	Too little	30	29	33
	Right amount or don't know	56	55	58
	Too much	14	17	9
	(n =)	(531)	(350)	(181)
	T-value = 1.21, df = 529, p = .24			
"Suppose the local public schools said they needed much more money. As you feel at this time, would you vote to raise taxes for this purpose, or would you vote against raising taxes?" [EDVOTE]	For taxes	47	47	49
	Don't know	4	2	8
	Against taxes	49	51	43
	(n =)	(496)	(310)	(152)
	T-value = .91, df = 441, p = .36			
"I think continued economic growth is good for my community." [ECOGROW]	Strongly disagree	—	—	—
	Disagree	7	5	9
	Don't know	3	3	2
	Agree	73	73	73
	Strongly agree	18	19	17
	(n =)	(495)	(311)	(151)
	T-value = −1.11, df = 460, p = .27			
"Some people get involved in local affairs through donating their time to voluntary organizations — that is working for no pay for non-profit groups or charity. In the last 12 months, have you volunteered time to any non-profit group or charities?" [CHARITY]	Yes	40	42	39
	No	60	58	61
	(n =)	(498)	(313)	(152)
	T-value = −.62, df = 463, p = .53			
"How many hours in an average month do you volunteer work for these types of organizations?" [HOURS]	Average	16	12	23
	(n =)	(180)	(112)	(67)
	T-value = −2.07, df = 171, p = .04			

Note. Not all percentages equal 100 due to rounding.

often appear to suggest significant generational differences in perception concerning the local impact of the aging.

The most surprising response patterns, however, involve the three items concerned with the aging's attitude about local government services. A majority, or near majority, of *both* age groups agreed with statements that the aging did not want to pay for local services benefitting others and did incite the opposition of younger citizens when they promoted policies to their own advantage. However, younger citizens were more likely to agree with these items than the aging, and the differences on one of these items [YOUNGOLD] were statistically significant. Responses to the third statement, a measure of the respondent's willingness to support increased local school taxes, indicate that a majority in *both* age groups was unwilling to support new taxes or was undecided. These latter responses suggest that while the aging may, as often supposed, resist school taxes, they are not radically different (even statistically) in this respect than younger community residents — which is not often supposed.

The remaining items concerning involvement in local volunteer activities also entail a surprise. The aging, it appears, are no more involved in volunteer work than are younger community members, although the older volunteers tend to serve more hours than younger persons. Thus, approximately 40% of both age groups report some voluntary work, yet this does not seem a notably large proportion of the aging in light of assertions that the aging are distinguished by their community volunteerism.

The Public Mind Mirrored: Elite Images of the Aging

Three items used in the BEBR survey were also used in an earlier study, previously described, concerning beliefs about the aging among Florida's state and local officials (Rosenbaum & Button, 1989). Comparing these surveys further clarifies the extent to which stereotypes of the aging have diffused among Florida's population and, more importantly, have affected perceptions of the political elite. In Table 2 the earlier responses of Florida public officials are compared with the public's BEBR survey response to three common survey items.

A similar, and very substantial, proportion of the public and the officials concurred in two statements critical of the aging and conducive to generational tensions. More than a majority of both groups agreed with the statement that the aging opposed local services not beneficial to them and approximately a third in each group agreed that the aging were more burden than benefit to the local community. The final item, concerning local generational cleavages incited by the aging, elicited somewhat different responses: a majority of citizens agreed with this statement compared with a third of the officials. While state and local officials were more divided on this matter than were their constituents, fully one in three — a significant proportion — agreed with the public majority. Thus, on one questionnaire item, attitudes and stereotypes conducive to generational conflict seemed to be widely shared between the political elite and the public. On the second item, a substantial minority of both groups seemed to share such opinions and, on a final item, more than half the public officials and a third of the Florida public concurred in opinions critical of the aging. These responses seem to imply that generational tensions, though far from crisis proportions, are nonetheless real in Florida's communities. In particular, many community leaders — those most strategically placed to influence public policies within the state — appear susceptible to the new, negative imagery of the aging as the average citizen.

The Social Correlates of Attitudes About the Aging

Using socioeconomic and demographic information about respondents in the BEBR survey, we attempted to evaluate, in a preliminary way, several plausible social explanations for differing perceptions of the aging among the sample population. It seemed to us that antipathy toward the aging: (a) might result from resentment of their perceived new economic status and therefore would relate inversely to the economic status of respondents; (b) might increase among younger persons as the size of the

Table 2. Citizen and Public Officials' Responses to Survey Questions About the Aging

Item	Response	Percent of respondents	
		BEBR survey	State and local officials
"The economic benefits brought to my community by older residents do not compensate for the burden they place upon local government."	Strongly disagree	4	37
	Disagree	51	26
	Don't know	9	5
	Agree	32	26
	Strongly agree	4	6
	N =	491	253
"Older persons in my community tend to oppose paying for local services which do not directly benefit them."	Strongly disagree	1	13
	Disagree	36	31
	Don't know	12	3
	Agree	47	38
	Strongly agree	4	16
	N =	495	252
"When older residents in my community advocate government policies that benefit themselves, this often creates political opposition from younger residents."	Strongly disagree	—	27
	Disagree	34	33
	Don't know	10	7
	Agree	51	29
	Strongly agree	4	4
	N =	492	252

Note. Not all percentages equal 100 due to rounding.

aging population in a respondent's community grows; (c) might relate inversely to a respondent's own age; and (d) might indicate lack of information, education, social awareness or other cognitive qualities associated with diminished social or economic status.

Socioeconomic data acquired for each respondent included age, sex, race, education, years of Florida residence, and income. Additionally, we obtained data concerning the population growth rate between 1980–1990 and the proportion of the population aged 65 + for each respondent's county, as well as the respondent's current voter registration status and political party affiliation. A multiple regression analysis was utilized in which each of the 9 BEBR items previously described was treated as a dependent variable and the respondent's socioeconomic and demographic characteristics were classified as independent variables. Among the independent variables, only education and income were highly intercorrelated. To resolve this problem of multicollinearity, we used only education as a measure of socioeconomic status in the regression equations. Our primary concern was to learn if the resulting statistics were consistent with any of the explanatory theories we have described. The results of this statistical analysis are summarized in Table 3.

The most important information in Table 3 involves the first 4 dependent variables — the attitude items concerning the community impact of the aging. *The one variable most consistently, significantly related to critical attitudes toward the aging was the proportion of aging (65 +) in the population of the respondent's county.* Stated differently, antipathy toward the aging appeared to grow within counties concurrently with the growth of the older population. (The average proportion of the aging in counties surveyed was 19% with a range of 8 to 35%.) Moreover, when the survey population was divided into older groups (55 +) and younger (less than 55), the relationship between the size of the older population within the respondent's county and critical attitudes toward the aging was much more significant for the younger survey group.

This contextual variable also was significantly associated with responses to the question on the second survey concerning the political power of the aging (SENPOWER). Among all respondents, those expressing a belief that the aging had "too much" political power were likely to come from counties where the average proportion of aging was significantly larger than that for the respondents who believed the aging had "too little" political power (the respective county averages for the aging were 20%

Table 3. Regression Results for Items in the BEBR Survey[a]

Independent variables	Dependent variables[b]								
	GOVBURDEN	QUALIFE	OPPGOVSV	YOUNGOLD	SENPOWER	EDVOTE	ECOGROW	CHARITY	HOURS
Age	− .012**	.016**	− .009**	− .004	− .019*	− .430	− .002	.052	.267
	(.003)	(.003)	(.003)	(.002)	(.009)	(.267)	(.002)	(.280)	(.158)
Sex	− .278**	.116	− .218*	− .305**	− .882**	− .360	− .106	− .396	− 1.21
(1 = male)	(.102)	(.092)	(.099)	(.096)	(.327)	(.290)	(.066)	(.304)	(5.22)
(2 = female)									
Race	.247	.023	− .270	− .056	− 1.23*	− .111	.056	1.40*	− 6.20
(1 = white)	(.195)	(.174)	(.190)	(.181)	(.599)	(.529)	(.125)	(.710)	(12.7)
(2 = non-white)									
Education	− .049*	− .010	.003	− .067**	.109	− .659	.025	− 2.33**	.573
	(.024)	(.021)	(.024)	(.022)	(.070)	(.632)	(.015)	(.745)	(1.20)
Years of residence	.004	− .005	.007*	− .000	− .048	.185	− .000	− .137	.390*
	(.003)	(.003)	(.003)	(.003)	(.399)	(.097)	(.002)	(.110)	(.161)
Population growth	− .000	− .000	− .000	− .000	− .005	.091	− .002	.085	.010
	(.002)	(.002)	(.002)	(.002)	(.009)	(.157)	(.001)	(.167)	(.096)
% 65 +	.002**	− .003**	.003**	.001*	.076**	− .177	− .000	.163	.013
	(− .000)	(− .000)	(− .000)	(− .000)	(.024)	(.251)	(− .000)	(.266)	(.038)
Voter registration	− .003	.134	.068	.136	—[c]	− .563	.087	− 1.18**	.358
(1 = No;	(.124)	(.111)	(.121)	(.115)		(.374)	(.080)	(.432)	(7.27)
2 = Yes)									
Party ID	.012	− .048	− .026	− .121	− .150	− .056	− .062	− .073	5.03
(1 = Dem.;	(.067)	(.061)	(.066)	(.063)	(.213)	(.229)	(.044)	(.238)	(3.20)
2 = Ind.; 3 = Rep.)									
R^2 =	.08	.09	.06	.06	.07	[d]	.04	[d]	.10

[a]Unstandardized regression coefficients are listed; standard errors are in parenthesis.

[b]For the first 5 dependent variables and for ECOGROW, "strongly agree" is coded 4. For EDVOTE, "for raising taxes" is coded 1, and for CHARITY "yes" is coded 1.

[c]Voter registration status not asked in 1991 survey.

[d]R^2 not reported because logit regression analysis was used for this dichotomous dependent variable.

*$p < .05$; **$p < .01$.

and 17%). Among the respondents under age 55, the same contrast was apparent and the disparity between the proportions of the county aging populations even larger (20% and 16%). Thus, the data offer support to the assumption that generational conflict may arise, and intensify, as the proportion of aging increases at local levels.

The second respondent attribute to be significantly associated with antipathy toward the aging was the respondent's age. Age was associated with 4 of the 5 attitude items, and this finding seems consistent with the idea that generational cleavages may account for growing hostility toward the elderly. This finding is especially noteworthy because it confirms a similar conclusion reached more than a decade ago in Douglas St. Angelo's study of public perceptions about the aging in 10 representative Florida counties (St. Angelo, 1981).

More puzzling is the correlation between sex and benign perceptions of the aging. On 4 of the attitude items relating to the aging (GOVBURDEN, OPPGOVSV, YOUNGOLD and SENPOWER), women were much more likely than men to evaluate the aging and their civic activities favorably. Any explanation is speculative because the literature on political gerontology is silent about such a gender issue. One or two explanations seem plausible. Since women constitute a large proportion of the aging — a proportion that grows steadily with advancing age — the gender association may reveal a natural empathy between women of all ages toward a population perceived as predominately female and variously handicapped. The gender association may also reveal another psychological dimension of the nurturing and caretaking role which women so often assume in American society (Gilligan, 1982; Welch & Hibbing, 1992).

The data in Table 3 related to the remaining dependent variables are noteworthy for what does *not* appear. There is no significant statistical association (controlling for other variables) between age, or any other respondent attribute, and propensity to oppose an increase in local school taxes — an apparent refutation of the "anti-education" bias attributed to older persons. In the first BEBR survey, both the younger and older groups were divided about equally over additional taxes for education, with a slightly larger proportion of the older respondents (49%) than younger (47%) supporting more taxes. So anomalous did this finding seem that we repeated the item on the second BEBR poll with very similar results. When other variables are controlled, however, age is not statistically significant. Thus, the aging are no more willing than younger respondents to favor or to oppose increased taxes for education. Equally unexpected was the finding that neither voluntary community service nor the amount of such service was associated with age when other variables were controlled. Contrary to another assumption about older Americans, they do not appear to be more involved in community service than their younger neighbors.

The relationship between socioeconomic status and hostility toward the aging is inconclusive in our data. Education, our measure of socioeconomic status and social awareness, was significantly related with negative perceptions of the aging on only 2 (GOVBURDEN, YOUNGOLD) of the 5 survey items directly involving such attitudes.

Discussion and Conclusion

Does Florida epitomize in any important way the political status of the aging elsewhere? Florida's aging, as demographer Brad Edmundson has observed, have reached a socioeconomic stage that an increasing number of older persons will reach in the future elsewhere and, for American business, the social styles and values of Florida's aging have become reliable indicators of national trends among the aging (Edmundson, 1987). Most important politically, Florida is on the leading edge of a profound urban demographic transformation in which the aging will become an increasingly large proportion, or a majority, of many communities and political constituencies. "Florida may not be the blueprint for the nation's future," notes Edmundson, but it "tells us what society looks like when age, not youth, is in charge" (Edmundson, 1987, p. 69). Thus, Florida suggests not only qualities of a civic culture in which the aging are "in charge" politically but also how this transformation may be greeted by those not empowered.

The most significant finding in our survey is the very substantial proportion of younger respondents, ranging from roughly a third to more than half this group, who agreed to a variety of statements suggesting that older residents in their county or city were variously an economic burden, an economically selfish voting bloc, a generationally divisive influence, or an unconstructive community element. Moreover, these proportions closely resembled responses we received a few years earlier to a similar survey of Florida's state and local public officials. These findings imply no imminent eruption of generational conflict. Indeed, we often found complimentary and beneficial images of the aging widely shared between the generations when, for instance, they agreed that older persons had "about the right amount of political power." But we also found a widely distributed, latent disaffection with the aging's community impact and civic behavior. The social breadth and depth of this negative image suggests that it ought to be considered at least as typical of the aging's community stereotype as more complimentary images.

Another important aspect of our findings is the statistically significant association between critical appraisals of the aging and the size of the aging population in the respondents' home counties. Generally, the respondents most likely to express critical views about the aging's civic impact came from the counties with the larger proportion of older residents. This relationship was especially noteworthy among the younger survey group (those under age 55).

Our findings challenge several articles of political faith among the public and their local officials. Our responses suggest that the aging may be no more likely than younger community residents to oppose new school taxes and that younger residents are themselves almost evenly divided (not strongly agreed) about supporting such taxes. Additionally, the older respondents in our survey were not significantly more involved in voluntary community activities than younger ones.

These findings beg the question of why generational tensions do not appear with similar clarity in the studies previously reviewed. One persuasive answer, we believe, is that the public policy questions do not usually ask whether respondents believe the older beneficiaries of entitlement programs need or deserve them. Also, the generational tensions we have observed may arise only in a community context, in relation to local issues, or arise at the local level first. Generational cleavages over national policies may gradually evolve if beliefs in the legitimacy of the aging's claims on entitlements, or other negative stereotypes of the aging, persist longer, as Cook and Barret suggest could happen in the case of Social Security (Cook & Barret, 1988).

Most importantly, we believe these survey findings should reinvigorate the debate over the eminence of generational conflict in America. It is notable, we think, that the critical appraisals we have documented among so many of Florida's younger residents arise at the *community* level, where respondents are often brought into daily, sustained relationship with the aging through the normal events of civic life. Here, where elderly persons are no abstraction but a daily reality, seen and heard, critical cross-generational antagonisms have evolved and persisted. Moreover, our data imply that this community-level antipathy to the aging among the younger population may be expected to increase as the size of the local aging population grows. One provocative implication of these data is that greater contact between generations in civic life arising from the increasing size of the aging population in America's cities and counties may exacerbate generational tensions and nationalize them as the aging become more prominent across the nation.

Moreover, the criticism of the aging we often encountered among younger persons was generalized and diffuse, unanchored to specific community acts or events. This strongly suggests a "standing verdict" among many younger Floridians, a propensity to perceive the aging and their behavior in critical, uncomplimentary terms. If a deteriorating image of the aging precedes a declining political status, then the unattractive images of the aging we have often documented would seem to bespeak an image degeneration that might anticipate, or promote, generational conflict. This image transformation seems analogous to a pattern that Torres-Gil suggests could be a provocation of generational tensions: change from an image of the aging as poor and needy with the "automatic legitimacy" implied for their political claims to an image as "selfish and concerned only with personal pension and income benefits" (Torres-Gil, 1992, pp. 76, 87). In short, we think there is good reason for continuing concern about generational tensions in the U.S.

References

Aaron, H. J., Bosworth, B. P., & Burtless, G. T. (1989). *Can America afford to grow old?* Washington, DC: Brookings Institution.

Barnes, J. (1991). Age old strife. *National Journal, 4* (January 26, 1991), 216–219.

Beck, P. A., & Dye, T. R. (1982). Sources of public opinion on taxes: The Florida case. *Journal of Politics, 44,* 172–182.

Berger, P. (1963). *Invitation to sociology.* Garden City, NY: Doubleday.

Bernstein, A. (1991). Is Uncle Sam shortchanging young Americans? *Business Week* (August 18), 85.

Button, J. W. (1992). A sign of generational conflict: The impact of Florida's aging voters on local school and tax referenda. *Social Science Quarterly, 73,* 786–797.

Button, J. W., & Rosenbaum, W. A. (1989). Seeing gray: School bond issues and the aging in Florida. *Research on Aging, 11,* 158–173.

Button, J. W., & Rosenbaum, W. A. (1990). Gray power, gray peril, or gray myth?: The political impact of the aging in local sunbelt politics. *Social Science Quarterly, 71,* 25–38.

Campos, C. D. (1986). *Political priorities of older Americans.* Paper delivered at the Annual Meeting of the Midwest Political Science Association, Chicago, April 10–12.

Cook, F. L., & Barrett, E. J. (1988). Public support for social security. *Journal of Aging Studies, 2,* 339–356.

Day, C. L. (1990). *What older Americans think: Interest groups and aging policy.* Princeton, NJ: Princeton University Press.

Edmundson, B. (1987). Is Florida our future? *American Demographics, 9,* 38–44.

Eagleton Institute of Politics (1987). *Eagleton Poll.* New Brunswick, NJ: Rutgers University.

Elder, C. D., & Cobb, R. W. (1984). Agenda-building and the politics of aging. *Policy Studies Journal, 13,* 115–130.

Foner, A. (1972). The polity. In M. W. Riley, M. Johnson, & A. Foner (Eds.), *Aging and society: A sociology of age stratification, Vol. 3.* New York: Russell Sage Foundation.

Freiman, M. P., & Grasso, P. G. (1982). Budget impact and voter response to tax limitation referenda. *Public Finance Quarterly, 10,* 49–66.

Gallup, G. H. (1978). *The Gallup poll: Public opinion 1972–77.* Wilmington, DE: Scholarly Resources, Inc.

Gilligan, C. (1982). *In a different voice.* Cambridge, MA: Harvard University Press.

Grubb, W. N., & Lazerson, M. (1982). *Broken promises: How Americans fail their children.* New York: Basic Books.

Haas, W. H. (1989). *The gray peril?: Implications for politics, health and service delivery.* Paper presented at the Conference on Migration and Elderly Population Change in Appalachia: The 1980s and Beyond. Asheville, NC.

Haas, W. H., & Serow, W. J. (1991). *An exploratory study of retirement migration decision making.* Research Report to the Appalachian Regional Commission.

Huddy, L. (1989). *Political attitudes in an aging society: Raising the specter of generational conflict.* Paper presented at the annual meeting of the Midwest Political Science Association, Chicago, IL.

Hudson, R. B. (1978). The 'graying' of the federal budget and its consequences for old-age policy. *The Gerontologist, 18,* 428–440.

Hudson, R. B. (1980). Old-age politics in a period of change. In E. F. Borgatta & N. G. McCluskey (Eds.), *Aging and society.* Beverly Hills: Sage.

Jencks, C., & Torrey, B. B. (1988). Beyond income and poverty: Trends in social welfare among children and the elderly since 1960. In J. L. Palmer, T. Smeeding, & B. B. Torrey (Eds.), *The vulnerable.* Washington, DC: Urban Institute Press.

Kingson, E. R., Hirshorn, B. A., & Harootyan, L. K. (1986). *Ties that bind: The interdependence of generations.* Cabin John, MD: Seven Locks Press.

Kingson, E. R. (1988). Generational Equity: An unexpected opportunity to broaden the politics of aging. *The Gerontologist, 28,* 765–772.

Longman, P. (1985). Justice between generations. *Atlantic Monthly, 255,* 73–81.

Longman, P. (1987). *Born to pay.* Boston: Houghton Mifflin Co.

Mullins, D. R., & Rosentraub, M. S. (1990). *Migrating dollars?: Elders, taxes and local budgets.* Special Issues Report No. 7, Heartland Center on Aging, Disability and Long Term Care, School of Public Administration and Environmental Affairs, Indiana University, South Bend, Indiana.

Oberhofer, T. (1989). The cultural discount rate, social contracts, and intergenerational tension. *Social Science Quarterly, 70,* 858–869.

Palmer, J. L, Smeeding, T., & Boyle, B. T. (1988). *The vulnerable.* Washington, DC: Urban Institute Press.

Petersen, J. E. (1991). All those goodies for the elderly, have they gone too far? *Governing, 4,* 79.

Philadelphia Inquirer (1989). February 1, pp. 1A, 4A.

8. SOCIAL POLICIES, PROGRAMS, AND SERVICES

Pifer, A. (1986). The public response to population aging. *Daedalus, 115,* 373–380.

Ponza, M., Duncan, G. J., Corcoran, M., & Groskind, F. (1988). The guns of autumn: Age differences in support for income transfers to the young and old. *Public Opinion Quarterly, 52,* 441–463.

Preston, S. H. (1984a). Children and the elderly. *Scientific American, 251,*

Preston, S. H. (1984b). Children and the elderly: Divergent paths for America's dependents. *Demography, 21,* 435–457.

Reeves, R. (1988). Seniors are wielding more clout. *Gainesville Sun,* March 23.

Rhodeback, L. A., & Fitzgerald, R. E. (1989). *The Politics of greed?: The dynamics of public opinion among the elderly.* Paper prepared for presentation at the Annual Meeting of the Midwest Political Science Association, Chicago, April 13–15.

Rosenbaum, W. A., & Button, J. W. (1989). Is there a 'gray peril?': Retirement politics in Florida. *The Gerontologist, 29,* 300–306.

St. Angelo, D. (1981). *Are senior citizens the next backlash target?* Paper presented at the Annual Meeting of the Midwest Association for Public Opinion, Chicago, October 24.

Schmidhauser, J. R. (1970). The elderly in politics. In A. M. Hoffman (Ed.), *The daily needs and interests of older people.* Springfield, IL: Charles C Thomas.

Schuck, P. H. (1979). The graying of civil rights law: The Age Discrimination Act of 1975. *Yale Law Journal, 89,* 27–93.

Skinner, M., & Kinney, L. (1991). 'We have a right to be heard.' *Gainesville Sun,* July 14, 6–7 (Supplement).

Smith, L. (1988). The world according to AARP. *Fortune, 117,* 96–98.

Tolchin, M. (1988). Aid to elderly divides young, old and politicians. *New York Times,* December 23.

Torres-Gil, G. (1992). *The new aging.* New York: Auburn House.

Walker, A. (1990). The economic 'burden of the aging' and the prospect of intergenerational conflict. *Ageing and Society, 10,* 377–396.

Welch, S., & Hibbing, J. (1992). Financial conditions, gender and voting in American national elections. *Journal of Politics, 54,* 197–213.

Credits/ Acknowledgments

Cover design by Charles Vitelli

1. The Phenomenon of Aging
Facing overview—United Nations photo by F. B. Grunzweig. 18-21—Illustrations by Harriet Greenfield. 23—Photo by John Goodman.

2. The Quality of Later Life
Facing overview—Photo courtesy of Louis Raucci Jr.

3. Societal Attitudes toward Old Age
Facing overview—United Nations photo by F. B. Grunzweig.

4. Problems and Potentials of Aging
Facing overview—United Nations photo by P. Sudhakaran. 130-131—Photos by the Illinois Department on Aging.

5. Retirement
Facing overview—United Nations photo by John Isaac.

6. The Experience of Dying
Facing overview—Photo courtesy of Louis Raucci Jr.

7. Living Environments in Later Life
Facing overview—United Nations photo by Shelly Rotner.

8. Social Policies, Programs, and Services for Older Americans
Facing overview—United Nations photo by John Isaac.

ANNUAL EDITIONS ARTICLE REVIEW FORM

■ NAME: _____ DATE: _____

■ TITLE AND NUMBER OF ARTICLE: _____

■ BRIEFLY STATE THE MAIN IDEA OF THIS ARTICLE: _____

_____

_____

_____

■ LIST THREE IMPORTANT FACTS THAT THE AUTHOR USES TO SUPPORT THE MAIN IDEA:

_____

_____

_____

_____

_____

■ WHAT INFORMATION OR IDEAS DISCUSSED IN THIS ARTICLE ARE ALSO DISCUSSED IN YOUR TEXTBOOK OR OTHER READING YOU HAVE DONE? LIST THE TEXTBOOK CHAPTERS AND PAGE NUMBERS:

_____

_____

_____

_____

_____

■ LIST ANY EXAMPLES OF BIAS OR FAULTY REASONING THAT YOU FOUND IN THE ARTICLE:

_____

_____

_____

_____

■ LIST ANY NEW TERMS/CONCEPTS THAT WERE DISCUSSED IN THE ARTICLE AND WRITE A SHORT DEFINITION:

_____

_____

_____

_____

_____

*Your instructor may require you to use this Annual Editions Article Review Form in any number of ways: for articles that are assigned, for extra credit, as a tool to assist in developing assigned papers, or simply for your own reference. Even if it is not required, we encourage you to photocopy and use this page; you'll find that reflecting on the articles will greatly enhance the information from your text.

ANNUAL EDITIONS:
AGING, Tenth Edition
Article Rating Form

We Want Your Advice

Here is an opportunity for you to have direct input into the next revision of this volume. We would like you to rate each of the 41 articles listed below, using the following scale:

1. **Excellent: should definitely be retained**
2. **Above average: should probably be retained**
3. **Below average: should probably be deleted**
4. **Poor: should definitely be deleted**

Your ratings will play a vital part in the next revision. So please mail this prepaid form to us just as soon as you complete it.
Thanks for your help!

Annual Editions revisions depend on two major opinion sources: one is our Advisory Board, listed in the front of this volume, which works with us in scanning the thousands of articles published in the public press each year; the other is you—the person actually using the book. Please help us and the users of the next edition by completing the prepaid article rating form on this page and returning it to us. Thank you.

Rating	Article	Rating	Article
	1. Can You Live Longer? What Works and What Doesn't		22. American Maturity
	2. Exercise Isn't Just for Fun		23. Older Persons and the Abuse and Misuse of Alcohol and Drugs
	3. Why We Get Old		24. Silent Saviors
	4. Why We Will Live Longer . . . and What It Will Mean		25. Retirement Prospects of the Baby Boom Generation: A Different Perspective
	5. Over *What* Hill?		26. School Days for Seniors
	6. Undercover among the Elderly		27. Rethinking Retirement
	7. A New Life for the Old: The Role of the Elderly in the Bahamas		28. Coping with Dying: Lessons That We Should and Should Not Learn from the Work of Elisabeth Kübler-Ross
	8. Sexuality and Aging: What It Means to Be Sixty or Seventy or Eighty in the '90s		29. The Right Way to Die
	9. Religiosity, Aging, and Life Satisfaction		30. Is Dying Young Worse than Dying Old?
	10. Roles for Aged Individuals in Post-Industrial Societies		31. Physician-assisted Dying: Contemporary Twists to an Ancient Dilemma
	11. Remarriage among the Elderly: Characteristics Relevant to Pastoral Counseling		32. A Comparative Study of Family Bereavement Groups
	12. Women in Our Aging Society: Golden Years or Increased Dependency?		33. The Story of a Nursing Home Refugee
	13. Live and Learn: Patient Education for the Elderly Orthopaedic Client		34. Board and Care Versus Assisted Living: Ascertaining the Similarities and Differences
	14. Men and Women Aging Differently		35. From 'Our Town' to 'Ghost Town'?: The Changing Context of Home for Rural Elders
	15. Saved by the Hand That Is Not Stretched Out: The Aged Poor in Hubert von Herkomer's *Eventide: A Scene in the Westminster Union*		36. A Room of One's Own: The SRO and the Single Elderly
	16. In Search of a Discourse on Aging: The Elderly on Television		37. Group Homes for People with Dementia: A Swedish Example
	17. Getting Older Is Getting Better		38. Canada's Health Insurance & Ours: Real Lessons, Big Choices
	18. What Doctors and Others Need to Know: Six Facts on Human Sexuality and Aging		39. Can We Afford Old Age?
	19. Amazing Greys		40. Heading for Hardship: The Future of Older Women in America
	20. How to Take Care of Aging Parents		41. The Unquiet Future of Intergenerational Politics
	21. Older Problem Drinkers—Long-Term and Late-Life Onset Abusers: What Triggers Their Drinking?		

(Continued on next page)

ABOUT YOU

Name_____ Date_____

Are you a teacher? ☐   Or student? ☐

Your School Name _____

Department _____

Address _____

City _____ State _____ Zip _____

School Telephone #_____

YOUR COMMENTS ARE IMPORTANT TO US!

Please fill in the following information:

For which course did you use this book? _____

Did you use a text with this Annual Edition?   ☐ yes   ☐ no

The title of the text? _____

What are your general reactions to the Annual Editions concept?

Have you read any particular articles recently that you think should be included in the next edition?

Are there any articles you feel should be replaced in the next edition? Why?

Are there other areas that you feel would utilize an Annual Edition?

May we contact you for editorial input?

May we quote you from above?

ANNUAL EDITIONS: AGING, Tenth Edition